CRITICS
&
CRUSADERS

A CENTURY OF AMERICAN PROTEST

CHARLES A. MADISON

Second Edition, Illustrated

What is man born for but to be a Reformer, a Re-maker of what
man has made, a renouncer of lies; a restorer of truth and good. . . .

— EMERSON

FREDERICK UNGAR PUBLISHING CO.
NEW YORK

TO THOSE WHO
CHERISH FREEDOM
PRACTISE EQUALITY
AND SEEK JUSTICE

Second Printing, 1964

PRINTED IN THE UNITED STATES OF AMERICA
LIBRARY OF CONGRESS CATALOG CARD NO. 58-14283

PREFACE TO THE NEW EDITION

CRUSADERS FOR INDIVIDUAL FREEDOM and the general welfare —the subjects of this book—cherish the Bill of Rights above all other fundamental documents. Since the first edition of this work was published a dozen years ago, the rights guaranteed by this charter have been under fiercer attack than ever before in their long existence. Freedom has had to retreat on all fronts. For a time in the early 1950's it indeed seemed as if the beacon of our liberties, made brighter by the New Deal in the 1930's, was to be dimmed by the destructive forces of McCarthyism. Fortunately for all of us, the common sense of the Senate, strengthened by an aroused public, discomfited the unscrupulous demagogue from Wisconsin; at the same time the liberalized Supreme Court under Chief Justice Warren resumed its traditional protection of the freedoms affirmed by the Constitution.

In preparing the new edition it seemed best to leave the original text intact, since little more can be said about the men and women treated therein, and to bring the subject up to date by adding a new section on the critics and crusaders of our own time. In recent years, however, we have been intolerant of dissidents and extremists. Whereas all through the nineteenth century it was permissible for radicals and reformers to speak their minds freely and to advocate their views openly, the emphasis of the present turbulent century—the New Deal period excepted—has been on conformity and acquiescence. With the

[iii]

beginning of the cold war Communists and their sympathizers have been disdained and damnified as enemies of our society; reformers have been actively discouraged, and those who persisted were harassed and hurt. In the new section, therefore, these trends and events were discussed both generally and from the point of view of representative critics and crusaders.

The background chapter begins with a brief summary of the achievements of the New Deal, delineates in some detail the antidemocratic activities of various governmental agencies and their conspicuous victims, and concludes with a survey of recent Supreme Court rulings in the field of civil liberties. The choice of Senator George W. Norris was' made in the belief that he best represents the positive aspects of contemporary liberalism. Henry A. Wallace was selected because he typifies the intransigent New Dealer who refused to acquiesce in the cold-war strategy and was driven from public life. The final chapter treats Justice Hugo L. Black as the spirited and persistent protagonist of the freedoms guaranteed by the Bill of Rights.

With this new section the book now contains a comprehensive review of the representative critics and crusaders who have striven courageously, each in his own way, to further our basic freedoms and the public good.

C. A. M.

New York City
July 1958

PHOTOGRAPH ACKNOWLEDGMENTS. Of the illustrations, all of which were added to the second edition, the following are used by courtesy of the original owners: Wendell Phillips and Brooks Adams, Massachusetts Historical Society; Henry George, from an oil painting by Harry Thurston See, Robert Schalkenbach Foundation; Daniel De Leon, Socialist Labor Party; Henry Wallace and Hugo L. Black, Mr. Wallace and Justice Black respectively.

PREFACE TO THE FIRST EDITION

THE QUEST FOR FREEDOM has been a basic characteristic of the American people from the very beginning. The Pilgrims braved the dangers of a hostile shore in order to worship God in their own way. Roger Williams founded the colony of Rhode Island to practise the freedom of thought denied him in Massachusetts. Puritans without number preferred the hardships of the wilderness to an oppressive conformity.

This assertion of conscience has shaped our national development ever since: there were always enough bold spirits ready to fight for the greater freedom of all. When the British tried to curb the liberties of the colonists, the happy consequences were revolution and independence. The Founding Fathers made the " self-evident truths " our rallying cry. The Bill of Rights, forced upon a reluctant gentry, became the lifeblood of the young nation and the faith of its greatest heroes.

Freedom is not, of course, a simple or static good. In its noblest aspects it reflects man's loftiest aspirations; hypocrites and knaves have sometimes flaunted it to their immediate gain; always it is the prize for which the subservient many join the powerful few in ever-renewed combat. Equally remarkable is its chameleon-like quality. Roger Williams called it religious liberty; to Sam Adams it was political independence; William Lloyd Garrison believed it synonymous with emancipation of the Negro; Thoreau extolled it as the absence of coercion; Eugene V. Debs defined it as economic equality. As the concept and content of freedom evolved through the years, the critics and crusaders fought for it over and over: each victory appeared glorious and final at the moment of triumph, only to disclose other and more complex aspects of the hydra-headed enemy.

This much is true: every battle for freedom has resulted in an expansion of human rights. The recoil from witch-hunting led to religious tolerance. Colonial rebellion ended in national independence. The triumph of Jacksonian democracy gave men political equality, and nearly a century later the agitation of the suffragettes extended this privilege to women as well. In 1835 Garrison was mobbed for being an Abolitionist; thirty years later the Thirteenth Amendment removed slavery from the land. A century ago the labor union was denounced as the devil's work, but now it is a common and legally sanctioned social instrument. Eighty years ago the agitation of the National Labor Union for the eight-hour workday was decried as outrageous; it is at present an accepted fact and already replaced by the demand for the thirty-hour week.

Each of these gains was achieved only after a long and bitter struggle. Men and women fought for them step by step, year after year, usually at great personal sacrifice. Driven by zeal of conscience and by a strong social idealism, these reformers and crusaders dedicated their lives to the greater good of all the people. While the frontier of the freedom they sought to extend differed with changing conditions and their own peculiar character, all were motivated by the common desire to improve the status of the exploited and underprivileged poor.

The story of these frontiersmen of freedom cannot be told too frequently; actually it is not narrated often enough. In this book I have selected for discussion a few of the nonconformists who have helped mightily to advance social and economic freedom during the past century. The choice was governed by limitations of space and the pattern of organization. The first group comprises the three outstanding advocates of Abolition. For decades Garrison and Phillips were thorns in the flesh of the government, and John Brown was hanged as a traitor. The utopians, who are treated next, were at the same time groping for the key to heaven on earth and establishing colonies as experimental laboratories for the new society. Of those active after 1830, Margaret Fuller best represents the Brook Farm Transcendentalists, Albert Brisbane the Fourier followers, and Edward Bellamy the later literary utopians.

The ideal of a society uncoerced by the rule of force has always appealed to certain free spirits. Thoreau, living in a fluid society, succeeded in both preaching and practising civil disobedience without having to drink the cup of hemlock; Benjamin R. Tucker, individualist anarchist, escaped notice in the hubbub of economic strife; Emma Goldman and Alexander Berkman, newcomers to a country insisting on conformity, preached their doctrine of anarchism at the cost of continuous persecution. The dissenting economists who focused their critical eye on our unbridled industrialism have an honored place in any study of American social progress, and of these Henry George, Brooks Adams and Thorstein Veblen have most ably analyzed the weaknesses of our economic society.

An increasingly rampant and rapacious capitalism could not but bring forth the caustic criticism of those who had read the Declaration of Independence — and believed it. Of the militant liberals dealt with here, Governor John P. Altgeld brought obloquy upon his memory by acting in consonance with the principles of the Bill of Rights; Lincoln Steffens muckraked American politics and never stopped seeking the truth; and Randolph Bourne died a social casualty because he refused to follow his fellow progressives in a militaristic debauch. The final section deals with the Marxians who advocated a social economy which eschewed profit, exploitation, and inequality. Of these Daniel De Leon represented the early missionary phase of socialism; Eugene V. Debs helped to bring it to its greatest flowering; and John Reed led it towards postwar communism.

These individual studies of critics and crusaders who are most responsible for the extension of our social and economic freedom, together with background sketches of the movements they had led, were undertaken in an attempt to depict and re-evaluate our social

PREFACE

progress of the past century without the rigor and formality of im-
personalized history. I have made no special effort at original research, but I have sought to familiarize myself with the work and
writings of each subject of study and to make the discussion true
to fact as well as to the spirit of American liberalism. The bibliog-
raphy indicates the material used in the preparation of each chapter.

C. A. M.

New York City
July, 1946

ACKNOWLEDGMENTS

The following specially qualified persons were kind enough to read
critically one or more chapters of the book: Charles A. Beard,
Henry Black, Van Wyck Brooks, Henry Seidel Canby, Saxe Com-
mins, Mrs. Anna George De Mille, George R. Geiger, Granville
Hicks, Harry W. Laidler, Wesley C. Mitchell, Arnold Petersen,
Arthur M. Schlesinger, Mrs. Pearl J. Tucker, Henry Garrison Villard, and Henry Weinberger. Each of them gave me valuable suggestions, and I take this occasion to express my deep appreciation.
I am also grateful to those who have read the printed studies and
have commented on them constructively. I am particularly in-
debted to Ralph Bates for his careful reading of the entire manuscript and for his numerous helpful suggestions. My wife and
daughter have also read each chapter with care and have assisted
me in the proofreading.

I am grateful to the editors of the following periodicals for pub-
lishing portions of the manuscript: *The American Scholar, The
Antioch Review, Ethics, Journal of the History of Ideas, The New
England Quarterly, The South Atlantic Quarterly, Twice a Year,
The University of Kansas City Review,* and *The Virginia Quar-
terly Review.*

CONTENTS

[ix]

CONTENTS

THE ABOLITIONISTS

WILLIAM LLOYD GARRISON   JOHN BROWN
WENDELL PHILLIPS

THE ABOLITIONIST BACKGROUND

CONTRARY TO COMMON ASSUMPTION the movement for the abolition of Negro slavery in the United States began in the South rather than in the North. The wave of freedom crested by the Declaration of Independence, and especially the increasing economic disadvantages of cotton-raising prior to Eli Whitney's invention of the gin in 1793, caused many of the leading Southerners to deprecate the system of slave labor as a moral and economic blight upon the young republic. Washington, Jefferson, Madison, Henry, to mention only the most eminent Virginians, believed that slavery was contrary to the genius of American liberty. " I can clearly foresee," Washington once said, " that nothing but the rooting out of slavery can perpetuate the existence of our union by consolidating it in a common bond of principle."

This anti-slavery sentiment in the South increased with the years, particularly among the poorer whites, and found strong expression from the pulpit and in print. By the end of the 1820's four-fifths of the emancipation societies and an even greater proportion of their membership were to be found in the plantation states. North Carolina alone contained more than ten times as many enrolled Abolitionists as all of New England and New York. It should be said, however, that at the time these Northern states had no more than 300 members — kindly souls who seconded the Southern formula for the liberation of slaves by means of gradual emancipation and African colonization.

The establishment of Garrison's crusading *Liberator* in 1831 and

[3]

Nat Turner's ominous revolt in the same year combined to revolutionize the character of the anti-slavery movement. Southern Abolitionists, already alarmed by the prospect of potential Negro uprisings, were all the more horrified by Garrison's radical doctrine of immediate emancipation. They denounced him as a fanatical meddler and argued that his fantastic demands were making impossible the gradual reforms which alone could solve the problem to the benefit of both master and slave. They resented especially his harsh and uncompromising language and what they believed to be his arbitrary simplification of an issue that reached to the deepest roots of Southern life. The Rev. Dr. Witherspoon of Charleston, South Carolina, writing to Dr. Lyman Beecher in 1832, spoke for most of them when he asserted: " I detest it [slavery] as the political and domestic curse of our Southern country and yet *I would contend to the death* against Northern interference with Southern rights."

This sectional pride, becoming swollen and sinister with the years, soon drove Abolitionism from the South. Of the numerous anti-slavery societies none remained in existence by the end of the 1830's, and one could not speak favorably of emancipation without risking a coat of tar and feathers — or even death itself. Most Southerners believed it their proud duty to insist upon the sanctity of slavery and to praise Calhoun's political vindication of slavocracy. Though inwardly aware of the moral and economic weaknesses of their slave culture, they persuaded themselves that slavery was based upon the laws of God and nature and that it alone, even as in ancient Athens, made possible the highest form of civilization. They insisted, moreover, that the Negro was unfit for freedom and the responsibilities of citizenship, that he was suited only to the menial tasks of the plantation. With Professor Thomas Dew of the College of William and Mary they argued that " the exclusive owners of property ever have been, ever will be and perhaps ever ought to be the virtual rulers of mankind. It is as much in the order of nature that men should enslave each other as that other animals should prey upon each other."

[4]

If the Abolition movement became anathema to Southerners after 1831, it was fostered energetically in the North by an increasing band of reformers. The crusade made a deep appeal to a sincerely Christian generation which could no longer accept the Calvinism of their fathers. To work for the liberation of Negroes moved them as much as the narrower view of churchly life inspired their orthodox brethren. Before long there were anti-slavery societies in towns from Maine to Ohio. Spurred by Garrison's weekly exhortations, by Phillips's impassioned eloquence, and by the inspiring example of other leaders, they collected funds, sheltered fugitive Negroes, and furthered the agitation for the immediate abolition of slavery.

At no time during the thirty-year campaign did this crusade become a mass movement. The Abolitionists, however, more than compensated for their lack of numbers by their earnestness, their strenuous activity, and their overflowing eagerness to do God's great work. Their zeal antagonized not only the Southerners but also the rich merchants and conservative churchmen of the North. In the press and from the platform and pulpit Garrison and his followers were excoriated as madmen and zealots who sought to tear up established society by the roots and bring chaos upon the land. In a book published in 1857 George Fitzhugh, Southern economist, stated the common sentiments of the anti-Abolitionists: " We warn the North that every one of the leading abolitionists is agitating the negro slavery question merely as a means to attain their ulterior ends . . . a surrender to Socialism and Communism — to no private property, no church, no law, to free love, free lands, free women and free children." As a consequence of this vilification the Abolitionists had their meetings broken up, their halls wrecked, and their presses thrown into rivers. Many suffered bodily injury and not a few lost their lives. As so often happens, however, this determined band thrived on oppression. So certain were they of the evil of slavery that opposition only strengthened their zeal to eradicate it from the land.

The Abolitionists living near the Mason and Dixon Line, having learned to hate slavery from their first-hand contact with it, were particularly eager to help fugitive blacks. Up to the very outbreak of war in 1861 thousands of zealous whites and free Negroes gave much of their time and goods to encourage the escape of slaves and to shelter them on their way to Canada and freedom. Their clandestine routes along the byways of the North soon became known as the Underground Railroad. Its " station-masters " and " conductors " — colored as often as white, since the hapless runaways first sought out their own kind — engaged on scheduled relayed runs from numerous points on the Southern border to several terminals in Canada. They protected and transported their " passengers " at great personal risk and frequently in the face of almost insuperable obstacles. Their ingenuity and daring kept the slave-hunters at bay when most certain of their quarry. Not a few were arrested and made to pay the full penalty of the law. But they were no sooner at liberty than they returned to their " underground " tasks, convinced that they were engaged in holy work and were not bound by laws made by slaveholders.

One of the first to succeed conspicuously in the establishment of the Underground Railroad was the stout-hearted Quaker, Isaak Hopper, who saved many Negroes from being overtaken by their pursuing masters. Most eminent among these crusaders was Levi Coffin, another energetic Quaker, who came to be known as the president of the Railroad and who was himself responsible for the safe conduct of more than 3000 fugitives. Some of the " conductors " were audacious enough to invade the South for their " passengers." Thus Laura Haviland, the Quakeress from Michigan, made a daring trip to a Kentucky plantation in order to help the wife of an escaped Negro join her husband. The incredible Harriet Tubman, herself a slave until her flight in 1849, became known as the Negro Moses because of her nineteen trips to the South, during which she transported over 300 slaves to freedom without losing a single soul. So successful were these men and women in their operation of the Underground Railroad that its branch lines netted the entire North and its " passengers " were counted in the tens of thousands. The loss of these millions of dollars' worth of " property " became an increasing drain upon the strength of slavocracy and caused more vexation among the planters than all the harsh talk of the extreme Abolitionists.

Meantime the Abolitionist movement acquired an indirect but increasingly powerful ally in the industrial development which was changing the face of the urban North during the second quarter of the nineteenth century. Manufacturers of infant industries clamored for the benefits of higher tariffs, internal improvements, more railroads, cheap and abundant labor — only to find themselves blocked by a government dominated by southern planters. Eager to avail themselves of the bounteous resources ready for their exploitation, they resented keenly the restraints of an inimical Washington. The wealthier they grew, the more insistently they claimed the privileges which they regarded as their due. In the words of Charles A. Beard: " By the middle of the century they were ready in numbers, in wealth, and in political acumen to meet in the arena of law or war the stanchest spokesmen of the planting aristocracy." Unlike the merchants who continued to appease their slave-owning clients in order to retain their lucrative trade, the industrialists began to work actively for the election of a government of their own choosing. Their pragmatic and powerful opposition to Southern agrarianism was of great advantage to the Abolitionists in the fight against slavery.

After 1850 the Abolitionist movement became an integral part of American history. Industrial expansion and a rapidly increasing population in the free states were making slavery an economic anomaly; that it was against our basic morality made it all the more abhorrent to men and women having a Puritan upbringing. Thus not a few mill-owners and bankers, while not scrupling to exploit their hired labor to the limit, condemned the evil of slavery and contributed generously to the treasuries of the several Abolitionist societies.

[7]

Three events in the early 1850's helped to dramatize the issue of slavery and to accentuate its urgency. The first was the passage by Congress of the Fugitive Slave Law, which violated the Bill of Rights and placed the full power of the federal government at the disposal of the slaveowners in search of escaped slaves. The oppressive provisions of the law shocked the Northern populace into active opposition. Indignant men and women everywhere met to urge the repeal of the Act. Law-abiding farmers and tradesmen, who hitherto had shown little interest in the agitation of the Abolitionists, denounced the arrogant aggressiveness of the Southerners and offered their services to the overworked Underground Railroad. In Boston, in Philadelphia, in Syracuse — wherever slave-hunters pounced upon their prey — the people rioted in their rebellious willingness to contravene the hated law.

Provoked by the cruel consequences of the Fugitive Slave Law, Harriet Beecher Stowe wrote *Uncle Tom's Cabin*. The spectacular success of the novel not only made the author famous but also popularized the sentiments of the Abolitionists the world over. The literary merits of the book were grossly exaggerated. Its phenomenal sale would have been impossible without the groundwork of the Garrisonians and the general detestation of the Fugitive Slave Law; yet the fact remains that time and circumstance combined to make it one of the most widely read books of the century. Hardheaded men wept as they pored over its pages; farmers and mechanics who seldom looked into a book and who disdained fiction on principle concentrated on the sentimental story of Uncle Tom and little Eva as if they were reading the Holy Bible. Many of them now saw the practice of slavery in a new light: instead of dismissing it as none of their affair they began to think of it as an evil to get rid of — and the sooner the better. Force of habit, however, made it difficult for them to cut across their lifelong predilections. Much as they now detested slavery, they were not yet ready to change their political allegiance in order to bring about its abolition. In the 1852 elections, with *Uncle Tom's Cabin* at the crest of its popularity, the Free Soil party actually received fewer votes than in the previous national election. But the anti-slavery spirit of the book left a definite impress upon its millions of readers and made them more receptive to the intensified agitation of the Abolitionists.

The logic of events compelled the Southerners to become more aggressive, and in 1854 they pushed through Congress the Kansas-Nebraska Bill, which repealed the Missouri Compromise and opened Northern territory to slavery. Senator Stephen A. Douglas, eager for the Presidency, had hoped with the aid of his magic formula of " squatter sovereignty " to win favor in the South and at the same time to extend his hold on the North. But the mischief of his plan quickly became obvious. Almost to a man Southern Congressmen of both political parties were for the Bill, while many Northern Democrats voted against it. Abolitionists vehemently denounced the measure as another attempt to spread slavery across the land. Industrialists were equally quick to see it as a threat to their legitimate sphere of exploitation. Men who had heretofore refused to commit themselves now joined the humanitarians in decrying the law. Nor were they shocked on learning that Garrison had burned a copy of the Constitution at a Fourth of July celebration. That same month the newly born Republican Party met in Michigan to demand the repeal of the pro-slavery laws and the abolition of slavery in the District of Columbia. For the first time since they had begun their crusade Garrison and Phillips became the leaders, not of a handful of zealots, but of millions of Northerners determined to overthrow the planter oligarchy in Washington.

In 1854 the territory of Kansas was opened for settlement on the basis of " squatter sovereignty." The neighboring Missourians, anxious to insure as well as to extend their slavery domain, at once enlisted enough " Border Ruffians " to enter the territory and take over the reins of government. But the free-soil settlers, who followed as fast as they could in steadily increasing numbers, refused to acknowledge the pro-slavery constitution. Both sides engaged in guerrilla warfare, and numerous pitched battles and acts of wanton brigandage earned the territory the title of " Bleeding Kansas." The dramatic arrival of old John Brown, following his five stalwart sons in 1855, gave the advantage to the free-soil settlers. The fiery Abolitionist's effective ruthlessness at Pottawatomie and his brave stand at Black Jack and Osawatomie made his name worth " an army with banners." When ague and disease compelled him to leave the scene of action at the end of the following summer, the free-soilers so definitely outnumbered the pro-slavery faction that they had little difficulty in gaining control of the government. The Southern majority in the Senate, however, blocked their efforts to achieve statehood, and not till 1862 was Kansas admitted to the Union.

The planters made their final attempt to insure their dominance early in 1857, when Chief Justice Taney announced the Supreme Court's rejection of Dred Scott's appeal for freedom, on the ground that the black man had no rights which the white man was bound to respect. Most significant was his pronouncement that " Congress has no power to abolish or prevent slavery in any of the territories." Only a few days earlier President Buchanan, apprised of the content of the decision, had urged in his inaugural address that the people leave the settlement of the slavery question to the Supreme Court. With seven of the Justices condemning the Negro to chattel bondage, the Southern leaders acclaimed the wisdom of the Court and hoped that the meddling Northerners would come to their senses.

But the Abolitionists and their sympathizers were outraged by this judicial turpitude. They attacked the Court with all the vehemence of their passionate anger. State legislatures and state courts denounced the decision and declared that so far as they were concerned the Negro was free the moment he set foot within their borders. Senator Seward made the most castigating attack of all, charging collusion between the President and the Supreme Court. Riots broke out afresh when federal marshals attempted to seize fugitive slaves. No wonder the Abolitionists soon came to regard the ruling as a godsend in disguise. As Frederick Douglass put it: " This very attempt to blot out forever the hopes of an enslaved people may be one necessary link in the chain of events preparatory to the complete overthrow of the whole slave system."

The crisis was reaching the point of explosion. All its legal and political victories notwithstanding, the South was perturbed and splenetic. The planters and their politicians in Washington knew only too well that they were losing ground rapidly in both wealth and numbers — that it was only a question of time before they would be overwhelmed by the force of industrial power and majority votes. They were equally aware of the obsolescent wastefulness of the plantation system. Yet they refused to acknowledge the realities of scientific progress and social change, and stubbornly insisted on the spread of slavery. The influential Northerners, on their part, while very eager for peace and willing to leave the aggravated problem of slavery to the states affected by it, were determined to keep the territories free. Moreover, the industrialists, enterprising and ambitious, demanded their rightful share of national power and were ready to spend millions to get it. Prejudice, pride, and politics thus combined to deepen the cleavage and wrench the two sections apart. And the federal government was blindly widening the breach. Each move by Washington in favor of the planters served to bring the nation nearer to " the irrepressible conflict." Americans everywhere felt the truth of Lincoln's insistence that " this government cannot endure permanently half slave and half free." But while north of the Mason and Dixon Line only the Abolitionists were urging separation, nearly all Southerners, dreading political eclipse, were resolved to secede from the Union the moment they lost control of the federal government.

The country was in this state of social ferment when John Brown startled the entire world with his spectacular raid on Harpers Ferry. Virginia and her sister states, aghast and desperate, interpreted this quixotic attack by a handful of fanatics as the spearhead of a Northern conspiracy to lay the South waste. The wounded zealot, weak of body but spiritually aflame, was tried within a week of his arrest and sentenced to be hanged. The appearance of vengeful haste, and even more the old man's saintly behavior during the interval between his capture and his execution, changed the shock and revulsion, which the raid had first aroused in most Northerners, into sympathy and adulation. The gnarled body of John Brown, hanging from the gallows in the prison yard on December 2, 1859, symbolized to his executioners the criminality of conspiring Abolitionists; but to an angered and agitated North it signified the dramatic martyrdom of a man who had dared to die for the sake of wretched slaves. As Garrison rightly judged the event, the hanging of John Brown showed that the time was high noon.

It is not very easy for our generation to imagine the intense excitement, the passionate rancor, and the deep heartache experienced by Americans in the year 1860. It was tragically evident to all that only a miracle could prevent civil war. Southerners, in Washington and at home, were feverishly preparing for it with sanguine fatalism. Most Northerners, with the exception of the extreme Abolitionists who approved secession, dreaded the prospect of war, and were groping desperately for a formula that would keep the Union intact. Yet no such solution appeared possible, and events were irresistibly driving the country towards the bloody abyss. The Republican party, combining the strength of aggressive industrialism and intensified Abolitionism, convened in Chicago and nominated Abraham Lincoln for the Presidency. With the Democrats quarreling amongst themselves, with the bankers and manufacturers backing the lanky lawyer from Illinois with lavish contributions, and with a majority of the voters living in the North, the election of Lincoln was practically certain. And a Republican victory meant Southern secession. When the votes were counted, Wendell Phillips exclaimed: "For the first time in history, the slave has chosen a President of the United States." Southerners for once agreed with him and began to secede.

The record of the war belongs to the main narrative of American history. The outbreak of hostilities was a signal for the Abolitionists to insist on immediate emancipation of the slaves. Disregarding Lincoln's desperate efforts to keep the border slave states in line and discounting the wisdom of diplomatic delay, they argued that only by coming out boldly and actively against slavery could the government work havoc within enemy territory and gain popular support at home. But the sad gaunt man in the White House kept his own prudent counsel and waited until the victory at Antietam in September 1862 before making public his Emancipation Proclamation. His erstwhile critics shouted hallelujah and praised him for his sagacity. Thereafter few doubted the final outcome.

The defeat of the Confederate army at Appomattox not only preserved the Union but also capped the long campaign of the Abolitionists with conspicuous success. At the annual meeting of the American Anti-Slavery Society in 1865 Garrison maintained that the work of the organization was done, and refused re-election to its presidency when he was outvoted. Phillips, his closest friend and fellow-worker throughout the long crusade, insisted that the task of the Society would remain unfinished until the Negro was given not only liberty but full citizenship, and agreed to lead the campaign for the additional laws. For five years more the agitation continued. It ended with the adoption of the Fourteenth and Fifteenth Amendments and the Society's formal dissolution.

While the story of the Abolition movement should take into account the many thousands of anonymous men and women who abhorred slavery and gave freely of their time and money in the struggle against it, major emphasis must be given to the few undaunted spirits who expounded its moral purpose and directed the campaign to a successful conclusion. Of these leaders, William Lloyd Garrison, John Brown, and Wendell Phillips are the most eminent. The first was in truth the founder and prime mover of Abolitionism, giving it backbone and moral urgency. "Osawatomie" Brown came upon the scene with the flash of a meteor and fired the conscience of Northerners with the poignant drama of his death. Wendell Phillips, golden-voiced aristocrat, gave up a life of leisure for the thorny reward of the reformer and together with Garrison led the agitation against slavery. The characters of these men, as well as their special place in the American annals, are discussed in the three following chapters.

WILLIAM LLOYD GARRISON

APOSTOLIC CRUSADER

ILLIAM LLOYD GARRISON, the most forceful reformer in our history, is perhaps the least known of great Americans. Nor is this strange. The most abused man of his time, the taint of this calumny continues to influence public judgment, though eighty years have passed since success crowned his lifework. Fortunately, he was not one to be affected by the opinion others had of him. From the very first he pursued his destined course with an inflexible will that made him, like the prophets of old, the scourge and conscience of his generation. Once convinced of the sin of slavery, he persisted in making it the paramount issue for thirty troubled years. And at last he compelled his countrymen to grapple with the problem to the bloody end. Then, having sacrificed the youth of the nation to free the slaves, they quickly forgot the man who was chiefly identified with the greatest social reform of the century.

Completely unlike his shiftless, seafaring father whom he scarcely remembered, very much the son of his hard-working Baptist mother, who remained a pious " dissenter " to the end of her brief life, young Garrison grew up under her guidance with an acute sense of justice and with the fanatic's readiness to fight doggedly for what he believed was right. The urge to reform the world, a dominant characteristic of his generation, agitated his mind while he was still a printer's apprentice. A number of his immature but forthright editorials on political and moral issues soon livened his employer's weekly, the Newburyport *Herald*.

In 1825, on his twentieth birthday, he completed his apprenticeship. His dynamic personality had won him a number of friends, and they encouraged him to become a journalist. It took little capital to begin a periodical in those days, and he had no difficulty in borrowing the necessary money. Early in 1826 he began to issue the *Free Press*, a small weekly sheet. At once he began to express his convictions freely. His editorials were Whiggish, naïve, but incisive, and in one of them he spoke out for the first time against what he regarded as the national evil of slavery. At the end of the same year, however, his publishing venture failed for lack of support and he went to Boston in search of employment. He worked for a while at odd jobs, but his ambition to put his thoughts down in writing sent him to Vermont to edit the *National Philanthropist*, a local temperance periodical. A few months later he became the editor of the *Journal of the Times*, another rural weekly with reformist leanings. In a short time he had made it, according to Horace Greeley, into " about the ablest and most interesting newspaper ever issued in Vermont."

When South Carolina passed a new law prohibiting Negroes from going to school, Garrison's indignation was aroused. Intolerant of half-measures, convinced that iniquity must be given no quarter, he wrote against the evil of slavery with fanatic harshness. Reflection intensified his crusading spirit. In November 1828 he stated editorially: " We are resolved to agitate the subject to the utmost; nothing but death shall prevent us from denouncing a crime which has no parallel in human depravity." Two months later he reiterated his crusader's avowal: " Before God and our country, we give our pledge that the liberation of the enslaved Africans shall always be uppermost in our pursuits." No wonder that pious little Lundy, coming upon these trenchant attacks, made his way on foot from Baltimore to Vermont in order to shake the hand of his spirited new ally and to offer him the co-editorship of *The Genius of Emancipation*. Garrison, twenty-three years old and aching for a platform of national scope, required little urging to follow along his destined path.

The zealous youth reached Baltimore in the summer of 1829. He wasted no time in expounding his basic views on Abolition. His inaugural editorial in the issue of September 2 was the first nationally published demand for "immediate and unconditional emancipation." A month later he went a step further in arguing against compensation to slaveowners. "It would be paying a thief for giving up stolen property, and acknowledging that his crime was *not* a crime. . . . No, let us not talk of buying the slaves — justice *demands* their liberation." His condemnation of everyone connected with slavery soon caused him to be tried for criminal libel and, when he could not pay the fine of fifty dollars and costs, to be sent to jail. "I am in prison," was his tart comment, "for denouncing slavery in a free country." After seven weeks' confinement he was released through the generosity of Arthur Tappan, a wealthy New York merchant who was also a warm Abolitionist. Confronted with another libel suit, the truculent youth decided to leave the hostile Southern city for more hospitable Boston. He was not sorry to part with Lundy, since from the very beginning he had been averse to the latter's gradualism. Moreover, his mind had begun to seethe with plans for an anti-slavery journal that would be fearless and outspoken.

A half-century after the Declaration of Independence first startled the world, this country experienced a spiritual and intellectual resurgence. In his *Life of Theodore Parker*, Frothingham remarked that at this time "all institutions and all ideas went to the furnace of reason, and were tried by fire. Church and state were put to the proof, and the wood, hay, stubble — everything combustible — were consumed." Emerson wrote: "The key to this period appeared to be that the mind had become aware of itself. Men grew reflective and intellectual. There was a new consciousness." The epoch that ushered in the industrial revolution also brought forth an eagerness to make heaven on earth. It was in truth an age swarming with reformers of every conceivable variety — from food faddists to the most visionary of utopians.

What distinguished Garrison from his fellow meliorists was his inspired tenacity and prophetic zeal. The printer to whom he had been apprenticed well defined his qualities: "His peculiar characteristics are an ardent temperament and warm imagination; his undeniable merits, pure purpose and unshaken courage." This burning spirit showed itself soon after his return to Boston. In order to enlist the local Abolitionists in the support of his projected periodical, he decided to hold an anti-slavery meeting. He was not long in learning that none of the public or religious buildings was open to a gathering of this nature. Though he was then a pious Baptist, he engaged the only hall at his disposal, the place used by the city's society of infidels. His audience on the appointed day was pitifully small, and the response was negligible. But so fervent and forceful was his address that Samuel J. May, who had come with Bronson Alcott and several others to learn of the new venture, was immediately impressed with Garrison's magnetic personality. "That is a providential man," he remarked to his companions; "he is a prophet; he will shake our nation to its center, but he will shake slavery out of it."

Garrison was not in the least discouraged. He proceeded with his plans to publish *The Liberator*. He turned his dingy room into a printing shop, and what he did not make with his own hands he managed to rent or borrow. On January 1, 1831, without a dollar of capital or a single advance subscriber, he brought out the first issue, a modest folio of four pages. Though unaware of Thomas Paine's earlier use of them, he chose for his motto the memorable words: "Our Country Is the World — Our Countrymen Are Mankind." In his opening editorial he stated his anti-slavery creed with clarity and passion. The final phrases have lost none of their bite:

I *will be* as harsh as truth, and as uncompromising as justice. On this subject I do not wish to think, or speak, or write, with moderation. . . . I am in earnest — I will not equivocate — I will not excuse — I will not retract a single inch — AND I WILL BE HEARD.

The intellectual maturity and inflexible purpose of this manifesto are all the more extraordinary when one remembers that it was written by a youth of twenty-five, with neither formal schooling nor other cultural advantages. Indeed, his Abolitionist doctrine was so complete and comprehensive at its first utterance that it remained unaltered throughout the long campaign. Twenty years later George Thompson, the English reformer, well said of the final passage: " I have met nothing in the language of any other Reformer that ever gave me so clear an insight into the soul of the man as these words into that of Mr. Garrison."

To Garrison's unsympathetic contemporaries, and they included all but a handful, the editorial read like the raving of a rank madman. Both Northern traders and Southern planters — to say nothing of the conservative clergy — were darkly aware of the dynamic combustibility of the slavery problem and wished to bury it in deep silence. They had no understanding of the strong missionary drive which impelled an apostolic zealot like Garrison to right a moral wrong regardless of the consequences, and strongly resented his meddling with a matter in which he had not the slightest material interest. With the first issue of *The Liberator*, therefore, this Puritanic protagonist of Abolition began a fight to the death with the vested interests of slavery.

At first Garrison's stinging editorials were outcries in the wilderness, unnoticed except by his Southern detractors. Even those on whom he had counted most for support, particularly the church groups, refused to heed his appeal. As he wrote to a friend, " I found the minds of the people strangely indifferent to the subject of slavery." So much so, indeed, that after *The Liberator* had been published a full twelvemonth it had only 500 subscribers; and although this number had quadrupled by 1834, no more than a fourth were whites. In view of the periodical's extraordinary influence throughout its existence, it is all the more interesting to note that the total of 3000 subscribers, reached in 1837, remained the average circulation to the end of its life in 1865.

The Liberator became anathema to Southerners with the very first issue. In 1831 a law was passed in Georgetown, D.C., prohibiting free Negroes from taking the weekly from the post office, under pain of twenty dollars' fine or thirty days' imprisonment; if they were unable to pay the fine or the jail costs they were to be sold as slaves for four months. Every Southern state quickly excluded the periodical, and Georgia put a price of $5000 on Garrison's head. In the North " men of substance and standing " publicly repudiated the new weekly and refused to associate their names with the cause it advocated. Gerrit Smith, shortly to become a prominent Abolitionist, wrote in 1835: " I should think that Mr. Garrison's influence on good minds at the North is very slight. Those who like ebullitions of wrath and columns of abuse, may like his paper."

This wrath and abuse could not but antagonize those who profited from the established order or who wished to effectuate reforms gradually and painlessly. Yet the vehement editor of *The Liberator* persisted in his unsparing indictment of slavery. For he was convinced that established institutions are not overthrown by polite pleading. " Has not the experience of two centuries," he argued, " shown that gradualism in theory is perpetuity in practice? Is there an instance, in the history of the world, where slaves have been educated for freedom by their taskmasters? " In his " Address Before Free People of Color," printed in June 1831, and reprinted thrice in two months, he declared bluntly: " I am determined, nevertheless, to give slaveholders and their apologists as much uneasiness as possible. They shall hear me, and of me, and from me, in a tone and with a frequence that shall make them tremble. There shall be no neutrals; men shall either like me or dislike me." Nor was his use of violent language a mere idiosyncrasy: he was keenly aware of the Herculean task before him and deliberately used the harshest language he knew in order to shock his readers out of their moral lethargy. " An immense iceberg," he explained at the outset, " larger and more impenetrable·than any which floats in the Arctic Ocean, is to be dissolved, and a little *extra heat* is not only pardonable, but absolutely necessary." Several years later, in reply to reiterated criticism not only from his professed detractors but also from his genuine sympathizers, he again insisted on his need of forceful language:

To carp at my composition, and yet confess the justness of my principles, as many do, is very much like sneering at the black man on account of his complexion, and yet conceding that he has all the marks and attributes of manhood. Fine and delicate phraseology may please the ear; but masculine truths are utterly divorced from effeminate words, and cannot be united without begetting a dwarfish progeny.

This fierce and feverish mode of expression characterized all his writing and lecturing to the end of his active life; as the anti-slavery crusade gained in strength and momentum, its participants accepted his style as part of the man and revered him for his spirited leadership. Amasa Walker well speaks for most of them: " We do not all feel perfectly pleased with all Mr. Garrison says. Like Martin Luther, his language is rough and sometimes violent. But Mr. Birney has said, ' My anti-slavery trumpet would never have roused the country — Garrison alone could do it.' "

In the early years, however, a number of disgruntled reformers refused to accept Garrison's leadership and accused him of weakening the anti-slavery movement by his intemperate speech and extreme arrogance. So ardent an Abolitionist as Lewis Tappan, brother of the man who had freed the young editor from his Baltimore incarceration, referred to him as " the Massachusetts Madman." When these opponents failed to dislodge him from his leadership, they combined with the anti-Garrison clergy to organize the American Union Against Slavery — a society " thoroughly imbued with the ' Hang Garrison spirit.' " For a decade the antagonistic factions warred more against each other than against the common enemy. Throughout this period, however, Garrison retained his flinty firmness of purpose. Nor did the loyalty of his followers diminish in the slightest; in their admiration of his sterling qualities they were, in the words of an unfriendly critic, " impervious to criticism and superior to argument." Years later Edmund Quincy voiced this faith in a letter to an English reformer: " It is a horrid trick he has of being *right*. . . . He is more often overruled on points of difference, and we have almost always had to acknowledge in the end, that he was right and we were wrong." In time the dissenting minority returned to the " old organization " and did yeoman work on behalf of Negro emancipation.

The hours Garrison did not give to *The Liberator* he devoted to organizing those sympathetic to Negro liberation. With the help of a few faithful followers he arranged meetings in private homes and rallied groups in outlying towns to form anti-slavery societies. As early as 1832 he succeeded in organizing The New England Anti-Slavery Society. Addressing the few delegates, he said: " We have met this evening in this obscure schoolhouse; our numbers are few and our influence limited; but mark my prediction, Faneuil Hall shall erelong echo with the principles we have set forth. We shall shake the nation with their mighty power." A year later Abolitionists from several Northern states met with him in Philadelphia to establish The American Anti-Slavery Society. Its famous Declaration of Sentiments, composed by him, spoke out as boldly for the Negro slaves as Jefferson had for the colonists in 1776. And so persevering were the efforts of this band of reformers that five years later the Society boasted 1350 local branches.

Very early in the campaign Garrison encountered the vehement opposition of The American Colonization Society, an association of complacent philanthropists who expected to abolish slavery by helping freed Negroes to settle in Africa. The apostolic Abolitionist was quick to discern the cruel fallacy of such a policy: by sending a few Negroes to the African jungle this group was in effect lulling the perturbed conscience of the American people and consequently furthering the perpetuation of slavery. He believed, moreover, that Negroes had become Americans by virtue of their native birth and training and had as much right to remain in this country as their white masters. To discredit the idea of colonization, Garrison wrote in 1832 his *Thoughts on African Colonization*, a pamphlet of 240 pages, in which he made effective use of the literature of the Colonization Society to expose its misleading and contradictory principles. His conclusion was that the way to abolish slavery was not to ship a few Negroes to Africa but to liberate immediately all slaves in the United States. The bulky brochure, the most significant tract produced in this country up to that time, had an enormous effect upon those interested in the subject. In the words of Elizur Wright, Jr., an active Abolitionist:

Mr. Garrison struck the greatest blow of his life — or any man's life — by publishing in a thick pamphlet, with all the emphasis that a printer knows how to give with types, his *Thoughts on Colonization.* . . . Hundreds of thousands of men who might never agree with Mr. Garrison in their mode of action in behalf of the slave, were thoroughly aroused to act, each in his own way, and they never ceased and never will cease to honor and revere the man whose brave words dispelled their daydreams.

Garrison next sailed to England, where anti-slavery sentiment had attained great intensity, to explain the purposes of the Abolitionists and to discredit the agent of the Colonization Society. The British humanitarians, having read his writings, had assumed that he was a Negro. Garrison was amused to find that even Buxton, Wilberforce's successor as leader of the anti-slavery advocates, " had somehow or other supposed that no white American could plead for those in bondage as I had done, and therefore I must be black." The youthful Abolitionist was received most cordially and quickly won the confidence of the prominent liberals. George Thompson, an outstanding reformer and orator, became his close friend and agreed to visit the United States in order to further the cause of Abolition.

Garrison's criticism of our pro-slavery government at a London meeting was severely criticized by New York newspapers, and on his return he was met at the pier by an unruly mob of about 5000. In Boston his reception was equally turbulent; handbills urging the use of tar and feathers against him were distributed freely. Somewhat later a stout gallows with two suspended ropes was erected one night before his house, with the superscription, " By Order of

Judge Lynch." When George Thompson arrived, the agitation against him became so violent that it was necessary to smuggle him onto a ship going to England to save him from bodily harm. Despite all this, Garrison persisted in his virulent attacks on the pro-slavery forces. "My friends are full of apprehension and disquietude," he wrote at that point, "but I *cannot* know fear. I feel that it is impossible for danger to awe me. I tremble at nothing but my own delinquencies, as one who is bound to be perfect, even as my heavenly Father is perfect." But though his will was unshaken, persecution had had some visible effect upon him. When Harriet Martineau interviewed him at about this time, she at once noticed his uneasy behavior: "The one thing I did not like was his excessive agitation when he came in, and his thanks to me for desiring to meet one 'so odious' as himself."

The defenders of slavery in both sections of the country were determined to stop the agitation of the Abolitionists. As a prominent Bostonian said to Garrison: "It is not a matter of principle with us; it is a business necessity; we cannot afford to let you succeed; we do not mean to allow you to succeed; we mean to put you down by fair means if we can, by foul means if we must." A number of slaveowners met in New York on July 20, 1835, to declare that slavery was "a question belonging solely to the states in which it is tolerated," and that the rights of property were sacred and would be maintained at all costs. A month later Faneuil Hall was crowded with the elite of Boston, and such luminaries as Peleg Sprague and Harrison Gray Otis denounced the Abolitionists with fiery eloquence. Ignoring the violations of the rights of free speech and free press in the South, they decried the activity and writings directed against the slaveholders. Criticizing this meeting in his *Diary*, John Quincy Adams remarked: "Slavery and democracy — especially democracy founded, as ours is, upon the rights of man — would seem to be incompatible with each other. And yet at this time the democracy of the country is supported chiefly if not entirely by slavery." Garrison naturally waxed sarcastic at the thought

of such a gathering within the hallowed walls of this historic hall:
" Call it no longer the *Cradle of Liberty*, but the *Refuge of Slavery*."
But, he continued prophetically, " *The cause of the bleeding slaves
shall yet be pleaded in Faneuil Hall*, in tones as thrilling, in language as stirring, in eloquence as irresistible, as were ever heard
within its walls."

The climax of this agitation occurred exactly two months after
the meeting, when these " gentlemen of property and standing from
all over the city " led a mob against the Abolitionists. Thompson
was still in this country, and placards appeared in the streets urging citizens to " snake Thompson out " and offering a hundred
dollars to " the individual who shall lay violent hands on Thompson, so that he be brought to the tar-kettle before dark." In the
afternoon the mob in broadcloth gathered before the makeshift
office of *The Liberator*, disrupted a meeting of the Female Anti-
Slavery Society, seized Garrison, tied a rope about his waist, and
began dragging him, hatless and disheveled, toward the City Hall.
There the irresolute mayor, with the help of his officers, finally succeeded in wresting the victim from his captors and placing him in
jail for safety. Wendell Phillips, then a young man of twenty-five,
witnessed the disgraceful scene and took an immediate and sympathetic interest in the victim and his cause.

This persecution of the enemies of slavery continued to the very
outbreak of the Civil War. Those who profited from slave labor
or who feared for the Union were ready to hang them wholesale in
order to preserve the existing social order. Helped by the venal press
and the federal government, they incited mobs against the reformers. Thus in 1837 Elijah P. Lovejoy was killed in Alton, Illinois,
while defending his printing press from pro-slavery ruffians. A year
later a mob attacked and burned the newly built Pennsylvania Hall
in Philadelphia and rioted for several days afterwards. In the same
year Senator Preston announced, to the applause of his colleagues,
that " if an abolitionist come within the border of South Carolina,
and we can catch him, we will try him, and, notwithstanding all the
interference of all the governments on earth, *including the Federal*

Government, WE WILL HANG HIM." For many years the Abolitionists could not meet in New York City without an organized disturbance, usually led by the notorious Captain Rynders, a leading political ruffian. James Gordon Bennett, the Hearst of his day, was largely responsible for these attacks. A typical example of his fulminations was the following: " Never, in the time of the French Revolution and blasphemous atheism, was there more malevolence and unblushing wickedness avowed than by this same Garrison." Even after the flagrant Fugitive Slave Law was rapidly converting the cause of Abolition into a mass crusade, many wealthy merchants and traders in the North persisted in defending slavery. Josiah Quincy had these men in mind when he wrote to Richard H. Dana, Jr.: "The Boston of 1851 is not the Boston of 1775. Boston has now become a mere shop — a place for buying and selling goods, and I suppose, also, of *buying and selling men.*" As late as 1860 meetings of Abolitionists were broken up by hoodlums in the pay of these Southern sympathizers.

Although the Abolition movement was motivated by moral and religious sentiments, it was for many years bitterly opposed by a large part of the clergy. At the outset Garrison had naturally assumed that these servants of Jesus would eagerly embrace the cause of Negro emancipation. A few ardent souls did heed his call and became his devoted lieutenants. But the large majority of divines rejected either his uncompromising principles or his leadership with unctuous scorn. Moreover, intimidated or cajoled by their church trustees, a number preached against the doctrine of immediate emancipation as if the ideal had emanated from Satan. Even those who professed anti-slavery views were antagonized by Garrison's forthrightness. Their hostility was noted by an anti-slavery agent who lectured in sixty New England towns during 1841. " All the opposition I have met with in the prosecution of my mission has originated with scarcely an exception with clergymen."

It is not surprising, therefore, to find Garrison stating that " the moral cowardice, the chilling apathy, the criminal unbelief and cruel skepticism that were revealed [by the clergy] filled me with rage." Believing as he did that "*God never made a tyrant, nor a slave,*" he was not long in denouncing the unsympathetic ministers as friends of slavery. At an Abolitionist gathering in Massachusetts he offered the following resolution: "That the indifference or open hostility to anti-slavery principles and measures of most of the *so-called* religious sects, and a great majority of the clergy of the country, continues THE MAIN OBSTRUCTION to the progress of our cause." In New York he worded the condemnation even more drastically: "Resolved, That the Church ought not to be regarded and treated as the Church of Christ, but as the foe of freedom, humanity and pure religion, so long as it occupies its present position. . . ." As late as 1850, addressing another New York audience in the presence of Captain Rynders and his mobsters, he again touched upon the defection of the clergy: "In this country, Jesus has become obsolete. A profession in Him is no longer a test. Who objects to His course in Judea? The old Pharisees are extinct, and may safely be denounced. Jesus is the most respectable person in the United States."

In impugning the Christianity of the non-Abolitionist ministers, Garrison took pains to stress his own deep devotion to the doctrines of its Founder. "My religious sentiments (excepting as they relate to certain outward forms and observances, and respecting these I entertain the views of 'friends') are as rigid and uncompromising as those promulgated by Christ himself." All his life, indeed, he trod the narrow and noble path of practical Christianity. J. Miller McKim spoke for many when he wrote:

He is eminently a religious man. This is the secret of his power, both as a speaker and in his private relations. He places the cause on a broad basis of Christianity, and his appeals are always made to the conscience and through the religious sentiment. His discourses are in this respect like sermons of the best models; and it is a quite common remark, that "there is something apostolic in his manner." In one respect he always reminds me of the Hebrew writers of the Old Testament: he speaks of everything in its relation to God.

As a son of his century, however, Garrison insisted on exercising his God-given right to brush away the cobwebs of tradition and on making use of his power of reasoning at all times. Although he was of a somewhat credulous nature — he inclined his ear to quacks of all kinds and believed in spiritualism " to a limited extent " — he gradually relinquished his belief in the supernatural part of the Bible and in the divinity of Jesus. When certain ministers denounced the Abolitionists for advocating their cause on Sundays, he claimed that such interpretation of the Sabbath was without the authority of either " Scripture or reason," and was in truth " a shameful act of imposture and tyranny." Nor was he satisfied with mere words. In due course he called conventions to discuss the validity of the Sabbath and the sanctity of the Bible. Shortly afterwards he explained his position on these matters in a letter to Elizabeth Pease, the English Quakeress:

We are led to perceive not only that there is no scriptural authority for the observance of the first day of the week as the Sabbath, but that time is sanctified only as we use it aright, without regard to particular days or seasons. . . . Your theological views of man's disparity, the atonement, eternal punishment, the divinity of Christ, the inspiration of the Bible, etc. . . . are all wrong (in my judgment, I mean, though I was brought up to believe them), admit of no satisfactory proof, much less of demonstration.

No wonder that he was called " the Prince of New England infidelity"! This absurd aspersion on a man who believed so firmly in the Christian doctrine of equality that he could not tolerate the idea of slavery, merited the following retort from Samuel J. May: " The infidelity of the anti-slavery movement consists in this simple thing, that it has outstripped the churches of the land in the practical application of Christianity to the wants, wrongs and oppressions of our age and our own country."

Even as Garrison did not scruple to criticize the Bible when it was used to sanction slavery, so he did not hesitate to contemn the Constitution of the United States when the anti-Abolitionists interpreted it in their favor. Perfectionist that he was, he came to regard it as "a blood-stained instrument" because it did not confirm the complete equality of men advanced by the Declaration of Independence. In an early issue of *The Liberator* he made his stand clear:

It was a compact formed at the sacrifice of the bodies and souls of millions of our race, for the sake of achieving a political object — an unblushing and monstrous coalition to do evil, that good might come. Such a compact was in the nature of things and according to the laws of God, null and void from the beginning. No body of men ever had the right to guarantee the holding of human beings in bondage. . . . They had no lawful power to bind themselves or their posterity for one hour — for one moment — by such an unholy alliance. It was not valid then — it is not valid now.

This doctrine he preached frequently and forcefully.

The question of secession, brought to the fore by South Carolina in 1832, was increasingly in the public mind during the following decades. Concerning it Garrison took as extreme a position as did the "fire-eating" Southerners. He asserted that "nothing can prevent the dissolution of the American Union but the abolition of slavery." If Negro emancipation could not be achieved within the Union, he was ready to let it fall apart. "Why not the Union resolved in form," he wrote to a friend, "as it is in fact — especially if the form gives ample protection to the slave system, by securing for it all the physical force of the North?"

The masthead of *The Liberator* became the index of Garrison's doctrines. In 1842 it was changed to read: "A repeal of the Union between Northern liberty and Southern slavery is essential to the abolition of the one and the preservation of the other." A year later this slogan was replaced by the following resolution passed at the meeting of the Massachusetts Anti-Slavery Society in Faneuil Hall: "Resolved, That the compact which now exists between the North and the South is 'a covenant with death and an agreement with hell' — involving both parties in atrocious criminality and should be immediately annulled." In 1845 the masthead was augmented by the motto, " No Union with Slaveholders! " This battle-cry remained at the head of *The Liberator* until December 13, 1861, when it gave way to the jubilant " Proclaim Liberty throughout all the land, to all the inhabitants thereof."

During the controversy over the annexation of Texas, Garrison was in the forefront of the violent opposition and was applauded by the incensed Boston whigs. At a protest rally in Concord he exclaimed: " I am for revolution, were I utterly alone. I am there because I *must* be there. I *must* cleave to the right. I cannot choose but obey the voice of God. . . ." The climax of his critical attitude towards the federal government occurred on July 4, 1854, when at a public celebration in Framingham, Massachusetts, he burned copies of the Fugitive Slave Law, some court decisions, and the Constitution. The last he condemned " as the source and parent of all the other atrocities." As the flames licked the crumpled papers he exclaimed: " So perish all compromises with tyranny! And let all the people say, Amen." And all the people did.

Notwithstanding his bellicose attitude towards the forces of slavery, which was gradually but surely fanning the fires of civil strife, Garrison remained throughout his life a strict Christian paci-fist. The doctrine of nonresistance appealed to him as right and logical. When twenty-four years old he was fined four dollars for the " failure of appearance on May muster." This presumed injus-tice strengthened his prejudice against any recourse to military force. After months of thought he arrived at the following decision: " I now solemnly declare that I will never obey any order to bear arms, but rather cheerfully suffer imprisonment and persecution. What is the design of military masters? *To make men skilful murderers.* I cannot consent to become a pupil in this sanguinary school."

His pacifism, like his Abolitionism, was the logical result of his belief in the Sermon on the Mount. He was as ready to offer the other cheek as he was willing to give his life for human equality. When in the heat of the crusade against slavery his harsh language caused him to be accused of fomenting war between the states, he declared his abhorrence of physical force at every opportunity. "I war with no man after the flesh," he wrote to Samuel J. May in 1838. "I feel the excellence and sublimity of that precept which bids me pray for those who despitefully use me; and of that other precept which enjoins upon me, when smitten upon the cheek, to turn the other also." That same month, as the moving spirit of the Peace Convention in Boston, he embodied the following doctrine in its Declaration of Sentiments: "We cannot acknowledge allegiance to any human government; neither can we oppose any such government by resort to physical force."

To emphasize his nonintercourse with a pro-slavery government he refrained from voting or from participating in any political campaign. When a number of prominent Abolitionists decided to take part in national elections in the hope of swaying candidates to their views, Garrison refused to countenance such action and argued that they were merely compromising their principles. Nor would he take any part in the organization of the Liberty party or lend his great prestige to its nominees. It was not until the campaign of 1860, when it was generally assumed that the election of Abraham Lincoln would bring about the end of slavery, that Garrison spoke out in favor of the candidates of the Republican party. Four years later, with the slaves liberated by executive proclamation, he advocated the renomination of President Lincoln and even went to Baltimore to attend the convention. From the gallery he witnessed the adoption of the resolution approving the abolition of slavery — to him "a full indorsement of all the abolition 'fanaticism' and 'incendiarism' with which I had stood branded for so many years."

Garrison adhered to his policy of nonresistance even when it became obvious that the issues which he had vitalized could be settled only in blood. When the anti-slavery struggle in Kansas became a focal point for the opposing forces, he refused to condone the acts of violence committed by John Brown and others. So far as he was concerned, moreover, the Kansan free-soilers were not true Abolitionists since they were interested only in excluding slavery from their territory and not from the country as a whole. "They are contending," he argued, " for their own rights *as white men,* not for the rights of all, without distinction of caste or color; they have pursued a shuffling and compromising policy throughout." Nor did he approve of John Brown's seizure of Harpers Ferry, although he sympathized with his underlying purpose. Professing his belief in " the peaceful abolition of slavery," he judged Brown to be an Old Testament hero, unaffected by the teachings of Jesus.

With the outbreak of the Civil War, Garrison's pacifism lost its unequivocal character. At first he refused to take sides, insisting that both factions were equally guilty. To his friend Oliver Johnson he wrote: " I would have nothing changed, for this is God's judgment-day with our guilty nation, which really deserves to be visited with civil and servile war, and to be turned inside out and upside down, for its unparalleled iniquity." Gradually, however, as the end of slavery appeared certain, his sympathy became obvious: " The weapons resorted to, on both sides, are the same; yet it is impossible not to wish success to the innocent, and defeat to the guilty party. But, in so doing, we do not compromise either our anti-slavery or our peace principles." Nevertheless, he counseled his followers to serve the government to the best of their ability, and urged even nonresisters to help to the limit of their conscience. When his favorite son enlisted in the army, he made no attempt to dissuade him and sent him away with his paternal blessing. President Lincoln finally won his complete loyalty with the issuance of the Emancipation Proclamation. " The government is, and must be, if true to itself, wholly on the side of liberty. *Such a government can receive the sanction and support of every Abolitionist, whether in a moral or military point of view.*"

Garrison directed and energized the Abolition movement to the very end of the Civil War. He worked dynamically and with complete concentration. At the twentieth-anniversary celebration of *The Liberator* he spoke truly when he remarked: " I have counted nothing too dear to peril in the cause to which my life is devoted. For that course I have sacrificed whatever is desirable in good reputation, or pleasant in human friendships, or alluring in worldly advancement." He was fortunate in having married a woman who was in hearty sympathy with all he believed. She was self-effacing and untiring in her devotion to his welfare. It was this devotion that enabled him to leave all household cares to her, and made of their modest home the spiritual center of the Abolition movement and a place of cheer for all who entered it. When in the course of his crusade Garrison became weary or discontented, he knew he could always refresh his spirit in the love and understanding of his wife.

His unrelenting agitation against slavery, seemingly impotent and futile at first, in time affected the conscience of the majority of Northerners. As economic and political events drove them nearer and nearer to "the irrepressible conflict," the more odious slavery appeared to them. The enactment of the Fugitive Slave Law and its enforcement only made more widespread the feeling that those in power were determined to perpetuate chattel property. John A. Dix, a former Senator from New York and no radical, wrote to a friend at that time: "Commercial interests rule the day. The prices of stocks and of merchandise are considered, by a large portion of the business men, as of more importance than the preservation of great principles." At a memorable mass meeting in Boston, Wendell Phillips excoriated Webster and the other politicians responsible for the passage of the obnoxious law. "We say that they may make their little motions, and pass their little laws, in Washington, but FANEUIL HALL REPEALS THEM, in the name of the humanity of Massachusetts." The crystallization of the struggle was greatly hastened by an expanding industrialism which demanded higher tariffs and a free and cheap labor market. Garrison, though unaware of the economic implications of his moral crusade, was quick to take advantage of the new ally. In a resolution which he presented at an anti-slavery convention in 1853 he wrote: "Emancipation can be as triumphantly defended on the ground of political economy and material prosperity, as it can be on moral and religious principles."

All kinds of people were beginning to crowd the Abolitionist meetings — not to jeer but to applaud. In 1854 Garrison spoke to a large gathering in New York in his usual vitriolic vein. Taking advantage of the definite antagonism towards the expansion of slavery in the Kansas-Nebraska territory, he argued against chattel bondage everywhere. " If it would be a damning sin for us to admit another slave state into the Union," he asked pointedly, " why is it not a damning sin to permit a slave state to remain in the Union? " The unexpected enthusiasm of the audience caused him to write to his wife: " My language was strong, and my accusations of men and things, religion and politics, were very cutting; but, strange to say, not a single hiss or note of disapprobation was heard from beginning to end, but some of my strongest expressions were most loudly applauded."

Public disapproval of slavery came to a boiling point with John Brown's martyrdom in Virginia. With the deadlock of the 1850's about to end in sanguinary combat, the hanging of the old Abolitionist was made the battlecry of an aroused people. Garrison could not but compare the excited approval of John Brown's raid with the early vilification he himself had met.

The sympathy and admiration now so widely felt for him, prove how marvellous has been the change effected in public opinion during thirty years of moral agitation — a change so great, indeed, that whereas, ten years since, there were thousands who could not endure my slightest rebuke of the South, they can now easily swallow John Brown whole, and his rifle into the bargain. In firing his gun, he has merely told us what time of the day it is. It is high noon, thank God!

The election of Abraham Lincoln was the signal for Southern secession and civil war. Once this conflict reached its sanguinary climax, Northerners everywhere reacted as free men to the issue of slavery. Abolitionists found themselves in the limelight of popularity, and Garrison was acclaimed as a national hero. On learning the results of the election, Wendell Phillips said, " Lincoln is in *place*, Garrison is in *power*."

The editor of *The Liberator* only intensified his campaign, now that his cause was in the hands of a friendly government. He wanted the slaves freed with the least delay, and would not wait until Lincoln decided on the propitious time for action. Reaching straight to the heart of the matter, sublimely confident in the triumph of righteousness, he refused to acknowledge the obstacles confronting the President. At a Fourth of July celebration in Framingham he urged his audience to " create a great Northern sentiment which shall irresistibly demand of the Administration, under the war power, the emancipation of every slave in the land." That fall he sent a memorial to Congress against slavery. At the same time he addressed himself editorially to Lincoln and his Cabinet: " *To refuse to deliver those captive millions who are now legally in your power, is tantamount to the crime of their original enslavement*; and their blood shall a righteous God require of your hands. Put the trump of jubilee to your lips! " Week after week his editorials exhorted the government to act, and his numerous lectures repeated the cry for emancipation with insistent zeal.

In time the demand for the abolition of slavery became as widespread as that for military victory. Early in 1862 Garrison wrote to his wife: " Our distinctive movement is nearly swallowed up in the great revolution in Northern sentiment which has been going on against slavery and slavedom since the bombardment of Sumter." When Lincoln finally made public his Emancipation Proclamation, thereby bringing to a successful end the long campaign for Negro liberation, Garrison hailed the news as a " great historic event, sublime in its magnitude, momentous and beneficent in its far-reaching consequences, and eminently just and right alike to the oppressor and the oppressed."

With victory in the field practically assured, the House of Representatives, on January 31, 1865, voted favorably on the Thirteenth Amendment, which abolished slavery forever. Garrison announced the glad tidings with " devout thanksgiving to God, and emotions of joy which no language can express." At the Jubilee meeting in Boston, where he was wildly applauded, he said; " Allow me to confess that, in view of it, and of the mighty consequences that must result from it to unborn generations, I feel tonight in a thoroughly methodistical state of mind — disposed at the top of my voice and to the utmost strength of my lungs, to shout, 'Glory!' 'Halleluia!' 'Amen and Amen!'" When the required number of states ratified the Amendment ten months later, the venerated Abolitionist set Secretary Seward's proclamation into type with his own hands. " Henceforth," he added, " personal freedom is secured for all who dwell on the American soil, irrespective of complexion or race. . . . It is, consequently, the complete triumph as well as utter termination of the Anti-Slavery struggle as such."

As always, Garrison meant what he said. To him the cause of Abolition was won and his campaign was at an end. At the next annual meeting of the American Anti-Slavery Society, of which he had long been president, he urged its dissolution. When he was outvoted, chiefly as a result of opposition on the part of his closest friend Wendell Phillips, he refused re-election to office. Nor was he dissuaded from discontinuing *The Liberator*, and the final issue appeared on its thirty-fifth anniversary. In his valedictory editorial he made his position clear:

The object for which *The Liberator* was commenced — the extermination of chattel slavery — having been gloriously consummated, it seems to me especially appropriate to let its existence cover the historic period of the great struggle; leaving what remains to be done to complete the work of emancipation to other instrumentalities (of which I hope to avail myself), under new auspices, with more abundant means, and with millions instead of hundreds for allies.

Garrison's lifework was done: the millions of Negro slaves were forever free. Now generally proclaimed as the outstanding reformer of his time, he found himself the object of special honors and esteem. Both he and his friend George Thompson, who was then in this country, were invited to address Congress as a mark of high respect. They were also the distinguished guests of the government at the flag-raising exercises at Fort Sumter on April 15, 1865. When Garrison was invited to speak on this significant occasion, he addressed his prominent auditors with characteristic frankness:

I have not come here with reference to any flag but that of freedom. If your Union does not symbolize universal emancipation, it brings no Union for me. If your Constitution does not guarantee freedom for all, it is not a Constitution I can subscribe to. . . . And now let me give the sentiment which has been, and ever will be, the governing passion of my soul: " Liberty for each, for all, for ever."

Early in 1866 a national testimonial was written by some of Garrison's ardent admirers, signed by the leading men of the day, and presented to the public with the object of collecting the sum of fifty thousand dollars as a gift of the nation. These friends knew that their leader and his devoted wife had given no thought to providing for their old age. Two years later the couple were presented with a bank draft for $31,000. Garrison was particularly pleased to learn that the contributions had come from every part of the country and from all classes of society. A number of eminent Englishmen were equally glad to share in the testimonial, and they likewise exerted themselves to honor its recipient when he visited their country in 1867.

On his return from Europe Garrison was urged to write the history of the anti-slavery movement. Willing though he was to undertake the task, he found himself too intimately connected with the subject to treat it objectively. He became instead a regular paid contributor to the New York *Independent*, and wrote some hundred articles on topics and problems of interest to him. Although he continued to write in behalf of the Negro, and although he favored such reforms as woman's rights, prohibition, and free trade, he was no longer the apostolic crusader. The newer and more complex issues were outside his moral ken. The fire in his soul which had blazed for more than thirty-five years with such intensity as to make every utterance bright with passion, having no longer a congenial subject to seize upon, was reduced to a flicker. Unlike his comrade Wendell Phillips he preferred to assume that with the abolition of slavery the country had become relatively free of social ills — with the result that long before his death in 1879 he was almost forgotten.

The Jubilee of Emancipation lifted William Lloyd Garrison to the pinnacle of popular esteem. Only Abraham Lincoln, after his martyrdom, was more admired by the mass of Americans. Then came the harsh period of Reconstruction, with the exploitation of the South, and of the country as a whole, by ruthless and greedy adventurers. It was during this period that Garrison's reputation suffered an eclipse that has persisted to the present. The generation of the Gilded Age was only too eager to forget the struggle against slavery. Few of the sons of Abolitionists possessed the moral fervor of their fathers. Most of them were subconsciously sick of the Civil War and the causes that had brought it about. They interested themselves in making money, in exploiting a continent opened to them by a lax and lavish government. As a consequence, and especially after the South had resumed its legitimate part in the affairs of the nation, the man who was most responsible for the liberation of millions of Negro slaves came to be remembered, if at all, not for his inspired leadership but for his querulous fanaticism.

The fact remains, nevertheless, that Garrison is among the very few great Americans who have succeeded in forcing a recalcitrant generation to do their bidding. His towering strength came from his moral earnestness — his " strange power of making himself believed." The magnetism of his personality drew men to him; once they came under his influence, his deep ethical fervor drove them to fight for the right. According to Oliver Johnson, one of his earliest and most ardent disciples, " his unselfish devotion to his work touched and opened the hearts of all who witnessed it." This striking ability to retain the allegiance of men appears conspicuously in his lifelong friendship with Wendell Phillips. The latter wrote in 1846: " I owe you, dear Garrison, more than you would let me express, and, my mother and wife excepted, more than to any other one. Since within the sphere of your influence, I trust I have lived a better man." Nineteen years later, when Garrison's refusal to lead the campaign to its logical conclusion was criticized by some of his erstwhile admirers, Phillips, who was his leading opponent at the meeting, quickly rose to his defense. Garrison, he insisted, " is, in

[37]

so true and full a sense the creator of the anti-slavery *movement*, that I may well say I have never uttered an anti-slavery word which I did not owe to his inspiration; I have never done an anti-slavery act of which the primary merit was not his."

As a contributor to human welfare Garrison ranks with the greatest — having headed the crusade that brought about the liberation of four million slaves. It was this positive achievement that caused the great novelist Leo Tolstoy, himself an eminent humanitarian and pacifist, to pass the following judgment:

Garrison understood that which the most advanced among the fighters against slavery did not understand: that the only irrefutable argument against slavery is the denial of the right of any man over the liberty of another under any condition whatsoever. . . . Garrison was the first to proclaim this principle as a rule for the organization of the life of man. In this is his great merit. . . . Therefore Garrison will forever remain one of the greatest reformers and promoters of true human progress.

JOHN BROWN

A FANATIC IN ACTION

T HE PHENOMENON of John Brown remains, after nearly ninety years, as exciting and inexplicable as it was when his lifeless body first swayed from the hangman's noose. The perpetrator of the Pottawatomie massacre and the desperate leader of the Harpers Ferry raid, the scourge of the Border Ruffians and the terrible saint of the Abolitionists, Brown became a legendary figure at the very outset of his anti-slavery activity. Men failed to see him as he was: they either condemned him as a fiendish criminal or revered him as " God's angry man."

One cannot fully appreciate his activity during the last four years of his life without a sympathetic understanding of his abomination of slavery. Born in 1800 of a family of pious and hardy pioneers, named after his grandfather who had died in the Revolutionary War, brought up in the primitive and challenging environment of the Ohio frontier, he early acquired a hatred of human bondage which in the end inflamed every fiber of his being. His father and their neighbors both in Connecticut and in Ohio worked for Negro emancipation as part of their Christian duty. Like so many youths of his day he grew up with a determination to love God and obey His commandments, and human equality was an essential part of them. He studied the Bible with such zeal that in time his speech and writing acquired the flavor of the Old Testament. As a youth he became a teetotaler, shunned dancing, and scorned card-playing; he did not hunt or fish because these sports tended to develop lazy habits of living; he refused to enlist in the army or carry firearms, and did not own a gun until, at twenty-six, he thought it necessary for protection against Free-Masons.

Deep piety increased his compassion for the enslaved Negro. At the age of twelve, while delivering cattle to the army during the War of 1812, the callous mistreatment of a boy slave he had befriended " made him a most *determined Abolitionist*: and led him to declare, *or swear: eternal war* with slavery."

His antipathy to what he termed " the sum of all villainies," while obviously strong, manifested itself only negatively for many years. Garrison had not yet appeared with his words of fire. No avenues for action had yet been charted. Like all the early Abolitionists he hoped that education would in time remove the blot of slavery from the land. Moreover, having married at the age of twenty and having soon to provide for a growing family — he had two wives and became the father of twenty children — he found himself too busy earning a living to think of much else. Of an optimistic temperament and confident of his own shrewdness in business, he involved himself in one commercial enterprise after another. He was in turn a farmer, a tanner, a land speculator, a breeder of sheep and race horses, a postmaster, and finally a wool merchant. Although " he *habitually expected to succeed* in his undertakings," he failed in every one and was frequently in financial straits. By the time he was forty-five he had figured as a defendant in twenty-one lawsuits in the Ravenna (Ohio) Court of Common Pleas. Preoccupation with partners and creditors explains why, notwithstanding his " unceasing and anxious care for the present and everlasting welfare of every one in my family," he was so often away from home and so often penniless.

All these years he continued to nurse his Abolitionist sentiments. Although there is no documentary evidence of his thoughts on the subject during his twenties, his later statements indicate that he must have brooded over the problem throughout this period. Only a man who has given deep thought to the question of slavery could write as he did to his brother Frederick in 1834: " I have been trying to devise some means whereby I might do something in a practical way for my poor fellowmen who are in bondage." In the same letter he discussed his wish to adopt a colored boy, even if he had to buy him, and bring him up together with his own children. Even more appealing to him was the idea of founding a school " for blacks " — which had been with him " a favorite theme of reflection for years." Shortly afterwards, however, new financial difficulties made it necessary for him to move from Pennsylvania, where he had made his home for some time, back to Ohio. There he at once became engrossed in business, and his melioristic projects went the way of many of his other schemes.

The dramatic murder of Elijah P. Lovejoy, which shocked the entire North, brought about a radical change in Brown's attitude towards slavery. The attack convinced him that the slaveowners would never willingly abolish an institution which was to their material benefit, and that it was necessary to fight force with force. Never a loquacious man, he made no effort to ally himself with the " ranting " Garrisonians. Brooding in solitude, he soon conceived the idea of invading " dark Africa " and freeing the slaves at the point of the gun. Some time in 1839, according to family testimony, he explained his purpose to his wife and three elder sons and swore them to secrecy. The illegality of his plan never occurred to him: How could he do wrong in fighting the battle of the Lord!

He was shrewd enough to realize that so daring a scheme could succeed only if carried out in complete secrecy and with the greatest enterprise and precision. For years, therefore, he kept his plans very much to himself. Outwardly he remained the active, sanguine wool merchant, but the forcible liberation of slaves had definitely become the task uppermost in his mind. On frequent trips east, ostensibly on business, he made the acquaintance of prominent Abolitionists and discussed with them the best means of effecting their common purpose. He also befriended numerous Negroes and tried to discover how many would accept his leadership in the effort to free their enslaved brethren. When he met Frederick Douglass and found him worthy of his confidence, he outlined to him his great plan: to enlist a small but determined band of Abolitionists, raid a number of plantations, probably beginning with those in Virginia, free their slaves and bring them to safety in the near-by mountains, and continue these guerrilla attacks until chattel slavery should be at an end. He admitted that this method of emancipation involved the shedding of blood, but insisted that the slaves could not be freed otherwise. The Negro leader was deeply affected by the white man's fanatic belligerency and assured him of his eager support.

The acceleration of the anti-slavery campaign in the late forties increased John Brown's eagerness to carry out his private plan. In 1848 he obtained from Gerrit Smith a parcel of land in the bleak Adirondacks on the promise of settling his family next to the Negro settlement established by the wealthy Abolitionist. With his usual insensibility to the discomfort of his wife and children he moved them to North Elba shortly before he himself left for Europe on a business venture. The trip proved a financial fiasco, but it gave him an opportunity to study battlefields at first hand.

About this time he issued *Sambo's Mistakes,* a brief pamphlet written in the form of an old black's reminiscences, in which he advised Negroes to be thrifty, practical, and virtuous in order that they might establish themselves as free men. When the Fugitive Slave Law was passed, he rallied the escaped Negroes to resist capture with their very lives. To his wife he wrote: " It now seems that the Fugitive Slave Law was to be the means of making more Abolitionists than all the lectures we have had for years. It really looks as if God had his hand in this wickedness also. I of course keep encouraging my colored friends to ' trust in God and keep their powder dry.' " To this end he organized the League of Gileadites and wrote for it his *Words of Advice,* in which he exhorted the members to keep in mind that " in Union there is strength," and to " make clean work " of anyone attempting to capture a fugitive slave. " Stand by one another, and by your friends, while a drop of blood remains; and be hanged, if you must, but tell no tales out of school " — counsel which he himself was later to follow so courageously. Nothing much came of this agitation. Some forty-odd Negroes joined the lone branch of the Gileadites in Springfield, Massachusetts, where Brown was then in business; but no member ever followed the tenets of his leader or risked his life on account of an escaped fellow Negro.

John Brown was too much of a fanatic to be discouraged by failure. Once an idea entered his mind he could not rid himself of it except by putting it into action. Beset by lawsuits and the worries of an insolvent business, and balked in his anti-slavery efforts, he tenaciously pursued his study of ways and means to accomplish " his greatest or principal object." His hair was graying rapidly and the toll of a hard life showed on his lined face, so that people began to think of him as aged. Yet his soul was more than ever actively dedicated to his lifework. He pored over the books of great military leaders; he studied detailed maps of the border terrain; he read the current periodicals, and his heart gladdened to note the rising tide of anti-slavery sentiment. By the time he finally unraveled the legal tangle which had kept him worried and wary in a business that no longer interested him, and was thus free to devote himself wholly to his great plan, he had completed his spiritual metamorphosis. The call from Kansas found him ready for his new role as guerrilla chieftain.

When the Kansas-Nebraska Bill was enacted, Senator Charles Sumner remarked: " [It] annuls all past compromises with slavery and makes all future compromises impossible. Thus it puts freedom and slavery face to face and bids them grapple." The contest began the moment the territory was opened to settlers. From Maine to Texas all kinds of men — hoodlums and adventurers, farmers and fanatics — hurried to test the validity of " squatter sovereignty." With many of them it was a desperate business, and they were ready to give their lives for their principles. Because the bordering state of Missouri had 50,000 slaves, its planters stopped at nothing to save themselves from the dreaded consequences of a free Kansas. According to Senator David R. Achison, their leader and chief of the Border Ruffians, " a horde of our Western savages with avowed purposes of destruction would be less formidable neighbors than the Abolitionists." General B. F. Stringfellow, another " fire-eater," thus addressed a troop of hirelings about to depart for Kansas: " I tell you to mark every scoundrel among you who is the least tainted with abolitionism and exterminate him. Neither give nor take any quarter, as the Cause demands it."

The Abolitionists were equally active in their efforts to gain control of the territory. The Emigrant Aid Society, organized in New England, did all in its power to encourage free-state men to hurry to Kansas. The Missourians, however, being nearer and less scrupulous, were the first to dominate the territorial government by the simple device of stuffing the ballot boxes. Moreover, since the most direct way to Kansas led through Missouri, they made it difficult for the Northerners to reach their destination and sought to intimidate those who did settle on the land. Within a few months, however, the free-soilers had arrived in sufficient numbers to challenge the authority of the pro-slavery officials. They called several conventions of their own, voted for a free-state constitution, and refused to recognize the acts passed by the existing legislature. The two governments fought desperately for control of the territory, and both resorted to intimidation, pillage, and bloodshed.

John Brown's elder sons were among the first to join the exciting crusade. When, in the fall of 1854, they informed their father of their decision to settle in Kansas, he replied: " If you or any of my family are disposed to go to Kansas or Nebraska, with a view to help defeat Satan and his legions in that direction, I have not a word to say; but I feel committed to operate in another part of the field. If I were not so committed, I would be on my way this fall." The following spring five of his sons reached Kansas, eager to cultivate their parcels of land and ready to do their share to keep the territory free. They came as men of peace, bringing with them fruit trees, grapevines, and farm implements, and having among them only one revolver and two small squirrel rifles. A band of Ruffians accosted them shortly after their arrival and wanted to know to which side the newcomers belonged. It did not take the Browns long to ascertain the state of affairs, and they were "thoroughly determined to fight" to keep slavery out of Kansas. The eldest of the brothers immediately requested his father to send them Minié guns and intimated that the free-soilers were badly in need of a leader to direct them in the fight against the pro-slavery forces.

At this news the fiery Abolitionist was ready to meet his destiny. Not yet prepared for his major action, he thought that a venture into Kansas would not only help keep the territory free but also test his skill as a guerrilla fighter. In his fifty-fifth year, gray and gaunt, he felt the fire in his soul flare with intense brightness. On taking leave of his wife he said:

For twenty years I have never made any business arrangement which would prevent me at any time answering the call of the Lord. I have kept my affairs in such condition that in two weeks I could wind them up and be ready to obey that call permitting nothing to stand in the way of duty — neither wife, children, nor worldly goods. That hour is now near at hand, and all who are willing to act should be ready.

He made no effort, however, to reach his sons directly, but tarried to preach his doctrine and to collect money and ammunition in various towns along his route. He did not reach Osawatomie till early in October.

John Brown had come to Kansas to wage war against the slavocrats, and was making no secret of it. With Hebraic fierceness he was ready to put the enemy to the sword. " *I am here,*" he declared, " *to promote the killing of American slavery.*" He was quick to discover, however, that few free-soilers were of his mind. Most of them were as determined to keep Negroes out of the territory as to keep it free. During his first visit to Lawrence, the seat of the free-staters, he was greatly chagrined by the timid treaty of peace arranged by the town leaders with the Border Ruffians. He mounted the platform immediately after them and urged the gathering to repudiate their spokesmen and to drive the pro-slavery forces out of Kansas. " I'm an Abolitionist, dyed in the wool," he announced, and offered to lead them in the attack. But none volunteered, and he left for Osawatomie in an angry but unyielding mood.

Meantime the proponents of slavery were busy strengthening their initial advantage. Early in 1856 Senator Achison exhorted them to make short work of the free-staters: " Get ready, arm yourself; for if they abolitionize Kansas you lose $150,000,000 of your property. I am satisfied I can justify every act of yours before God and a jury." A fortnight later the *Squatter Sovereign,* one of the local periodicals engaged in the controversy, had this to say regarding the Northerners who were arguing for a government of their own choosing: " In our opinion the only effectual way to correct the evils that now exist is to hang up to the nearest tree the very last traitor who was instrumental in getting up, or participating in, the celebrated Topeka Convention." The wounding of Sheriff Jones by free-staters two months later caused the same weekly to write: " We are now in favor of leveling Lawrence and chastising the Traitors there congregated, should it result in total destruction of the Union." And after another week: " In a fight let our motto be, ' War to the knife, and knife to the hilt, asking no quarters from them and granting none.' *Jones' Murder Must be Revenged!!* " Jones was not dead; but that spring several free-soilers were killed and scores were robbed and beaten as a consequence of this agitation.

Old Brown was familiar not only with these inflammatory speeches and editorials but also with the outrages and misdeeds perpetrated by the Ruffians. Rumor brought the news of each attack, of every insult and threat, on the wings of fervent hate. The Kansas atmosphere was charged with the electricity of internecine conflict, ready to discharge with the first disturbance. The reports, exaggerated in the telling, greatly perturbed the impetuous Abolitionist. He ached to repay the Ruffians in their own coin, " to strike terror into the hearts of the pro-slavery people." As Oswald Garrison Villard has pointed out: " Brown was prepared to meet violence with violence, to do to the Border Ruffians what they were doing to Free-Soilers. To accomplish this, he was ready to take from the pro-slavery men their chattels, living and immovable, and even their lives." It was his hope that by doing this work of the Lord he would

not only help make Kansas a free state but also precipitate the
conflict which was to give slavery its deathblow."

His opportunity came late in May when the volunteer troop led
by his eldest son was called to defend Lawrence against imminent
attack. Learning on the way that the free-state town had already
been sacked, the company decided to return home. But not old
John Brown. He told Weiner, one of the men, that "now something *must* be done. We have got to defend our families and our
neighbors as best we can. Something *is going to be done now*. We
must show by actual work that there are two sides to this thing and
that they cannot go on with impunity." When someone urged
caution, he exclaimed impatiently: "Caution, caution, sir. I am
eternally tired of hearing that word caution. It is nothing but the
word of cowardice." Thereupon he set out with four of his sons
and three others — "a little company by ourselves" — to perform
his duty as he saw it. Holding back in hiding till after Saturday in
order to do the Lord's work on the Lord's Day, he led his band in
the dead of night to the small pro-slavery settlement on the Pottawatomie, wakened the men named on a list he had previously obtained, and had five of them killed in cold blood. He had no previous traffic with these victims. Nor were they to his knowledge
guilty of any overt act against their free-soil neighbors. It was enough
for the vengeful fanatic that they had favored slavery and therefore
had committed murder in their hearts. To him they were merely a
means of putting the fear of God into the slavocrats — of fighting
the Ruffians with their own ruthlessness; the mutilated bodies in
the Pottawatomie were his way of giving notice to the advocates of
slavery that Old Brown had declared war upon them and would
stop at nothing to drive them out of Kansas.

The news shocked and horrified everyone. Free-staters were
quick to condemn the crime and to disclaim any foreknowledge of
it. Posses of enraged Ruffians scoured the vicinity in vain for the
murderers and wreaked vengeance upon their cowering opponents.
Among the numerous victims were John Brown, Jr., and his brother
Jason, the two sons who had not taken part in the massacre; when

they protested their innocence, the Rev. Martin White, bellicose pro-slavery preacher who was later to kill their brother Frederick without provocation, told them that " we hold every man a scoundrel till he is proven honest."

But the Ruffians failed to find the " little company." Indeed, Old Brown soon proved himself their master not only in ruthlessness but in daring as well. In addition, he had the advantage of his intensive study of guerrilla tactics. Immediately after leaving Pottawatomie he hid with his companions in a thick wood near by. Never admitting his part in the massacre, he prepared for war as if he were a general in a holy crusade. He bore hardship as a matter of course, and imbued the youths under him with the glory of fighting for the right. To James Redpath, the New York *Tribune* correspondent, who sought him out in his hideout, he said: " Give me men of good principles; God-fearing men; men who respect themselves, and with a dozen of them I will oppose any hundred such men as these Bufford ruffians." His chance to prove this boast came a few days later. At Black Jack he succeeded, with a much smaller force, in defeating and capturing Captain H. C. Pate and his troop. This victory, gained by courage and cunning, so astonished everyone in Kansas that he found it possible to come out in the open and assume his unchallenged role as the anti-slavery champion. For the free-soilers now perceived the pragmatic effect of Pottawatomie and were prepared to overlook its moral implications. As Governor Robinson, their foremost leader, subsequently explained: " He was the only man who comprehended the situation, and saw the absolute necessity of some such blow and had the nerve to strike it."

Old Brown now regarded himself at war with the pro-slavery forces and did not scruple to raid their settlements for supplies and horses — asserting that he was merely taking back what had originally belonged to the free-soilers. Since the Ruffians were equally adept at robbery, both sides terrorized the more peaceful settlers during this period. The climax of this open warfare came at the end of August with the battle at Osawatomie. It began with the shooting of huge Frederick Brown as he went out at dawn to feed the horses. The shot was a signal for attack, and General Reid and his Ruffians opened fire on the free-soilers in the immediate vicinity. John Brown, then some distance away, was notified of the murder of his son and he at once hurried to engage the enemy. He commanded only about forty men in all, most of them without experience in fighting. One of the youths, having never before been under fire, wanted to know what he should do. " Take more care to end your life well than to live long," was his leader's quick rejoinder. Brown's men fought spiritedly, but had to retire before a force six times as large. Yet the rare courage displayed that day by the old warrior had forever joined his name with Osawatomie.

Brown's fanatical fierceness and ruthless audacity made him an ogre in the eyes of the Ruffians and a " terrible saint " to the free-soilers. Anti-slavery raids were credited to him even when he had not the slightest connection with them. So widespread had his fame become and so feared was he by the enemy that his admirers boasted at the time that " Old John Brown's name is equal to an army with banners."

The hero of Osawatomie, however, was a very sick man during the late summer months. Prolonged privation and intensive exertion had sapped his strength and finally brought him down with dysentery and ague. Unable to remain in the saddle further, knowing that his efforts had strengthened the free-staters, and certain that the coming of winter would interrupt the fighting, Brown decided in October to leave Kansas for quieter quarters, in order to rest and recover.

John Brown's interest in Kansas must have begun to wane as soon as he believed it safe from Southern domination. His " greatest or principal object " was, after all, not so much to make the territory free as to eradicate slavery from the land. " I have only a short time to live," he had stated after Osawatomie, " and only one death to die, and I will die fighting for this cause. There will be no peace in this land until slavery is done for. I will give them something else to do than to extend slavery. I will carry the war to Africa."

After about a week in Tabor, Iowa, he felt strong enough to proceed to Chicago. Ostensibly his trip eastward was being made for the purpose of collecting funds and arms for the struggle in Kansas. Actually he was exploiting the fighting in that territory and his part in it as a means of furthering his undisclosed plan. His begging of money from town to town, his hoarding of ammunition, his efforts to enlist and train " volunteer regulars " under a formal drillmaster — everything he was to do from this time to the futile raid on Harpers Ferry, pertained to his preparation for the " African invasion."

The dilatoriness, the distrustfulness, and the downright niggardliness of the affluent Abolitionists in the East nearly broke Old Brown's heart during the extended period between Osawatomie and Harpers Ferry. He reached New England in December, 1856, and at once began a round of visits to men of wealth and influence. Wherever he could obtain a hearing he addressed public meetings. Although he made a favorable impression on almost everyone he met, and such men as Emerson and Thoreau were pleased to speak favorably of his courage and volcanic energy, the net result in money and guns was scant indeed.

One reason for this failure was his secretiveness. When he was asked in 1857 whether the funds he was then collecting would be used to invade slave territory, Brown's reply was characteristically evasive: " I do not expose my plans. No one knows them but myself, except perhaps one. I will not be interrogated; if you wish to give me anything I want you to give it freely. I have no other purpose but to serve the cause of liberty." Even to so sympathetic a friend as Theodore Parker, whom he had asked to help finance the training of his little band of volunteers in Iowa, he would say no more than that he needed the money " for secret service, and no question asked." That most Abolitionists were also pacifists and did not wish to encourage Brown in the shedding of blood was another reason for failure. Most important, perhaps, was the general assumption that the free-soilers in Kansas were no longer in need of self-protection, since they were by that time a strong majority and progressing rapidly towards their rightful control of the government machinery of the territory. The meagre response galled the irascible fighter, who was still suffering from chronic ague and fever as a consequence of the Kansas campaign. He felt that since he was prepared to give his life in fighting the battle of the Lord, others should provide him at least with the necessary means.

In November 1857, Brown was back in Kansas for a fortnight, "keeping very quiet, and looking about to see how the land lies." When he satisfied himself that the prevailing truce would continue through the coming winter, he did little more than try to procure volunteers for his "African invasion." Late next June, however, after another disappointing sojourn in the East, he again returned to Kansas, this time under the name of Shubel Morgan, and remained as an active participant in the renewed fighting until the end of the year. Soon after his arrival he witnessed the conclusive defeat of the slavery forces at the polls. But Hamilton's brutal massacre of a number of free-staters renewed the guerrilla warfare, and Brown-Morgan, despite his recurring malarial fever, was at hand wherever trouble was brewing. That his belligerence was motivated only by his hatred of slavery is attested by his refusal to kill the murderer of his son Frederick when he had him in his power. "I do not harbor the feelings of revenge," he told his followers. "*I act from a principle*. My aim and object is to restore human rights."

The chance to test his long-nurtured plan of "African invasion" came late in December, when a Negro appeared in his camp to plead that he and other slaves on a near-by Missouri plantation be saved from removal to the deep South. The impulsive Abolitionist acted with characteristic promptness. As George Gill, one of his followers, explained: "I am sure that Brown, in his mind, was just waiting for something to turn up; or in his way of thinking, was expecting or hoping that 'God would provide him a basis of action.' When this came he hailed it as heaven-sent." Again choosing the

Sabbath, he and several of his men raided the plantation as well as a neighboring one, took eleven slaves and all the valuables they could cart away, and returned safely to their hiding place in Kansas. Unfortunately, his lieutenant Stevens, who had ventured forth with a few volunteers on a similar mission, killed the owner in freeing a Negress. There was a hysterical outcry against the crime, and Border Ruffians and federal soldiers set out to capture the raiders. Rewards for the apprehension of the gang were immediately offered by both the President of the United States and the Governor of Missouri. But at no time was Brown in danger of seizure or betrayal: he was more than a match for his pro-slavery enemies and too popular among the free-soilers to fear treachery. It took him three months to bring the eleven slaves to safety in Canada, since he could not resist the temptation to appeal for funds on the way; but he accomplished this feat without a mishap, despite the reward of $3,250 posted within view of his auditors at a number of public meetings.

After hearing John Brown speak in Boston, Bronson Alcott remarked: " He did not conceal his hatred of slavery, and less his readiness to strike a blow for freedom at the fitting moment. I thought him equal to anything he should dare: the man to do the deed necessary to be done with the patriotic zeal, the martyr's temper and purpose." More and more Brown's fanaticism began to overflow the confines of reality. He had come to think of himself as the new Moses whom God had chosen as " the deliverer of slaves." In February 1858, shortly after he had divulged his plan of invasion to B. F. Sanborn and Gerrit Smith, he wrote to the former that " the whole world during the present and future generations *may reap* " from the successful execution of his scheme. " I have only had," he continued, " *this* one opportunity in a life of nearly sixty years, and could I be continued ten times as long again, I might not again have an equal opportunity." This febrile fervor was evident in his behavior during his final sojourn in Kansas. William Hutchinson, the New York *Times* correspondent who had visited him a few days after the Missouri raid, wrote later: " I am sure he talked on that till the small hours, and his all absorbing theme was ' my work,' ' my great duty,' ' my mission,' etc., meaning of course, the liberation of the slaves. He seemed to have no other object in life, no other hope or ambition. The utmost sincerity pervaded his every thought and word."

When the old warrior learned of the effectiveness of his Missouri raid — the slaveowners in that vicinity had had to go to the expense of keeping a strong guard over their Negroes — he ached to make a similar attack on a much larger scale and in a different region. So bent was he on this " African invasion " that, when his brother Jeremiah, whom he visited in Ohio on his way east, urged him to return to his work and his family interests, he insisted he could not since " he knew he was in the line of his duty and he must pursue it though it should destroy him and his family." In his final desperate efforts to collect funds for his momentous mission he appeared to many people to be insane.

Like most Abolitionists, Brown thought of slavery in terms of abstract morality. Because human bondage was to him " the sum of all villainies," he was certain that all slaves yearned to be delivered and would eagerly do his bidding the moment he called on them to rebel. When Colonel William A. Phillips tried to point out that Negroes were actually a meek and intimidated lot, Brown assured him to the contrary: " You have not studied them right, and you have not studied them long enough. Human nature is the same everywhere." His failure to organize free Negroes into Gileadite groups had not weakened this belief. Nor was he in the slightest disillusioned by the pitifully small attendance at the convention in Chatham, Canada, which he had called for the purpose of obtaining Negro support for his campaign. Of the many thousands of blacks then living in the British Dominion only thirty-four appeared at the meetings. With his customary forcefulness he proceeded to explain his plan of organization, to read the constitution that he himself had written, and to appoint the staff that was to carry the war to Africa. He was totally unaware of the fantastic and pathetic aspects of the enterprise. Nor did it occur to him that the possible refusal of the slaves to stampede to his standard would mean failure and death to himself and his volunteers. In his final secret interview with Frederick Douglass he urged the Negro leader to take part in the raid in order to give courage to the freed slaves. "When I strike," he explained, "the bees will begin to swarm, and I shall want you to help me hive them." But the shrewd and realistic former slave, after vainly pleading with Brown to forsake his mad scheme, deliberately refused to place his head in the hangman's noose.

Having overcome his friend Sanborn's objections that the invasion was "desperate in its character, wholly inadequate in its provision of means, and of most uncertain result," John Brown was ready for his final firm action. So strong was his conviction that "something startling was needed" to bring the issue of slavery to a head, that he could no longer wait until he had enough men and means. On June 30, 1859, he arrived in Hagerstown, Maryland, with two of his sons and the faithful Jeremiah Anderson to spy out the land. Under the name of I. Smith he rented the Kennedy farm, situated about five miles from Harpers Ferry, and began to study the terrain and to prepare the attack. Throughout the summer he worked anxiously, brooding over the timidity of his wealthy supporters and the failure of his lieutenants to recruit the required number of volunteers. Desperate yet sanguine, he proceeded to carry out his self-imposed task to the best of his ability. With Andrew Jackson be believed that "one man with courage is a majority."

His plan was to capture Harpers Ferry by sudden attack, open its richly stocked arsenal to the slaves — who were certain to flock to him on learning the glad tidings — close the mountain passes and drive ever southward with his swelling forces of white and black volunteers until the country was rid of slavery. With twenty-one men in all — sixteen white and five black — he started out on the night of October 16, once more on the eve of the Sabbath, in the direction of Harpers Ferry. By daybreak he was in complete control of the town and the federal arsenal. He had also taken a number of prominent hostages. When asked by what authority he was taking possession of public property, he answered: " By the authority of God Almighty." Although he knew he was committing treason and was with his little band challenging the military might of an inimical federal government, he had made no provision for retreat. Trusting in God's might, he neglected to cover a river that separated him from the safety of the hills, allowed a train to pass through and sound the alarm, and scattered his scant forces. Once the mad venture became known, it was crushed with tragic ruthlessness. Brown and his troop fought bravely to the last moment, defying the proud Virginia Guard and a detachment of the United States army commanded by Colonel Robert E. Lee; but after two days of desperate resistance ten of his men, including his two sons, lay dead or dying, Brown himself and four others were under arrest, and the remainder were in flight.

News of the event exploded on the pages of the nation's press. Southerners, fearful of the portent, clamored for the immediate hanging of the culprits. As after Pottawatomie, the first reaction in the North was one of recoil and condemnation; only a few extreme Abolitionists approved treason as a means of achieving Negro emancipation. Yet within a few days most Northerners became warmly sympathetic towards the ill and aged fanatic.

Virginia's almost spiteful haste to dispatch its notorious prisoner from this world gave impetus to the radical shift in Northern opinion. Regardless of his wounds and objections, Brown was tried a week after his arrest, and quickly condemned to die within a month. Even more influential was the old man's brave deportment. His simple yet moving eloquence in court and his remarkably effective letters convinced even his enemies of his patriarchal probity. His utter fearlessness and complete unselfishness likewise added greatly to his stature in the public imagination. Bronson Alcott spoke the minds of many when he said: " This deed of his, so surprising, so mixed, so confounding to most persons, will give an impulse to freedom and humanity, whatever becomes of its victim and of the States that howl over it."

Wendell Phillips and other men of prominence began to agitate for John Brown's liberation; Northern newspapers lionized him in their columns; table-talk everywhere dwelt upon his self-abnegation and his impending martyrdom. The court proceedings were described in minute detail in periodicals of every sort. Indeed, up to that time no American trial had aroused such controversy and bitter feeling. By the time it was over and the expected sentence was pronounced — a matter of several days — the entire North and many in Europe hailed the doomed old fanatic as the martyred hero who, almost single-handed, had tried to destroy the monster of slavery.

" I am ready for my fate," John Brown told the court at the outset. " I do not ask for a trial. I beg for no mockery of a trial — no insult — nothing but that which conscience gives, or cowardice would drive you to practice." Several days later he wrote to his family: " Under all these terrible calamities; I feel quite cheerful in the assurance that God reigns; and will overrule all for his glory; and the best possible good. I feel *no* consciousness of *guilt* in the matter: nor even mortification on account of my imprisonment; and irons. . . ." Before sentence was pronounced he addressed the court with a homely eloquence that moved deeply the hearts of his Northern sympathizers and lovers of liberty and justice the world over:

Had I so interfered in behalf of the rich, the powerful, the intelligent, the so-called great . . . it would have been all right. Every man in this Court would have deemed it an act worthy of reward rather than punishment. . . . I believe that to have interfered as I have done, in behalf of His despised poor, I did no wrong, but right. Now, if it is deemed necessary that I should forfeit my life for the furtherance of the ends of justice, and mingle blood further with the blood of my children and with the blood of millions in this slave country whose rights are disregarded by wicked, cruel and unjust enactments, I say, let it be done. . . .

Sentenced to be hanged on December 2, Brown felt no regret or self-pity. He tended to identify his plight with that of Jesus, saying: "Jesus of Nazareth was doomed in like manner. Why should I not be?" Eager for a martyrdom that would strike hard against slavery, he refused his counsel permission to take advantage of the streak of insanity in his family which might have saved him from the gallows. He likewise frowned on all efforts to help him escape. Throughout the trial he concentrated not on saving his life but on fighting the "enemy." On one such occasion he remarked: "I think I cannot now better serve the cause I love so much than to die for it; and in my death I may do more than in my life." What buoyed his spirit most was the satisfaction that his life's work was done. "As I believe most firmly that God reigns, I cannot believe that anything I have done, suffered, or may yet suffer, will be lost to the cause of God or of humanity. And before I began my work at Harper's Ferry I felt assured that in the worst event it would surely pay." Throughout his last weeks he remained sanguine and benign, greatly pleased with the admiration and praise of his Northern followers. To one of them he said: "I have enjoyed remarkable cheerfulness and composure of mind ever since my confinement, and it is a great comfort to feel assured that I am permitted to die for a cause, not merely to pay the debt of nature — as all must."

To the very last day of his life, in letter after letter and in numerous interviews — his keepers permitted him this much freedom — he was preoccupied with the struggle against slavery. That the conflict had indeed become inescapable he now saw clearly, and he exhorted his family and friends to engage in it with all their might and not to rest until the abomination was eradicated from the land. In the last letter to his family he bequeathed them this legacy: "John Brown writes to his children to abhor, with undying hatred also, the sum of all villainies — slavery." Finally, in a note handed to his keeper on the way to the scaffold, he prophesied: "I John Brown am now quite *certain* that the crimes of this *guilty land: will* never be purged *away*; but with Blood. I had *as I now think: vainly* flattered myself that without *very much* bloodshed; it might be done."

John Brown's remarkable equanimity in the face of death, and even more his complete devotion to the Abolition cause, greatly endeared him to the people in the North and made him a symbol of inspiration long before his body began to molder in the grave. "The innate nobility of the man," wrote Mr. Villard, "his essential unselfishness and his readiness for the supreme sacrifice, all heightened the impending tragedy, and brought to many the conviction that, misguided as he was, here was another martyr whose blood was to be the seed, not of his church, but of his creed." Shortly before his death and long after, the leading reformers at every opportunity extolled his services to the cause of Abolition. George L. Stearns, wealthy Boston businessman and liberal, believed him to be the "representative man of this century, as Washington was of the last." Emerson referred to him as "that new saint who will make the gallows glorious like the cross." Wendell Phillips, in his moving funeral oration, asserted that the man whose body they were about to bury had killed slavery in this country as surely as Warren's death at Bunker Hill had severed our ties with England. In fact, the soul of John Brown was at once on the march — quickening the outbreak of the Civil War and sending young men to an eager death to complete the work to which he had given his life.

John Brown's immortality was attained by this chain of circumstances: the nation had become economically ripe for the change to our present industrial society; the people were deeply stirred by the agitation of the Abolitionists; it was not generally known that Brown had instigated and supervised the Pottawatomie massacre; the self-sacrificing zeal that inspired the raid on Harpers Ferry tended to minimize his guilt in the subsequent bloodshed; Governor Wise's undue haste to deal him Virginia's justice could not but react in the victim's favor; most of all, his final saintly behavior helped to cover his previous reprehensible acts with the martyr's mantle. An unfavorable shift of events might easily have deprived him of historical significance. If, for instance, the Abolitionist leaders had known in 1856 of what had taken place at Pottawatomie — only many years later was Brown's part in the murders fully confirmed — it is more than likely that they would have recoiled from any contact with him and thus condemned him to the obscurity to which time has relegated the other Kansas outlaws.

But speculation is now pointless. Even his detractors concede that John Brown, by the power of his fanatical faith and audacious action, succeeded in dramatizing the conflict between industrialized North and slavocratic South and in precipitating the war which was to doom the system of society based on chattel labor. This achievement, untarnished by the bloodshed of which he was certainly guilty, has forever illumined his name in the annals of American history.

WENDELL PHILLIPS

AGITATOR FOR THE COMMON GOOD

UNLIKE EITHER GARRISON OR BROWN, Wendell Phillips, born in 1811, grew up in an atmosphere of cultural sufficiency. He belonged to one of Boston's most distinguished families, being the seventh in direct line of descent from the Rev. George Phillips who had come to Salem in 1630 to practise the Puritan way of life. As the attractive and gifted son of the city's first mayor, he had as his early companions the sons of leading families. Thomas G. Appleton, J. Lothrop Motley, and Charles Sumner were among his closest boyhood friends. On completing his preparatory studies in the famous Boston Latin School, he entered Harvard at the age of sixteen, where he made his mark as a brilliant student, the leader of his aristocratic set, and an outstanding athlete. He was also the first orator of his class, and proceeded with the study of law as a matter of course. With the eminent Judge Story as his mentor, he easily learned the fine points in the writings of Coke and Blackstone and displayed an intellectual vigor that promised a successful career. In 1834 he was admitted to the bar of Massachusetts with the cordial blessings of his teachers and elders.

" At this time," writes his biographer Carlos Martyn, " there was nothing of the radical about him — hardly a flavor of democracy. He seemed to be the predestined leader of American conservatism, the inevitable champion of class distinctions and elegant leisure." The truth is not quite so obliging. Young Phillips was a genuine aristocrat, but he was also an authentic son of the American Revo-

[60]

lution. Puritan in thought and in his way of life, a conscious believer in the inalienability of human rights, inherently generous and forthright, he took it for granted that the law of the land was based upon the principles of the Declaration of Independence. In his sheltered existence at home and in school, however, he had met with nothing to jolt his equanimity. Until his twenty-fifth year he had found it easy to assume that he was living in the best of all possible worlds.

On the warm afternoon of October 24, 1835, while sitting before an open window of his office, the young lawyer's attention was attracted by angry street noises. On going out he discovered that a disorderly and abusive mob was dragging a disheveled man by a rope fastened around his waist. A bystander told him the victim was William Lloyd Garrison, "the damned Abolitionist." Phillips saw that the attackers were men he had known all his life — some of them members of his own regiment. The shocking injustice outraged his sense of right; the thought that it was being enacted by men of civic prominence — men he had highly respected — struck at the very foundations of his social morality. Deeply thoughtful, he returned to his office. He simply could not square the doctrines of the Constitution, which he had sworn to uphold, with the sight of " gentlemen of property and standing" trying to lynch a man for exercising his legal prerogatives.

The experience shattered young Phillips's proud faith in the essential democracy of his social set. The image of the victimized Abolitionist remained before his mind's eye, and the more he thought of him the more he admired Garrison's courage and convictions. That a man should be ready to die for a cause made both very attractive to his idealistic nature. It was not easy for him, however, to shed forthwith the habits and prejudices that he had acquired in childhood. It was only after he had come under the beguiling influence of Ann Terry Greene, an active member of the Female Anti-Slavery Society and one of the women driven from the hall at the time Garrison had been seized by the mob, that he began to break with his conservative past. His friendship, indeed, quickly became love and the enamored couple married on October 12, 1837. Years later he remarked in this connection: "My wife made an out-and-out Abolitionist out of me, and she always preceded me in the adoption of the various causes I have advocated."

In the 1830's Bostonians were in the main uninterested in the slavery question. The number of Abolitionists was still small, while most of the leaders of public opinion were conservative and ready to disregard issues of a disturbing nature. But in 1837 the murder of Elijah P. Lovejoy in Illinois was too shocking to be ignored. Several men of eminence, led by Dr. William Ellery Channing, publicly wished to protest against this egregious violation of a free press and organized a meeting in Faneuil Hall. The attendance was large, and the majority appeared to favor Dr. Channing's denunciatory resolutions. One of the invited speakers, however, was James T. Austin, the conservative attorney-general of Massachusetts, and his harangue succeeded in turning a large part of the audience against the victim of the pro-slavery mob, who in the words of his detractor had "died as the fool dieth." The tirade was no sooner over than the hall began to ring with the uproar of contending factions. Just then young Wendell Phillips, who had come to the meeting with his wife, leaped upon the rostrum, overcame the interference of Austin's followers, and refuted the attorney-general's arguments in a strong, clear voice and with a logic at once simple and persuasive. It was this speech that established him as Boston's greatest orator. Oliver Johnson, who was in the hall, remarked later: "Never before, I venture to say, did the walls of the old 'Cradle of Liberty' echo to a finer strain of eloquence." When the deafening applause had finally died down, and Dr. Channing's motions had been adopted by acclamation, Phillips found himself both a hero and a social outlaw. His great speech had lost him the friends of his boyhood, the favor of his powerful elders; but it had won him what he began to prize much more — a clear conscience and leadership in the Abolition movement.

Wendell Phillips's ethical fervor, dormant throughout a happy yet uneventful youth but now galvanized into action by the enemies of Abolition, represented the Puritan conscience at its finest flowering. As a true Christian he felt impelled to practise the precepts of the Sermon on the Mount; as a genuine democrat he believed that the Declaration of Independence was and should be the guiding star of our republic. There were, of course, many like him during the first half of the nineteenth century: men and women who were close enough to the Nazarene and the Founding Fathers to insist that a human being has an inalienable right to life, liberty, and the pursuit of happiness. But Phillips towered over them by virtue of his extraordinary spiritual zeal and his great eloquence. The kindliest of men in his daily conduct, he was always rigorously uncompromising in his denunciation of wrongdoers, not sparing even his closest friends when it became a choice between them and his convictions.

Thinking over the problem of slavery after the mobbing of Garrison, Young Phillips discovered to his consternation that, in the words of John Quincy Adams, "a knot of slaveholders give the law and prescribe the policy of the country." He refused to accept a condition that furthered such iniquity, and determined to fight it with all his strength. Encouraged by Garrison's righteousness and his wife's love, he ignored ostracism and the estrangement of his family — all of them, except his mother, broke with him. Fortunately provided with a modest income, he gave up the practice of law in order not to be bound by his oath to a Constitution that permitted the existence of chattel slavery.

After a pleasant and instructive sojourn in Europe during the years 1839–41, in the vain hope of relieving his wife's increasing invalidism, he returned to this country eager to further the anti-slavery movement. He read assiduously to equip his alert mind with the facts of history and the essentials of the human thought of past ages. Thus he developed the effective flow of wit and argument which were to make his lectures so pungent and persuasive.

Wendell Phillips spoke unwittingly for himself when he said:

"The reformer is careless of numbers, disregards popularity, and deals only with ideas, conscience, and common sense." For he was a strong believer in the supreme power of ideas, in the great advantages of education, and in the essential goodness of mankind. "The people always mean right," he insisted, "and in the end they will do right." Taking ready advantage of the popularity of the lyceum, he made the public platform the center for the freest discussion of the questions of the day. With Faneuil Hall as his headquarters, and with every lecture room in the North packed on his arrival, he was able to broadcast his denunciations and exhortations to his eager Northern audiences. More than any other man of his generation, he fought for social reforms and exercised his golden voice and irrefutable logic in behalf of the common good.

Wendell Phillips stood shoulder to shoulder with Garrison in his opposition to the forces that fought immediate emancipation. None escaped his scathing castigations. Thus, although he remained to the end an orthodox Christian and would not accept the prevailing liberal creed of Unitarianism, he fiercely attacked the clergy for condoning slavery. Nor was he intimidated by the veneration with which his fellow Americans had come to regard the Constitution. He believed firmly that whatever favored the slave system was noxious and argued that "the Constitution and government of the country is worth nothing, except as it is or can be made capable of grappling with the great question of slavery." To him the Bible was infinitely more sacred than the Constitution, and the final authority on the issue of human bondage. Speaking in 1842 in behalf of Latimer, an escaped slave to whom Judge Shaw had refused to grant a trial by jury, he said: "We presume to believe that the Bible outweighs the statute-book. When I look on those crowded thousands and see them trample on their consciences and on the rights of their fellowmen, at the bidding of a piece of parchment, I say, my curse be on the Constitution of these United States!" A decade later, when the government had ceased to protect Negroes even in the North and was helping to harry fugitive

slaves out of their hiding places, the outraged orator defied it publicly and proclaimed his non-allegiance: " I am not to be bullied
by institutions. I am not to be frightened by parchments. Forms
and theories are nothing to me. Majorities are nothing." Only human freedom mattered, and for that right he was ready to fight to
his last breath.

This extraordinary courage and firmness of purpose Phillips displayed most effectively immediately after John Brown's raid on
Harpers Ferry. A wave of panicky condemnation beat against the
captured and wounded fanatic. Even the prominent Abolitionists
who had backed him with a full knowledge of his quixotic plans
either disowned him or went into hiding. Phillips, however, along
with Thoreau, at once perceived the full significance of Brown's
action. Although he had known nothing of it beforehand, and
would not have approved of it if he had, he insisted that the prisoner receive full and impartial justice. On the Sunday following
the raid he stood before an unsympathetic audience in Beecher's
church in Brooklyn and spoke out boldly for Brown's right to violate the laws that kept men enslaved. His eloquent defense, featured in Northern newspapers the next morning, helped materially to turn the tide of public opinion in favor of the man whom
Virginia was determined to hang. And at John Brown's open grave
in bleak North Elba, Phillips uttered the prophecy that was to be
realized even sooner than he himself knew:

History will date Virginia's Emancipation from Harper's Ferry. True,
the slave is still there. So, when the tempest uproots a pine on your hills,
it looks green for months, — a year or two. Still it is timber, not a tree.
John Brown has loosened the roots of the slave system; it only breathes,
— it does not live, — hereafter.

Confronted from the beginning with a condition which kept the
United States half slave and half free and its government in the
hands of pro-slavery men, Phillips did not hesitate to take his stand.
When the charge was made that the Abolition movement was disrupting the Union, he declared:

[65]

If lawful and peaceful efforts for the abolition of slavery in our land will dissolve it, let the Union go. Love it as we may, and cherish it as we do, equally with the loudest of our opposers, we say, Perish the Union when its cement must be the blood of the slave! — when the rights of one must be secured at the expense of the other!

With the intensification of the sectional struggle Phillips regarded the separation of the states as inevitable; so far as he could see, that was the only way of avoiding the terrible bloodshed of civil war. " As to disunion," he declared confidently, " it must and will come. Calhoun wants it at one end of the Union, Garrison wants it at the other. It is written in the counsels of God."

The shift in opinion brought about by time and changing economic forces made the preservation of the Union a closed issue to the millions of Northerners who disapproved of slave labor and yet were determined to curb it without disrupting that Union. When Lincoln's election in 1860 precipitated the secession of the Southern states, civil war was the obvious consequence. Phillips disregarded his previous opposition to the Union and immediately devoted his great eloquence to the support of the government, perceiving that victory would bring about the abolition of slavery. In explanation of his change of mind he said:

I did hate the Union, when union meant lies in the pulpit and mobs in the streets, when union meant making white men hypocrites and black men slaves. . . . But now — when I see what the Union must mean in order to last, when I see that you cannot have union without meaning justice, and when I see twenty million people, with a current as swift and as inevitable as Niagara, determined that the Union shall mean justice, why should I object to it?

During the first period of the war, when the need to keep the border states in line made it necessary for the government to play down the slavery issue, Phillips became " a whip and a spur." He urged the principle of Abolition upon everyone in a position of power. and insisted that only an ideal of such nobility and magnitude would imbue the army with the spirit of victory:

No man can fight Stonewall Jackson, an honest fanatic on the side of slavery, but John Brown, an equally honest fanatic on the side of freedom. They are the only chemical equals, and will neutralize each other. You cannot neutralize nitric acid with cologne water. William H. Seward is no match for Jefferson Davis. You must have what they have — positive convictions. Otherwise the elements of the struggle are unequal.

When President Lincoln finally decided to make public his Emancipation Proclamation, heralding the end of Negro slavery in the United States, the great Agitator rejoiced in the certainty of victory. He did not, however, slacken his zeal or his vigilance in behalf of the Negroes. In the following year he aided in the formation of two colored regiments in Massachusetts. Later he fought the readmission of those conquered Southern states which did not give the blacks complete equality. " No emancipation can be effectual," he maintained, " and no freedom real, unless the Negro has the ballot and the states are prohibited from enacting laws making any distinctions among their citizens on account of race or color."

When Garrison insisted in 1865 that the American Anti-Slavery Society had achieved its purpose and should disband, Wendell Phillips replaced him as president of the organization. During the next five years, in the words of Carlos Martyn, he " watched every move of the slippery gamesters at Washington with unflagging vigilance, criticising, suggesting, analyzing, insisting; and by directing universal attention to the game, made them play fair and square." These were the years of the bitter Reconstruction Period, when intrigue and chicanery were exploited to the utmost in a desperate effort to deprive the liberated Negroes of the substance of freedom. Phillips now had to do Garrison's work in addition to his own, and his writings in *The Standard* ably supported his public speeches and personal appeals to the leaders in Congress. Senator Henry Wilson, who was in the best possible position to judge the effectiveness of the Agitator's great work, wrote to Senator Charles Sumner: " More than to any other, more than to all others, the colored people owe it that they were not cheated out of their citizenship after emancipation, to Wendell Phillips."

When on March 30, 1870, President Grant proclaimed the adoption of the Fifteenth Amendment, which crowned the fight of the Abolitionists for the personal freedom and political equality of the Negro in the United States, Phillips was ready to disband the American Anti-Slavery Society and did so at its annual meeting in New York City. The economic aspect of the freed slaves interested him no more than the political aspect had interested Garrison.

As leaders in the Abolition movement, Phillips and Garrison complemented each other very advantageously. Garrison was the organizer, the vitriolic editor; Phillips was the galvanic orator, the inspired advocate. For three decades the two were inseparable in their devotion to the cause of Negro emancipation. Although Phillips continued to the end to regard Garrison as his leader, he was generally thought of as the more influential of the two during the final phase of the Abolitionist struggle. His impassioned speeches against the Fugitive Slave Law echoed sympathetically in the hearts of his fellow Northerners. His defiance of those in authority was stated with the fire and firmness of the powerful tribune.

The final triumph of the anti-slavery movement was brought about not by one man alone, nor by a single group, but by a ripening of social conditions which were making the radical change inevitable. The fact remains, however, that a few fanatic reformers, aided by economic mutations which were making the slave plantation an obsolete institution, had in time succeeded in forcing their indomitable will upon an entire nation. Phillips expressed this fact very aptly, and with a modesty that becomes him, shortly after victory was assured:

The reason why the Abolitionists brought the nation down to fighting their battle is that they were really in earnest, knew what they wanted, and were determined to have it. The leading statesmen and orators of the day said they would never urge Abolition; but a determined man in a printing office said that they should, and they did it.

After the enactment of the Thirteenth Amendment in 1865, Garrison, Edmund Quincy, and scores of other prominent Abolitionists relaxed their labors and enjoyed the fruit of a well-earned triumph. Slavery was abolished, the millions of Negroes were free, and the battle-scarred Union was now truly "the land of the free and the home of the brave." One by one these weary warriors returned to the life they had forsaken thirty and more years previously, and all received the homage due to honored elders. Sooner or later one after another found himself relegated to a respectable obscurity.

Not so Wendell Phillips, however. Instead of reaping the rewards of victory, he decided "to put out into the underbrush." From the beginning he had not limited his efforts to a single reform. While the fight against slavery had engrossed his attention till the end, he had worked concurrently in behalf of prohibition and women's rights and against capital punishment. The woes of the Irish and the factory workers had likewise enlisted his active sympathy. Indeed all suffering, all inequality, all oppression had always moved him deeply. It was not surprising therefore that at the final meeting of the American Anti-Slavery Society, after having received a tremendous ovation, he should have ended his remarks with the following declaration: "We will not say 'Farewell,' but 'All hail.' Welcome new duties! We sheathe no sword. We only turn the front of the army upon a new foe." To him the foe was the increasingly powerful capitalist, whom he regarded as an even more ruthless enemy than the slavocratic planter. Accordingly, he readily espoused the cause of labor — and thereby antagonized State Street even more than his Abolitionism had alienated Beacon Street.

Even in his maiden speech at Faneuil Hall Phillips had "felt that he was speaking for the cause of the laboring man." Nearly thirty years later, when slavery was no more, he delivered in the same hall the first of his powerful labor lectures, "The Eight-Hour Movement." He remarked at the time, conscious of the coldness with which his latest agitation was being received by his fellow reformers: "Let it not be said that the old Abolitionist stopped with the Negro, and was never able to see that the same principles claimed his utmost effort to protect all labor, black and white, and to further the discussion of every claim of humanity." Garrison, Quincy, Emerson, Gerrit Smith, and other leading humanitarians, shied away from the new crusade: they were either tired old men or too intimately a part of the group under attack to see the need of it. But to Phillips the lords of the loom were as unconscionable as the lords of the lash. He had seen too many New England mill towns not to be impressed by the drab and degraded condition of the workers inhabiting them. And having fought mightily to eradicate bond-slavery, he now felt impelled to agitate for the abolition of wage-slavery. Of all the reformers of his time he alone, acting upon the implicit logic of his Christian humanitarianism, joined forces with the socialists in preaching the overthrow of capitalism.

There is no evidence that Phillips was familiar with the writings of Karl Marx and other prominent socialists. By 1870, however, when he organized the Labor Reform Convention in Worcester and presided at its sessions, it was obvious that he had assimilated the seminal ideas of the *Communist Manifesto* — so much is indicated by the following excerpts from the platform which he read to the delegates and of which he was the sole author:

We affirm, as a fundamental principle, that labor, the creator of wealth, is entitled to all it creates.

Affirming this, we avow ourselves willing to accept the final results of the operation of a principle so radical, such as the overthrow of the whole profit-making system, the extinction of all monopolies, the abolition of privileged classes, universal education and fraternity, perfect freedom of exchange, and, best and grandest of all, the final obliteration of that foul stigma upon our so-called Christian civilization, the poverty of the masses.

Resolved, That we declare war with the wage system, which demoralizes alike the hirer and the hired, cheats both, and enslaves the workingman; war with the present system of finance, which robs labor, and gorges capital, makes the rich richer, and the poor poorer, and turns the republic into an aristocracy of capital. . . .

Phillips had not become a Marxian doctrinaire. In condemning the conspicuous evils of capitalistic exploitation, he was always the bold humanitarian ready to destroy the power and privilege of the few for the greater good of all. He made this clear a year later in his decision to accept nomination for the governorship of Massachusetts on the Labor ticket — a decision made in spite of his unwillingness to take political office and purely for its agitational possibilities. Capital and labor, he maintained, were partners and not enemies, and must share fairly in the common profits. This view he stated even more emphatically on another occasion: " There is no antagonism between Man and Money — between Capital and Labor; they are friends, not foes, partners, not competitors; they are the two parts of one scissors — each useless without the other. Whatever harms one or helps one, must, *on any just system*, harm or help the other." To this non-Marxian assumption he added another: an implicit trust in the might of the ballot. If the workers united politically, they could by means of their voting power bring justice to all and thus greatly improve their economic status. " I am fully convinced," he claimed, " that hitherto legislation has leaned too much — leaned most unfairly — to the side of capital. Hereafter it should be impartial. Law should do all it can to give the masses more leisure, a more complete education, better opportunities, and a fair share of the profits."

Always thinking things through to a logical conclusion, ever ready to act according to principle regardless of the consequences, Phillips began to devote himself completely to the betterment of the poor workers. In a number of powerful addresses he expounded his ideas of social organization and human happiness.

Basically a man of the eighteenth century and always a Jeffersonian democrat, he preferred the simple town life of New England before it was blighted by the drabness and disparity of industrialism. " My ideal of civilization," he explained, " is a very high one: but the approach to it is a New England town of some two thousand inhabitants, with no rich man and no poor man in it, all mingling in the same society, every child at the same school, no poorhouse, no beggar, opportunities equal, nobody so proud as to stand aloof, nobody so humble as to be shut out."

Life in the America of the 1870's, however, was the antithesis of the idyllic society of his dream. He was confronted, indeed, by a rampant capitalism which heedlessly trampled upon the democratic institutions he held dear. Railroad manipulators were corrupting state legislatures, Wall Street speculators were mulcting innocent investors, greedy employers were exploiting their unorganized workers, the power of government was " ever shifting from the many to the few." To an English friend he wrote:

Wealth, with you, governs; but its power is, I suppose, somewhat masked, sometimes countervailed or checked by other forces. With us it rules, bare, naked, shameless, undisguised. Our *incorporated* wealth, often wielded by a single hand, is fearful with direct, and still more with indirect, power.

In his lectures on labor he lashed out against this abuse of power. Singling out notorious malefactors to prove his thesis, he insisted that the safety of our democracy and the weal of our people required the curbing of incorporated wealth. " The great question of the future," he asserted, " is money against legislation. My friends, you and I shall be in our graves long before that battle is ended; and unless our children have more patience and courage than saved this country from slavery, republican institutions will go down before moneyed corporations. Rich men die, but banks are immortal, and railroad corporations never have any diseases." In his notable address on " The Foundations of the Labor Movement " he carried his criticism of predatory capitalism to its obvious conclusion:

I confess that the only fear I have in regard to republican institutions is whether, in our day, any adequate remedy will be found for the incoming flood of the power of incorporated wealth. No statesman, no public man yet, has dared to defy it. Every man that has met it has been crushed to powder; and the only hope of any effectual grapple with it is by rousing the actual masses, whose interests permanently lie in an opposite direction, to grapple with this great force. . . . Now, gentlemen, to me the labor movement means just this: It is the last noble protest of the American people against the power of incorporated wealth.

Unwilling to accept the Marxian doctrine of the class struggle, unable to view society without his reformer's spectacles, Phillips argued that the effective antidote to the abuse of capitalistic power was education and organization of the masses of workers. Because he believed that a reduction in the manual laborer's hours of work would enable him to broaden his social perspective and make him a worthier citizen, Phillips was one of the first Americans to advocate the eight-hour work day. He was also an enthusiastic promoter of the labor union. In his talks to workers he insisted that only by combination could they " put in a united force to face the organization of capital." Trade unionism would offset the fact that in a dispute time was usually on the employer's side. " Capital can wait to win; labor cannot without being starved into submission — unless it organizes." He told them also that capital, the labor of yesterday, " gets twice the protection and twice the pay that labor of today gets." The remedy, he exhorted, was self-evident: workmen must organize; they must learn to take full advantage of their civic prerogatives; they must make intelligent use of their mass power at the polls. Once they elected their own candidates to the state legislatures and to Congress, they could easily destroy the hold of the rich on government.

We'll crumple up wealth by making it unprofitable to be rich. The poor man shall have a larger income in proportion as he is poor. The rich man shall have a lesser income in proportion as he is rich. You will say, " Is that just? " My friends, it is safe. Man is more valuable than money. . . . Land, private property, all sorts of property, shall be so dearly taxed that it shall be impossible to be rich; for it is in wealth, in incorporated, combining, perpetual wealth, that the danger lies.

Wendell Phillips was in his time the foremost defender of our democratic rights. He knew only too well how easy it was for those

[73]

in power to forget that the law of the land gave the people certain inalienable rights, how ready were the mighty to crush those who questioned their prerogatives or denounced their arrogation of privilege. "When a nation sets itself to do evil," he said in connection with his Abolitionist work, "and all its leading forces, wealth, party, and piety, join in the career, it is impossible but that those who offer a constant opposition should be hated and maligned, no matter how wise, cautious, and well planned their course may be." He fervently acclaimed the rights of the dissenter and the insurgent, maintaining that not to give free scope to an opponent was evidence of a lack of faith in one's own opinions. To act otherwise was to nullify the creed upon which our nation was founded: " Men are educated and the State uplifted by allowing all — everyone — to broach their mistakes and advocate all their errors. The community which dares not protect its humblest and most hated member in the free utterance of his opinions, no matter how false or hateful, is only a gang of slaves."

This noble sentiment, uncommon in his own day and even less met with in our own, Phillips championed to the end of his life — and never more courageously and eloquently than in " The Scholar in a Republic," his Phi Beta Kappa address at Harvard in 1881. Already a septuagenarian, yet never more energetic in his lifelong struggle for freedom and justice, he stood on the hallowed rostrum of his alma mater, which for fully fifty years had completely ignored him and now honored him only grudgingly. There, before a distinguished audience, he extolled the principles and ideals which it preferred to disdain. James Freeman Clarke, who heard the lecture, afterwards reported:

He gave an oration of great power and beauty, full of strong thought and happy illustrations, not unworthy of any university or academic scholar. It was nearly, though not wholly, free from personalities; but it was also one long rebuke for the recreant scholarship of Cambridge. It arraigned and condemned all scholarship as essentially timid, selfish, and unheroic.

Holding, according to T. W. Higginson, who was also present, "an unwilling audience spellbound, while bating nothing of his radicalism," Phillips developed his theme with rare felicity. First he discussed the process by which the United States had become the most successful experiment in self-government known to man.

We have done what no race, no nation, no age, had before dared even to try. We have founded a republic on the unlimited suffrage of the millions. We have actually worked out the problem that man, as God created him, may be trusted with self-government. We have shown the world that a church without a bishop, and a state without a king, is an actual, real, every-day possibility.

This trust in the people, he stated, laid a great responsibility on those possessed of "strength, wisdom, and skill." The very purpose of a democracy, indeed, made it incumbent upon those capable of leadership to lift their neighbors to their own level. Yet the "book-educated," the men of intellect and erudition, with few honorable exceptions had not only shirked this responsibility but had tried to limit this trust in the people, thus betraying "their lack of distinctive American character." The truth was, he continued, that "a chronic distrust of the people pervades the book-educated class in the North; they shrink from that free speech which is God's normal school for educating men." Then he must have painfully shocked his Brahmin audience with the challenging exhortation: "Trust the people — the wise and the ignorant, the good and the bad — with the greatest questions, and in the end you educate the race. At the same time you secure not perfect institutions, not necessarily good ones, but the best institutions possible while human nature is the basis and the only material to build with."

Phillips next made clear the need for men of education to join in the fight for social and political reform. "I urge on college-bred men that, as a class, they fail in republican duty when they allow others to lead in the agitation of the great social questions which stir and educate the age." Not that the common people cannot get along without them; "by sovereign and superabundant strength they can crush their way through all obstacles." But by abstaining from this agitation the educated and the gifted not only were recreant to their duty as Americans but were actually neglecting their "opportunities and the means God offers us to refine the taste, mould the character, lift the purpose, and educate the moral sense of the masses, on whose intelligence and self-respect rests the State." Already they had missed several great occasions: the crusade against slavery, the reform of penal legislation, the attack on intemperance, the movement for woman suffrage, and the appeal for Ireland's freedom. Instead of forming the front ranks in each of these campaigns for social advancement, as was their right and duty, they had held back willfully, scornfully, keeping their skirts clean and their minds decorous and ineffectual.

His final remarks proved a veritable bombshell. To defend democracy and the people before the conservative elders of Harvard University was audacious enough; to vindicate Russian Nihilists at a time when they were assassinating high Imperial officials — only three months after they had killed Czar Alexander II — was perhaps even more courageous than his championship of John Brown. It should be understood that he broached the unpopular subject not merely to shock the smug Brahmins before him but as the logical climax to his exposition of the principles for which he had been agitating throughout his life. For to him Nihilism was merely the Russian manifestation of the struggle for human freedom.

Nihilism is the righteous and honorable resistance of a people crushed under the iron rule. . . . It is crushed humanity's only means of making the oppressor tremble. . . . I honor Nihilism; since it redeems human nature from the suspicion of being utterly vile, made up of only heartless oppressors and contented slaves. . . . [In a country such as ours] where discussion is free, the press untrammelled, and where public halls protect debate . . . he is doubly and trebly guilty who, except in some most extreme cases, disturbs the sober rule of law and order. But such is not Russia. In Russia there is no press, no debate, no explanation of what Government does, no remonstrance allowed, no agitation of public issues. . . . In such a land dynamite and the dagger are the necessary and proper substitutes for Faneuil Hall and the *Daily Advertiser.* . . . I at least can say nothing else and nothing less — no, not if every tile on Cambridge roofs were a devil hooting my words.

No wonder that, again to quote Higginson: " Many a respectable lawyer and divine felt his blood run cold, the next day, when he found that the fascinating orator whom he had applauded to the echo had really made the assassination of an emperor seem as trivial as the doom of a mosquito."

Wendell Phillips was unquestionably the greatest orator of his time. Though his voice thinned out in its highest register, it was in its middle and lower notes as pliant and penetrating and expressive as a fine violin. He was able to modulate it so exquisitely as to fit it to a wide range of mood and meaning. His enunciation was distinct and cadenced without being studied or elocutional. His stage presence was natural, graceful, and impressive. He was never at a loss for words, yet there was nothing glib or effusive about his platform delivery. Indeed, the keynote to his remarkable success as a speaker lay in his ability to raise the conversational quality of his voice to its highest power.

Phillips's forensic powers were ever the means to a known end. When on the platform, he thought of himself not as the eminent orator but rather as the zealous reformer eager to bend his audience to his will. Thoroughly sincere, believing with all his heart in the reforms he advocated, often addressing crowds bitterly hostile to his views, he frequently had to exercise his unparalleled intellectual and rhetorical resources to the utmost in order to gain the sympathy of his hearers. His ability to employ the most pertinent approach equaled his skill to fit his words to the level of his auditors. Learned and sagacious, he coated his barbs of satire and his shafts of condemnation with apt allusions, felicitous quotations, and humorous anecdotes. These witticisms and metaphors issued from his tongue with remarkable profusion, and have added up to more than a hundred in a single lecture. An exceptionally quick thinker on his feet and in command of a tremendous range of historical and contemporary information, he was able frequently to present his views with the power of self-evident finality.

Phillips seldom made use of notes on the platform. He was at his best when speaking extemporaneously, with a general topic to guide him and an audience to stimulate him. " The chief thing I aim at," he said, " is to master my subject. Then I earnestly try to get the audience to think as I do." When he was eventually induced to prepare a volume of his speeches, however, he could not revise and polish them enough, and was never quite content with the result. For he believed that speaking and writing require different habits of mind and that few great orators have won laurels in the field of literature.

His popularity as a lecturer was truly extraordinary. In spite of his unwelcome and disagreeable subjects, he was for many years, especially after the Civil War, the favorite speaker of lyceum audiences from Maine to California. Year after year he would begin his tour in the early fall and remain on the road, except for brief intervals, till April or May. He called himself a " vagabond lecturer " and traveled during some seasons as much as twelve thousand miles to deliver more than sixty addresses. His large repertoire contained a wide variety of topics, but none of his lectures was intended for entertainment only. And although his fees were relatively high — bringing him during his later period as much as fifteen thousand dollars a year — he had always more invitations than he could accept.

Wendell Phillips achieved his eminent place in American history not by virtue of his profound intellect or original genius, but by a combination of noble zeal and prime eloquence. He was not an innovator of a moral movement, as Garrison was; nor had he, like John Brown, captured the imagination of a nation by a timely act of fanatic daring. But he was supremely the fighter for social justice. More than any other man of his generation he devoted himself unselfishly and passionately to the welfare of his people and of humanity everywhere. No suffering left him unmoved; no oppression escaped his condemnation. For above all he championed the rights of the masses and the efficacy of genuine democracy. Like so many Americans before his time and after, he believed thoroughly in the ideal of democratic society and devoted his life to give it national reality.

George William Curtis has well said of him: "A student of history, and a close observer of men, he rejected that fear of the multitude which springs from the feeling that the many are ignorant while the few are wise; and he believed in the saying, too profound for Talleyrand, to whom it is ascribed, that everybody knows more than anybody." This intense faith in the people made Phillips, in George Woodberry's epithet, the "perfect American." Essentially a Puritan in that he thought he knew and knew he was right, he led the fight to make the Bill of Rights the living law of the land. After the Civil War, when the downfall of slavocracy initiated the Gilded Age of a strident industrialism, he broadened his protest — but his criticism became more and more a cry in the wilderness of moral hypocrisy. But to the very end, and with undiminished vigor, he persisted undauntedly in his advocacy of the principles of freedom and justice and in laying the foundation for the rights of the mass of Americans which have made the United States the chief democracy in the world.

THE UTOPIANS

MARGARET FULLER   ALBERT BRISBANE

EDWARD BELLAMY

THE UTOPIAN BACKGROUND

HROUGHOUT THE AGES utopian dreamers, impractical and often fantastic in their altruistic efforts, have nevertheless fought in the vanguard of social progress. They are charged with a divine unrest which is not satisfied until they have settled upon a prospect of the ideal world. Critics of their generation and of the ways of men, they envision a society purged of the evils they abhor. Their utopias know no poverty, pain, or persecution; the foundation pillars of their imagined societies are peace, plenty, and complete happiness. These perfect communities remain, of course, a beautiful dream. Yet their ardent creators frequently have succeeded far better than they knew, since in stirring the imagination of many thousands they have initiated movements for reform which in time have brought at least a good part of their utopias down to earth. "The Utopian dreamers of social justice," William James remarked, "are . . . analogous to the saint's belief in an existent kingdom of heaven. They help to break the edge of the general reign of hardness, and are slow leavens of a better order." Anatole France, a keen critic of human foibles, was even more positive in his estimate: "Out of generous dreams come beneficial realities. Utopia is the principle of all progress and the essay into a better future."

Most utopians have started from the belief that man is naturally good and that a favorable environment is bound to bring him to a condition of perfection. Their chief task therefore has been the provision of plans for the good life. Here they differed considerably in aim and method. The Hebrew prophets envisioned a society quite unlike the one prescribed by Plato. The utopias delineated by More and Bacon had little resemblance to the spiritual regimens evolved by Luther and Calvin. Nor was there much connection between the various Protestant sects that broke away from the dominant Church to insure the life of their members after death and the host of social utopias in the early nineteenth century. Yet all these dreamers of perfect societies had this in common: they were sublimely confident of the perfectibility of their ideal communities and were not in the least discouraged by the ridicule heaped upon them. To the very end they clung to the belief that their detractors would yet live to see the advent of the ideal society.

The United States has been from the very beginning the popular proving ground for the better life. With a new continent available for the taking, religious and social dreamers were quick to make use of it in their efforts to try out their particular panaceas. Thus the Pilgrims, harried out of their native England by an intolerant state church and finding their haven in Holland cramped and difficult, braved the stormy Atlantic in order to establish their theocratic community in the new land. Lord Baltimore and William Penn founded their colonies not so much for their personal gain as for the relief of their harassed co-religionists. As the years passed, scores of other idealists and visionaries reached these shores with similar intent. Indeed, for three centuries this country has been known everywhere as a refuge for the oppressed and the land of opportunity for those in want.

During the first two centuries, with Christianity continuing to dominate Western thought, utopian colonies were founded by religious prophets who believed they had discovered the mode of life leading to eternal salvation. Some of these settlements have become a vital part of our culture, contributing rich elements to the bloodstream of this country's thought. Since they are part of our history, this discussion is not concerned with such efforts, the supreme example of which is the early Puritan community. Others had briefer lives or more restricted influence. In 1684 the followers of Jean Labadie, a Catholic priest who advocated a communistic system of society based upon rigorous religious principles, set up in Maryland one of the first of the sectarian societies outside of New England. The Ephrata Society in Pennsylvania, which was organized in 1732 by Anabaptists under the leadership of Conrad Beisel, one of the most successful of these sectarian groups, established its first settlement in Watervliet, New York. Half a century later this movement spread from Maine to Kentucky and counted about five thousand members in its prosperous villages. Several hundred of them continue to this day in the frugal pacifism of their fathers. In 1805 George Rapp, a visionary from Württemberg, founded Harmony in western Pennsylvania. Nine years later he moved his community to a 30,000-acre tract in Indiana, only to sell the well-developed colony in 1824 to Robert Owen for $150,000 and return with his followers to a new settlement in Pennsylvania. The Zoar colony in Ohio, which began its existence in 1818, was led by Joseph Bimeler, like Rapp a Württemberger and a Separatist. The communities of Bethel in Missouri and Aurora in Oregon owed their existence to Dr. Keil, a German who practised "magnetic cures" until he experienced a revelation and began to preach his special doctrine of the good life, and both were dissolved shortly after his death in 1877. Metz, another German visionary, organized the True Inspiration Society and established the Amana community near Buffalo in 1842; thirteen years later the settlement moved to Iowa, where it prospers to this day.

The first purely American sectarian community was begun in 1834 by John Humphrey Noyes, a religious eccentric, in his native town of Putney, Vermont. His first few adherents were limited to his own immediate family, but in time his perfectionist doctrines attracted a number of his neighbors. In 1848 Noyes moved with his followers to Oneida, New York, where they hoped to practise their particular mode of the good life without external interference.

The misunderstood doctrine of sexual promiscuity — a dutiful promiscuity based on personal liberty and " holiness of heart " — gave the colony considerable notoriety until the authorities forced moral conformity upon it. After a slow start the group, never exceeding a few hundred in number, prospered notably and its commercial products became favorably known throughout the United States.

The Mormon Church was the most notorious and the most successful of the sectarian settlements. Founded in 1830 by Joseph Smith, who claimed to have discovered the Book of Mormon and to be the recipient of revelation for the guidance of his followers, the new religion soon gained many adherents. After unfortunate efforts at settlement in Ohio, Missouri, and Illinois, during which persecution was climaxed by the mob murder of Joseph Smith, the Mormons in 1847 followed their new leader Brigham Young to the wilderness of Utah. Within a few years their number grew to 60,000 and their energy transformed the arid territory around Salt Lake into one of the most prosperous sections of the entire country. In the early years especially, Brigham Young ruled the Mormons with a remarkable combination of strictness and sagacity. The Church was in complete control of the economy of the province. The members bought their supplies and sold their produce through the common store. The co-operative principle ruled in all activities where it was practicable. Young and his Elders believed that everyone was entitled to a fair living — and no more; consequently no man who worked was poor and none was permitted to accumulate riches. Sobriety, industry, piety, and general well-being characterized this largest sectarian experiment. In time, however, the intrusion of " Gentiles," the intensified agitation against the practice of polygamy, and the inevitable softening that comes with increasing prosperity brought about the deterioration of the rigorous discipline and with it the weakening of church control of the community's economy.

All these sectarian communal experiments, notwithstanding their vagaries and divergent doctrines, were inspired by a common yearning for the good life on earth and for spiritual salvation after death. All practised some form of collective economy, and all were noted for their pacifism, sobriety, extreme simplicity of manner, industriousness, and relative prosperity. The membership of all these communities, whether those of German origin or of American ancestry, was made up of farmers and mechanics and was held together by strong inspirational bonds. After the Civil War, however, the slackening of religious fervor and the pressure of external materialistic forces caused these utopian colonies either to disband or to shrink to their present relative insignificance.

The utopian experiments of the social type began early in the nineteenth century. The prime movers in each instance were humanitarians eager to alleviate the suffering of the poor and eliminate the gross social inequalities of a rising industrialism. Unlike the religious utopians they were interested not in spiritual salvation but in the humanization of daily life. As social dreamers they did not approach the problem with the practical shrewdness of the realistic reformer, but merely concentrated their efforts on devising plans for the regeneration of mankind. Influenced by Rousseau and the ideals of the French Revolution and stimulated by the noble sentiments of the Declaration of Independence, they sought to abolish poverty, establish complete equality, and lift mankind to heights of happiness.

The first and by far the largest and best-known of these utopian communities was established by Robert Owen early in 1825. An Englishman of great business acumen and one of the outstanding humanitarians of his time, Owen bought the Rappite colony in Indiana in order to found the first of a series of communities with the aim of transforming society into "a new empire of peace and good-will to men." The settlement began under very favorable auspices: it had a village ready for occupancy, cultivated land for farming, several eminent educators among the early members, and the financial backing of its wealthy proprietor. Owen hoped that the success of New Harmony would spread "from Community to

Community, from State to State, from Continent to Continent, finally overshadowing the whole earth, shedding light, fragrance and abundance, intelligence and happiness upon the sons of men."

This sentimental altruism, which befuddled Owen's practical business sense, led to the inevitable doom of the experiment. So great was his enthusiasm for the project and so confident was he of its success that he did not trouble to supervise the establishment of the colony or to limit the membership to a balanced group of farmers, artisans, and professional men. Instead he left the place in charge of one of his young sons and went on a long lecture tour to advertise New Harmony to his audiences and to urge those interested to join him in the glorious enterprise — at his expense. As a consequence the community was soon inhabited by as mixed a collection of nonconformists as one is ever likely to find. Nine hundred arrived in all, and all were accepted without test or qualification. Nor was there anyone to take them in hand and train them for the work that needed to be done. Seven constitutions were adopted and tried out in rapid succession but none was able to overcome the increasing dissension. Failure was inevitable, and after three painful years Owen admitted defeat — and the loss of four-fifths of his fortune. The post-mortem was well stated by his son Robert Dale Owen: " At New Harmony there was not disinterested industry, there was not mutual confidence, there was not practical experience, there was not union of action, because there was not unanimity of counsel; and these were the points of difference and dissension — the rocks on which the social bark struck and was wrecked."

Owen's ideas and influence were evident in a number of other settlements formed in the 1820's. The best-known of these utopian efforts was the Yellow Springs Community in Ohio. Its members were a group of Swedenborgian intellectuals who had heard Owen lecture and were converted to his scheme of communal living. All of these experiments began with the usual high hopes and lack of equipment. While they lasted, the members enjoyed the pleasures promoted by their leaders; but, lacking the men to do the essential work and unprovided with the capital put into New Harmony, they failed all the sooner.

About the time that Owen was negotiating the purchase of the Rappite tract another native of England was planning the Nashoba experiment that was intended to lead to the peaceful abolition of slavery in the United States. Frances Wright, radical reformer and stormy petrel of her time, was so distressed by the practice of slavery, as she saw it during her travels as Lafayette's companion in 1824, that she bought a 2000-acre farm in Tennessee and began to settle it with Negro slaves bought by her or donated by generous planters. It was her idea that the profits made from the labor of the colony would help liberate other slaves, and that this procedure would eventually rid this country of its greatest social evil. The plan was praised by many prominent persons and put into operation with the unreserved enthusiasm of those connected with it. At first all went well, and at one time as many as thirty liberated slaves were living on the plantation. But all the hard work of the white members went for naught when they were unable to persuade the Negroes to follow their example. Newly freed from the overseer's whip, unable to appreciate the idealism motivating the plan, interested only in taking advantage of their unexpected good fortune, they made the most of their opportunities to loaf and indulge themselves. When Frances Wright became seriously ill and had to leave Nashoba for a cooler climate, the colony deteriorated rapidly and was brought to an inglorious dissolution when its sexual laxness antagonized the unsympathetic Southerners. To Miss Wright's credit it must be added that she personally supervised the resettlement of the Negro members on land bought for them in free Haiti.

These utopian failures notwithstanding, the longing for perfection continued to stir the hearts of thousands of Americans who loved life and hated its evil aspects. Everywhere men and women, liberated from the restrictions of orthodox religion and buoyed by a belief in progress, eagerly enlisted in the numerous movements for social and moral reform. Abolition, prohibition, woman's rights, Bible study, trade unionism — these and other manifestations of the same urge for the better life were each advocated as basic to the conversion of society. In the vicinity of Boston, then the hub of intellectual America, scores of altruists wrestled with the problems of the universe even as Jacob had with the Angel — neither prevailing against them nor letting them go. The sturdier minds evolved the comforting philosophy of transcendentalism, which John R. Commons defined as "a combination of the religious spirit of puritanism and an individualism that sought independence from social relations." Others, more sensible of the ugly features of the new industrialism, sought to escape to a world of their own making. Brook Farm became the haven for those who wished to prove to themselves and to mankind that it was possible to live nobly and fruitfully without adding to the miseries of the less fortunate. Of these New England idealists, Margaret Fuller was without doubt the outstanding representative. A leading transcendentalist, an active well-wisher of Brook Farm, a pioneer advocate of women's rights, a spirited soldier in the army for liberation — she exemplified the romantic humanitarians who had dedicated themselves to the good life without erecting altars to Utopia.

The economic depression that followed the panic of 1837 gave fresh impetus to utopian experimentation. Albert Brisbane had recently returned from France, where Charles Fourier had indoctrinated him with his theory of Association. The idea of making work attractive and life enjoyable appealed irresistibly to thousands of Americans who yearned for the security and comforts of the good life. Years later Emerson wrote ironically of Brisbane's infectious enthusiasm: "As we listened to his exposition, it appeared to us the sublime of mechanical philosophy; for the system was the perfection of arrangement and contrivance. . . . Poverty shall be abolished; deformity, stupidity and crime shall be no more. Genius, grace, art, shall abound." No wonder that some of the idealistic reformers in New York and in Boston were converted by Brisbane and joined him in advocating the advantages of Association. Their voices carried as far as the wilds of the frontier and phalanx after phalanx was soon organized by Associationists whose enthusiasm outran their practical sense. The movement gained its greatest momentum after Brook Farm was reorganized according to Fourierist principles. For a brief period it appeared as if Association were taking root. But the same fallacies that had undermined the Owenite communities soon began to disrupt the phalanxes. The lack of capital and necessary skills, aggravated by emerging dissension, forced most of these settlements to disband shortly after they had made their brave beginning.

Etienne Cabet's utopian novel, *Voyage en Icarie*, which showed the influence of Owen and the more rigorous socialistic thinkers, brought into being the French Icarian communities. Cabet planned to settle a million workers on a million-acre tract in Texas, but the revolution in 1848 dampened the enthusiasm for the project and only a few scores of the most faithful adherents left France for the new venture into utopia. Misfortune attended them from the very first, and according to Morris Hillquit they "were in a constant process of disintegration and reorganization." After their disastrous efforts in the swamps and woods of Texas, they rented a part of Nauvoo from the evacuating Mormons and succeeded in establishing their communistic colony. But discord and other difficulties caused some of the members to break away and organize new settlements. All these colonies struggled heroically for survival, but the last of them disappeared during the early 1890's.

The final decade of the anti-slavery agitation and the years of the Civil War and Reconstruction were not conducive to further utopian experimentation. The issue of Negro emancipation dwarfed every other reform movement for a generation. In the meantime the urge toward communal panaceas was dissipated by two emerging forces: on the one hand the rise of Marxism deprived utopianism of its appeal, since the workers, little attracted by social visions and interested primarily in increased wages and shorter hours, began to unite in their own behalf; on the other the remarkable industrial expansion after 1860, bringing with it a crop of multimillionaires and powerful trusts, made the small utopian settlements mere drops of oil on the rough sea of economic strife. Intensified social abuses called forth a new band of reformers, but they were realistic enough to perceive the full scope of the problem and to advocate more appropriate measures.

Yet the longing for utopia was by no means dead. As social conditions during the Gilded Age created a proletariat, in violation of the principles of the Declaration of Independence, there was greater need than before for the vision of a better world. Among the dreamers who clung to the ideal of true democracy and sought to establish it in every field of human endeavor, Edward Bellamy towers as a social thinker and writer. Eager to see the tenets of Jefferson prevail, not only in the voting booths, but in the factories and counting houses as well, he preached his doctrine of complete equality in the guise of entertaining fiction. *Looking Backward,* picturing a United States freed from the evils of poverty and inequality and blessed with all attributes of a perfected social order, became a literary sensation and brought its message of cheer to more men and women than all the communal experiments put together. Tens of thousands of Americans who believed with Bellamy that it was high time for the people to fight for their inalienable rights quickly organized groups to work for the nationalization of our entire economy. For several years these Nationalist Clubs gathered momentum and appeared within reach of their goal. But the passing of the economic depression of the middle 1890's, and the intense gold vs. silver controversy which followed it, cut short this new utopian agitation, so that Bellamy's plan was soon forgotten.

The social utopians failed of practical achievement because of the very nature of their panaceas. All of them began with idealistic blueprints for the complete regeneration of mankind. They tended to think of society as more or less of a mechanism, to be taken apart and reassembled to fit their particular program, and not as a living organism that cannot undergo mutation without violent shock. They took little or no account of the milieu in which they found themselves and sought to establish model microscopic societies on the assumption that the success of these communities would lead inevitably to universal adoption. They oversimplified human behavior. In assuming the natural goodness of man they disregarded the chief stumbling block in the path before them. Thus, while the sectarian settlements generally restricted their membership to persons of common belief and similar aspirations, the social utopians welcomed all comers. The result is aptly described by the disillusioned Horace Greeley:

Along with many noble and lofty souls, whose impulses are purely phil-anthropic, and who are willing to labor and suffer reproach for any cause that promises to benefit mankind, there throng scores of whom the world is quite worthy — the conceited, the crotchety, the selfish, the headstrong, the pugnacious, the unappreciated, the played-out, the idle, and the good-for-nothing generally; who, finding themselves ut-terly out of place and at a discount in the world as it is, rashly conclude that they are exactly fitted for the world as it ought to be.

The utopian movement, however, did leave a definite impress on the social progress of the past century. Fantastic though the schemes of its leaders seemed to their detractors, and futile though its attempts at economic mutation were, its advocacy of the good life and its championship of individual reforms hastened a marked improvement of economic conditions. The extent of this progress may be seen in the fact that the social standards of the New Deal appear utopian when contrasted with those of the early nineteenth century.

The individual studies that follow are intended to stress the three most representative utopian trends of the past century. Mar-garet Fuller, blue-stocking and social rebel, is notably typical of those inchoate idealists who sought a better world but could not quite reach the heights of Pisgah. Albert Brisbane is obviously the chief of the American utopians who looked backward to a golden past for the panacea of mankind's ills. Edward Bellamy, on the contrary, tried to harness the future to a perfected society of his own making and to incorporate into it all the comforts of an ad-vanced industrialism.

MARGARET FULLER

TRANSCENDENTAL REBEL

To us, nearly a century after her death, Margaret Fuller's enduring eminence seems inexplicable when considered in the light of her published work; while much of it is still vigorous and readable, even the most finished of her essays lacks the depth and directness of distinguished writing. We soon discover, however, that her fame derives from her remarkable personality rather than from her books. Only the husks of her brilliant mind went into print. This she knew better than anyone else. " I feel within myself an immense power," she remarked with her usual candor, " but I cannot bring it out." It was this torrential power, which became quick and magnetic in the heat of conversation, that made her the sibylline voice of her generation and gained her lasting renown. But this leading role in the Transcendental ferment was not the sum of her achievement. Moved by an unquenchable unrest, stirred by an irresistible passion for freedom, she forsook the tranquillity of her native New England for the barricades of a Europe in revolt. And although the French invaders defeated Garibaldi's Legion and restored Rome to the Pope, her heroic efforts in behalf of the shortlived Roman Republic capped the glorious adventure of her tragic life.

In Cambridge, where Margaret was born in 1810, her father Timothy Fuller was known as a stubborn nonconformist. He had definite ideas on politics and education, and decided to test his pedagogical theories on his firstborn, even though she was not the son he had expected. As soon as Margaret was able to quit the nursery he took complete charge of her. He bought her clothes, and supervised her every activity. Early aware of her precocity, he forced her mental development to the utmost. He taught her English grammar and Latin in her sixth year; in her seventh he had her read Virgil, Ovid, and Horace for their Roman virtues. At the same time he gave her the freedom of his compact library closet, and she took joyous advantage of it during the hours she was not preparing her arduous lessons. He insisted on accuracy in her daily recitations, and often kept her until long past her bedtime before he was satisfied with her progress. As a consequence she sometimes left him feeling so excited and unstrung that she dreaded closing her eyes and finally would fall asleep only to experience terrifying nightmares. Yet she accepted her solitude and her intensive training as a matter of course, and later wrote of this period of her life without rancor and with little regret.

Margaret matured like a forced plant. Without regular playmates, with little opportunity to vent her normal animal zest, she devoted most of her childhood to study and reading. In the realm of classical and modern literature she roamed from peak to peak with exceptional ease. The heroes of mythology and the great characters of Shakespeare, Fielding, Cervantes, and Molière engrossed her imagination. Her father, however, who treated her as " a living mind " and precious instrument, was closest to her heart and she yearned to have him all to herself. She sometimes dreamt " of following to the grave the body of her mother," and " of horses trampling over her " — evidences of her sexual precocity. Indeed, at the age of thirteen she appeared physically and mentally full-grown and was accepted as such by her elders. When her father sent her to a finishing school in her fourteenth year, she had great difficulty in adjusting herself to the less mature ways and views of her classmates and, after two years, was greatly relieved to return to the comforting solitude of her father's library.

Throughout her teens ambition coursed through her consciousness like a burning fever. In her eagerness to acquire superior knowledge and understanding, she read as avidly as Gibbon: history, metaphysics, and foreign languages and literatures became her steady diet. For a time she went to a boys' school to study Greek; what man could do she would do. When the more serious Harvard freshmen of the class of 1829 began to take note of her, she enjoyed matching wits with them and made lifelong friends of several of them. She also began to appear in society, and assisted her father in entertaining a large and distinguished gathering at a reception in honor of President John Quincy Adams. But her arrogant impatience with polite small talk and her uncouth manners alienated many Cambridge matrons, and she was glad to place herself under the tutelage of Mrs. Eliza Farrar, author of A *Manual for Young Ladies*.

The tragedy of Margaret's life now began to cut into her sensitive heart. Of an intensive nature, her need for emotional fulfilment was strong and irrepressible. She craved not only admiration but affection. Yet no young man appeared to pay court to her. Harvard students were eager to converse with her, to enjoy the sparkling brilliance of her wit, to open their secret thoughts to her — but it never occurred to them to make love to her. For Margaret lacked physical charm: her bony face and blinking eyes failed to invite amorous glances. Not that she was homely. Emerson, who was at first disagreeably impressed by her appearance, soon found that " when she was intellectually excited, or in high animal spirits, as often happened, all deformity of features was dissolved in the power of expression." Yet the knowledge that she was not attractive was wormwood to her colossal ego. " I hate not to be beautiful," she confessed years later.

She would gladly have exchanged all her intellectual attainments for the normal joys of the wife and mother. If she " was not born to the common womanly lot," however, she was determined to be admired as a sibyl. To this end she intensified her studies during the next few years and adopted the maxim: " Make the emotions the servant, not the master of the soul." Because the *Weltschmerz* of the German Romantics fitted her mood, she zealously studied their writings and later became the "Germanico" of her Transcendental circle. Goethe's genius impressed her most deeply. She became one of his early American disciples, and for years prepared herself to write his biography.

For a long time her compensating conceit strove with her Goethean "extraordinary generous-seeking" for mastery. "There is no modesty or moderation in me," she admitted to T. W. Higginson. Fully aware of her great gifts, yet always conscious of her plain face, she was at all times eager to assert her intellectual superiority. Her queenly bearing and her romantic predilections helped her to idealize herself as a sovereign of the mind. "I now know all the people worth knowing in America," she once asserted, "and I find no intellect comparable to my own." Nor was this an idle boast, as Emerson and other eminent thinkers were soon to discover.

Her eagerness to lift human beings to her own high level caused her to castigate them for their shortcomings and to spur them with her caustic wit. This forthrightness, softened by an outgoing generosity of spirit, drew to her the discerning youth of Cambridge. Her magnetic personality encouraged them to overlook her obtrusive conceit and her sharp tongue in order that they might enjoy her exciting intellect. Regarding her more as a disembodied intelligence than as a girl of flesh and blood, they shared with her the woes of the world and communicated to her their innermost thoughts and feelings. And she helped them to unfold their powers and solve their personal problems with rare unselfishness. Those she cared for particularly she cultivated with a tender solicitude that bound them to her for life. "The friends whom her strength of mind drew to her," Emerson declared, "her good heart held fast; and few persons were ever the objects of more persevering kindness."

Margaret was twenty-three when her father, disappointed politically and professionally, decided to move with his family to a farm near Groton. The change was repugnant to her, but she knew better than to oppose it. For the next two years she led a secluded and unrewarding existence: she helped her mother with the housework, tutored her younger brothers and sisters, and assisted her father in his study of American history. Hard work and inner fretting made her an easy victim of an attack of brain fever, and for nine days she was in mortal danger. She had hardly regained her health when her father fell ill of Asiatic cholera and died within twenty hours. The blow was as severe as it was sudden, but she bore up under it with remarkable courage. With her mother self-effacing and unfitted to deal with the outside world, Margaret accepted her new duties as head of the family and reconciled herself to the deep disappointment of having to give up a trip to Europe with Harriet Martineau, who had recently befriended her.

Grief and discontent had shaken her to the roots; her Journal of that period gives evidence of severe soul-searching. But by the following summer she had regained her emotional stability and decided to seek a teaching position in order to improve the family income. In September 1836 she was engaged by Bronson Alcott to teach in his Temple School in Boston and was delighted to quit the farm where she had " to give up all which my heart had for years desired."

Margaret Fuller's coming to Boston was both a resurrection and a flowering. She was so happy to live once again in a center of culture that she did not mind the loneliness of the first weeks or the hard work that sapped her strength throughout that winter. For she was not only teaching Latin and French at the school but also giving private lessons in German and Italian and reading German aloud to Dr. William H. Channing one evening a week; in addition, of course, she continued her omnivorous reading and study. Yet she rejoiced in this " incessant toil," since it brought her in contact with the choicest spirits of the land. Although her brusque manner and caustic tongue discouraged the more tender minds, enough persons of prominence had befriended her to give her the satisfaction of having become an integral part of Boston's circle of intellectuals.

Her greatest conquest was Ralph Waldo Emerson, to whom Harriet Martineau had introduced her and whom she had visited in Concord during the previous summer. The young philosopher was at first on the defensive: her plain face and blinking eyes only accentuated her "rather mountainous ME." After their initial meeting he recorded: "We shall not get far. . . . I am a little afraid of her, she has such an overpowering personality." But she was not easily discouraged. She knew his worth, was certain that friendship would stimulate both of them, and made no secret of her wish to gain it. Before her visit was ended she thawed his inhospitable prudery. Repeated meetings only strengthened their bond of sympathetic understanding. Margaret opened his eyes to a vision of truth and universality that added to his own; Emerson instilled in her a sense of serenity and assurance that she had not known before meeting him and that helped her fully to unfold her idealistic self.

Happy though she was in Boston, she was too much in need of a larger income not to accept the offer from the Greene Street School in Providence at the unprecedented annual salary of a thousand dollars. During the two years that she held the post she continued to regard Boston as her spiritual home and maintained a large correspondence with the friends she had left behind. She also kept up her studies in European literature and philosophy and translated Eckermann's *Conversations With Goethe* for George Ripley's new series of standard foreign works. Her holidays were spent in the Massachusetts capital, where she attended art exhibits and classical concerts and exchanged views with a growing circle of intellectuals who were searching their souls for the key that would unlock the secret of philosophical certainty. In 1839 she decided that teaching children was not her final vocation — that it was time to strike out for her appointed place in a broader world.

The Boston to which Margaret returned was in the full career of a seething cultural upsurge. The Puritanism that had confined the life of New Englanders for two centuries had been thrust aside by an impatient generation which knew not the Calvinistic Mathers and which found Dr. Channing's Unitarianism pale and ineffectual. Not religion but philosophy, not salvation but social reform, became the goals of the young men and women who had tasted of European Romanticism and found it good. Perfection appeared to them a feasible reality; education a talisman with which to acquire all that the imagination conceived. Everyone was engaged in study: mill hands and chambermaids were as preoccupied with self-improvement as were their wealthy employers. Lecture-going had become a passion, and the Lyceums were crowded with eager audiences. Those who had become aware of the businessman's crass materialism began to hatch utopian schemes to rid the world of greed and inequality; others preferred to dwell in the clouds of soulful talk and educational fantasy.

Margaret, culturally in full flower and with a mind that probed deeper and ranged farther than those of her contemporaries, was quick to assert her superior gifts. Her eloquence and passionate vitality made her the center of every discussion in which she participated. Emerson, with whom she frequently shared honors at these gatherings, admitted that she " always appeared to unexpected advantage in conversation with a circle of persons, with more common sense and sanity than any other, — though her habitual vision was through colored lenses." This notable success as a moderator led her, logically enough, to decide upon the career of a " paid Corinne."

She had long been fretting at the restrictions laid on women. Brought up by her father as the equal of any man, conscious of her worth and yet vexed by her lack of beauty, she chafed at the thought of being deprived of certain rights and privileges simply because she was a woman. " I have often had reason to regret being of the softer sex and never more than now," she wrote at the time when, as the nearest male kin, her dour uncle took charge of her father's estate. It was therefore natural for her, in capitalizing upon her speaking ability, to wish to further the cause of equal rights.

She decided upon a feminine audience and upon topics of special benefit to it. But she did not want to lecture to her hearers: she wished rather to discuss with them such questions as, " What were we born to do? and how shall we do it? "; to bring these women out of their stuffy parlors and help them acquire the knowledge and self-reliance that would compel men to accept them as their equals. Her first course of ten Conversations began on November 6, 1839. Twenty-five women attended, among them the most intelligent in Boston. The respect which the most eminent men of the city had for Margaret's gifts made it possible for their wives and daughters proudly to venture into a public activity previously open to them only at their peril. The topic was Greek Mythology, and the praise of heathen Greeks at a Christian meeting so disturbed her inexperienced audience that she had to do most of the talking at first. But she soon enlivened everyone with her volcanic personality; her penetrating analysis of myths hitherto accepted uncritically opened the minds of her hearers to new and exhilarating vistas. Before the course was far along they were actively participating in the discussions and gaining that firmness of intellect which speeded the organization of the feminist movement.

The notable success of these Conversations led immediately to a second course, this time on the fine arts. Again these novel two-hour discussions attracted a maximum audience, and once more Margaret's regal manner and brilliant talk made the women her grateful debtors. At their urging she prepared new courses of Conversations and gave them regularly until she left for New York in 1844. In March 1841 she opened the Conversations to men as well, and a number of the intellectual leaders paid two dollars an evening for the privilege of discussing literary and philosophical prob lems with the queen of conversationalists.

Margaret Fuller's determination to achieve fame was now realized. Alcott, himself a fountain of eloquence, extolled her as " the most commanding talker of her day." After attending one of her discussions, Dr. Channing wrote that " she blended feminine receptiveness with masculine energy. By the intensity of her concep-

tions, she brought out in those around her, *their own consciousness.*" Emerson likewise averred that her conversation was "in ele-
gance, in range, in flexibility, and adroit transition, in depth, in
cordiality, and in moral aim, altogether admirable, surprising and
cheerful as a poem, and communicating its own civility and elevation like a charm to all hearers." No wonder that she preened herself as the most celebrated woman in Boston!

All this admiration yielded her nothing of the emotional fulfilment she craved. To her Journal she confided her anguished
heart: "With the intellect I always have, always shall, overcome;
but that is not half the work. The life, the life! O, my God! shall
the life never be sweet?" Nor did she know that her very self-
consciousness drove men away from her. Even Samuel Gray Ward,
who had come closest in his admiration of her, was in the end discouraged by her equivocal and neurotic behavior. All she could do
was to express this sense of failure in one of her frequent prayers:
"I am weary of thinking. Oh God, take me! take me wholly! . . .
No fellow being will receive me. I cannot pause; they will not de-
tain me by their love. . . ."

Margaret's next venture was the editing of the *Dial*, the organ
of the Transcendentalists. The latter were a small group of thinkers and reformers who, after 1836, met irregularly and infrequently
to discuss the ideas and problems uppermost in their minds. Emerson, Alcott, Theodore Parker, and·George Ripley were among the
leaders; Margaret and about a dozen others joined the conversations
at one time or another. These idealists had no common philosophy
and no definite program. They all believed, however, in "the inalienable integrity of man" and in his "birthright to a universal
good." Many of them were ministers in reaction against Puritan
orthodoxy; others showed the influence of Greek philosophy and
German metaphysics; all were humanitarians recoiling from the
materialism about them. Margaret's mind was enthusiastic rather
than reflective; but she compensated this deficiency by her powers
of analysis and expression and by her great knowledge of modern

writing. These qualifications made her the logical choice as editor when the group decided to issue a quarterly that would reflect the latest trends in philosophy and literature.

The first issue appeared in July 1840, and she herself had to fill space reserved for procrastinating contributors. But the immediate success of the periodical enabled her thereafter to publish the best contemporary writing without paying for it. Especially noteworthy was her ability to seek out the timid neophytes and nurse their talents to rapid fruition. Yet her policy of letting everyone have his say, even to the magazine's hurt, soon met with the inevitable disapproval. The conservatives condemned the quarterly for its very existence. But even its friends found fault: the radicals did not like its conventional part; the social reformers complained it was impractical; and the literary critics were annoyed by the uneven style. Most of them, moreover, could not accept the idea of a woman editor and insisted that what the periodical needed most of all was a masculine emphasis. The circulation, small at best, had dwindled to fewer than one hundred copies at the end of the second year. Margaret saw no advantage in continuing her thankless task and gave over the editorship to Emerson, who accepted it reluctantly in order not to let it fall into the hands of the " Humanity and Reform men." With young Thoreau's help the number of subscribers rose to about 250, but after two years more the *Dial* was suspended. It had served its purpose well as a vehicle for the rising generation and the new philosophy, and Emerson had other work to do.

About the time the *Dial* was launched George Ripley began to plan for a utopian farm community, based on the Transcendental principle of plain living and high thinking. Numerous similar phalanxes were then being operated by foreigners who had come to this country in the hope of bringing heaven upon earth. Ripley's Brook Farm was the first venture into utopia by native Americans. When the idea was broached to the group of Transcendentalists, Emerson was cool, Alcott thought the plan not severe enough, while Margaret, though sympathetic, remembered too well the dreary years on the Groton farm to chance a similar experience. Moreover, as an advocate of self-reliance she objected to " doing things in crowds." " Why bind oneself to a central or any other doctrine? " she asked rhetorically. " How much nobler stands a man entirely unpledged, unbound! Association may be the great experiment of the age, still it is only an experiment."

Nevertheless she was too much the utopian idealist not to favor the attempt at human betterment. It was only her esthetic recoil from the " rabid and exaggerated " behavior of the Abolitionist leaders that had kept her from joining the reform which was then most in the limelight; later, from the vantage point of the Roman Revolution of 1848, she came to appreciate the high motive of the Garrisonians — " it was really something worth living and dying for to free a great nation from such a terrible blot " — and to regret her inactivity. Likewise, while she frowned upon the mechanical disciplines of Fourierism, she sympathized with its humanitarian aspirations. It was her belief that " every noble scheme, every poetic manifestation, prophesizes to man his eventual destiny." She was therefore glad to visit Brook Farm whenever she could. Several of her Conversations were given there. The grateful community honored her as one of its distinguished guests. Only Hawthorne, whom she had met at Brook Farm and who had seemed eager enough to be friends with her, wrote disparagingly of her as " the stump-oratress " in *The Blithedale Romance*, which he published after her death. This novel of the utopian experiment is probably chiefly responsible for the much closer association of her name with Brook Farm than is warranted by the facts.

An unexpected but welcome invitation in the spring of 1843 made it possible for her to visit the Great Lakes country and to observe life on the frontier at first hand. She recorded her impressions in *Summer on the Lakes*, her first work, which in form is reminiscent of Heine's *Reisebilder* and which reveals clearly her interests and sympathies. She deplored the tendency of farmers to send their children to schools in the East and thus to unfit them for life on the prairie. She also deprecated the "comfortless and laborious life" of most of the women; by comparison she found the Indian squaw enjoying a higher social status within the tribe. The raw injustice towards the Indians evoked her strongest condemnation — "The white man as yet is a half-tamed pirate, and avails himself as much as ever of the maxim, 'Might makes right.'"

Horace Greeley, a West enthusiast and reformer, was so favorably impressed by the little book that he offered Margaret the position of literary critic on the *Tribune*. She was delighted with this opportunity to make her way in the American metropolis, as the trip west had made her aware of Boston's parochial limitations. First, however, she wished to complete the expansion of an essay on equal rights into a volume, and did not begin her journalistic career until December 1844.

Woman in the Nineteenth Century, published early in 1845, was the first book on feminism in this country and was praised and denounced with equal heat. Essentially Margaret argued for the right of women to develop their talents in accord with their inherent natures. She defended as persons worthy of honor Mary Wollstonecraft and George Sand, at that time scorned as immoral freaks. Drawing upon her enormous reading, she demonstrated that her sex had always been stultified and conditioned against "originality of thought and character." She urged women to stand firmly on their own feet, to develop "self-subsistence in its two forms of self-reliance and self-impulse." So far as she was concerned, women were capable of filling any office — even that of "sea-captains" — and had in fact already "taken possession of so many provinces for which men had pronounced them unfit, that although these still declare there are some inaccessible to them, it is difficult to say just *where* they must stop."

Yet she was too much the reformer and Transcendentalist to advocate mere equality. Perfection was to her the ultimate goal. Denying that love encompassed woman's whole existence, she exhorted her sex to clear their "souls from the taint of vanity" and to cultivate their potent moral power in order to achieve nobility in themselves and to lift men to their own level.

You see the men [she counseled], how they are willing to sell shamelessly the happiness of countless generations of fellow-creatures, the honor of their country, and their immortal souls for a money market and political power. . . . Tell these men that you will not accept the glittering baubles, spacious dwellings, and plentiful service they mean to offer you through these means. Tell them that the heart of Woman demands nobleness and honor in man, and that if they have not purity, have not mercy, they are no longer fathers, lovers, husbands, sons of yours.

Horace Greeley soon had reason to congratulate himself on his choice of Margaret Fuller as his literary critic. The quality of her reviews made them one of the *Tribune's* special features. With the possible exception of Poe, she was the first American to write of books with objectivity and deep critical acumen. Her thorough study of European literature and of Goethe in particular enabled her to expose the provincialism, the imitativeness, and the general mediocrity of much American writing. She dissected the books under scrutiny without fear or favor, and she shocked many of her readers by devastating criticisms of such popular poets as Lowell and Longfellow. Only Emerson's verse and Hawthorne's fiction appeared to her to measure up to the best work of European writers. Margaret's evaluation of the leading English and Continental authors was equally penetrating. In all her reviews she adhered to the principle that " a great work of Art demands a great thought, or a thought of beauty adequately expressed." She tried her utmost to develop the literary taste of her readers and to wean them from the prevailing pedantry and prudery. When her representative reviews were collected and published in 1846 under the title of *Papers on Literature and Art*, they constituted a volume of the most distinguished criticism to appear in this country up to that time.

The realities of a newspaper office and the broader associations of the metropolis soon rubbed off a good deal of the mystic sentimentalism — " cant and nonsense " to Greeley — which she had cultivated in Boston. She became keenly interested in the improvement of the city's charitable and reformatory institutions. The women prisoners at Sing Sing and Blackwell's Island attracted her particularly, and she spent days with them in intimate discussion. Convinced of their inherent goodness, she wrote about them with compassion at a time when social tabus excluded them from the ken of women of respectability, and so brought a new note into the incipient agitation for penal reform.

Margaret was soon as popular in New York as she had been in Boston. But no amount of adulation could fill the void in her yearning heart. " I am alone, as usual," was her reply when asked why she had sighed so deeply at the end of a Valentine Day party. That same month, however, she met James Nathan, a German-Jewish merchant of cultural predilections, and fell in love with him. Flattered by her attention, he encouraged her interest in him. In her usual impetuous manner Margaret soon contrived to see him often. She wrote to him almost daily and made no secret of her affection for him. For the first time in her life she thought she was being wooed for herself and felt too grateful and too happy to bother with formalities and reticences. Nathan was not equal to her passionate ardor, but for a time did his best to reciprocate. They had many ups and downs, yet went deeper right along. Nathan was becoming frightened; he could think only of flight, and sailed for Europe in June.

Margaret now knew " how wounds can burn and ache." She would have been disconsolate in her humiliation and misery had not her friends exerted themselves to help her to forget. On her return in October from a short vacation in Massachusetts she busied herself with her work and did her best to put the unhappy experience out of mind. Thus the winter passed and the spring, and in the summer came the opportunity she had sought for so many years — a grand tour of Europe with dear friends, plus a correspondent's assignment from the New York *Tribune,* her country's most exciting daily.

Margaret's reputation as a feminist and critic had preceded her to Great Britain, and she was everywhere received with marked cordiality. Her visits to the centers of manufacture and commerce — " burning focuses of grief and vice " — made it easy for her to join the cause of Reform and to associate with the liberals and Continental exiles who came her way. Mazzini, whom she met at the Carlyles', became one of her closest friends. The Carlyles received her many times, and although she found her Scottish host arrogant and overbearing — he was her match as a talker and shouted her down at will — she admired his great talents and powerful personality.

In November she went to Paris and made the rounds of the galleries, theaters, and celebrities, and was greatly stimulated by her interview with George Sand. Here, too, she studied the life of the workers and was keenly affected by their wretched poverty. The sight of this misery made her overcome her earlier distaste for Fourier's doctrines. " I should pity the person," she wrote, " who, after the briefest sojourn in Manchester and Lyons, the most superficial acquaintance with the population of London and Paris, could seek to hinder a study of his thoughts, or to be wanting in reverence for his purposes."

The Italians quickly impressed her with their " capacity for pure, exalting passion." In Rome, which she reached the following April, she absorbed the imposing richness and dignity of its antiquities and churches with the zeal of a pious pilgrim. Here again, however, she was not satisfied to remain merely the disinterested tourist. She was quick to note the incipient restiveness of the people and soon became an active participant in their agitation for national independence. Her frequent letters to the *Tribune* and to friends reveal a deepened awareness of the world, an eagerness to bring about the rebirth of a new society. " I see the future dawning," she wrote to William Channing in May 1847; "it is in important aspects Fourier's future."

Shortly after coming to Rome, while visiting St. Peter's, Margaret met Giovanni Angelo Ossoli and was immediately attracted to him. He was of a noble family, but of little education and less means; moreover, he was only twenty-six years old and she was nearing her thirty-seventh birthday. But he made himself very useful to her as a guide and gazed upon her with a yearning that made her quick with happiness. What mattered age or station, she wondered, so long as there was understanding and affinity? "Woman is born for love," she asserted about that time, "and it is impossible to turn her from seeking it." With George Sand as her model and with the long-repressed woman in her crying for affection, it was easy for her to welcome Ossoli as her destined lover. When she returned to Rome in October, after a tour of other parts of Italy, her erstwhile guide was waiting for her and made himself her almost inseparable companion.

The movement for Italian liberation was gaining momentum. Revolution was in the air. The downfall of Louis Philippe in France and of Metternich in Austria encouraged the Italians to seek the overthrow of their own despots. Pope Pius IX at first led them to expect political reforms in the Roman States, but the aggressive mood of the people frightened him and he withdrew his support of the liberals. Mazzini and Garibaldi, however, proceeded without his approval.

More than any other English-speaking resident in Rome, Margaret Fuller knew the unhappy history of the divided country and was very eager to work for its national unity. But she expected more than political freedom; she wanted to see social betterment as well. Indeed the socialistic agitation appealed to her as just and commendable. "Our age is one where all things tend to a great crisis," she wrote in October 1847; "not merely to revolution, but to radical reform." So preoccupied had she become with the thought of a better world that on the first day of what she knew would be a momentous year she could not help reflecting on the pitiful state of Europe after eighteen centuries of Christian culture. "Where is the genuine democracy to which the rights of all men are holy? . . . If we consider the amount of truth that has really been spoken out in the world, and the love that has beat in private hearts . . . the public failure seems amazing, seems monstrous." Nor did she exclude the United States from this indictment, excoriating it as "the darkest offender because with the least excuse." It was at this time that she expressed her admiration for the Abolitionists, whose rabid behavior she could not endure while at home but whose moral motive now appealed to her as noble and heroic.

The flame of revolution which spread so rapidly through Western Europe during the early months of 1848 warmed her responsive heart. "It is a time such as I always dreamed of," she wrote to Channing in April. And a month later she excused herself to Emerson for not accepting his invitation to take ship with him from London: "I should like to return with you, but I have much to do and learn in Europe yet. I am deeply interested in the public drama, and wish to see it *played out*. Methinks I have *my part* therein, either as actor or historian." It was her intention to be both. Her letters to the *Tribune*, giving a clear and acute analysis of the prevailing political and social conditions in Europe, served well as material for her history. At the same time she participated actively in the increasing agitation in Rome, and when Mazzini returned to it after seventeen years of exile she became his associate and confidante.

But now there was crisis in her private life: she became pregnant. Her first reaction was one of despair. "This incubus of the future" caused her to write to Caroline Sturgis: "I have no reason to hope that I shall not reap what I have sown, and do not. Yet how I shall endure it I cannot guess." But her good sense kept her buoyant and balanced. She married Ossoli privately, and shortly thereafter left for Rieti to await the birth of her child. The baby came early in September and Margaret had a difficult and anxious time with the doctor and the wet-nurse. Two months later, badly in need of money and eager to resume her part in the social drama, she arranged for the care of her infant son and returned to Rome. To her mother she wrote cryptically: "In earlier days I dreamed of doing and being much, but now am content with the Magdalen to rest my plea hereon, '*She has loved much.*'"

Her return to the city almost coincided with the Pope's flight from it. The subsequent establishment of the Roman Republic gave her great joy. "I pass whole days abroad," wrote the erstwhile bluestocking and bookworm; "sometimes I take a book, but seldom read it: — why should I, when every stone talks?" But the forces of revolt were still too weak to oppose the French army which Napoleon had ordered to restore the Pope to his throne. When General Oudinot began the attack on Rome in April, Margaret took charge of a hospital and worked day and night to minister to the wounded. The tragedy of the siege drained her vitality even more than the physical strain. "O Rome, *my* country," she cried to Emerson that June. "Could I imagine that the triumph of what I held dear was to heap such desolation on my head!" And a month later, after the defeat of the Garibaldi Legion, she confessed to Channing: "Private hopes of mine have fallen with the hopes of Italy. I have played for a new stake and lost it. Life looks too difficult." She was "*tired out* — tired of thinking and hoping — tired of seeing men err and bleed."

Friends helped her and Ossoli to reach Rieti, where they found their son half-starved and ill. He reacted very quickly to their tender nursing, however, and the little family settled in Florence for the winter. Margaret now had to appear before her friends as a wife and mother and was greatly relieved to find them accepting her new role as a matter of course. For the next few months she worked on her history of the Roman Revolution. In the spring the lack of means and a reluctance to remain in an Italy no longer congenial to her speeded her decision to return to the United States. Numerous difficulties, real and fancied, confronted her — the most immediate being the high cost of travel for the three of them. But with the help of solicitous friends she succeeded in arranging for their passage on the *Elizabeth*, a small and slow ship, and sailed from Gibraltar on June 19. As the vessel approached Fire Island exactly a month later, a storm smashed it against a sandbar within a few hundred yards of the shore. No help came during the gale, and in the confusion Margaret and her husband and child were washed into the sea and drowned. Most of her belongings, including the manuscript on the Roman Revolution, were lost with her.

It was a striking tribute to Margaret's personality that her tragic death should have caused such genuine grief among so many persons on both sides of the Atlantic. The Brownings, who had befriended her in Florence, were deeply shocked; Landor wrote a long poem to her memory; Lowell and Longfellow, forgetting the hurt of her criticism, were quick to extol her genius; Mazzini, again in London, was disconsolate. Even the dour Carlyle was moved to praise her in his characteristic fashion: " Such a predetermination to *eat* this big universe as her oyster or her egg, and to be absolute empress of all height and glory in it that her heart could conceive, I have not before seen in any human soul." Emerson, with whom she had been most intimate, recorded the sad tidings in his Journal: " To the last her country proves inhospitable to her; brave, eloquent, subtle, accomplished, devoted, constant soul! . . . I have lost in her my audience." With several of her other lifelong friends he proceeded at once " to build her a cairn " — which materialized early in 1852 in the two-volume *Memoirs of Margaret Fuller Ossoli*, a somewhat bowdlerized but deeply moving account of her life and character.

Time has made secure her prominent position in the cultural history of the United States. Although her tragic death cut off her productivity before it had reached its maturest fruition, her personality had impressed itself indelibly upon her generation. Her great intellectual vigor, her extraordinary generosity of spirit, and above all her passionate criticism of the parochialism and materialism about her, made her the effective leader of those who resented the restraints of their Calvinistic environment and sought to enthrone the precious freedoms of civilized man. It is this championing of human rights, this abhorrence of oppression and inequality of any kind, that still endears her name to all lovers of liberty and democracy.

ALBERT BRISBANE

SOCIAL DREAMER

MOST ENCYCLOPEDIAS, the Britannica included, make no mention of Albert Brisbane, although they pay homage to his son Arthur's journalistic attainments. The only published study of his life and work remains his wife's " mental biography," which appeared shortly after his death in 1890. Yet throughout the 1840's he was widely acclaimed as an eminent social philosopher. As the interpreter and promoter of Fourier's grand scheme of Association he became the leader of a reform movement that swept across the United States. Horace Greeley was one of his first converts and opened to him the columns of the influential *Tribune*; Parke Godwin, of the New York *Evening Post*, became one of his ardent admirers; the Transcendentalists of Brook Farm swallowed Brisbane's doctrine whole. About 8000 Americans in all invested their goods and their future in Fourieristic phalanxes. These enthusiasts believed that the success of their experimental communities would speedily bring the millennium, and united in national conventions to hasten the coming of the glorious day. Their dreams were of short duration; one after another the phalanxes collapsed like pricked balloons.

Yet although Fourier's utopia went the way of all panaceas, it stirred the enthusiasm of many Americans for more than a decade and made a definite impress upon the nineteenth-century movement for social reform. Brisbane's reputation rests squarely on the importance of Association in the history of American culture.

Born in 1809 in the frontier environment of Batavia, New York, young Albert Brisbane was more interested in outdoor life than in his school work. His intelligent and well-to-do parents permitted him the freedom of the forest, and he spent much of his early adolescence in hunting and fishing. While on one such excursion at the age of fifteen a " spontaneous intuition " suddenly revealed to him that he " belonged to a vast army in which each individual had his place and function, and that those who left its ranks to attend to individual concerns could not advance in the great achievement to which they were destined." This vision of the duty of man never left him. The belief that " it is not right for the individual to work for himself " motivated all his future study and striving.

That same year his father sent him to a school in New York. The friendship of one of his teachers, an ingenious and independent pedagogue, enabled him not only to acquire a solid knowledge of foreign languages but also to familiarize himself with the exciting intellectual ferment of the Continental capitals. As a consequence he conceived a great eagerness to study philosophy and the theory of social progress at their sources and persuaded his parents to let him go to France. In May 1828 he sailed for Paris in the hope of finding an answer to the question: " What is the destiny of man and what can I do to accelerate it? "

A year later, while eating ice cream during an intermission at the Paris Opéra, young Brisbane received his second " intuition ": " that a certain class in society lived on the labor of the masses." He had found his teachers, among the leading French thinkers, unsatisfactory guides. The lectures of Victor Cousin led him to Hegel — then the fountainhead of philosophy — and he went to Germany to seek enlightenment. After another year of intense study, this time with the acknowledged leaders of civilized thought, he found himself no nearer to a solution. As a democratic American he refused to accept Hegel's smug assumption that the Germans had attained the highest form of social development. But if young Brisbane could not subscribe to the tenets of German philosophy, he was delighted with the society of Berlin and took full advantage of the welcome that was given him as the only American student then in the Prussian capital.

More eager than ever to learn the ways of men, he left Germany in 1830 for a tour that took him to Vienna, Turkey, Greece, Italy, France, England, and Ireland. Everywhere he observed the life of the people and was pained to note the poverty and inequality that existed universally and that seemed especially acute in Greece and Ireland. In France he was attracted to the Saint-Simonian movement, but could not fully accept the teachings of its leaders. Before returning to Berlin to study the social sciences he took stock of his intellectual acquisitions and summed them up as follows: (1) At fifteen he had discovered that " man had a work to perform on this earth — a collective work — the function of the race." (2) At nineteen he had " speculated on the source of wealth." (3) He had "learned absolutely nothing" from Cousin and Hegel. (4) On the elevation of woman depends the elevation of the race. (5) " *Political* reforms are of secondary importance, — that the reality is in the social organization and in the institutions of society." (6) " The source of wealth — the prosperity — of a nation is in its industrial organization . . . the equipment of productive labor."

Like so many other Americans of his generation, young Brisbane grew into manhood with a messianic compulsion. He reasoned that it was not God's will that men should suffer, that there must be a way of eliminating squalor from the world. It was his eagerness to learn the thoughts of great minds on this problem that caused him to return to Berlin. But the eminent lecturers on social science satisfied him no more than Hegel had done the year before.

While in this state of perplexity he began one day to look over Fourier's new work, *L'Association Domestique-Agricole*, which a Parisian friend had sent him. The book made " an indescribable impression " upon his receptive mind. The very thought of " dignifying and *rendering attractive* the manual labors of mankind " struck the excited youth with the force of a revelation. He began at once to discuss the work with his German friends, to convey to them his enthusiasm for the author's great discovery; their complete indifference only deepened his zeal to learn more about the radical reform and he left for Paris to make Fourier's acquaintance.

Charles Fourier was sixty years old when Brisbane arranged with him for private instruction. As a young man he had been deprived of his inheritance by the French Revolution and deeply frightened by the excesses of the Terror. Later his dealings with fraudulent and greedy tradesmen had developed in him a strong antipathy towards bourgeois businessmen. The social anarchy brought about by the Industrial Revolution made him yearn for a world free from the rule of force and injustice. Influenced by the " positive " and meliorist thinkers of his day — a period marked by great intellectual energy and emotional confusion — he began to devise a system of society in which every man lived in comfort and security. Of a precise yet uncritical turn of mind, he studied the scientific as well as the pseudo-scientific theories of his contemporaries with equal zeal and planned to organize " the collective life of man on strictly scientific principles." He believed that human motives and passions were on the whole good; that commerce corrupted human nature; that our civilization, however faulty, was unwittingly preparing the forces which would raise mankind to the next stage of society's development — harmonious Association. This system — at once efficient and efficacious — would render manual labor dignified and attractive, would abolish poverty and inequality, and would make possible the highest scientific development and general human perfection. So deeply did he impress his views on the receptive Brisbane during their two years of almost daily contact that the young disciple came to regard him " among those bold and original geniuses, like Columbus, Copernicus and Newton, who open new paths to human science, and who appear upon the stage of the world to give it a new impetus, and exercise an influence, which is to be prolonged for ages."

In 1834, after six years abroad, Albert Brisbane returned to the United States. He was overflowing with faith in Fourier's social system and eager to familiarize his fellow Americans with his great discovery; yet he was too much the dreamer and philosopher not to follow Fourier's practice of reflection rather than action. Moreover, he had undermined his health during his sojourn in Europe and needed time to regain his strength. For the next few years he remained in seclusion, pondering the work of his master, relating the details of Association with man's activity throughout his historic development, preparing himself for the glorious task ahead. Yet he was at no time averse to making his views known to friends and sympathetic inquirers. By 1839 he had organized Fourier study groups in New York and Philadelphia. To these societies he lectured as often as he was able. All the while he was at work on his vigorous study of Association, *The Social Destiny of Man.*

This work, which appeared in 1840, contains a persuasive discussion of Association, partly in Fourier's own words and partly in Brisbane's. The zealous disciple was the ideal interpreter. He had so merged his views with those of his master that it was difficult to discern what he had borrowed from that which was his own. As a consequence Fourierism in the United States became synonymous with Brisbane's writings.

The thesis of Association is thus stated by Brisbane: " We assert that the evil, misery and injustice, now predominant on the earth, have not their foundation in political or administrational errors, in this defect or that institution, but in the *False Organization of Society Alone.*" To abolish the existing evils, therefore, it was necessary to reorganize society completely on a plan which would eliminate poverty and inefficiency and provide each human being with " an *ennobling and pleasing activity.*" Living in an age still largely agricultural, loathing the abuses of an emergent industrialism, seeking a solution that would obviate human exploitation and the defacement of nature, Fourier had hit upon the idea of associative unity. His ideal was a small compact community living in harmony and comfort. In deliberating on the desirable size of the phalanx or group, he made use of prevailing statistical estimates that " among every 810 persons Nature distributes all the talents necessary for excelling in the different branches of human activity." To make sure that these self-contained communities should not suffer from any chance lack of necessary talent, he determined that each phalanx should contain at least twice that many members. This Association, "which would replace the desultory action of individuals by combined efforts of masses, distribute judiciously and appropriately the capacity, talent and labor of the different sexes and ages, introduce method and a scientific system of cultivation in the place of waste and ignorance, would conflict with no rights or principles, but, on the contrary, would forward greatly the interests and welfare of all classes, both rich and poor." To insure its success, he insisted that no phalanx must be begun with less capital than half a million dollars. Indeed, he had announced early in his career that at a certain hour he would wait daily in his study for the philanthropist ready to invest this amount of money to prove the validity of his theory, and for thirty years he continued to expect his rich visitor — in vain. Brisbane, taking American conditions into account, thought a community of as few as four hundred members could thrive, provided it began with adequate capital.

To demonstrate the superiority of Association over the existing form of "incoherent industry," Brisbane presented the following comparative table:

Result of Combined, Attractive Industry	Results of Incoherent, Repugnant Industry
1. General and graduated riches	1. Indigence
2. Practical truth in business and social relations	2. Fraud
3. Real and effective liberty	3. Oppression
4. Constant peace	4. War
5. Equilibrium of temperature and climate	5. Derangement of climate
6. System of preventive medicine	6. Diseases artificially produced
7. Opening offered to all ameliorations and improvement	7. Vicious circle without any opening for improvement

Brisbane's eloquence and enthusiasm made the plan of Association plausible and persuasive to those of his readers in the early

1840's who were themselves in quest of a panacea. Even the more hard-headed had to admit that a phalanx of 300 families would be a more efficient economic unit than the same number of families living apart and in their own particular ways. To mention only the most elemental needs, the disunited families require 300 individual homes with the same number of kitchens, stoves, fires, sets of kitchen utensils, and women to do the work — "which is the essence of complication and waste"; the phalanx would meet these same needs much more satisfactorily with one great palace, three or four huge kitchens, a few large ranges and fires, and several expert cooks. This saving of labor and equipment would make possible a vastly increased productivity. The normal non-producers, such as women, children, servants, the idle rich and others, would become productive workers. In addition each person, stimulated by congenial tasks and naturally eager to excel within his own group, would tend to increase his output. Brisbane made this point forcefully:

Hired labor between man and man, as it exists in civilization, is degrading, besides being a source of petty tyranny, persecution, quarrels and litigation without end. In the combined order the individual has no superior but the Phalanx; if he performs duties for so high an employer, there is something ennobling in it; if he obeys the calm decision of the mass, there is something honorable in it.

The proper and able direction of this increased production would augment the income of the phalanx manifold and thus make possible undreamt of benefits and enjoyments to each member. In his enthusiasm Brisbane went so far as to assert that " if Association raised every product to its highest degree of perfection, man should attain at least to a treble increase in strength, longevity and intelligence."

The keystone of Association was, of course, the promise to make labor attractive. *The Social Destiny of Man* begins with this assurance: " We assert, and will prove, that Labor, which is now *monotonous, repugnant, and degrading*, can be *ennobled, elevated* and made *honorable;* — or in other words, Industry can be rendered *Attractive!* " It was obvious that to achieve this laudable goal it was

necessary to fit the work to be done to man's " Passional System."
After many years of study and reflection Fourier had discovered a
total of twelve human passions or instincts: the five senses, four
affective passions (friendship, love, ambition, paternity), and three
distributive or directive passions. " Happiness," he argued, " consists in the continued satisfaction of the twelve passions harmoniously developed." This satisfaction can be attained within the phalanx by a proper and voluntary division of labor: each member
would join the Groups and Series of workers which best suited his
passional nature. The actual work of the phalanx was to be divided
into three classes: necessary labor, useful labor, and pleasing labor;
to insure a proper distribution of workers to each class, the highest
wages were to be paid for necessary work and the lowest for pleasing
work. To eliminate the element of repugnance from any sort of
productive or " useful " labor, three conditions would be strictly
observed: " 1. Compact scale among Groups. 2. Short duration of
occupations, and free choice of the same. 3. Parcelled exercise in
occupations and functions." The right of members to choose the
nature of their work and to change their occupations every hour or
two would eliminate the distasteful elements of employment —
compulsion and monotony.

Fourier knew that even the highest wages would not attract volunteers to perform the uncleanly yet unavoidable tasks of the phalanx.
To solve this difficulty he made use of his discovery that boys between the ages of nine and sixteen have little antipathy to " dirty
or offensive contacts." He therefore provided that these youngsters
be organized into a " Sacred Legion " to assume the repulsive labors
and be awarded the highest honors at the disposal of the phalanx.
The work would be so arranged, of course, that no boy would be
so employed more than two hours a day.

An important element of Association was the scheme of education for children from infancy through adolescence. According to
Fourier, " Nature demands the education of children in masses, as
well for their own good as for the comfort of the parents." In order
that mothers might be as free and productive as the other adults of

the phalanx, skilled nurses and teachers were to be provided for the care of the children, who would be separated into the quiet, the restless, and the turbulent. Refinement of the senses would begin at the age of six months; the suckling of infants would cease on their first birthday. During their second year they would be regarded as the Weaned, and as Little Commencers during their third. In their fourth year they would enter the first order of the Initiated and would begin to earn their maintenance by doing work according to their capacities. As they grew older and gained in skill they would advance from one order to the next until they reached the sixth at maturity. Since admission to each order was conditioned upon increased skill and knowledge, the children would voluntarily solicit instruction in both. Upon reaching the age of nine they would be induced to seek the welfare of the phalanx as a whole in order that they might willingly undertake the tasks that were repugnant to their elders.

The distribution of income was considered carefully by both Fourier and Brisbane. The latter, the greater humanitarian, was the less tolerant of capitalist enterprise. " The tyranny of capital," he asserted hopefully, " one of the last relics of tyranny, and the most repulsive, will be swept from the face of the earth by Association." Even Brisbane, however, believed in individual property and in the right of capitalists to a handsome profit. It was the hope of both men that the benefits of their plan would so appeal to the powerful and the rich as to turn them into " the true leaders of the world, instead of its oppressors." To attract wealthy investors to his scheme Fourier provided for a relatively high share to be paid to capital out of the annual income of each phalanx. Brisbane put it as follows:

The total product of a Phalanx from all sources, agriculture, manufacture, etc., is divided into three parts, or dividends, bearing to each other the following proportions: 5/12 to labor, 4/12 to capital, 3/12 to skill. Every man, woman and child receives on the day of the yearly settlement, a portion of one, two or all the above dividends, according to his or her labor, capital or skill.

An account would be kept with each individual member, from the four-year-olds in the first order to the most skilled or wealthy adult, and against it would be charged all purchases and services. Members would live modestly or luxuriously, according to their means and wishes, since they would be free to use their earnings as they pleased. To provide for these differences in taste and expenditures, the phalanx would offer meals, accommodations, and goods at several levels of cost.

There is little point in going further into the detailed plan of Association. Brisbane's writings described its minutest aspects. His powerful will-to-believe imparted to the phalanx an impress of assured success. How could any social system fail which provided for "convenient and labor-saving machinery . . . healthy, even elegant workshops . . . short sessions of labor . . . bringing the play of sentiments into industry, and identifying the social and the productive life of man?" So unrestrained was his enthusiasm for Association during the early 1840's that his claims for it, as recorded in his reminiscences, assumed cosmic proportions:

I saw humanity united in a great whole — united in all the details of its material life: unity of language; unity in the means of communication; unity in all its enterprises, in its weights and measures, in its currency; concert and combination everywhere. I saw this associative humanity working with order, with concert, to realize some great purpose. I had a vivid conception of a great function as the destiny of this humanity; I saw the association of our globe and the humanities upon it to the Cosmic Globe to which they belong; I felt an instinctive pride in the great human race and an ambition to serve it — an ambition to be a part, however small and humble, in the vast organism.

Albert Brisbane was not a leader of men. He had neither the fanatic drive nor the forceful personality of the successful crusader. Very mild-mannered and modest in deportment, uncompromising in his adherence to principle, always the student and dreamer rather than the man of action, he became the chief propagandist for Association only because he happened to be the first American to have brought Fourier's plan with him from Europe and to have presented it in explicit and appealing terms. *The Social Destiny of Man*, with its detailed and glowing exposition of the new utopia, appeared just as the victims of the panic of 1837 were emerging from economic distress and were favorably disposed towards a way of life that promised to be both stable and pleasant. Association offered them all this and much besides, and those who wished to learn more about it naturally turned to Brisbane.

The first important convert was Horace Greeley who had read *The Social Destiny of Man* at the behest of the author and was completely won over by the humanitarian aspects of the plan. As he made clear during his journalistic controversy with Henry J. Raymond of *The Courier and Enquirer* over the merits of Association, he favored it because it promised its members a comfortable home, a good education, the opportunity to labor at a just and adequate recompense, agreeable social relations, and cultural opportunities. " Its grand aim," he added, " is to effect a Reconciliation of the interests of Capital and Labor, by restoring the natural Rights of the latter without trenching on the acquired Rights or Interests of the former."

Greeley being a man of zeal, he at once joined forces with Brisbane. For two months the pair issued *Future*, a weekly devoted to Industrial Association. When Greeley established *The Tribune*, he made it possible for Brisbane to print a daily column in that newspaper at a charge of $150 per week. He also took pains to call the attention of his many interested readers to this special column, and thus helped Brisbane spread the idea of Association over the entire country. A contemporary said of the effect of the column: " The rich were enticed! the poor were encouraged; the laboring classes were aroused; objections were answered; prejudices were annihilated, etc." The angry attacks upon him from the conservative pulpit and press were proof of the wide influence of Brisbane's writings. Parke Godwin, George Ripley, William H. Channing, and Charles A. Dana were among the leading converts during the two years in which the column appeared. Brisbane also edited *The Chronicle*, wrote twice weekly for *The Plebeian,* and contributed articles to *The Democrat* and *The Dial.* In addition he established *The Phalanx, or Journal of Social Science,* which appeared regularly from October 1843 until it was absorbed by *The Harbinger* some two years later.

The years 1843–45 witnessed the formation of a great number of phalanxes throughout the northern half of the country — more by far than in all the rest of the world. One of the first was Sylvania Phalanx, organized by workers in western Pennsylvania. Its ardent leaders proceeded without Brisbane's approval, and having neither the capital nor the necessary skills they had to disband within six months. North American Phalanx, situated near Red Bank, New Jersey, was the most ambitious experiment of all. Brisbane gave it only his reluctant approval, but the other leading Associationists backed it with money and encouragement. At no time, however, did it have even a sizable fraction of the members and capital stipulated by Brisbane as the permissible minimum; counting 77 persons a the end of the first year, a little more than a hundred somewhat later. Lack of money, morever, narrowed its enterprise and kept its income at a low level. Yet despite recurring internal dissensions the phalanx persereved for more than twelve years; ceasing to exist as an organized unit only after a fire had consumed its buildings.

The Fourierist movement in the United States attained its greatest effectivcness with the conversion of Brook Farm into a phalanx in 1844. The high cultural standards of this New England colony had given it a prestige far above that of any other existing community. Its reorganization on Fourierist lines could not but stimulate enthusiasts everywhere. The Friends of Association formed a national organization and elected George Ripley as their first president. Brisbane became known among them as the Great Disciple and his free-flowing eloquence warmed the hearts of his followers at the various assemblies. He was especially influential among the Brook Farmers and his visits with them were sympathetically recorded in numerous diaries. The vision of Utopia so carried away many of the members that W. H. Channing spoke their minds when he wrote in *The Harbinger*:

We have a solemn and glorious work before us: 1. To indoctrinate the whole people of the United States with the principles of Associative unity. 2. To prepare for the time when the nation, like one man, shall reorganize its townships upon the basis of perfect justice. A nobler opportunity was certainly never opened to men, than that which here and now welcomes Associationists.

The very next year, in 1847, a fire destroyed the newly built phalanstery and with it went the hopes and dreams not only of the Brook Farmers but of the entire Association movement.

About fifty other phalanxes were started during these years. All of them were begun by enthusiasts who gloried in the alluring goal but ignored the hard road leading to it. They lacked enough capital and members, proper skills and favorable conditions. Greeley stated later that these experiments were " destitute alike of capacity, public confidence, energy, and means." Only the Wisconsin Phalanx, which endured for six years, ended its existence with a profit to its members; two others lasted for four years; the remainder broke up after a struggle of two years or less. By the end of the 1840's the vogue of Association was completely dead. At the outset Brisbane had done his utmost to discourage these premature efforts — the consequence largely of his own enticing promises — and had urged the necessity of patient and prolonged preparation. When his advice was politely ignored he disassociated himself from the experiments, and at a later date constantly asserted that their failure in no way called in question the essential validity of his principles.

Late in 1843, perturbed by the thought that he had initiated a movement which he could not control, Brisbane returned to Paris to complete his study of Fourier's unpublished writings. He remained in France more than a year; there he copied the treasured manuscripts, and attended courses in musical theory and the " practical execution of the art " in order to appreciate more fully the underlying harmony of the world order. Likewise to understand more clearly the processes of living nature, he took lessons in embryology.

When he returned to New York in December 1844, the wildcat popularity of Fourierism had already begun to decline. The failure of several phalanxes, although caused by a flagrant disregard of the conditions set down plainly and emphatically in Brisbane's writings, was beginning to deflate the optimism of those interested in the idea of Association. Moreover, some of the orthodox editors and preachers were attacking Fourierism as atheistic and immoral and concentrating their abuse on its chief advocates. Brisbane was anything but a fighter. Though he refused to swerve a jot from his principles, he recoiled from the hurly-burly of public controversy. Unlike Garrison and Phillips who were at that time fighting slavery with belligerent persistence, he lacked the drive of fanatic faith. Instead of joining in the debate he left for Batavia, New York. In the peaceful wilds of the Alleghenies he resumed his study of Fourier's manuscripts and pondered the fundamental problems of society.

His probing of the theory of harmony had convinced him that nothing exists in isolation and that all things and thoughts are related to one another. To find the binding threads of our social system he began to examine the significant and recurrent features of the historic past. Fourier's speculations had not completely satisfied him on this point. At one time he even stated that " if ever a man deserved to be hanged for intellectual rashness and violence, it is Fourier." And although this was uttered more in admiration than in reproof, Brisbane pursued his researches in the hope of finding scientific proofs of his master's theories. His reflections led him to the conclusion that there must be " a *Great System of Laws* which, when integrally discovered, would constitute, like the parts of the human body, a complete whole; each one being the unvarying impression of some force in the Universe."

He kept aloof from the existing phalanxes, Brook Farm excepted, and would not invest his money in any of them. These experiments in Association were to him pathetic caricatures of the phalanxes that Fourier and he had envisioned. What grieved him most was the knowledge that the inevitable failure of these foolhardy efforts at Association was making impossible the establishment of a phalanx under favorable circumstances. As late as 1870 he insisted that not one of the half-hundred communities organized during the forties followed the basic conditions of Association — " no practical trial, and no approach to one, has yet been made of Fourier's theory of Social Organization."

In the spring of 1848 and again in the summer of 1851 Brisbane went to Europe to observe the effects of the revolutionary movement on the public mind. He sojourned in the several centers of unrest and fraternized with the leading radicals in each. A close study of the nature and failure of the various uprisings led him to remark that " reform movements which produce an effect are those which enter into our real wants and interests, and take into account the misery and sufferings of the people." He also met Karl Marx and interested himself in the German's social doctrines. Since he was convinced that Association was based upon scientific principles and that there could be no clash of classes within the phalanx, he never became a Marxian socialist. Yet he acknowledged that both Fourier and Marx were at one in their aims to eliminate economic exploitation and establish social equality. Speaking many years later of his sympathy with socialism, he said:

The property of the nation must be controlled by the nation — the Collective Mind represented by its government; thus securing to all members of the great national family the right to engage freely in all those branches of labor for which they feel themselves adapted, and with the full enjoyment of the product of their labor.

When his father, who had always shielded him from material cares, died in 1851, Brisbane for the first time had to enter into the family realty business. He was so ill-adapted to his new role, however, that his younger and more practical brother soon relieved him of it without reducing his generous allowance. Two years later he married Sarah White, and in time became the father of five children. Yet so intent was he on his scholarly pursuits and so oblivious at times to the real world about him that his wife had to bear the entire burden of the household. When she died in 1867, shortly after the birth of her fifth child, he did his best to care for his infant sons all by himself; but he made a poor nurse and permitted the children to fend for themselves a good part of the time. In 1876 he married Redelia Bates, a young admirer of his published writings, and she quickly brought order and comfort into the completely neglected home. In the same year he published his *General Introduction to the Social Sciences*, a philosophical recapitulation of Association. During his last years he traveled abroad, continued his inquiries into various phases of the social order, and tinkered with such mechanical inventions as the steamship, compressed wood pavement, and a vacuum cooking oven. On the day before he died, late in April 1890 — alone and forgotten, an ineffectual dreamer who had been all his life " impelled by a single absorbing passion, the social redemption of the *collective* man " — his one concern was that he would not live to witness the workers' holiday on May First.

General Introduction to the Social Sciences, the fruit of forty years of contemplative effort, claims to be the " philosopher's stone " for the transformation of a disorganized civilization into a free and happy society. Unlike Brisbane's earlier writings, this work contains neither a detailed blueprint of the ideal phalanx nor the proselyting zeal which had brought thousands of enthusiasts to his cause. Instead it dwells upon the scientific principles governing society, the universal laws which, in Brisbane's belief, Fourier was the first to discover. His investigations, stimulated by a strong admiration for Newton's laws, had first led this pedantic Frenchman to the conclusion that everything was subject not only to its own laws but also to the laws of the universe. This assumption made it possible for him to arrive at his theory of social reorganization, not by speculation but by " a Deduction from the Laws of Nature." This emphasis on the universality of laws impregnated the entire discussion of the principles of Association.

[129]

The Universe is governed by Fixed and Mathematical Laws, which distribute, coordinate, classify, in a word, regulate its phenomena, and establish in it the reign of Unity and Order. . . . The Plan of Social Organization which Fourier proposes is a deduction from these Laws, and is not therefore an arbitrary, capricious creation of his intellect, but a scientific theory based upon the principles which govern the Universe.

Brisbane asserted that the human race was still in its infancy, comparatively speaking, and therefore ignorant and subject to evil. In its various stages of development — savage, patriarchal, barbarian, civilized — mankind had evolved social institutions which were of necessity imperfect. The closer it came to natural law, the nearer would it approach to the life God had ordained for it. The next stage in human development, which Fourier regarded as by no means the final one, was " a system of society in which the general incoherence and conflict of individual interests will tend to disappear in a spirit of collectivity which will lead to an understanding among men for the proper adjustment of all interests both public and personal." This system is Guarantism or Association.

In defense of the principle of attraction, upon which the theory of Association was based, Brisbane offered much evidence from the working of nature. Most persuasive, of course, was the fact that nature, or God, relies upon attraction for the perpetuation of life. " He governs the Universe by this power alone; he impels all beings to fulfil their Destiny from the pleasure, the charm, the delight, he connects with it, and not from the fear of pain or punishment." Since the aim of Association was " *to dignify Industry and to render it honorable and attractive,*" it followed that in making it the principle of society mankind would give evidence of having accepted the great law of nature. In his advocacy of this principle Brisbane described at length how Association guaranteed individual property, free choice of one's mode of living and occupation, ample remuneration, and all social pleasures and privileges.

Neither Fourier nor Brisbane progressed very far beyond the individual phalanx. Both rebelled against the complexity and bigness of urban industrialism and would have done away with it if they could. They would have preferred to limit society to as many self-contained phalanxes as were needed. They realized, however, that this would be impractical and so approved of a voluntary federation of communities. As the prophets of a new social order they even felt impelled to give it worldwide scope and to outline a global federation of phalanxes. Because they assumed that Constantinople occupied a geographically central position, they chose it as " the great capital of the Globe," but proposed to limit its population to 300,000. Again, since there would be many public tasks beyond the capacities of the individual phalanx to perform and since war would be outlawed, they anticipated William James by proposing to use the manpower of the abolished armies for these special activities.

Industrial armies — or great collective industrial organizations, of which our destructive armies present an inverted image — will execute all works of a collective character. They will open brilliant spheres of action to true devotion and heroism, to the display of genius, and the acquisition of fame, far exceeding anything which the *inverted armies of our inverted societies* can now possibly offer to man.

By providing this moral equivalent for war and by directing the vast energies spent on the fields of battle into channels of productive labor, they capped their plan for turning the earth into a paradise for all living men.

Albert Brisbane was completely the social dreamer. He belonged to the group of humanitarians who refused to accept the ruthless and anarchic industrialism of the period. These thinkers condemned the spoliation of thousands of human beings for the sake of larger profits; they grieved to think of the abject poverty of the slum dwellers, and they were appalled that the mass of mankind should remain in brutish ignorance at a time when science and invention had made it possible to put knowledge within reach of all men. Groping for a quick remedy for these social ills, they naturally favored nostrums that satisfied their peculiar natures. Albert Brisbane, having resolved in his teens that it was the duty of the individual to devote his life to the betterment of humanity and having the means and the zeal to heed the voice of his conscience, became one of the first Americans to travel half across the world in search of a panacea. Fourier's plan for social reorganization fired his imagination because it fitted his idealistic conception of society better than any other scheme for human meliorism. And having once adopted it he could not but devote himself to its realization with all the gentle fervor of his generous spirit. It never occurred to Brisbane that Association went against the grain of industrial society and was therefore impossible of realization. This belief that the plan was logical and beneficial made it desirable and feasible as well.

The early response to his writings exceeded his most hopeful expectations. " I had contemplated," he insisted long after, " years of patient, careful propagation before the means of a single Association could be obtained." Had not Fourier himself waited thirty years in vain? The mushroom growth of the phalanxes during the 1840's revealed his pathetic inability to cope with reality. Instead of exercising leadership and forcing his guidance upon the starry-eyed Associationists, he merely voiced his disapproval of their ill-advised efforts and left them to their quick doom. John Humphrey Noyes was justified in blaming him " for spending all his energy drumming and recruiting, while, to insure success, he should have given at least half his time to drilling the soldiers and leading them in actual battle. One example of Fourierism carried through to splendid realization would have done definitely more for the cause in the long run, than all his translations and publications."

The effect of Brisbane's Fourierism on the history of American social reform is not easy to ascertain. From the point of view of concrete results, it was of only ephemeral significance. After the failure of the phalanxes in the 1840's the Association movement disappeared, leaving little trace of its existence. The term " utopian " with which the Marxists had dubbed the several idealistic social plans of the period helped to give Fourier its philosophical quietus. Brisbane continued to propagate the idea for another forty years, but he remained unheard and forgotten. Yet in a more fundamental sense it cannot be said that the theory of Association was devoid of influence. For more than a decade and more effectively than the other utopian experiments, it caught the imagination of American social meliorists. Its vision of a society in which work was rendered dignified and attractive inspired all later schemes for the improvement of the laborer's lot. Equally appealing was the doctrine of efficiency by means of the division of labor. Moreover, the thousands of men and women whom Brisbane had drawn into the Association movement did not forget the lessons of social justice. Long after the collapse of the phalanxes, these reformers continued to preach the gospel of human welfare and made it a significant part of the movements they entered. It was this intangible yet undeniable influence that made Albert Brisbane a positive factor in the advancement of social reform in the United States.

EDWARD BELLAMY

SOCIAL PLANNER

EXPLAINING THE GENESIS of his extraordinary novel in the first issue of *The Nationalist* (May 1889), Edward Bellamy remarked: " In undertaking to write *Looking Backward* I had, at the outset, no idea of attempting a serious contribution to the movement of social reform. The idea was of a mere literary fantasy, a fairy tale of social felicity. There was no thought of contriving a house which practical men might live in, but merely of hanging in mid-air, far out of reach of the sordid and material world of the present, a cloud palace for an ideal humanity." Bellamy's critics took him at his word. They assumed that he had merely stumbled on his plan of economic equality in his effort to write a romance of social fantasy. Even so friendly an admirer as William Dean Howells, who placed Bellamy's fiction alongside that of Hawthorne, was of the opinion that *Looking Backward* was pretty much of an accident. Following the author's modest self-appraisal, he paraphrased him as follows: " He had come to think of our hopeless conditions suddenly, one day, in looking at his own children, and reflecting that he could not place them beyond the chance of want by any industry or forecast of providence; and that the status meant the same impossibility for others which it meant for him."

Yet the facts of Bellamy's life argue against this assumption. He had his roots in the melioristic environment of New England, having been born in 1850 in Chicopee Falls, Massachusetts, where his father served for many years as the minister of the Baptist Church.

[134]

The atmosphere of his home helped to develop in him the ethical fervor characteristic of the idealistic puritan. Sensitive and introspective, he grew up eager to promote justice and mitigate poverty and suffering. Living through the excitement of the defeats and victories of the Civil War at a highly impressionable age, he became absorbed in the study of military strategy and studied the Napoleonic Wars with special attention. No doubt he perceived himself as a great general, succeeding where Napoleon and Lee had failed. It was this adolescent passion for generalship that later led him to seek admission to West Point Academy. His rejection on physical grounds deeply disappointed him. Like so many other youths who daydream of romantic careers totally different from their life's work, Bellamy, never thinking of battles as anything more than games of chess, later became a strict pacifist. His interest in military science, however, led him to develop his utopia on a foundation of universal service in an " army of production."

Shortly after his rejection at West Point, while uncertain of the next step, he joined his older brother at Union College and took a course in English. The following year, at the strong urging of his parents, he accompanied a wealthy cousin of his to a German university. He did little study, but he did visit several countries. The destitution and drabness of the Continental slums only deepened his dissatisfaction with the existing social system. " It was in the great cities of Europe," he wrote in his Journal, " that my eyes were first fully opened to the extent and consequences of man's inhumanity to man." This humanitarian attitude no doubt predisposed him to the socialism of Karl Marx, which was then erupting among the urban workers; it is equally probable that he followed the exciting debates at the annual conference of the First International during his sojourn in Germany.

On his return home in 1870 he decided to study law and a year later he was admitted to the bar. The more he learned about the ways of lawyers, however, the less he wished to be one of them. What he thought of them may be gathered from the hyperbole uttered by one of his characters in *The Duke of Stockbridge*: " I calc-late ye could cut five tories aout o' one lawyer an' make a dozen skunks aout o' what waz left over." As a man of principle he could not practise a profession he disdained.

Now fully " aroused to the existence and urgency of the social problem," the earnest youth of twenty-one found himself face to face with the brash rapaciousness of the " robber-barons " of his day. The prevailing low wages and long workdays seemed to him no better than slavery. Had he had the opportunity, he would un-doubtedly have taken an active part in reforming a society that per-mitted the existence of both grasping millionaires and penniless tramps. But there was then no organized reform movement. Nor was he fanatic enough to initiate a crusade. It was more in keeping with his character to express his dissenting views in a lecture with the telling title of " The Barbarism of Society." One of the points he stressed was that " the great reforms of the world have hitherto been political rather than social. In their progress classes privileged by title have been swept away, but classes privileged by wealth re-main." His logical conclusion was that wealth is at the root of all social injustice: " I ask only that none labor beyond measure that others may be idle, that there be no more masters and no more slaves among men. Is that too much? Not so, for nothing that is unjust can be eternal and nothing that is just can be impossible." Here in brief is the full kernel of the idea of equality which he later developed so persuasively in *Looking Backward*.

Unable to find a ready outlet for his ethical zeal, determined to begin earning his own living, already timidly nursing the ambition to become a writer, young Bellamy decided to obtain work on a newspaper. His first job was with the New York *Evening Post*. After about a year he left it to become an editorial writer and book reviewer on the Springfield (Mass.) *Union*. His successful career as a journalist ended suddenly some five years later when he suf-fered a physical breakdown. As soon as he was able he took a leisurely trip to Hawaii via Panama, and felt much improved on his return across the continent late in 1877. Loath to jeopardize his frail health, he thought it best not to return to a newspaper desk but to try to write salable fiction. His first novel, *Six to One: A Nantucket Idyl,* was completed within a year and received with considerable favor. *Dr. Heidendorff's Process* and *Miss Ludington's Sister* were published in 1880 and 1884 respectively, and his short stories appeared in the leading periodicals. He combined a fertile inventiveness with a gentle realism to create a whimsy world of his own, and when his setting was not in the realm of fancy it was located in the small-town milieu he knew so well. His characters were drawn with the clarity and acuteness of sympathetic understanding. Reviewers in this country and in England appreciated his imaginative style of writing, and more than one spoke of him as a lineal descendant of Hawthorne. In the meantime he had married and had become the father of two children. It was after the birth of his second child, in 1886, that his thoughts turned to a romance in which injustice and insecurity were known only as a part of the abolished capitalistic system.

Bellamy had not, of course, shuttered his vision of a better world during the previous fifteen years. Indeed, time had increased his dislike of the poverty and greed which, to his thinking, blighted our great economic development. Only, like so many other diffident men of good will, he lacked the zeal to fight inequality openly. Fiction became his means of expression, and he endowed a number of his characters with intrinsic goodness and a predilection for the right. Very early in his career as a novelist, moreover, he gave free vent to his social indignation in *The Duke of Stockbridge: A Romance of Shays' Rebellion,* one of the first American novels to treat the problem of the class struggle with the directness and passion of the ardent reformer. Since he depended on his writing for a livelihood, however, he was loath to see it published at that time. After it had appeared as a serial in the obscure *Berkshire Courier* in 1879 the novel remained in his drawer until it was issued in 1900, two years after the author's death.

The Duke of Stockbridge has its setting in the western part of

Massachusetts. In 1786 the acute economic depression which followed the Revolutionary War drove the impoverished populace to desperation. Hard money was practically unobtainable, so that commerce was almost at a standstill. High taxes and harsh creditors were subjecting the farmers to beggary and incarceration by the cruel process of foreclosure. Throughout Massachusetts " men talked of nothing else but the hard times, the limited markets and low prices for farm produce, the extortions and multiplying numbers of lawyers and sheriffs, the oppression of creditors, the enormous grinding taxes, the last sheriff's sale." The more vocal of the villagers insisted that " the only work that pays nowadays is picking the bones of the people." Since many of the sufferers were yeomen who had fought in the war to establish their inalienable human rights, they could not but consider themselves oppressed by a greedy gentry. In their wrath they defied the authorities and stopped the courts from victimizing them; and although they were cowed into submission before very long, they forced a frightened government to institute appropriate reforms.

Bellamy chose this historic incident because it enabled him to stress the deep social gulf between the hard-fisted squires and the destitute farmers. In his research and reflection preparatory to writing the novel he was distressed to discover that the inequality between the two classes showed no signs of abatement during the century in which the wealth of the country had multiplied manifold. His sympathy with the poor is seen in the pithy expression which his yeomen give to their rightful grievances. One of them, referring to the tenfold rise in taxes at a time when money was unobtainable, remarks sarcastically: " It seems darn curis, bein' as we fit ag'in the redcoats jest to rid o' taxes." The same villager says on another occasion: " Wal, we licked the redcoats, and we got lib'ty, I s'pose; lib'ty to starve, — that is, if we don't happen to git sent to jail fust." At still another time he speaks his mind, Yankee-fashion, to one of the powerful squires: " They said, ye'd got no more compassion fer the poor than a flint stun . . . an' would take a feller's last drop o' blood sooner'n lose a penny debt. They said, them fellers did, that yer hands, white as they look, wuz red with the blood o' them that ye'd sent to die in jail."

The gentry are equally outspoken in their insistence on their God-given right to govern the country for their own good. Many of them think of their indigent townsmen as a team of horses which they may use at will. At the first sign of rebelliousness they crack the whip. One of them expostulates: " This presumption of the people to talk concerning matters of government is an evil that has greatly increased since the war, and calls for sharp castigation. These numskulls must be taught their places or 't will shortly be no country for gentlemen to live in." Another squire is equally frank: " We must look to it, gentlemen, or we shall find that we have ridded ourselves of a king only to fall into the hands of a democracy, which I take it would be a bad exchange." When we consider that the sentiments of these men, some of them about to draft our federal Constitution, are quoted from their own writings, we can appreciate Bellamy's warm compassion for their debt-ridden victims.

The novel does not hold up to the end. The narrative begins well, the thesis is stated with pointed clarity, and the characters are limned sharply against a realistic background. But the development of events gradually becomes lost in the thickening layer of conventional romance, and the progress of the rebellion gives way to the mawkish love story in the latter half of the book. To the very end, however, there is no mistaking the author's zeal for reform.

Although Bellamy's social conscience appeared to have become quiescent after its crusading venture in *The Duke of Stockbridge*, he was too much the humanitarian not to be deeply troubled by the rapacity of industrialism. The existence of a group of multimillionaires who manipulated the economic life of the nation for their private advantage was to him the negation of democracy; nor was he underestimating the angry mutterings of millions of workers who were groping blindly yet with increasing insistence for the means of a better livelihood. He had learned that "wealth is power in its most concentrated, most efficient and most universally applicable form" — and he abominated the greed it engendered. Exploited labor, on the other hand, he envisaged as an undeveloped giant capable of great eruptive strength — and he dreaded the wanton destructiveness of social revolution. As he observed the two antagonistic forces girding for battle — and the bloody strikes of the period seemed to him mere skirmishes — he became convinced that unless a way were found to eliminate the evils of capitalistic exploitation, the nation was certain to be plunged into another civil war.

Looking Backward, according to Dr. Arthur E. Morgan written after a detailed study of the Inca civilization, presented Bellamy's way out. The book vividly describes the working of a society based upon the system of co-operative equality. Yet it is not merely another story of elusive utopia. Indeed, the great appeal of the novel inheres in the fact that Bellamy emulated Defoe in his deliberate effort to keep within the bounds of credibility. This air of realism enabled him to look back from the vantage point of the year 2000 and describe with prophetic certitude such novel scientific and social advances as the radio, the airplane, television, paper clothes, and complete economic equality.

Looking Backward [he tells us in a later postscript], although in form a fanciful romance, is intended, in all seriousness, as a forecast, in accordance with the principles of evolution, of the next stage in industrial and social development of humanity, especially in this country; and no part of it is believed by the author to be better supported by the indications of probability than the implied prediction that the dawn of the new era is already near at hand, and that the full day will swiftly follow.

Bellamy evolved the social system of the year 2000 naturally and logically out of the presumed ultimate abolition of the present order. He begins with the premise that monopolistic capitalism, which in his day was spreading its financial tentacles in every direction and rapidly gaining control of the nation's entire economy, was strangling the mass markets on which its existence depended and thereby making it possible for the final merger of all trusts into one Big Trust. This unification of all the means of production and distribution under the aegis of the government must, of course, be brought about gradually and by the will of the people. The economic transformation, once begun, will become consummated more rapidly than might be expected. For instance, if the majority of voters were persuaded of the advantages of public ownership, what was to stop them from directing the government to take over and operate the large utilities? Why could not the railroads, practically bankrupted by watered-stock manipulations, be run on the same basis as the postal service? And if once these utilities were managed for the benefit of the entire nation, would not the collapse of capitalistic enterprise become inevitable? Once the industrial system was nationalized, the subsequent program of equalization was certain to eliminate the present social ills and transform the country into an earthly paradise.

The great appeal of Bellamy's plan lay in its cogent presentation as an accomplished fact. The reader is confronted not by an imaginary social scheme which is obviously impracticable but by a perfected way of life based on the existing industrial system. Dr. Leete, Julian West's mentor in the new society, informs him that the change from monopolistic capitalism to co-operative equality occurred early in the twentieth century. At that time

the people of the United States concluded to assume the conduct of their own business, just as one hundred odd years before they had assumed the conduct of their own government, organizing now for industrial purposes on precisely the same grounds that they had then organized for political purposes. . . . There was absolutely no violence. The change had been long foreseen. Public opinion had become fully ripe for it, and the whole mass of the people was behind it. There was no more possibility of opposing it by force than by argument.

Once the country's economy became nationalized and the profit motive was eliminated, the prime function of the government became the protection of the people from " cold, hunger and naked-ness" rather than from foreign aggression. To this end it divided the total national income equally between all citizens. Unemploy-ment vanished as if by magic. " When the nation became the sole employer, all the citizens, by virtue of their citizenship, became employees, to be distributed to the needs of industry." Indeed, everyone of a certain age had to work: work or starve. Service to the state was made a necessary concomitant to the equality of in-come.

To speak of service being compulsory [Dr. Leete explained] would be a weak way to state its absolute inevitableness. Our entire social order is so wholly based upon and deduced from it that if it were conceivable that a man could escape it, he would be left with no possible way to provide for his existence. He would have excluded himself from the world, cut himself off from his kind, in a word, committed suicide.

In its efforts to provide work for everyone and thus to bring about the greatest possible productiveness, the government found it convenient to adapt the plan of military service to its civil needs. The reasoning was that, even as every able-bodied young man owed his country a term of service in the army for the protection of all from an outside enemy, so every citizen of the co-operative state is required to work for a definite period to insure a common abun-dance of the necessities of life. Experimentation led to the decision that twenty-four years of work will suffice for the lifetime well-being of all. Since the period of youth is required for education and that of late maturity " sacred to ease and agreeable relaxation," the interim of service begins on one's twenty-first birthday and ends on the forty-fifth. On every October 15 those who have served twenty-four years are mustered out, to be called back only in emergencies, and all youths of twenty-one are enlisted for their term of service.

In the new society the hit-or-miss way of doing things under capitalism was replaced by a system based upon scientific skills and certainties. The greatest possible caution is exercised in guiding each individual in the development of his capacities and aptitudes. " The principle on which our industrial army is organized," Dr.

Leete pointed out, " is that a man's natural endowments, mental and physical, determine what he can work at most profitably to the nation and most satisfactorily to himself." Children are carefully trained by both parents and teachers, and all are thoroughly familiarized with all kinds of trades and occupations. As a consequence young men and women know what they prefer to do long before they are mustered into service and are only too eager to begin working. To avoid overcrowding in some occupations and a shortage of applicants in others, the administration seeks " constantly to equalize the attractions of the trades, so far as the conditions of labor in them are concerned, so that all trades shall be equally attractive to persons having natural tastes for them. This is done by making the hours of labor in different trades differ according to their arduousness." Since this apportionment of work-time will not necessarily eliminate the greater appeal of certain occupations, everyone is required to develop a second or even a third choice, so that if one's first preference is unavailable one " can still find reasonably congenial employment. This principle of secondary choices as to occupation is quite important in our system."

First, however, one has to undergo a period of hardening and leveling. To make sure that work of a necessary but unpleasant nature is performed as needed, everyone is required to devote the first three years of service to common labor. With the advance of science it became possible to reduce the distastefulness of much of this work to a minimum; even sewers lost their offensive odors, and ditch-digging became a relatively simple mechanical task. At the completion of this period of service a young man is free " to choose, in accordance with his natural tastes, whether he will fit himself for an art or profession, or be a farmer or mechanic." If he wishes to prepare himself for a profession, and if his previous record favors such preparation, he enrolls in the school offering the required course. Should he prove himself unable to keep up with his class, he is required to leave the school and obtain employment of a less taxing nature. He is permitted, however, to apply for special training up to the age of thirty.

Under capitalism, when business was conducted by " irresponsible individuals, wholly without mutual understanding or concert," there were various kinds of waste: mistaken undertakings, cut-throat competition, periodical gluts and crises, strikes and lockouts, etc. — any one of which sufficed to keep a nation economically inefficient. In the co-operative society, with all industry under unified control and with the proficiency of every worker developed to the utmost, production soon exceeded all expectations. It became possible for the administration to provide each citizen, in return for his twenty-four years of labor, with a lifelong annual income of about $4000 in addition to many free services. As a consequence " no man any more has any care for the morrow, either for himself or his children, for the nation guarantees the nurture, education and comfortable maintenance of every citizen from the cradle to the grave."

Bellamy defended this guarantee of complete equality of income on two grounds: our common humanity and industrial efficiency. In the first place, since civilization is our common inheritance, its fruits should be shared by all alike. From the days of our savage ancestors, when no man acquired more than his essential needs, to our own time with its marked discrepancy of income, all that a man earns above his bare living he owes to the accumulated skills and inventions of the past. By himself even the most successful capitalist would soon relapse into savagery.

Every man, however solitary may seem his occupation, is a member of a vast industrial partnership, as large as the nation, as large as humanity. The necessity of mutual dependence should imply the duty and guarantee of mutual support. . . . The right of a man to maintenance at the nation's table depends on the fact that he is a man, and not on the amount of health and strength he may have, so long as he does his best.

He fortified this ethical principle by an appeal to general economic advantage. Under capitalism, competition and greed lowered the efficiency of production. Economic equality, on the contrary, stimulates industrial combination and increases production. Thus, " even if the principle of share and share alike for all men were not the only humane and rational basis for a society, we should still enforce it as economically expedient, seeing that until the disintegrating influence of self-seeking is suppressed no true concert of industry is possible."

One of the first things the new order abolished was money. Under capitalism it was an essential commodity — the key to all doors in the hands of the wealthy and the whip over the poor. With the establishment of economic equality, money became superfluous. In Bellamy's utopia buying and selling are considered anti-social transgressions, encouraging " self-seeking at the expense of others." Nor is there any need for trading. Direct distribution from national and local storehouses has completely replaced the old system. In these public depositories an individual orders what he needs by means of a credit card. " A credit corresponding to his share of the annual product of the nation is given to every citizen on the public books at the beginning of each year, and a credit card issued him with which he procures at the public storehouses, found in every community, whatever he desires whenever he desires it." (It may not be amiss at this point to mention that our wartime experience with rationing is a ready reminder of the feasibility of the plan.)

Bellamy stressed the encouragement of individual differences in his equalitarian society. The cultivation of personal taste is one of the features of the new order, since everyone may use his ample credit card in any way he wishes. Indeed, the aim of education is to develop a child's special capacities to their highest degree not only for his own sake but also for the pleasure of others. Women are given the same opportunities as men in order that they may exercise their particular talents to the advantage of the entire nation. These and other aspects of the perfected social system are described with such matter-of-fact plausibility that one is favorably prepared for Dr. Leete's assertion that " in the time of one generation men laid aside the social traditions and practices of barbarians, and assumed a social order worthy of rational and human beings. Ceasing to be predatory in their habits, they became co-workers, and found in fraternity, at once, the science of health and happiness."

Looking Backward was published in January 1888, and was immediately recognized as a work of extraordinary significance. Many Americans were at the time painfully perturbed by the combination of capitalistic aggrandizement and industrial conflict. They were vaguely aware of the new economic speculation abroad, but preferred an American expression of it. The new utopia, describing a system of reform at once appealing and seemingly practicable, served as a clarifying catalyist. Bellamy knew this. "A work of propaganda like *Looking Backward*," he explained, "produces an effect precisely in proportion as it is a bare anticipation in expression of what everybody was thinking and about to say." A few conservative critics scorned the book as a fantastic concoction; several learned economists proved it fallacious and impertinent; but many thousands of enthusiastic readers, thoroughly dissatisfied with inequality, were ready to use the novel as a blueprint for the new society. Ten thousand copies were sold in 1888; 200,000 the year after; and about a million copies in all were in active circulation during the early 1890's. Frank B. Tracy, writing in *The Forum* of May 1893, stated: "Copies of *Looking Backward* are in every community. Probably every village has at least one man who is a thorough Nationalist, while hundreds of his neighbors are in sympathy with its principles." Measured by its popularity as well as by its effectiveness, the volume is undoubtedly one of the most influential books ever published in this country and on a par with *Uncle Tom's Cabin* and *Progress and Poverty*.

Almost at once *Looking Backward* became a focal point for the Nationalist groups which sprang up everywhere with the sole aim of advocating the new social system. The first Nationalist club was organized in Boston shortly after the book appeared. Within two years, without aid or stimulation from any central authority, more than 150 similar clubs had come into existence, most of them west of the Mississippi. These groups published periodicals, conducted forums, participated in political campaigns. They appeared to be a real threat to the capitalistic order. They called themselves Nationalists because their aim " was to nationalize the functions of production and distribution," to bring " the entire business system of the country under the same popular government which now extends only to a few comparatively trifling functions called political." In the Presidential campaign of 1892 they united with the Populists and exerted a considerable influence among the Western farmers and organized labor.

The great popularity of *Looking Backward* forced upon Bellamy the role of a leader and reformer. Shy man that he was, and afflicted with " weak lungs," he found himself drawn into the public arena. As the acclaimed head of a vigorous social crusade he had to lecture before Nationalist audiences, reply to belligerent critics, and write expository articles for popular periodicals. During 1891–93 he also edited *The New Nation* and gave to it much of his time and thought. In addition, since he was not a professional economist and yet had to cope with academic adversaries, he found it necessary to make a thorough study of economic theory.

On the platform and in his writings he excoriated the cankerous evils of capitalism and urged the need of economic reform. On the masthead of *The New Nation* he repeated weekly the following credo:

The exercise of irresponsible power, by whatever means, is tyranny, and should not be tolerated. The power which men irresponsibly exercise for their private ends, over individuals and communities, through superior wealth, is essentially tyrannous, and as inconsistent with democratic principle and as offensive to self-respecting men as any form of political tyranny that was ever endured. As political equality is the remedy for political tyranny, so is economic equality the only way of putting an end to the economic tyranny exercised by the few over the many through the superiority of wealth. The industrial system of a nation, like its political system, should be a government of the people, by the people, for the people. Until economic equality shall give a basis to political equality, the latter is but a sham.

One of his first demands was public ownership of the railroads, the telephone and telegraph systems, the express companies, the coal mines, and the essential municipal utilities. He insisted that " the brute principle of competition " must be replaced by " the nobler principle of association "; that " the nationalization of industry presents the logical, conclusive, and complete form of evolution from competition toward combination which is now in progress." It was his belief that, if no unforeseen reaction set in, all business in the United States would become the property of the state early in the twentieth century and that responsible public agents would operate it for the benefit of all the people.

Again and again he took pains to point out that he was no Marxian and that he abominated the ideas of violent revolution and the dictatorship of one group over all others. Nationalism was to him synonymous with " economic democracy " — a principle implicit in the Declaration of Independence and rooted deep in the heart of every true American. " We seek the final answer to the social question not in revolution, but in evolution; not in destruction, but in fulfilment, — the fulfilment of the hitherto stunted development of the nation according to its logical intent." He was obviously no Marxian even when he expounded socialistic doctrines. His quest for economic equality was in truth an attempt to restrain a colossal industrialism with the reins of Jeffersonian democracy.

Although Bellamy had implicit faith in the principles he advocated and would gladly have given his life to abolish the existing inequalities, he was wanting in the driving energy and political shrewdness to force his will upon the nation. Powerful economic forces also kept him from harnessing the tremendous popular enthusiasm generated by *Looking Backward* for the purpose of voting Nationalism into power. His " principle of human brotherhood," coming at a moment of national economic crisis, appealed greatly to the oppressed farmers and exploited urban workers. They flocked to his standard eager for the benefits of his panacea — only to lose heart when they found nothing solid to get their teeth into, nothing

[148]

to gird them for Armageddon. The passing of the panic of 1893 and the new spurt of industrial expansion swept the Nationalist movement into oblivion.

By nature a dreamer rather than a doer, yet unable to accept defeat, Bellamy thought he could bolster Nationalist sentiment by strengthening and enhancing the edifice he had erected in *Looking Backward*. To this end he wrote *Equality*, a more thorough exposition of the economic and ethical principles that formed the pillars of the new society. This second book, while lacking the spontaneous imaginative appeal and emotional warmth of the earlier volume, is replete with cogent accounts of every aspect of economic equality. A good part of it is also concerned with an incisive criticism of capitalism. It was his strong belief that a more comprehensive report of his proposed social order could not but persuade all persons of normal intelligence and good will.

Equality discusses the evils of capitalism with satiric effectiveness. Julian West is treated to a classroom demonstration of the irrational basis of the economic system of the nineteenth century. One of the best chapters in the book is " The Parable of the Water Tank," which epitomizes the senselessness of an economy in which a few aggressive men exploit the necessities of life for their private gain without regard to the suffering of the mass of mankind. Equally effective is the re-examination of the inefficiency of capitalism, in which the profit motive tends to curb the very mass markets on which industrialism depends. Nor does he overlook the chicanery of businessmen. " The desperate rivalry of the capitalists for a share in the scanty market which their own profit taking had beggared drove them to the practice of deception and brutality and compelled a hard-heartedness such as we are bound to believe human beings would not under a less pressure have been guilty of."

Much more than in the earlier book, capitalism is indicted as undemocratic. Dr. Leete quotes statistics on the grave inequality of wealth towards the end of the nineteenth century and argues that the possession of political freedom without economic equality is like the occupation of the outworks without taking the citadel. "The Revolution came when the people saw that they must either take the citadel or evacuate the outworks. They must either complete the work of establishing popular government which had been barely begun by their fathers, or abandon all that their fathers had accomplished." This combination of political democracy with economic equality is stated again and again as the basic principle of Nationalism. "The primal principle of democracy is the worth and dignity of the individual. That dignity, consisting in the quality of human nature, is essentially the same in all individuals, and therefore equality is the vital principle of democracy." Since capitalism is obviously anti-democratic, it is necessary to overthrow it by a peaceful revolution which will destroy "the last vestige of the system by which men usurped power over the lives and liberties of their fellows through economic means."

Equality described the transition period in full detail. Once the efficiency of public ownership had been demonstrated to the satisfaction of the majority, the people themselves insisted that the government take over all industries and services. This initial step both decreased unemployment and enhanced the standard of living. When scrip was given to government employees in lieu of cash and made the only means of purchasing goods at the public stores, it soon "became a currency which commanded three, four, and five hundred per cent premium over money which could only buy the high-priced and adulterated goods for sale in the remaining stores of the capitalists." Before long the value of money disappeared entirely and the rich found it advisable to give up their useless wealth to the government and become members of the new economic order. At this point the state was able to "assume the responsibility of providing for all the people." Wages ceased to be paid, and every citizen began to receive an equal share of the total annual income. Poverty and ostentatious wealth disappeared simultaneously, as if by magic.

Those who feared that the lack of a money incentive would destroy initiative and slacken production were soon convinced of their error. The people were so enthusiastic over their new sense of security and their improved living conditions that they tripled the total product of the country during the first full year of the new order and doubled that amount during the next year. In time, Dr. Leete assured Julian West, "the hunger motive died out of human nature and covetousness as to material things, mocked to death by abundance, perished by atrophy, and the motives of the modern worker, the love of honor, the joy of beneficence, the delight of achievement, and the enthusiasm of humanity, became the impulses of the economic world."

In reply to earlier criticism on this point, Bellamy maintained that his plan provided for full individual initiative. Under capitalism, he argued, a man is driven by dire need. Yet fear, the lash of want, is "on the whole the weakest as well as certainly the cruelest of incentives." Even under the wage-system, moreover, a well-provided employee is a more efficient worker than one who has to worry over his next meal. Nationalism, he claimed, giving each person an equal share of the total income and rewarding special effort with prized degrees of rank and prestige, is certain to develop a healthy and desirable kind of initiative.

He answered with equal force the objection that Nationalism would abolish private property. He stated that his plan would not eliminate private property but would equalize it among all citizens. "The Revolution made us all capitalists," Dr. Leete observed. It had merely destroyed private capitalism. The direction of the business of the nation was taken away from irresponsible individuals and given to carefully chosen public agents. True enough, the few rich were thereby deprived of their wealth; but this change made all citizens equal partners in the riches of their country. "The change created an entirely new system of property holding, but did not either directly or indirectly involve any denial of the right of private property." Indeed, Nationalism placed the private and personal property rights of every citizen on an incomparably more secure and extensive basis than they had had under capitalism. For by this pooling of property into one Big Trust, each individual became " entitled not only to his own product but to vastly more — namely, to his share of the product of the social organism, in addition to his personal product, but he is entitled to this share not on the grab-as-grab-can plan of your day, by which some made themselves millionaires and others were left beggars, but on equal terms with his fellow capitalists."

When *Equality* appeared in 1897, the crucial Presidential campaign of the previous year had become a part of American history. Mark Hanna and his Big Business henchmen had succeeded in befuddling enough workers, fearful of unemployment and tempted by the promise of " a full dinner pail," to insure McKinley's election. And with Bryan's defeat went the hopes of millions of poor men who had voted for him in the hope of keeping this country economically free. The blow was fatal to the army of Populists and Nationalists. The wave of reform, thus blocked, was thereupon completely broken by a new industrial expansion that included billion-dollar trusts and initiated an imperialist drive which led to the war with Spain and turned the United States into a world power. For a few years prosperity made any attempt at social melioration a futile undertaking. Bellamy's loyal followers received *Equality* with great enthusiasm. Ten thousand copies were quickly bought and discussed with sanguine appreciation. But the book failed to attain the mass popularity of *Looking Backward*.

Bellamy, who had long been in frail health, had contracted tuberculosis while writing *Equality*. As soon as it was finished he went with his family to Colorado, but by then his lungs were too ravaged by the disease to benefit from the climate. He was, however, greatly cheered by the praise of his simple admirers on the farms and in the mining towns of that part of the country. In the early spring he knew his end was near and decided to return to his home in Chicopee. He died on May 22, 1898, in his forty-eighth year.

Edward Bellamy, small-town editor, writer, and dreamer, was an outstanding American reformer. He possessed the social conscience characteristic of a long line of New England Puritans — from Roger

Williams to Wendell Phillips. He was not of those who accepted the world for what it was and busied themselves feathering their own nests. As a true believer in the teachings of both Jesus and Jefferson he felt impelled to cry out against oppression and inequality, to expound " the principles of human brotherhood — the enthusiasm of humanity." He did this in the way he knew best: by writing *Looking Backward* and *Equality* and by dedicating his life to the realization of his equalitarian society. He envisioned a world in which all men were equal; in which hunger was non-existent, greed a forgotten evil, and complete education the birthright of every child; in which criminals were unknown, drones an anomaly, and inordinate luxury impossible; a world in which intelligence reigned supreme and every man lived to his fullest capacity. It was a beautiful mirage: a utopia so vivid and noble, so cleverly woven out of the warp and woof of daily life, that it could not but fascinate those who perceived it with him.

Uncounted thousands the world over, in want and fearful of the days ahead, read *Looking Backward* and were ready to join the new millennium. But they soon discovered that panaceas were possible only in the imagination and scurried back to their meager fleshpots. Yet a half-century later we have greater equality than the skeptics of Bellamy's day thought possible. Many of the evils of that time are now forgotten or greatly mitigated, and a number of the reforms then considered fantastic are now embodied in the law of the land. In Soviet Russia the Communism of Lenin has marked resemblance to the social order outlined in *Equality*; and although Stalin's regime is generally pointed out as a horrible example of what happens when the capitalistic order is meddled with, that country, freed from the fear of external enemies and fully industrialized, may yet realize the economic equality of Bellamy's dream. Science, accelerated by war, is changing the face of civilization before our very eyes. Who knows what reforms it will bring or what the world will be like a half-century hence? All we can say with certainty is that much of the advance made by society is the result of new social ideas percolating to the minds of the majority of the people. These ideas are mostly the visions of such dreamers as Bellamy. Ida M. Tarbell, referring to *Looking Backward*, placed its author among the leading social dreamers: " Of all Utopias which men, revolting against the bitter world in which we live, have created to stir the imagination and raise the hopes of the people of the earth, none has ever been so substantial, so realistic, so seemingly practical. A dream — yes — but a dream built upon materials in our hands."

THE ANARCHISTS

HENRY DAVID THOREAU   BENJAMIN R. TUCKER

EMMA GOLDMAN

THE ANARCHIST BACKGROUND

THE SEED of anarchism was imbedded in the first established state. It was immanent in the individual's natural reaction against his forced compliance to the will of the tribe. Later it became the cry of the rebel who refused to bow to authority; the credo of the idealist who discovered that power corrupts and must be destroyed at the source. These anarchists, cherishing liberty more than life, dreamed of a society in which the individual was completely free to live by himself if he so wished or to join his neighbors in voluntary association for the common good. Since it was in the very nature of government to exercise constraint, they were opposed to any communal organization which arrogated authority over its members. Peter Kropotkin, perhaps the most persuasive exponent of this doctrine, defined it as "a principle or theory of life and conduct under which society is conceived without government — harmony in such society being obtained not by submission to law, or by obedience to any authority, but by free agreements to conclude between the various groups, territorial and professional, freely constituted for the sake of production and consumption, as also for the satisfaction of the infinite variety of needs and aspirations of a civilized being."

While the attitude of mind that gives rise to anarchism is as old as recorded history, the development of the concept into a social doctrine is a relatively modern phenomenon. One of the first formally to criticize the state was the hedonist Aristippus, who urged his fellow citizens not to yield any of their liberties to the government. Zeno, the great Stoic, likewise enlarged upon the idea of anarchism when he repudiated the omnipotence of Plato's ideal republic. These views, however, found little sympathy among the thinkers who followed them during the next two millennia. Here and there an isolated and obscure libertarian appeared to refute the prevailing authoritarianism, but his voice was readily stifled by the proper officials. The Catholic Church in particular saw no advantage from such heretical speculations and discouraged them with a finality that endured as long as its temporal power.

With the flowering of the Age of Reason in the late eighteenth century, anarchistic ideas again became current. Voltaire, Diderot, Rousseau, and others decried the abuses of authority and played gingerly with the notion of a society without a government. Some of the Jacobins likewise advanced the alluring ideal. But the first systematic exponent of anarchism was William Godwin, whose *Inquiry Concerning Political Justice* appeared in 1793. Strongly influenced by the sentiments of the French Revolution, he argued that since man was a rational being he must not be hampered in the exercise of his pure reason. All forms of government have irrational foundations, are consequently tyrannical, and must be swept away. Laws, being not the product of wisdom but the result of fear and greed, should be replaced by the decisions of reasonable men. Accumulated property, being a means of exploitation, must also be abolished; in a later edition, however, Godwin changed his mind about the pernicious effect of property. The book, for all its indebtedness to Aristippus and in spite of the weasel words of the final revision, was a work of fresh stimulation and became a beacon to generations of rebels.

A half century later Pierre Joseph Proudhon, who popularized anarchism, created a sensation with the publication of *What Is Property?* in 1840. His answer — " property is robbery " — became a rallying cry for radicals everywhere. His fundamental credo was that " justice is the central star which governs societies." He rejected all institutions that did not square with his conception of justice, and chief among these were the state and the church. He realized, however, that the state could not be abolished in the foreseeable future and advocated increasing decentralization as a practical approach to his goal. His adherence to the utopian communism of his day was of brief duration. He soon came to favor private property as a means to freedom, and opposed only the accumulated possessions of the rich because they were used to exploit the poor. His solution for the evils of capitalism was the abolition of interest, which he regarded as the cause of our economic ills. To this end he proposed the establishment of banks which would serve, at cost, as places of exchange for producers and which would give workers checks representing the hours of labor required to produce a commodity. This system of mutualism, which provided free credit and equitable exchange, would stop exploitation and make possible the simultaneous existence of individual sovereignty and voluntary co-operation — the basic principles of anarchism. " The ideal republic," he stated, " is a positive anarchy. It is liberty free from all shackles, superstitions, prejudices, sophistries, usury, authority; it is reciprocal liberty and not limited liberty; liberty not the daughter but the Mother of Order."

While Proudhon was gaining a mass following for his principles of mutualism, Caspar Schmidt, better known as Max Stirner, was developing the doctrine of egotistical anarchism in his provocative book, *The Ego and His Own*. Repelled by the sentimentalism of the utopian socialists as well as by the authoritarianism of Hegel's absolute state, he stressed the complete supremacy of the individual. He argued that the highest form of civilization is predicated upon the assumption that each human being is a sovereign unto himself and free to follow his own bent. In elaborating upon this extreme form of individualism he formulated a philosophy of egoism which disdained all social and ethical standards.

A fig for good and evil! I am I, and I am neither good nor evil. Neither has any meaning for me. The godly is the affair of God, and the human that of humanity. My concern is neither the Godly nor the Human, is not the True, the Good, the Right, the Free, etc., but simply my own self, and it is not general, it is individual, as I myself am individual. For me there is nothing above myself.

Thus he, as egoist, laughed at the claims of others when they conflicted with his own needs and desires; nor did he scruple about property rights or law or common decency when his own wants were involved. His proposed League of Egoists was in truth the utopia of a petty bourgeois in revolt. Ironically enough, it was the hard selfishness of his individualist anarchism that logically justified the " rugged individualism " which characterized the rampant capitalism of the nineteenth century. *The Ego and His Own* remained hidden in obscurity for several decades, but was rediscovered in the 1880's and achieved considerable popularity, particularly among writers and artists who rebelled against the smugness of Victorian society. Benjamin R. Tucker, the American individualist anarchist, was deeply moved by Stirner's work and became his chief exponent in this country.

Michael Bakunin, upon his return from Siberian exile in 1861, replaced Proudhon as the leader of the anarchist movement. A romantic and extremist, his chief doctrines were an aggressive atheism, the destruction of the state, and the social revolution. He advocated complete freedom in all spheres. In his view the state was a necessary evil in a lower form of civilization but has subsequently become an instrument of oppression that prevented the emergence of a nobler form of society. It "was born historically in all countries of the marriage of violence, rapine, pillage, in a word, war and conquest. . . . Even when it commands what is good, it hinders and spoils it, just because it commands it, and because every command provokes and excites the legitimate revolts of liberty." A believer in the natural solidarity of mankind, he desired to supplant the state — the organ of oppression — with a free federation of autonomous associations from every sphere of social activity.

Bakunin's prison experiences developed the strain of mysticism in his nature and he became the exponent of conspiracy and secret strategy. He rejected political action as a means of abolishing the state, asserting that only a social revolution could achieve so radical a change. Since a revolution was predicated upon a universal uprising of the masses, and since this was possible only by means of an active and disciplined membership, he developed the doctrine of leadership along Jesuitical principles: absolute and complete obedience to the head of the revolutionary organization. That this doctrine was the antithesis of anarchism did not trouble him at all; what mattered to him was that it squared with practical revolutionary politics. Accordingly, in 1868, he founded the Alliance of Social Democracy, a secret revolutionary society headed by the Hundred International Brothers whose " only country was universal revolution and whose only enemy reaction." Fundamentally opposed to the principles of centralization and political action which Karl Marx had succeeded in establishing as the policy of the First International, Bakunin made use of his society in an effort to wrest control from Marx. This scheming led to his expulsion from the International in 1872. His approval of violence as a weapon against Czarist oppression, which stimulated nihilism in Russia, later also encouraged individual acts of terrorism elsewhere. In Latin countries particularly his influence remained strong for many years and was in large part responsible for the development of strong anarchist and syndicalist movements in France, Spain, and Italy.

Peter Kropotkin was undoubtedly the most likable if not the greatest of the anarchist leaders. Unlike Bakunin, he was no schemer, being gentle, pacifistic, frank, genuinely altruistic. Of a princely family, in pursuit of a career as geographer he found himself facing this choice: either he must selfishly pursue his work, or he must do what he could to mitigate the miserable lot of his people. A trip to Switzerland brought him into contact with Bakunin and other radicals, and he subsequently embraced the cause of anarchism. Like other social rebels he suffered incarceration and persecution during the first years of his activity. Early in the 1880's, however, he settled in England and there he pursued his social and scientific studies until his return to Russia after the revolution in 1917.

One of the kindest of men, Kropotkin opposed the state as the agency of oppression and misrule. He likewise criticized egoistic individualism as a philosophy that permitted the strong and selfish to exploit their less aggressive neighbors. "Individualism," he explained, "narrowly egoistic, is incapable of inspiring anybody. There is nothing great or gripping in it. Individuality can attain its supreme development only in the highest common social effort." In his desire to further this principle in a positive and appealing manner, he put forth the theory of mutual aid — the free federation of men for the benefit of all. "Mutual aid is, to say the least, as much a fundamental principle in Nature as mutual struggle; while for progressive evolution it is without doubt the more important of the two." He believed that the practice of mutual aid would inevitably lead to the abolition of capitalism and the establishment of communal anarchism. "If plenty for all is to become a reality, this immense capital — cities, houses, pastures, arable lands, factories, highways, education — must cease to be regarded as private property, for the monopolist to dispose of at his pleasure. . . . There must be Expropriation. The well-being of all — the end; expropriation — the means." Unlike Bakunin, however, he rejected the employment of force and depended upon education as a means of persuading mankind of the great benefits of communal anarchism. George Bernard Shaw came close to an evaluation of Kropotkin's anarchism when he called him "an advocate of free Democracy" and suggested that his radicalism was in the nature of a recoil "from a despotism compared to which Democracy seems to be no government at all." For Kropotkin was primarily the great humanitarian eager to abolish oppression and suffering by the establishment of absolute equality for all.

At the outbreak of World War I all advocates of anarchism were driven from the marketplace, and the subsequent emergence of authoritarianism — communist and fascist — has further eclipsed, in a large part of the world, the philosophy of the sovereign individual.

While in Europe the idea of anarchism came as a reaction against oppressive despotisms, in this country the frontier made it a practical necessity long before it was used as an intellectual weapon against British tyranny. The pioneer living in isolation and the scattered settlers in outlying communities managed as best they could without benefit of government. Even in the established towns along the Atlantic coast the rule of political authority had little of the arbitrary constraint common throughout the older continent. Native Americans grew up in an atmosphere of comparative freedom. They learned early to rely on their own powers rather than on the protective might of the state. When George III attempted to force his will upon them as he had on his subjects in England, he found himself faced with a determined rebellion. Thomas Jefferson and other Revolutionary leaders, influenced by English and French libertarian theories, spoke for both the townsmen and backwoodsmen when they insisted that the people are the source of all sovereignty. The belief in a minimum of government became a fundamental article of faith of the new nation. Americans everywhere affirmed Jefferson's " eternal hostility to every form of tyranny over the mind of man."

Since that time this love of freedom has now narrowed to a lazy trickle and now surged forward like a raging cataract. The half-century between the final war with England and the conflict between the states witnessed a plethora of reform movements. Most vociferous were the Abolitionists, to whom the existence of slavery was a crying iniquity. When the federal government adhered to the letter of the law in its effort to effect a compromise between the antagonistic sections, it was condemned as an oppressive tyranny. Men like Garrison and Phillips renounced their allegiance to it, John Brown openly declared war upon it, and thousands of others regarded is as unfit to command their respect and loyalty.

While many of the Abolitionists carried their defiance into the highroad of anarchism, the leading Transcendentalists developed their doctrine of individualism with a boldness that led to a like condemnation of governmental authority. Emerson's cadenced encomiums of self-reliance and the sovereignty of the individual were echoed in all the crowded lyceums from Maine to the frontier. His young friend and follower Henry D. Thoreau brought the doctrine to its logical extremity with a clarity and conviction that gave classical expression to the philosophy of anarchism. His refusal to compromise with or conciliate the agents of government and his successful demonstration at Walden Pond of his ability to live apart from organized society made him pre-eminent among the political dissidents of the United States.

Garrison, Phillips, Emerson, and Thoreau remained within the Jeffersonian orbit, even if straining at its outer edge. Josiah Warren, who began as a follower of Robert Owen at New Harmony and who was for many years an active Abolitionist, became the first avowed anarchist in America. Owen's utopian communism irritated his independent spirit and led him to the doctrine of extreme individualism. " Everyone," he asserted, " must feel that he is the supreme arbiter of his own [destiny], that no power on earth shall rise over him, that he is and always shall be sovereign of himself and all relating to his individuality. Then only shall men realize security of person and property." To illustrate the practicality of his theory he opened his Time Store in Cincinnati in 1827, many years before Proudhon proposed the formation of his exchange banks. Here he sold goods at a cost, plus four percent for overhead, plus the time spent on the sale. The customer was required to pay for this time with an equivalent amount of work. Thus, if Warren gave a half-hour of his time to a sale, the purchaser obligated himself to return thirty minutes of his own work; in the society planned by Warren all occupations were equally remunerative and all services were paid in kind. The store remained in operation for two years and demonstrated to the owner that " equity and justice in human relations would promote happiness to a degree unattainable in the present selfish scramble for place and power." The experiment also convinced him that " there is no service undertaken by government that could not be more efficiently and more economically performed by associated or individual effort springing naturally to meet the needs of society."

In 1850, after considerable further study and reflection, he founded the colony Modern Times on Long Island to prove that a group of individuals could live together amicably and advantageously by observing the principle of "mind your own business." Labor notes facilitated the exchange of products of farming and industry. Each member followed his own bent, and all voluntarily co-operated in performing the social tasks of the community. The village persisted for about twelve years, but the venture could boast no greater success than dozens of other utopian colonies. Warren's interest in it ceased soon after he had satisfied himself that men can be individualist anarchists and still perpetuate the human race. From that time till his death some twenty years later he devoted himself to the advocacy of his doctrine.

Stephen Pearl Andrews, Lysander Spooner, and William B. Greene were among Warren's better-known followers. Discussion of Proudhon's views, similar to their own yet broader and clearer, enriched their conclusions. Greene's *Mutual Banking*, appearing in 1850, presented the American version of mutualism in its most systematic form. He argued that while we are all dependent on one another, mutualism "coordinates individuals without any sacrifice of individuality, into one collective whole, by spontaneous confederation and solidarity." Andrews's *The Science of Society*, published in 1852, was regarded by Warren as the most lucid and complete exposition of his own theory. The first part explained the political doctrine of "the sovereignty of the individual as the final development of Protestantism, Democracy, and Socialism"; the second part treated the theory of cost as the limit of price and described it as "a scientific measure of honesty in trade," as one which in turn would "inevitably bring about cooperation and mutual aid." In their narrow concern with political liberty they disregarded or condoned the wage system. In *The Science of Society* Andrews declared: "It is right that one man employ another, it is right that he pay him wages, and it is right that he direct him absolutely,

[165]

arbitrarily in the performance of his labor." All that he and other individualists anarchists demanded was that "all natural opportunities requisite to the production of wealth be accessible to all on equal terms," and that "monopolies arising from special privileges created by law" be abolished. It is not surprising therefore that they failed to impress their views upon a nation dominated by an aggressive capitalism. The authorities either ignored or tolerated them, and the mass of workers either knew not of their existence or disdained them as impractical dreamers.

Communist anarchism reached the United States on a wave of strikes and riots in the late 1870's. A number of radicals, mostly German immigrants, became disgusted with the political views of the Socialist Labor Party and broke away from it in order to create an organization of their own. For a while they floundered in the doctrinal turbulence within the labor movement. Then in 1882 John Most, the dynamic exponent of Bakuninism, arrived in New York and quickly established his leadership of the dissident groups.

Born in Germany in 1846 of an illegitimate mating and suffering from the spiritual scars of a wretched childhood as well as from facial disfigurement, Most grew up hating those in authority. He joined the Social Democrats during his teens and was elected to the Reichstag in the 1870's. His experience as a lawmaker convinced him of the futility of political action and he went over to the Bakunin faction. After several terms of imprisonment he left Germany and settled in London, where he began to edit *Die Freiheit*, an anarchist weekly. An editorial approving the assassination of Czar Alexander II caused Most to be sent to jail for a term of sixteen months. As soon as he was released he sailed for the United States to resume his radical activities in the new world. At the age of thirty-six he was at the height of his forensic powers and already a legend among radicals. His platform addresses electrified his audiences. Because of his provocative and sarcastic editorials, his weekly, *Die Freiheit*, appealed to his readers more effectively than any of the other labor periodicals. Within a few months he had persuaded many of his admirers that " propaganda of the deed " was the surest way of achieving the social revolution. As practical instruction he published a pamphlet with the self-explanatory title: *Science of Revolutionary Warfare: A Manual of Instructions in the Use and Preparation of Nitroglycerine, Dynamite, Gun-Cotton, Fulminating Mercury, Bombs, Fuses, Poisons, etc., etc.*

In 1883, after a year of intensive agitation he called a congress of communistic anarchists in Pittsburgh. Twenty-eight delegates from twenty-two cities gathered in solemn session and produced the following platform:

1. Destruction of the existing class rule by all means; i. e., energetic, relentless, revolutionary and international action.
2. Establishment of a free society, based upon co-operative organization of production.
3. Free exchange of equivalent products by and between the productive organizations, without commerce and profit-mongering.
4. Organization of education on a secular, scientific, and equal basis for both sexes.
5. Equal rights for all, without distinction of sex or race.
6. Regulation of all public affairs by free contracts between the autonomous (independent) communes and associations, resting on a federative basis.

The delegates returned to their locals determined to spread the gospel among their fellow workers. The focal center became Chicago, where Albert Parsons and August Spies were the energetic leaders. The unemployment crisis, a flurry of strikes, and the agitation for the eight-hour day strengthened the hands of the anarchists, and in 1885 Parsons claimed a total membership of seven thousand. His weekly, *Alarm*, expounded the use of dynamite as the best available weapon against the oppressors of labor. " A pound of this good stuff," he wrote, " beats a bushel of ballots all hollow, and don't forget it." The inflammatory language of the anarchist periodicals, coinciding with sporadic strikes and violence, alarmed many businessmen and public officials. The fact that most of the anarchists were recent immigrants — Germans, Russian Jews, and Italians — tended to intensify the prejudice against them. The newspapers, always eager to capitalize on matters of public interest, began to play up the threat of anarchism and reported each strike or labor disturbance as if it were the first blow for the social revolution. Preachers and politicians joined in the attack with an eagerness compounded of fear and pharisaism. In a short time a large part of the nation was converted to the belief that labor agitators must be exterminated if the American way of life was to be retained.

The eight-hour-day movement was to reach its culmination in a general strike on May 1, 1886. On the appointed day tens of thousands of workers absented themselves from their shops in order to enforce their demand for the shorter workday in public meeting. No disturbance worthy of notice occurred during the demonstrations. On May 3, however, some of the strikers of the McCormick Harvester Company attacked the strikebeakers as they were leaving the factory. The police reserves were called out and in the melée one striker was killed and several were seriously wounded. August Spies, who witnessed the clash, immediately wrote a " revenge " circular, to be distributed among various groups of workers. The next evening a meeting of protest was held at Haymarket Square. The speakers were mostly anarchists, but the gathering was peaceful until police reserves appeared on the scene and the officer in charge ordered instant dispersal. Before any protest could be made, a bomb exploded with terrific impact among the men in uniform, killing one and wounding several others. The unharmed police became panicky and fired upon the startled crowd. Some of the workers made quick use of their own revolvers. When the shooting ceased a couple of minutes later, seven policemen were dead and sixty wounded: the casualties among the laborers were never determined but the number was probably much higher.

The disastrous explosion and riot shocked the entire nation. The loose and flamboyant talk of the anarchists now assumed a terrifying ominousness in the eyes of the adversaries of labor. In their hysterical fright they saw themselves deprived of their privileges and even of their lives. To stave off bloody revolution they determined to act quickly to destroy the aggressive leaders of labor. Editors, preachers, and politicians — the molders of public opinion — needed no urging to intensify their campaign of abuse and condemnation of all radicals, and particularly the anarchists. The wild-eyed, bushy-bearded, bomb-throwing agitator — a caricature of Most — became a familiar character in the cartoonist's repertory. The very idea of radicalism was everywhere execrated as an alien doctrine which sought to destroy the fundamental American liberties.

Although the anarchists who addressed the Haymarket meeting had been deliberately mild in their criticism of the police, and although no evidence was ever uncovered to connect them with the unidentified thrower of the fatal bomb, they and several others were arrested, tried for murder, and sentenced to death under conditions that made impartial justice impossible. All the emphatic protest of liberal Americans against this violation of fair play was of no avail in the face of an aroused mob spirit bent on legal lynching. Of the seven defendants condemned to die, one committed suicide, four were hanged, and two had their death sentences commuted to life imprisonment.

The event shook the entire nation, and with a vehemence that tore at its social roots. The arbitrary procedure of the police and the hysterical incitement of press and pulpit stung the conscience of those Americans who believed in democracy and feared capitalistic monopoly. William Dean Howells, Henry Demarest Lloyd, and scores of other liberals spoke out repeatedly, and with exemplary courage, for the acquittal of the condemned anarchists. Several years later Governor John P. Altgeld, more interested in " doing right " than in public applause, pardoned the surviving victims in a notable message exonerating the defendants and exposing the prejudice of judge and jury.

From the time of the Haymarket bombing until our own day, the term anarchism has been generally regarded as synonymous with social depravity and its adherents have been branded with the stigma of Cain. Although few of them ever preached terrorism, and although John Most and his followers had early renounced it in favor of peaceable propaganda, all were execrated as detestable desperadoes. The shooting of Henry C. Frick by Alexander Berkman in 1892 and the assassination of President McKinley by Leon Czolgosz nine years later — both isolated *attentats* by hot-headed youths — unfortunately served to intensify the common belief in the inherent criminality of all anarchists. Congress responded by passing an act forbidding their admission to this country. The police treated them as dangerous enemies of the state, breaking up their meetings at every opportunity and arresting their leaders at the slightest provocation. Emma Goldman, the most aggressive of the advocates of anarchism, suffered more harassment and violence from officers sworn to maintain law and order than any other woman of her time. Made of the stuff of martyrs, however, she carried her message to tens of thousands from one end of the country to the other, until her opposition to the war in 1917 caused her imprisonment and subsequent deportation.

It should be stressed that communist anarchists, unlike individualist libertarians, were mostly workers and closely connected with labor organizations. They thought of themselves as the extreme left wing of the mass movement seeking the abolition of capitalism; they did not hesitate to go along with the socialists, whom they otherwise disdained as confused doctrinaires, in any direction that might lead to the social revolution. They were also among the first to respond to the call of strikers who needed help, and their zeal often proved the deciding factor in achieving victory. Frequently they embarrassed the more conservative labor leaders by their mere presence on the picket line or at workers' demonstrations, but the rank and file usually appreciated their devotion. As was to be expected, they were especially interested in the activities of the I. W. W. (Industrial Workers of the World), which followed a syndicalist program, and took a major part in their strikes and in their clashes with the police and the courts.

The anarchist movement in this country suffered almost complete disruption during the war years 1916–21, when the government attempted to destroy all radicalism by sheer force. Hundreds of anarchists were jailed and deported, and those who remained free were cowed into outer acquiescence. By the time Attorney-General Palmer retired to a deserved obscurity and the opponents of capitalism were again permitted to make themselves heard, the surviving anarchists lacked the strength and leadership to resume their former agitation. Individuals and small groups maintained here and there at least a modicum of anarchist propaganda, but the nationwide lecture tours were no more.

The last flare-up of anarchist activity was caused by the tragic Sacco-Vanzetti case. The two Italian radicals, one a shoemaker and the other a fish peddler, were accused of killing two men in a payroll robbery and sentenced to die in the electric chair. This grievous miscarriage of justice, like the Haymarket and the Mooney-Billings cases, was the poisonous fruit of acute anti-radical prejudice. Again, however, the forces of liberalism, dormant for nearly a decade, hurried to the aid of the radicals in their long and bitter fight to save the two victims from electrocution. The struggle was in vain, but it brought to light a large number of Americans who believed in freedom and justice as passionately as had their Abolitionist fathers and grandfathers. And with them were arrayed the few zealous anarchists who fought for the lives of their hapless comrades with the determination of despair.

In the 1930's a number of the surviving anarchists, with Carlo Tresca at their head, became involved in the factional strife among the communists. In their natural opposition to the dominant Stalinists, a number of them embraced the cause of the Trotskyists — ironically the group which Emma Goldman and Berkman had found most obnoxious during their unhappy sojourn in Soviet Russia. With the assassination of Tresca, the small anarchist group in this country lost its chief spokesman.

When the thick crust of prejudice is removed from the popular conception of anarchism, the doctrine assumes an idealistic character bordering on utopianism. As Bertrand Russell put it: " Liberty is the supreme good in the Anarchist creed, and liberty is sought by the direct road of abolishing all forcible control over the individual by the community." In their opposition to the state the anarchists assume that men can live together without it. Yet they do not conceive of a society without order, but of an order maintained by self-governing groups. Nor do they ignore the advantages of economic combination; they merely insist that such combination must be wholly voluntary. From their standpoint every individual is a sovereign who finds it desirable to co-operate with his peers for the common good. "In this sense," remarked Thomas Huxley, "strict anarchy may be the highest conceivable grade of perfection of social existence; for, if all men spontaneously did justice and loved mercy, it is plain that all swords might be advantageously turned into plowshares, and that the occupation of judges and police would be gone."

In plucking anarchism from the clouds of egotistical philosophy and thrusting it into the turmoil of the marketplace, Bakunin and his followers have turned it from a daydream into a challenge. They stressed the abolition not so much of the state as of capitalism; they sought to establish a society by means of social revolution and based on the principles of voluntary association. Judged by their place in the political arena they were, willy-nilly, cheek by jowl with the Marxian socialists; if anything, they were more aggressive in their agitation against the exploitation of labor. Yet their position was largely and necessarily negative. Their philosophy made it impossible for them to bridge the gap between complete individual liberty and social obligations. Until men become angels or are possessed by fanatical zeal they cannot be expected to do voluntarily tasks which are not to their liking. Nor are anarchists wholly realistic in their conception of a society fostering at once unrestricted liberty and a limited, simplified economy in a civilization as complex as ours. Max Netlau, the leading historian of anarchism, was keenly aware of this impractical position.

I have been struck for a long time [he declared] by the contrast between the largeness of the aim of Anarchism — the greatest possible realization of freedom and well-being for all — and the narrowness, so to speak, of the economic program of Anarchism, be it Individualist Anarchism or

Communist. . . . I feel myself that neither Communism nor Individualism, if it became the sole economic form, would realize freedom, which
always demands a choice of ways, a plurality of possibilities.

The three chapters that follow deal at length with leading representatives of the different schools of anarchism. Henry D. Thoreau
is unquestionably the keenest exponent of the theory that man and
not the state is sovereign. Benjamin R. Tucker, while not the
founder, was certainly the most influential advocate of individualist
anarchism. Finally, Emma Goldman was for many years the dynamic leader of the anarchists who worked zealously for the social
revolution. A study of their lives and beliefs makes clear the nature
and scope of the anarchist movement in the United States.

HENRY DAVID THOREAU

TRANSCENDENTAL INDIVIDUALIST

PERHAPS no other major writer has concerned himself so consciously and so effectively as Henry David Thoreau with the ever-pressing problem of how one might earn a living and yet remain free. This is understandable: poverty abetted principle in accentuating his keen yearning for the full life. The son of an unsuccessful pencil-maker, he discovered quite early in life that most men cannot provide for their daily needs without giving up what seemed to him the better part of themselves. Concord born and bred, of a rebellious, reflective nature, an earnest admirer and later an intimate friend of Emerson, he was readily influenced by the ideals of transcendentalism which had become current during his adolescence. While still a student at Harvard he underwent a spiritual revolution after reading Emerson's essay on " Nature." " In the woods is perpetual youth," he read. " Within these plantations of God, a decorum and sanctity reign, a perennial festival is dressed, and the guest sees not how he should tire of them in a thousand years. In the woods, we return to reason and faith." After this exhilarating vision, college studies became even more barren and fatuous than before. He longed to become a guest at nature's festival, to take to the woods rather than follow his classmates in the beaten groove of custom.

It was easier to dream than to do. When Thoreau graduated from Harvard College in 1837 he had to begin earning his living and so became a teacher in the Concord public school. After a fortnight, however, he resigned rather than submit to the school committee's insistence that he use corporal punishment instead of moral suasion. For months thereafter he helped his father with his pencil-making. His difficulty in adjusting himself to the smug materialism of his neighbors only intensified his yearning for a life entirely different from theirs.

" How shall I help myself? " he asked himself in his Journal the following year. His answer was: " By withdrawing into a garret, and associating with spiders and mice, determining to meet myself face to face sooner or later." Meantime he visited Emerson at every opportunity. That the older and already famous man appreciated his new friend is shown by the following entry in his 1838 Journal: " I delight much in my friend, who seems to have as free and erect a mind as any I have ever met." It was at this time that Thoreau, following Emerson's suggestion, began to keep a Journal and to nurture the ambition of becoming a writer.

He still needed to support himself, and in June 1838 he joined his older brother John in organizing a private school based on advanced pedagogical principles. They soon had all the pupils they could accommodate, and the school flourished until March 1841, when it was closed as a consequence of John's illness. Thoreau was again at loose ends, outwardly as far as ever from his goal of self-sufficiency. He was determined, however, not to permit necessity to deprive him of adequate leisure. The next month he accepted Emerson's invitation to live with him as a member of the family. He helped edit the *Dial* and did many of the chores about the house and garden. Much of the time he was able to enjoy the solitude of his hall bedroom or to saunter in the near-by woods.

After two years his conscience began to chafe at the thought of his dependence upon another, even if that other were Emerson. He had just read the latter's essay on" Self Reliance " — " It is only as a man puts off from himself all external support and stands alone that I see him to be strong and to prevail " — and he wanted complete independence. Emerson thereupon arranged with his brother William, who lived in Staten Island, to employ the youth as a tutor for his son. The removal to New York was to give Thoreau the opportunity of finding a place for himself as a writer. During the next six months he tried hard to market his essays and reviews. But the editors and publishers he called upon gave him little encouragement. Lonely for the serenity of the Concord woods and concluding in his disappointment that " the pigs in the street are the most respectable part of the population," he decided to leave the indifferent metropolis and return to his beloved native haunts.

As unable as he was unwilling to make his way in the large city, he now insisted on living his own life. During the years with Emerson and while in New York he had read widely and pondered deeply on the meaning of human existence. His inherent tendency to shun compromise, to shy away from dogma and custom, and to seek the truth behind the event, had become a rebellious resolve to follow his own bent without regard to the opinion of others. The decision was not made in haste. While still a senior in college he had written: " The fear of displeasing the world ought not in the least to influence my actions. Were it otherwise, the principle avenue to Reform would be closed." Several months later he had asserted in his Commencement Speech that " the characteristic of our epoch is perfect freedom — freedom of thought and action." During the years of groping he recorded in his Journal the thoughts that became stepping-stones to a mature philosophy of life.

As to conforming outwardly, and living your own life inwardly, I have not a very high opinion of that course. . . . If I were confined to a corner in a garret all my days, like a spider, the world would be just as large to me while I had my thoughts. . . . Perhaps I am more than usually jealous of my freedom. I feel that my connections with and obligations to society are at present very slight and transient. . . . If I should sell both my forenoons and afternoons to society, neglecting my peculiar calling, there would be nothing left worth living for. I trust that I shall never thus sell my birthright for a mess of pottage.

On his return to Concord towards the end of 1843 he yielded completely to the allure of the neighboring woods, fields, and waters. To minimize his working time he stripped his needs to the bone. He wore corduroy clothes, ate simply and frugally, and denied himself the indulgences that cost money. Indeed he soon pursued poverty as others do wealth. Simplicity of life gave him what he desired most — leisure, peace of mind, freedom. Reversing the Biblical injunction, he labored one day a week and made of the other six a prolonged Sabbath. For the next year and a half he worked at odd jobs, helped build his father's house, and prepared for the experiment that was to prove his ability to live as he pleased and to write immortal prose.

I went to the woods because I wished to live deliberately, to front only the essential facts of life, and see if I could not learn what it had to teach, and not, when I came to die, discover that I had not lived. I did not wish to live what was not life, living is so dear; nor did I wish to practise resignation, unless it was quite necessary. I wanted to live deep and suck out all the marrow of life, to live so sturdily and Spartan-like as to rout all that was not life, to cut a broad swath and shave close, to drive life into a corner, and reduce it to its lowest terms, and, if it proved to be mean, why then to get the whole and genuine meanness of it and publish its meanness to the world; or if it were sublime, to know it by experience, and be able to give a true account of it in my next excursion.

The foregoing celebrated passage from *Walden* suggests nothing quixotic or altruistic in Thoreau's experiment in solitude. He was neither running away from life nor improvising a new panacea. Even more than Emerson he scorned the social reformers. Extreme individualist that he was, he refused to join Brook Farm, asserting that he "would rather keep bachelor's hall in hell than go to board in heaven." Nor could his personal solution be regarded as eccentric in a nation whose undaunted pioneers were then conquering a continental frontier.

The details of Thoreau's two years and two months of solitary life at Walden Pond are to be found in the book which spread his fame to the ends of the earth. Possessed of manual skill, he built himself a substantial hut for twenty-eight dollars and lived in it at an average cost of twenty-seven cents a week. He enjoyed living alone, a mile from the nearest neighbor, amidst the tranquillity of nature.

" I thrive best on solitude," he told his Journal. " My fairies invariably take to flight when a man appears upon the scene." Time, to him the most precious of man's possessions, was all his own and he luxuriated in this leisure to the utmost. He read stimulating books, wrote much and thought even more; he studied nature with keen attention, visited the village and received visitors at his hut. In his own estimation, the experiment was entirely successful: he had learned the secret of life and had found it truly sublime.

Thoreau came to Walden Pond a probing and perturbed youth; he left it a man profoundly aware of the working of both nature and the mind. The Concord townsmen still regarded him as queer, " a Harvard graduate turned loafer and handyman." But Emerson and Channing and Alcott, who had visited him and had read his writings, greatly respected the wildwood freshness of his acute intellect. While at the Pond Thoreau had completed A *Week on the Concord and Merrimac Rivers*, an account of the excursion he and his brother John had taken in 1839, replete with nature lore and the reflections of a poetic youth in search of his soul. He had also written the greater part of *Walden* and many pages of his Journal. By the time he left the hut he had developed a prose style that centered in the epigrammatic phrase and sparkled with the luster of the subtly cadenced sentence. The interval also served to clarify his views on economics which, particularly in *Walden*, were to become the most eloquent, if unavailing, protest against materialistic domination ever uttered by an American.

Having satisfied himself that man can live on very little and be the happier for it, Thoreau spoke out firmly and frequently for the simple life. He abhorred the greediness of men, their zeal to accumulate wealth, their slavish devotion to things. In his Journal and in his famous essay, " Life Without Principle," he wrote scathingly of businessmen and others who valued money above everything else and profaned their minds in the unscrupulous pursuit of it. He maintained caustically that " most are engaged in business the greater part of their lives, because the soul abhors a vacuum, and they have not discovered any continuous employment for man's nobler faculties." The rush to acquire California's new-found gold struck him as a fine example of the processes of enrichment which "almost without exception head downward." "I know of no more startling development of the immorality of trade, and all the common modes of getting a living. . . . It is not enough to tell me you worked hard to get your gold. So does the Devil work hard."

Thoreau had proved to his own satisfaction that no man needed to be a slave to work. It was his firm belief, indeed, that "a man had better starve at once than lose his innocence in the process of getting his bread." Yet he knew that most men lacked his love of independence; that the urge to live reconciled them to slavery. Against this increasing dehumanization he directed his keenest shafts. "Even if we grant that the American has freed himself from a political tyrant, he is still the slave of an economic and moral tyrant." He particularly regretted the spread of industrialism and the plight of the workers in the mills and factories. "It is remarkable," he wrote, "that there is little or nothing to be remembered written on the subject of getting a living; how to make getting a living not merely honest and honorable, but altogether inviting and glorious; for if *getting* a living is not so, then living is not."

Again and again he returned to his attack upon those who were forfeiting their souls in the mad scramble for material possessions. Wealth, he argued, was truly impoverishing because it enslaved one to things. Genuine wealth was not possession but enjoyment. "It is the greatest of all advantages to enjoy no advantage at all. I find it invariably true, the poorer I am, the richer I am. . . . I am reminded often that if I had bestowed on me the wealth of Croesus, my aims must still be the same, and my means essentially the same." Not luxury, but the edification of the spirit was man's greatest good. It was far better to forgo physical comfort than the pleasures afforded by nature and the nobler faculties. "The most glorious fact in our experience," he wrote in *A Week*, "is not anything we have done or may hope to do, but a transient thought, a vision, or dream, which we have had. I would give all the wealth of the world, and all the deeds of all the heroes, for one true vision."

In his quest for economic freedom Thoreau developed a profound hostility to authoritarianism. He was not alone, of course, in placing the individual above the state. The pioneering spirit was of necessity individualistic: willy-nilly the early settlers had to shift for themselves, and many of those who subsequently established their claims on the frontier did so to avoid the restraints of an organized society. The followers of Jefferson favored their leader's assumption that that government was best which governed least. Nearer home were Abolitionists like Garrison and Wendell Phillips who repudiated the federal and state governments as well as the Constitution for condoning the existence of slavery. Thoreau, however, went even beyond these in his extreme stand against political power. In "Civil Disobedience" and in later writings he propounded his opposition to the state with such eloquence that like-minded men the world over have acclaimed him as their spokesman ever since.

Inevitably Thoreau gravitated towards philosophical anarchism. He was, according to Emerson, "a born protestant. . . . He interrogated every custom and wished to settle all his practice on an ideal foundation." This practical pursuit of his ideals strengthened his character. Emerson's conspicuous practitioner of self-reliance, he again and again rebelled against the claims and conventions of society. Asking little, he wanted to give even less. To him most institutions embodied "the will of the dead" to oppress the living; he would neither respect them nor accept any part of them unless they passed his test of relevancy. Nor did he dread standing alone. "To some men their relation to mankind is all important," he recorded in his Journal. "I feel myself not so vitally related to my fellowmen. I impinge on them but by a point on one side. It is not a Siamese-twin ligature that binds me to them. It is unsafe to defer so much to mankind and the opinions of society, for these are always, and without exception, heathenish and barbarous, seen from the heights of philosophy." Not that he disdained his neighbors; he simply felt no need of their fellowship and resented constraint, whether put on him by an individual or by the state.

So long as he was left alone he was perfectly willing to remain a passive rebel. His civil disobedience was precipitated in 1846 by the demand of a poll tax which he believed was to further the pro-slavery war with Mexico. He did not object to paying taxes as such, and he was not in arrears with his highway tax; but as a strong opponent of slavery he would do nothing that furthered that iniquitous institution. When he came into town one day to have a shoe mended he was put in jail. The next morning his mortified family paid the tax without his knowledge and he was released.

" Civil Disobedience " grew out of his reflections upon his imprisonment. On leaving the town jail he felt the darts of antagonism. Certain he was right, he regarded those who disapproved of his defiance as enslaved to their prejudices and superstitions. For he believed that he could not as a free man have done otherwise. Basing his stand on the transcendental esteem of the individual, he reasoned that he and not society was the better judge of right and wrong. Thus he had refused to pay church tithes and to attend religious services because he had a low opinion of the organized church. Again, since he preferred poverty and freedom to comfort and economic subjection, he insisted on living his own life in his own way. He refused to vote because he regarded the ballot as a feeble political instrument: by voting for the available candidates one merely furthered the work of the demagogues. Nor would he submit to the will of the majority in matters of principle, since he saw " but little virtue in the action of the masses of men." And while he did not advocate fighting wrong, he certainly would not support wrong by his acquiescence. To pay the poll tax was to his mind equivalent to abetting the government in furthering slavery. This he would not do. The next step was civil disobedience. " I simply wish to refuse allegiance to the State, to withdraw and stand aloof from it effectually. . . . In fact, I quietly declare war with the State, after my fashion, though I will still make what use and get what advantage of her I can, as is usual in such cases." Always the practical Yankee, he saw no reason to decline the benefits of government merely because he refused its ignoble demands.

He did not shirk the consequences of his action. If governmental iniquity, he asserted, " is of such a nature that it requires you to be the agent of injustice to another, then, I say, break the law. . . . Law never made men a whit more just, and, by means of their respect for it, even the well-disposed are daily made the agents of injustice." He therefore submitted to incarceration rather than help strengthen slavery, knowing that he would feel freer in jail with a clear conscience than at large with a burdened one. This insistence on acting from principle motivated his entire behavior. Nor was he unaware of his radicalism. " Action from principle, the perception and performance of right, changes things and relations; it is essentially revolutionary, and does not consist wholly with anything which was. It not only divides states and churches, it divides families; ay, it divides the individual, separating the diabolical in him from the divine." It was his firm belief, moreover, logically deduced from his transcendental view of society, that if enough men passively resisted injustice, the government would soon be driven to capitulate. Such action on the part of a resolute minority would lead to a "bloodless revolution." " If the alternative is to keep all just men in prison, or to give up war and slavery, the State will not hesitate which to choose."

Along with Godwin, Emerson, and the extreme Abolitionists, Thoreau was not concerned with the fate of society subsequent to the collapse of government. He did not conceive of the state in the abstract; to him it was the power of government used by politicians for ends that were usually deplorable. Since its power was originally derived from individuals, their rights were of necessity superior to those conceded to the state. Man was not born to be forced; his first duty was to his conscience. If the state attempted to ride roughshod over the rights of its citizens, the latter must without compromise resist this breach of compact. The sooner the oppressive state was shorn of its power, the better. " Government," he asserted, " is at best an expedient; but most governments are usually, and all governments are sometimes, inexpedient."

Not that Thoreau was opposed to the state as such. He knew that so long as men were subject to greed and passion they needed policing by public authority. What he objected to was the arrogation of power by the state to the detriment of its citizens. In his view this censure applied as much to the weak, liberal government under which he lived as to the most oppressive tyranny: their respective clashes with the upright individual differed in degree rather than in kind. From this standpoint " that government is best which governs not at all." Since such government was not yet in existence, he outlined his conception of the ideal state:

There will never be a really free and enlightened State until the State comes to recognize the individual as a higher and independent power, from which all its own power and authority are derived, and treats him accordingly. I please myself with imagining a State at least which can afford to be just to all men, and to treat the individual with respect as a neighbor; which even would not think it inconsistent with its own repose if a few were to live aloof from it, not meddling with it, nor embraced by it, who fulfilled all the duties of neighbors and fellow-men. A State which bore this kind of fruit, and suffered it to drop off as fast as it ripened, would prepare the way for a still more perfect and glorious State, which also I have imagined, but not yet anywhere seen.

" Civil Disobedience " was written primarily to vindicate the ethical principles which led to its author's imprisonment. It is a vigorous essay, full of strong feeling and lofty rebelliousness, and bristling with pointed epigrams. Neverthless it was a self-conscious performance: his indignation was simulated; his philosophy of idealistic anarchism was an exercise in moral contemplation. It was his reaction to a situation forced on him against his will. Nor was it a work of originality — the basic ideas having had political currency for nearly a century. That the essay should have become the classic statement of the ever-present conflict between the individual and the state is a tribute to the rhetorical effectiveness of Thoreau's style.

It should be stressed that the provocation in this instance was personal and relatively unimportant. A night in jail served Thoreau as an opportune springboard; being the man he was, he was bound to give expression to his anti-authoritarian views sooner or later. He therefore minimized the prison incident and dwelt mainly on the philosophical aspects of the problem. Yet as a thorough individualist he shied away from the implications of practical reform. He had a very poor opinion of both society and its institutions, and preferred to live the hermit rather than try to lift men to his own lofty level. He had himself in mind when he wrote: " The true poet will ever live aloof from society, wild to it, as the finest singer is the wood thrush, a forest bird." The turmoil and turpitude of the marketplace were not for him. " What is called politics," he was to write in " Life Without Principle," " is comparatively so superficial and inhuman, that, practically, I have never fairly recognized that it concerns me at all."

It was easy enough for Thoreau to keep aloof from the fussy reform movements such as Temperance and Woman's Rights, since they seemed to him of little consequence in a society suffering from economic and moral slavery. "The wisest man preaches no doctrine," was his motto. Nor was he much interested in the Abolition movement so long as it remained on the level of virtuous talk. It was simply not in his philosophy to crusade for the betterment of mankind. Moreover, from his high ethical perch the cotton-mill owners in his own state were no less guilty of human subjugation than the cotton planters of South Carolina. If he were to devote himself to fighting iniquity and oppression wherever he came upon them, he would have no time to live his own life. " It is not a man's duty, as a matter of course," he argued in " Civil Disobedience," " to devote himself to the eradication of any, even the most enormous wrong; he may still properly have other concerns to engage him." Among these concerns were excursions to Cape Cod, the Maine woods, Canada, nature studies in the vicinity of his beloved Concord, and above all the writing, with scrupulous stylistic care, of the volumes that were to place his name alongside of Emerson's.

The passage of the Fugitive Slave Act of 1850, which brought slavery to his very door, greatly irritated his conscience. In the past he had more than once helped his family to shelter runaway slaves. The new law, however, not only made such succor a criminal act but also directed him, as a citizen, to assist public officials in tracking down fugitive Negroes. That was too much. His conscience gave him no peace. In his Journal his excited indignation filled page after page. When Thomas Sims was taken in Boston and returned to his one-time owner, Thoreau felt as if he himself had, by virtue of his passivity, participated in the crime against the innocent victim. Had he been in the Massachusetts capital, he would probably have opposed the slave-catchers with more than words of wrath. As it was, his saunterings became even more solitary, and his assiduous study of nature appeared almost a flight from reality.

Three years later the arrest and deportation of Anthony Burns shocked Thoreau into action. As a man of strict principle — and he was then writing " Life Without Principle " — he could no longer ignore the ignoble behavior of his native state. " Who can be serene in a country where both the rulers and the ruled are without principle? The remembrance of my country spoils my walks. My thoughts are murder to the State, and involuntarily go plotting against her." On July 4, 1854, he left his seclusion and delivered a philippic that exploded in the face of proud Boston Brahmins. The address, " Slavery in Massachusetts," was made at Framingham before an enthusiastic Abolitionist audience. It said little of Negro slavery and less of the South. Instead it dwelt on the moral laxity of the North, the degrading influences of the city, the venality of the press and the courts, and the general evasive loyalty to the letter of the Constitution.

What perturbed Thoreau most deeply was the subservience of his native state to a federal government bent on preserving slavery. The politicians had indeed degraded it to " a drab of State, a cloth-o'-silver slut." Such a state undermined the moral integrity of its citizens and endangered the liberties gained with the blood of their grandfathers in 1776. " I want my countrymen to consider that whatever the human law may be, neither an individual nor a nation can ever commit the least act of injustice against the obscurest individual without having to pay the penalty for it." In returning Anthony Burns to his former master, Massachusetts was not merely depriving a Negro of his freedom but was making mock of the political principles upon which it had been founded. Of such a state he could not be a citizen. " I have lived for the last month — and I think every man in Massachusetts capable of the sentiment of patriotism must have had a similar experience — with the sense of having suffered a vast and indefinite loss. I did not know at first what ailed me. At last it occurred to me that what I have lost was a country." If Americans were again to live as free men they must fight to regain the Revolutionary inheritance which they had foolishly tossed away.

More than William H. Seward or any of the other exponents of the " higher law " doctrine Thoreau affirmed the supremacy of conscience. The mistreatment of Anthony Burns having given fresh evidence of the egregious nature of the Fugitive Slave Act, he appealed to the citizens of Massachusetts to disavow their blind allegiance to man-made law, to stop quibbling as to the legality of slavery under the Constitution, and to heed the inner voice of conscience.

The question is, not whether you or your grandfather, seventy years ago, did not enter into an agreement to serve the Devil, and that service is not accordingly now due, but whether you will not now, for once and at last, serve God, — in spite of your own past recreancy, or that of your ancestors, — by obeying that eternal and only just CONSTITUTION, which He, and not any Jefferson or Adams, has written in your being.

If the government insisted on forcing the demoralizing proslavery law upon its citizens, resistance was the only remedy. He urged his auditors to trample the law as one did a snake.

This law rises not to the level of the head or the reason; its natural habitat is the dirt. It was born and bred, and has its life, only in the dust and mire, on a level with the feet; and he who walks with freedom, and does not with Hindoo mercy avoid treading on every venomous reptile, will inevitably tread on it, and so trample it under foot, — and Webster, its maker, like the dirt-bug and its ball.

His final thrust was that this country needed men, " not of policy, but of probity," men who will obey the spirit rather than the letter of the law. " The law will never make men free," he insisted; " it is men who have got to make the law free." If the federal government persisted in its promotion of slavery, it was up to Massachusetts to leave the Union; otherwise it was incumbent upon its citizens to refuse allegiance to the state " as long as she hesitates to do her duty."

Thoreau's transcendental individualism attained a dramatic climax in his defense of John Brown. Five years earlier, having delivered his indictment of Massachusetts and thereby having cleared his conscience, he had gone back to his woods to experience the peace of soul which no man could give him. Season after season he observed the miracle of nature with joyous gratitude. His Journal recorded the minute details of his studies and discoveries, of his sensitive reactions and reflections. The renown that came to him after the publication of *Walden* had no effect upon his social status; to most Americans he remained " the hermit of Concord." Yet at no time did he turn his mind from the events that were rapidly shaping the future. When John Brown, the hero of Osawatomie, visited Concord in 1857 to collect funds for his anti-slavery enterprises, Thoreau contributed his mite. He was strongly impressed by the man's flinty character and firm idealism. When Brown again lectured in Concord two years later, shortly before leaving for Virginia, Thoreau was once more present and rejoiced to find the old Abolitionist so determined in his righteous resolve. Here at last was the ideal man of action.

The following October came the electrifying news of John Brown's attack at Harpers Ferry. The first general reaction was dismay and indignation. Even most of the Abolitionists were shocked by the folly of the raid and were quick to disassociate themselves from it. Not so Thoreau. He at once perceived the heroic stature of the man and exulted to be his contemporary. For several days and nights he filled his Journal with excited thoughts on the singular event. Then, disregarding the active antagonism of his townsmen, he organized a meeting in the vestry of a church and delivered his defense of John Brown. According to *The Liberator,* "he spoke with real enthusiasm for an hour and a half. A very large audience listened to this lecture, crowding the hall half an hour before the time of its commencement, and giving hearty applause to some of the most energetic expressions of the speaker."

"A Plea for Captain John Brown" was not made in an effort to save the life of the condemned raider. "I plead not for his life, but for his character — his immortal life." It was a warm and forthright defense of the principles which Thoreau had been asserting all his adult life and for which John Brown was about to be hanged. There was this difference, however. The author of "Civil Disobedience," faced with a new and desperate situation, had come to realize that passive resistance was not enough. When a state trampled on human rights and individual integrity — and these abstract things assumed the guise of a human being in danger of his life — violent rebellion was the only effective method of resistance. And he was as ready philosophically, as John Brown was actually, to face the expected consequences. "I do not wish to kill or be killed," he wrote during the trial in Virginia, "but I can foresee circumstances in which both of these things would be by me unavoidable. In extremities I would even be killed."

A man of the garret and the woods, he admired all the more the fanatic idealist who was also a daring and dangerous man of action. He thought no other American could measure up to John Brown's noble stature; indeed the old rebel was "firmer and higher principled" than the best of men of 1776. Only a Cromwell might be regarded as his peer.

He was a superior man. He did not value his bodily life in comparison with ideal things. He did not recognize unjust human laws, but resisted them as he was bid. For once we are lifted out of our trivialities and dust of politics into the region of truth and manhood. No man in America has ever stood up so persistently and effectively for the dignity of human nature, knowing himself for a man, and the equal of any and all governments. In that sense he was the most American of us all.

One need only think of this rock-hewn old man with his six sons and few devoted followers dedicating themselves to a task that meant certain death " without expecting any reward but good conscience," to understand why Thoreau called their attack upon a government arsenal " a sublime spectacle."

In his plea for John Brown he lashed out against the state with all his intellectual might. " The only government that I recognize, — and it matters not how few are at the head of it, or how small its army, — is that power which establishes justice in the land, and not that which establishes injustice." He pointed out that Brown's body was of little worth, but that in snuffing out its life the government was making the gallows glorious as the cross. " You who pretend to care for Christ crucified, consider what you are about to do to him who offered himself to be the savior of four million men." So deeply agitated was he by John Brown's sublime daring, that he predicted the triumph of righteousness. " When a government takes the life of a man without the consent of his conscience, it is an audacious government, and is taking a step towards its own dissolution." Right and justice, he asserted, will prevail long after the mightiest of governments have passed into oblivion.

Thoreau was the first to speak in praise of the condemned Abolitionist, the first to recognize his singular spiritual drive. For months after John Brown was hanged Thoreau found no peace. The death of his hero so perturbed his mind as to alter his outlook on life. The woods lost their appeal, solitude ceased to attract him. " I was so absorbed in him as to be surprised whenever I detected the routine of the natural world surviving still, or met persons going about their affairs indifferent." While in this disconcerted state — and the oncoming " bronchitis " did not help his disposition — he paid little heed to the surging passions which Brown's death had helped to swell into an irresistible tide. The election of Abraham Lincoln and the outbreak of the Civil War, good omens though they were, roused in him not a fraction of the enthusiasm generated in his heart by the raid at Harpers Ferry. His hero had acted from strict principle; the country at war was a maelstrom of prejudice and hate.

On July 4, 1860, Thoreau came to North Elba to lecture before the martyr's family and neighbors. In "The Last Days of John Brown" he related the now familiar events with simple and sincere admiration, praising the natural nobility of the man's spirit. Other Abolitionists, he pointed out, had been hanged in the South without disturbing the peace of the nation; in Brown's case the revolution of opinion came not after the lapse of years but within a few days. This extraordinary phenomenon testified not only to his exceptional firmness of principle but also to the innate morality of the people; in learning from the possibility of living and dying for an ideal they were lifted to a nobler level. "When a noble deed is done, who is likely to appreciate it? They who are noble themselves. I was not surprised that certain of my neighbors spoke of John Brown as an ordinary felon, for who are they? They have either much flesh, or much office, or much coarseness of some kind." And although the state took the life of him who "appeared the greatest and best in it," the very sacrifice served to fire men's conscience. That was John Brown's contribution to mankind and it had gained him immortality.

Less than two years later, after considerable illness, Thoreau himself was counted among the immortals.

It would be unfair, if not futile, to evaluate Thoreau's social philosophy by contemporary standards. He was peculiarly the product of an America at the beginning of its industrial development. One need only consider how gratuitous his accentuated individualism would have appeared to the signers of the Declaration of Independence, and how unrealistic it seems in our era of statism, to realize that it could have flourished only during the early laissez-faire era of inchoate capitalism. Thoreau was indeed the last great American exponent of the Rousseauistic doctrine of the natural rights of man. It was just because he could foresee the final subjugation of the individual by the Leviathan State that he spoke out against it with such uncompromising idealism. Yet even now, for all the present impracticality of his anarchistic principles, there is an essential appeal in his philosophy which endears him to all freedom-loving peoples.

Thoreau's nonconformity was compounded of Emerson's principle of self-reliance, the teachings of Hindu scripture, the necessary individualism of the frontiersman. Like so many of his contemporaries he grew up to question the mores and manners of his generation; unlike them, however, he was, in Emerson's phrasing, " stubborn and implacable " in his adherence to his principles. He found life beautiful, reflection exhilarating, and he wanted nothing more. When he discovered that earning a living left no time for life, he rebelled. He scorned as monstrous the gospel of work which was part of the Puritan way of life and which was eagerly propagated by an emerging industrialism. Wealth he regarded as an incubus that corrupted the body and degraded the soul. A Yankee hedonist, he argued that man's goal was enjoyment, not property. The success of his experiment at Walden Pond validated his transcendental economics. Nor is it fair to maintain that he was able to live on six weeks' work a year because he had the assistance of Emerson and his family. The fact is that the account with his mother was kept to the half-penny, and that the service he rendered the Emerson household easily balanced the cost of his room and board and the rent on the lot at Walden. So far as he was concerned, it was merely a matter of preferring personal leisure to physical comfort, spiritual ease to social approval, and no man had a greater right to such a decision. The residual significance of this preference lies rather in his thoroughgoing criticism of a materialistic society which made such a choice necessary, and this criticism is as relevant now as it was in his day.

Solitude and soul-searching nurtured an acutely critical opinion of society. It pained him to see men ignore or degrade the values which alone made life meaningful. A strong believer in the principles of Sam Adams and Jefferson and Tom Paine, he resented the

curbs placed upon the rights of the individual, the increasing arrogation of power by the government. More and more he saw the
United States changing from the agricultural, politically weak state
of his childhood to the slave-ridden, compromising government of
Webster and Calhoun — with the industrial vanguard in the East
threatening ominously to transform the country into a huge mech-
anized mill — and his sharp protest became a desperate last cry
against the inevitable. His rejection of the state was in effect a refusal to submit to " the freedom of the prison-yard." In possession
of greater literary power and firmer principles than the other dissidents of his day, he championed the rights of the individual with
such persuasive eloquence that his " Civil Disobedience " became
the classic expression of philosophical anarchism.

Thoreau's indictment of the state was obviously the hyperbole of
the advocate. He did not approve of license. " To speak practically
and as a citizen, unlike those who call themselves no government
men, I ask for, not at once no government, but at once a better government." Although he believed that the ideal society needed no
government — and in this he was the philosophical anarchist — he
was too wise ever to expect perfection. In denouncing the state he
aimed at assuring the individual the freedom to which he was entitled. And if his anarchistic direction leads to a blind alley, his bold
method of moral resistance is still pertinent.

His antipathy to politicians who preferred palliatives to principles
having burst into trenchant wrath at the passage of the Fugitive
Slave Act, he put the issue of slavery where it belonged: upon the
conscience of those who adhered submissively to the letter of the
Constitution. His outburst was provoked not so much by the capture of a few slaves as by the moral lassitude which made such an
event possible. He wanted the men of Massachusetts to be worthy
of their inheritance. " O for a man who is a *Man*, and, as my neighbor says, has a bone in his back which you cannot pass your hand
through." Even Emerson seemed to him not firm enough.

Then came John Brown's dramatic raid, and Thoreau at last had
his hero. In his estimation no other of his contemporaries had acted

so purely from principle. While other Abolitionists merely ranted, Brown had the great courage to precipitate action; in giving his life for an ideal he helped to destroy the roots of slavery. And " the hermit of Concord " was gratified to learn before his death in 1862 that the soldiers of the North were marching to battle with the name of John Brown on their lips.

Henry David Thoreau excelled as a writer of trenchant prose and as a poet of nature. But it is as the eloquent spokesman of noble principles and the superiority of conscience that he is best remembered the world over. Many of his admirers, influenced by the estimates of his two most distinguished disciples, Tolstoy and Gandhi, have thought of him primarily as the outstanding practitioner of passive resistance. He was far more than that. His attitude toward the state remained negative and inactive so long as it left him in peace. But when it acted in a manner to trouble his conscience, he at once became aggressive in his attack against it. He was ready to " kill or be killed " in behalf of his ideals. Were he living in our time, he would not merely have secluded himself or have fasted in protest; he surely would have breasted the rising tide of authoritarianism and would have suffered martyrdom rather than compromise his conscience. This love of liberty, this boldness of spirit, this loyalty to principle, rather than his doctrine of nonresistance, we might take to heart as his most valuable contribution to our moral heritage.

BENJAMIN R. TUCKER

INDIVIDUALIST ANARCHIST

BENJAMIN R. TUCKER, chief exponent of individualist anarchism or the doctrine of the stateless society, had his roots deep in Yankee idealism. Of Colonial and Quaker ancestry, born in Dartmouth, Massachusetts, in 1854, when the agitation for the abolition of Negro slavery was reaching its crest, he grew up in an atmosphere of social reform. He was a very bright child and was early stimulated by the radical preaching of the Unitarian minister whose church he attended. He became " a daily devourer of the *New York Tribune* from the age of twelve," when Horace Greeley was at his best as the journalistic spokesman for American liberalism. During his early teens he studied the writings of Darwin, Spencer, Buckle, Mill, Huxley, and Tyndall, and all of them strengthened his nonconformist tendencies. He also went regularly to the winter lectures at the New Bedford Lyceum, and heard such advanced speakers as Wendell Phillips, Garrison, and Emerson. By the time he graduated from the Friends School in 1870 he was, much more than his fellows, eager to reform the world. His parents persuaded him to attend the Massachusetts Institute of Technology, where he remained for three years, more absorbed in social problems than in the study of engineering. A chance meeting with the aged Josiah Warren, the pioneer anarchist, so sharpened his interest in individual liberty that he decided to make it his prime concern. Many years later he had this to say of his adolescent zeal:

I naturally took a decided stand on all religious, scientific, political and social questions, and cherished a choice collection of chaotic and contradictory convictions, which did not begin to clear until I reached the age of eighteen, when a lucky combination of influences transformed me into the consistent anarchist that I have remained until this day. In the meantime I had been an atheist, a materialist, an evolutionist, a prohibitionist, a free trader, a champion of the legal eight-hourday, a woman suffragist, an enemy of marriage, and a believer in sexual freedom.

For all his intellectual aggressiveness, at eighteen Tucker was a very shy youth. He was, moreover, too busy with philosophical studies and too preoccupied with the establishment of the newly organized New England Labor Reform League to suffer for the lack of feminine friendship. It was as a representative of the League that he met the still alluring Victoria Woodhull, notorious socialist and feminist. She was having difficulty in obtaining permission to lecture in Massachusetts towns on "The Principles of Social Freedom." When Tucker heard of this denial of free speech he at once joined her manager in the fight for her constitutional rights. After considerable exertion he succeeded in browbeating the mayor of one city into granting the required permit. A few days later Victoria delivered her speech. When her young champion was introduced to her, she was at once attracted to him. Though she was then twice his age, he found her charming. Some months later, when she again visited Boston, she invited him to call on her and promptly seduced him. Shortly thereafter he went to New York to meet with radical groups, and while there he resumed his intimacy with Victoria. Nor, when his father sent him abroad for study, did he think it odd that she and her family should accompany him. After several weeks, however, Victoria returned to New York and the two went their separate ways.

Early in 1875 young Tucker, now an enthusiastic anarchist, was back in Boston and eager to broadcast his beliefs to his fellow Americans. While in Paris he had continued his reading of Proudhon's writings. In his view Proudhon's mutualism complemented Warren's individualism, and these two doctrines became the twin pillars of his belief in equal liberty. For more than a year he assisted

Ezra Heywood in editing *The Word*, a progressive periodical. He also translated Proudhon's *What Is Property?* and managed to publish the book with his own meager funds. All this time he planned to edit a journal of his own. In May 1877 he issued the first number of *The Radical Review*, a quarterly aiming to serve, according to the Prospectus, as an " adequate literary vehicle for the carriage and diffusion of the most radical thought of our time." This standard he maintained in the four issues that he published. Among the contributors were leading contemporary libertarians, men such as Lysander Spooner and Stephen Pearl Andrews, whose essays on literary, religious, and economic topics were the product of solid effort. Tucker's own contribution was his translation of Proudhon's *System of Economic Contradictions*.

His own money having run out and being unable to obtain more from his parents for radical ventures, Tucker went to work for the Boston *Daily Globe*. For eleven years he was a regular and highly regarded member of the editorial staff, although he refused to write on any topic that might compromise his anarchistic principles. During this stormy and prejudiced era he became the acknowledged leader of the individualist anarchists, so that the mutual respect that existed between Tucker and his employers reflects favorably on his ability and their liberalism.

As soon as he had established himself at the *Globe* and had accumulated a little money, Tucker began to plan for the publication of a periodical that would become an effective organ of anarchist opinion. In August 1881 the first issue of *Liberty* appeared. The title and masthead of this weekly were made up of Proudhon's challenging assertion: " Liberty not the daughter but the mother of order." The top of the first column was headed by the following lines from John Hay:

> For always in thine eyes, O Liberty!
> Shines that high light whereby the world is saved;
> And though thou slay us, we will trust in thee.

Tucker's own pungent paragraphs, under the title of "On Picket Duty," extended across the first page. These comments, as well as his longer editorials and polemical articles, usually dealt with current events or with ideas and problems that seemed to him to need theoretical discussion. The remainder of its eight large pages were devoted to contributed essays on a variety of topics, letters from correspondents and replies by the editors, excerpts or complete pieces from other publications, and occasional book reviews. As the magazine became better known it received voluntary contributions from men of international reputation.

The salutatory announcement in the first number ended with the following declaration: " Monopoly and privilege must be destroyed, opportunity afforded, and competition encouraged. This is *Liberty's* work, and ' Down with Authority ' her war-cry." These principles Tucker expounded with regularity and with forthright earnestness throughout the long life of the periodical. The polemics that he carried on with all comers became one of its exciting features. He had no patience with lukewarm partisans, and gave no quarter to sophists and hypocrites. His usual procedure was to print the communication or article of his adversary and then hack it to shreds. His logic was incisive and devastating, and his style was often caustic and invariably clear and concise. George Bernard Shaw in *The Impossibilities of Anarchism* had to admit that " an examination of any number of this Journal will show that as a candid, clear-headed and courageous demonstration of Individualist Anarchism by purely intellectual methods, Mr. Tucker may safely be accepted as one of the most capable spokesmen of his party." Voltairine de Cleyre, who differed with Tucker in principle, praised him for " sending his fine hard shafts among foes and friends with icy impartiality, hitting swift and cutting keen, and ever ready to nail a traitor." Other eminent libertarians the world over were attracted to *Liberty*, and in time it exerted an influence for beyond its circulation, which never exceeded six hundred subscribers. As Eunice M. Schuster wrote in her objective study, *Native American Anarchism:* " Benjamin Tucker won the attention and sympathetic interest of the American people more than any other anarchist in the United States."

Although Tucker had valuable and devoted editorial assistance most of the time, *Liberty* was as much his personal publication as the *Liberator* was Garrison's, and he brought it out as regularly and as frequently as he was able. When he lacked the means or went abroad or was too preoccupied with his other publishing ventures, the magazine was temporarily suspended. Upon his removal to New York in 1892 to work for *Engineering Magazine*, the office of *Liberty* was transferred as a matter of course. Two years later he adopted what he termed the " ragged-edge " style of typography on the ground that no justification of lines made possible better spacing between letters and was cheaper than orthodox alignment. In 1906, owing to difficulties with the postmaster but primarily as a consequence of his enlarged publishing plans, he began to issue *Liberty* bimonthly and changed its format to a small pamphlet. Fiction and poetry, some of it by writers of international eminence and all of it libertarian in emphasis, occupied a good many of its 64 pages. The periodical came to an abrupt end early in 1908 when a disastrous fire destroyed its office and stockroom and hastened Tucker's decision to make his home in France. The publication of *Liberty* from abroad remained a vain hope.

A pacifist and intellectual, Tucker believed in the efficacy of the written word. While making *Liberty* the hub of his activity, he was ever busy planning and publishing books and pamphlets to further the cause of individual liberty. Since most of this literature was of European origin, he went to great trouble to familiarize himself with the writings of prominent radicals and journeyed several times to the Continent to make advantageous arrangements with authors and publishers. The job of translating the works he decided to issue often became an additional responsibility, and his numerous adaptations from the French were highly praised. Thus, in addition to the two books of Proudhon already mentioned, he translated and published Felix Pyat's *The Rag Picker of Paris*, Claude Tellier's *My Uncle Benjamin*, Zola's *Money* and *Modern Marriage*, Octave Mirbeau's *A Chambermaid's Diary* and Alexandre Arsène's *The Thirty-Six Trades of the State*. He also translated and published French versions of Bakunin's *God and the State*, Chernishevsky's *What's to be Done?* and Tolstoy's *Kreutzer Sonata*. In addition he issued many books and pamphlets by American and English libertarians, such as Stephen Pearl Andrews's *The Science of Society*, William B. Greene's *Mutual Banking*, Lysander Spooner's *Free Political Institutions*, Shaw's *The Quintessence of Ibsenism* and *The Sanity of Art*, and Oscar Wilde's *The Ballad of Reading Gaol*. One of his last ventures was to bring out an English translation of Paul Eltzbacher's *Anarchism*. All these volumes were priced to fit the purse of the literate worker; and since financial loss was practically inevitable in each case, the size of the editions depended upon Tucker's means.

Tucker managed this publication program with a minimum of money. His own earnings were never large, and his parents disapproved of his anarchistic views and refused to finance any of his projects; after his father's death his mother occasionally paid the expenses of a trip to Europe but continued — with one exception — to disassociate herself from his radical activities. Nor were monetary contributions from friends and sympathizers either frequent or considerable; only around 1900 did Henry Bool give him substantial assistance. As a consequence he had to do most of the editing and sometimes even the typesetting after a full day's work at his regular employment. When his savings were spent and his credit was refused, he had to wait until he could accumulate money or obtain it from friends. The result was that a number of his projects were either abortive or shortlived. For a number of years he planned to edit a periodical which would make available in English the best of European writings. When in 1889 he did succeed in launching *The Transatlantic*, a first-rate literary monthly, he could not keep it going for more than a year. Shortly thereafter he began to issue *Five Stories a Week*, but this magazine had an even briefer existence. Undismayed by this lack of popular response, he continued with individual book projects until, with the help of a few devoted sympathizers, he succeeded early in 1900 in organizing The Tucker

Publishing Company, which was to issue pamphlets weekly and books at frequent intervals. Nine months later, however, the company was liquidated at a small fraction of its original capital. More than a year elapsed before Tucker had money enough to resume the publication of *Liberty*.

The settlement of his mother's estate provided him with a sum of money large enough to give him relative independence. After investing the larger part in annuity shares, he put aside about ten thousand dollars for his publication projects. Now he was able to develop a plan that had long been maturing in his mind: a non-profit mail-order bookshop containing " the most complete line of advanced literature, in the principal languages, to be found anywhere in the world." For this purpose he made an extended trip to Europe in order to make the necessary arrangements with friendly publishers. On his return he opened the Unique Book Shop. An inclusive descriptive catalogue of books in English was soon made available, and annotated lists of foreign-language publications were in preparation. For the first time in his long and laborious career Tucker felt himself on solid footing.

In January 1908 occurred the fire which destroyed practically his entire stock. Since he had — his place of business being in a fire-proof building — " deliberately refused to insure, because of the absurdly high rates now prevailing (the rate for the stock in my book shop exceeds four per cent a year), the loss was total, amounting to at least ten thousand dollars." A few friends tried to collect money to set him up in business again, but the financial depression of that year made contributions few and inadequate. Tucker had by then made up his mind. As soon as their child was born he and his young companion, Pearl Johnson, with whom he had recently set up a ménage, would settle in France, where he had long wished to live and where his annuity would give him twice as much as in New York. " It is my intention," he wrote in the last issue of *Liberty*, " to close up my business next summer, and, before January 1, 1909, go to Europe, there to publish *Liberty* (still mainly for America, of course) and such books and pamphlets as my remaining means enable me to print. In Europe the cost of living and of publishing is hardly more than half as much as here."

Benjamin R. Tucker was the advocate rather than the innovator. He arrived at his anarchistic beliefs not, like Josiah Warren, through a pioneering effort of the imagination but through a study of those advanced doctrines which appealed most to his lofty idealism. When the aged Warren befriended him and taught him his principles of " the sovereignty of the individual " and " cost the limit of price," the eighteen-year-old youth became his ardent disciple. Two years later, while in France, he reread Proudhon and compounded the principle of mutualism with his other economic beliefs. Finally, in full maturity, his moral views were sharply modified by Max Stirner's *The Ego and His Own*, which he published in this country and which in the first flush of his enthusiasm he regarded as " the greatest work of political philosophy and ethics ever written."

He was convinced that individualist anarchism was inherent in the political thinking of the Founding Fathers. They believed that that government was best which governed least; he followed Thoreau in the logical preference for a government which did not govern at all. " The anarchists," he asserted, " are simply unterrified Jeffersonian Democrats." Hating the very thought of compulsion, he defined anarchism as " the belief in the greatest amount of liberty compatible with equality of liberty." Such propitious anarchy, he pointed out, already prevailed in the arts, in religion, and in social intercourse; why then should it not function in other spheres of human activity?

To Tucker individual liberty, with its nineteenth-century emphasis on economic laissez-faire and personal self-reliance, was " both the end and means " of human happiness. So certain was he of the evil effects of force and of the efficacy of liberty as " a sure cure for all vices," that he readily argued for " the right of the drunkard, the gambler, the rake, and the harlot to live their lives until they shall freely abandon them." Whatever seemed to him inimical to equal liberty for all, he fought unfalteringly. Since the state was the most formidable practitioner of aggression and constraint, he advocated its ultimate abolition. Individualist anarchism, he emphasized in italics, is " *the doctrine that all the affairs of men should be managed by individuals or voluntary associations, and that the State should be abolished.*"

He argued eloquently that human beings are capable of living together amicably and advantageously and that they have no need whatsoever to subject themselves to the rule of an aggressive government. In answer to those who regarded the state as synonymous with society and feared that the dissolution of the one would destroy the other, he explained:

Society is a concrete organism. . . . Its life is inseparable from the lives of individuals . . . it is impossible to destroy one without the other. But though society cannot be destroyed, it can be greatly hampered and impeded in its operations, much to the disadvantage of the individuals composing it, and it meets its chief impediment in the State.

Once this obstacle was removed, society would enjoy a rich efflorescence.

The problem of how to maintain equal liberty for all without resorting to force proved a stumbling block to all individualist anarchists. Although Tucker, following Stirner, rejected the idea of moral obligation or the existence of inherent rights and duties, he did acknowledge the duty of society to restrain and punish the invasive individual. " Anarchism," he stated, " does not recognize the principle of human rights, but it recognizes human equality as a necessity of stable society." The protection which will assure this equality was " a thing to be secured, so long as it is necessary, by voluntary association and co-operation for self-defence, or as a commodity to be purchased, like any other commodity, of those who offer the best article at the lowest price." This voluntary association " will restrain invaders by any means which may prove necessary." Although such restraint entailed the force of police power, Tucker insisted that it did not violate the principle of anarchism since it was exercised to protect peaceful and noninvasive individuals. He also asserted that in a free society crime and perverseness would be reduced to a minimum and that voluntary juries would deal with the few aggressors. He overlooked the fact that the mere employment of restraint and punishment, involving a form of police power, must in actual practice entail the use of organized force and thus become the negation of anarchism.

In the stateless society all association was to be absolutely voluntary. An individual was free to do as he pleased, providing he did not invade the liberties of others. If he preferred to evade the communal tasks on which the life and safety of the group depended, nobody would compel him to do his share. For the individualist anarchist, being opposed to compulsion as such, regarded the decision of the majority as repugnant as the commands of the state itself. " Rule is evil," Tucker explained, " and it is none the better for being majority rule." Acting on this premise, he refused to vote and never entered a polling booth. His extravagant criticism of this basic democratic right suggests more the Nazi *Ja* elections than our own exercise of suffrage: " What is the ballot? It is neither more nor less than a paper representative of the bayonet, the billy, and the bullet. It is a labor-saving device for ascertaining on which side force lies and bowing to the inevitable. The voice of the majority saves bloodshed, but it is no less the arbitrament of force than is the decree of the most absolute of despots backed by the most powerful of armies."

Since religion presupposes man's submission to the will of a Supreme Being, the anarchists would have nothing to do with it. They professed atheism and scorned the rites and precepts of churches. Their rejection of the bonds of marriage and the curbs on divorce was an obvious corollary. To the anarchists, Tucker wrote, " legal marriage and legal divorce are equal absurdities. They look forward to a time when every individual, whether man or woman, shall be self-supporting, and when each shall have an independent home of his or her own, whether it be a separate house, or rooms in a house with others; when the love relations between these independent individuals shall be as varied as are individual inclinations and attractions; and when the children born of these relations shall belong exclusively to the mothers until old enough to belong to themselves." This sexual freedom among anarchists, made notorious by their detractors, did not actually result in any flagrant profligacy. Many of them lived with their companions and children on the same monogamous level as the most devoted of legally married couples. Tucker himself loved his companion, Pearl Johnson, and lived with her and their daughter till the day of his death.

Tucker was fully aware of the fundamental position of economics in modern society. Even as other reformers of his day he was strongly affected by the spread of urban slums and the existence of mass poverty in a land of abundance. Much as he sympathized with the aims of social reform, however, he rejected all those proposals which implied governmental interference or the socialization of the means of production and distribution. He was of the opinion that socialism would merely replace a laissez-faire capitalism with a large-scale bureaucracy which might prove even more burdensome to the great majority of the people. As an anarchist he maintained that even the best of economic systems would become oppressive and obnoxious if it involved the arbitrary distribution of goods according to statute law. He demanded liberty above all, including the liberty for man to control what he produced, as " the surest guarantee of prosperity." The policy of complete noninterference — enabling everyone to mind his own business exclusively — would permit wealth to " distribute itself in a free market in accordance with the natural operation of economic law." Such truly free competition, he maintained, would enhance the welfare of society without curbing the initiative of the ambitious and the capable.

As an advocate of free competition Tucker condemned all forms of monopoly. He called the monopolists " a brotherhood of thieves " and ascribed all economic ills to their state-sanctioned practices. All our millionaires, he insisted, owed their wealth to plunder and ruthless exploitation. " The State is the servant of the robbers, and it exists chiefly to prevent the expropriation of the robbers and the restoration of a fair and free field for legitimate competition and wholesome, effective voluntary co-operation." To solve the economic problems which have long plagued civilized society, he advocated the abolition of the state and with it the four major types of monopoly — those of land, money and banking, trade, and patents and copyright.

Tucker urged the " abolition of landlordism and the annihilation of rent," and proposed the occupancy-and-use formula as the only valid title to land. Such observance would free millions of unused tillable acres and unoccupied valuable city parcels. The needy farmers would then take possession of as much land as they could cultivate and the poor city workers would obtain their dwellings for a fraction of the current rent. Yet he insisted that no forcible measures must be taken against the large landlords. He fought Henry George's Single Tax plan because it entailed arbitrary and compulsory state regulation. He likewise opposed the nationalization of rent on the ground that it " logically involves the most complete State Socialism and minute regulation of the individual." His solution was education: if most of the people were taught to accept the validity of the occupancy-and-use principle, the rich laggards would in time see the wisdom of giving up the land which they themselves were not using. He argued that since land reform would occur not in isolation but as part of a general social revolution, the landlords would not prove so obdurate as they now seemed.

The most radical change proposed by individualist anarchists concerned money and banking. Assuming that the monopoly of money was responsible for most of the economic inequities within our society, they urged the complete liberalization of all monetary functions. Tucker condemned the high interest rates which the government permitted. " The usurer is Somebody, and the State is his protector. Usury is the serpent gnawing at labor's vitals, and only liberty can detach and kill it. Give laborers their liberty, and they will keep their wealth. As for the Somebody, he, stripped of his power to steal, must either join their ranks or starve." In his enthusiasm he asserted that free money was " the first step to Anarchy." He argued for " the utter absence of restriction upon the issue of all money not fraudulent." Thus anyone in need of money would have the right to issue it — the paper bills with his signature having the value of promissory notes and their acceptance depending upon the assets and standing of the issuer. Once this practice became general, lending and borrowing, and consequently interest, would virtually disappear. " If the holders of all kinds of property," Tucker elucidated, " were equally privileged to issue money, not as a legal tender, but acceptance only on its merits, competition would reduce the rate of discount, and therefore of interest on capital, to the mere cost of banking." This practice would break up the present monopoly of money, enable every man to be his own banker and enjoy the full product of his labor, and abolish poverty along with conspicuous wealth.

In the field of business Tucker followed Proudhon in asserting that without the co-operation of the state it would be impossible to amass great fortunes and establish monopolies. He made clear, however, that in a free society private property was legitimate and everyone had the right to own what he could gain by his own enterprise and efficiency. This antagonism to monopoly made him an outstanding exponent of free trade and free competition. Anarchists, he stated, believed in " competition everywhere and always." Joseph A. Labadie, writing in *Liberty* in 1897, agreed with the editor on the advantages of laissez-faire economics: " Personal responsibility and private enterprise in business and industry produce the best results. . . . There is no doubt at all in my mind that liberty has a good effect in economics. Free competition is the soul of progress." Tucker, in a speech on trusts made two years later, observed that he had no objection to large corporations as such, but only to their throttling of competition. Free competition, he argued, would ensure the well-being of all men. " When interest, rent, and profit disappear under the influence of free money, free land, and free trade, it will make no difference whether men work for themselves, or are employed, or employ others. In any case they can get nothing but that wage for their labor which free competition determines."

His opposition to patent and copyright laws was based on his desire to see the principle of liberty prevail in every field of human endeavor. He had no objection to a fair compensation to the inventor of a useful device or to the author of a book, but he saw no reason why the public should be penalized to the extent permitted by the established laws. Particularly he protested against those corporations that enriched themselves by exploiting cheaply bought patents.

It was axiomatic that Tucker disapproved of government ownership. He regarded state control as the most complete and therefore the most obnoxious form of monopoly. "The government," he claimed, "is a tyrant living by theft, and therefore has no business to engage in any business." He believed, moreover, that the bureaucrat was usually less able than the private entrepreneur and too irresponsible to be trusted. Again and again he condemned the inefficiencies of the post office and praised the presumably superior service of the competing express companies. "The government has none of the characteristics of a successful business man, being wasteful, careless, clumsy, and short-sighted in the extreme." As a consequence he strongly opposed the agitation of the Populists for state-owned granaries and of the urban liberals for the government ownership of the essential public utilities.

Tucker's economic views were not presented systematically or at length. His only published volume, *Instead of a Book, By a Man Too Busy to Write One,* issued at the request of his admirers and only after they had sent him advanced orders for six hundred copies, was merely a compilation of material from *Liberty.* As a consequence he has said little or nothing on aspects of our economy which are important for a fuller understanding of life under individualist anarchism. In fairness it should be said that he was not interested in blueprints for the future society, and that all his social views converged in a worship of pure liberty. He had a right to his utopian vision, of course, and to criticise it would be a thankless task. One can perhaps do no better than to quote the following summary of his economic credo:

Liberty will abolish interest; it will abolish profit; it will abolish monopolistic rent; it will abolish taxation; it will abolish the exploitation of labor; it will abolish all means whereby any labor can be deprived of any of his product; but it will not abolish the limited inequality between one laborer's product and another's. . . . Liberty will ultimately make all men rich; it will not make all men equally rich.

Tucker disapproved of communism even when it was to be practised within the stateless society. In his numerous polemics with anarchists who advocated communistic living he maintained that while voluntary organization for specific tasks was desirable and even advantageous, the socialized community could not but deprive its individual members of certain precious liberties. Why subject oneself to the restraints of socialized duties and obligations, when one could live in peace and plenty without such limitations? One needed only to learn to abide by the motto: Live and let live.

Of Quaker background and inclination, he was a thorough pacifist and deprecated violence in any form, except in self-defense. He insisted that nothing good or lasting was ever accomplished by force, and that violence only tended to multiply itself. Much as he desired the abolition of the state, he refused to achieve it by means of terror. He believed that it was neither possible nor desirable to dissolve the state before the people had learned to live freely and fruitfully without it. The premature and violent overthrow of government would only retard the advent of anarchism. "If government should be abruptly and entirely abolished tomorrow, there would probably ensue a series of physical conflicts about land and many other things, ending in reaction and a revival of the old tyranny." He therefore preached widespread education and ultimately a passive resistance that was to take such forms as the refusal to pay taxes, the evasion of jury duty and military service, and the nonobservance of other types of compulsion. Consequently, when

John Most came to this country to further the " propaganda of the deed " as a means of achieving anarchism, Tucker criticised him on the ground that the end never justified immoral means. For many years these two leaders of rival factions carried on a contentious polemic in their respective periodicals.

Yet Tucker's political philosophy never affected his promptitude in attacking injustice. Whether it was a Massachusetts law against syphilitic prisoners, or the protective arrest of known pickpockets in New York just prior to Grant's funeral services, or the ill-treatment of individuals who refused to conform to the mores of the majority — he was ever the alert crusader bent on combating organized force and defending the rights of the minority.

A striking instance of his love of justice was his stand during the Haymarket hysteria in 1886. Much as he disapproved of terroristic doctrines, he was convinced that the defendants were innocent of the charges against them and that they were being tried not for what they had done but for what they believed. He therefore condemned their conviction in forceful editorials. When the Illinois supreme court upheld the action of the trial judge, he wrote: " The judges say that Spies and his comrades must hang, though they cannot prove them guilty of murder. It is for the people now to say that the judges must go, there being no doubt as to their guilt." When Henry George, at that time an influential liberal, refused to join the distinguished defenders of the condemned men and readily accepted the verdict of the higher court, Tucker attacked him as a traitor; for " to him perhaps more than to any other single person did lovers of liberty and friends of labor confidently look for willing and effective aid and leadership through and out of a crisis pregnant with results beyond all human vision." Nor did *Liberty* cease to decry the crime committed against the victims until Governor Altgeld had courageously done his best to make amends.

When several years later Alexander Berkman, a young Russian anarchist, shot and wounded Henry Clay Frick to avenge the workers who had lost their lives in the bloody Homestead strike, Tucker refused to join the defense of the imprisoned anarchist. As an opponent of violence he could not condone murder as a means of propaganda. "The hope of humanity," he wrote, "lies in the avoidance of that revolution by force which the Berkmans are trying to precipitate. No pity for Frick, no praise for Berkman — such is the attitude of *Liberty* in the present crisis." Some time later he was urged by friends of Berkman to use his influence in an effort to obtain a pardon for the prisoner. Tucker told them that he would do so only if Berkman would agree to abstain from acts of terrorism in the future; since these friends could not expect the prisoner thus to bind himself, Tucker declined to proceed further.

Long before the fateful fire in 1908 which precipitated his decision to settle in France, Tucker had come to see that the tide of affairs was running counter to his philosophy of liberty. With the passing of the years he could not avoid the realization that his dream of anarchism had lost its appeal to those engaged in the struggle against a powerful capitalism. Never popular within labor circles, after 1900 individualist anarchism began to dwindle rapidly. Some of its adherents joined the more aggressive faction led by Emma Goldman and Alexander Berkman; many others favored the rising socialist movement as the only effective weapon against billion-dollar corporations. All this depressed Tucker, and he began to think of withdrawing from the social conflict. The burning of his bookstore hastened his decision.

On leaving the United States at the end of 1908 Tucker had no idea that he was never again to see his native land. Since his modest income made traveling a luxury, he planned first to take root in his new home and accumulate a cash reserve before taking the costly trip. By the time he found it feasible to visit America, the outbreak of war in 1914 made the voyage practically impossible. He did go to England with his family and remained there until France became safe enough for their return.

While in England, Tucker disappointed a number of his followers by supporting the war against Germany. These men and women, far from the scene of battle, perceived the struggle as a battle for markets between rival imperialisms, and refused to take sides. Not so Tucker, who deeply appreciated the French way of life and hated Prussian arrogance and brutality. As far as he was concerned, the German armies had to be driven back or civilization would collapse. In a letter to Joseph Labadie dated December 23, 1914, he explained his stand:

I favor the Allies because I pity the Belgian people, because I admire the British influences that make for liberty, because I feel some (though I regret to say a declining) concern for the future of the American people, because I have a considerable sympathy for the *people* of Russia, and because I hate and fear the German people as a nation of domineering brutes bent on turning the whole world into a police-ridden paradise on the Prussian pattern. I have numerous other reasons for favoring the Allies, but the above is the main reason and a sufficient one.

Shortly after the United States entered the war in 1917, Tucker learned of the mistreatment of conscientious objectors. True to his libertarian beliefs, he wrote a long letter to *The Masses*, the leading radical magazine, protesting against this brutality on the part of the government and pointing out why he, a pacifist, felt impelled to support the cause of the Allies. Max Eastman, the editor, published the protest but omitted the remainder, thus making it appear that Tucker was as much against the war as were the editors of *The Masses*. To rectify this false impression Tucker wrote to a number of his friends to explain the incident. The uncommon prescience of the man, not to mention his persuasive logic and good sense, may be noted in the following extract from one of these letters:

Germany's onslaught on civilization in August, 1914, confronted all liberty lovers with a horrible alternative: either to offer no resistance, and thereby suffer, at Germany's hand, a well-nigh total and probably permanent annihilation of our liberties, or to resist, and, to make the resistance effective, suffer, at our own hands, a partial and possibly only temporary annihilation (or suspension) of those liberties. I take it that any earnest man who could hesitate in his choice must be blinded or dazzled by idealism, as to be incapable of interpreting the march of events with even the smallest degree of realism. For me, at any rate, there was but one road, and I took it promptly. From the start I have favored war to the limit — war till Germany (rulers and people alike) shall be so whipped and stripped that never more shall she have the will or the power to renew aggression. In choosing this course I deliberately accept, though with soreness of heart, the evils involved in it, to none of which I am more blind than Max Eastman himself or any other pacifist. Among those evils I accept conscription, though conscription, which must commend itself to every believer in the State equally with taxation so far as principle is concerned, is entirely counter to my political philosophy. I accept also the incidental evil of having to cooperate for a limited time with a considerable number of brutes. But I reserve the right to square accounts with brutality after the liquidation of l'union sacrée.

Always an omnivorous reader of newspapers, he spent his declining years perusing the important journals of many lands and clipping the items which interested him. His plans to resume the publication of *Liberty,* to bring out various books, and to write about his philosophy of life were deferred from day to day by a lassitude which the years aggravated. After going through the various papers he had neither time nor energy for anything else. Although he lived for twenty years after the Peace of Versailles and witnessed the rise of a fascism far worse than the Prussianism which he had condemned so vehemently, he lacked the drive to throw off his strange lethargy. The newspapers alone interested him, and before his death in 1939 he had collected enough clippings to fill twenty-odd volumes. These news items, dealing with a variety of topics of social interest, properly arranged and indexed, are now awaiting the hospitality of a library.

A deep pessimism possessed him during his old age. He felt himself in the grip of irresistible forces: a dominant monopolistic capitalism, a madly aggressive nationalism, and a worldwide social conflict were brutally stifling the enfeebled cries of individual liberty. Twentieth-century authoritarianism was riding roughshod over the ideals of human freedom cherished by the previous century, and the first victim was anarchism. Benjamin R. Tucker, unable to quicken his wan ideal and unwilling to nurse a delusion, was reduced during his final years to become an onlooker rather than a participant: to cut topical clippings and dream of the distant day when mankind will at last bask in the bright and enduring glories of a free society.

EMMA GOLDMAN

ANARCHIST REBEL

T HE HANGING of several anarchists in 1887 as a consequence
of the Haymarket bombing in Chicago caused many Americans to sympathize with the gibbeted radicals. Youths
swathed in bright idealism, men and women rooted in equalitarian
democracy, workers trusting in the rectitude of their government —
all doubted the guilt of the condemned prisoners and were deeply
perturbed by the egregious miscarriage of justice. Many of them for
the first time became aware of the state's ruthless arrogation of
power, and scores upon scores remained to the end of their lives
inimical to government and apprehensive of all forms of authority.

Emma Goldman was one of these converts. Resentment against
the restraints of authority was no new experience for this spirited
girl. As far back as she could remember she had hated and feared
her father, a quick-tempered and deeply harassed Orthodox Jew
who had vented his emotional and financial vexations on his recalcitrant daughter. Unable to get from him the love and praise she
craved, she had refused to submit to his strict discipline and had
preferred beatings to blind obedience. Consequently she grew up
in an atmosphere of repression and acrimony. "Since my earliest
recollection," she wrote, "home had been stifling, my father's
presence terrifying. My mother, while less violent with her children,
never showed much warmth."

At the age of thirteen she began to work in a factory in St. Peters-
burg, and her life became doubly oppressive. She soon learned of
the revolutionary movement and sympathized with its agitation

against Czarist autocracy. To escape from the tyranny of her father, the irksomeness of the shop, and the repressive measures of the government, she fought with all her stubborn strength for the opportunity to accompany her beloved sister Helene to the United States. Early in 1886 the two girls arrived in Rochester to live with their married sister, who had preceded them to this country.

Like other penniless immigrants, the seventeen-year-old Emma had no alternative but to follow the common groove to the sweatshop. Paid a weekly wage of two dollars and a half for sixty-three hours of work, she naturally resented the social system which permitted such exploitation. Together with other immigrants she had dreamed of the United States as a haven of liberty and equality. Instead she found it the home of crass materialism and cruel disparity. This disillusionment was deepened by the hysterical accounts of the trial in Chicago. She was quick to conclude that the accused anarchists were innocent of the charge against them; and the vilification not only of the prisoners but of all radicals merely hardened her hatred against the enemies of the working poor.

It was easy enough for her to believe John Most's claim in *Die Freiheit* (which chance had brought her way) that Parsons, Spies, and the other defendants were to be hanged for nothing more than their advocacy of anarchism. What this doctrine was she did not quite know, but she assumed it must have merit since it favored poor workers like herself. When the jury found the men guilty, she could not accept the reality of the dread verdict. Her thoughts clung to the condemned anarchists as if they were her brothers. In her passionate yearning to do something in their behalf she attended meetings of protest and read everything she could find on the case; and she sympathetically experienced the torment of a prisoner awaiting execution. In her autobiography, *Living My Life*, she wrote that on the day of the hangings " I was in a stupor; a feeling of numbness came over me, something too horrible even for tears." The very next day, however, she became imbued with a surging determination to dedicate herself to the cause of the martyred men, to devote her life to the ideals for which they had died.

In the meantime, discouraged and lonely, she had welcomed a fellow worker's show of affection. She felt no love for him and, as a result of an attempted rape at the age of fifteen, she still experienced a " violent repulsion " in the presence of men, but she had not the strength to refuse his urgent proposal of marriage. She soon learned to her dismay that her husband was impotent and not at all as congenial as she had thought. However, the very suggestion of a separation enraged her father, who had recently come to Rochester. After months of aggravation she did go through the then rare and reprehensible rite of Orthodox divorce, but she had to leave town to avoid social ostracism. When she returned some months later, her former husband again pursued her, and his threat of suicide frightened her into remarrying him.

Emma now felt herself thwarted and trapped. Twenty years old and yearning to make life meaningful, she chafed at the very thought of her drab and dreary existence. Her anxiety to elude her father's abuse, to free herself from a loveless marriage, to escape the dullness of her oppressive environment, only intensified her longing for freedom and affection. Consequently she began to nurture her dream of dedicating herself to the ideal championed by the Chicago martyrs. One day in August 1889 she broke relations with her husband and parents and left for New York with money supplied by her ever-devoted sister Helene.

In the metropolis Emma felt herself gloriously free. For the first time in her life she was completely independent. On the teeming East Side a new and wonderful world emerged before her, and she embraced it with passionate abandon. Alexander Berkman, a determined doctrinaire at eighteen, made her acquaintance the day she arrived and the pair at once established an intimate comradeship which endured through many vicissitudes to the day of his death. John Most, the impetuous anarchist leader, became her lover as well as her mentor and opened new and fascinating vistas of the mind. " Most became my idol," she wrote. " I adored him." Under his tutelage she read seminal books and learned about significant men and ideas. Anarchism assumed definite meaning; the struggle by the many in want against the few in power, then so pathetically feeble, became to her a war unto death; the goal of social freedom appeared tangible and alluringly near. For months her voracious hunger for knowledge seemed insatiable, her capacity for emotion inexhaustible. This tremendous release of energy was in truth the expression of long-pent-up zeal. She threw herself into the radical movement of the East Side with the enthusiasm of an inspired visionary.

Her first years in New York were a period of preparation. Along with her work in sweatshops, which she had to do to earn her living, she found time to familiarize herself with the latest libertarian literature and to spend hours on end in intellectual discussion. Nor was she able to remain a passive onlooker even during her early apprenticeship. With John Most's helpful guidance she went on her first " tour of agitation " only a few months after reaching New York. She addressed several meetings in as many cities on the eight-hour day, then a timely topic, and discovered that she was able to hold the attention of an audience and to think quickly while facing its inimical questioning.

That winter the newly formed Cloakmakers' Union called its first general strike. Emma immediately "became absorbed in it to the exclusion of everything else." Her task was to persuade the timid girl workers to join the strike. With prodigious energy she exhorted them at meetings, encouraged them at dances and parties, and thus influenced many to partake in the common effort to improve working conditions in the sweatshops. The strike leaders were greatly impressed by her dynamic qualities as an organizer and public speaker.

Emma's association with John Most became strained to the breaking point when she perceived that he esteemed her more as a lover than as a fellow anarchist. His arrogance irritated her and, much as she admired his impassioned eloquence and incisive mind, she could not accept the acquiescent role he had assigned her. When his high-handed behavior resulted in a factional split, she sided with those who rejected his domination. Some time later, when Most derided Berkman's attempt to kill Henry C. Frick and disavowed the theory of " propaganda of the deed" of which he had been the chief exponent, she came to hate him. At the first opportunity she lashed him with a horsewhip at a public meeting and denounced him as a renegade. Nor did time bring about a reconciliation.

Emma, Alexander Berkman, and a youthful artist were living together in congenial intimacy. They worked at their menial tasks during the day and devoted their evenings to agitation. Because the progress of anarchism in this country was too slow for them, the news of increased revolutionary activity in Russia filled them with a romantic nostalgia for their native land. They decided to engage in some business until they should have saved enough money for the journey back. In the spring of 1892 chance brought them to Worcester, Massachusetts, where they were soon operating a successful lunchroom.

The bloody consequences of the lockout at the Homestead plant of The Carnegie Steel Company inflamed the minds of these youthful idealists. The plan to return to Russia was abandoned with little regret. They agreed it was their duty to go to the aid of the brutally maltreated workers. Berkman insisted that their great moment was at hand, that they must give up the lunchroom and leave at once for the scene of the fighting. " Being internationalists," he argued, " it mattered not to us where the blow was struck by the workers; we must be with them. We must bring them our great message and help them see that it was not only for the moment that they must strike, but for all time, for a free life, for anarchism. Russia had many heroic men and women, but who was there in America? Yes, we must go to Homestead, tonight! " Taking with them the day's receipts and their personal belongings, they left immediately for New York. Berkman, eager to emulate the Russian nihilists who were then fighting hangings with assassinations, determined to make Frick, the dictatorial general manager, pay with his life for the death of those who had worked for him. Unable to perfect a bomb, he decided to use a pistol. Emma wanted to accompany him to Pittsburgh, but remained behind for the lack of railroad fare. A few days later the resolute youth of twenty-one made his way into Frick's office, discharged three bullets into his body, and stabbed him several times before being overpowered and beaten into unconsciousness.

Prior to the attempt on his life Frick had been severely criticized for harsh and arbitrary treatment of his employees. His determination to break their union and his reckless use of Pinkertons had antagonized even those who normally favored the open shop. Berkman's attack, so alien and repugnant to our democratic mores, completely changed the situation. Frick became the hero of the day. Journalists and public men vied in praise of the victim and execration of the assailant. The fact that the latter was of Russian birth and an anarchist only served to strengthen his guilt. Although Frick recovered from his wounds with extraordinary rapidity and was back at his desk within a fortnight, and although the law of Pennsylvania limited punishment for the crime to seven years, the defendant was tried without benefit of legal counsel and sentenced to twenty-two years' imprisonment.

The ascetic youth was thoroughly dismayed by the calamitous turn of events. He regarded Frick as " an enemy of the People," a cruel exploiter of labor who had to be destroyed as a concrete warning of the oncoming revolution. He gloried in this opportunity to serve the American workers in the manner of the Russian nihilists. It pained him therefore to think that he owed his failure to kill Frick to the interference of the very workers for whom he was ready to die. The attack upon him by John Most was distressing enough, but the scornful repudiation by the strikers and the coolness of labor everywhere cut him to the heart. Suffering the anguish of a living death in one of the worst prisons in the United States, he sought comfort in the thought that he was a revolutionist and not a would-be murderer. " A revolutionist," he later explained, " would rather perish a thousand times than be guilty of what is ordinarily called murder. In truth, murder and *Attentat* are to me opposite terms. To remove a tyrant is an act of liberation, the giving of life and opportunity to an oppressed people." Some years afterwards he came to believe that even such shedding of blood " must be resorted to only as a last extremity." It was this faith in the ideal for which he was prepared to die that kept him alive through fourteen years of physical torture and mental martyrdom. One need only read his *Prison Memoirs of an Anarchist*, a work of extraordinary acumen and power, to appreciate the high purpose that had motivated him and the strength of character that enabled him to turn his prison trials into spiritual triumphs.

Emma, his lover and accomplice, from the very first defended him with passionate abandon. To her he was " the idealist whose humanity can tolerate no injustice and endure no wrong." The excessive punishment dealt to him by the state struck her as barbarous and cowardly. " The idealists and visionaries," she asserted years later, " foolish enough to throw caution to the winds and express their ardor and faith in some supreme deed, have advanced mankind and have enriched the world." At the time, however, she grieved to think of her noble companion doomed to waste the best years of his life in execrable confinement.

Unable to lighten his suffering, she resolved to double her effort towards the realization of their common ideal. A physical breakdown, however, forced her to seek rest and medical care. Her sister Helene welcomed her back and helped her to regain strength. But the aggravation of the unemployment crisis in 1893 caused her to disregard the doctor's warning and to return to her post on the East Side. " Committee sessions, public meetings, collection of foodstuffs, supervising the feeding of the homeless and their numerous children, and, finally, the organization of a mass-meeting on Union Square entirely filled my time." As the main speaker at this large gathering she excoriated the state for functioning only as the protector of the rich and for keeping the poor starved and enslaved, like a giant shorn of his strength. Commenting on Cardinal Manning's dictum that " necessity knows no law," she continued: " They will go on robbing you, your children, and your children's children, unless you wake up, unless you become daring enough to demand your rights. Well, then, demonstrate before the palaces of the rich; demand work. If they do not give you work, demand bread. If they deny you both, take bread. It is your sacred right." For this speech she was arrested, charged with inciting to riot although the meeting was peaceable, and sentenced to one year in Blackwell's Island Penitentiary.

She went to prison in a defiant mood. She was now the avowed enemy of the corrupt minions of the state and she knew they would stop at nothing to keep her from agitating for a better world — the world for which she and Berkman were then in jail. She resolved to fight back and fight hard. So long as breath remained in her lungs and strength in her body, she would deliver her message to the oppressed masses! No amount of torture in prison or persecution outside would deter her in the struggle against the state and the powerful rich!

While in prison Emma learned the rudiments of nursing. She liked the work better than sewing, and upon her release she persuaded several doctors to recommend her as a practical nurse. Wishing to qualify herself, she accepted the aid of devoted friends in order to study nursing in the Vienna Allgemeines Krankenhaus, a hospital of very high repute. While in Europe she lectured in England and Scotland and met the leading anarchists in London and on the Continent. She also made first-hand acquaintance with the contemporary social theater, on which she was later to lecture and write with penetrating insight. In the summer of 1896 she returned to this country, qualified as a nurse and midwife.

Once back in New York, she immediately resumed her anarchist activity. Her first concern was to promote an appeal for Berkman's pardon, and keen was her sorrow and resentment when it was refused. More than ever eager to further their common ideal, and greatly moved by the sporadic attacks upon the more aggressive workers, she undertook her first continental lecture tour.

Everywhere workers were slain, everywhere the same butchery! . . . The masses were millions, yet how weak! To awaken them from their stupor, to make them conscious of their power — that is the great need! Soon, I told myself, I should be able to reach them throughout America. With a tongue of fire I would rouse them to a realization of their dependence and indignity! Glowingly I visioned my first great tour and the opportunities it would offer me to plead our Cause.

Her opportunities fell far short of her expectations, but her words of fire ignited the hearts of many who came to scoff.

For the next twenty years she devoted most of her time to lecturing. She spoke wherever there were comrades enough to organize a meeting; and in scores of cities, from Maine to Oregon, there were libertarians ready to suffer great inconvenience for their cause. At first most of her talks were given in Yiddish and German; later, as she attracted more Americanized audiences, she spoke mainly in English. Her topics ranged widely in content. She expounded the doctrine of anarchism whenever possible, but her lectures dealt mainly with current social problems and the modern European drama. Shortly before World War I she discussed birth control with a frankness that sent her to jail for a fortnight. She usually keyed her talks to the intelligence of her auditors, and always she spoke with clarity and enthusiasm.

Throughout her years of agitation she exercised extraordinary tact and exceptional physical courage. No other woman in America ever had to suffer such persistent persecution. She was arrested innumerable times, beaten more than once, refused admission to halls where she was to speak. Often the police dispersed her audience. Intimidated owners frequently refused to rent her meeting places or cancelled contracts at the last minute. On various occasions she was met at the train and compelled by sheer force to proceed to the next stopping place. In 1912 she and Ben Reitman, at that time her manager and lover, were driven from San Diego and the latter was tarred and tortured.

It must be said that the lawbreakers and defilers of liberty were not Emma Goldman and her harassed followers but the sworn guardians of the law and leading local citizens. The latter and not the anarchists were guilty of violating the rights of free speech and free assembly, of beating their victims without cause and of jailing them without warrant. It was after one such instance of unprovoked brutality that Emma wrote:

In no country, Russia not exempt, would the police dare to exercise such brutal power over the lives of men and women. In no country would the people stand for such beastliness and vulgarity. Nor do I know of any people who have so little regard for their own manhood and self-respect as the average American citizen, with all his boasted independence.

The newspapers abetted the police in the lawless treatment of Emma and her fellow rebels. They sometimes perverted a grain of truth into columns of muck and made " Red Emma " a symbol of all that was dangerous and despicable. The rank injustice of this abuse caused the staid New York *Sun* to protest on September 30, 1909: " The popular belief is that she preaches bombs and murder, but she certainly does nothing of the kind. Bombs are very definite things, and one of the peculiarities of her doctrine is its vagueness. The wonder is that with a doctrine so vague she managed to strike terror into the stout hearts of the police."

Nor were the police and the press the only perpetrators of this modern witch hunt. President Theodore Roosevelt expressed the attitude of many persons of privilege and respectability when he blustered: " The Anarchist is the enemy of humanity, the enemy of all mankind, and his is the deeper degree of criminality than any other." When William Buwalda, a soldier in the United States Army and the recipient of a medal for bravery, shook hands with Emma Goldman at one of her lectures in 1908, he was courtmartialed and sentenced to five years' imprisonment. It was only as a consequence of numerous public protests that Buwalda was pardoned after he had served ten months. The Red Hysteria of 1917–21 merely climaxed decades of ill-treatment of a militant minority in a nation founded on the principles of human rights and individual liberty.

If this ugly chapter in recent American history was the work of men of property and of public officers, there were numerous other Americans, less powerful but of greater probity, who cherished the fundamental freedoms of our Founding Fathers. These liberals spoke out forcefully against the violation of rights guaranteed by the Constitution. They gladly gave of their time and money to the defense of the harassed radicals. Because Emma Goldman suffered most from police brutality and because her dynamic personality attracted those who came in contact with her, she was befriended by scores of Americans in every part of the country. These Jeffersonian liberals admired her courage and sincerity and helped her to organize her lecture tours and to finance her propagandistic and literary ventures.

Emma reached the nadir of her career during the aftermath of President McKinley's assassination. With the memory of Alexander Berkman's fate still festering in her heart, she said: " Leon Czolgosz and other men of his type . . . are drawn to some violent expression, even at the sacrifice of their own lives, because they cannot supinely witness the misery and suffering of their fellows." Even before her attitude was known, she was arrested as an accomplice of Czolgosz and treated with extreme savagery before being released for lack of evidence.

Even more painful to her was the obtuseness of those anarchists who condemned Czolgosz's act as wanton murder. Ironically enough, even Berkman wrote from prison to disapprove of the shooting and to differentiate it from his own attack upon Frick; in his opinion the killing of McKinley was individual terrorism and not a deed motivated by social necessity. Emma was shocked by this argument, since to her both acts were inspired by the same high idealism and spirit of self-sacrifice. Unlike Berkman, who had come to see the futility of terrorism in a country like the United States, she was more interested in the incentive than in the effectiveness of an assassination. She was ostracized for her loyalty to Czolgosz and, as a consequence of his execution, suffered severe depression.

Once Emma Goldman had mastered the English language, she was not long in wishing to establish a periodical that would carry the message of anarchism to those whom she could not reach in person. Outbreaks of strikes in this country and increased revolutionary activity in Russia only made her more eager for a magazine of her own. In 1905 she was serving as manager and interpreter for Paul Orleneff and Alla Nazimova, who had come to the United States for a theatrical tour. When Orleneff learned of Emma's ambition to publish a periodical, he insisted on giving a special performance for her benefit. Although a pouring rain kept the audience to a fraction of the expected number, the receipts sufficed to pay for the first issue of *Mother Earth*.

The scope and purpose of the new monthly, which began to appear in March 1906, were explained at the outset:

Mother Earth will endeavor to attract and appeal to all those who oppose encroachment on public and individual life. It will appeal to those who strive for something higher, weary of the commonplace; to those who feel that stagnation is a deadweight on the firm and elastic step of progress; to those who breathe freely only in limitless space; to those who long for the tender shade of a new dawn for a humanity free from the dread of want, the dread of starvation in the face of mountains of riches. The Earth free for the free individual.

Emma Goldman edited the monthly throughout its eleven years of existence. In all this time it reflected her views, her interests, her dynamic liveliness. Her fellow editors at one time or another were Max Baginski, Hippolyte Havel, and Alexander Berkman, but the character of the periodical underwent no change as a consequence. Each issue contained at least one poem, brief editorials on the events of the month, articles on current aspects of anarchism, comments on labor strikes and radical activities the world over, reports by Emma on topics of interest to her or on her frequent lecture tours, and finally appeals for money. Many prominent libertarians contributed essays of a philosophical or hortatory nature. It emanated a youthful vigor and an exuberance not found in any other contemporary periodical. Its several thousand readers were devoted to it and supported it with their limited means until the postal censor put an end to the monthly shortly after the declaration of war in 1917.

Mother Earth was not Emma Goldman's sole publishing activity. A firm believer in the efficacy of educational propaganda, she printed and sold a long list of inexpensive tracts. Her table of literature became a prominent feature at all her meetings. When no commercial publisher would accept Berkman's *Prison Memoirs of an Anarchist*, she collected funds and issued the book herself. The volume has since become a classic in its field, and stands to this day as a living reminder of the dominance of a keen and determined mind over all physical obstacles. Emma also brought out her own collection of lectures, *Anarchism and Other Essays*. She was able, however, to find a publisher for her impressive volume of lectures on *The Social Significance of the Modern Drama*, which deals incisively with the European plays that dissect the common failures and fallacies of bourgeois society.

Face to face with an audience, Emma Goldman was a forceful and witty propagandist. Frequently she lifted her rapt hearers to heights from which they envisioned a world wholly free and completely delightful. In cold print, however, her lectures reveal little of her dynamic appeal. They are primarily the work of a forceful agitator: clear, pointed, spirited, but without originality or intellectual rigor.

The faithful disciple of Bakunin and Kropotkin, Emma perceived civilization as " a continuous struggle of the individual or of groups of individuals against the State and even against ' society,' that is, against the majority subdued and hypnotized by the State and State worship." This conflict, she argued, was bound to last as long as the state itself, since it was of the very nature of government to be " conservative, static, intolerant of change and opposed to it," while the instinct of the individual was to resent restriction, combat authority, and seek the benefits of innovation.

Her definition of anarchism first appeared on the masthead of *Mother Earth* in the issue of April 1910: " The philosophy of a new social order based on liberty unrestrained by man-made law; the theory that all forms of government rest on violence, and are therefore wrong and harmful, as well as unnecessary." In her oft-repeated lecture on the subject she warmly described the benefits to ensue from social revolution:

Anarchism stands for a social order based on the free grouping of individuals for the purpose of producing real social wealth; an order that will guarantee to every human being free access to the earth and full enjoyment of the necessities of life, according to individual desires, tastes, and inclinations.

To the end of her life Emma avowed the soundness and practicality of her doctrine. As late as 1934 she declared in *Harper's Magazine:* " I am certain that Anarchism is too vital and too close to human nature ever to die. When the failure of modern dictatorship and authoritarian philosophies becomes apparent and the realization of failure more general, Anarchism will be vindicated." It was her belief that sooner or later the mass of mankind would perceive the futility of begging for crumbs and would take power into its own hands. Since she scorned political means, she expounded the validity of direct action. This method she defined as the " conscious individual or collective effort to protest against, or remedy, social conditions through the systematic assertion of the economic power of the workers." Once the state and capitalism were destroyed, anarchism would assume the form of free communism, which she described as " a social arrangement based on the principle: To each according to his needs; from each according to his ability." It must be stressed that although the wording is common to all forms of communism, that of Marx and Lenin implies strict centralized authority, while that of Kropotkin and Emma Goldman envisions complete decentralization and the supremacy of the individual.

No man who has pondered the concept of the good life will fail to appreciate the ideal propounded by the anarchists. And one who has observed the results of modern dictatorship cannot but sympathize with a vision of the future in which the individual is the prime beneficiary of all social activity. Yet life often makes mock of man's noblest dreams. Emma may have been " the daughter of the dream "; her doctrine remains as utopian as it is alluring. There is no gainsaying the fact that modern conditions still favor national and industrial centralization. The philosophy of anarchism appears less tenable today than ever.

Though in no sense a pacifist, Emma Goldman was intensely opposed to wars between nations. The very idea of human slaughter on the battlefield appeared to her as barbaric and criminal. And to her the culprit was the state. Without governments to lead their subjects to battle wars would be as unthinkable as duels are now. " No war is justified unless it be for the purpose of overthrowing the Capitalist system and establishing industrial control for the working class."

Her first contact with war occurred in 1898, when the United States attacked Spain. While she abominated the medieval monarchy which oppressed the Cubans, she did not want our politicians and industrialists to use the liberation of that island as a pretext for their imperial aggrandizement. She therefore agitated against the war at every one of her lectures, and did not cease to expose our imperialist intentions until the end of the fighting. Fortunately for her, the liberties of the people were not curbed as a result of the war, and the police did not consider her lack of patriotism more provoking than her advocacy of anarchism.

In 1914, when war broke out in Europe, she immediately perceived its catastrophic nature and condemned its instigators as monstrous criminals. Alexander Berkman, who had been enjoying uneasy liberty since 1906 and who worked closely with her despite their intermittent personal and ideological differences, at once joined her in the attack. Both did their utmost to rouse the people against our involvement. It was a hard and increasingly thankless fight against deep-seated prejudices. Consternation struck their hearts when they learned that Peter Kropotkin and other eminent anarchists had embraced the cause of the Allies and were participating in the propaganda campaign against Germany. Resolved to retain their sanity in a world gone mad, they repudiated all " warmongers " regardless of their previous professions and intensified their efforts to keep the United States out of the European holocaust.

When events moved· us in the direction of belligerency, the government sought feverishly to regiment the nation for the war struggle. Emma, Berkman, and numerous other radicals resisted this martial hysteria with all the force at their command. *Mother Earth* blasted the proponents of preparedness in issue after issue and denounced the government for trampling upon the Bill of Rights in its hypocritical pretence of making the world safe for democracy. Emma denounced the capitalist basis of war before crowds of enthusiastic sympathizers. As late as March 1917 she wrote:

I for one will speak against war so long as my voice will last, now and during the war. A thousand times rather would I die calling to the people of America to refuse to be obedient, to refuse military service, to refuse to murder their brothers, than I should ever give my voice in justification of war, except the one war of all the peoples against their despots and exploiters — the Social Revolution.

She and Berkman organized the No-Conscription League for the purpose of encouraging conscientious objectors to resist induction into the army. Writing in behalf of the League, Emma explained: " We will resist conscription by every means in our power, and we will sustain those who, for similar reasons, refuse to be conscripted." At several mass-meetings she and Berkman expressed these sentiments, knowing that government agents were taking notes on their speeches. On June 15, 1917, both were arrested and charged with " conspiring against the draft."

The two rebels did not flinch from the ordeal awaiting them.

" Tell all friends," Emma wrote shortly before their trial, " that we will not waver, that we will not compromise, and that if the worst comes, we shall go to prison in the proud consciousness that we have remained faithful to the spirit of internationalism and to the solidarity of all the people of the world." In court they conducted their own defense with a facility and frankness that gained the admiration of even their detractors. They shrewdly used the court-room as a forum. In addressing the jury they were eloquently polemical.

It is organized violence on top [Emma asserted] which creates individual violence at the bottom. It is the accumulated indignation against organized wrong, organized crime, organized injustice, which drives the political offender to his act. . . . We are but the atoms in the incessant human struggle towards the light that shines in the darkness — the ideal of economic, political, and spiritual liberation of mankind!

The dramatic trial was in a sense another re-enactment of the age-old tragedy in which the rebellious idealist is condemned by the gross guardians of society. The obdurate defendants were each given the maximum penalty of two years in prison and a fine of ten thousand dollars.

Time passed in dreary monotony for Emma in Jefferson City and Berkman in Atlanta. The war was fought and won, the millions of American soldiers were back from Europe, and peace again prevailed over the earth. But to conservatives the specter of Bolshevism had replaced the ogre of Prussianism as the enemy of established society. In this country Attorney-General Mitchell Palmer, a Quaker and God-fearing man, led the manhunt against those who were suspected of sympathy with the Russian Revolution. Thousands of men and women were made the victims of an Anti-Red hysteria, and hundreds were deported as undesirable aliens. When Emma and Berkman were released, they also became subject to expulsion. Although she had long been a naturalized citizen by virtue of her marriage to a citizen, the Department of Labor ruled otherwise. On the night of December 21, 1919, the two rebels together with 247 other undesirables were hurried aboard the ancient troopship *Buford* for passage to Russia.

Thirty years of struggle and suffering on this side of the Atlantic had so Americanized Emma and Berkman that they could not think of themselves as belonging to another country. The ignominy of expulsion and the loss of their friends wounded them deeply. Yet they were comforted by the thought of the adventure that lay ahead. As the battered *Buford* plowed its billowy way to the shores of Finland they reflected on the ironic turn of events which had transformed Czarist Russia into a land of revolution and converted the free United States into a citadel of reaction. While still in jail they had approved the Bolshevik coup as a necessary safeguard of the revolution. They believed that Lenin and his fellow leaders, while Marxists and therefore advocates of a strong centralized government, were devoted to the principles of freedom and equality and therefore deserved the support of all workers and libertarians. Now, outcasts from the capitalist stronghold, they longed to join their Russian comrades in the defense of the revolution. When she reached the Soviet border, Emma later wrote, " my heart trembled with anticipation and fervent hope."

Dismay darkened their days throughout the twenty months of their sojourn in Russia. Their official welcome quickly spent itself. They began to look about for themselves, to speak privately with fellow anarchists, and to seek explanations of events and practices not to their liking. The twin demons of inefficiency and stupidity — judged by their American and anarchist standards respectively — leered at them wherever they went; the black walls of bureaucracy rose before them at every turn. Perverse cruelty on the part of the government came to their attention with distressing frequency. All their early efforts at rationalization failed to excuse the needless hunger, the mass arrests, the arbitrary executions. They discussed these events with prominent Bolshevik leaders, including Trotsky and Lenin, in the hope of persuading them to mitigate conditions injurious to the revolution. In each instance the response was either enigmatic or equivocal. Angelica Balabanova, then secretary of the

Third International and later as disaffected an exile as herself, told Emma that life was " a rock on which the highest hopes are shattered. Life thwarts the best intentions and breaks the finest spirits." Alexandra Kollontay, the hard-headed diplomat, chilled her with the advice to stop " brooding over a few dull gray spots." Even Lenin impressed her and Berkman as callous and unsympathetic.

Time only deepened their perturbation. After eight months of life in Russia, Emma began to doubt the revolution itself. " Its manifestations were so completely at variance with what I had conceived and propagated as revolution that I did not know any more which was right. My old values had been shipwrecked and I myself thrown overboard to sink or swim." The climax of her quarrel with the Bolsheviki came a year later during the attack upon the mutinous Kronstadt sailors. That hundreds of true sons of the revolution should be shot down for sympathizing with striking workers seemed to her a crime worse than any committed by the Czarist regime. Neither she nor Berkman could any longer stomach such ruthless authoritarianism and both left the country as soon as they were able to obtain visas.

Their disillusionment was as absolute as it was inevitable. Having for thirty years, as Emma admitted later, " fought the Marxian theory as a cold, mechanistic, enslaving formula," they should have known that the Bolsheviki, fighting desperately to establish their hold upon the country and grappling with crucial problems without benefit of outside sympathy or experience, would hardly endanger their regime by accepting the anarchist conception of freedom.

Emma and Berkman had naïvely assumed that the Russian Revolution, even though directed by extreme Marxists, would create the libertarian utopia. Moreover, as leading American radicals they had expected positions of eminence. Finding themselves merely tolerated — treated as poor relations rather than admired as expert revolutionists — they magnified the " dull gray spots " until they could see nothing else. As lifelong rebels, ever hounded by the minions of authority and always defying them, it was easy for them to revert to their old dissidence. And because, like themselves, the Bolsheviki were workers and revolutionaries, their brutal and arbitrary behavior seemed even more intolerable than that of the American officials whom the couple had fought so bitterly. As Emma stated subsequently, " it was impossible for me to speak dispassionately about Russia."

Once past the Soviet border, the hapless pair became true Ishmaelites, without either home or country. No government offered them asylum, and few were willing to provide them with even temporary visas. Devoted friends had great difficulty in getting Swedish officials to permit the two refugees a long-enough stay in Stockholm to procure visas for a sojourn in Germany.

Their one great mission now became the unmasking of the Bolsheviki, and their attacks were more virulent and hysterical than those of the most extreme reactionaries. Berkman's *The Bolshevik Myth* and Emma's *My Disillusionment in Russia* and *My Further Disillusionment in Russia* (the book was published in two separate volumes as a result of an inadvertent misunderstanding) are charged with fanatic hatred. Both insisted that Lenin and his monstrous crew were perverting the Russian Revolution to their own sinister purposes and must be destroyed at all costs. They made no effort to view the situation objectively. They failed to realize that social revolutions, once unloosed, do not proceed smoothly along the groove of beneficent innovation but turn into avalanches that carry everything before them with an irresistible and infernal force; that, had the anarchists seized power, they might have been equally cruel and incompetent under the drastic circumstances; that, in truth, the gap between theory and practice is frequently the grave of the loftiest human aspirations. Ironically enough, they forgot that Bakunin, the founder of modern anarchism, was — in the words of his biographer, E. W. Carr — " the first originator of the conception of a select and closely organized revolutionary party, bound together not only by party ideals, but by the ties of implicit obedience to an absolute revolutionary dictator."

In 1924 Emma was permitted to make her home in England. At once she busied herself with plans to rouse the people against the Bolsheviki, but found herself either snubbed or scorned. The liberals refused to support her for fear of endangering Soviet Russia's precarious relations with Great Britain; the radicals insisted on the need of bolstering the Bolsheviki during the period of revolutionary experimentation. Her lectures were poorly attended; her audiences failed to be impressed. After two years of discouragement she decided to leave England altogether. Shortly before her departure she married James Colton, an old rebel, for the convenience of British citizenship.

A vacation in France preceded a lecture tour through Canada. Again on American soil, she resumed the old pattern of agitation. But the Dominion did not provide sufficient scope for her seething energy. And when friends, who had long urged her to write her autobiography, provided her with funds for that purpose, she returned to France.

Living My Life appeared in 1932. It is a lively story, palpitating with strong feeling and epitomizing the blazing years of her anarchist activity. The writing is vivacious, forceful, exciting. The narrative is colorful and wholly uninhibited. Emma's strong personality stamps every page. She was as dynamic in her numerous amours as in her work for human freedom, and she discusses both with equal zest. Her unrepressed egotism prompts her to relate personal incidents which have little bearing on her own development and none on that of anarchism — incidents that sometimes reveal petty malice and that might better have been left unrecorded. The final impression, however, is of her generous character, her profound devotion to the ideal of liberty, her extraordinary energy, her great courage, and her successful insistence on living her life in her own way.

When Emma had completed her long book and was ready to resume her role as lecturer and agitator, the menace of fascism drove the Bolshevik betrayal from the forefront of her mind. A tour through Germany and other parts of Europe convinced her that the Nazis were the greater threat to freedom and must be fought without let. Late in 1933 she returned to Canada and addressed large audiences on such topics as "Hitler and His Cohorts," "Germany's Tragedy," and "The Collapse of German Culture." With Cassandra-like foresight she argued that England and Germany's neighbors were blind to the danger confronting them and that if the Nazis were not ousted from power they would destroy civilization.

In January 1934 she was granted permission to visit the United States for ninety days. Friends arranged for a two-month lecture tour. Her audiences were large, though a good percentage came more out of curiosity than to pay homage to her anarchist leadership. Some hotels refused to admit her, and detectives and policemen were as conspicuous within the halls as in former times. Communists heckled her, but there was comparatively little of the excitement and defiance of her previous "tours of agitation." In truth neither Emma nor her hearers bothered much about the doctrine of anarchism. The immediate menace had become not the capitalistic state but fascist authoritarianism (to Emma, Bolshevism was "only left-wing fascism"); and she attacked it not as the apostolic anarchist but as the passionate libertarian. The end of April came all too soon, and again she had to depart from the land in which she had spent her best years. Nor did the fact that she was an old woman without roots elsewhere make leavetaking any easier.

The following year she sojourned in Canada, lecturing, writing, hoping in vain for readmission to the United States. In the spring of 1935 she went to France. Berkman was already there, and the two old friends again saw much of each other. The day after her sixty-seventh birthday their lifelong intimacy was abruptly ended by his suicide; he had been ill for some time and characteristically preferred death to a wretched old age. The tragic event oppressed her grievously.

The Spanish Civil War, beginning shortly after, provided her with much-needed distraction. With energies renewed she at once went to Spain. Her previous friendly association with Spanish anarchists made her a welcome addition to their ranks. For the next two years she devoted herself to bolstering the cause of the Loyalists. Since England's sympathy was of crucial importance, she went to London to work in behalf of the Spanish government. The callous and undiscerning attitude of the ruling Tories deprived her of the last atom of hope. She returned to Spain in 1938, wishing to stand beside her comrades during their final futile efforts to hold back the fascist inundation.

Early in 1939, with darkness rapidly enveloping the whole of Europe, Emma returned to Canada. There she died on May 13, 1940, clinging tenaciously to the shreds of her revolutionary ideal until her last gasp.

Emma Goldman was unquestionably the most active and audacious rebel of her time. An idealist to the core of her being, cherishing liberty as the most precious of human possessions, completely dedicated to the full and free life for all mankind, she early became the object of concentrated contumely and brutal abuse on the part of the defenders of the status quo. Her threat to society lay not so much in her revolutionary doctrine as in her attacks upon the abuses of capitalism. B. R. Tucker and other individualist anarchists were equally opposed to authority, but they were not molested so long as they did not concern themselves with economic exploitation. Emma, however, had made it her duty to fight against injustice toward the worker and the nonconformist. Consequently she organized mass-meetings and marches against unemployment; she became a picket-leader and fund-raiser, and protested openly and persistently against violations of free speech and against police brutality. This activity, especially effective because of her untiring zeal and bold eloquence, gave her pre-eminence as a dangerous enemy of capitalism and subjected her to persecution by the authorities until she was driven out of the country.

Quite a few Americans, however, respected her for her honest idealism and valued her as a goad stinging the social conscience of our complacent public. One of them, William Marion Reedy, called her " the daughter of the dream " after a meeting with her in 1908 and added: " She threatens all society that is sham, all society that is slavery, all society that is a mask of greed and lust." Floyd Dell spoke for many in the blithe year of 1912 when he wrote: " She has a legitimate social function — that of holding before our eyes the ideals of freedom. She is licenced to taunt us with our moral cowardice, to plant in our souls the nettles of remorse at having acquiesced so tamely in the brutal artifice of present-day society."

For all her courage and iconoclasm, she was deeply feminine in outlook and behavior. Her strongest attribute was of an emotional rather than intellectual nature: she felt first and thought afterwards. She had an extraordinary capacity for believing whatever suited her ideological or personal purposes. Rationalization and ratiocination merged in her mind very readily. Thus in her autobiography she was punctilious in recording the details of her love affairs, presumably in the belief that everything she did and felt affected her revolutionary development. Yet at all times she was ready to sacrifice her own happiness for the good of anarchism.

On her fiftieth birthday, while in prison for obstructing the draft, she took stock of her past. " Fifty years — thirty of them on the firing line — had they borne fruit or had I merely been repeating Don Quixote's idle chase? Had my efforts served only to fill my inner void, to find an outlet for the turbulence of my being? Or was it really the ideal that had dictated my conscious course? " She had not the slightest doubt, however, that her life had not been lived in vain. She had fought valiantly, and was to remain on the firing line for another twenty years. And while it is in the very nature of an ideal to fail of achievement, its mere existence gives life its impetus and its reward. Emma's quotation from Ibsen, made while waiting for deportation in 1919 — " that it is the struggle for the ideal that counts, rather than the attainment of it " — may well be her epitaph.

THE DISSIDENT ECONOMISTS

BROOKS ADAMS   HENRY GEORGE

THORSTEIN VEBLEN

THE ECONOMIC BACKGROUND

VICTORY at Appomattox gave a tremendous impetus to American business enterprise. In 1865 the United States, licking its wounds, was largely an undeveloped agricultural country; a half-century later its amazing industrial growth gave it first place among the great world powers. Its phenomenal expansion may be measured in terms of the evolution from the typical independent oil driller to the gigantic Standard Oil Company, or from the modest iron foundry employing a few men to the enormous United States Steel Corporation. Never in the history of mankind has a nation grown at once so fast and so powerful. This fabulous rate of economic expansion will become evident from a few samples of statistical data.

In 1860 the federal government possessed more than a billion acres or more than half of the total area of the country. Fifty years later relatively little of this land was not owned privately, and much of it was in the hands of the railroads and large landowners. During this same period, however, the number of individual farms had tripled and their annual production of such staples as corn, wheat, and cotton had more than tripled. A good indicator of the vast conversion of the public domain into private property is to be found in the production and sale of barbed wire, which rose from 10,000 pounds in 1874 to 300,000,000 pounds in 1900.

The rate of expansion for industry is even more striking. From the end of the Civil War till 1900 the number of factories — disregarding enlargements and consolidations — increased fourfold; the number of workmen, fivefold; the value of the products, sevenfold; the amount of available capital, ninefold. Railways covered the country with nearly 200,000 miles of track, about one-third of the world's total mileage. The annual production of pig iron increased sixteenfold, and that of steel expanded from an insignificant amount to more than 10,000,000 tons. Other products showed similar rates of increase. Inventions, new production techniques, and adequate capital were combined by men of great energy in the exploitation of the country's vast natural resources. The even more amazing achievements after 1900 — in some instances multiplying production tenfold — are too familiar for comment.

Political conditions after the Civil War greatly favored this extraordinary industrial development. The government was in the hands of politicians who saw eye to eye with the men bent on utilizing the country's wealth to the utmost, and they gave them every possible benefit — knowing that they too would share in the rich harvest. Protective tariffs were enacted, immigration was encouraged, the building of railroads was expedited, land containing natural resources was given away almost for the asking, labor unions were discountenanced, and a sound currency was established. As Parrington remarked: " In the tumultuous decades that followed there was to be no bargaining with corporations for the use of what the public gave; they took what they wanted and no impertinent questions were asked."

The courts were even more solicitous than the legislators for the protection of the individual and the corporation in their pursuit of profit. The Supreme Court majority, in its effort to safeguard private property and individual enterprise, defined the word " person " to include corporations and maintained that the Declaration of Independence and the Constitution gave the individual the right to accumulate what property he could and to use it as he saw fit. Justice Field in 1883 proclaimed " the right of men to pursue their happiness, by which is meant the right to pursue any lawful business or vocation, in any manner not inconsistent with the equal rights of others, which may increase their prosperity or develop their faculties, so as to give them their highest enjoyment." Ten years later Justice Brewer stated that the Supreme Court " simply nails the Declaration of Independence, like Luther's theses against the indulgences, upon the doors of the Wittenberg church of human rights and dares the anarchist and the socialist, and every other assassin of liberty to blot out a single word." These spokesmen for the Supreme Court, assuming that the day laborer and the president of a large corporation had equal rights and opportunities before the law and in the marketplace, interpreted the principles of human rights and individual liberty as synonymous with the nineteenth-century gospel of wealth.

The men who effected this industrial transformation were mostly of humble origin and without adequate discipline or training but with ability and the will to power that well fitted them for the task. They were, in Parrington's estimation, " primitive souls, ruthless, predatory, capable; single-minded men; rogues and rascals often, but never feeble, never hindered by petty scruple, never given to puling or whining — the raw materials of a race of capitalistic buccaneers." They were indeed — taken together — ingenious, shrewd, enterprising, thrifty, dominated by a gospel of get-and-grab which justified their lack of scruple and their sharp dealing. Their Calvinistic conscience saw no discrepancy between cheating their competitors and customers on weekdays and endowing churches and colleges on the Sabbath.

One of the best of them, Andrew Carnegie, had the drive and the imagination to make millions out of steel by riding the crest of industrial expansion. His steel company was organized in 1873 with a capital of $700,000. In twenty years the company's profits added up to $40,000,000. In 1900 the company was reorganized and recapitalized at $300,000,000 — the current value of its assets — and was geared to produce 3,000,000 tons of steel annually. Even more successful, though much less scrupulous, was John D. Rockefeller, whose Standard Oil Company became the first and most notorious of the gigantic trusts. In the *Atlantic Monthly* of March 1881,

Henry D. Lloyd first told about the corrupt, illegal, and fraudulent methods by which Standard Oil achieved its monopoly of the oil industry. It crushed its competitors by any means at its disposal, chiefly by obtaining unlawful control of transportation facilities.

The refineries at New York had often to lie idle while the oil was running on the ground at the wells, because they could not get transportation. The monopoly of the pipe lines which the railroad gave it made the Standard the master of the exits of oil from the producing districts. Producing themselves but one-fiftieth of the oil yield, they stood between the producers of the other forty-nine-fiftieths and the world. There was apparently no trick the Standard would not play.

Consequently Rockefeller and his several partners had maneuvered themselves into a position from which they were able to force competitors either to sell out below cost or face bankruptcy. " Refiner after refiner in Pittsburgh, buying his crude oil in the open market, manufacturing it at his works, shipping it to the seaboard, met with a continued succession of losses, and was forced into bankruptcy or a sale of his works to the Standard, who always had a buyer on the spot at the right time."

An absence of scruple and a sense of largeness marked almost all business enterprise of the post-Civil War decades, aptly called the Gilded Age. The federal, state, and local governments encouraged this philosophy of get-and-grab. Political bosses in every large city trafficked brazenly with favors and franchises — often beating the industrial buccaneers at their own game. Graft affected many of the votes of public officials — from petty aldermen to mighty members of the United States Senate. The corruption of city councils and state legislatures became a public shame, yet exposure and censure had little effect.

Perhaps the most notorious instance of fraud is to be found in the disposal of public lands. Immediately after the Civil War the federal and state governments began to squander the public domain in their ostensible efforts to encourage railroad building and land settlement. By 1873, when public protest checked this extravagance,

economists, however, were staunch exponents of the princip
natural rights and the gospel of wealth. They ignored crying al
and declared that every man had the inalienable right to a
property and to use it as he wished. "As men now are," Presi
Mark Hopkins of Williams stated in *Lectures on Moral Scie*
" it is far better that they should be employed in accumulating pr
erty honestly, to be spent reasonably, if not nobly, than that th
should be encouraged any sentimentalism about the worthlessn
of property, or tendency to a merely contemplative or quietistic li
which has so often been either the result or the cause of inefficien
or idleness." As late as 1875 President James McCosh of Princet
asserted in *Christian Ethics* that "God has bestowed upon us ce
tain powers and gifts which no one is at liberty to take from us
to interfere with. All attempts to deprive us of them is theft.
Shortly afterwards President Hadley of Yale, while admitting tha
to the medieval economist the businessman was a licensed robber
insisted that to the modern economist he was " a public benefac
tor " to whom the community freely gave the chance to direct its
productive resources. And at about the same time Professor J. Laurence Laughlin, soon to head the economics department of the new
University of Chicago endowed by John D. Rockefeller, argued
that one could gain wealth only by " sacrifice, exertion and skill "
and that the rich man therefore " has the right to enjoy the products of his exertion to the exclusion of everyone else."

These academic apologists maintained that the poor have no one
to blame for their indigence but themselves and that, in their efforts
to amass wealth, men of enterprise were certain to benefit the people
as a whole. Several of the small minority of economists who criticized laissez-faire practices as inimical to public welfare, suffered
the consequences of their dissidence. Thus Professor Henry C.
Adams was dismissed from Cornell in 1886, Professor Edward W.
Bemis was not reappointed at the University of Chicago in 1895,
and Professor John R. Commons was asked to leave Syracuse University in 1899 — and in each instance academic freedom was violated in order to appease rich patrons.

[248]

Congress alone had donated considerably more than a hundred million acres to land-grant railroads. Those who undertook the construction of these railways practised deceit and chicane on a gargantuan scale. Thus the four partners of Crocker and Company,
who completed the first transcontinental railway, received $121,-
000,000 for construction costs totaling around $58,000,000 at the
highest estimate. Smaller organizations and many individuals emulated the railroad companies in getting what they could out of a
bountiful government. They were fraudulent in filing their homestead claims — some even rented movable miniature log cabins in
order to swear that they were complying with the requirements of
the Pre-emption Act. Cattlemen helped themselves to large tracts
of land by means of illegal enclosings. Shrewd speculators unlawfully pre-empted timber and mineral lands which later yielded them
large fortunes. The guardians of the law did little or nothing to
check this chicane, and indeed often conspired with the speculators.
The general assumption was that the continent in the possession
of the government was an inexhaustible horn of plenty and everyone was welcome to its fruits so long as he was instrumental in populating the frontier or in developing the land.

If manufacturers and merchants and mineowners did not measure up to our present standard of ethics, they nevertheless succeeded in bringing the industrial capacities of the country up to
their present efficiency. This much cannot be said for many of the
bankers and brokers of Wall Street, who were interested not in production but in profits and who became the notorious robber-barons
of the period. They cheated and swindled and robbed and ruined
— at times one another, but mostly the innocent and gullible investors. It was these buccaneers who were responsible for the gold
corner in 1867, the Credit Mobilier scandal, the various financial
panics, the stockwatering of the railroads and industrial corporations, the organization of trusts and holding companies, and the
vast and unscrupulous stock manipulations which caused Carnegie
to say that " they throw cats and dogs together and call them
elephants." It was they, to cite only two of their exploits recorded

[245]

Congress alone had donated considerably more than a hundred million acres to land-grant railroads. Those who undertook the construction of these railways practised deceit and chicane on a gargantuan scale. Thus the four partners of Crocker and Company, who completed the first transcontinental railway, received $121,000,000 for construction costs totaling around $58,000,000 at the highest estimate. Smaller organizations and many individuals emulated the railroad companies in getting what they could out of a bountiful government. They were fraudulent in filing their homestead claims — some even rented movable miniature log cabins in order to swear that they were complying with the requirements of the Pre-emption Act. Cattlemen helped themselves to large tracts of land by means of illegal enclosings. Shrewd speculators unlawfully pre-empted timber and mineral lands which later yielded them large fortunes. The guardians of the law did little or nothing to check this chicane, and indeed often conspired with the speculators. The general assumption was that the continent in the possession of the government was an inexhaustible horn of plenty and everyone was welcome to its fruits so long as he was instrumental in populating the frontier or in developing the land.

If manufacturers and merchants and mineowners did not measure up to our present standard of ethics, they nevertheless succeeded in bringing the industrial capacities of the country up to their present efficiency. This much cannot be said for many of the bankers and brokers of Wall Street, who were interested not in production but in profits and who became the notorious robber-barons of the period. They cheated and swindled and robbed and ruined — at times one another, but mostly the innocent and gullible investors. It was these buccaneers who were responsible for the gold corner in 1867, the Credit Mobilier scandal, the various financial panics, the stockwatering of the railroads and industrial corporations, the organization of trusts and holding companies, and the vast and unscrupulous stock manipulations which caused Carnegie to say that " they throw cats and dogs together and call them elephants." It was they, to cite only two of their exploits recorded by Lloyd, who burdened the New York Central and the Erie railroads with watered stock amounting to $53,507,000 and $63,963,381 respectively. Another conspicuous instance of such manipulations was the merger of several steel companies into the United States Steel Corporation, which was achieved by the Morgan Company at a clear profit of $62,500,000. While this particular feat represented finance capitalism at its best, other transactions produced not even the semblance of a real elephant.

Throughout the nineteenth century and later American business enterprise was defended by the most eminent academic economists. Their pragmatic approach to economic theory made it relatively easy for them to justify the activities of an untrammeled capitalism.

Alexander Hamilton was the first eminent economic spokesman for the new American nation. His effective advocacy of a financial system and of a specific policy of tariff protection for new industries fitted so well the evolving needs of capitalistic industrialism that his views prevailed throughout the nineteenth century and into our own time. His principle of protection became, in its application, largely an American doctrine. Economists like Frederick List, John Ray, Henry C. Carey, and numerous others refined it for current acceptance.

American economic theory began primarily as a protest against the presumed universality of classical economics. Circumstances forced the more venturesome economists to a reluctant acknowledgement that earlier theories based on English conditions did not answer the requirements of a frontier people. Loyalty to Adam Smith and David Ricardo, their respected masters, did not blind them to the fact that these Englishmen had based their doctrine on the principle of scarcity; that their theories of production and distribution lost validity when applied to a country operating on the principle of abundance. Several economists likewise criticized the Malthusian theory of population as irrelevant to the United States where population growth meant expansion and wealth and not crowding and misery. Henry C. Carey, the outstanding American economist before the Civil War, was typical in considering himself a disciple of Adam Smith while espousing the principle of protection as necessary to the healthy development of a growing industrialism.

Political economy was not a serious subject of study in American colleges until considerably after the Civil War. Most men were too busy developing the economy of the country to concern themselves with its underlying principles. Consequently the first courses in this field were taught for the most part by doctors of divinity who sought to fit political economy into the all-embracing scheme of their cosmic theology. Thus towards the middle of the century, when the Smith-Ricardo-Mill school was at the peak of its popularity in England, its doctrines were given the authority of Holy Writ. American students were taught, among other things, that liberty and property were the keystones of any rational economic order; that economic freedom would consequently yield a greater total benefit than any form of governmental control; that wages were that price which would enable laborers to subsist and perpetuate themselves; and that profit was the socially beneficent reward of abstinence and enterprise. These doctrines were explained on hedonistic and utilitarian grounds: every man knew that in the long run his own happiness was bound up with the happiness of his neighbors; that since everyone knew best what profited him most, his freedom from governmental restraint in the pursuit of happiness was the best means of securing happiness for all. Francis Wayland's *Elements of Political Economy*, which presented these views as obvious truths, was for many years the most popular college text in this country. This book was succeeded in turn by such widely used texts as those written by General Francis A. Walker and President Arthur T. Hadley, leading orthodox economists who had adapted English doctrine to current American conditions.

Many academic economists, loyal to their English masters and yet loath to antagonize the wealthy benefactors of their institutions, veered enough from the doctrine of laissez-faire to deny the benefits of free trade in a country in process of development. All economists, however, were staunch exponents of the principle of natural rights and the gospel of wealth. They ignored crying abuses and declared that every man had the inalienable right to amass property and to use it as he wished. " As men now are," President Mark Hopkins of Williams stated in *Lectures on Moral Science*, " it is far better that they should be employed in accumulating property honestly, to be spent reasonably, if not nobly, than that there should be encouraged any sentimentalism about the worthlessness of property, or tendency to a merely contemplative or quietistic life, which has so often been either the result or the cause of inefficiency or idleness." As late as 1875 President James McCosh of Princeton asserted in *Christian Ethics* that " God has bestowed upon us certain powers and gifts which no one is at liberty to take from us or to interfere with. All attempts to deprive us of them is theft." Shortly afterwards President Hadley of Yale, while admitting that to the medieval economist the businessman was a licensed robber, insisted that to the modern economist he was " a public benefactor " to whom the community freely gave the chance to direct its productive resources. And at about the same time Professor J. Laurence Laughlin, soon to head the economics department of the new University of Chicago endowed by John D. Rockefeller, argued that one could gain wealth only by " sacrifice, exertion and skill " and that the rich man therefore " has the right to enjoy the products of his exertion to the exclusion of everyone else."

These academic apologists maintained that the poor have no one to blame for their indigence but themselves and that, in their efforts to amass wealth, men of enterprise were certain to benefit the people as a whole. Several of the small minority of economists who criticized laissez-faire practices as inimical to public welfare, suffered the consequences of their dissidence. Thus Professor Henry C. Adams was dismissed from Cornell in 1886, Professor Edward W. Bemis was not reappointed at the University of Chicago in 1895, and Professor John R. Commons was asked to leave Syracuse University in 1899 — and in each instance academic freedom was violated in order to appease rich patrons.

While a number of the leading professional economists of the Gilded Age dissented from classical theory in their interpretation of or departure from one or another of its specific doctrines, they all adhered wholeheartedly to its major premise of individual liberty of action. Differ as they might with their theological adversaries in other respects, they vied with them in their praise of thrift and enterprise and in their condemnation of idleness and radicalism. Whether they were for or against free trade, for or against the gold standard, for or against a mild form of social-welfare service, they were united in the hedonistic justification of capitalism and in their righteous abuse of labor organizations and of governmental regulation of business.

One of the most eminent of these economists, General Walker, described the captain of industry as the great engine of industrial progress. As an ardent classicist he maintained that capital was always the product of abstinence and savings; consequently its owner had the right to employ it as he wished. He also asserted that profits were not wrested from labor, as the socialists insisted, but were the reward of efficient enterprise. " The gains of the employer are not taken from the earnings of the laboring class, but measure the difference in production between the commonplace or bad, and the able, and shrewd, and strong management of business." He denied, however, the validity of the wages-fund theory and asserted that labor received in wages whatever was left from rent, interest and profit — assuming the existence of a " full and free competition." Since rent and interest were fixed charges, wages tended to rise with profits. He therefore condemned labor unions and strikes as futile, vicious, and un-American, and dealt summarily with the radical views of Karl Marx, Henry George, and Edward Bellamy by impugning the honesty of these dissidents.

Professor William Graham Sumner of Yale, another outstanding economist of the time, was equally harsh in his denunciation of the critics of capitalism. A disciple of Darwin and Spencer, he believed that social evolution was an automatic process which could not and therefore must not be disturbed. He linked the dog-eat-dog practices of many businessmen with the theory of the struggle for survival which led to a higher form of life. " The truth is," he asserted, " that the social order is fixed by laws of nature precisely analogous to those of the physical order. The most that man can do is by his ignorance and conceit to mar the operation of these social laws." Consequently he saw only harm as the result of any effort to regulate business enterprise. Why interfere with a process which brought wealth to men of merit and poverty to the indolent and the dissolute? That he did not find complete favor with the class he championed was due to his persistent advocacy of free trade as a long-run economic policy.

Towards the end of the nineteenth century Professor John Bates Clark of Columbia established himself as the leader of those economists who extolled the virtues of free individual enterprise. His economic theories, expressed with force and precision and ostensibly opposed to classical doctrine, were nevertheless based on what Thorstein Veblen termed " the pre-evolutionary ground of normality and ' natural law.' " Hedonistic in character, this economics was primarily interested in the theory of distribution — the distribution of ownership and income. It concerned itself chiefly with

the definition and classification of a mechanically limited range of phenomena, [being] confined, in substance, to the determination of the refinements upon the concepts of land, labor, and capital, as handed down by the great economists of the classical era, and the correlate concepts of rent, wages, interest and profit. Solicitously, with a painfully meticulous circumspection, the normal, mechanical metes and bounds of these several concepts are worked out, the touchstone of the absolute truth aimed at being the hedonistic calculus.

As a hedonistic economist Professor Clark asserted optimistically that men behave rationally and respond without prejudice to the stimulus of anticipated pleasure and pain. While he veered from the position of earlier classical economists in his assumption that society was dynamic and not static, he maintained that man is naturally good, and not bad, even in his economic relationships. He therefore stressed the importance of free competition in an open market. Such competition, he declared, would make prices conform to " standards of cost," wages to " the standard of the final productively of labor," and interest to " the marginal product of capital." It would moreover tend to make the rich richer and the poor better off — since that was the natural law which controlled the distribution of the income of society.

Aware that existing monopolies limited free competition, he condemned them as an economic evil and proposed that the state, which existed chiefly to protect property, take steps towards their elimination. " No description," he asserted, " could exaggerate the evil which is in store for a society given hopelessly to a regime of private monopoly." And by a private monopoly he meant not only the large trusts and corporations but also what he termed the selfish labor unions. To the very end of his life, which reached into our own time, he refused to recognize the inevitable monopolistic tendency of business enterprise and preached a competitive individualism of free and honorable men.

Not all economists, however, were optimistic exponents of the gospel of wealth. Professors R. T. Ely and John R. Commons shocked many of their colleagues and outraged leading businessmen by their declaration that labor unions were a necessary concomitant of powerful trusts and corporations. A few sociologists were equally concerned with the welfare of the mass of the people. Lester Ward was among the first to decry the deleterious results of dog-eat-dog practices. He argued that it was the duty of the state to deal with the problem of poverty by regulating the economic forces of production and distribution. Somewhat later Professors E. A. Ross of Wisconsin and C. H. Cooley of Michigan were even firmer in their opposition to uncontrolled individualism and in their contributions to the theory of social welfare. These and a few other liberal social scientists felt distressed by the increasingly acute strife between the struggling labor unions and the ruthless industrialists; they discarded the blinders of classical economics and viewed the realities of a growing capitalism with a critical mind.

If Professor Clark was the leading exponent of laissez-faire economics, his friend Professor Simon N. Patten of Pennsylvania was for a time its chief critic. A product of the generous Illinoisian prairie and the easy-going German university, he began his mature study of economics from a pragmatic standpoint. He was not long in discovering serious discrepancies between classical theories and current economic practices. Further inquiry convinced him, even more firmly than some of the earlier American economists, that the views of the Smith-Ricardo-Mill school, having their basis in a scarcity economy resulting from a niggardly nature, had been invalidated by the scientific conquest of nature and a concomitant social progress. A statistical analysis of the vast rise in the production of staple commodities made obvious that the scarcity economy of the early nineteenth century had been replaced by an economy of abundance. " We no longer live in an age of deficit and pain," he pointed out, " but rather in an age of surplus and pleasure when all things are possible if we will but keep our eyes turned towards the future and strip our intelligences for their tasks."

Professor Patten, convinced of the inapplicability of classical theories in an economy of abundance, maintained that the problem of diminishing returns, and indeed the entire theory of production, demanded much less attention than the question of consumption. In this discussion of capital he pointed out that since abstinence and hardship were no longer necessary in a highly developed industrial society, the rewards for saving had lost their essential justification. The wages-fund theory he dismissed as presumptuous. " The reasoning of the wages-fund theorists was a selfish upperclass view of those who wished to pose as humanitarians without being so." From this rejection followed logically his criticism of the classical theory of distribution, with its static and sharply defined divisions of income. " There is but one social surplus for which all industrial classes contend and among whom it is divided not in definite funds but in parts altered by each new alignment of economic forces." He further broke with laissez-faire theory by his stand that a protective tariff was advisable if it furthered the national economy. Finally he argued that competition was not a basic and desirable social good. "Competition," he wrote, "is not a human trait but an unsocial tendency. It fails in large-scale production because this is the first to be socialized."

Professor Patten was one of the first American economists to declare that industrial depressions were caused by the loss of mass-purchasing power. To avoid such disaster, he contended, it was necessary on the one hand to stress the value of efficiency and thus assure an economy of abundance and on the other to equalize the distribution of income with a view to abolishing poverty. He believed that poverty could be eradicated. Unlike other economists he did not subscribe to the Biblical assertion that the poor will always be with us, nor did he believe that indigence was caused by innate moral deficiences. This view, he maintained, confused cause with effect. "Abolish poverty, transform deficit into surplus, fill depletion with energy, and the ascribed heredity of the poor will vanish with its causes."

To achieve the efficient working of an economy of abundance Professor Patten recommended the curbing of unrestrained individualism in business, the control of chaotic competition, and a planned economy — measures which presumed general governmental supervision of our economic structure. He did not elaborate his outline for a planned society, and there is no notion of socialism in his writings. All he wanted, as an economist, was a society functioning in an economy of abundance for all its members.

If Professor Patten was a severe critic of classical economics, Thorstein Veblen, the chief founder of institutional economics, was its executioner. He approached economics from the standpoint of the evolutionary sciences. He had made a thorough study of the Darwinian method, of the biological experiments of his colleague Jacques Loeb at the University of Chicago, and of the latest researches in the relatively new sciences of anthropology and psychology. It was in the light of his findings in these fields that he established the institutional approach to economics in a series of articles and books published in the 1890's and 1900's. In his view, economic activity was not an independent entity, to be analyzed in the manner of the classical economists, but a part of general human activity which was best understood if examined as an evolutionary process. This process made evident that institutions were decisive factors in influencing human behavior. Consequently social science, of which economics was a part, must deal with human beings rather than with rationalized human nature, with facts rather than with their normalized aspects. Since men, however, adapted their institutions to the changing needs of human nature and general progress, social scientists must consider these institutions from an evolutionary rather than a normative standpoint.

Institutional economists, and their number has become large, thus concern themselves with things in flux and employ those methods of study which best analyze the processes of economic change. They criticize orthodox economists for their continued dependence upon an outworn hedonistic psychology, an inaccurate postulate of individualistic competition, and a static view of economic organization. They make a virtue of their disinclination to develop new economic laws, and favor monographic work on single topics. Professor Wesley C. Mitchell's *Business Cycles*, published in 1913, became a model and manual for a generation of institutional economists. They continue to concentrate on the specific aspects of our economy, seeking not speculative syntheses but a knowledge of processes and statistics, not normality but the nature of social change. By shunning the dogmatism and generalizing of the classical economists, they have fertilized economic thinking and have come closer to economic realities.

American academic economists of the nineteenth century, whether they accepted classical theory without question or rejected one or more of its tenets, all functioned within the orbit of industrial capitalism. While some of them criticized the malpractices of business enterprise and urged government regulation as a means of keeping industrial buccaneers within the bounds of legality, all agreed that modern society was served best by a capitalistic system of economy. It was only in our own time that a few institutional and Marxian economists questioned this assumption. The large majority of economists, however, continued to reject socialism as fallacious if not vicious, even as their forerunners had dismissed the Populist, single-tax, and other similar movements as muddle-headed versions of panacea.

Outside of the academic cloisters, however, men took a more realistic attitude towards the rapacity of capitalistic enterprise. Most of them, tempted by the opportunities for profitable business ventures, readily joined the stampede to the national money trough. Many sons of Abolitionists, utopians, prohibitionists — scions of first families and children of radical immigrants — put aside their ideals in the mad effort to get rich quick. But not a few men recoiled from this dog-eat-dog scramble. Like some of their fathers before them, they dedicated themselves not to private wealth but to public welfare. Wendell Phillips, Edward Bellamy, John Swinton and the sons of Charles Francis Adams and William Lloyd Garrison in the East, Henry George in California, Henry D. Lloyd and Clarence Darrow in Chicago, and Robert M. LaFollette in Wisconsin, were merely a few of the more conspicuous liberal critics of the unscrupulous exploiters of our land and people.

In the cities thousands of workmen, driven desperate by arrogant and arbitrary employers, again and again engaged in strikes and riots that blotched the social history of the period. The farmers also, swindled by land speculators and victimized by brokers, bankers, and the railroads, fought back furiously. The cause of these workmen and farmers was taken up for the most part by men who loved justice and hated wrong — men who cherished the ideals of the Declaration of Independence and wanted to make them prevail. A few of them, having come under the influence of the writings of Karl Marx, ascribed all social evils to capitalism and urged its abolition; a much greater number, less doctrinaire and less radical, sought redress by means of labor unions and political reform. They exposed the nefarious practices of the railroads and larger corporations and campaigned for government regulation. In time this pressure upon state legislatures and Congress resulted in laws aiming to curb the more flagrant malpractices. And while politicians and judges, who favored the corporations rather than the nation's welfare, tried to minimize the effectiveness of these laws, they could not indefinitely hold back the forces of social progress.

Of the three critics of capitalistic economics chosen here for detailed study, Henry George attacked the existing order because it increased want along with wealth; as a Jeffersonian idealist he wanted to establish economic justice by means of land reform. Brooks Adams, aristocrat and Puritan in the best sense of these terms, struck out against a rapaciously selfish capitalism in a Jeremian effort to prevent the decline of the United States from its primacy as a world power. Thorstein Veblen, perhaps our most original economist, analyzed capitalistic precepts and practices with an ironic incisiveness that exposed their faults and fallacies and indicated their underlying weaknesses.

HENRY GEORGE

PROPHET OF HUMAN RIGHTS

OUR PROFESSIONAL ECONOMISTS, anxious to lift their studies to the high objective plane of the natural sciences, have disregarded Henry George as an unerudite tamperer with matters which are their special concern. As a consequence most Americans who have heard of him associate his name only with a confiscatory and unworkable single-tax panacea. This has obscured the fact that his books once excited the imagination of millions and that his energetic crusading gave them a new vision and fresh hope. A familiarity with his work shows indeed that he had the greatness of soul to sublimate his early experience with grinding indigence into a passionate drive to obliterate want from the face of the earth. Without the advantages of a formal education, he evolved a philosophy of society, at once prophetic and melioristic, which has placed him among the pre-eminent social thinkers of our time.

George was born in Philadelphia on September 2, 1839, the second of ten children. His father was at one time a publisher of religious books and later a clerk in the customs house, but he was never quite able to provide for his large family. Young George went to work before he was fourteen. Ambitious and restless, interested in ships like his grandfather before him, he sailed in 1855 as foremast boy on a voyage that took him to Australia and as far as India and back. When he returned to Philadelphia about a year later he obtained work in a printing shop, but his weekly earnings of two dollars were wholly inadequate for the alert youth who had seen the world and knew of the high wages paid in California. The lure of the West gave him no peace, and before long he again went to sea, on a government ship bound for San Francisco. But conditions in that city had greatly deteriorated since the early years of the Gold Rush. There was no pot of gold at the end of the rainbow for the newcomer, but he was too young and too ambitious to feel discouraged. Unable to find work, he joined some miners on their way to Fraser River in search of the precious metal. Again he met with disappointment, and after several months of futile effort he returned to San Francisco. Penniless and in debt, he was ready to take the first job that came his way, but there was no work of any kind available in the city which a few years before had paid the highest wages in the world.

Determined to improve himself, he read considerably and joined a reading circle. On July 21, 1859, he wrote to his sister Jennie: " I try to pick up everything I can, both by reading and observation, and flatter myself that I learn at least something every day." He was also beginning to dream of heaven on earth, and in a letter to his sister two years later he expressed his longing for the time

when each one will be free to follow his best and noblest impulses, unfettered by the restrictions and necessities which our present state of society imposes on him; when the poorest and meanest will have a chance to use all his God-given faculties and not be forced to drudge away the best part of his time in order to supply wants but little above those of the animal.

All this time he was living hapazardly on odd jobs as a printer's substitute, and he was never free of debt. His situation became more precarious when he fell in love with a young orphan from Australia, Annie Corsina Fox, and married her on December 4, 1861. Shortly afterwards he found work in Sacramento and soon became the father of a son. Early in 1864 he lost his job and returned to San Francisco. Nothing seemed to come his way no matter how hard he tried. " I came near starving," he recalled years later, "and at one time I was so close to it that I think I should have done so but for the job of printing a few cards which enabled us to buy a little corn meal. In this darkest time in my life my second child was born." So frantic was he on that particular day that he was ready to kill a man for five dollars if the latter had not given him the money voluntarily. A month later, greatly in debt and still without regular employment, he confided to his diary, "Am in desperate plight. Courage."

Although George was able to improve his condition somewhat after 1865, and at times even lived in relative comfort, he never forgot the dreadful months of utter despair. He had long given up the dream of riches, but the memory of dire poverty kept him "in perpetual disquiet" and turned his mind to social problems. Groping in the darkness of ignorance and inexperience, yearning to make the world a better place for his children to live in, keenly conscious of the fire in his heart and the power of his pen, he began to read voraciously and to practise writing at every opportunity. Lincoln's assassination moved him to express his admiration of the martyred President in two stirring editorials which were printed in *Alta California*, the newspaper for which he was then a typesetter. The completion of the first transcontinental railway gave him the occasion to write down the thoughts about land and wealth which had long been simmering in his mind. "What the Railroad Will Bring," which appeared in *Overland Monthly* in 1868, stressed the idea that material progress was not necessarily beneficial to the people as a whole and that increased wealth tended to accentuate want.

High wages and high interest were indications that the natural wealth of the country was not yet monopolized, that great opportunities were open to all. . . . Those who have land, mines, established business, special abilities of certain kinds, will become richer for it and find increased opportunities; those who have only their own labor will become poorer, and find it harder to get ahead — first because it will take more capital to buy land or get into business; and second, as competition reduces the wages of labor, this capital will be the harder for them to obtain.

Here, in bare outline, George expressed the basic idea which he was a decade later to incorporate in *Progress and Poverty*.

George was by this time an established journalist. His zeal for justice and his sharp pen made him at once known and notorious throughout California and prevented him from remaining long on one newspaper. He became preoccupied with civic affairs, and his editorials were charged with the indignation and zest of the aggressive reformer. Yet his deepest thought was reserved for the problem which in his view affected the very foundations of modern society: the simultaneous increase of wealth and want in a civilization capable of providing the comforts of life to all mankind. In possession of a creative intelligence that perceived relationships where the ordinary mind saw only isolated events, he began to gather the evidence for those principles upon which a better society might be built. He recalled that, years before, a lot in San Francisco had doubled in price upon the arrival of a ship carrying supplies. He remembered what the old miner had told him about wages going down with the growth of population. In 1869, while in New York trying in vain to establish a news service in opposition to the Associated Press and Western Union, he felt the full impact of the kind of society he was determined to abolish: " I saw and recognized for the first time the shocking contrast between monstrous wealth and debasing want." Shortly after his return to California, while riding on horseback in the neighborhood of Oakland, he noticed that the completion of the railway had caused a land boom far outside of the urban limits. Land, previously of little worth, had been subdivided into acre lots, and these were being offered at a thousand dollars apiece. " Like a flash it came upon me that there was the reason of advancing poverty with advancing wealth."

His mind seethed with the discovery, but he was not yet prepared to formulate it. At this time Governor Haight, too honest a man to condone the land-grabbing of the railroads, decided to put an end to the corrupting machinations of the Central Pacific Railroad. He engaged George to edit the Sacramento *Reporter* and campaigned for re-election on an anti-railroad platform. Central Pacific was more than a match for these two doughty warriors. It bought the *Reporter*, depriving George of his job, and paid for enough votes to swamp the recalcitrant governor.

The experience gave George the proper impetus to express his views on land monopoly and its consequences. He was then wholly unfamiliar with the literature on the subject and did not know that the French Physiocrats and several individual thinkers in other lands had preceded him in the exposition of similar conclusions. *Our Land and Land Policy, National and State*, which he wrote and published in 1871, was a 48-page pamphlet presenting his solution of the land problem. In sketchy outline the booklet explained the pertinent issues and proposals which he was later to discuss in persuasive detail in *Progress and Poverty*: the exhaustion of the nation's public lands, the dependence of the laborer on land, the viciousness of land monopoly, and the need to socialize land by taxing its unearned increment to its full value. George sent copies to various men of prominence and was gratified by the response.

In December 1871 he became editor and part owner of the newly established *Daily Evening Post*, the first newspaper in California to be sold for a penny — a coin not then in free circulation on the Pacific Coast. Its editorial page gave George opportunity to excoriate the abuses of privilege and to expound his economic ideas on the causes of poverty and land values. Although the daily was to be " the organ of no faction, clique or party " it came out for Greeley in the election of 1872, championed the cause of labor, and forced the prosecutions of political grafters and wealthy criminals.

Late in 1875 the *Post* was sold and George was once again without a job. He did not, however, seek work on another newspaper. The urge to propound his economic views and social ideals gave him no peace. Since he had worked for Governor Irwin's election he applied to him for a sinecure that would provide his family with bread and afford him the leisure to write. Early in January 1876 he was appointed state inspector of gas meters, a post that paid him a fee for each inspection and that therefore became less lucrative as fewer meters were installed during the years of depression. This position he kept until he was deprived of it by the next governor — long enough to have enabled him to complete his great work.

George now had his own well-stocked collection of books as well as access to several public and private libraries. To his mother he wrote on November 13, 1876: "I propose to read and study; to write some things which will extend my reputation, and perhaps to deliver some lectures with the same view. If I live I will make myself known, even in Philadelphia. I aim high." For all his eagerness to concentrate on his main task, he could not abstain from speaking his mind on the affairs of the day. No longer having access to an editorial page, he began to voice his views from the public platform. During the Hayes-Tilden campaign he became known as one of the best political speakers in California. While not a prepossessing figure on the rostrum — he was a rather short, bald, untidy man with a reddish beard — he more than made up for this deficiency in the logic of his thought and the fervor of his delivery.

The following March he was invited by the University of California to deliver a lecture on political economy. His friends on the faculty were hoping that he would be appointed to the first professorship in this subject. But George was not the man who aimed to please. He spoke his mind with a frankness and an iconoclasm which precluded his consideration for the chair. Addressing himself to the students, he insisted that the study of political economy required not so much teachers and textbooks as the ability to think straight and to the root of things.

All this array of professors, all this paraphernalia of learning cannot educate a man. They can help him to educate himself. Here you may obtain the tools, but they will be useful only to him who can use them. A monkey with a microscope, a mule packing a library, are fit emblems of the men — and, unfortunately, they are plenty — who pass through the whole educational machinery and come out learned fools, crammed with knowledge which they cannot use — all the more pitiable, all the more contemptible, all the more in the way of real progress, because they pass, with themselves and others, as educated men.

Several months later he was the chief orator at San Francisco's celebration of Independence Day. Here was his opportunity to speak on the meaning of liberty — the subject dearest to his heart — and he had prepared for it with exceeding care. His address was polished, pointed, passionate. His apotheosis of liberty, rising to metaphysical loftiness, was no doubt beyond the grasp of his sweltering audience, and belongs more fittingly to the pages of *Progress and Poverty* where he later inserted it. But the people did not fail to appreciate his deep sincerity and his glowing praise of the principles upon which our republic had been founded. And not a few understood and applauded when he said:

Wealth in itself is a good, not an evil; but wealth concentrated in the hands of a few, corrupts on the one side, and degrades on the other. No chain is stronger than its weakest link, and the ultimate condition of any people must be the condition of its lowest class. . . . In the long run, no nation can be freer than its most oppressed, richer than its poorest, wiser than its most ignorant.

In 1878, even while deeply engrossed in writing his masterpiece, he took the time not only to deliver two important lectures but also to campaign for political office. So overflowing was he with the theme of poverty and its abolition by means of taxing land values that it crept into everything he did. Even in his address on Moses — a fervent and highly finished piece of writing — he could not help reverting to it again and again:

For all this wonderful increase in knowledge, for all this enormous gain in productive power, where is the country in the civilized world in which today there is no want and suffering — where the masses are not condemned to toil that gives no leisure, and all classes are not pursued by a greed of gain that makes life an ignoble struggle to get and to keep?

The grievous depression of 1877 with its widespread suffering and sporadic labor strikes impelled George to begin the writing of *Progress and Poverty*. He was then in debt again, his income from inspecting meters was dwindling, and he had to pawn his watch for some ready cash; but the theme of his book had taken complete possession of him. For eighteen months he devoted most of his waking hours to the great task, and when the last page was finished he wept like a child at the thought of having accomplished his life's major work. He knew he had written a capital book and said so to his father and friends. To John Swinton, the New York reformer, he stated that it was " the most important contribution to the science of political economy yet made."

In any evaluation of *Progress and Poverty* it is important to remember that the book was completed in 1879, when the Ricardian principles of political economy were still widely accepted, and that George was right in regarding Mill as the outstanding exponent of these principles. Nor should it be forgotten that George was wholly self-taught, that there were obvious lacunae in his knowledge of economic literature, and that he arrived at his doctrine deductively and philosophically. His aim was to demolish those principles which he believed false and detrimental to the welfare of mankind and to replace them with others which would explain the causes of poverty and the means of abolishing it.

George began with the problem which had long tormented him.

Where the conditions to which material progress everywhere tends are most fully realized — that is to say, where population is densest, wealth greatest, and the machinery of production and exchange most highly developed — we find the deepest poverty, the sharpest struggle for existence, and the most enforced idleness.

Before he could come to grips with this basic problem, however, he felt compelled to clear away the theoretical obstacles which the economists before him had erected as valid reasons for the perpetual existence of poverty. Of these, the chief were the so-called iron law of wages and the Malthusian doctrine that population tends to increase faster than the means of subsistence. Familiar with some of the attacks made upon these theories by later economists, he proceeded to disprove them anew with such irrefutable logic and slashing statement that nothing remained of them except the prejudices at their source.

In opposition to these pessimistic doctrines, which condemned the mass of mankind to a subsistence level and political economy to a state of hopelessness, George argued persuasively that man was an intelligent and ingenious creature and therefore able to meet any situation he might come up against. If laborers lived in want, it was not because their great number made the share of each in the available wages fund a mere pittance. This wages-fund theory, he pointed out, was a mere figment, since "wages, instead of being drawn from capital, are in reality drawn from the product of the labor for which they are paid." Nor had the Malthusian doctrine any basis in fact since, as he proved by a forceful analysis of the theory of population, "the law of population accords with and is subordinate to the law of intellectual development, and any danger that human beings may be brought into the world where they cannot be provided for arises not from the ordinances of nature, but from social maladjustments that in the midst of wealth condemn men to want." He asserted, moreover, that "in a state of equality the natural increase of population would constantly tend to make every individual richer instead of poorer."

Having removed the negative obstacles which in his view explained nothing and merely obscured the basic causes of poverty, George proceeded to examine the laws which govern the distribution of wealth. Here he followed Ricardian economics fairly closely. Land included "all natural opportunities or forces"; labor embraced "all human exertion," being "the active and initial force . . . the raw material of wealth"; capital consisted of "wealth used to produce more wealth" and therefore "not a necessary factor in production," since it must first be produced by labor before it became available. Rent from land was the price of monopoly and was "determined by the excess of its produce over that which the same application can secure from the least productive land in use." Consequently rent tended to increase as production increased and thus served to keep down wages and interest—a crucial factor in the distribution of wealth.

His inquiry into the causes of the increase of rent disclosed that the growth of population was not a basic cause, since rent advanced even where population remained stationary. The true cause inhered in the private monopoly of land. For any increase in the production of wealth inevitably stimulated the demand for land — with a consequent rise in rent. The landlord thus tended to receive the greater share of this increased wealth, which in turn resulted in a maladjustment of wealth and recurrent economic depressions. As George summarized his finding:

The great cause of the inequality in the distribution of wealth is inequality in the ownership of land. The ownership of land is the great fundamental fact which ultimately determines the social, the political, and consequently the intellectual and moral conditions of a people.

The remedy was to abolish the private ownership of land. Despite its radical implications, George found " that nothing short of making land common property can permanently relieve poverty and check the tendency of wages to the starvation point." To justify such drastic action against the present owners of land, he investigated the nature of property and concluded that " there is a fundamental and irreconcilable difference between property in things which are the product of labor and property in land." While one was obtained by honest human effort and therefore had the sanction of justice and equity, the other was originally seized by force and fraud and was indefensible. Moreover, the recognition of individual ownership of land " always has, and always must, as development proceeds, lead to the enslavement of the laboring class." Justice therefore demanded that landowners be curbed and that the land be restored to the people as a whole. " When a title rests but on force, no complaint can be made when force annuls it. Whenever the people, having the power, choose to annul these titles, no objection can be made in the name of justice."

He next met the expected objection that the socialization of land was detrimental to its best use. He pointed out that the private ownership of land frequently blocked its improvement and use — the vacant lots in crowded urban centers and large estates in the country being obvious examples — while land held in common was generally improved and used for the good of all. Having demonstrated the greater utility of land belonging to society over that owned by private individuals, he next discussed the most desirable method of abolishing the monopoly on land. To his mind neither nationalization nor confiscation was advisable. In order to disturb the status quo as little as possible, he was willing for the owners to retain the shell — provided they were deprived of the kernel. To this end he suggested a tax on the full value of the land, explaining that such a tax would not only help remove iniquity from society but would also suffice for all public needs and thus make all other taxes superfluous.

What I propose, therefore, is the simple yet sovereign remedy, which will raise wages, increase the earnings of capital, extirpate pauperism, abolish poverty, give remunerative employment to whoever wishes it, afford free scope to human powers, lessen crime, elevate morals, and taste, and intelligence, purify government and carry civilization to yet nobler heights, is — to appropriate rent by taxation.

Such a tax, bearing lightly on production, collected easily and cheaply, unshiftable, certain, and equitable, was in his belief not only the most just of all taxes but the only one bound "to stimulate industry, to open new opportunities to capital, and to increase the production of wealth."

George devoted the final section of *Progress and Poverty* to the law of human progress. He argued persuasively that economic disparities in civilization were due, not to differences in individuals, but to differences in social organization; that progress, stimulated by association, tended to be checked by the emergence of inequality. "Association in equality" was therefore the law of progress, and our own civilization, already showing signs of decay caused by inequality, must eliminate its social maladjustments if it was not to suffer the fate of earlier civilizations. Since the basic source of inequality lay in land monopoly, the taxation of land values would not only assure justice and equality to all men but would also provide fresh impetus toward greater progress.

The foregoing summary of the contents of *Progress and Poverty* gives but an indication of the book's scope and purpose. Even now, nearly seventy years later, one cannot read it without being moved by its clear style, the cogency of its logical exposition, the prophetic vision of its social message. The work has its obvious limitations, and its proposed remedy may be impugned as unfair and inadequate, but the reader cannot fail to be impressed by its high purpose and passionate sincerity. For the problem of poverty has continued to plague our civilization, and no other reformer has attacked it so fundamentally and so eloquently. Having felt its grievous effects to the despair of starvation, George perceived it as " the open-mouthed, relentless hell which yawns beneath civilized society. . . . For poverty is not merely deprivation; it means shame, degradation; the searing of the most sensitive parts of our moral and mental nature as with hot irons; the denial of the strongest impulses and sweetest affections; the wrenching of the most vital nerves." It was to remove this social cancer from the body of mankind that he wrote the book; and it was this high aim, expressed with compelling forcefulness, that inspired many of its multitude of readers to join him in the great effort. What appealed to them most was the simplicity of the remedy: no bloody revolution, no radical overthrow of government, no disruption of industrial enterprise — only a change in taxation which would right a long-standing wrong.

In an obvious sense *Progress and Poverty* was, as Parrington has indicated, George's reaction to " the policy of pre-emption, exploitation, and progress of the Gilded Age." In his own state of California he witnessed grants of land to the railroad companies amounting to 16,387,000,000 acres, or sixteen percent of the total area. Also, within eighteen years of the first pre-emption act in 1863, the state disposed of all its vast public lands. This misappropriation of common property, with its consequent social maladjustments, struck fire in George's heart and gave him no rest until he had exposed the wrong and pointed out the remedy. An even deeper purpose of the book was, in the words of Parrington, " to

humanize and democratize political economy, that it might serve
social ends rather than class exploitation." For in George's day
economists regarded poverty as "the result of an inevitable law,"
and thus sanctioned the grievous exploitation of the laborer as well
as the ruthlessness of laissez-faire enterprise. As a genuine democrat
he refused to accept such a "law" and expounded to his fellow
men a glorious future: the identification of "the law of social life
with the great moral law of justice: a vision of progress without
poverty, material enrichment based on equality, man rising to new
spiritual heights."

Eastern publishers did not share George's opinion of the book
and none would at first undertake to bring it out. It was only after
a friendly printer in San Francisco had agreed to make a set of
plates and run off an author's edition of five hundred copies that
D. Appleton and Company were persuaded to use the plates for
a trade edition. George sent a number of copies to leaders of public opinion in this country and abroad, and most of these responded
promptly and appreciatively. The book sold very sluggishly, and
the English publisher was able to dispose of only twenty copies
during the first few months.

Meantime George, considerably in debt and desperately in need
of work, borrowed the fare to New York in the hope of finding
employment on one of the city's newspapers. Failing in this effort,
he undertook whatever odd jobs he came upon. His strong concern
with the land problem caused him to interest himself in the current
agitation against landlordism in Ireland. The Irish in New York
welcomed him and engaged him to lecture on the land question.
Ever ready with his pen, he decided to review the situation in Ireland in the light of the universal land problem; and the resulting
brochure, *The Irish Land Question* (subsequently retitled *The Land
Question* because of its general implications and conclusions),
made him something of a hero among the Irish and led them to give
the booklet wide circulation. This publicity reacted favorably on
the sale of *Progress and Poverty* and induced many newspapers and

magazines in this country and in Great Britain to review the book seriously and at length. A five-column leader in the London *Times* helped the volume to spectacular popularity. Labor leaders, with Powderley of the Knights of Labor at their head, recommended the work enthusiastically to their followers. Cheap editions soon outsold the most popular fiction. Before long everyone seemed to be reading and discussing *Progress and Poverty*, and George found himself famous. In Ireland and England, where he went as a correspondent for the New York *Irish World* in October 1881, he was widely acclaimed.

This extraordinary enthusiasm for a book dealing radically with a fundamental social problem — around three million copies have been disposed of to date, a runaway record for a book in economics — greatly perturbed the academic guardians of the science of economics. In the judgment of these scholars, who were just then making a great effort to replace the theories of the Smith-Ricardo-Mill school with views consonant with the latest scientific principles, George's indebtedness to that school stamped him as a lay meddler. His deliberate, almost evangelical fusion of economics with ethics struck them as rank heresy — being contrary to their painful attempts to divorce the two disciplines. His proposed remedy of taxing land values to the exclusion of all other taxes appeared to them unscientific, highly unjust, and, in view of its great popular appeal, dangerously demagogic. Alfred Marshall, soon to become their chief spokesman, and the dying Arnold Toynbee each tried to demolish the book in three analytical lectures; Herbert Spencer, Lord Bramwell, the Duke of Argyll, and practically all American economists scorned him as an ignorant intruder into their special field of knowledge.

The socialists, in the 1880's struggling for public attention, were likewise critical of George's proposed remedy for the social maladjustment which they regarded as their special concern. They approved, of course, of his castigation of the existing order and sympathized with his desire to abolish poverty, but they insisted that a tax on land values would affect only a fraction of the surplus value created by labor and could not therefore accomplish all that George claimed for it. They moreover disparaged what they considered his misunderstanding of the nature of capital and his rejection of the doctrine of the class struggle. His remedy, they contended, might suffice for the primitive agricultural society, in which land was the " primary, all-inclusive element," but was wholly inadequate in our era of monopolistic industrialism. When Karl Marx was given a copy of *Progress and Poverty*, he looked it through and remarked that it was " the capitalists' last ditch."

Ironically enough, George was largely responsible for the rise of socialism in England, which he had visited at an opportune time. Most of the liberal and labor intellectuals of the discontented 1880's, who later gravitated towards socialism, crowded first to his standard. " Henry George," wrote John A. Hobson, " may be considered to have exercised a more directly formative and educative influence over English radicalism of the last fifteen years [1882–1897] than any other man."

George, in turn, was quite contemptuous of socialism, and regarded Karl Marx as " a most superficial thinker, and entangled in an inexact and vicious terminology." The American reformer was indeed a genuine individualist, a product of the eighteenth-century equalitarianism. Thomas Jefferson was his patron saint, and the Declaration of Independence his revered Decalogue. In an address in Baltimore on " The Democratic Principle " he stated: " Our belief is that of Thomas Jefferson; our aim is his aim and our hope his hope." He regarded the doctrines of natural law and natural rights as sacrosanct and argued that even if these rights had no actual historical basis, they were so obviously the higher goal of human striving that one should work for their realization as a matter of simple justice. He assumed that a true understanding of natural laws would lead to the establishment of equality and justice and bring society to a state of blessedness. His theory of reform, as expounded in *Progress and Poverty*, was based upon these moral

[271]

principles and was thus "but the carrying out in letter and spirit of the truth enunciated in the Declaration of Independence — the 'self-evident' truth that is the heart and soul of the Declaration — 'That all men are created equal; that they are endowed by their Creator with certain inalienable rights; that among these rights are life, liberty, and the pursuit of happiness!'"

His great book having initiated a social movement, George became acutely conscious of his responsibilities as the prophet of social reform. The popularity of *The Irish Land Question* made it possible for him to visit Great Britain, and he took advantage of the opportunity to preach his philosophy in that country. The enthusiasm of the growing host of British admirers was balm to his soul, and he was glad in the course of the next few years to make several missionary excursions to England.

When George returned to New York after his first trip, he had already acquired an international reputation. The bounty of one of his admirers and his success as a lecturer and writer at last freed him from the drag of poverty. A whole-hearted believer in education, he took every opportunity to apply his philosophy to problems of current interest. Again and again he lectured before labor and other groups on the cause and cure of social maladjustments. Since politicians were then advocating tariffs as a means of raising wages, he exposed their pretenses and indicated the true source of higher wages.

He interrupted this work, however, when *Frank Leslie's Illustrated Newspaper*, eager for a feature to counterbalance Professor W. G. Sumner's articles in *Harper's Weekly*, asked him to write a series of thirteen essays on "Problems of the Times." These discussions he revised and expanded into a book which he published in 1883 under the title of *Social Problems*. In essence a popular application of his land doctrine to current questions, its central thesis was that "at the root of every social problem lies a social wrong." Most essential in righting these wrongs was a just distribution of wealth, which he defined as follows:

To secure to each the free use of his own power, limited only by the equal freedom of all others; to secure to each the full enjoyment of his own earnings, limited only by such contributions as he may be fairly called upon to make for purposes of common benefit.

Since men now lacked such economic justice, he argued, they behaved like hungry hogs before a pail of swill; with wealth justly distributed, men would behave everywhere with the ease and grace of those seated at a banquet table. Moreover, without economic justice, political democracy remained a myth.

Democratic government in more than name can exist only where wealth is distributed with something like equality — when the great mass of citizens are personally free and independent, neither fettered by their poverty, nor made subject by their wealth.

This equality, he insisted, could be attained only by the land reform — truly " the greatest of social revolutions." He declared that our great material development necessitated a higher moral standard.

Civilization, as it progresses, *requires* a higher conscience, a keener sense of justice, a warmer brotherhood, a wider, loftier, truer public spirit. Failing these, civilization must pass into destruction. . . . For civilization knits men more and more closely together, and constantly tends to subordinate the individual to the whole, and to make more and more important social conditions.

While in the British Isles in 1883, addressing large audiences under the auspices of the Land Reform Union, he was attacked by the Duke of Argyll in an article, " The Prophet of San Francisco," published in *Nineteenth Century*. This titled critic termed George a " Preacher of Unrighteousness " because of his uncompromising attitude towards landowners. On his return to New York the " Prophet of San Francisco " composed a reply, published in the same periodical, which slashed to shreds the Duke's argument that landlords have a right to the monopolistic use of their land regardless of the manner in which it was originally acquired or of the nature of property in land.

George next devoted himself to writing his book on the tariff problem. So popular had he become by this time that he was able to obtain $3000 for several of the finished chapters of *Protection or Free Trade*, and this money enabled him to publish the volume during the summer of 1886. The work had a tremendous circulation, owing largely to the efforts of Tom L. Johnson, who had become converted to George's views. In 1890 Johnson, then in Congress, succeeded, with the aid of several fellow Congressmen, in placing the entire contents of the book in the *Congressional Record*. Hundreds of thousands of copies were sent to constituents of these and other members of Congress, and the total distribution, including various cheap editions, exceeded two million copies.

Protection or Free Trade contains some of George's most lucid writing and is undoubtedly one of the clearest and most cogent discussions of free trade ever published. In it he argued from general principles to the logical conclusion that not only was protection based on a fallacy but that genuine free trade involved the abolition of all tariffs and taxes and led to the confiscation of land values. He attacked the prevailing tariffs as a hidden tax on labor, " the producer of all wealth "; as conducive to " corruption, evasion, and false swearing "; as antagonistic to " improvements in transportation and labor-saving devices." In brief, " the restrictions which protection urges us to impose upon ourselves are about as well calculated to promote national prosperity as ligatures, that would impede the circulation of the blood, would be to promote bodily health and comfort." Protection, moreover, could not be of more than temporary benefit to any class of producers except monopolists because of the fact that competition within a country tended to keep profits to a common level.

George asserted that the principle of free trade derived from the right of each man to the full produce of his labor. Consequently, to insure this right, free trade required " the sweeping away of all tariffs . . . the abolition of all indirect taxes of whatever kind . . . as well [as] all direct taxes on things that are the produce of labor." There remained only the taxes on ostentation and land values. To justify the land tax George reiterated the ethical argument for the common ownership of land.

Land in itself has no value. Value arises only from human labor. It is not until the ownership of land becomes equivalent to the ownership of laborers that any value attaches to it. And where land has a speculative value it is because of the expectation that the growth of society will in the future make its ownership equivalent to the ownership of laborers.

From a moral standpoint, therefore,

Property in land is as indefensible as property in man. It is so absurdly impolitic, so outrageously unjust, so flagrantly subversive of the true right of property, that it can only be instituted by force and maintained by confounding in the popular mind the distinction between property in land and property in things that are the result of labor.

George was opposed, however, to the nationalization of land. He believed that " all men have equal rights to the use and enjoyment of the elements provided by Nature," and that any form of communism must interfere with these rights. He criticized the socialists for not thinking the matter through — asserting that their views were " a high-purposed but incoherent mixture of truth and fallacy." To him any dependence on government for the insurance of justice and equality was shortsighted so long as mankind was dominated by greed and force.

All schemes for securing equality in the conditions of men by placing the distribution of wealth in the hands of government have the fatal defect of beginning at the wrong end. They presuppose pure government; but it is not government that makes society; it is society that makes government; and *until* there is something like substantial equality in the distribution of wealth, we cannot expect pure government.

In 1886 George was invited by the united labor unions of New York to become their candidate for mayor. He had not thought of entering politics, and had made definite plans for a lecture tour and for the publication of a weekly journal of opinion; but when the labor leaders, who hoped to capitalize on his popularity, met his stipulation by obtaining thirty thousand bona fide signatures, he decided to enter the campaign. To a friend he wrote: " If I do go into the fight, the campaign will bring the land question into practical politics and do more to popularize its discussion than years of writing would do."

It was the first election in New York to be fought on social issues. George gave no quarter and attacked his rivals with all his forensic power, speaking as often as twelve and fourteen times daily. His opponents, Abram S. Hewitt and young Theodore Roosevelt, took full advantage of the fact that he was backed by radical groups and asserted that the horrors of the French Terror would seem mild in comparison with the hell that would be let loose by George's election. The Catholic hierarchy likewise opposed his candidacy and brought about the excommunication of the Rev. Edward Mc-Glynn when he insisted on speaking in George's favor. When the votes were counted, Tammany emerged victorious — but only because its henchmen had thrown many George ballots into the East River. George himself was gratified by his large vote and believed that the land question had become a political issue. His position in the campaign was well stated by his eldest son:

Rather than a seeker for office, he was a man with a mission, preaching the way to cast out involuntary poverty from civilization. Rather than a politician ready to pare away and compromise, he pressed straight for equality and freedom, and in a breath-taking way struck at the ignorant prejudices of his own followers as sharply as at those of his fiercest antagonists.

Several days after the election he spoke encouragingly to a large gathering of his followers. " It is not the end of the campaign," he assured them, " but the beginning. We have fought the first skirmish." The following year he ran as candidate for Secretary of State and campaigned across the state with unabated zeal. But his unwillingness to compromise alienated the socialists and brought about the disruption of the tenuously united labor party. The final vote for George was disappointingly small, and both the candidate and his labor backers decided they had had enough of politics.

Immediately after the mayoralty election George began to organize the staff for his long-projected weekly newspaper, *The Standard*, and employed such experienced journalists as William T. Croasdale and Louis F. Post. The first issue appeared on January 8, 1887, and because it was devoted to the flagrant case of Father McGlynn it achieved a circulation of 75,000 copies; subsequently it maintained a level of about 25,000 copies. During its five years of existence *The Standard* was very actively concerned with the reforms of the day. George's pungent editorials put him in the forefront of political journalism. The weekly also sponsored and devoted much space to the Anti-Poverty Society, which was headed by Father McGlynn and which aimed to spread the doctrine that "God has made ample provision for the need of all" and that poverty is caused by man-made laws. In 1890, however, shortly after his return from a triumphant but exhausting tour of Australia by way of Europe, George suffered a mild stroke. Thereafter the periodical declined, and in August 1892 it ceased publication.

A sojourn in Bermuda helped George to recover at least the appearance of health. He at once began to work on a book that would round out his principles of political economy and establish his doctrine on a philosophical foundation firm enough to withstand all the assaults of his academic opponents. The following remark in a letter written on April 28, 1891 suggests that, despite his insistence to the contrary, he was very sensitive to their criticism: "How persistent is the manner in which the professors and those who esteem themselves the learned class ignore and slur me; but I am not conscious of any other feeling about it than that of a certain curiosity."

As was the case with his two other major works, he interrupted his efforts on his new book in order to attend to controversial matters of more immediate importance. Pope Leo XIII's encyclical letter on "The Condition of Labor," while criticizing all radical means of improving the lot of labor, appeared to George to aim its shafts particularly at the theories of land reform. His reply, extending to about 25,000 words, politely and modestly analyzed the Pope's fallacious reasoning and reaffirmed the sound Christian basis of his own doctrine. He submitted that, because the essence of religion was equality before God, " the social question is at bottom a religious question." Consequently his economic remedy was offered " not as a cunning device of human ingenuity, but as a conforming of human regulation to the will of God." He also elaborated upon the justness and advantages of the tax on land values. And, while he joined the Pope in condemning the " forcible communism " of the socialists, he asserted that in his view " voluntary communism might be the highest possible state of which man can conceive."

George's vehement attack on Herbert Spencer was occasioned by the latter's presumed apostasy from the views on the land question which he had expressed in *Social Statics*. This book, published in 1850, was one of the seminal studies of the nature of property in land. George had come upon it at the time when he was first struggling with the problem, and its forceful logic had helped him to formulate his conclusions. George sent Spencer a copy of *Progress and Poverty*, but received no acknowledgment. Two years later, when they met in London, Spencer's defense of the Irish landlords irritated the American. Then came the controversy between Spencer and his critics in which the author of *Social Statics* virtually repudiated his own book and merely confused the issue by his effort to differentiate between absolute and relative ethics. This was followed by a new edition of the book, with the disputed chapter on land entirely omitted and the sections on property revised to accord with the author's later views. Since this recantation was not accompanied by an offer of new evidence but rested upon a reinterpretation of the original premise, George concluded that his one-time mentor had committed intellectual treason.

A *Perplexed Philosopher*, published in 1892, while bitter and almost scurrilous in the sections dealing with Spencer's apostasy, presents an incisive review of the latter's treatment of the land problem and a critical analysis of synthetic philosophy. By way of illustration George reiterated his own belief in Jeffersonian democracy.

The sphere of government begins where the freedom of competition ends, since in no other way can equal liberty be assured. But within this line I have always opposed governmental interference. I have been an active, consistent and absolute free trader, and an opponent of all schemes that would limit the freedom of the individual. I have been a stauncher denier of the assumption of the right of society to the possessions of each member, and a clearer and more resolute upholder of the rights of property than has Mr. Spencer. I have opposed every proposition to help the poor at the expense of the rich.

However, while he held " the rights of property to be absolute," he insisted that land values lacked the rights inherent in the produce of labor. As a concrete example of this distinction he pointed out that " if the population and business of London could be transported to a newly risen island in the Antipodes, land there would become as valuable as land in London now; and that, though all improvements were to be left behind, the value of land in London would disappear." Since land values were created by society and not by individual labor, the inequity arising from the individual ownership of land might be removed without doing violence to the rights of legitimate property.

So far from the destruction of those spurious and injurious rights of property which have wound around the useful rights of property, like choking weeds around a fruitful vine, being calculated to injure that respect for property on which wealth and prosperity and civilization depend, the reverse is the case.

These interruptions over, George returned to his work on *The Science of Political Economy*, which he did not live to complete and which his eldest son edited and published in 1898. His primary aim was to " put the ideas embodied in *Progress and Poverty* in the setting of a complete economic treatise, and without controversy." He wanted to relate the science of political economy to all human activity, to make clear the principles deriving from nature and affecting the life of man. He began with the familiar axiom that " men seek to gratify their desires with the least exertion," and broadened it into a fundamental law:

This disposition of men to seek the satisfaction of their desires with the minimum of exertion is so universal and unfailing that it constitutes one of those invariable sequences that we denominate laws of nature, and from which we may safely reason. It is this law of nature that is the fundamental law of political economy.

From this central principle he developed the scientific structure of our modern economic society into which he fitted every aspect of economic life. He restated and amplified his views on the nature of land and labor, wealth and capital, production and distribution. He stressed " the distinction between the productive power derived wholly from nature, for which its term is land, and the productive power derived from human exertion, for which its term is labor." Value was determined by labor but measured by effective demand; " thus it is not exchangeability that gives value, but value that gives exchangeability." Wealth he defined as " the embodiment or storage in material form of action aiming at the satisfaction of desire, so that this action obtains a certain permanence." Capital " is but a part of wealth, differing from other wealth only in its use, which is not to satisfy desire, but indirectly to satisfy desire, by associating in the production of other wealth." Consequently wages were paid not out of capital but out of the product of labor, and interest became the wages of capital. Production was obtained by means of adapting, growing, and exchanging — their importance being in the order given. " Production and distribution are in fact not separate things, but two mentally distinguishable parts of one thing — the exertion of human labor in the satisfaction of human desire." Money he defined as the common medium of exchange used in any time and place.

From the point of view of the rising generation of economists, who stressed data and facts rather than standards and values, the book was out of date before it was published. They therefore ignored it in their teaching and thus prevented it from exerting any influence on the subsequent development of economic theory. Despite this neglect, however, the work remains a milestone in American economic thought. It was the most ambitious undertaking attempted by an American up to that time and it towers as a contribution to the understanding of how men make their living. For George did not limit himself to the mechanics of economic activity, but sought to discover the causes of social maladjustments as well as their remedy — the establishment of equality and justice as the guiding principles of society. It was indeed this prophetic vision plus his remarkable ability as a writer of lucid prose that, all his limitations notwithstanding, give his major books the stamp of greatness.

In 1897, while devoting to his writing all the time that his precarious health would permit, he again received a call to become candidate for mayor of New York City, this time from the " Party of Thomas Jefferson." The appeal of duty was irresistible. He knew that the liberal groups had no other man around whom they could unite, and he could not fail them. Nor was he unaware of the stimulus his election would give to the cause to which he had devoted his life. When the doctors warned him that the rigors of the campaign would probably prove fatal, he answered: " How could I do better than die serving humanity? Besides, so dying will do more for the cause than anything I am likely to be able to do in the rest of my life." For a while the excitement of the campaign seemed to invigorate him, but after three weeks of strenuous exertion he began to show signs of collapse. On October 28, five days before the election, he found himself unable to go on after his fourth speech. Fatigued and overworked, he died that night of a stroke of apoplexy.

New York was genuinely shocked by the tragedy. For the moment the election was forgotten. The loss of one of its greatest citizens completely overshadowed the normal activities of the metropolis. More than a hundred thousand mourners filed past George's bier, and an equal number, unable to enter the building, crowded the streets near by. A vast funeral procession followed the body to the City Hall and across Brooklyn Bridge to the cemetery. No other private citizen had ever received greater tribute from his fellow New Yorkers.

There are a number of things about Henry George's land doctrine with which one might disagree. Essentially, any social remedy that depends upon a single factor is almost certain to fail. While the tax on land values might have been of paramount importance in an agrarian economy, in a more complex society it can be considered only in association with other factors. One may doubt whether the common ownership of land can by itself give man the full produce of his labor in a monopolistic industrial society. For it is hardly true that the landlord now victimizes both the laborer and the capitalist; the latter himself is frequently a landlord and is, in any event, too powerful for anyone's exploitation. Thus a Henry Ford or a Du Pont is neither subject to the landlord's exaction nor at the mercy of a tax on land values. In this respect Karl Marx was more realistic in regarding ground rent as merely " a portion of the surplus value produced by industrial capital."

In considering the practicality of the single tax one must take into account the nature of the opposition. While George justified his remedy on moral grounds — at least to the satisfaction of his admirers — he disregarded the powerful opposition of the wealthy landlords and made little effort to mollify the small farmer who could not help fearing a confiscatory tax on the means of his livelihood. This shortcoming becomes all the more glaring when it is remembered that, although the farmers a half-century ago were a far more potent element of our population than the urban laborers, George concentrated his attention upon the grievous lot of the latter group.

It is not at all strange to find the professional economists disdaining George's land doctrine as the teaching of an untrained and confused layman. Even the more liberal insisted that economics was, like all sciences, descriptive and correlative and not normative and evaluative. In their view his reliance on the old, classical theory invalidated his writings. Certain aspects of his economic thought are no doubt open to criticism and have been dealt with by some of his discerning disciples. Yet his work taken as a whole places him in the very forefront of American economic thinkers. His system of political economy is, for all its flaws and " unscientific " emphasis, an original and positive formulation of a body of principles which has been condemned as a whole or in part by a number of the keenest academic minds but invalidated by none. And while the remedy of the single tax has failed to make its impress upon society, the philosophy underlying it has withstood the attacks of the acutest critics.

George's greatness, however, lies not in his originality as a political economist but in the combination of broad social vision with a passionate concern for the welfare of mankind. The love of liberty and equality spurred him to probe deeply into the causes of poverty and to discover the means for its alleviation. He had the opportunity to see, in the words of George Bernard Shaw, " in a single lifetime the growth of the whole tragedy of civilization from the primitive first clearing," and the creative intelligence to make use of this experience in arriving at a true understanding of the nature of society. He perceived that " the poverty which in the midst of abundance pinches and imbrutes men, and the manifold evils which flow from it, spring from a denial of justice "; that the source of poverty lies in the private monopoly of land; that economic equality was the essential criterion of true progress. He therefore preached that men

must have liberty to avail themselves of the opportunities and means of life; they must stand on equal terms with reference to the bounty of nature. Either this, or Liberty withdraws her light! Either this, or darkness comes on, and the very forces that progress has evolved turn to powers that work destruction. This is the universal law. This is the lesson of the centuries. Unless its foundations be laid in justice, the social structure cannot stand.

These are the words of a prophet. And his voice in behalf of righteousness rang out around the world, and many men blessed him while others scorned him. He became the protagonist of the rights of man — his one lapse in connection with the Haymarket anarchists was caused by misunderstanding — and he fought for them with all his mind and all his heart. John Dewey no doubt had in mind this combination of prophetic vision and passionate crusading when he stated: " It is the thorough fusion of insight into actual facts and forces, with recognition of their bearing upon what makes human life worth living, that constitutes Henry George one of the world's great social philosophers."

BROOKS ADAMS

JEREMIAN CRITIC OF CAPITALISM

T HE RECENT REISSUE of Brooks Adams's *The Law of Civilization and Decay*, with a long and illuminating introduction
by Charles A. Beard, is tardy recognition of a work of seminal significance. Published over a half-century ago, it was one of the
first efforts by an American scholar to study the roots of Western
civilization in order to discover the basic law which governed the
movement of society and to which mankind must pay heed if it was
to escape catastrophe. Although the book was received with greater
favor, both in England and in this country, than the author had anticipated — and Theodore Roosevelt's discerning analytical review
in *The Forum* was very gratifying to him — it made little impress
upon the thought of his contemporaries. Nor was this surprising.
The work appeared during the heated bimetallist controversy and
was at once branded by the " gold-bugs" as a defense of silver. Its
larger implications were overlooked by both factions, and the leading Brahmins of his own state of Massachusetts scorned the author
as the last and least worthy of the captious Adams tribe.

Yet this youngest son of Charles Francis Adams was in some essential respects the most original and profound member of that
highly distinguished family. His great-grandfather and grandfather
had been Presidents of the United States; his father had been the
extraordinarily capable minister to Great Britain during the crucial
period of the Civil War; the leading men of England and America
were the intimate friends of his family. He himself was in every

respect a true Adams. He grew up intensely proud of his heritage, and pride of family spurred his keen intelligence. Nor was it mere conceit. He and his brothers more than justified their acute sense of self-importance. In the words of the late Professor Parrington: "Intellectually curious, given to rationalism, retaining much of the eighteenth-century solidity of intellect and honest realism, refusing to barter principles for the good will of men, the Adams line produced no more characteristic offshoots than came in the fourth generation." But the defects of personality were equally prominent. According to James Russell Lowell, " the Adamses have a genius for saying even a gracious thing in an ungracious way." From the very first the family had always been prone to dramatize themselves. They had put themselves in leading positions, for which their intellects and their pride well fitted them, but which they had not the resolution to maintain. In debate and in their writings they were ever ready to exaggerate the hostility of their opponents. Misunderstanding, injurious to most men's pride, appeared also to flutter the pride of the Adamses. As if to conceal an innate shyness, they usually appeared brusque, often arrogant. None of the exceptionally able sons of Charles Francis Adams would deign to fit himself to the political hurly-burly of the post-Civil War decades; proud and disdainful men, and natural dissenters, they all turned from the making of history to writing about it.

Brooks, born in 1848, was a thoroughbred Adams. He was certain of his high intellectual capacities; he was driven by an acute social conscience and tormented by extreme shyness, as much the prig as his brother Henry. Both of them, according to the latter, " were used to audiences of one " — and suspicious of the motives of others. Brooks resented not being a member of the ruling class to which he belonged by right of birth, and he scorned those in power for their egregious lack of social responsibility. Brought up by a father whose puritanic severity had made his sons' childhood monotonous and dreary, to the end of his life Brooks took things very much to heart and became zealous for the sanctity of truth and justice. As his brother Henry wrote to him in 1910: " I have known you for sixty-odd years, and since you were a baby I've never known you when you weren't making yourself miserable over the failings of the universe. It has been your amusement, and a very good one."

Following the family tradition, Brooks studied at Harvard and became a lawyer. Jealous of his considerably older brothers and wishing to make his way unaided, he opened an office for himself and for eight years he waited for a practice that failed to materialize. It was not that he was deficient as a lawyer; his knowledge of the law in time became immense. Nor was he handicapped by an aristocratic scorn for material success; indeed, the idea of failure was wormwood to his inflated vanity. The truth was that even less than his brothers was he able to adapt himself to the grasping and often unscrupulous ways of his thriving contemporaries. He could no more truckle to clients than stoop to the deceitful tricks of his profession. It was not surprising therefore that his adherence to an ideal integrity soon gained him a reputation for eccentricity. " Brooks," wrote his brother Henry some years later, " irritated too many Boston conventions ever to suit the atmosphere." And to a friend he confided: " Brooks is too brutal, too blatant, too emphatic, and too intensely set on one line alone, at a time, to please any large number of people."

If Brooks never became a denizen of the marketplace, he was quick to note the principles and practices of those who dominated it. To his puritanic mind these practices were the abominations of Baal. He shuddered to think that the leading men of the state which his fathers had cradled and preserved had forfeited their spiritual birthright in the mad scramble for wealth. Before long State Street became to him, even more than to the other Adamses, the symbol of all that was crass and iniquitous. The more he detested this crassness, however, the more his mind became preoccupied with it, and he struggled with it during the remainder of his life even as the orthodox Puritan contended with sin. Having early inherited from his maternal grandfather enough money to keep him in comfort to the end of his days, he decided in 1881 to close his law office and to devote himself to his favorite study of economic history.

The next forty-odd years of his life — he died in 1927 — were outwardly uneventful to a singular degree. He married in 1889, traveled abroad a good deal, and taught law at Boston University from 1904 till he was dismissed for his dangerous ideas in 1911. Reading and writing were his chief occupations. His few friends delighted in conversing with him but usually rejected his ideas as eccentric. The following comment by Justice Holmes is characteristic of this attitude: " I have found him more suggestive than almost anyone, generally with propositions which I don't believe."

Toward the end of his days he sometimes felt the need of spiritual certainty. Proud dissenter that he was, he once stood up in the Stone Church at Quincy and, in the manner of his Puritan forefathers, made public profession of his faith: " Lord, I believe, help thou mine unbelief." But his prayer was of little avail. To the last he was too honest with himself to nurse a faith which was not in him.

Brooks Adams first turned to the history of the early years of his native state in order to trace the transference of power from the priesthood to the merchant class. An enterprising Boston publisher heard of his project and contracted for the publication of the manuscript. In 1886, after years of intense research and hard thinking, he completed his work on *The Emancipation of Massachusetts*. The book aroused considerable controversy, and was damned and praised with equal promptitude. It was in truth an iconoclastic appraisal of our Colonial past — one of the first histories to treat persons and events with the critical objectivity of the scholar rather than with the gloss of the sentimental chronicler. He thus struck a body blow against the time-honored prejudices that had pervaded historical writing up to that time. " From that day," his friend W. C. Ford testified, " the filiopietistic school of history was laughed out of court."

If documentary evidence formed its basis, the book throbbed

with passion for freedom of thought. Shocked to find that there had been so much cruelty, persecution, and greed in the early life of Massachusetts, Brooks unfolded the terrible record with relentless severity. He had nothing but scorn for a clergy who had perverted the Puritan Commonwealth — child of the Reformation and predicated on the assertion of the freedom of the mind — into a "cesspool of iniquity" more intolerable than the one they had fled. Nor had he anything to retract when he issued a new edition some thirty years later, regretting only the "acrimonious tone" of certain passages.

For the rule of the clergy in early Massachusetts resembled all other clerical exercises of temporal power.

The power of the priesthood [Brooks declared] lies in submission to a creed. In their onslaughts on rebellion they have exhausted human torments; nor, in their lust for earthly dominion, have they felt remorse, but rather joy, when slaying Christ's enemies and their own. The horrors of the Inquisition, the Massacre of St. Bartholomew, the atrocities of Laud, the abominations of the Scotch Kirk, the persecution of the Quakers had one object, — the enslavement of the mind.

In chapter after chapter Brooks described in factual detail how, in the fanatic pursuit of conformity, the Puritan clergy and elders cruelly persecuted Anabaptists, Quakers, women accused as witches, and religious liberals — basing their criminal code on Pentateuch law and turning their parishioners into neurotic censors and vindictive zealots. Although the life of the Puritan Commonwealth was allegedly based on the freedom of worship, "this great and noble principle is fatal to the temporal power of a priesthood, and during the supremacy of the clergy the government was doomed to be both persecuting and repressive." Indeed, the petty state was "ruled by an autocratic priesthood whose power rested upon legislation antagonistic to English law," and "the elders clung obstinately to every privilege which served their ends, and repudiated every obligation which conflicted with their ambition."

The leaders are drawn to life. Governor Winthrop, John Cotton, the Mathers — these and numerous others Brooks quoted to their own condemnation as cruel and conceited bigots. Increase Mather was pictured as having " an inordinate love of money and flattery," as a preacher who " delighted to blazon himself as Christ's foremost champion in the land." And of his son Cotton's pious attempts to justify the burning of witches, Brooks remarked: " It is not credible that an educated and a sane man could ever have honestly believed in the absurd stuff which he produced as evidence of the supernatural." Father and son were quoted at length on their opposition to Leverett's appointment to the presidency of Harvard, and only after reading their epistles to Governor Dudley and their diary notations can one appreciate Brooks's satisfaction in their final discomfiture: " But these venomous priests had tried their fangs upon a resolute and able man. Dudley shook them off like vermin."

The Boston Brahmins never forgave Brooks Adams for his scathing portrayal of their Puritan ancestors. But he was ready for the role of Ishmael, and disdained the society of those whom he did not respect. He had the stimulating companionship of his wife, his brothers, and friends like Holmes and Ford, and he had no desire for more. His researches in the field of religion had greatly exercised his imagination and provided him with intimations of the nature of civilization, and these he was determined to develop. He began to read history backwards and to examine the elements of social organization, from period to period, from modern times to the darkness of antiquity. He also traveled in those countries which, once civilized, had since relapsed into barbarism or insignificance. Everywhere he gathered material and gained new impressions; everywhere he studied the relation between man and his environment. On his return home to Quincy, he was ready to organize his newly gained information and note the result.

When Henry Adams came to spend the summer of 1893 in Quincy he found Brooks absorbed in bringing his conclusions on the nature of civilization into coherent form. The two brothers gave many hours to comparing views and clearing up points on which they differed. After Henry had read the first version of his brother's manuscript he noted:

Brooks had discovered or developed a law of history that civilization followed the exchanges, and having worked it out for the Mediterranean was working it out for the Atlantic. Everything American, as well as most things European and Asiatic, became unstable by this law, seeking new equilibrium and compelled to find it. Loving paradox, Brooks, with the advantages of ten years' study, had swept away much rubbish in the effort to build up a new line of thought for himself, but he found that no paradox compared with that of daily events. The facts were constantly outrunning his thoughts. The instability was greater than he calculated; the speed of acceleration passed bounds.

That winter and the following year Brooks worked hard on the revision of his manuscript. When he submitted the finished version to Henry, the latter assured him that it was much improved and ready for publication. Being essentially a timid man, however, Henry not only refused to have the book dedicated to him but warned his brother not to publish it if he had any thought of taking part in public life. "The book is wholly, absolutely, and exclusively yours. Not a thought in it has any parentage of mine. Not only am I not in it, but it is strongly contrary to my rigid rules of conduct. . . . I do not care to monkey with a dynamo. If you choose to do it, well and good! " Brooks was not in the least intimidated. He would state the truth as he saw it, come what may. In reply he wrote: " So be it. I have no ambition to compete with Daniel Webster as the jackal of the vested interests. And, as for me, I am of no earthly importance. I had rather starve and rot and keep the privilege of speaking the truth as I see it, than of holding all the offices that capital has to give from the presidency downward."

The Law of Civilization and Decay was first published in England in 1895. The revised American edition appeared a year later, and the enlarged French version was brought out in 1899. Essentially, the thesis of the book is that human society oscillates " between barbarism and civilization " or moves " from a condition of physical dispersion to one of concentration "; that civilization is the product of such social concentration; and that society is constantly moving from barbarism to civilization and back again to dispersion and barbarism. Moreover, the velocity of this social movement is proportionate to its energy and mass, and its centralization is proportionate to its velocity. Thus the greater the acceleration, the greater the centralization. A corollary of this formula pertained to the conspicuous roles played by man's two basic drives, fear and greed, during the different periods of civilization.

In the early stages of concentration, fear appears to be the channel through which energy finds the readiest outlet; accordingly, in primitive and scattered communities, the imagination is vivid, the mental types produced are religious, military, artistic. As consolidation advances, fear yields to greed, and the economic organism tends to supersede the emotional and martial. . . . When surplus energy has accumulated in such bulk as to preponderate over productive energy, it becomes the controlling social force. Thenceforward, capital is autocratic, and energy vents itself through those organisms best fitted to give expression to the power of capital. In the last stage of consolidation, the economic, and, perhaps, the scientific intellect is propagated, while the imagination fades, and the emotional, the martial, and artistic types of manhood decay. . . . At length a point must be reached when pressure can go no further, and then, perhaps, one of two results may follow: A stationary period may supervene, which may last until ended by war, by exhaustion, or by both combined, as seems to have been the case with the Eastern Empire; or, as in the Western, disintegration may set in, the civilized population may perish, and a reversion may take place to a primitive form of organism.

To demonstrate the validity of this thesis, Brooks traced in vivid detail the development of European civilization from the earliest times to the end of the nineteenth century. His brilliant observations illumined as much the dark recesses of human nature as the law itself. His study of the rise and decline of the various centers of population revealed the similarity of the elements of growth and decay in each instance. In the Christian era, with which the book is most concerned, the fall of Rome initiated a period of decentralization which lasted a thousand years — a millennium during which men, motivated by the fear of the invisible, yielded to the rule of the organized clergy.

The power of the imagination, when stimulated by the mystery which, in the age of decentralization, shrouds the operations of nature, can be measured by its effect in creating an autocratic class of miracle-workers. Between the sixth and the thirteenth centuries, about one third of the soil of Europe passed into the hands of the religious corporations, while the bulk of the highest talent of the age sought its outlet through monastic life.

With the development of trade and science, however, fear gave way to greed. Commerce and skepticism have always gone hand in hand, and in time they brought about the Reformation, the separation of church and state, and the supremacy of the moneyed classes. The merchants and traders, once they began to accumulate wealth, refused to give it up to the Church. Soon there arose among them those who argued that certain sacred writings, which could be consulted without fee, were an effective substitute for the innumerable costly fetishes and masses. This deification of the Bible, while it resulted in enormous savings to the mercantile class, led to the disintegration of the Church as a temporal power and to the subsequent confiscation of ecclesiastical property in all Protestant countries. England, having gone farthest along the path of concentration, best illustrated this passing of power from the monk to the merchant. The Tudors plundered the churches and monasteries to strengthen the Crown and to fill their coffers. The clergy, reduced to an adjunct of the civil power, were granted salaries in order to inculcate obedience to the Crown and to break their allegiance to Rome.

Perhaps, in all modern history, there is no more striking example of the rapid and complete manner in which, under favorable circumstances, one type can supersede another, than the thoroughness with which the economic displaced the emotional temperament, in the Anglican Church, during the Tudor dynasty.

From the Reformation to the revolution of 1688 England was ruled by " a comparatively few great landed families, forming a narrow oligarchy which guided the Crown." The decline of Spain and the conquest of India in the eighteenth century opened the stores of gold and silver of these two countries to the plunder of venturesome Englishmen and enabled them to make London, through the Bank of England, the world's center of economic enterprise. The extension of credit — " the chosen vehicle of energy in centralized societies " — spurred the exploitation of mechanical inventions as a means towards greater capitalistic production. The merchant adventurers, " bold, energetic, audacious," were quick to take full advantage of the natural and fortuitous opportunities which the emergent industrial revolution opened to them, and from 1688 to 1815 they ruled England as capably and as aggressively as the landed oligarchy had before them. So successful, however, were they in the accumulation of wealth that the mass of their riches became a force which brought the modern bankers into being.

With the advent of the bankers, a profound change came over civilization, for contraction began. Self-interest had from the outset taught the producer that, to prosper, he should deal in wares which tended rather to rise than to fall in value, relatively to coin. The opposite instinct possessed the usurer; he found that he grew rich when money appreciated, or when the borrower had to part with more property to pay his debt when it fell due, than the cash lent him would have bought the day the obligation was contracted.

Early in the nineteenth century the bankers established the gold standard. This permitted an inelastic currency to rise in value with the expansion of trade, and the bankers exploited this advantage to their great gain. As creditors they had little difficulty in wresting economic control from the debtor industrialists.

Another corollary of the law of civilization was the relative nature of law itself. " Law is merely the expression of the will of the strongest for the time being, and therefore laws have no fixity, but

shift from generation to generation." At each stage of civilization
the class in power always sought to perpetuate itself by means of
legislation. When the imagination was vivid and fear held sway
over the minds of men, ecclesiastical law prevailed. As trade developed and competition sharpened, the merchants, more interested
in sales than in salvation, sought to enact " civil codes for the enforcement of contracts and the protection of the creditor class."
With the further acceleration of society, the bankers emerged in
control and adopted legislation to suit their special ends. Law,
therefore, had always favored the group in power and was changed
with each social mutation.

When *The Law of Civilization and Decay* was published in 1895,
its provocative ideas and original concepts were obscured by the author's views on the then embittered silver question. Few men knew
of its appearance and fewer took the trouble to read it. But the
keener minds who did read it were quick to appreciate its suggestive
qualities. Justice Holmes, Brooks's shrewd and skeptical friend, read
the book as soon as he received it and at once wrote to his friend Sir
Frederick Pollock in England:

I only received it two days ago but read it in a flash. It is about the most
(immediately) interesting history I ever read. . . . It hardly strikes me
as science but rather as a somewhat grotesque world poem, or sym-
phony in blue and gray, but the story of the modern world is told so
strikingly that while you read you believe it.

Theodore Roosevelt's appreciative, if patronizing, review in *The
Forum*, while disapproving strongly of Brooks's political and economic radicalism, frankly admitted that the volume was " a marvel
of compressed statement " and " a distinct contribution to the philosophy of history." However one-sided the author's discussion
sometimes became and however melancholy were his conclusions,
both contained truths which no thinking man could deny. And
Adams's deep sympathy equaled his strong prejudices. " Through
the cold impartiality with which he strives to work merely as a re-
corder of facts," Roosevelt declared, " there break through now and

then flashes of pent-up wrath and vehement scorn for all that is mean and petty in a purely materialistic, purely capitalistic, civilization."

For obvious reasons Henry Adams was the chief admirer of his younger brother's book. He referred to it again and again in his correspondence. He spoke of it as "a great book," and added caustically: "Luckily our society is too far gone in Byzantium to understand how great it is, so it will not need notice." To Brooks he wrote that the thesis of the volume might be stated in the fewest possible words as follows:

> All Civilization is Centralization.
> All Centralization is Economy.
> Therefore all Civilization is the survival
> of the most economical (cheapest).

On another occasion he stated: "Your economical law of History is, or ought to be, an Energetic Law of History. Concentration is energy, whether political or industrial."

That Henry was influenced in his thinking by a study of Brooks's book is obvious to anyone familiar with his later work. As Professor Beard puts it: "A comparison of Henry's writings before 1893 with his writings after that year shows that during the period 1893–1899 he acquired certain fundamental conceptions of history, explicit in *The Law*, which subsequently bulked large in his historical thought and writing. Of the fact there can be no doubt." Nor was Henry averse to acknowledge this indebtedness. In a letter to Brooks about the time the book was first published he wrote:

That it must have a strong and permanent effect on the treatment of history, and probably on politics as a science, I cannot doubt; but it may be slow and devious. All I can say is that, if I wanted to write any book, it would have been the one you have written.

The truth is that the brothers had independently adopted nearly parallel lines of thought as to the development of civilization, and that each had influenced the other in the refinement of their final conclusions.

To the end of his life Brooks Adams continued his study of the flux of civilization. Having completed the final version of *The Law of Civilization and Decay*, he began to investigate the principles of modern economic concentration. He had just witnessed the sudden emergence of the United States as a world power, and he wanted to ascertain whether or not this crucial transference of economic power proved the validity of his theory of civilization. *America's Economic Supremacy* and *The New Empire*, collections of essays published in 1900 and 1902 respectively, present his considered findings on this point.

His chief interest in these essays was the problem of the transmission of energy from one center of concentration to another. He traced the development of the main trade routes of the past and indicated their controlling effects upon the flow of social activity. Decades before the appearance of Spengler's work on the decline of Western civilization, Brooks demonstrated the constant movement of power and empire from east to west, from south to north, until they had gone half around the earth and had at the turn of the twentieth century established themselves in the United States. After considering all the available information, he concluded that the centers of concentration had developed in places containing an abundance of food and useful metals, and that when these means of wealth were depleted the seat of power migrated to a more suitable location — sometimes at the cost of a social cataclysm. " Most of the greatest catastrophes in history," he stated in the preface to *America's Economic Supremacy*, " have occurred because of the instinctive effort of humanity to adjust itself to changes in the conditions of life, wrought by the movement from point to point of the international centre of empire and wealth." In this connection it should be mentioned that he was among the first to stress the value of geopolitics for social theory: " I am convinced that neither history nor economics can be intelligently studied without a constant reference to the geographical surroundings which have affected different nations."

His general survey of the great movement of empire from one

center of concentration to another was preparatory to his detailed analysis of the economic conditions in Europe during the final quarter of the nineteenth century. His examination of the status of the leading nations led him to conclude that France, as a consequence of her defeat by Prussia, had definitely entered a phase of eclipse; that Germany, for all her explosive energy, lacked the resources for world dominance. Of Russia he was less certain. A vast country potentially capable of great economic development, it could only be impelled in that direction by " a social reorganization which will put her upon a cheaper administrative basis." In the light of what has actually occurred, his clear-sightedness was truly noteworthy: " What a social revolution in Russia would portend transcends human foresight but probably its effects would be felt throughout the world." In his view England, having maintained the seat of power and empire for more than a century, began to decline about 1870. His sojourn in England convinced him that its people were exerting less initiative, less energy; they were depending too much on the income from their colonies, and indulgence was causing them to become mentally sluggish.

At the turn of the century, Brooks observed, the ascending curve of economic power in the United States was clearly evident. In every field of major industrial endeavor American enterprise and American capital dwarfed the efforts of competing countries. What impressed him most forcefully about this transfer of the seat of energy was the extraordinarily accelerated velocity of its migration.

The phenomenon is not new, as similar perturbations have occurred from the earliest times; its peculiarity lies in its velocity and its proportions. A change of equilibrium has heretofore occupied at least the span of a human lifetime, so that a new generation has gradually become habituated to the novel environment. In this instance the revolution came so suddenly that few realized its presence before it ended. Nevertheless, it has long been in preparation, and it appears to be fundamental, for it is the effect of that alteration in mental processes which we call the advance of science.

It is not surprising that Brooks regarded the rapid rise of his native land to economic supremacy with grave apprehension. He knew well the type of men who headed the gigantic corporations and huge banking establishments, and did not trust them. Aware also that prosperity made men blind to all signs of adversity, he could not help fearing that the cupidity of our business leaders would hasten the migration of economic power from our shores to the next seat of concentrated energy across the Pacific — Japan. "Supremacy," he reflected, "has always entailed its sacrifices as well as its triumphs, and fortune has seldom smiled on those who besides being energetic and industrious, have not been armed, organized, and bold."

The problem of America's destiny acutely perturbed Brooks Adams for years on end. The prospect greatly depressed him. In an article published in 1910 in *The Atlantic Monthly* he said:

Within the last decade, step by step and very reluctantly, I have been led to suspect that not only the tranquility of life, but the coherence of society itself, may hinge upon our ability to modify, more or less radically, our methods of thinking, and, as I tend toward this conclusion, I look at these questions more seriously.

The fate of Rome had taught him that the cost of centralization was very high and tended to engulf any civilized nation which could not meet it with freshly created wealth and self-controlled energy. It was the latter function that worried him so far as the United States was concerned. "We are abundantly inventive and can create wealth, but we cannot control the energy which we liberate. Why we fail is the problem which perplexes me." Continuing his study of the greatly accelerated velocity of our economic concentration, and observing closely the type of mind of our leading businessmen, he came gradually and unwillingly to believe that, unless we direct our energy more wisely, "the expansion of the social core within would induce an explosion which we call a revolution."

In 1913 he published the result of this reflection and research in a collection of essays entitled *The Theory of Social Revolutions.* His main thesis was that our intensely centralized society required exceptional administrative capacity, and that our present ruling class, the capitalists, were psychologically incapable of coping with the complex problem of democratic government and must be replaced with men able to adapt themselves to modern conditions. Two things should be noted at the outset: he presented the proposition not as a law but as a theory, and by social revolution he meant not the violent deposition of a sovereign government but an active phase in the evolution of society. Such a revolution, he explained, had occurred, on the average, once in every two generations since the rise of industrialism about 1760. " Every advance in applied science has accelerated social movement, until the discovery of steam and electricity in the eighteenth and nineteenth centuries quickened movement as movement had never been quickened before." In his judgment we were, in 1913, on the verge of another such radical change, and he wrote the book to make clear the dangers ahead and to stress the need for intelligent direction. This exposition and indictment were his salient contribution to the attack upon trusts and bankers that characterized the decade in which the essays were written.

His analysis of our complex economic system, which occupies a good part of the volume, was detailed and incisive, if oversimplified. He declared that moneyed capital — " stored human energy, as a coal measure is stored solar energy " — had become extremely fluid and compressible and lent itself to monopolized control. As a consequence " in a community like the United States, a few men, or even, in certain emergencies, a single man [he had in mind J. P. Morgan in the financial crisis of 1908], may become clothed with various of the attributes of sovereignty " without the sovereign's responsibilities. Especially reprehensible was the misuse of monopolistic privileges for private gain. Thus throughout history roads have been the responsibility of the state and cared for in one way or another in the interests of all. The railroads, in our industrial era es-

sentially the roads of commerce, are in this country privately owned
and exploited for the benefit of their manipulators at the expense of
the public. The capitalist, he maintained, " is too specialized to comprehend a social relation, even a fundamental one like this, beyond
the narrow circle of his private interests." A variety of other functions, which in the past were either monopolized by the community
or carried on by competitive individuals, had in our time been taken
over by powerful trusts and manipulated to their special advantage.

Since 1871, while the area within which competition is possible has
been kept constant by the tariff, capital has accumulated and has been
concentrated and volatilized until, within this republic, substantially
all prices are fixed by a vast moneyed class. This mass, obeying what
amounts to being a single volition, has its heart in Wall Street, and pervades every corner of the Union.

Brooks Adams's indictment of these capitalists is thorough and
severe. He delineated them as a crass, greedy, unprincipled, and
antisocial body of men without vision or the capacity for communal
leadership, clinging selfishly to the economic power thrust upon
them by the sudden and fortuitous change in social concentration.

The modern capitalist not only thinks in terms of money, but he thinks
in terms of money more exclusively than the French aristocrat or lawyer
ever thought in terms of caste. . . . He may sell his services to whom he
pleases and at what price may suit him, and if by so doing he ruins men
and cities, it is nothing to him. He is not responsible, for he is not a
trustee for the public.

To illustrate the capitalist's obtuseness, Brooks pointed to his scorn
for the very laws upon which his security depended.

In spite of his vulnerability, he is of all citizens the most lawless. He
appears to assume, that the law will always be enforced, when he has
need of it, by some special personnel whose duty lies that way, while he
may evade the law, when convenient, or bring it into contempt, with
immunity.

An even more glaring deficiency, in Brooks's opinion, was the capitalist's failure to rise above his sordid position as the exploiter of money and men and become a benefactor of mankind. Not that Brooks did not regard him as a consciencious man. More than earlier dominant types, however, the capitalist tended to become overspecialized and insensitive to his environment. Thus, while in the past the great soldiers and priests had often been famous statesmen also, Brooks was unable to discover one capitalist in English and American history of great merit as a statesman.

Certainly, so far as I am aware, no capitalist has ever acquired such influence over his contemporaries, as has been attained with apparent ease by men like Cromwell, Washington, or even Jackson.

Brooks's analysis of modern economic society led him to conclude that the capitalist class, having in the past — like all ruling groups — served its social purpose while advancing along the path to power, like them had become stricken with fatuity upon reaching the crest. Yet if the civilization which that class had developed was to cohere, it

must have a high order of generalizing mind, — a mind which can grasp a multitude of complex relations, — but this is a mind which can, at best, only be produced in small quantity and at high cost. Capital has preferred the specialized mind and that not of the highest quality, since it has found it profitable to set quantity before quality to the limit which the market will endure. . . . It is hard to resist the persuasion that unless capital can, in the immediate future, generate an intellectual energy, beyond the sphere of its specialized calling, very much in excess of any intellectual energy of which it has hitherto given promise, and unless it can besides rise to an appreciation of diverse social conditions, as well as to a level of political sagacity, far higher than it has attained within recent years, its relative power in the community must decline.

He had not the slightest doubt that the capitalist class would neither succeed in developing the intelligence and the ability with which to perpetuate itself nor submit peacefully to the group destined to supplant it. He feared, therefore, that the resulting struggle for power would be as fierce and formidable as all previous similar contests, since " the rise of a new governing class is always synonymous with a social revolution and a redistribution of property."

Brooks was equally outspoken in his censure of the politico-economical nature of our court system. He anticipated J. Allen Smith and Charles A. Beard in demonstrating the class bias of our Constitution and the special interpretation given to it by lawyers elevated by the group in power. A profound student of our legal development, he presented a wealth of irrefutable evidence to prove not only that our federal courts function politically but that this character was given to them deliberately at the beginning of our national existence. At the time of the Constitutional Convention this compromise had seemed the only feasible solution of the conflict between the frail federal republic and the jealous and obstinate states.

As a consequence of this basic adjustment, the courts, presided over by men who wished to use them (in the words of *The Federalist*) as " a barrier to the encroachments and oppressions of the representative body," have arrogated to themselves the right to control the political branches of the government. Thus,

under the American system the Constitution, or fundamental law, is expounded by judges, and this function, which, in essence, is political, has brought precisely that quality of pressure on the bench which it has been the labor of a hundred generations of our ancestors to remove. On the whole the result has been not to elevate politics, but to lower the courts to the political level.

It was his belief that our courts tended to become legislative chambers and a menace to order.

This propensity in the court system irritated Brooks as much as any other deficiency in our national life. He argued that " a court should be rigid and emotionless " and that any attempt on the part of judges to use the courts to control legislation must result in disaster.

[303]

When plunged into the vortex of politics, courts must waver as do legislatures, and nothing is to me more painful than to watch the process of deterioration by which our judges lose the instinct which should warn them to shun legislation as a breach of trust, and to cleave to those general principles which permit of no exceptions.

To prove his point he analyzed numerous decisions, from that of *Marbury vs. Madison* down, in which the judiciary had interfered with the will of Congress in favor of a special class. It was his conviction that a society organized under the modern industrial conditions which have created trusts and monopolies in the manufacture and distribution of the essentials of life cannot indefinitely be administered under an outmoded code of law.

Law is the frame which contains society, as its banks contain a river; and if the flow of a river be increased a thousandfold, the banks must be altered to correspond, or there will be a flood overwhelming in proportion to the uncontrollable energy generated. . . . Courts, I need hardly say, cannot control nature, though by trying to do so they may, like the Parliament of Paris, create a friction which shall induce an appalling catastrophe.

Anxious that the nation should circumvent the danger confronting it, eager to see justice done and truth prevail, Brooks was wrathful at the thought that those best able to accomplish this end were instead selfishly bolstering the status quo. Of a family of lawyers and himself a profound student of law, he excoriated the limited and rigid mentality of the legal practitioners who were more interested in benefiting their clients — and hence themselves — than in upholding the laws of the land; men who employed their ingenuity and cunning in behalf of capitalists bent on sordid aggrandizement. It was these lawyers, he argued, who had deliberately turned the Constitution into a fetish, as if it had " some inherent and marvellous virtue by which it can arrest the march of omnipotent Nature," in order to make it a bulwark against the efforts of social reformers to adapt the existing economy to changing conditions for the benefit of the people as a whole.

Brooks Adams was the first American economic historian to occupy himself with the basic problem of our industrial civilization: how to adjust contemporary society to the ever-increasing velocity* of economic concentration. The more he observed the effect of our economy upon the mass of mankind, the more he was persuaded that capitalism must either develop a greater social intelligence or be superseded by a ruling group able to cope with the strains and stresses of scientific centralization. Only thus could we avoid an internal explosion and remain the world's seat of energy. Believing that every ruling class was struck blind once it passed the zenith of its development, he was full of foreboding: " I am full of gloomy fears," he wrote to W. C. Ford in 1897. " I do not know where we are going, nor do I see any light ahead. There seems to me to be no headway on the ship, and that we are going on the rocks. I hope I may be wrong." Further study of our economy and our politics as they functioned at the turn of the century only intensified his fears.

It is easy to dismiss his admonitions as the alarms of a disgruntled pessimist, as some have done, or to decry his indictment of capitalism as the arraignment of a deluded socialist. Brooks Adams was neither. True, he had the temperament of a Jeremiah. Influenced by the scientific speculation of his day, he came to the conclusion that society was " an organism operating on mechanical principles," and that without an understanding of these principles we were no better than novices tinkering with a complex machine. His determinism became more rigid with the years. In 1919, in his introduction to Henry's *The Degradation of the Democratic Dogma*, he wrote:

I learned, as a lawyer and as a student of history and economics, to look on man, in the light of the evidence of unnumbered centuries, as a pure automaton, who is moved along the paths of least resistance by forces over which he had no control.

This pessimistic attitude, however, was merely the negative aspect of his passion for social justice, of his devotion to truth. Motivated in all his thinking by an acute puritanic conscience, he was impelled to rise in wrath against the crassness, the selfishness, and the greediness which characterized so many dominant capitalists of his generation. If he generalized too freely and if his conclusions were at times too sweeping, his basic analysis of tendencies is as valid today as it was when first made. Indeed, his original and acute intellect perceived trends and relationships long before they became apparent to his contemporaries. It took the cataclysm of two world wars to bring home the truth of his assertion that capitalistic civilization had failed to devolp the intelligence necessary to cope effectively with the velocity of scientific centralization.

In his criticism of our capitalistic society Brooks was of course on the side of the socialists. He was familiar with much of their thinking and sympathized with their economic interpretation of history. His brother Henry, who disliked the popular implications of socialism but was convinced of " the logical necessity for society to march that way," in 1899 indicated to him the similarity between his view of history and that of Karl Marx.

The Marxian theory of history I take to be the foundation of yours: that is, when you assert an energy always concentrating, you assert economy as the guiding force, and the acceleration of mass and motion as consequence of accelerating economy — and reciprocally reacting. The assertion of the law of economy as the law of history is the only contribution that the socialists have made to my library of ideas.

Yet Brooks had too keen and unequivocal a mind to absorb the ideas of another uncritically. If he agreed with the socialists in important respects, he was too definitely an individualist and an intellectual aristocrat to join them in any of their activities.

Politically he was, if anything, in the words of his favorite brother, " a Jeffersonian Jacksonian Bryonian democrat " and a sincere admirer of George Washington, " the whole man." Yet he was not an uncritical exponent of laissez-faire democracy. In his introduction to *The Degradation of the Democratic Dogma* he accused democracy of deifying competition — " preaching it as the highest destiny and true duty of man " — and thereby encouraging an unbridled capitalism. It was this worm at the heart of democracy that had brought disappointment to his grandfather John Quincy Adams and to liberals in later years who fell victims " to that fallacy which underlies the whole theory of modern democracy — that it is possible by education to stimulate the selfish instinct of competition, which demands that each man should strive to better himself at the cost of his neighbor, so as to coincide with the moral principle that all should labor for the common good." From this standpoint, if his brother's nomenclature is translated into contemporary usage, Brooks might be termed a left-wing New Dealer. Essentially, however, he was a true descendant of the Adamses who had helped mightily to give our nation its present democratic character.

THORSTEIN VEBLEN

ICONOCLASTIC ECONOMIST

ONE of our foremost social thinkers, deeply interested in man's welfare, Thorstein Veblen never crossed the periphery of American life. One of our most original economists, providing new leads in basic theory for an entire generation, he was at best merely tolerated in the universities in which he taught and received neither the advancement nor the honors commensurate with his contributions to knowledge. A stylist of extraordinary power, a phrase-maker of remarkable felicity, a master of ironic indirection, he produced books that are little read because he is reputed to be a ponderous and prolix writer.

Nor did Veblen ever seek the leadership that was his by virtue of his acutely original mind. There was indeed something perverse in his character which led him to intensify his peculiarities and to conceal his feelings under a mask of impassive aloofness. Outwardly he appeared indifferent to friends, uninterested in his students, and unconcerned with the world around him. Except to a few intimates he seemed nearly always companioned by loneliness and mastered by silence. It was only in his writings that his towering intellect found free scope; there his pointed irony punctured the inflated fallacies of our business economy. His analyses of the capitalistic structure show that breadth of perception and critical acumen which have made him unique among modern economists.

The fact that Veblen was a "Norskie" at a time when Norwegians were still the butt of popular humor goes far to explain the aloof and alien aspects of his character. He was born in 1857 on a frontier farm in Wisconsin, one of twelve children of a Norwegian immigrant, and reared in a Minnesota Norwegian settlement which clung to its native tongue and custom. Very early, conscious of his intellectual precocity and eager to excel his older brothers, he made himself the " oddest " of the Veblens; he kept a good deal to himself, read much, defended unpopular causes, and gave the impression of being conceited.

He spoke almost no English until he entered Carleton College Academy at the age of seventeen. This linguistic handicap only accentuated his uncouth appearance and prejudiced his classmates against him. To compensate his vanity he exercised his sardonic humor at their expense, which only alienated them the more. Nor was his social status improved when he began his collegiate studies three years later. He was already twenty, eager to make the world of knowledge his own, and he was impatient with the puerile interests of the other students. Only Ellen Rolfe, niece of the president and equally a misfit, befriended him; only John Bates Clark, then one of his teachers, perceived and praised his acute mind. Like so many other bright, eccentric college youths, he read widely, pondered deeply, and made his mark on the campus as a critic of conventional conceits and defender of liberal ideas. In his last year at Carleton he not only did the work of two years but found the time to read George's *Progress and Poverty* and to keep up with developments in the agrarian Populist movement.

After teaching for a year at the parochial Monona Academy in Wisconsin, he decided to join his older brother Andrew in graduate study at Johns Hopkins. Dissatisfied with its system of pedagogy, he transferred to Yale University in order to study philosophy under its eminent president, the Reverend Noah Porter. During the next two and a half years Veblen plowed through several fields of advanced knowledge and impressed his teachers with his intellectual perceptions. In 1884, shortly before he was graduated as a doctor of philosophy, he won the $250 John A. Porter prize for the best English essay on the problems of a federal tax surplus.

Veblen was now twenty-seven years old and exceptionally well qualified to teach philosophy and kindred subjects. But no college wanted him. For all the enthusiastic letters of recommendation from his eminent teachers, college presidents shied away from him. They did not want him for two very good reasons: he was not a doctor of divinity — the degree was then almost a prerequisite to the teaching of philosophy — and he was a Norskie suspected of agnosticism.

His disappointment was intense. It embittered him to see less able men obtain desirable posts while he was not even considered. He returned to his parents' farm a self-confessed failure, sick in body and soul. But he persisted in his wide reading and in his search for a teaching position. Four years later, discouraged and anxious to get away from his unsympathetic brothers, he decided to marry Ellen Rolfe and make his home on her father's farm in Iowa. There he continued with his reading and research. Everything was grist to his capacious mind. Philosophy, anthropology, Norse sagas, Bellamy's *Looking Backward* — whatever book he could lay his hands on he added to his store of knowledge. He was still the student, still yearning to satisfy his gargantuan curiosity, still anxious to find employment as a college teacher.

In 1891, after seven years of outward idleness but actually of intense intellectual fermentation, Veblen decided to resume formal study in a renewed effort to obtain an academic post. Because of his active interest in economic problems, he went to Cornell University to work under Professor J. Laurence Laughlin. The latter at once noted the newcomer's agility of mind and helped him get a much-needed fellowship. His favorable opinion was soon strengthened by a reading of Veblen's paper, "Some Neglected Points in the Theory of Socialism," which revealed a remarkable grasp of the working of industrial society. When Professor Laughlin was called the following year to head the economics department of the newly organized University of Chicago, he arranged to have Veblen go with him on a fellowship paying $520 a year.

At the age of thirty-five, Veblen was at last a member of a university faculty. True, he was only on the first rung of the ladder and his hold was still precarious, but at least he had ceased being a ne'er-do-well. As he was to teach a course in socialism, he lost no time in preparing for his assignment.

He was not long at the university before he arrived at two important conclusions: that his conception of political economy differed radically from that of other economists; and that President Harper would not jeopardize the success of his institution by encouraging ideas unpalatable to its benefactors. Since he was loath either to compromise with truth as he saw it or resign his fellowship, he learned to resort to a mode of expression that encased his ideational barbs in sheaths of irony and indirection. His very slow drawl and his outwardly impassive demeanor helped him to maintain an academic objectivity in his classroom teaching, so that in his course in socialism it was difficult to tell which side he favored. In his writings he resorted to illustrations from anthropology rather than from contemporary society and employed words in their original meanings rather than in their modern connotations, thus veiling them with the innocuousness of the pedant. He also leaned backward in his aloofness from current industrial conflicts and gave no intimation of his reactions to such significant events of the day as the Homestead and Pullman strikes.

His earnest effort to avoid giving offense proved of little avail. Although he wrote addresses for President Harper and translated needed materials from the German for the economics department, and though he wrote for and edited *The Journal of Political Economy*, he received scant encouragement. Only in 1895 was he made an instructor, and not till after the publication of *The Theory of the Leisure Class* in 1899 did he become an assistant professor. President Harper considered him a doubtful asset to the university and was ready to have him go at any time. This Veblen decided to do in 1906, when he received an offer from Stanford University.

Veblen's fourteen years at the University of Chicago were for him a period of notable efflorescence. He saturated his mind with the speculation of his time, but his own thought was entirely original. His study of the nature of capitalistic society convinced him of the ineptitude of prevailing economic theories. They struck him as refinements and elaborations of ideas based upon the handicraft economy and pre-Darwinian science, and therefore inapplicable to a machine technology. The expounders of this normative and hedonistic system of economics tended to ignore or disregard the fundamental difference between the "industrial" and the "pecuniary" employments. They continued to assume — more than a century after Adam Smith and in the face of gigantic corporations and vast absentee ownership — that all normal, legitimate activities which serve a materially useful end are lucrative to the extent that they are socially productive. Veblen considered such views anachronistic and worthless. He argued that economics was not a normative but an institutional science.

Any science, such as economics, which has to do with human conduct, becomes a genetic inquiry into the human scheme of life; and where, as in economics, the subject of inquiry is the conduct of man in his dealings with the material means of life, the science is necessarily an inquiry into the life-history of material civilization, on a more or less extended or restricted plan.

The results of such an inquiry he published in numerous reviews and articles. In command of an extraordinary store of general and specialized knowledge, he traced man's means of making a living, from his first social emergence to the present. In the process he developed his basic economic theories, which constitute the greatest contribution to the subject yet made by an American. These theories he later developed at length in his larger works.

The Theory of the Leisure Class is Veblen's first and most widely read book. Its striking terminology, which seemed peculiar until many of its epithets entered common usage, its novel and eccentric approach, its perturbing comparisons and conclusions, and most of all its bold combination of implicit criticism and ironic indirection gave the volume an exotic flavor which both attracted and repelled its early readers. Lester Ward, Howells, and other liberals lauded its originality and incisiveness; the more conservative economists attacked it as vicious; still others simply dismissed it as a freakish specimen of inept pedantry.

Veblen studied the leisure class genetically, tracing its diverse manifestations from its first appearance in history down to modern times. He found that leisure was from the very beginning the conspicuous accompaniment of property, or — to use Veblen's term — of pecuniary power. This power was first obtained in the era of predatory barbarism as reward for prowess in battle. In time the mere possession of goods became a mark of merit.

Ownership began and grew into a human institution on grounds unrelated to the subsistence minimum. The dominant incentive was from the outset the invidious distinction attaching to wealth, and, save temporarily and by exception, no other motive has usurped the primacy at any later stage in the development.

The possessors of wealth, having no need of remunerative employment, made abstention from it a requisite of decency. Conversely, as productive labor became the task of the poor and the enslaved, it was made " inconsistent with a reputable standing in the community." Thus wealth and leisure became synonymous with social superiority. The leisurely rich set their manner of life and standards of worth as the norm of reputability for the entire group. Those aspiring to belong to their class had to display both conspicuous consumption of goods and abstention from useful labor. They engaged in refining their tastes and manners " because good breeding requires time, application, and expense, and can therefore not be compassed by those whose time and energy are taken up with work." They also took over the predatory employments, " such as government, fighting, hunting, the care of arms and accoutrements, and the like," because these came to be regarded as noble and honorific.

This test of social superiority remained valid through the ages. Those wishing to prove their pecuniary power showed it by the conspicuous and consequently wasteful consumption of goods. Such extravagance tended to drive the standard of living of all classes to the limit of their earning capacities. Display was always the thing, with the costliness of a product being its chief criterion of value. Where men, such as modern merchants and industrialists, cannot personally display conspicuous leisure and consumption, they do so vicariously through their wives, children, servants, and the like. Thus, until recently women constricted their waists, deformed their feet, and wore long skirts and long hair to indicate their social superiority. Both sexes wore clothes designed to show the wearer's ability both to bear the cost and to abstain from useful work.

The second half of the book deals with the more modern and more critical aspects of leisure-class economics. Its retarding effect upon the evolution of society is discussed in provocative detail. The point is made that, while human institutions change slowly because of mental inertia, this resistance is strengthened by the natural conservatism of the dominant group. "The office of the leisure class in social evolution is to retard the movement and to conserve what is obsolescent." The result is a maladjustment of social and economic institutions.

From the point of view of the economic process, the leisure class is interested in acquisition rather than in production, in exploitation rather than in serviceability. Those engaged in predatory activities — and the barbaric chieftain, the medieval robber baron, and modern captain of industry are of the same lineage in this respect — have always sought to gain and retain control of the substance within their reach. Their effect "upon the growth of institutions is seen in those enactments and conventions that make for security of property, enforcement of contracts, facility of pecuniary transactions, vested interests." Their employments and characteristics lead to "an unremitting emulation and antagonism between classes and between individuals. . . . Freedom from scruple, from sympathy, honesty, and regard for life, may, within fairly wide limits, be said to further the success of the individual in the pecuniary culture." The traits of probity, diligence, altruism, and the like, which best serve the collective interest, are discouraged as detrimental to personal success; those wishing to get ahead are compelled to cultivate the habits of mind that best serve shrewd trading and aggressiveness. Those who succeed in acquiring wealth and power enter the leisure-class employments and behave as members and enjoy the privileges of the ruling group.

In our contemporary society the leisure class, in its unremitting pursuit of conspicuous waste and pecuniary emulation, in effect " acts to lower the industrial efficiency of the community and retard the adaptation of human nature to the exigencies of modern industrial life." In clinging to its privileges the leisure class preserves archaic traits and traditions. While disdaining the industrial process, it furthers the barbaric employments of prowess and predation in its modern forms of war, sports, and the pecuniary occupations. Its encouragement of gambling and devout observances — both survivals of the archaic temperament — likewise hinders the natural functioning of the industrial process. Equally harmful is its influence on higher education, since the high repute which it attaches to the humanities and the classics cultivates an aversion to what is useful.

A more direct and far more devastating analysis of modern business is to be found in Veblen's second book, *The Theory of Business Enterprise*, published in 1904, which contains in integrated form the ideas he had been expounding for a decade in magazine articles and in the classroom. It begins with a discussion of the intrinsic differences between the industrial process and business enterprise. The first is characterized by mechanical accuracy, which in turn leads to " a standardization of services as well as goods." This standardization stimulates efficiency and facilitates the meeting of current wants. A corollary of the machine process is the interdependence of production and service units not only within the branches of a single industry but also among all highly developed industries.

A disturbance at any point, whereby any given branch of industry fails to do its share in the work of the system at large, immediately affects the neighboring or related branches which come before or after it in sequence, and is transmitted through their derangement to the remoter portions of the system.

Such dislocation causes idleness, waste, and hardships, and must be avoided for the good of the community.

In modern society, however, industry is controlled by businessmen who find it to their advantage to disturb the industrial balance. Veblen stressed the fact that this had not been the case before the emergence of industrial capitalism, when business, whether handicraft or trade, was carried on primarily to earn a living and not to make a profit from investment. Indeed, gain from investment was considered a fortuitous matter, neither wholly legitimate nor reducible to a standard rate. " Under no economic system earlier than the advent of the machine industry does profit on investment seem to have been accounted a normal and unquestionable legitimate source of gain." With the development of capitalism the motive of production became pecuniary profit. Industry was regarded not as a means of earning a livelihood or of providing for the needs of the community, but as a source of financial gain. " Industry is carried on for the sake of business and not conversely; and the progress and activity of industry are conditioned by the outlook of the market, which means the presumptive chance of business profits." Since it is to the interest of leading businessmen to control large portions of industry, the better to manipulate the market, they try deliberately " to upset or block the industrial process at one or more points " with a view to removing competition and discomfiting business rivals. The result is frequent industrial unbalance. " This chronic state of perturbation is incident to the management of industry by business methods and is unavoidable under existing conditions." Such disturbances, imposing financial distress and bankruptcy on some businessmen and idleness and want on their employees, stimulates the consolidation of industrial units under a single business management.

Veblen next traced the basic business principle of the private ownership of property. He showed that it was John Locke who developed the first philosophical system to regard ownership as a natural right — taking his cue from the prevailing era of handicraft, when productive work was the rule and things were usually at the disposal of him who had made them. " It became a principle of the natural order of things that free labor is the original source of wealth and the basis of ownership." Out of this principle developed such practical props of competitive enterprise as the freedom of contract and the security and ease of credit engagements.

In his discussion of the use of loan credit Veblen explained that since " the business man's object is to get the largest aggregate gain from his business . . . it is accordingly to his interest to extend his credit as far as his standing and the state of the market will admit." Borrowed funds, however, available to all competitors alike, do not necessarily increase the aggregate industrial equipment or the aggregate earnings of the industrial community. " Funds of whatever character are a pecuniary fact, not an industrial one; they serve the distribution of the control of industry only, not its materially productive work."

With the development of business enterprise the strategic use of credit extended in the direction of increased capitalization in the form of stocks and debentures. The promoters and financiers, in their striving for personal gain, sought to expand the business capital of industrial corporations to the limit of their putative earning power. Whatever gave these corporations a differential advantage was capitalized in the form of good will, and their total capitalization was figured, not according to the value of their industrial plant, but according to the market quotations of their securities. " The business capital of a modern corporation is a magnitude that fluctuates from day to day; and in the quotations of its debentures the magnitude of its credit extension also fluctuates from day to day with the course of the market." These manipulations of salable capital have enabled industrialists and financiers to amass fortunes greater than any known in history.

The rule of business capital has grave consequences for the conduct of industry and so for the community as a whole. Because prosperity is thought of primarily as business prosperity and not as industrial efficiency, the great productive capacities of modern technology had not hindered the recurrence of hard times. Both prosperity and depression have come to be business phenomena, with expansion and contraction occurring " primarily in the intangible items of wealth, secondarily in the price rating of the tangible items." In their persistent quest for profits, businessmen bring about industrial depressions when they " do not see their way to derive a satisfactory gain from letting the industrial process go forward on the lines and in the volume for which the material equipment of the industry is designed." Consequently, as our technological resources grew, chronic depression has tended to become a normal concomitant of competitive business enterprise, checked only by such accidents as lower prices, war, or new industries. Veblen maintained that under capitalism only monopoly can offer relief to depression — " the more nearly complete the monopoly, the more effectually is it likely to serve its purpose."

Businessmen by common consent have assumed the management of the community at large. Law and politics " are chiefly concerned with business relations, pecuniary interests, and they have little more than an incidental bearing on other human interests." The dogma of natural rights, appropriate to a society in which craftsmen competed on an equal footing, was carried over into the present business era to uphold " freedom of contract " and the inviolability of property in a society in which there is far less equality. In the United States the sacredness of pecuniary obligations has come near to " being the only form of obligation that has the unqualified sanction of current common sense." Court decisions have abetted this principle.

In the view of these higher adepts of the law, free contract is so inalienable a natural right of man that not even a statutory enactment will enable a workman to forego its exercise and its responsibility. . . . A business man is looked upon as the putative producer of whatever wealth he acquires. By force of this sophistication the acquisition of property by any person is held to be, not only expedient for the owner, but meritorious as an action serving the common good.

Veblen described the peculiar kind of intelligence required by the machine process. In operating a machine a workman must develop qualitative·precision or fail at his job. In the course of time his thinking becomes habituated to terms of mechanical efficiency or to precisely adjusted cause and effect. Other intellectual faculties tend to suffer neglect or disparagement, because the machine, now master of men, " is no respecter of persons and knows neither morality nor dignity nor prescriptive right, divine or human; its teaching is training them into insensibility of the whole range of concepts on which these ministrations proceed." Businessmen, on the other hand, while unavoidably affected by modern technology, persist in thinking in terms of profit on a natural-rights plane. They adhere to the conventional assumptions and defend the institutions based upon these postulates. Thus " the two classes come to have an increasing difficulty in understanding one another and appreciating one another's convictions, ideals, capacities, and short-comings."

The standardization of the schemes of work and life for laborers within the machine process has brought forth what may be termed the spirit of trade unionism, or the effort to adapt working conditions to the new exigencies and disciplines of industry. This in effect negates the spirit of natural rights. "Trade-unionism denies individual freedom of contract to the workman, as well as free discretion to the employer to carry on his business as may suit his own ends." Its primary concern is not with natural liberty and individual property rights but with a standardized livelihood and mechanical necessity; not with business expediency but with technological standard units and standard relations. This disregard for the natural-rights doctrine — found chiefly, of course, among the highly skilled urban workmen — must in time lead to socialistic disaffection, or to the demand for the effective disappearance of property rights as such.

Veblen concluded this provocative volume with an incisive exposition of the basic incompatibility between the discipline of the machine process and the aim of business enterprise. " In the nature of the case the cultural growth dominated by the machine industry is of a skeptical, matter-of-fact complexion, materialistic, unmoral, unpatriotic, undevout." Modern business enterprise must sooner or later be confronted by this dilemma: either it must oppose the machine process and thereby impoverish itself, or it must extend the process and thereby fall into abeyance.

The foregoing paragraphs give only a partial indication of the scope and originality of Veblen's writing up to 1904. For all their repetition, circumlocution, and lack of integration, his books are undoubtedly among the most profound treatments of business economics produced in this country. Fresh ideas, ironic implications, startling statements, verbal sallies, and shafts of savage wit imbue their pages with the excitement of dramatic narrative. The themes are developed with symphonic richness and variation; the boldness of Veblen's mind invests even his casual asides with significance. His analyses and conclusions, now widely current, were so heterodox forty years ago that only a few liberals grasped their full meaning and appreciated their revolutionary significance.

Veblen approached the prevailing system of economics with a mind free from conventional prejudices. Combining his vast knowledge of the social sciences with his extraordinary powers of theoretical synthesis, he traced the existing economic institutions to their archaic sources and laid bare the inner drives that motivated man's practical activities. He studied the origin and nature of what he termed the instinct of workmanship, the leisure class, the natural-rights doctrine, the machine process, and business enterprise. Lacking the urge of the reformer and aware of his precarious academic standing, he developed his themes deviously and inferentially and in a style that glossed over their radical implications. Consequently his ideas at first appeared too incredibly novel for sympathetic consideration or criticism. But time was on his side. Although the profit system is still operating in high gear forty years after he had predicted its ultimate downfall, many discerning economists agree that despite his tendency to drive an idea to its extreme limits Veblen's long-run conclusions seem more valid now than when they were first published.

Veblen's career at Stanford University was brief and disappointing. He seldom had more than a dozen students in his classes, and toward the end the number dwindled to three. He also proved very trying to those who sought to improve his standing with the administration. His long silences embarrassed people and discouraged friendships. It was only during his frequent visits to the socialistic Arnotts, whose humble home was a center for visiting radicals, that he relaxed and at times even became loquacious. His relations with Mrs. Veblen, never wholly congenial, deteriorated during the years at Stanford and on several occasions she left him. He refused to discourage his feminine admirers and was deliberately careless with their letters to him. One of these women moved into his home during Mrs. Veblen's absence — causing a campus scandal. When a friend suggested that the affair might cost him his job, he asked: "What is one to do when the woman moves in on you?" In December 1909 he was forced to resign.

For a year Veblen was unable to find another academic post. Finally Professor H. J. Davenport, a former student of his, made a place for him in his own department at the University of Missouri. There he remained as a lecturer for seven years, no happier than he had been at Chicago and Stanford. He received a maximum salary of $2400 during his last year, was never fully appreciated, and always refused to accommodate himself to the mores of academic life. In 1911 Mrs. Veblen agreed to divorce him. Three years later he married a Mrs. Bradley, who looked after him devotedly until 1918 when she suffered a mental breakdown and was removed to a sanitarium.

Veblen's written work declined markedly after he had left the University of Chicago. His articles and reviews, which lost nothing of their quality, appeared less frequently. His third book, *The In-*

stinct of Workmanship and the State of the Industrial Arts, was not ready till 1914. Like his other longer works, it was essentially a careful elaboration of an early essay on man's natural bent for work. A study of prehistoric society showed that in the relatively peaceable culture of primitive tillage and cattle-breeding the individual labored not for himself alone but for the group to which he belonged. Conditions developed in him a proclivity for taking pains and for avoiding waste as well as a concern for the welfare of those with whom he lived. Intimately related with this sense of workmanship was the impulse to "idle curiosity," which in the long run and because of its concentration in sporadic individuals has made possible the intellectual progress of the race.

As man learned to produce by indirect methods and thereby increased production, he began to accumulate wealth. The result was an institutional revolution. The temptation to obtain food and other effects by force led to wars, devastation, subjugation. Ownership implied mastery over man as well as over goods. It "is commonly found, in the barbarian culture, to be tempered with a large infusion of predatory concepts, of status, prerogative, differential respect of occupations." In the predatory society the individual ceased to concern himself with the welfare of his group and aimed instead at his own advancement. In the process there emerged the warrior chief who arrogated to himself power over his community.

The history of Western civilization lies within this predatory-pecuniary culture. The institution of ownership flourished throughout this period, "and the rights of ownership are of a personal, invidious, differential, emulative nature." The sense of workmanship and curiosity as well as concern for the group, while of an intrinsic nature, became subjugated "to the rule of the self-regarding proclivities that triumphed in the culture of predation." As the institutional ground shifted with the passing of time from barbaric predation to pecuniary gain, the sense of workmanship became "combined and compounded with ownership" and found expression in that meritorious regard for wealth through work characteristic of the middle class. When society had become stratified, the upper or predatory class no longer worked but possessed both wealth and leisure; the middle or commercial class gained wealth by working for it; while the lower or industrial class labored but possessed neither wealth nor leisure. This differentiation between social groups, based on a dissociation of workmanship from sales-manship, " grew into a ' division of labor,' between industry and business, between industrial and pecuniary occupations — a dis-junction of ownership and its peculiar cares, privileges and profi-ciency from workmanship."

In Europe the rise of the handicraft class put an end to Chris-tian feudalism with its " cult of fearsome subjection and arbitrary authority." These workmen, becoming in time " masterless men," demanded and finally obtained " an equitable livelihood for work done." Their scheme of life led to the theory of natural rights; but by the time it became established " as a secure principle of enlight-ened common sense . . . the handicraft system was giving way to the machine industry." Since industrialism and its accessory finan-cial mechanisms and credit loans were an outgrowth of the handi-craft system, they continued to function within the institution of natural rights. The result of this social lag was confusion between the industrial and the pecuniary functions. As in the older predatory cultures, wealth and not work remained the criterion of achieve-ment. " The business man who gains much at little cost, who gets something for nothing, is rated, in his own as well as in his neigh-bor's esteem, as a public benefactor." This confounding of disci-plines, values, and interests has tended greatly to deteriorate the in-stinct of workmanship.

Veblen had implicit trust in evolutionary anthropology and con-tinued to believe in it even after Boas and others had largely dis-credited its unrealistic emphasis. Likewise, his acceptance of Mc-Dougall's theory of the instincts persisted long after it had been discarded by later psychologists. His assertion that the era of peace-able savagery was characterized by a system of primitive commu-nism and an absence of exploitation was denied by John Dewey and other thinkers. As Dewey summarized the matter in *Human*

Nature and Conduct: " No system has ever as yet existed which did not in some form involve the exploitation of some human beings for the advantage of others." Yet this criticism does not invalidate Veblen's view of workmanship as a creative and nonpecuniary process. All productive activity is creative in the sense that it is self-satisfying. The neolithic savage was no doubt conditioned by his environment to find satisfaction in producing for the group that sustained him. So, too, the modern craftsman often finds pleasure in doing his job well. The acquisitive element, however, has been an equally potent motive throughout history. If the acquisitive drive remained dormant during the perhaps dubitable era of peaceable savagery, it has certainly dominated the activities of many men ever since. The joy in work as work and the drive for pecuniary power flourished fairly equally during the centuries of handicraft production. It was only with the establishment of the machine process, when work began to be measured quantitatively with a stop watch, that the acquisitive drive achieved dominance over the sense of workmanship.

While Veblen's evolutionary anthropology and his emphasis on instincts are therefore open to criticism, he has in *The Instinct of Workmanship* achieved the remarkable intellectual feat of clarifying the interaction of instinct and habit, the basic interrelationships between the industrial and the pecuniary processes, and the effects of the prevailing cultural lag. His analysis of the origin and nature of the natural-rights doctrine and its insidious persistence in the machine era is fundamental to a realistic understanding of capitalistic incompatibilities.

While in Europe during the summer of 1914, Veblen was able to observe the outbreak of war at first hand. He was so impressed with German aggressiveness that on his return to the University of Missouri he immediately began to work on his next book, *Imperial Germany and the Industrial Revolution,* and completed it in time for publication during 1915. As in all his major writings, the first chapters deal with the fundamental characteristics of early man and their subsequent development under conditions peculiar to different groups. The Germans, he demonstrated, are " in point of native productivity and aptitude" no different from their neighbors. What placed them apart from the French and especially from the English, who derive from the same stock, was their retarded medievalism. While the Germans, until the nineteenth century, remained steeped in the "feudalistic animus of fealty and subservience," and with habits of mind "suitable to a coercive, centralized, and irresponsible control and to the pursuit of dynastic domination," the countries of Western Europe had for several centuries concentrated on those material realities which led to the industrial revolution and the democratic state. Thus, while the Germans were disciplined by petty courts and bureaucracies, the English-speaking peoples in particular were conditioned by the town meeting and the machine shop. As a consequence the two groups developed radically different attitudes toward personal liberty and political responsibility. "The German conception of this liberty is freedom to give orders and freely to follow orders, while in the English conception it is rather an exemption from orders — a somewhat anarchistic habit of thought."

In the time that England and her neighbors were developing the mechanistic way of life — the only concept in which, according to Veblen, modern society advanced over earlier civilizations — Prussia persevered in her feudal ambitions.

Prussia came in with no cultural traits other than a medieval militarism resting on a feudally servile agrarian system, and made its way forcibly as a political power of ever increasing potency among an aggregation of small and feeble quarreling neighbors.

When the German lands were finally united under Prussian domination in 1871, sovereignty resided not in the people but in the state. Germany began at once to seek a place in the sun. It took over modern technology ready-made — without the handicaps which encumbered it in the countries of its early development but also without the cultural discipline attending the machine process.

The vaunted German philosophy, idealistic in character, was peculiarly ineffective in bridging the gap between feudal habits of mind and the cultural demands of modern industry, since it found "no application in the scheme of thought within which modern science and technology live and move." The result was that Germany grafted a highly efficient technology upon a medieval culture and made use of it, not for pecuniary gains, as other countries did, but for dynastic ends. The government, instead of functioning as the agent of business enterprise, "guided the economic policy of the Empire along mercantilistic lines. Warlike power was its prime consideration." Under these conditions war was inevitable. And Veblen believed that war would continue to haunt mankind so long as the German people persevered in their feudal habits of mind. He pointed out, however, that in the long run the ends of dynastic government must clash with the inexorable demands of the machine process. "Coercion, personal dominion, self-abasement, subjection, loyalty, suspicion, duplicity, ill-will — these things do not articulate with the mechanistic conception." The modern imperial state, no longer able to get along without technological production, will in the end be undermined by the habits of thought fostered by the industrial system.

Twenty-five years after the book was written Henry A. Wallace, discussing the new edition in the *Political Science Quarterly*, stated that it "is probably the most acute analysis of modern Germany which has ever been written." Certainly no other thinker of our generation has analyzed this greatest political problem of our time so astutely and so forcefully. Germany's unreadiness to articulate with the democratic nations, which has already resulted in two devastating world wars within a quarter of a century, is basic to Veblen's view of the conflicting elements of our mechanistic system. And what held true for Germany in 1915 he demonstrated at the same time to be equally valid for Japan. Yet his conclusions were not only ignored but officially condemned in 1917 when the book was denied mail privileges by Postmaster-General Burleson.

When it became obvious that the United States was about to

enter the war against Germany, Veblen decided to present his views of war and peace in *An Inquiry into the Nature of Peace and the Terms of Its Perpetuation,* which he published in 1917, largely at his own expense. He examined at length the conceptions of patriotism and dynastic loyalty in order to explain the basic motives of warfare. The first he defined "as a sense of partisan solidarity in respect of prestige" which "lives on invidious comparison and works out in mutual hindrance and jealousy between nations." Patriotism is thus kin to the spirit of pecuniary gain, antagonistic to the normal processes of life and capable of subjecting them to its own purposes. It is essentially " of the nature of habit, induced by circumstances of the past and handed on by tradition and institutional arrangements into the present." The way to overcome it is to develop conditions "which will set the current of habituation the contrary way."

Veblen's analysis of the nature of the state made obvious its ambiguous relation to peace. " At the best, the State, or the government, is an instrumentality for making peace, not for perpetuating it." For the state, like the feudal chieftain, always strives for self-perpetuation and will stop at nothing to achieve that end. If peace does not serve this purpose it will be terminated on short notice. The dynastic states are by their very nature more aggressive and warlike than the democratic governments. In 1917 Germany — and Japan also — was an egregious example of the dynastic state bent on disturbing the peace in order to strengthen its Empire. Its aim was the fruits not of pillage but of perpetual usufruct, and it was able to pursue its imperialistic ambitions at will because of the feudal habits of thought of its subjects. " No other people comparable with the population of the Fatherland has so large and well-knit a body of archaic preconceptions to unlearn." In taking over modern technology and in using it to further dynastic ambitions, the arrogant Germans have become an even greater danger.

The perpetuation of peace does not, however, depend only on " the unconditional surrender of the formidable warlike nations."

That is only the beginning. In the long run war will not cease while competitive capitalism prevails. So long as " free income, that is to say income not dependent on personal merit or excursion of any kind, is the breath of life to the kept classes," and so long as the latter are in control of the several governments, the drive to retain and to enlarge this free income will lead to war. Again in the long run, however, wars result in social upheavals which tend to undermine the right to free income and vested privileges. The common man, who has most to lose and least to gain out of war, will sooner or later learn to distrust his betters. After a period of sanguinary crises " it is at least conceivable that the vested right of owners might fall so far into disrepute as to leave them under a qualified doubt on the return of ' normal ' conditions."

Writing before the League of Nations was officially projected, Veblen made clear that any effective league to enforce peace would have to eliminate not only " all monarchical establishments, constitutional or otherwise, from among its federated nations," but also modern capitalism with its international scramble for markets. In other words, peace can be kept only at the price of a social revolution:

either the price-system and its attendant business enterprise will yield and pass out; or the pacific nations will conserve their pecuniary scheme of law and order at the cost of returning to a war footing and letting their owners preserve the rights of ownership by force of arms.

Veblen's two books on war and peace are monumental testaments to his profound grasp of the working of modern civilization. His acute analysis of the anomalous nature of the dynastic state in contemporary society and of its virulent manifestations in Germany and Japan has been fully substantiated by recent tragic events. Still of the utmost importance to the future weal of mankind is his repeated and emphatic insistence that, first, technological processes will in the long run disintegrate the political and economic forces favoring war; second, unless this happens relatively soon, society may not be able to avoid self-destruction. During World War I these warnings were ignored or scorned. Nor are they being heeded now.

In 1917 Veblen left the University of Missouri by mutual agreement. His half-hearted efforts to find another teaching position were unsuccessful; no university wanted him in spite of his great achievements in the field of economic theory. Nor did he realize his hope of assisting the government in working out the terms of peace; only the Food Administration employed him on a mission to the Middle West, which resulted in a paper favorable to the I.W.W. farm workers. Later that year Helen Marot, an admirer of his, took over the management of *The Dial* and asked him to edit it in collaboration with John Dewey and others. He readily accepted, and wrote for it a number of timely and provocative articles.

Now that he had lost all expectation of further connection with a university he decided to bring out *The Higher Learning in America,* which he had begun many years back and which he had not planned to publish during his lifetime. It was his way of paying back the academic administrators for their obtuse, pusillanimous, and prudish behavior toward him, and his coin was savage satire. The first version was so fiercely critical that his friends persuaded him to moderate his attack. He began by insisting that the university was a seat of learning for men eager to pursue their scholarly studies. He excluded from it the undergraduate college and the professional and business schools, since their purpose was " to afford a rounded discipline to those whose goal is the life of fashion or of affairs." The university man, he argued, was interested in knowledge for its own sake. The results of his scholarly and scientific inquiries might be, and often were, of great benefit to society, but they were only incidental to his main purpose. He was interested in having students, but he welcomed only those who knew what they wanted and went after it without compulsion.

He knew of no such university in the United States. The existing institutions, public and private, were controlled by businessmen for business interests. The boards of trustees, self-perpetuating bodies or political appointees, represented the point of view of the dominant business group. " The intrusion of business principles in the universities goes to weaken and retard the pursuit of learning, and therefore to defeat the ends for which a university is maintained." The trustees engaged as presidents men who were " captains of erudition " and willing to conduct their institutions in the spirit of business enterprise — which Veblen defined as " a spirit of quietism, caution, compromise, collusion, and chicane." Eager to attract both students and men of wealth, these administrators sought a faculty that would " serve as coadjutors and vehicles of executive policy." Consequently they tended to value men more for their committee work than for their scholarship and gave preference to those who demonstrated their " administrative facility, plausibility, proficiency as public speakers and parliamentarians, ready versatility of convictions, and a staunch loyalty to their bread."

Veblen's castigation of business trustees and businesslike administrators, however exaggerated, dealt with conditions prevalent in many of our universities. His attack on the spirit of business enterprise, fiercer and franker than in any of his previous writings, was motivated by his idealistic view of scholarship, as well as by personal resentment. His insistence on the abolition of both the boards of trustees and the captains of erudition was in line with his belief that our system of business enterprise fails to satisfy man's higher ambitions and must give way to a nobler scheme of life.

Early in 1919 Veblen published *The Vested Interests and the State of the Industrial Arts,* a small volume consisting of the series of articles which had appeared in *The Dial* during the previous fall and winter. Writing for the general public and stimulated by the common hope of a better world, he threw off his habitual restraint and developed his thesis with the freedom of the journalist. The first chapters reviewed his basic theme of the increasing divergence between business enterprise and modern technology, between the facts of science and industry and the established system of law and order. Little was being done to remedy this discrepancy, " inasmuch as settled habits of thought are given up tardily, reluctantly, and sparingly." Consequently, notwithstanding the demands of the machine, free income from investment remained sanctioned as a natural right.

The free income which is capitalized in intangible assets of vested interests goes to support the well-to-do investors, who are for this reason called the kept classes and whose keep consists in an indefinitely extensible consumption of superfluities.

Veblen pointed out that while over half of the net income went to the vested interests, even more than that amount was taken from the community by business enterprise in its effort to limit production and increase the cost of salesmanship in order to obtain the greatest rate of profit. This was made possible by the existence of obsolete laws and customs. " The great distinguishing mark of the common man is that he is helpless within the rules of the game as it is played in the twentieth century under the enlightened principles of the eighteenth century." The emergence of auxiliary vested interests, comprising clergymen, military officers, judges and law-yers, the police, union officials, and the like — men of relatively small means but with sufficient stakes in " a capitalized claim to get something for nothing " — tended to perpetuate the power and privileges of the vested interests. According to Veblen, this condition cannot continue indefinitely, since the mechanistic logic of the machine and science will sooner or later discard the right to free income even as the natural-rights doctrine had earlier done away with feudal privileges.

In 1921 Veblen published in a small volume another group of essays from *The Dial* entitled *The Engineers and the Price System*. The book begins with an examination of the prevalence of sabotage in our economy. Veblen insisted that in any capitalistic society " habitual unemployment of the available industrial plant and work-men, in whole or in part, appears to be the indispensable condition without which tolerable conditions of life cannot be maintained." In the absence of this sabotage, capitalism would suffer from over-production, depression, and bankruptcy. This sabotage took various forms, and the best known was the protective tariff.

Modern specialization had brought forth the industrial engineer and the investment banker. The function of the first was to secure production; that of the second was to control it in the interest of profit. Since the captain of finance found the engineer indispensable, and therefore treated him relatively well, the latter bothered little with the larger problems of society. These productive specialists, however, have become the key men in our economic system. Although they at present helped to maintain an industrial dictatorship, sooner or later they must follow their normal inclination as productive engineers. Thereupon a general strike on their part "would swiftly bring a collapse of the old order and sweep the timeworn fabric of finance and absentee sabotage into the discard for good and all."

In these two brief works Veblen is more the reformer than the scholar. He wrote them at a time of social crisis and great expectations: when Wilson's Fourteen Points, the Russian Revolution, and the declarations of the British Labour Party augured well for the New Economic Order. For once Veblen, yielding to the hope that the war had accelerated the process of institutional change, dropped his objective aloofness and his ironic indirection and spoke out with the eager enthusiasm of the social crusader. In his criticism of the vested interests he sought to bring about the overthrow of capitalism; in his praise of the industrial engineer he tried to point the way to production for use and not for profit. Under the influence of the Russian experiment in communism he even envisioned a soviet of engineers in the United States. But he soon perceived the folly of his wishful thinking and made an end of his excursion to the marketplace. Nevertheless the two slender volumes, though they lack the originality and depth of his earlier work, testify eloquently to the ardent social hopes of the armistice period.

Veblen's connection with *The Dial* terminated at the end of a year, when the periodical changed ownership and policy. In the same year, however, the New School for Social Research was established and he, John Dewey, Charles A. Beard, James Harvey Robinson, Wesley C. Mitchell, and other eminent scholars were engaged as teachers and lecturers. Veblen, as previously, made no effort to attract students. Some time later, when the school lost a good part of its financial support, his position became precarious and he remained on its faculty only because one of his former students paid his salary and because he was unable to find employment elsewhere.

Absentee Ownership and Business Enterprise in Recent Times, which appeared in 1923, was Veblen's last and in some respects his keenest analysis of our modern economic system. His thesis was that "absentee ownership has come to be the main and immediate controlling interest in the life of civilized men." The first part repeated, with many refinements and elaborations, his illuminating summary of the economic circumstances which led to the establishment of the laws and customs governing the activities of present-day businessmen. The cultural lag was stressed. "In the nature of things, the scheme of law and custom is always archaic, at all points, in some degree; always out of date more or less." Thus the natural-rights principle of ownership, established by masterless men for purposes of equality, was in the nineteenth century made the legal foundation for the contrary doctrine of absentee ownership. In our own century the corporation and the captain of industry, products of accelerated business enterprise, achieved control of industrialized society.

Nowhere else does the captain of big business rule the affairs of the nation, civil and political, and control the conditions of life so unreservedly as in democratic America, as should be the case, inasmuch as the acquisition of absentee ownership is, after all, in the popular apprehension, the most meritorious and the most necessary work to be done in this country.

This worship of wealth made it possible for the absentee owner of natural resources "to withhold them from use until his charge for them is allowed him," which was always the largest net return. "It is always sound business practice to take any obtainable net gain, at any cost and at any risk to the rest of the community." Everywhere, and particularly in our smaller towns, this practice was regarded as entirely ethical and even exemplary.

The second half of the book discusses the dominance of industry by absentee ownership and the crucial position of credit in contemporary business enterprise. Primarily interested in net gain, business strategy tended to practice "a conscientious withdrawal of efficiency, with whatever tactics of artifice and effrontery may be required to give it effect." The key industries, administering the staple natural resources, "exercise a decisive control over the industrial system at large . . . by owning the right to retard or curtail the supply of necessary power and materials that goes to the manufacturing industries." They likewise dominated the country's farming, the primary source of human livelihood, by virtue of their command of machinery and credit. But if the financier had become the paramount factor in the management of our business system, the technician was emerging as an equally potent director of its mechanical operation. The latter, interested in productive efficiency and requiring co-ordination and mutual aid, in practice had to serve owners who habitually resorted to "afterthoughts and guesswork." Likewise the technology of physics and chemistry, upon which our major industries depend for their operation, now functioned "in an institutional environment imbued with a logical bias that is alien to its bent and inhospitable to its free growth." Sooner or later, if technological progress was not to continue at an uneven and clipped rate, the industrial engineer must seek liberation from capitalistic control.

It was Veblen's contention that "the larger use of credit" had become the pivotal element in the rule of absentee ownership. While the roots of credit were firmly established in the nineteenth century, its current large-scale efflorescence began with the rise of the investment banker and the holding company.

The holding company and the merger, together with the interlocking directorates, and presently the voting trust, were the ways and means by which the banking community took over the strategic regulation of the key industries, and by way of that avenue also the control of the industrial system at large.

The bankers, commanding the country's credit resources, took over the capitalization and credit of corporations and for these services received bonuses of stock which " represented no new acquisition of capital " and therefore stimulated the creation of new credit values. The result was a credit economy ever more complex and unstable, with control gravitating " into the hands of the massive credit institutions that stand at the fiscal center of all things." Yet these institutions require stability and confidence for the success of their operations. " The fabric of credit and capitalization is essentially a fabric of concerted make-believe resting on the routine of the business community at large." A lack of confidence, puncturing this make-believe, will unavoidably disturb the credit structure and even cause its collapse. While the bankers ever seek to strengthen this confidence, they are continually endangering it by depriving the bulk of the population of " an enlarged allowance of livelihood." Sooner or later, consequently, the technicians on the one hand and the organized industrial manpower and farm population on the other will clash with these custodians of absentee ownership and disturb the stability of the entire business structure.

Absentee Ownership is in a true sense a recapitulation of Veblen's previous writings as well as his final effort to strip the glamor from business enterprise and to expose it in all its crassness and contradictions. It is a work of ripe wisdom, mellow in its acerbation, garrulous in its sparkling rhetoric, somber in its acute analysis. Veblen was disappointed in the postwar turn of economic affairs, disheartened by the persistent unintelligence of the mass of mankind, and his last book, for all its castigation of business enterprise, breathes a pessimism that questions his long-run prediction of the overthrow of capitalism.

In 1926, ill and aging, disdainful of the artificial prosperity of the period, discouraged by his failure to obtain another teaching position, he decided to move to California. There he lived in his simple and crude shack, feeling alone and neglected, until his death three years later at the age of seventy-two.

Thorstein Veblen's great achievement was his removal of the underpinnings from the static structure of classical economics. In the 1890's, when he first surveyed the literature, the practising economists were still pre-Darwinian in their thinking and unscientific in their uncritical acceptance of ideas that no longer squared with experience. Most of them still made use of a hedonistic psychology which other sciences had discarded. They identified acquisition with production, and dogmatically expounded the doctrine of natural rights. Consequently they persisted in asking the wrong questions and so arrived at the irrelevant conclusions. Impatient with their obtuse smugness, yet in no position to make a formal attack, he used an exaggerated form of their own jargon to disguise the directness of his criticism. Thus, parodying the pseudo-scientific style of the pedant, he asked satirically:

What does all this signify? If we are getting restless under the taxonomy of a monocotyledonous wage doctrine and a cryptogamic theory of interest, with involute, loculicidal, tomentous and moniliform variants, what is the cytoplasm, centrosome, or karyokinetic process to which we may turn, and in which we may find surcease from the metaphysics of normality and controlling principles?

No wonder that, to quote Professor Paul T. Homan, " so far as one man can be held accountable it can hardly be denied that Veblen has been the arch-disturber of the economist's academic peace of mind."

An intensive study of the writings of Karl Marx and his followers persuaded Veblen that the socialists were at several important points out of line with reality in their interpretation of the economic process. Because Marx's antecedents were " the Materialistic Hegelianism and the English system of Natural Rights," his habits of thought were pre-Darwinian and dialectical. For all his efforts at scientific objectivity, Marx could not free himself from some of the preconceptions of the classical economists. Consequently his theory of the class struggle — which follows Bentham rather than Hegel — in its emphasis on self-interest depended upon an unsound hedonistic psychology. Even less tenable was the doctrine of increasing misery, upon which Marx had predicated the overthrow of capitalism, as time had convincingly demonstrated.

While the theory of value and surplus value are Marx's explanation of the possibility of existence of the capitalistic system, the law of the accumulation of capital is his exposition of the causes which must lead to the collapse of that system and of the manner in which the collapse will come. . . . In Marx's theory, socialism will come by way of a conscious class movement on the part of the propertyless laborers, who will act advisedly in their own interest and force the revolutionary movement for their own gain.

Veblen found, however, that Marx's logic, while impeccable theoretically, was hardly borne out by events. The intensification of capitalism brought forth not abject misery and social revolt but a trade unionism determined " to deal with questions of capitalistic production and distribution by business methods, to settle the problems of working-class employment and livelihood by a system of non-political, businesslike bargains." While this procedure was contrary to Marxian theory, the socialists willy-nilly had to deal with the trade unions in the hope of gaining a mass following and thereby repudiated the doctrine of increasing misery. Much as Veblen admired Marx's profound intellect and much as he sympathized with his criticism of capitalism, he never became a socialist.

Veblen developed his own economic theory with singular brilliance. For all its extravagant generalization and invalidated particulars, it remains an extraordinary intellectual achievement and has exerted a profound influence on our economic thinking. While his use of the term instinct has been effectively criticized by psychologists, none has questioned his basic assumption that man's aversion to work as work is more a convention than an innate condition. His differentiation between the sense of workmanship and pecuniary activity, stated eloquently in all his major writings, is fundamental to a clear understanding of the nature of our economic society. Similarly significant is his repeated insistence on the disciplinary demands of the machine process and of their long-run effect on industrial workmen. Another of his main contributions is his exposition of the anachronistic basis of the natural-rights doctrine; since this doctrine forms the chief means for the perpetuation of vested interests and absentee ownership, his analysis of its unwarranted exploitation for pecuniary advantage has given the critics of capitalism their most effective weapon. Equally important was his criticism of the antisocial nature of business enterprise, in which he was even more condemnatory than Marx. Doubtless his habit of generalization and long-run predictions led him to exaggerate the influence of technology on our thought, but this did not invalidate his basic thesis.

Veblen's style is characteristic of the man he was: precise yet ponderous, incisive yet indirect, witty yet long-winded. So striking and so significant were the phrases he coined that many of them have entered into our common speech. He made his most cutting thrusts in verbose footnotes, but few readers overlooked them. By limiting his examples largely to the archaic past, he was able to express a withering contempt for the shams and chicane of the present. His polysyllabic jargon, which irritated many of his readers, was his deliberate means of speaking his mind without suffering the consequences. For he regarded language as " an instrument of precision " and used it deliberately to produce specific impressions — often intentionally heightening or obfuscating them for his own amusement. "Veblen loved producing literary effects," wrote Professor Wesley C. Mitchell. "He was an archphrasemaker. He took a naughty delight in making people squirm. His aloofness, his objectivity were partly stage make-up."

In his later work, however, he felt sufficiently free of academic restraint to write simply and directly. Always, even when deliberately ponderous, he composed with scrupulous care. Although he frequently took much space to get going, he rewrote every page until it satisfied his hypercritical eye; and he permitted no editor to tinker with his sentences even when their elephantine appearance cried for emendation. He knew what he wanted to say and he insisted on saying it in his own particular way. There is no doubt that his singular style has deprived him of readers, but he could no more change it than he could alter the fiber of his thought.

Veblen has from the very first attracted ardent disciples — keen students who readily perceived the greatness of his intellect. Though the orthodox economists tried to ignore him, they could not keep his work from their younger liberal colleagues. In time the growing number of institutional economists came to regard him as their leader. Many prominent publicists, particularly those of liberal bent, have given evidence of his influence upon their thought. Professor Homan, writing two decades ago, asserted: " It falls little beyond the truth to say that almost all the new leads in economic thinking which have been fruitfully followed during the past twenty years are in some degree directly traceable to him." Time has not deprived Veblen's ideas of their stimulating quality. Indeed, they have become basic to a clear grasp of our economic society. The outstanding advocates of the New Deal since 1933 — men like Henry A. Wallace, Isador Lubin, and R. G. Tugwell — have been close students of Veblen's writings. And his stature has grown accordingly.

THE MILITANT LIBERALS

LINCOLN STEFFENS   JOHN PETER ALTGELD

RANDOLPH BOURNE

THE LIBERAL BACKGROUND

FOR A GENERATION and more the crusade against Negro slavery had dominated the activities of American liberals. The various progressive movements of the 1830's and 1840's had been almost completely eclipsed by the concentrated Abolitionist effort of the succeeding decade. Once the Civil War had ended, however, it appeared as if all zeal for reform had died with the slavery issue. With the Negroes nominally free, even the extreme Abolitionists — Wendell Phillips excepted — acted as if the millennium had arrived.

Yet the voice of liberal protest was sorely needed in the years following Lee's surrender at Appomattox. For the end of chattel slavery coincided with the intensification of economic inequality. The Civil War had not only stimulated Northern businessmen to develop machine industry at an accelerated pace but had also enabled bankers to concentrate and control the liquid capital of the nation. When peace came, these two groups had the means and the techniques for the exploitation of the continent that lay open before them. Nor did they hesitate to make the most of their boundless opportunities. With an arrogance and callousness that matched their energy and enterprise, they established new industries, covered the country with a spider web of iron rails, and exploited the nation's vast natural resources — all to their great personal advantage. In their compulsive efforts to get rich quick they ruined competitors by ruthless and dishonest means and deceived their unsuspecting and helpless customers. To obtain franchises and special privileges they bribed legislators and corrupted high officials without the least scruple. They did not hesitate to make the government serve their private advantage because they believed that the state's prime function was to expedite business enterprise. " It was an anarchistic world," wrote Professor Parrington, " of strong, capable men, selfish, unenlightened, amoral — an excellent example of what human nature will do with undisciplined freedom. In the Gilded Age freedom was the freedom of buccaneers preying on the argosies of Spain."

The farmers were among the early victims of rapacious businessmen. Unlike those who had lived off the land before 1860 — pioneers who had turned to the frontier in their quest for economic independence — the Civil War veterans and European immigrants who were lured to the virgin prairies by the prospect of a free homestead were neither independent nor self-sufficient. Mostly without means, forced to outfit their farms with capital borrowed at a usurious rate of interest, wholly dependent on the railroads for the shipment of their crops and on a falling price level for their gross income, the large majority of these hard-working farmers failed pathetically in their efforts to free themselves of debt. For years the objects of exploitation on the part of the railroads and the grain elevators, the meat packers, the local bankers and storekeepers, they became in effect the drudges of an industrialized society. The phrase " ten-cent corn and ten-percent interest " truly expressed their plight.

It was this harsh adversity that drove the farmers into politics. In the early 1870's they turned their Granges, which they had founded several years earlier as a nonpolitical and secret social organization, into forums, in which much was said against unscrupulous railroads and extortionate bankers. Although natural individualists, they were forced by necessity to turn to the government for redress. Their gatherings were not part of an organized revolt but the spontaneous and sporadic expression of despair. The

Granges quickly multiplied in number and soon counted a million and a half members. Their leaders called on the legislatures of their respective states for laws curbing monopolies. In 1873 the Illinois Grange demanded that the despotic railroad, which " defies our laws, plunders our shippers, impoverishes our people, and corrupts our government, shall be subdued and made to subserve the public interest at whatever cost." The following year the National Grange expressed its strong condemnation of " the tyrannies of monopolies." As a consequence of this widespread agitation, state after state in the Middle West enacted " Granger " laws regulating the railroads and other monopolies. But the federal courts quickly nullified most of this legislation on the ground that interstate commerce could be regulated only by the federal government. This unforseen blow brought about the precipitous decline of the Grange; most of the members, eager for immediate relief, dropped away soon after the courts had frustrated their first attempt to obtain redress by political means.

Meantime urban liberals, outraged by the corruption that characterized President Grant's administration, began to consider means of purging national politics. They believed that improvements in the machinery of government plus upright officials would recapture the state from " the interests " and again provide equal opportunity for all. Led by Carl Schurz, Horace Greeley, Charles Francis Adams, Salmon Chase, and others of national prominence, they convened in 1872, organized the Liberal Republican party, chose Greeley as their Presidential candidate, and campaigned on a platform of honesty and efficiency in government. But the Grant political machine rode over them with the force of a steamroller. The young party of reformers failed miserably at the polls. Nevertheless the insurgents persevered in their attacks upon political corruption and business brigandage. It was largely through their efforts that such misfeasances as Credit Mobilier, the Salary Grab, the Whiskey Ring, and the Belknap Scandal were exposed to public condemnation.

The panic of 1873 and the subsequent economic depression spurred liberals and reformers to intensified activity. Wendell Phillips spoke out with powerful eloquence against the ill-treatment of wage laborers. To save workmen from enforced idleness and suffering, which he came to regard as worse than chattel slavery, he was ready to abolish the burgeoning system of capitalism. A few labor representatives agreed with him. Most liberals, however, were unwilling to consider so radical a proposal. Concrete immediate reforms appealed to them most. Because of their deep suspicion of bankers and brokers, they were most alarmed by the government's deflationary policy. They criticized the resumption of specie payments and the continued withdrawal of Greenbacks from circulation as flagrantly bad measures certain further to squeeze the debt-ridden farmers and poor city workers. After considerable discussion they united to form the Greenback party in time to put a ticket in the 1876 campaign, with the patriarchal Peter Cooper at its head. In the election two years later the party reached its greatest strength, polling nearly a million votes. Powerless, however, to effect the social and monetary measures it advocated, it too began to decline with the passing of the economic depression at the end of the 1870's.

The grievous poverty of the period called into question the fundamental pattern of our government. Men wanted to know why such privation and suffering should exist on a continent blest with untold wealth. Where, they asked, was our vaunted equal opportunity for all? When President Hayes ordered federal troops to break up the railroad strike without troubling to learn the wretched conditions which had driven hard-working men to desperate measures, Robert Ingersoll spoke for thousands when he condemned this use of soldiers against civilians.

I sympathize with every honest effort made by the children of labor to improve their condition. That is a poorly governed country in which those who do the most have the least. There is something wrong when men are obliged to beg for leave to toil. We are not yet a civilized people; when we are, pauperism and crime will vanish from our land.

Henry Demarest Lloyd, a Jeffersonian liberal, was the forerunner of the "muckraking" journalists of the 1900's. Unlike E. L. Godkin of *The Nation*, whose liberalism was narrowly Manchesterian and whose social criticism was directed more against the vulgarity than against the chicane and ruthlessness of the rich, Lloyd was profoundly perturbed by the rapacious ruffianism of our leading businessmen. Because the Standard Oil Company was the most notorious of the firms engaging in unscrupulous practices in the 1870's, he selected it for special study. What he uncovered turned him into a social crusader. The company's unrestrained lawlessness, its brutal extermination of honest competitors, its deceitful practices — the means which enabled it to reach a production of 6,000,000 barrels of oil annually and a capitalization of $200,000,000 in ten years' time — appeared to him as the total negation of the principles upon which our nation had been founded. The factual article incorporating his findings, published in *The Atlantic Monthly* in 1881, was, in the words of his biographer, "a turning point in our social history; with it dawned upon Americans the first conviction that this industrial development of which we had been so proud, was a source, not of strength, but of fatal weakness, and that the Republic could no more endure an oligarchy of capitalists than an oligarchy of slaveholders." So great was the demand for this essay that seven printings of the issue containing it had to be ordered in quick succession. Judged by the testimony of Charles Edward Russell, the article struck fire in the minds of many Americans who cleaved to the ideals of the Declaration of Independence.

Lloyd persevered in his investigation of the criminal methods employed by large corporations to ruin competitors and to plunder the public. For years he pored over the reports of legislature investigations, trial records, and court decisions — gathering his data from sworn evidence and judicial findings in order to make his indictment the more devastating. In 1894 he published his monumental work on the subject, *Wealth Against Commonwealth*. Appearing during the nadir of a new and severe depression, when armies of hungry unemployed crowded the cities and tramped the country-side on the way to Washington, the book emphasized the callous cupidity that brought about this human suffering. After presenting a detailed and documented exposition of the manner in which the large corporations achieved monopolistic power, Lloyd declared that the Rockefellers, the Carnegies, and the Morgans were merely the beneficiaries of a state of mind which confused social self-interest with individual self-interest. Ever since Adam Smith we had assumed that these two interests were in effect identical — that the individual's pursuit of personal gain would inevitably benefit society as a whole. In practice, however, capitalist enterprise has tended to encourage selfishness and to thwart the pursuit of the common good.

In industry we have been substituting all the mean passions that can set man against man in place of the irresistible power of brotherhood. . . . We have overworked the self-interest of the individual. The line of conflict between individual and social is a progressive one of the discovery of point after point in which the two are identical.

Grasping businessmen, however, have accepted the principle of "the public be damned." They have regarded themselves as responsible to none but themselves.

Without restraint of culture, experience, the pride, or even the inherited caution of class or rank, these men, intoxicated, think they are the wave instead of the float, and that they have created the business which has created them.

Yet their arrogance cannot stay the tide of social progress. For all their concentration of power they cannot indefinitely escape the wrath of an outraged people. "Monopoly is business at the end of its journey. It has got there. The irrepressible conflict is now as distinctly with business as the issue so lately met was with slavery." As a sanguine liberal Lloyd had no doubt of the outcome. But he knew that it could be achieved only when the mass of mankind understood the issue and insisted on the establishment of a self-interest that identified the individual with society. "The new self-interest will remain unenforced in business until we invent the forms by which the vast multitudes who have been gathered together in modern production can organize themselves into a people there as in government."

Wealth Against Commonwealth was read by thousands with the excited interest which a pirate adventure story arouses. It easily withstood the attacks of the lawyers and lackeys of the businesses it pilloried. Yet it attained only a mite of the effect one might have expected. The large middle class, upon whom changes in governmental policy largely depended, was horrified by Lloyd's arraignment of big business but was loath to accept the alternative of social democracy. The book, however, became a quarry and a source of inspiration for the succeeding generation of liberals, and thus became a milestone on the road to social reform.

The poor and disgruntled farmers were indifferent to the advocates of civil service reform and were distrustful of, if not hostile to, Henry George's single tax, but they readily followed the critics of monopolies and banks. When the Grange and the Greenback party failed them, they flocked to the Farmers Alliance. The aim of this organization was to improve the lot of its members and to right pressing social wrongs. Its leaders argued that while the railroads and banks and industries prospered, farmers were the victims of " some extrinsic baleful influence "; they, " the bone and sinew of the nation," the producers of the largest bulk of necessities, were receiving a mere pittance in return. The restless and discontented, wrote Professor John D. Hicks, " voiced their sentiments more and fled from them less. Hence arose the veritable chorus of denunciation directed against those individuals and those corporations who considered only their own advantage without regard to the effect their actions might have upon the farmer and his interests." This critical attitude among farmers served to stimulate interest in the Alliance groups, both in the South and in the West. Local branches soon united into statewide organizations and in 1882 they formed a national Farmers Alliance. Thereafter membership rose from

100,000 to 2,000,000 in 1890, when the Alliance reached its peak of activity and influence.

Throughout the 1880's farmers, like the city-dwelling workers, were becoming increasingly class-conscious. It was a decade noted on the one hand for the rapid growth of big business and on the other for such evidences of discontent as Lloyd's articles against monopolies, the publication and popularity of *Progress and Poverty* and *Looking Backward*, the strikes which culminated in the Haymarket hysteria, the Anti-Monopoly party in 1884, and the National Union Labor party in 1888. Each of these events furthered the farmers' interest in politics. Poverty and continued debt made them more vociferous in their demands for help from government agencies. Frederick Jackson Turner stated that by 1890 " the defenses of the pioneer democrat began to shift from free land to legislation, from the ideal of individualism to the ideal of social control through regulation by law." In the 1890 elections the Alliance sent two of its members to the Senate, eight to the House, and scores to state legislatures. Many other elected officials, particularly in the South, while nominally of the major parties, were openly in sympathy with Alliance demands.

The next logical step was greater political concentration. Alliance leaders in the West and South, roused by the widespread dissatisfaction among their followers, became sharply insistent in their demands for reform. Mary Elizabeth Lease of Kansas, famous for her advice to farmers to raise less corn and more hell, expressed the sentiments of many thousands when she declared: " We want money, land and transportation. We want the abolition of National Banks, and we want the power to make loans direct from the government. We want the accursed foreclosure system wiped out." " Sockless " Jerry Simpson, another popular agitator, was especially vehement in his attacks on the railroads because of their large land holdings. An admirer of Henry George, he argued that " man must have access to land or he is a slave. The man who owns the earth, owns the people, for they must buy the privilege of living on his earth." Leaders of even greater eminence were James B.

Weaver, who had been the Greenback Presidential candidate in 1880 and who was generally trusted by those who sought reforms rather than a revolution; Ignatius Donnelly of Minnesota, an outstanding orator and versatile politician; William A. Peffer, Senator from Kansas; and Ben Tillman, L. L. Polk, and Thomas E. Watson — popular liberal spokesmen for the agricultural South.

In 1891 these and other representatives of Farmers Alliance groups met at a preliminary session in Cincinnati for the purpose of uniting their forces in the coming election. After many efforts at conciliation and combination, they agreed to hold an organizational meeting at an early date. This convention took place in St. Louis the following February. Delegates from twenty-two organizations, including a number of Congressmen from the major parties, sang and shouted their acclaim of the newly formed People's party. The rostrum, according to a current periodical, " was filled with leaders of the Alliance, the Knights of Labor, the single tax people, the Prohibitionists, the Anti-Monopolists, the People's party, the Reform Press, and the Women's Alliance." On the Fourth of July Populist delegates from nearly every state in the Union convened in Omaha to prepare a platform and nominate the national candidates. They were an evangelical, solemn, idealistic body of dissident reformers. " We believe," they asserted in their platform, " that the time has come when railroad corporations will either own the people or the people must own the railroads." In addition they demanded the government ownership of the telegraph and telephone lines, government loans to farmers at low rates of interest, the free coinage of silver at the ratio of 16 to 1, a graduated income tax, the reduction of the tariff, postal savings banks, shorter hours of labor, the popular election of Senators, and the adoption of the initiative and referendum. Although most of these planks have since been incorporated into our fundamental political pattern without in the least affecting our form of government, they seemed truly revolutionary to the conservatives of 1892 and were denounced as such by the leaders of both major parties. The Populist campaign was extremely vigorous. In the Western states numerous speakers, headed by the Presidential candidate Weaver, were received with enthusiastic approval. The aggravated Negro problem, however, kept most of the Southern farmers within the Democratic fold. When the votes were counted in November, Weaver's share exceeded a million. Populist voters had also elected three Senators, ten Congressmen, four governors, and 345 state legislators.

The economic depression which ushered President Cleveland into his second term of office only intensified the wretched condition of the poor farmers and laborers. Nor were they mollified by the government's apparent indifference to their plight. In the 1894 state elections this discontent was evidenced by a greatly increased vote for the Populist candidates — about a million and a half in all. Populist leaders were in a sanguine mood and began to plan for the national election two years hence. On the eve of the campaign their executive committee boldly declared that the main issue confronting the nation was the struggle between the people and big business.

There are but two sides in the conflict that is being waged in this country today. On the one side are the allied hosts of monopolies, the money power, great trusts and railroad corporations, who seek the enactment of laws to benefit them and impoverish the people. On the other side are the farmers, laborers, merchants, and all others who produce wealth and bear the burdens of taxation. . . . Between the two there is no middle ground.

The tide of events, however, made naught of the hopes of the radical Populists. Always eager for a plausible panacea, the mass of farmers and small merchants were readily persuaded by the silver advocates that their salvation lay in a reformed currency system. The immense popularity of W. H. Harvey's *Coin's Financial School*, which appeared in 1894 and contained a simplified exposition of the free-silver doctrine, proved a godsend to the bimetallist politicians. Shrewdly nurtured by them, the currency issue soon assumed first place in the minds of the majority of the people west and south of the Alleghenies. H. D. Lloyd, who was an ardent radical Populist, protested that free silver was becoming the cowbird of the reform movement and was laying its eggs in the nest painstakingly built by the proponents of genuine liberalism. But his voice remained a cry in the wilderness. Another blow to the Populists was the refusal of co-operation by the young and lusty American Federation of Labor on the ground that inflation would bring higher wages. Equally serious was the unresolved Negro question which was plaguing Southern insurgents and forcing them to remain within the Democratic party. Confronted by these difficulties and confused by internal dissent, the Populists committed the fatal error of postponing their national convention until the major parties had held theirs. After Altgeld and Bryan had captured control of the Democratic party and committed it to silver reform as well as to a thoroughly progressive platform, the Populists had no alternative but to align themselves with Bryan and become a mere faction of the unsuccessful older party.

It should be noted that such outstanding radicals and reformers as Henry George, Edward Bellamy, W. P. D. Bliss of the Christian Socialists, Victor Berger, and Eugene V. Debs worked enthusiastically for the success of the Democratic ticket. The platform, which Godkin denounced as anarchistic, was indeed a revolutionary document in that it expressed a people's declaration of economic independence against plutocracy. That Bryan was not the leader to establish it as the law of the land was evident to those who were not completely hypnotized by his mellifluent oratory. But its principal proposals, for which Altgeld was mainly responsible, had only to wait for the march of democracy to catch up with them.

Big business, temporarily frightened but doubly secure in victory, accelerated its rate of combination and expansion, with the blessing of the McKinley administration. The economic stimulus given by the Spanish-American War opened worldwide vistas to the business venturers bent on completing the circle of financial enterprise. Dollar diplomacy abroad and a free hand at home cleared the way for their manipulations. John Chamberlain declared that around 1900 " the United States was definitely committed to the welfare of plutocracy." This policy was ratified by the people on election day, when they voted down Bryan's second endeavor to gain the Presidency.

Yet the great wave of Populism, while it broke vainly against the walls of chicane and reefs of gold adroitly constructed by the astute Marcus A. Hanna, did not recede without leaving agitated pools of liberalism behind. Everywhere, and particularly west of the Alleghenies, men without number could not forget the vision of the democratic apocalypse which had stirred them deeply and which, even in adversity, continued to brighten their hearts. And wherever they could find a strong leader they persevered with him towards the gates of victory. Professor H. U. Faulkner stated that whereas Altgeld was the only notable liberal state executive in the 1890's, " within a decade of Altgeld's retirement to private life amidst a storm of abuse, the people of the various states were placing in the gubernatorial chairs men whose schemes of reform were more radical than Altgeld's." The most eminent of these progressives was Robert M. La Follette, who became governor of Wisconsin in 1900. His radical reforms in the fields of public utilities, education, taxation, industry, and labor, transformed Wisconsin into the most liberal state in the Union.

Equally significant were the eddies of revolt in a number of cities. For decades American urban centers had been notoriously honeycombed with political graft. Again and again improvised parties of reform failed to budge the entrenched bosses from their control of the corrupted city governments. In the 1890's, however, civic reformers began to gain victories at the polls. One of the first of these notable liberals was Hazen S. Pingree who, as mayor of Detroit and governor of Michigan, had for a decade fought the public utilities openly and effectively. In 1897 Toledo chose as mayor " Golden Rule " Samuel M. Jones, a wealthy sucker-rod manufacturer who had turned Tolstoyan and practised the teachings of Christ with a stubborn perseverance which antagonized the rich and respectable citizens but which won him the devotion of the poor and lowly voters. It was these simple folk, who knew a friend when they saw one, who kept him in office till he died in 1904; after which they voted Brand Whitlock, his secretary and successor, into office, till he begged off after his fourth term. In neighboring Cleveland, Tom L. Johnson became in 1901, according to Lincoln Steffens, " the best mayor of the best governed city in the United States." Johnson, like Jones, was a successful businessman before he became a reformer. " We ourselves have created monopoly by law," he argued, echoing Henry George, his mentor. " Take away special privilege, and competition will reappear." Johnson fought vigorously against the monopolies, and he too was re-elected again and again in the face of powerful opposition on the part of the " best " citizens. And his distinguished successor, Newton D. Baker, likewise maintained a reform administration.

Throughout the 1900's social reform received its greatest support from a group of editors and journalists whose sensational reports of business chicane and political corruption kept the nation on edge from month to month. These writers, termed " muckrakers " by President Theodore Roosevelt in 1906 in a vain effort to discredit them, were motivated by the traditional concepts of American democracy. They assumed that men in the mass were essentially good and that it was only necessary to expose wrongs for them to be righted by the might of public indignation.

Lincoln Steffens was the most eminent of these muckrakers. His articles on bosses and boodle — penetrating expositions of the politics which came to be known as " invisible government " — written in a clear and urbane style, made him the most influential journalist of the period. Ida Tarbell brought Lloyd's study of the Standard Oil Company up to date, and her book indicted the Rockefeller corporation with a finality unshaken by its adroit apologists. James Howard Bridge's *The Inside History of the Carnegie Steel Company*, which appeared concurrently with the Tarbell chapters on Standard Oil in 1902, was equally objective and damnatory. It was not long before the flagrantly rapacious practices of other large companies were described in ugly detail by such conscientious journalists as Ray Stannard Baker, Samuel Hopkins Adams, Mark Sullivan, and Charles Edward Russell.

While even the staid " quality " magazines succumbed during the 1900's to the general demand for articles of exposure and criticism, the periodicals most closely identified with muckraking were *McClure's, Munsey's, Everybody's, The Arena, American Magazine, Leslie's* (later the *Cosmopolitan*), and *Collier's*. Improvements in printing and lithography, which enabled publishers to reduce the price of the monthlies to ten cents a copy, put these journals within the reach of a large public. Time and again the publication of an important article brought a periodical hundreds of thousands of new readers. To keep these enormous gains, editors vied with one another in the quality as well as the sensational nature of their reading matter. S. S. McClure led the field by going to great expense in obtaining the best writers and by his insistence on a " high degree of truthfulness, accuracy, and interest " in the articles he published. The phenomenal popularity of his magazine spurred rival publishers to similar activity and to seek new fields of exploitation.

In 1904 both *Collier's* and *The Ladies' Home Journal* began a campaign against patent medicines which exposed the fraudulent nature of these quack nostrums. At about the same time Charles Edward Russell began his series of articles on the criminal practices of the meat packers. Upton Sinclair's sensational novel, *The Jungle,* climaxed the public revulsion against the producers of rotten food. The agitation for a pure food and drug act, for years carried on in vain by public-spirited doctors and scientists, suddenly forced itself upon a recalcitrant Congress with such irresistible clamor that the measure was made the law of the land despite the powerful lobbying of the affected corporations. Also in 1904 *Everybody's* began to print Thomas W. Lawson's chapters from *Frenzied Finance,* which described in sensational detail the fraudulent manipulations of some of the leading bankers and businessmen of the day. The enormous popularity of this series for a time made the monthly the most widely read of the magazines. Life insurance and the railroads were next placed in the pillory by the muckrakers. These articles brought about public investigations and enabled La Follette, now in the Senate, to ram through the Hepburn bill for the revitalization of the Interstate Commerce Commission. It was with David Graham Phillips's papers on "The Treason of the Senate," which began to appear in Hearst's *Cosmopolitan* in 1906, that the literature of exposure reached its most sensational effectiveness. Although the series was suddenly stopped and was never reprinted in book form, it generated such public indignation that the citadel of reaction was forced wide open and the constitutional amendment favoring the popular election of Senators was made inevitable.

Phillips's uncompromising assault upon the most strongly entrenched supporters of big business initiated a counterattack upon muckraking and reform. Conservative editors, preachers, and politicians began to confuse the issues and to vilify the aggressive liberals. Businessmen set out to intimidate the popular periodicals by threatening to withdraw their advertising, and in several instances they gained control of editorial policy by outright purchase. The American News Company added its weight against the progressive monthlies by impeding their newsstand sale. As a result one after another of the muckraking magazines disappeared or changed its editorial policy.

Equally decisive was the fact that the writers themselves were losing their zeal for the public good. Most of them were true freelances. While a few of them became socialists and did their best work after that, the majority lacked the inspiration of a strict political philosophy. All of them were exposed to constant pressure, if not coercion — and sooner or later they could not but grow tired and gravitate towards safety and comfort. John Chamberlain described their position succinctly when he remarked that Lincoln Steffens's "generation tried valiantly, throughout the fifteen-year period of the quest for social justice, to understand plutocratic, industrial, monopolistic America by means of Jeffersonian, agrarian, individualistic shibboleths." It remained for the generation of liberals after them to adjust Jeffersonian democracy to monopolistic industrialism and bring forth the doctrine of the New Deal.

The writings of the muckrakers, especially of Lincoln Steffens, helped to keep public interest in politics at the boiling point. In city after city, large and small, in many states, and in the nation as a whole, voters were sufficiently provoked by the exposures of graft and special privileges to unite in a determined effort to clean up corrupt government. A number of boss-ridden administrations were driven out and replaced by reformers and public-spirited businessmen. Where the elected officials were honest, progressive and energetic — mayors like Brand Whitlock and Newton D. Baker, governors like Joseph W. Folk of Missouri and Hiram Johnson of California, and Senators like La Follette of Wisconsin and Albert Beveridge of Indiana — they served the people well and protected them from the anti-social aims of big business. Even more numerous, however, were those officials who meant well but who had neither the strength nor the idealism to stand up against the insidious maneuvers of the professional politicians and suave lobbyists.

Throughout the 1900's Theodore Roosevelt, first as President and then as elder statesman, posed as the nation's leading liberal. A man of wide culture, at once an advocate of social reform and a practical politician, a colossal egoist who despised the selfish rich, gifted with a zest for the strenuous life and a coiner of striking phrases, he employed a combination of evasive compromise and bold statement to further his assumed role as a champion of the people. This he was not. Although his accomplishments while President were not so insignificant as some of his critics have maintained — time tends to tarnish achievements which at first seem lustrous — they do not measure up to his claim for them. He was clear-sighted enough to know when to bow to an inevitable reform, but his letters and his behavior during the last few years of his life mark him, not as the genuine liberal, but as a politician who loved popularity more than the people.

President Taft's aloofness and his respect for the established order of things kept him from succeeding his mentor as leader of the liberal Republicans. Although he adhered closely to his constitutional conception of public welfare and furthered legislation that compared favorably with that enacted during Roosevelt's administration, he early antagonized the men who worked for the liberalization of American government. The voters in the 1910 election further weakened his authority by sending a Democratic majority to Congress. His estrangement from Roosevelt, who was playing shrewd politics, also added to his general unpopularity. Early in 1912 it became evident that Roosevelt and not Taft was the choice of the Republican majority. When the political bosses forced the renomination of the latter, the large number of liberal delegates bolted the convention, organized the Progressive party, and nominated Roosevelt with an enthusiasm that reminded many of the early Populist gatherings.

The Progressive party was indeed the People's party in a new dress. Their platforms were essentially alike. Both denounced the corrupt condition of the old parties and urged the return to popular government; both favored greater control of business and measures intended to benefit laborers and farmers. Roosevelt endorsed every plank and exhorted the people to strengthen his hand at Armageddon — but primarily as a means to political victory. For he had only a vague understanding of political theory and only a tithe of the deep faith in the people which Senator La Follette, who had refused to accept his leadership, possessed in natural abundance. It was Roosevelt's opportunistic attitude that enabled him, without a change of heart, to acclaim in 1912 the reforms which sixteen years earlier he had decried as anarchistic and un-American — and which he discarded readily enough when the outbreak of war in 1914 altered the social atmosphere.

Roosevelt and La Follette had repelled each other from the first. While one gave his heart and mind to the cause of social welfare and fought the reactionaries in the Senate with a stubborn persistence which beat down all opposition, the other could not even appreciate such dogged devotion to an ideal.

La Follette [John Chamberlain pointed out] was deeds and words in close tandem; Roosevelt was words — and an occasional deed for the sake of the record, or to save face. La Follette was a man who sought to make strict economic analysis the basis of his laws; he never talked without facts, the best available facts, and the University of Wisconsin faculty came, characteristically enough, to replace the lobby in his home state.

When Roosevelt, eager for the Presidential nomination on a regular or insurgent ticket, induced the liberal Republicans to follow him rather than La Follette, their rightful leader, the latter chose to remain with the Republican party.

In the three-cornered race in 1912 Taft was ignominiously defeated, running far behind Roosevelt, and Woodrow Wilson won the election by a minority vote. The Progressives were jubilant in defeat because their strong showing presaged victory in the near future. But they did not take cognizance of their leader's attitude. Defeat had dampened Roosevelt's enthusiasm for social reform: he was not eager to act the crusader except as a means to political success. In 1913 he left for Brazil and gave complete charge of the party's affairs to George W. Perkins, a Morgan partner and Wall Street trader who had become associated with the Progressives. According to Harold L. Ickes, Perkins held the party " in the hollow of his hand " and kept it from capitalizing on the popular enthusiasm it had generated during the campaign. Nor did he relinquish his control after Roosevelt's return, and he further weakened the party by his desultory leadership during the 1914 election. From that time till the political conventions in 1916 Perkins maneuvered for a reunited Republican party — with Roosevelt as its standard-bearer if feasible and with a compromise candidate if necessary. Roosevelt abetted these tactics by his obvious indifference to the fate of the party which he had brought into being. And his refusal to accept the renomination, made by acclaim despite Perkins's opposition, deeply disillusioned his followers and caused the quick disintegration of the Progressive party.

If the liberal Republicans were thwarted by defective leadership, the Jeffersonian Democrats were led to victory by a man who fathered a remarkably progressive body of legislation which in all likelihood exceeded by far the reforms Roosevelt might have promoted. Under Wilson's firm guidance Congress lowered the tariff, improved and broadened the currency and banking systems, passed the anti-trust Clayton Act, established a Federal Trade Commission to supervise business practices, enacted favorable labor laws, and provided lower interest rates to farmers by means of the Farm Loan Act. This was his " New Freedom " — the fruition of long agitation for a more equitable distribution of the country's bounties.

We are going to climb the slow road [he declared in 1913] until it reaches some upland where the air is fresher, where the whole talk of mere politicians is stilled, where men can look in each other's faces and see that there is nothing to conceal; and whence, looking over the road, we shall see at last that we have fulfilled our promise to mankind. We had said to the world " America was created to break every kind of monopoly, and to set men free, upon a footing of equality " and now we have proved that we have meant it.

Wilson realized his program of reform because he sincerely believed in the necessity of these measures and had the ability to channel the prevailing progressive mood of the people in the direction of a heedful Congress. But the outbreak of war in Europe in 1914 forced him to concern himself more and more with international affairs and military preparedness. Not the welfare but the safety of the nation became his chief care. In the process his economic liberalism yielded to the ideal of world security. The carnage across the Atlantic inspired him to seek ways and means of making future wars impossible. For this noble purpose he agreed to bring the United States into the war — a war to end war and make the world safe for democracy. Once the die was cast, victory over the enemy became his major pursuit. He was so possessed by the lofty ideals for which he believed the war was being fought that he stopped at nothing in his efforts towards their realization. Although a great many liberals, blinded by the brilliance of his rhetoric and unable to meet stubborn facts face to face, eagerly joined him in the crusade against Prussianism, he insisted on complete national unanimity. " Woe to the man or group of men," he warned in 1917, " that seeks to stand in our way in this day of high resolution." The more amenable critics he silenced by taking them into the government; the handful of pacifists and radicals who dared to question the wisdom of his actions he persecuted without mercy.

Never in the history of this country were civil liberty and the basic rights of the individual so cruelly and arbitrarily violated as during Wilson's second administration. The high idealism of his speeches contrasted strangely with his increasingly intolerant contempt for the freedom of conscience and opinion guaranteed by the Constitution. And what he did on a lofty plane and out of principle, the bureaucrats under him emulated with stupid brutality. Conscientious objectors were not merely imprisoned but tortured. Espionage and sedition laws, enacted at Wilson's request, enabled the Department of Justice to force long prison terms on men and women for the mere expression of dissident opinion. Newspapers and magazines that printed anti-war material were barred from the mails and their editors tried for sedition. Mass raids were staged in crowded streets and at packed meetings on the pretense of catching a few draft evaders. Aliens who were suspected of radical views were hounded and jailed and many of them were deported without regard to family ties and personal hardship. Radical unions such as the Industrial Workers of the World were persecuted and disrupted. The Bolshevik Revolution in Russia helped to initiate a " Red " scare which was exploited by various dominant groups to serve their own ends. Thus Southerners used it to keep down Negroes whom the war had made restless; employers exaggerated the communist bogey in order to weaken labor unions; and members of the American Legion turned upon radicals as scapegoats for their postwar discontent. All in all, the years 1917–21 became the most illiberal period in our history.

Yet American democracy was too deeply rooted in the spirit of the nation to suffer permanently from the violent blast of war. Even as the squall of reaction blew over the land, forthright liberals clung fast to the ideals of the Declaration of Independence. The Civil Liberties Bureau, headed by Roger Baldwin and Albert De Silver, fought valiantly to safeguard the rights of innocent individuals. The editors of *The New Republic* headed by Herbert Croly, although among the early advocates of war on Germany in the belief that the defeat of the Kaiser would strengthen the forces of liberalism the world over, struggled persistently, if ineffectually, against the flood of reaction which they had helped to unloose. Oswald Garrison Villard, pacifist individualist, bought *The Nation* in 1918 and converted it into an outspoken and comprehensive medium of liberal protest. At about the same time Francis Neilson, Albert Jay Nock, Van Wyck Brooks, and others began to issue *The Freeman*, perhaps the best written and certainly the most refined and genteel of the weeklies, for the purpose of expounding the principles of philosophic anarchism and the single tax. In the 1920 election campaign leading liberals formed the Committee of Forty-Eight to reaffirm the ideals of democracy in the midst of a hysterical witch-hunt; and although their Presidential candidate, P. P. Christensen, polled a pitifully small vote, their speakers and literature did bring the message of freedom and human rights to the attention of many thousands. Meantime a number of dissatisfied farmers in North Dakota and neighboring states organized the Non-Partisan League on Populistic principles. In the 1918 elections they sent more than two hundred of their representatives to the legislatures of five states and later boasted of a Senator, a governor, and several Congressmen.

After several years of Harding " normalcy," during which time liberalism was eclipsed by postwar prosperity, the glaring corruption of his administration again stirred the conscience of honest citizens. Although politics was eschewed by the millions who were for the first time riding in their own automobiles, tinkering with their radio receiving sets, or dreaming of getting rich by speculating in stocks, enough Americans were concerned for the future of their country to want to do something about it. The availability of the aging La Follette induced these democrats to convene for the purpose of nominating him for the Presidency on a third-party ticket. Progressives, farmers, workers, and even socialists united to carry the banner of insurgency to the White House. Their platform was Populism brought up to date, and the campaign was carried on with gusto and sanguine militancy. But the political climate was decidedly unfavorable to change. Most voters preferred "Coolidge prosperity" to La Follette liberalism. Although the Wisconsin Senator received nearly five million votes, the overwhelming majority clung to the fleshpots of the Republican status quo.

The great financial boom of the late 1920's was followed by the severest depression in our history. President Hoover's administration, as confused and credulous as the bankers and industrialists whose advice it heeded, and forever seeing prosperity "around the corner," was inclined to let matters drift on the assumption that sooner or later things were bound to improve. By 1932 the depression reached bottom and eagerness for change was so strong and widespread that the Democratic candidate, Franklin Delano Roosevelt, was elected by an overwhelming majority.

Roosevelt's New Deal program was composed of many of the planks of the 1896 Altgeld platform. Both men had indeed one purpose: to restore the government to the people and to give them a more equitable share of the national income. An unprecedented crisis confronted Roosevelt at the very outset, and he acted with such dispatch and determination, and with such disregard for the accustomed amenities towards big business, that he quickly banished fear and dejection and effected a definite economic upswing. Even more important was his affirmation that it was the function of the government to stimulate employment and to assist those in need.

In a very real sense the New Deal brought to copious fruition the desires and dreams of generations of liberal Americans. Although it did not achieve the millennium, it brought about a greater measure of social democracy than many of the Grangers and Populists and Progressives had thought feasible. Within an extraordinarily brief period it placed on the federal statute books laws which stabilized and strengthened our credit and banking systems, safeguarded bank deposits, and protected innocent investors; gave labor the right to organize and to deal with employers on an equal footing; relieved farmers of their economic burdens and insecurity; provided work for the unemployed and educationally productive activity for the idle youth; initiated the TVA as a yardstick for cheaper power and the improvement of our land resources; stimulated better and abundant housing by means of easier loans and lower interest rates; and instituted social insurance against unemployment, old age, and other types of insecurity. By these and other similar measures the New Deal has gone about as far as is possible under our capitalistic system of government towards the realization of the liberal principles of democracy advocated by progressive Americans from Jefferson to Franklin Delano Roosevelt.

The three chapters that follow are devoted to representative spokesmen for liberalism. More than any other political leader of his day Governor Altgeld fought for justice and equality when other powerful Americans were willing to wink at violations of these inalienable rights in their common scramble for wealth and prestige. Lincoln Steffens led his fellow journalists in a campaign for clean politics and fair dealing in business; but he early came to believe that reform was necessarily ineffective because it did not dry up the source of all political corruption and economic inequality — special privilege. Randolph Bourne, eloquent interpreter of idealistic youth, held fast to his vision of the American promise at a time when most liberals yielded to the temptation of saving the world by martial means. In the lives and thoughts of these three men are embodied the aims and ideals of modern American liberalism.

JOHN PETER ALTGELD

PIONEER PROGRESSIVE

J OHN PETER ALTGELD was the most reviled man of his generation.
Nearly all of the country's newspapers and journals of opinion
and many of the nation's leading citizens at one time or another
exhausted the Billingsgate dictionary in their vituperative attacks
upon him. In the minds of millions of people his name was synonymous with anarchy and depravity for a decade. Yet Altgeld withstood all abuse with the courage of a man who knew he was doing
right. Moreover, his uncompromising persistence and political proficiency scattered his enemies and planted the ideals of social liberalism in the field of national government. He was indeed the first
American in high office to denounce the greed of monopolies and
the graft of politicians and to proclaim the reforms needed to
bring back social justice to our newly industrialized nation. And
while he died a poor and broken man and became the " forgotten
eagle " of the succeeding generation, the logic of history must
sooner or later place his name close to that of his illustrious fellow
Illinoisian Abraham Lincoln.

Like Lincoln, Altgeld was born and reared in poverty and made
his way to the highest office within his reach by sheer ability and
strength of character. He was an infant of three months when his
parents brought him here from Germany in the spring of 1848. The
family settled on a farm near Mansfield, Ohio, where Mrs. Altgeld's brothers had already established themselves. Although Mr.

Altgeld was a hard-working farmer and plied his trade as wagon maker in addition, he was unable to earn more than a bare living. He was a harsh and bigoted man, a strict disciplinarian, and was satisfied to have his children remain on his own low level. Since John Peter was his eldest son, he had him help on the farm from his earliest years. At the age of thirteen the boy was doing a man's share in the field and the chores of the farm as well. He had very little schooling but early showed a marked eagerness for reading. Years after his death his friend Charles A. Towne testified: "Throughout his life he showed the results of this early experience; and while, as a lawyer and public man, he carried on extensive and careful special studies, his reading continued wide and various, storing his mind with useful incidental knowledge. He became one of the best-read men I have ever known."

The outbreak of the Civil War wakened John Peter's patriotism. Too young to fight, he eagerly followed the battles from afar. In 1864, when only sixteen, he enlisted as a substitute for one of the Ohio Home Guards. Of the hundred dollars he received as a bonus he gave his father ninety. While patrolling the swampland along the James River he contracted a fever which kept him at the field hospital for a fortnight and from which he was to suffer recurrently in later years. After a hundred days of service his regiment was mustered out and he returned home.

Life on the farm now became increasingly irksome to him. His social horizon having been widened by a visit to the nation's capital and by stories of adventure told by his fellow soldiers, he began to chafe at the German parochialism of his home environment. He read a great deal about American life and was strongly attracted by Jefferson's character and by his social and political ideals. Much against his father's will John Peter insisted on attending the Mansfield high school for a term and later Gailey's seminary in near-by Lexington. Once equipped to teach school, he did so for two years at thirty-five dollars a month and gave most of the money to his father. At twenty-one he fell in love with Emma Ford, a fellow teacher, but her father objected to him because of his poverty.

Thereupon the disappointed youth went westward in search of his fortune.

He worked his way along from farm to farm, with a brief interlude as a railroad section-hand in Arkansas, where he was laid low with a virulent recurrence of fever. Finally, ill and penniless, he reached the small town of Savannah, Missouri. There his eagerness to work impressed people favorably. In a short time he was teaching school and helping on a farm by day and studying law at night. In 1871 he was admitted to the bar and the next year he became city attorney. To hide a slight harelip as well as to add to his official dignity he now grew a beard. In another two years he was sufficiently established in the community to receive the nomination and to be elected as state attorney for the county on a combined Democrat-Granger ticket. In the campaign he first articulated his liberal views. Addressing Granger audiences, he denounced the violators of Jeffersonian social justice. The work of public prosecutor did not prove congenial to him, however, and late in 1875 he resigned his office and left Savannah for Chicago.

Altgeld was twenty-eight years old when he arrived in the Illinois metropolis to begin his career anew. He knew no one in the large bustling city. The first thing he did was to rent an office for six months with half of his hundred dollars of capital. To save expenses he made part of it his living quarters as well. After several months of increasing hardship he began to attract the notice of other lawyers and to get a few clients. Intensive work and a keen power of analysis helped him win cases which other attorneys had refused. In another year he was not only earning his expenses but saving money. In 1877 he renewed his wooing of Emma Ford, this time successfully. Though childless, the marriage was a happy one. Mrs. Altgeld was an intelligent and sensitive woman and became her husband's devoted companion to the end of his agitated life.

Chicago was growing fast. Real estate values boomed. Altgeld was quick to perceive the possibilities of large profits in land transactions. In 1879 he invested five hundred dollars in a lot. One advantageous deal led to others and before long he was giving a good deal of his time to his realty business. His farsighted and shrewd enterprise gained him considerable wealth. After a few years he turned his talents to the erection of office buildings. Each new structure gave him the pleasure of creative achievement, becoming a means of sublimating his strong parental craving.

Altgeld also resumed his interest in politics. His known liberal views and his knowledge of German made him a welcome speaker at labor rallies. In 1884 he ran for Congress, but lost because Illinois went Republican. Early the following year he was highly regarded as a potential Democratic candidate for United States Senator. Success came to him in 1886, when he was elected as judge in the Cook County Superior Court with the open support of labor.

One very good reason for labor's faith in Altgeld was the publication in 1884 of his important volume, *Our Penal Machinery and Its Victims*. In this book he was the earnest reformer, urging the removal of the causes of crime. He condemned the prevailing penal system as a tragic failure. " For it seems, first, to make criminals out of many that are not naturally so; and, second, to render it difficult for those once convicted ever to be anything else than criminals; and, third, to fail to repress those that do not want to be anything but criminals." He stressed the facts that most criminals come from the poor, with broken homes or none, and that the police stimulated crime by their brutality and needless arrests. " Brutal treatment brutalizes the wrong-doer," he argued, " and prepares him for worse offenses." He was particularly critical of the indiscriminate arrests and imprisonment of young offenders. " It is essential to a reformatory prison treatment that the self-respect of the prisoner should be cultivated to the utmost extent, and that every effort be made to give to him his manhood. Hence all disciplinary punishment that inflicts unnecessary pain or humiliation should be abolished as of evil influence."

Among the reforms he advocated were a more intelligent system of fines, paid work for prisoners, indeterminate sentences, and the abolition of grand juries. His discussion of each proposed improvement was based on facts and figures gathered from many sources and buttressed by a humane and persuasive logic. The ten thousand copies which he printed and distributed brought him numerous favorable responses from readers in every part of the country, invitations to address gatherings of professional groups, and the devoted, lifelong friendship of George A. Schilling, a young Chicago labor leader. If the guardians of the law in Illinois and elsewhere chose to ignore these suggested penal remedies, the more liberal citizens of his state were grateful to Altgeld for his courageous stand and remembered him on election day.

Altgeld served as judge for five years. While on the bench he became known for his fair and fearless conduct and was highly respected by lawyers and ligitants alike. In 1890 his associates on the bench honored him with the office of chief justice. The following year, however, he resigned. Court procedure had begun to irritate him; the judicial robes proved tawdry and confining. In an interview he explained that he regarded officeholders as " a cowardly hanging-on class, always careful to see how the wind blows before daring either to have or to express an opinion, and therefore a negative class." He preferred to belong to the group of successful private individuals "who mold public opinion and whose favor and support are sought by the politicians, and who, in the end, secure legislation and shape the policy of the country, using the officeholding class simply as an instrument by which to carry out a purpose."

He had by now acquired assets worth around a million dollars. Eager to become one of the successful private individuals, he decided to erect " the finest and best office building on earth." When asked why he should risk $400,000 of his own money on the venture when the interest on that amount would yield him more income annually than he normally spent, he replied: " Because I have no children. I have to create something, and so I am creating buildings." He was very proud of this enterprise, which he named Unity Building, and spared no expense in its construction. So confident was he of success that he not only put his private bank account into it but arranged for its financing with John R. Walsh, a banker-politician who was as unscrupulous as he was vindictive and who later effected Altgeld's financial ruin.

Despite his preoccupation with the rising Unity Building and his extensive law practice, Altgeld continued to participate in public affairs. He took his stand as a liberal each time, never forgetting his lowly origin and his Jeffersonian ideals. As early as 1886 — the year of great labor unrest, capped by the Haymarket riot — he wrote in favor of the arbitration of strikes and criticized the laissez-faire doctrine which held " that the State, as the embodiment of society, has no power to prevent or to remove those conditions which, if left alone, would lead to its own overthrow." He argued that society owed certain rights to each of its members and must protect the weaker from exploitation by the stronger. When Cardinal Manning's statement about the right of the poor to still their hunger was attacked in the press, Altgeld insisted that it merely expressed " a principle which society has long recognized, viz., that it is the duty of society to take care of its indigent, by lawful means of course." He also advocated legislative reforms, the Australian ballot, the abolition of the sweatshop system, and the enactment of the eight-hour workday. As a meliorist he believed that the world was gradually getting better. In connection with the current labor strikes and disorders, he wrote:

Honest investigation into the conditions of the poor will produce beneficial results, and if this agitation shall serve to enlighten the public at large in regard to the real character and condition of our poorer classes, then remedies will soon be found which will without violence and without revolution greatly improve this condition and serve to increase the greatness, the prosperity, and the happiness of our country.

These and other of his papers he published in the first edition of *Live Questions*, which appeared in 1890 and was subsequently reissued to include his later addresses. The book established him as a vigorous and intelligent critic of current social maladjustments. The liberals in Chicago eagerly claimed him as their own, while the Chicago *Tribune* was the first to disparage him as a follower of Karl Marx.

The Populist movement was on the march in 1892. Throughout the agricultural states and particularly in the Middle West farmers were in the mood " to quit raising corn and begin raising hell." The oncoming depression had hit them first and they were in a rebellious temper. After suffering for more than twenty years from high freight and interest rates and low prices for their produce, they clamored for a government that would favor, not the monopolistic corporations, but the people at large. And at last they were in a position to assert themselves. Their years of political effort were bearing fruit. Early in 1892 the politicians of each of the major parties in the affected states knew that they could not win in the coming election without the Populist vote. Since the Republicans were generally regarded as the party of the large corporations, the Democrats tried to capitalize on their favorable opportunities by picking candidates able to win the allegiance of the People's party.

It was this political exigency which forced the Illinois Democrats to nominate John Peter Altgeld as its candidate for governor. At the urging of his friends, who believed that as the state executive he would be able to effect needed social reforms, Altgeld campaigned vigorously from one end of the state to the other. In order to be under no obligation to anyone he bore all expenses himself — amounting to nearly $100,000. As in previous elections, he proved a master of attack. Ignoring the charges against him, he concentrated on the obvious weaknesses of the Republican incumbent. He also assailed the trusts, the convict labor system, and police brutality, and advocated the right of workmen to organize and to strike. When the votes were counted in November he had won by a sizable majority.

The strenuousness of the campaign had exhausted his energy and brought on a physical breakdown. For weeks it was doubtful if he would be able to assume office. He forced himself, however, to be present at the inauguration. In his prepared speech he insisted that justice must prevail. " The State must do justice to both employer and employee; it must see to it that law and order are maintained, and that life and property are thoroughly protected. All weakness in this regard would be pusillanimous and invite incalculable evil." This was regarded as a pious and pharisaical gesture. It was not long, however, before people in Illinois and all over the world realized that Governor Altgeld meant every word of it; that he was the first executive to see that justice was done to weakly organized workers as well as to powerful corporations.

His friends assumed that one of his first official acts would be to pardon the surviving Haymarket anarchists. But he seemed in no hurry to make up his mind. Although he had procured the records of the case within ten days after his inauguration, he gave no inkling of his decision. Instead he busied himself with the replacement of Republican officeholders by deserving Democrats and able reformers. To Schilling and Darrow, who prodded him about the pardon, he said that he would act when he was ready and that he would do what he thought was right. April and May passed, and June was winding its days, and still he kept his own counsel. On June 3 he condemned the lynching of a Negro in Decatur in an official proclamation that made a stir over the nation. Four days later he delivered his notable address to the graduating class of the University of Illinois, in which he told the students, among other things, to think of justice realistically as " a struggling toward the right." He pointed out that the men who administer justice take their biases with them onto the bench and that " the wrongs done in the courts of justice themselves are so great that they cry to heaven." He therefore urged them to become reformers; not to be satisfied with things as they are but to work for their betterment. " All great reforms, great movements, come from the bottom and not the top. . . . Wherever there is a wrong, point it out to all the world, and you can trust the people to right it."

On June 26 he issued his pardon of the three Haymarket anarchists. He made public his reasons in an 18,000-word document which analyzed and exposed the enormity of the judicial outrage. Citing the record and many affidavits he demonstrated that the jury was chosen not by chance (as required by law) but from a panel collected personally by a special bailiff who boasted that he had called only those men who " he believed would hang the defendants," and that Judge Joseph Gary had upheld the bailiff and had assisted in selecting the prejudiced jury.

No matter what the defendants were charged with [Altegeld declared], they were entitled to a fair trial, and no greater danger could possibly threaten our institutions than to have the courts of justice run wild or give way to popular clamor. . . . When in all the instances the trial judge ruled that these [admittedly prejudiced] men were competent jurors simply because they had, under his adroit manipulation, been led to say that they believed they could try the case fairly on the evidence; then the proceeding lost all semblance of a fair trial.

He showed further that much of the evidence was " a pure fabrication " on the part of the police officials who had terrorized and bribed witnesses; that it was Captain Bonfield's sadistic brutality which was chiefly responsible for the Haymarket riot. Finally he pointed out that " the State has never discovered who it was that threw the bomb that killed the policeman, and the evidence does not show any connection whatever between the defendants and the man who did throw it." Yet the record revealed " that every ruling throughout the long trial on any contested point was in favor of the State; and further, that page after page on the record contains insinuating remarks of the judge, made in the hearing of the jury, and with the evident intent of bringing the jury to his way of thinking."

Governor Altgeld knew the consequences of his outspoken condemnation of this judicial wrong. He knew also that he could have issued the pardon as a matter of mercy and received the plaudits of the public. But he refused to compromise with justice. A study of the record had convinced him that the anarchists had been hanged and imprisoned unjustly by a prejudiced judge and jury and his conscience impelled him to rectify the wrong done to the dead and living victims. Even more important to him was the need to expose and nullify a judge-made precedent which would have deprived the people of a trial by a jury of their peers. To Louis F. Post he said: " As for myself, no man has a right to allow his ambition to stand in the way of the performance of a simple act of justice." And when his friend Judge S. P. McConnell cautioned him that the pardon of the anarchists would end his political career, he replied: " If I decide they were innocent I will pardon them, by God, no matter what happens to my career."

The expected happened. The storm broke with exceeding violence. With very few minor exceptions the newspapers of the country followed the lead of the Chicago *Tribune* in a protracted outpouring of personal vituperation. Over night Altgeld had become to them a public enemy, a depraved anarchist, an instigator of evil and bloodshed. The very eminent citizens who had earlier petitioned him for the pardon now execrated him for impugning the sanctity of the courts. These men of wealth and power could not deny that Judge Gary was biased and unfair, that the jury was packed, that the evidence was largely faked, that the prosecution was prejudiced, and that the sentences were unjustified. Nor would they admit even to their own consciences that in 1886 they had been frightened by labor disorders and radical propaganda and consequently had fomented the hysteria against the defendents, so that the blood of the victims was on their own heads. Unwilling to concede their unsavory part in the case and finding Altgeld's legal position impregnable, they struck back at their nemesis by covering his good name with the foulest abuse. As for the public at large, the readers of newspapers, " very few," to quote Darrow, " knew anything about the facts, and fewer cared anything about them. Governor Altgeld was in the way of forces that control the world, and he must be destroyed."

John " Pardon " Altgeld faced the storm without flinching. " It was the crowd on one side and John Peter Altgeld on the other," as he was to remark more than once. Armed with a clear conscience, he stood firm. In public statements he said: " The reasons I gave for signing the pardon have been published and they must stand or fall by themselves. To those who ascribe mean motives in an act of public character, I have nothing to say." When asked if he regretted the pardon, he quickly exclaimed: " Never! If I had the matter to act upon again tomorrow, I would do it over again." As to the repeated charge that he was an anarchist, he dismissed it as nonsense. Referring to his detractors, he added: " In view of the facts, the talk of a few hangers-on around clubs, who spend other people's money, and of some gentlemen who have never done anything in their lives except suck blood from the public — who, if they own property usually manage to shirk paying taxes on it — the talk of this kind of individuals is not worthy of notice."

But he was deeply resentful of the scurrilous invective which the gentlemen of the press and the clubs continued to publish against him — and his heart hardened against them. Hereafter he would have no traffic with them. They feared the truth; he would work to make it prevail. Like his great fellow Illinoisian he would dedicate his talents to the benefit of the people. The wageworkers and the farmers needed him in their struggle against the greedy corporations and he would not disappoint them. The thought gave him strength and the will to fight. Instead of shrinking into obscurity, as his enemies had expected, he emerged from the slanderous onslaught firmly resolved to battle for the right as he saw it. Nellie Bly of the New York *World*, who had come to scoff, perceived the true Altgeld during her interview with him: " I am glad to say that I have met and talked with Governor Altgeld, who is going to do as he thinks right every time, if the whole world stands still."

The deepening economic depression forced Governor Altgeld to act in a manner that nonplused and irritated the heads of corporations and their vociferous mouthpieces. In June, strike riots in Lemont, causing the death of several workmen, made it necessary for him to send state troops to the scene of disorder. Unlike pre-

vious executives, however, he followed them at once to make sure
that justice was done. In his report he put the blame for the killings
on the employer. " The only men who seem to have violated the law
yesterday, and that in cold blood, were the men who had been
armed by the contractor and who did the shooting." The following
Labor Day he told Chicago workmen candidly that hard times were
ahead and that while he as governor would not let them down, constitutional provisions would make it impossible for him to give
them much assistance. He urged them to organize along lawful lines
in an effort to help themselves. " For the world gives only when it is
obliged to, and respects only those who compel its respect. The
earth is covered with the graves of justice and equity that failed to
receive recognition, because there was no influence or force to compel it, and it will be so until the millennium." He also addressed
the state militia to impress upon them their duty to keep law and
order above all things and to kill only as a last resort. " A soldier
cannot fight wrongs between individuals, but he becomes a murderer if he needlessly kills."

Arbitrary wage cuts and high-handed treatment caused many
sporadic strikes. Early in 1894 the soft-coal miners went out on a
nationwide strike. In sending militia to the Illinois strike scenes
Governor Altgeld instructed the officers that " it is not the business
of the soldiers to act as custodians or guards of private property.
. . . Troops can be used only for the purpose of quelling disturbance or of suppressing riot or in some other way enforcing the laws."
His readiness to send the militia promptly and his insistence on
law and order helped to prevent bloodshed.

The Bourbon obstinacy and callous greed of George Pullman
and his chief stockholder Marshall Field forced the employees of
the Pullman factories to strike in May 1894. Their wages had been
cut a quarter, while their rent in the company-owned houses remained about a quarter higher than elsewhere, and when a committee called on the management for relief three of the group were
fired. Pullman was indignant at this ingratitude. " Why," he told
reporters, " the average wage being earned is $1.87 a day! " He made

no mention, however, of the reserve of $4,000,000 that remained in the company's treasury from the profits of the previous year, or of the $26,000,000 it possessed in undivided earnings. The union was anathema to him and he was determined to drive it from his factories.

For more than a month the strike remained almost unnoticed in the excitement of more acute labor disturbances. Late in June, however, the American Railway Union, of which most of the Pullman strikers were members, began a boycott against trains containing Pullman cars. This action was taken after Pullman, despite the urging of business and political leaders, had flatly refused to arbitrate; it was voted also against the pleas of the union's president, Eugene V. Debs, who feared the consequences of a general railroad strike. So effective was this boycott at first that few trains were in operation. The strike quickly developed into a trial of strength between the American Railway Union and the illegal General Managers' Association, which represented the twenty-four railroads serving Chicago. The union appeared to be on the verge of victory.

At this point Attorney-General Richard Olney, formerly counsel for the Chicago, Burlington and Quincy Railroad and still on intimate terms with the railroad managers, determined to break the strike. Although in 1875 he had vigorously protested against federal interference in the affairs of a state except at the request of local officials, and although only two weeks earlier he had instructed a federal marshal in Illinois to apply to the state authorities for the protection of mail trains, he now completely ignored the powers of the state in his maneuvers against the strikers. He knew the mind of Governor Altgeld and decided to act without him. In appointing Edwin Walker, also a railroad attorney, as his representative in Chicago, he advised him " to go into a court of equity and secure restraining orders which shall have the effect of preventing any attempt to commit the offense." Since the strikers had been orderly and had done their best not to interfere with mail trains, the prime purpose of the injunction was to make the strike illegal. Judges Grosscup and Woods helped Walker to revise the sweeping injunction for greater effectiveness before granting it. Olney then ordered the Chicago marshal to engage several thousand deputies. These armed officers, who were paid by the railroads and whom the Chicago superintendent of police characterized as " thugs, thieves, and ex-convicts," at once acted to incite disorder and thus gave Olney the excuse to call out federal troops.

All this time the state authorities were being deliberately and contemptuously disregarded, even though Governor Altgeld had earlier demonstrated his readiness to send the state militia at once wherever it was needed to preserve order. While he was kept informed about conditions in Chicago and held several regiments in readiness, he could not legally interfere so long as the city remained relatively quiet. The arrival of the federal soldiers, however, quickly resulted in severe rioting and several deaths. At that point the mayor, largely at Altgeld's initiative, made the request for state troops. The militia arrived promptly and readily restored order.

On July 10 Debs and three other union leaders were indicted for violating the Sherman Anti-Trust Act. It was the first prosecution under this four-year-old law — a law passed to curb, not labor unions, but monopolistic businesses like the Pullman Company and the large railroads. A week later, however, realizing that action under this law would result in a long-drawn-out legal battle, Olney was instrumental in having the four defendants rearrested for disobeying the federal injunction. Debs was sentenced to six months in jail and the others to three for contempt of court. Once they were safe in the penitentiary the Department of Justice conveniently dropped the earlier indictment. But by that time the strike was already lost.

Altgeld was deeply angered by this brazen and unconstitutional interference with his duties as executive officer of the state of Illinois. He had been sending state troops to strike centers in other parts of the state at the slightest sign of disorder, although he knew that in most instances the trouble was fostered by the railroads who were unable to get crews to run their trains. Olney's machinations to break the strike at all costs appeared to him as the antithesis of democratic government. In Springfield he learned, with increasing irritation, of the injunction, of the hired deputy marshals and their criminal record, and finally of the arrival of the federal troops and the bloody rioting.

On July 5, the day of the fatal clashes, Governor Altgeld sent a long telegram to President Cleveland protesting against the unwarranted and unconstitutional federal interference in the local affairs of the state of Illinois. He reminded him that the Constitution gave the President no right to send troops into a state unless there was obvious proof of need or unless requested by local officials. He further pointed out that the state of Illinois was able not only to look after its own obligations but to furnish help to the federal government.

If any assistance were needed, the State stood ready to furnish a hundred men for every one man required, and stood ready to do so at a moment's notice. Notwithstanding these facts the Federal Government has been applied to by men who had political and selfish motives for wanting to ignore the State Government. . . . To absolutely ignore a local government in matters of this kind, when the local government is ready to furnish assistance needed, and is amply able to enforce the law, not only insults the people of this State by imputing to them an inability to govern themselves, or an unwillingness to enforce the law, but is in violation of a basic principle of our institutions.

President Cleveland's guarded reply briefly denied these allegations and insisted that the federal government had acted within its rights. His supercilious attitude only intensified Altgeld's concern for the fundamental principles of our democracy. He immediately telegraphed his detailed accusation that the President was evading " the question at issue — that is, that the principle of local self-government is just as fundamental in our institutions as is that of Federal supremacy." Point by point he demonstrated that the action of the federal government served to undermine local self-government and encourage dictatorship.

It will be an easy matter under your construction of the law for an ambitious executive to order out all the military forces of all the States, and establish at once a military government. The only chance of failure in such a movement could come from rebellion, and with such a vast military power at command this could readily be crushed, for, as a rule, soldiers will obey orders.

The President's second reply was curt and final. His dogmatic assertion of authority and his refusal to discuss the issue in question put an end to the controversy — but not before Altgeld had stated fully and unequivocally the basic problems raised by Olney's successful efforts to break the railroad strike.

Again the press and the politicians resumed their campaign of calumny and imprecation against Governor Altgeld. Without bothering to ascertain the facts or to consider the principles involved, they attacked him with intensified ferocity and condemned him as a traitor and scoundrel. Again the Chicago *Tribune* led the pack: " This lying, hypocritical, demagogical, sniveling Governor of Illinois does not want the laws enforced. He is a sympathizer with riot, with violence, with lawlessness and with anarchy. He should be impeached . . . because he is an anarchist opposed to all law." The highly respectable *Nation* was equally abusive, calling him " boorish, impudent, ignorant," a " professional blatherskite." Even so eminent a constitutional authority as Justice T. M. Cooley, at the time a federal officeholder, added his senile censure; ironically forgetting that twenty years earlier he, like Olney, had spoken clearly for the principle of local self-government: " By the terms of the Federal Constitution, there must be a demand for assistance from the State legislature or executive before it could be rendered."

All these agents of public opinion, representing both major parties, lauded President Cleveland's part in the controversy; not because he was right but because he had presumably preserved law and order by breaking the strike. Yet the facts as stated by Colonel Carroll D. Wright, chairman of Cleveland's own investigating committee, vindicated not the federal government but Governor Altgeld. To a Boston editor Wright confided " that not even hood-

[381]

lums instigated the burning of the mass of cars, but that it was instigated by the railway managers themselves as the surest way to bring the Federal troops and defeat the strike." He and later investigators agreed that Altgeld was correct in his insistence that the newspaper accounts of violence before the arrival of federal soldiers were mostly either pure fabrications or wild exaggerations. Nor were Cleveland and Olney able to substantiate their claim that the strike had held up the mail trains — their chief excuse for interference. Three days before they ordered the troops to Chicago, L. L. Troy, Superintendent of Mails, summarized the situation as follows: " No mails have accumulated at Chicago so far. All regular trains are moving nearly on time with few slight exceptions." He subsequently further stated that throughout the strike " the greatest delay to any outgoing or incoming mails probably did not exceed from eight to nine hours at any time."

It is now generally established that conditions in Chicago were at no time out of the control of local officials. In ordering troops to the city at Olney's advice, President Cleveland had clearly acted outside of the authority of the Constitution. Yet a decade later, in the face of all the evidence to the contrary, he wrote about the Pullman strike as if nothing had been uncovered to contradict his original assertion. By that time, however, passions had cooled, Altgeld had been dead two years, and Cleveland's belated effort at self-justification merely revealed his confirmed conservatism.

In 1894 Governor Altgeld's detractors were certain that they had killed him off politically. But they were thoroughly mistaken. They had merely kindled his righteous anger. Convinced that his cause was just and that the corporations and their henchmen in office were robbing the people of their heritage, he determined to fight them with all his might. As governor he was in a position of power. When the victorious Pullman Company arbitrarily refused to take back a number of the strikers and thereby forced them into destitution, he described the plight of these employees to the people of Illinois and appealed to them for funds. The ready response was a triumph for the governor and a defeat for George Pullman. Shortly thereafter Altgeld made public his letter to the tax commissioners in which he called their attention to the fact that the Pullman Company was paying taxes on only a small fraction of its revealed assets and was thus defrauding the state of large sums annually. Finally he compelled the company to dispose of its quasi-model village which it was operating illegally and oppressively.

In his biennial message to the legislature of January 1895, Governor Altgeld spoke frankly and forcefully in favor of labor. He singled out the coal company at Spring Valley, whose cupidity had resulted in repeated strikes and bloodshed.

This company has been a curse and a bill of expense to the State from the time it commenced operation. Almost every administration for a number of years has had to send a military force there to preserve order and protect the property of this concern that was really causing the trouble. . . . While we welcome every honest enterprise and industry, we cannot allow our State to become merely a forage ground for wolfish greed.

In his detailed and trenchant review of the Pullman strike he lashed out against the enemies of labor. His attack upon the malpractices of corporations and the " usurpation of power " by the courts was probably the most devastating ever made by a high executive. " At present the status seems to be this: Combinations of capital against the public and against labor have succeeded, no matter by what means, and the men who accomplished it are now patriots; while combinations among laborers for self-protection have failed, and the men who advocate it are enemies of society (i.e., ' anarchists ')." The danger to the country came, however, not from these so-called anarchists but " from that corruption, usurpation, insolence, and oppression that go hand in hand with vast accumulation of wealth, wielded by unscrupulous men."

Symptomatic of this danger, Governor Altgeld continued, was the " new form of government " effected by the judiciary — " *government by injunction.*" The first state executive to bring the ominous issue into the open, he discussed the origin and effect of labor injunctions with incisive clarity:

The judge issues an ukase which he calls an injunction, forbidding whatever he pleases and what the law does not forbid, and thus legislates for himself without limitation and makes things penal which the law does not make penal, makes other things punishable by imprisonment which at law are only punishable by fine, and he deprives men of the right of trial by jury when the law guarantees this right, and he then enforces this ukase in a summary and arbitrary manner by imprisonment, throwing men into prison, not for violating a law, but for being guilty of contempt of court in disregarding one of these injunctions.

Eager to make the nature of his criticism unmistakable, he added: "These injunctions are a very great convenience to corporations when they can be had for the asking by a corporation lawyer, and these were the processes of the court to enforce which the President sent the federal troops to Chicago!"

A few months later, in its decisions against the income tax rider and the Debs petition, the Supreme Court fully validated Altgeld's arraignment. For many years a federal income tax had been regarded as legal by the courts. Such a tax helped greatly to finance the Civil War. In 1894 Congress restored a federal tax on incomes as a rider to the Wilson-Gorman tariff bill. The following year the eminent corporation lawyer Joseph H. Choate persuaded a majority of the Supreme Court headed by Chief Justice Fuller, who had been Marshall Field's attorney, that a tax on incomes " is communistic in its purposes and tendencies and therefore unconstitutional." This specious legalism was criticized by Altgeld in a public statement charged with scorn. He pointed out that the unexpected reversal would save millions of dollars to " the Standard Oil kings, the Wall Street people, as well as the rich mugwumps" at the expense of the producing classes. The burden of the latter " is made a little heavier and the whip has made a new welt on their backs, but what of it? In fact, what are they for, if not to bear burdens and to be lashed?" As for the growing discontent on the part of these bearers of burdens, no doubt the Supreme Court " will have other opportunities from time to time to solidify our institutions and to teach patriotism by coming down with terrific force upon some wretch whose vulgarity and unpatriotic character will be proven by the fact that he is poor."

The wretch first to suffer the wrath of the Supreme Court was Eugene V. Debs. In denying his appeal the Justices unanimously upheld not only the use of injunctions but also the employment of federal troops to enforce them. Altgeld's comment on this decision was reminiscent of Garrison's and Phillips's reactions to the pro-slavery verdicts prior to 1860. He observed that " for a number of years it has been marked that the decisions of the United States courts were nearly always in favor of corporations." This power of capitalism has caused, among other evils, " that corrupt use of wealth, which is undermining our institutions, debauching public officials, shaping legislation and creating judges who do its bidding." This denunciation of the rapacious rich and a reactionary court, while motivated as much by personal resentment as by crusading zeal, made him widely known as the protagonist of the poor and the champion of the underdog.

Despite the persistent vilification in the newspapers and the open opposition of the Cleveland administration, Governor Altgeld grew politically stronger from month to month. A shrewd judge of men, he was favored by the logic of events. The current economic depression deepened the restiveness of large numbers of Americans. The Populist movement, now centering its attention upon the money problem, was still gaining in strength. Altgeld was too close to this political disaffection not to perceive its trend and its tremendous potentialities. While he had not previously considered the silver question to be of prime importance he was quick to use it as a weapon against the Cleveland faction and the corrupt city bosses. With the aid of the free-silver forces he hoped not only to rid the nation of the plutocratic bankers but also to even accounts with his enemies. He soon familiarized himself with the history and basic principles of money. His skillful use of facts, figures, and financial logic made him the most formidable opponent of the eminent " goldbugs." At the same time his sagacity and drive in building up the silver forces brought him to the fore as their effective spokesman. At his instigation free-silver Democrats met at special state conferences in order to make known their views and to prepare for the national convention in 1896. The keynote of his advice to them was: " The time has come when the Democratic party must again stand for Democracy, and no longer for plutocracy! " The Illinois Democrats enthusiastically adopted his free-silver plank and made him chairman of the state delegation.

When the Democrats gathered in Chicago for the national convention, most of them turned to Governor Altgeld for leadership. His " no compromise " stand became their source of strength, and they clung to it as the rock of their salvation. For the time being even the newspapers treated Altgeld with respect, although *Harper's Weekly* continued to perceive in him the " agitator who, when the bludgeon had failed of its full work, would be ready with his poisoned knife, and who, in leading a victory-drunken mob, would not hesitate to follow pillage with the torch." The " gold " Democrats, followers of President Cleveland and the party bosses, found themselves without influence. Their machinations and threats were of no avail. The delegates adopted the most radical major-party platform on record. The reform planks on labor, the courts, injunctions, civil and personal liberties, money, and the income tax were Altgeld's to the letter; while he was not on the drafting committee, he dominated it by virtue of his towering political and intellectual stature.

The opening paragraph well summarized not only the spirit of the convention but also the ideals for which Altgeld was then fighting:

We the Democrats of the United States in national convention assembled, do reaffirm our allegiance to those great essential principles of justice and liberty, upon which our institutions are founded, and which the Democratic party has advocated from Jefferson's time to our own — freedom of speech, freedom of the press, freedom of conscience, the preservation of personal rights, the equality of all citizens before the law, and the faithful observance of constitutional limitations.

The direct slap at Cleveland in the last phrase was repeated more emphatically in a notable section:

We denounce arbitrary interference by Federal authorities in local affairs as a violation of the Constitution of the United States and a crime against free institutions. . . . And we especially object to *government by injunction* as a new and highly dangerous form of oppression by which Federal judges, in contempt of the laws of the States and the rights of citizens, become at once legislators, judges and executioners.

The magnitude of Altgeld's triumph was truly extraordinary. In 1894 practically alone in his stand against President Cleveland and the federal courts, in two years he had succeeded in getting the Democratic delegates, who had come to Chicago to press the free-silver plank, to spurn their party bosses and to vindicate him completely in a platform which, practically in his own words, affirmed his political and social beliefs. In the opinion of many observers he would certainly have received the nomination for President had he been born in this country. As it was, he helped to select William Jennings Bryan, whose "Cross of Gold" speech had won the hearts of the delegates.

The campaign was noteworthy for its intense acrimony and violent passion. Marcus A. Hanna, wealthy businessman and William McKinley's manager, collected millions of dollars from rich contributors on the issue that a victory for the Republicans would save the country from economic chaos. This money he spent lavishly in "educating" the voters concerning the merits of his candidate. He cleverly avoided the main monetary question. Instead he concentrated the attack on the radicalism of the Democratic platform and Bryan's "rattle-pated" youthfulness. Because Governor Altgeld was obviously the effective leader of the opposition, he was assailed with renewed fury. All the Republican dailies and weeklies delineated him as the vicious and anarchistic boss of his party, with Bryan as his pliant dupe. *Harper's Weekly* called him "the ambitious and unscrupulous Illinois communist . . . the brain and inspiration of the movement for which Bryan stands." The New York *Tribune* insisted that Bryan " was only a puppet in the blood-imbued hands of Altgeld, the anarchist, and Debs, the revolutionist, and other desperados of that stripe." The brash Theodore Roosevelt — who sixteen years later was himself to speak Altgeld's language — went to Chicago to denounce him as " one who would connive at wholesale murder " and who "would substitute for the government of Washington and Lincoln, for the system of orderly liberty which we inherit from our forefathers and which we desire to bequeathe to our sons, a red welter of lawlessness . . . as fantastic and as vicious as the Paris Commune itself."

Governor Altgeld, though ill and weary, fought back with leonine courage. He neglected his own campaign for re-election in order to devote himself to national issues. In speeches and interviews he argued for the liberalism of the Democratic platform with consummate cogency. At Henry George's request he went to New York to present his side of the Pullman strike and to clarify the principles involved. The large crowd at Cooper Union stood up to honor him, shouting, " We love you for the enemies you have made." He also presented the case for free silver with such commonsense forcefulness that none of his Republican opponents — not even the eminent Carl Schurz who was sent to Chicago for this purpose — succeeded in vitiating his premises. Yet the forces under Marcus Hanna, aided by an endless supply of money and the aura of respectability and safety, managed to intimidate enough voters to win at the polls. It was our first *class* election. According to Tom Johnson of Ohio, it became a question not of free silver but of free men — and the powers of the purse feared nothing more than free men.

Altgeld lost his own election as well. But he was not discouraged. His party, despite its radical stand and the defection of the Cleveland group, had obtained more votes than ever before. More, it did this while " confronted by everything that money could buy, that boodle could debauch, or that fear of starvation could coerce."

That it did not succeed in routing the plutocratic forces was owing to the short time it had in which to impress its views upon the public. Surely " at the next general election of the people, the Democrats will triumph."

Altgeld's last day as governor fittingly climaxed his turbulent term of office. In accord with long custom he prepared a message of farewell for delivery at the inaugural of his successor. On the morning of the appointed ceremony he released his address to the newspapers. But the incoming executive refused to respect the traditional courtesy and gave his predecessor no opportunity to speak. The insult was all the more gratuitous because of the generous amiability of the valediction.

When Altgeld became governor in 1893 he was worth more than a million dollars and highly esteemed as a civic leader; when he ended his term four years later he was nearly penniless and one of the most abused men in the history of our country. Again the Chicago *Tribune* led in the gloating over his defeat and congratulated the citizens of Illinois on having rid themselves of the greatest threat to their welfare. The record, however, reveals a contrary situation. In truth the first effective reformer in high office, he was according to Professor H. U. Faulkner practically the only " state executive who stood out during the nineties as the representative of a better day." Handicapped by corrupt and antagonistic legislatures that fought his recommendations with every trick at their command, he nevertheless pushed through the following reforms: a civil service law, an inheritance tax law, laws providing for the indeterminate sentence, parole, and probation of prisoners; acts regulating the sweatshop system and child labor, limiting the period of work for women to eight hours; and acts installing factory inspection and a state board of arbitration for industrial disputes. He was untiring in his efforts to protect and promote the rights of the poor, to put an end to public corruption and to tax evasion on the part of the rich corporations, to build up the University of Illinois and the Chicago park system, to further the ends of justice by tempering, it with mercy — although he deliberately exercised his pardoning power very sparingly.

His use of the executive veto is best seen in his fight against the "Eternal Monopoly Bills," which the state legislators were bribed to pass in 1895. When the public utilities corporations learned of his attitude towards these bills, their agents tried to gain his good will by offering him upward of a half-million dollars. And he might have let the bills become laws by default or even by vetoing them perfunctorily. Instead, as in the Haymarket case, he followed his conscience. His vigorous veto exposed the evil of these measures, terming them "a flagrant attempt to increase the riches of some men at the expense of others by means of legislation." He also excoriated the corruption of the legislators and fought energetically against the defeat of his veto — succeeding by the grace of one vote.

This record of positive achievement is all the more extraordinary in view of the fact that he had to effect each reform by a violent wrench of tradition and by browbeating graft-ridden politicians. As Waldo R. Browne has well summarized the net result:

No governor before or since his time has done more, if as much, to improve and extend the public facilities of Illinois in its penal, charitable, and educational institutions; none has been more tireless in initiating legislative measures of social reform and amelioration; none has served the humble masses of the people more zealously and incorruptibly.

Altgeld left the governor's office an old man at forty-nine. The four years of intense struggle for the right had sapped his strength and impaired his health. Nor were his troubles at an end. Bank failures involving men he had trusted, his impoverished condition, the illness of his wife, and the continued persecution in the press served further to depress his spirit. In May 1897, he confided to his friend Judge Lambert Tree that he was having a wretched time. "During my whole public career I have never been pursued with so much venom as during the last four or five months. I had long been used to facing the frown of the Fates, but this time they assumed the aggressive and I have felt the sting of their irony." After years of great

political and intellectual exertion he could not get used to inactivity. Nor were his spirits lifted by the few speeches he made during the next few years. He was especially disappointed in the defection of young Carter Harrison, whom he had helped elect mayor of
Chicago in 1897. Sick body and soul, he wrote to Henry D. Lloyd
late in 1898: " I have been living on the dry dust of the road so
long that I need a change." He was still in this dark mood when
his friends persuaded him to run against Harrison the following
spring. The latter had aligned himself with the reactionary Democratic bosses in an effort to scrap the 1896 platform and return the
party to Cleveland conservatism. Since Harrison was in control
of the city political machine, it was necessary for Altgeld to place
himself on an independent ticket. Lacking both the money and the
physical energy to put up a strong campaign, the weary crusader
failed to dislodge Harrison from office.

Defeat acted as a powerful prophylactic. The fear that his enemies were about to seize control of the Democratic party strengthened Altgeld's combative spirit. He began a strategic campaign that
once more revealed his great skill as a politician and his uncompromising devotion to progressive reform. To Bryan he wrote: " In my
judgment the wisest course for us to pursue is to serve notice on the
trimmers and traders all over the country that the Chicago platform of America cannot be trifled with. . . . Once let this feeling
get abroad in the land and we will have no more trouble." In
speeches, interviews, and personal conferences he helped to acquaint the people with the designs of the scheming politicians. The
latter tried to choke his influence at the source by getting Carter
Harrison to keep him from being a delegate to the state and national
Democratic conventions of 1900. Altgeld, however, attended both
gatherings as a member of the party. In each hall the spontaneous
cheers of the delegates made it possible for him to address them
from the rostrum and subsequently to exert a major influence over
the deliberations of their committees. In the end the 1896 platform
was reaffirmed and Bryan was again the nominee for President.
Altgeld's triumph was complete when his proposed plank against

imperialism was readily adopted as " the paramount issue of the campaign."

Altgeld and Bryan fought strenuously and effectively, visiting many states and rousing the voters to a consideration of the important issues. But prosperity was over the land again and the " full dinner pail," for which the Republicans claimed credit, was a more potent argument than any offered by the Democrats. McKinley's majority was even greater than in 1896.

Altgeld felt deeply the sting of defeat. Yet he continued to believe in the rightness of his principles and in the ultimate triumph of social justice. Shortly after the election he resumed the practice of law and formed a partnership with his friends Clarence Darrow and W. H. Thompson. His zeal was remarkable and his achievements in the courtroom renewed his reputation as a great lawyer. He did not, however, slacken his strong interest in public affairs and continued to address audiences on topics of timely importance.

In the last year of his life Altgeld published a small book entitled *Oratory: Its Requirements and Rewards*. It was a clear, practical manual based on his own successful efforts as a public speaker. Its favorable reception pleased him deeply. To his friend Lloyd he wrote: " It is one of my children that the world is not frowning on."

For all his preoccupation with legal work and civic affairs, he was able to complete another short work immediately before his death which he called *The Cost of Something for Nothing*. Friends brought it out posthumously. The thesis of this hortatory volume of essays is well explained by the title. While each chapter dwells on a different topic, all of them concentrate on the admonition that in the long run one cannot get something for nothing; " that a man cannot indulge in a mean trick, be it ever so small, without lowering his moral status." For under " the law of balances, which governs alike the heavenly bodies and the lives of men . . . when more is taken than is given, destruction follows."

Altgeld was most severe on those who prized wealth and personal success above the rights of their fellows. Even the most affluent of them, he insisted, those who laid claim to fabulous wealth, were in truth failures and victims of moral leprosy if their millions were tainted by injustice. He excoriated the unscrupulous employer who took unfair advantage of his workmen — no doubt having in mind such men as George Pullman and the mine owners at Spring Valley. " If we keep," he warned, " that which, under the eternal equities, was earned by another, the poison of injustice will enter our households." The shrewd and shifty banker — of the ilk of John R. Walsh, who ended his career in prison shortly after Altgeld's death — likewise received his heavy lashing. " The cold truth remains that every time a banker drives a sharp bargain, every time he takes advantage of another's necessities, he gets something for which he has not paid full value, and here the first seed of moral death is sown. From the moment he gets something for nothing, the microbe of injustice enters his soul and begins its deadly work." Lawyers fared no better on his moral scale. The fallacy " that a man may do things as a lawyer that he could not do as honorable citizen . . . has ruined more lawyers than any other thing." As was to be expected, he was harshest on judges who abused the spirit of our laws to the hurt of the people. " The judge who gives way to pressure, and allows his high office to be used for purposes of oppression and of wrong, is a curse to this country."

If Altgeld excoriated the greedy, the unprincipled, and the corrupt, he lavished praise on the honest and the upright — those who cherished true democracy and worked to make it prevail. He assured these lovers of justice that " to establish liberty for mankind is the highest mission on earth." No doubt thinking of his own agitated career and of the agony he had suffered over and over, he asserted that " he who has deep down in his soul the knowledge that he has always fought for the right and that he never knowingly has wronged another, could not be unhappy though the whole world were arrayed against him."

The Cost of Something for Nothing, for all its naïve moralizing and vague mysticism, truly expresses his distilled thoughts on the values and vices of human existence. One cannot read these didactic essays without being moved by their complete sincerity, their eloquent idealism, their prophetic nobility of spirit. In these pages the whole man emerges life-size. His career is clearly reflected in his ethical conclusions. His deep hatred of injustice and oppression bred in him the belief in moral retribution, and made him, in the words of Brand Whitlock, " one of the forerunners of the newer and better time of the moral awakening in America."

On March 11, 1902, after a fatiguing day in court defending a hackmen's union against a strike injunction, he went to Joliet to speak in behalf of the Boers who were then at war with England. He discoursed for about forty-five minutes, ending with the words: " Wrong may seem to triumph. Right may seem to be defeated. But the gravitation of eternal justice is toward the throne of God. Any political institution which is to endure must be plumb with that line of justice." He sat down and was applauded enthusiastically. Two minutes later, feeling dizzy, he left the stage and collapsed in the wings — the victim of a cerebral hemorrhage. He died early the next morning. For once the newspapers united in praise of their erstwhile adversary. For once his friends and foes joined together in honoring his memory. Civic leaders and tens of thousands of common citizens stood for hours in the cold rain to pay their respects to the man who in Darrow's words " dies as he had lived, fighting for freedom."

American historians have still to rescue John Peter Altgeld from his undeserved oblivion. Few people outside of Illinois know of him at all, and most of these remember him as he was pictured in his lifetime: an obnoxious radical who had tried to undermine the foundations of our government. The crucible of time has not yet wholly melted down the vituperation and vilification with which his enemies besmirched him. Sooner or later, however, his reputation will be completely vindicated and he will appear in his full stature as one of our great crusaders for human freedom and social justice.

LINCOLN STEFFENS

MUCKRAKER'S PROGRESS

STEFFENS," wrote Ella Winter, " cared passionately about right-ing the evils his muckrake had uncovered." His prime concern, however, was not so much to expose political corruption as to discover its cause and cure. While no fanatic, he could not acqui-esce in mere palliation. Because he early came to understand the reasons for the failure of political reform, he did not, like so many of his fellow muckrakers, either resort to the fleshpots of the status quo or take flight into the obscurity of inaction. Instead he devel-oped inductively the thesis that it was special privilege which bred corruption and not the reverse; that only a revolution which would abolish all privilege could eradicate graft in politics. Consequently he studied the Mexican and particularly the Russian revolutions with scientific care. And when he found that these political erup-tions, for all their cost in blood and suffering, presaged the better society, he dedicated the remainder of his life to missionary work in their behalf. Like Moses he had looked into the future and found it good.

Lincoln Steffens, born in California in 1866, was permitted by his wise and considerate father to follow pretty much his own bent. As a boy he had " horses, guns, dogs, and the range of the open country." He learned by doing. What interested him he mastered, in and out of school; although there was little in the classroom that appealed to his imagination and he was usually at the bottom of his class.

Throughout his childhood he was perturbed by the discrepancy " between what was and what seemed to be." As a boy he attended the sessions of the California legislature and was shocked to realize how much its practice differed from what he had been led to believe concerning it. What made his discovery more shocking was the fact that neither his father nor his friends " had any strong feeling about the conflict of the two pictures. I had. I remembered how I suffered."

As an undergraduate at the University of California he neglected the courses that failed to interest him and concentrated on those that held his attention. His class standing was therefore very poor. Yet he was among the very few students who acquired a respect for pure knowledge. " Rebel though I was, I had got the religion of scholarship and science; I was in awe of the authorities in the academic world." He persuaded his father to let him go to Europe to study with the high priests of learning in German universities and in Paris, and for three years he steeped himself in philosophy and art. Ethics was his chief pursuit, but in the end he realized that he could not truly know it before he had practised it in daily life. " The thing for me to do, I decided, was to leave the universities, go into business or politics, and see, not what thinkers thought, but what practical men did and why." Meantime he had fallen in love with Josephine Bontecou, a fellow American student, and the two were married secretly during a brief visit to London.

In the summer of 1892 Steffens wrote to his father that he was ready to return home and work in a bank. It was his assumption that such employment would not only pay well but also give him at once an insight into the heart of business and the time to write his book on ethics. On his return to this country in October, however, he found a letter from his father containing one hundred dollars and the suggestion that he use this money to make his way in New York as best he could. Too proud to inform his family that he had a wife to support, he for the first time suffered the fear of poverty. After several weeks of discouraging effort he was engaged by *The Evening Post* as a reporter on a space-rate basis. It did not take him long to master the technique of newspaper reporting; his stories soon became feature articles. He was a success.

The forced return to England of the *Post's* regular financial reporter sent Steffens to Wall Street during the 1893 depression. His forthright and sympathetic manner gained him the confidence of the leading bankers and gave him an inside track to news reports. He never abused their trust in him. Yet they were not his heroes. Seeing them in action and uninterested in making a lot of money, he could not join in the general admiration for those who were successful at getting rich quick. For he learned early that the leading men of business worked by "hunches" rather than by reason. "Men of exaggerated success like Russell Sage, J. Pierpont Morgan . . . are all, all incapable of logical thought *even in* business matters. . . . They simply feel that such a thing will go. They do not reason it out carefully."

He soon unlearned another precept: that sincerity was not nearly so important as people thought it was. What the world needed most, he discovered, was "someone who was not sincere but intelligent." James B. Dill, author of the notorious New Jersey trust law and "a great name in Wall Street," was the first "bad" man to impress him with his keen intelligence. From him he learned the realities of modern economic life — what corruption was and how it made rogues out of honest men. "Trusts are natural, inevitable growths out of our social and economic conditions," Dill explained. "You cannot stop them by force, with laws. They will sweep down like glaciers upon your police, courts, and States and wash them into flowing rivers." His young admirer never forgot this lesson.

Late in 1893 Steffens became the first regular reporter to be assigned by the *Post* to police headquarters. The Rev. Dr. Charles H. Parkhurst was then carrying on his crusade against crime and corruption, and the city editor of this august daily decided to take cognizance of police activities in its news columns. Steffens at once resorted to his Wall Street method of learning what he needed to know. He allied himself with Parkhurst, who valued the *Post* connection, and the two began to exchange news and confidences. He was also befriended by Jacob Riis, the famous reformer and reporter, who initiated him into the mysteries and machinations of the police department. The brazen and ubiquitous system of graft and collusion between the officers of the law and lawbreakers shocked him, and he could not understand why so many good and respectable people were bitterly opposed to Parkhurst — until he became aware of their vested economic interests in the system which this crusader was trying to eradicate.

Contact with business and political bosses taught Steffens a basic lesson in social organization. From Dill, whom he continued to visit, he learned to distinguish between the principals and the figureheads in the financial world. " All directors are dummies," his mentor explained. " Most presidents too. Chairmen of Boards, managers, and heads of departments are real enough, but the bosses of business are the bankers and financial operators; they have no office at all in the company, but they run it through — dummies." At that time he also became friendly with Tammany boss Richard Croker, who was then under severe attack from reformers. Steffens found this notorious politician a man of his word, " true to his professional ethics . . . intellectually and morally a citizen of the civilization of New York." From him he ascertained that most political officials served the same purpose as dummy directors in business. Both systems " had unofficial, irresponsible, invisible, actual governments back of the legal, constitutional ' fronts.' " Croker told him also why elected or appointed officials had to be controlled by political bosses: " A business man wants to do business with one man, and one who is always there to remember and carry out the business."

By the time the Lexow Police Investigation began to uncover the scandalous corruption of the police, Steffens had already established himself as a fearless and formidable journalist and a pillar of strength to the reformers. He became interested in Captain Max Schmittberger, who was the first to confess his prominent part in the nefarious and hydra-headed system of graft, won his confidence, and later helped him to a distinguished career as police commissioner. Riis and Steffens worked closely with Theodore Roosevelt, the reform head of the police board, in cleaning up the police department.

All through this period he kept stumbling into cavernous depths which most reformers avoided. Croker had assured him that "the business men who have business with the city government and so know about the Tammany administration — they are with us." Yet the reformers were seeking to destroy Tammany in order to supplant it with a government of businessmen. It took him many years to "see through the appearances of things to the facts . . . past the lie to the truth," but his intimate association with various reformers taught him soon enough that the good man in business often turned out the bad man in politics — compromise, incompetence, and arrogance being his chief faults.

I saw enough of it to realize that reform politics was still politics, only worse; reformers were not so smooth as the professional politicians, and it seemed to me they were not so honest — which was a very confusing theory to me.

He also noticed that while waves of reform came and went, the sea of organized politics kept rolling along. Circumstances, however, temporarily turned his attention from this perplexing phenomenon.

In 1897 he became the city editor of the run-down *Commercial Advertiser*, which several of the executives on *The Evening Post* had decided to take over and enliven with their brand of reformist-literary journalism. In order to develop a repertorial staff that would depict New York "as it was: rich and poor, wicked and good, ugly but beautiful, growing, great," he engaged the pick of college graduates and trained them to see things clearly and to describe what they saw accurately and vividly. The ideal he presented to them was "to get the news so completely and to report it so humanly that the reader will see himself in the other fellow's place." In a relatively short time his staff of talented novices — most of them later became prominent writers and editors — succeeded in producing the livest and best-written newspaper in New York. Steffens's own chief interest remained the game of politics. During this period he strengthened his intimacy with Theodore Roosevelt and retained it throughout the latter's career as colonel of the Rough Riders, as governor of New York, and finally as President.

After four years of hard work on *The Commercial Advertiser* Steffens became managing editor of *McClure's Magazine*. For three months he tried to master his new job, but the result was disappointing. " I simply was not an editor. As I wandered around that magazine office looking for work, I realized that I was a false alarm." When McClure returned from Europe he sized up his new executive and suggested that he go out on a trip and learn his job away from the office.

Steffens went to Chicago because the magazine had credit with a railroad serving that city. He had no definite plan of action, but he hoped to discover ideas for articles and men to write them. A casual suggestion that he might get something out of the corruption scandal then agitating St. Louis sent him there with the celerity of a fireman at the sound of the gong. A day later he was learning the facts from Joseph W. Folk, the plucky prosecuting attorney who was fighting the city's powerful political machine in his effort to jail bribers and grafters. " It is good business men that are corrupting our bad politicians," Folk explained; " it is good business that causes bad government — in St. Louis." Steffens's imagination was on the run. He knew well the way of corruption and its evil effects; he was attracted to Folk and saw in a flash that he could serve his new friend as well as the cause of reform by exposing " boodle " politics in a popular magazine of national circulation. He was still thinking of himself as managing editor, however, and engaged an able local reporter to write the article on St. Louis graft.

When the manuscript reached him in New York some weeks later he found in it certain conspicuous omissions and a rather gentle treatment of Boss Butler. Remonstrance brought the reply that the complete unvarnished account would mean the end of the writer's usefulness in St. Louis. Steffens had no alternative but to rewrite the paper and take full responsibility as co-author. The article, which appeared in October 1902, was the first of its sort in the history of American journalism. It was received with surprising favor.

Encouraged by his colleagues, Steffens decided not to depend on others but to investigate and describe a series of metropolitan governments with a view to testing Folk's assertion " that bribery is not a mere felony, but a revolutionary process which was going on in all our cities." Minneapolis, St. Louis (again), Pittsburgh, Philadelphia, Chicago, New York — in each of these cities he worked hard with his muckrake and discussed his findings in lively and revealing papers which created a national sensation. In 1904 they were published in a volume, *The Shame of the Cities*, and established Steffens as the country's foremost journalist — at least he was the only one to have a cigar named after him.

In each city he visited he found that — as later proved to be true of all municipalities, large and small — the system of graft reached into every department of government. Graft was controlled by political bosses for the enrichment of the few principals and was condoned and encouarged by various leading citizens who thrived on the special privileges it afforded them. In each instance he discovered that the city administration was not an independent unit but was closely connected with, if not completely controlled by, the state government.

Since " the State was the unit of action for good or for evil," he next studied the governments of Missouri, Illinois, Wisconsin, Rhode Island, Ohio, and New Jersey. As he had expected, the multifarious systems of corruption in these states (La Follette's Wisconsin was an honorable exception) differed little, if at all, from those of the cities — " the same methods, the same motives, purposes, and men, all to the same end: to make the State officials, the Legislature, the courts, parts of a system representing the special interests of bribers, corruptionists, and criminals." He saw that this ubiquitous venality was transforming the basic democracy of our towns and states into a boss-ridden oligarchy. This condition he described in a series of frank and incisive articles on state government. The book containing these studies, issued in 1906 under the title of *The Struggle for Self-Government*, greatly accelerated the movement for political reform.

This Steffens knew: the current explanations of political corruption were superficial and false. " It is not a temporary evil," he explained, " not an accidental wickedness, not a passing symptom of the youth of a people. It is a natural process by which a democracy is made gradually over into a plutocracy." Chiefly responsible for this process were the businessmen who sought special rights and franchises and obtained them by corrupting public officials because it was easier and cheaper that way. " Not the politician, then, not the bribe-taker, but the bribe-giver, the man we are so proud of, our successful business man — he is the source and sustenance of bad government." Worse still was the resulting vicious circle which blighted both briber and bribed. Thus, to obtain certain rights for less than they were worth, public utilities bribed bosses and legislators to enact the necessary laws. But this was only the beginning. These corporations had to continue their political chicane to make sure that their privileges — and the stock they had watered on the strength of this " good will " — were properly protected from honest officials and slippery double-dealers. " A railroad," Steffens pointed out, " must govern, somehow, the State or the commission that otherwise would govern the railroad." Other businesses were equally involved in the practice of corruption.

After what I have seen in Chicago, St. Louis, Pittsburgh, and in Missouri and Illinois and the United States, I am almost persuaded that no honest official in power can meet the expectations of great corporations; they have been spoiled, like bad American children, and are ever ready to resort to corruption and force.

He was not surprised to find that these businessmen continued to think of themselves as good and patriotic citizens. Neither public opinion nor their own conscience pointed to the enormity of their guilt. To them, " treason " was to betray your country overtly to the enemy; but to destroy " the fundamental institutions of your country and the saving character of American manhood — that is not treason, that is politics, and politics is business, and business, you know, is business." When he pointed this out to a lawyer who handled " boodle " for his rich clients, the man was genuinely distressed.

I never realized how wrong we were. You understand, we thought we were after only this law or that franchise. We never stopped to think that other men also wanted this or that, and that all of us together were doing something rotten. We never saw it whole the way you see it. It's fierce when you take it all in at one gulp like this.

But he made no effort to reform. The lure of large fees and the grip of long habit were too much for this lawyer's crippled conscience.

Steffens's writings and lectures helped to bring political corruption to the forefront of national issues. The masses of people, shocked by the exposure of graft in high places, clamored for action. Assuming that political reform was the sovereign remedy, they met everywhere to " throw the rascals out." In almost every instance reform proved itself an ephemeral phenomenon in American life. Even where most successful it did not last long — and the politicians had only to bide their time until they were returned to office. This happened largely because of the defection of the " good " citizens. These civic leaders were either naïve men who believed that their duty ended with the election of reform canadidates or businessmen who reneged as soon as reform laws began to tamper with their special privileges. Their withdrawal usually brought the movement for reform to a full circle.

Aware as he had become of the weaknesses of reform, Steffens was not yet ready to give up the fight. By writing a series of essays on some of the outstanding reformers he hoped to encourage those honest citizens who were continuing their campaign against corrupt government. Having already enlarged upon the achievements of Folk, La Follette, Tom Johnson, "Golden Rule" Jones, and others, he now told the stories of Mark Fagan, the little Republican undertaker who "carried Democratic Jersey City three times running"; Everett Colby, the rich young Wall Street broker who beat the New Jersey bosses in a final showdown; Ben Lindsey, the Democratic "kids' judge" in Denver whose applied Christianity in the courtroom antagonized the rich of both parties but who was kept in office by the votes of the poor; W. S. U'Ren, the Colorado blacksmith who became a people's lobbyist in Oregon and hammered out "legislative tools for the use of democracy everywhere"; and Rudolph Spreckels, the millionaire capitalist who led the fight on vice and corruption in San Francisco. He depicted their devotion to truth, their trust in democracy, their deep humanity, their essential goodness. It is of these reformers that he wrote in italics: "*The happiest men I know in all this unhappy life of ours, are those leaders who, brave, loyal, and sometimes in tears, are serving their fellow men.*" The five sanguine studies of different types of reformers were published in *McClure's* and later in a book entitled *Upbuilders*.

These Davids in politics, Steffens emphasized, trusted the people and forged ahead with their help. They knew that the mass of citizens were not beyond temptation, but they regarded them as "better than their ' betters ' " just because their economic stake was so small. "They are not in on any graft, so they can be fair. . . . They are ignorant, and they can be and often are corrupted, but not many educated individuals are as wise as the mass of men when individuals haven't tampered with them." And while they tended to be suspicious or indifferent because they have been betrayed so often by leaders they had trusted, they were ever ready to listen to anyone who appealed to their sense of humanity. This fundamental truth of democracy is stressed in the Foreword:

Wherever the people have found a leader who was loyal to them, brave, and not too far ahead, there they have followed him, and there has been

begun the solution of our common problem; the problem of the cities,
states, and nations — the problem of civilized living in human communi-
ties.

In the late 1900's Steffens was at the peak of his influence. His
writings were widely quoted and discussed. He was in great demand
as a lecturer. His advice and assistance were sought by all types of
people, who turned to him as the expert in graft and government.
And he did not spare himself. To his father he boasted: " I like
best what I'm doing now, simply because I'm getting an influence
far beyond that of any newspaper editor, to say nothing of the
monthlies."

For all his prestige and power, and for all his eagerness to improve our democratic form of government, he remained the ques-
tioner and the critic. He was not made of the stuff of a popular
leader or of a social crusader. The urge to right a wrong seldom
impelled him to act overtly. His indignation was too often tempered
by an effervescent humor: the ironist's view of the foibles of humanity. He was more frequently impressed by the inherent decency of the unscrupulous boss than by the pinchbeck righteousness
of a civic leader. It took him years to realize that what mattered
was not so much the crook as the conditions that made his crime
possible. He was equally long in learning that the key to corruption was privilege. " It is privilege that causes evil in the world, not
wickedness, and not men." Yet his attacks on corruption were written to amuse as well as to deprecate, and few readers saw the significance of his basic conclusions. He was satisfied to let others un-
sheathe their swords against the monster.

After nearly seven years of political muckraking he felt he had
reached a journalistic dead-end. He was not interested in turning
the same muck all over again. Having given up his job with *Mc-
Clure's* in 1906 and his connection with *The American Magazine*
a year later, he decided to remain a free-lance and write as he pleased.
His articles on the Presidential candidates in 1908 helped him
maintain his eminence as a political reporter.

It was at this time that Edward A. Filene, the prominent Boston

merchant and philanthropist, asked Steffens to make a study of the
New England metropolis. The terms were very attractive: a year's
residence, a good salary, and a free hand. He accepted the more
readily because he had long thought of investigating Boston in
order to verify his theory that the older the city the more steeped
it was in privilege and hypocrisy. Nor was he disappointed: business and politics functioned as a unit. " Gentlemen attended to all
the politics." Consequently there was little obvious scandal and no
boss in Boston. But while it seemed better governed than other
cities, its bribery and corruption were merely more subtly concealed.
" Boston has carried the practice of hypocrisy to the nth degree of
refinement, grace, and failure."

From the point of view of the Boston reformers and businessmen,
Steffens's analysis of their city's politics was a complete failure. His
recommendation that they get rid of hypocrisy by yet more hypocrisy struck them as frivolous. Yet he was never more serious. What
he found was a deep, subconscious conflict between the city's Puritanic heritage and its gross industrialism. His remedy was

to draw a plan for its reform that would lead the community as a whole to
see that something was making them all do what they did not want to
do . . . to produce a city of people *on to* themselves, and so uncom-
fortably " on " that they would either change the conditions or become
a community of conscious crooks, or, best of all, give up their old ideals
and form new ideals which would fit modern life and save the United
States from hypocrisy and the fate of nations.

Yet he was too much the idealist to accept his own conclusions
with an easy conscience. It took him several years to write the report, which so dissatisfied him that it was never published. For by
this time he had learned another lesson: " The reformation of politics and business by propaganda and political action was impossible.
Nothing but revolution could change the system."

On his return to New York late in 1909 Steffens indeed thought
of himself as a radical and became interested in the prominent social rebels of the day. But he joined with none of them, finding

them creed-bound, doctrinaire. " I proposed to play with all of them, and work with some, as I did, experimentally." This attitude marked him as the true liberal, which he was, and therefore no better than any other bourgeois in the eyes of the extremists. Nor could he repress the feeling that he was indeed ineffectual, played-out. He refused several generous offers from magazines on the ground that he had nothing to offer them. Meantime his wife began to ail and died early in 1911. Her loss grieved him deeply and he felt himself adrift, homeless and helpless. His efforts to keep himself profitably occupied only accentuated the awareness that he was merely marking time. Only the study of the New Testament brought him a measure of solace.

Steffens was in that frame of mind when the sensational McNamara labor dynamiting case in Los Angeles broke in the newspapers. What aroused his interest was not whether or not the two brothers were responsible for the *Times* Building explosion which had caused the death of twenty-one lives but why a conservative trade union should feel compelled to fight unco-operative employers with dynamite. He had no difficulty in getting a syndicate of newspapers to send him to the trial as their special correspondent.

He very quickly surmised that the McNamaras had done the dynamiting and that Clarence Darrow, their chief counsel, was fearful that they would be convicted and hanged. He perceived as well that the opening of the trial was bringing the prolonged bitter struggle between organized labor and the united Los Angeles employers to the point of open class war. Eager to help avoid a costly and bloody clash, hoping to effect a working understanding between the antagonistic groups, and stimulated by his acute vanity, Steffens hit upon the idea of converting both sides to the Golden Rule. Ever at heart a true admirer of Jesus, his imagination hugged the thought of applying the balm of Christianity to a deep social wound. His plan was to get the McNamara brothers to plead guilty on the condition that the Los Angeles business leaders would agree to join with labor in making their city a model of co-operation between employer and employee — a sheer utopian dream.

When he explained his plan to the prisoners, they assured him that they would be willing to hang for its success. Darrow was skeptical but agreed to let him try. When he broached the idea to several of the principal businessmen, each one, affected by Steffens's sincere eloquence, agreed to take part in the social experiment but doubted if the others would even hear of it. He then invited them and a number of others to a meeting, explained his plan in full, and urged them to act generously for the good of their city. They did — justifying his " theory that there is enough good in all men of imagination and power to do any good, hard job, even if it is not obviously in their own selfish interest." One of them got the prosecuting attorney to agree to the plan as well as to obtain the judge's consent to the procedure.

When the story broke in the courtroom the shock of surprise was more than the human mind could assimilate suddenly. Some men, unable to apprehend the underlying motive, became angry — as if they had been cheated. Union leaders were confused. The ministers of the city's churches failed completely to recognize the Golden Rule in action. Their Sunday sermons were preachments of " hate and disappointed revenge "; their vindictive outbursts " came like the cries of a lynching mob and frightened all the timid men who had worked with us — and the judge." The next day the plan was repudiated. The agreements with labor were not kept. Steffens " felt defeated, disgraced somehow, and helpless." He had to admit that " Christianity won't work long in our day. The organization of society is against it." For years he was known as " Golden Rule " Steffens, derided by both sides alike for meddling in a matter that he did not understand.

The next three years were for him a period of decline and disillusionment. His popularity and influence reached their lowest ebb. But his conscience was clear — at least he believed that his scheme was a good one and could have worked. He faced his labor detractors openly and defended himself with a frankness and eloquence that earned the respect of hostile workmen. His lectures and debates on the McNamara case persuaded thousands of his hearers that the defeat of his plan was a great loss to the weal of the entire nation. Later, on completing his abortive book on Boston, he visited Europe on the chance that he might wish to muckrake its various governments. He found, however, that the system of graft was accepted there as a matter of course — with English gentlemen standing up for their privileges as Americans would for their rights. On his return to New York he hit upon another quixotic plan: an amnesty for all labor prisoners. None of the executive officials, however — from President Wilson down — showed a willingness to brave the consequences of public misunderstanding.

Steffens was in Italy when World War I began. He was not surprised. Nor did he care to become a war correspondent — a task he considered as futile as muckraking Europe. " The firing line *isn't* the line of most interest," he wrote. Instead he went to Mexico, where the revolution was reaching to the roots of the country's social system. It was his theory then " that the inevitable war would bring on the inevitable revolution," and he wanted to see for himself whether or not the civil strife in backward Mexico was the real thing. He soon sensed that it was. Nor was he long in discovering that the revolution was neither caused nor started by the radicals. Madero and Carranza were not revolutionists: all they wanted at first were mild reforms. The established order had become so rotten, however, that it collapsed at the first impact of rebelliousness on the part of a few liberals. The phenomenon appealed to his imagination. He gained Carranza's confidence and joined his retinue on a trip across the country. Months of intimacy with the leaders of the revolution enabled him to perceive that revolution had a basic similarity to reform: both tended to complete the circle. A wave of reform usually ended with the same privileged groups in control. A revolution merely took longer to dissipate its greater impetus. " But the tendency is to form a complete circle back to the starting-point, and there is progress or, at least, change only when the return misses the starting-point and forms a spiral." Carranza knew social history and was making a sincere effort to form this spiral.

For nearly two years Steffens made himself Mexico's unofficial interpreter and advocate. While American interventionists did their utmost to crush the revolution, he toured the United States in an effort to rally the country to a sympathetic understanding of events in Mexico. He also lobbied the administration in Washington and finally gained the ear of President Wilson — thereby helping to avoid a war which at the time seemed inevitable. Years later he regarded this interview as his most successful undertaking.

A chance meeting with his old friend Charles R. Crane, who was about to leave for Russia on a diplomatic mission, made it possible for Steffens to accompany him to that country within two weeks after the revolution in Petrograd had begun. Here, too, he found that the established government had been overthrown not by revolutionists, who were mostly in exile or in Siberia, but by its own corruption and decrepitude. For days he watched and studied the crowds of Russian workers and peasants milling in the streets: inarticulate, groping for the truth, dimly aware of their political liberation — yet dominating the situation by their multitudinous and persistent presence. They were the revolutionists! Milyukov and especially Kerensky rose to power because they " expressed the feelings — fear, faith, hope — of the people "; they were the first emotional mouthpieces of the masses in motion. As early as May, however, after watching the temper and direction of the increasingly restive crowds, Steffens knew that their real leader was not the ebullient Kerensky but the calm and clearheaded Lenin.

Overflowing with the urgency and importance of his message, Steffens returned to this country with the new Russian ambassador. After he had delivered confidential oral and written reports to President Wilson, he devoted himself to lecturing on the meaning of the Russian Revolution. Although his audiences were large and sympathetic, he found the nation as a whole increasingly hostile towards the revolution and particularly towards the emerging Bolshevik leaders. Men in positions of importance began to frown upon him as a radical, and for the first time in twenty years he was unable to sell an article to a popular magazine under his own name. This unsavory reputation later almost kept him from going to Europe for the peace conference; officials in the State Department refused to give him his passport — until he made use of the good offices of his friend Colonel House.

In February 1919, Steffens accompanied the young, dashing William Bullitt to Russia on a semiofficial mission. Again he had the opportunity to study the dynamic direction of the revolution. He noted with deep interest that the Bolshevik plan was " not by direct action to resist such evils as poverty and riches, graft, privilege, tyranny, and war, but to seek out and remove the causes of them." Nor was he unaware that the Soviet leaders were not practising what they had formerly preached; that in Russia, as elsewhere, theories tended to lose themselves in the welter of reality. Thus the once vital questions of political rights and personal liberty had become academic in the ruthless striving for economic democracy and national security. Indeed, the war on its several borders helped to intensify the emerging dictatorship — which the leaders admitted but made no effort to modify. " It was a new culture, an economic, scientific, not a moral, culture " — one that Steffens understood and wished well. Chiefly he admired Lenin's active intelligence. After an interview with him he was convinced that this Bolshevik chief was " cautiously applying to the social life of Russia the best we know of the science of government." More, he possessed greater perspicacity and acumen than the leaders of the Versailles Peace Conference. They were mere seamen on the stormy seas of history, sailing without compass toward no certain port; he was a fully equipped navigator, with his eye upon the chart of a long-planned voyage.

The truth of this comparison was emphasized by the cavalier repudiation of the Bullitt mission on the part of the Allies and by their refusal to face the reality of Bolshevik domination. The more Steffens watched the actual working of the peace conference the more it seemed to him " to be a case of a lot of great little human beings wabbling around in the throne of God." These politicians were blind to the underlying causes of the war and to the nature of its aftermath. And much as he sympathized with President Wilson, he could not help thinking of him as " the most perfect example we have produced of the culture which has failed and is dying out." Later Steffens wrote to his friend Filene:

Lenin understood, you remember, better than the members of the Peace Conference themselves what they did and failed to do. This simply means that there is another culture in the world than this immoral, so-called moral culture which your business men and statesmen prate about and march their armies all over. . . .

Steffens remained on the Continent for sixteen months after the peace conference had ended. He visited a number of countries, studying their abortive revolutions, their pathetic efforts at social and economic readjustments, and their general futile striving for a vanished sense of security. He wrote little — perhaps because no American editor was interested in his work — but he thought and " unlearned " a lot. Much as he preferred peaceful evolution to Bolshevism — he recoiled from class war even when he accepted it intellectually — he knew no alternative; men in power everywhere were too selfish to evolve — " not while they have their special privileges to protect." Before leaving for the United States in the fall of 1920 he wrote, as an afterthought:

Europe is fighting, waiting, starving. I have seen hell. But I saw light too; the dawn, and I would like to spend the evening of my life watching the morning of the new world.

Again he lectured to eager and interested audiences in many cities and towns, telling them about his impressions of Europe. He also revisited Mexico to see what the years had done to the revolution. The following summer he tried, unsuccessfully, to enter famine-stricken Russia. On his return to this country he became the executive secretary of the committee for Russian relief. At the same time he renewed his drive for the amnesty of American political and labor prisoners. He interested Postmaster-General Hays and might have prevailed with President Harding, but Hays's sudden illness permitted Secretary Hoover to frighten the easy-going Harding. Eugene V. Debs was the only conspicuous prisoner to be pardoned. Whereupon Steffens, prevented by Great Britain from visiting India, sailed once more for Europe, satisfied " merely to watch social processes."

More than a year later he joined Senator La Follette's party in a tour of Russia. His heart leaped at the sight of the progress achieved by the Soviet government. It was obvious that the revolution was spiraling to its original goal. Talks with some of the Bolshevik leaders made it easy for him to understand why so many liberals feared and detested them. He found them " as ruthless, arrogant, hard-boiled, as prisons, tortures, sufferings and failures can make them. They are terrible in their determination to stick it out." He left Russia convinced that its government " owns and means to control all those economic interests which own and control every other government in the world." Yet glad as he was to see the Bolsheviks validating his theory of modern society, he felt too old and too much the liberal to join them as his young friend John Reed had done. As he wrote afterwards:

I am a patriot for Russia; the Future is there; Russia will win out and will save the world. That is my belief. But I don't want to live there. It is too much like serving in an army at war with no mercy for the weak and no time for the wounded.

With his wonted humor he admitted that he was like the good Christian who believed in Heaven but was in no hurry to get there.

Some years ago Steffens had ceased muckraking because of his belief that nothing short of a spiraling revolution could abolish corruptive privilege. Now he began to grope for a means of presenting his theory in a clear and effective manner. His study of the Mexican and Russian revolutions excited his imagination but did not at once crystallize his conclusions. Events kept interrupting his reflections. For nearly a decade he was more the observer than the reporter and analyst. Then, even as he had saturated his mind with the New Testament after his muckraking experience, he turned to a perusal of the Old Testament subsequent to his final visit to Russia. And in the story of Moses he found the prototype of social revolutions.

Moses in Red, which he completed in 1924 and published two years later, narrates the events leading to the liberation of the Jews from Egyptian servitude in such a manner as to illustrate the causes and characteristics of a typical revolution. In discussing the various steps leading to the successful rebellion he develops "a serious essay on the laws of revolution." First of all he makes clear that nobody likes revolutions — not even revolutionists. "They are violent, messy, stormlike affairs which are almost impossible to manage and direct." They are usually forced upon the antagonists of the status quo by those in power who insist on blocking imperative changes. In such cases revolutions are "as natural and as understandable as a flood, a fire or a war." Yet the outside world, noting only the excesses and fearful of being affected by them, is quick to condemn the revolutionists and to seek their defeat.

The thing that people deplore most about revolutions is their perversely undemocratic direction. Yet that is inherent in all great social crises. In time of war or natural cataclysm governments tend in effect to become dictatorships; if most men do not feel oppressed on such occasions it is only because they willingly, if unconsciously, forgo their normal rights and prerogatives for the good of the entire nation. In a revolution, however, the defeated privileged groups will fight until they are crushed; where they are permitted to exist they will seize power at the first opportunity — as they did in Hungary and Bavaria in 1919; neither side can tolerate the slightest degree of individual freedom. As Steffens stated emphatically:

In revolutions, in wars and in all such disorganizing, fear spreading crises in human affairs, nations tend to return to the first, the simplest, and perhaps the best form of government: a dictatorship.

Human liberty, in truth, rises with the general sense of security and falls with the general sense of danger — "regardless of man-made laws and soul-felt idealism." Consequently individual freedom will be one of man's last achievements. Viewed from this standpoint, the excesses and excrescences of the revolution in Russia become not the work of depraved fanatics, as maintained by its victims and enemies, but the unavoidable concomitants of a grave social crisis; and Lenin's conscious acceptance and forceful direction of the consequences of the social storm mark him as a realistic historian and revolutionary genius.

These premises were confirmed in Steffens's mind by Mussolini's rise to power. This fascist leader struck him as a new kind of political boss. What impressed him particularly was the Italian's skilled adaptation of Lenin's revolutionary method to his own selfish ends.

Mussolini has no worth-while purpose that makes his policy an experiment in politics; but he did watch the Russian Revolution, as I would have such things watched, drew some conclusions scientifically and, acting upon them, confirmed some theories of Lenin as to political method.

Fascism at work proved some of Steffens's own contentions as well: that " our culture of good and evil does not contain a solution, cannot even visualize the problem, which is economic and not moral "; that any serious social crisis which poses class against class will bring forth a dictatorship — either of the Left or of the Right; that while a radical oligarchy is motivated by social ideals and looks to the future, a fascist autocrat tends to increase the powers of the privileged few and therefore to aggravate the social crisis. And when Steffens saw the capitalist statesmen, who scorned to deal with the Bolsheviks, ingratiating themselves with the blustering Mussolini, he knew that Europe was doomed to suffer another war.

At the peace conference in Versailles, Steffens fell in love with Ella Winter, a young English student of economics. Although he was then intermittently living with the woman he had cared for during his undergraduate days and had met again after his wife's death, he could not suppress his affection for the bright-eyed girl. In vain were the appeals to his conscience, the reminder of the great disparity in their ages. When he learned in 1923 that Ella loved him too, he married her. Their union was secret until he discovered, to his ineffable delight, that he was to become a father. He then made the marriage known to his friends and took his wife to Italy. There "Pete" was born and there they lived most of the time until in 1927 they made their home in California. Father of a firstborn in his fifty-ninth year, Steffens immersed himself in the duties and pleasures of parenthood. He became in truth the most affectionate and painstaking father in modern literature. And although he knew he had acted like a cad to his former lover, his strong sense of guilt failed to mar his new and overflowing happiness.

In 1925 he began to divide his time between Pete and the writing of his autobiography. For years he had wanted to present the lessons of his fruitful experience in a book. But the form eluded him. What he wished to bring out lent itself neither to fiction nor to political treatise. He experimented with the fable, but *Moses in Red* at best dealt with only one of the lessons. His choice of Satan as a mouthpiece failed to satisfy him. Then he hit upon the idea of telling his story in autobiographical form. Once he saw his way clearly, he wrote with enthusiasm and fastidious care. It was a labor of love, and it was very good. He knew he had a vivid and valuable story to tell and he told it with a freedom and verve and humor that gave his work pre-eminence among modern autobiographies. The book pulsates with the vitality of the whole man. The charm of his personality imbues every page; his moral earnestness thrusts through the veneer of soft humor. And if the style fascinates, the sagacity of his "unlearning" steals upon one almost imperceptibly. Never again can the reader of the book forget his "lessons" on the nature and technique of political corruption, the failure of reform, and the character and significance of social revolution.

It took Steffens five years to write the book. When it was published in 1931, its success exceeded everyone's expectations. A first large printing at $7.50 per copy was sold within ten days. A lower-priced edition brought the total sale to 65,000 copies by the end of the year. His name recovered its magnetic appeal, and his lecture schedule became as crowded as in the days of his muckraking eminence. In December 1933, however, he suffered a heart attack and his doctor put an end to his public appearances.

In 1931, refusing commercial offers, he began to write a column of brief paragraphs successively for *The Carmelite, Controversy,* and *Pacific Weekly,* all local periodicals. He spoke his mind freely and pithily on matters of interest to him. He also indulged in reminiscence, and gave many revealing sidelights on his political experiences. Although he himself had failed to foresee the economic depression, and had for a little while believed that the " new " capitalism of the 1920's might do indirectly what the Bolsheviks were achieving by frontal attack, his most caustic shafts were directed against the advocates of " rugged individualism." Paragraph after paragraph indicted the beneficiaries of special privilege. Only " a fearless, unprivileged economic system," he insisted, could secure for the people the good things they wanted. While he never became a communist, he continued to defend Soviet Russia and to sympathize with the aims and aspirations of communism. Yet he was never splenetic in these comments, for he believed that " the only thing worth having in an earthly existence is a sense of humor." He lived long enough to learn of the civil war in Spain, and one of his last paragraphs, written a few days before his heart stopped beating, reveals a prescience and wisdom characteristic of his deep understanding of the world he lived in: " Spain's is the first, the opening battle of man for man; perhaps it is the most decisive battle. Anyway it is ours, as they must know and we must. I say we do, and that we realize as they fight that we have to finish what they are starting." *Lincoln Steffens Speaking,* containing his own choice of the best of these columns, was published shortly after his death in 1936.

Two years later Ella Winter and Granville Hicks edited a two-volume collection of Steffens's letters. Spanning his entire adult life of nearly fifty years, these letters both complement and augment his *Autobiography.* In the latter he was too eager to dwell on the lessons of his experience and too handicapped by his promise not to mention the woman he had ill-treated to reveal significant aspects of his personal life. In his letters, however, he wrote freely and naturally. And the editors, confronted with the task of selection and omission, wisely included those letters which at once fill the gaps and enrich the portrayal of the *Autobiography*. The result is a book that deepens one's understanding of his warm and vivid personality. For here Steffens unfolds himself as a most devoted son and brother, the sympathetic and valued friend to scores of well-known men and women, the joyous lover who suffered deep anguish at his inability to control his affection, and the wise and watchful man of the world who retained to the end his childlike eagerness for "finding things out." Ever with him was the ability to laugh — a characteristic, much more evidenced in his personal letters than in his public writings, which spread joy across the path of his life. Equally remarkable about these hundreds of letters is their consistent stylistic excellence. Never written for publication, they are a free outpouring of finely phrased ideas and feelings. As Carl Sandburg wrote: "In this collection of letters there are moments when he surpasses in sheer writing, in vivid human utterance, the best spots in the books hitherto published." In these personal communications he was the man himself, unhampered and unselfconscious, making ready use of his great gift of verbal expression, revealing a personality firm in fundamentals and rich in overtones — a truly wise and cultivated man. .

RANDOLPH BOURNE

THE HISTORY OF A LITERARY RADICAL

Writing to a friend in 1913, while still a student at Columbia University, Randolph Bourne outlined his brief but turbulent future with exceptional insight:

I can almost see now that my path in life will be on the outside of things, poking holes in the holy, criticising the established, satirizing the self-respecting and contented. Never being competent to direct and manage any of the affairs of the world myself, I will be forced to sit off by myself in the wilderness, howling like a coyote that everything is being run wrong.

If this self-estimate was overmodest, it described accurately his unhappy role during the stormy years of World War I. Earlier his eagerness to deepen and purify the cultural stream and his impatience with muddling and meandering forced him to rebel against his smug elders and to proclaim the ideal of the American promise. He was equally energetic in his advocacy of progressive methods of education, new literary values, and economic democracy. In each field his voice rang true and strong — but not loud enough to shake the walls of Jericho. And when the claws of war fastened on the United States and men scorned the thought of peace, Bourne fought desperately against what seemed to him a disastrous betrayal of American culture. Driven into the wilderness, he remained there to the end of his untimely death a few weeks after the Armistice, feeding on the anguish in his heart and holding fast to his vision of the American promise.

[419]

Randolph Bourne's painfully crippled body affected every facet of his brief career as a writer and radical. Of an old American family living in Bloomfield, New Jersey, he was born in 1886 with a slight curvature of the spine and a twisted face that caused him to grow up a hunchback with a large head and asymmetrical features. As a child he was just strong enough to participate in boys' games but never able to compete successfully. His rigid Calvinistic training forced him to regard his failures as the consequence of moral weakness. " I never resigned myself to the inevitable," he wrote later, " but overtaxed myself constantly in a grim determination to succeed." The more he tried the deeper became his feeling of inadequacy. Yet, eager to excel, he unconsciously concentrated on the things he could do well. In time he exhibited a degree of precocity at the piano and at his studies. He took little pleasure in these accomplishments, however, and all through his childhood he was humiliated by his physical abnormality.

The years of adolescence intensified his misery. He was of a sociable nature and liked to be with girls. To see other youths dance and flirt excited and tormented him. Yet, to judge by the diary he kept in his fifteenth year, his daily life passed fairly pleasantly. For years he read the New York *Tribune* with interest if not with full understanding, and he later asserted that it educated him far better than his school textbooks. If his home and social environment were narrowly bourgeois, the books he read in his teens were mostly classics of his own choosing, and these quickened his critical sense. By the time he graduated from high school in 1903, well near the head of his class, his intellectual maturity and range of interests were far above those of his classmates.

Poverty now combined with deformity to aggravate his feeling of frustration. An unexplained adverse turn in the family fortunes not only cut short his hope of going to college at this time but forced him to begin earning his living without further preparation. The ordeal of looking for work became fixed in his memory. The knowledge that he was " unable to counteract that fatal first impression " and that people either pitied or put him off, tormented him long after the event. "This sensitiveness," he later said of himself, "absolutely unfits him for business and the practice of a profession, where one must be 'all things to all men,' and the professional manner is indispensable to success."

After several months of secretarial work he was employed by a musician to cut perforated music rolls for player-pianos. He was paid five cents a foot, or one-third of what his employer received. As his skill increased, his rate of pay was cut ten percent. When he protested he was told to leave if he was dissatisfied. "Fear smote me. This was my only skill, and my timorous experience filled the outside world with horrors. I returned cravenly to my bench." But he now knew the meaning of exploitation. The experience pushed him in the direction of radicalism. He began to read the literature of dissidence. Henry George's *Progress and Poverty* and other similar books provided him "with the materials for a philosophy which explained why men were miserable and overworked . . . and which fixed the blame." Further study turned him to the ideal of socialism.

This social philosophy has not only made the world intelligible and dynamic to me, but has furnished me with the strongest spiritual support. . . . Life will have little meaning for me except as I am able to contribute toward some such ideal of social betterment, if not in deed, then in word.

In the meantime his employer's business failed and, with no other work available to him near Bloomfield, Bourne went to New York. For two anguished years he tried everything at which he had the slightest chance. The giving of a few music lessons alone kept him from starving. This again deepened his sense of frustration, and he later wrote:

There is a poignant mental torture that comes with such an experience — the urgent need, the repeated failure, or rather the repeated failure even to obtain a chance to fail, the realization that those at home can ill afford to have you idle, the growing dread of encountering people.

After six years of struggle he became convinced that he could win security only by fitting himself for work which required neither a good appearance nor physical exertion. At the urging of a friend he applied for a Columbia University scholarship. To his surprise he not only received it but was admitted with advanced standing. In September 1909, in his twenty-fourth year, he resumed his formal education — with his body more crooked than ever, but with a mind straight and strong and eager for knowledge.

Life as a student was not easy for Bourne. He still had to provide for his room and meals and jobs were still as elusive as before. It was only after great effort that he obtained work as a piano accompanist. From the first, however, he rejoiced in his new mode of existence. The intellectual atmosphere of Columbia exhilarated him. The great books, classic and modern, which he soon read with avidity, wakened his latent powers of literary expression. While the stuffiness of his English courses changed his mind about majoring in literature, he began to write for *The Columbia Monthly* and later became its editor-in-chief. His admiration of such men as John Dewey, Charles A. Beard, F. A. Giddings, and Frederick Woodbridge led to his concentrating on the social sciences. It was with these teachers in mind that he later described the ideal professor as " the man who, while he knows one branch thoroughly, is interested in a wide range of subjects." They in turn readily appreciated his incisive mind and his literary talents, and went out of their way to befriend him.

Early in 1911, in his second year at college, he achieved the rare distinction for an undergraduate of getting an article accepted by the august *Atlantic Monthly* — largely through the assistance of Dean Woodbridge, who not only suggested the topic but sent the essay to his friend Ellery Sedgwick, the editor. The latter was so impressed with the cogency and craftsmanship of the paper — which contained a challenge of youth to their elders — that he arranged a meeting with Bourne and subsequently published a number of his articles. Before long, other widely read periodicals began to print his writings.

A number of his "high-brow" classmates, attracted to him because of his literary success, soon became his close friends. "At college I met for the first time not only one person but many who thought as I did, and formed an interesting social group in which members constantly stimulated each other." As a self-conscious, if vague, radical he joined the Intercollegiate Socialist Society and eagerly participated in its activities. The Paterson strike of 1913 stimulated him to write a poem, " Sabotage," in which he identified himself with the " slaves " of the industrial machine.

In his senior year his essay, " Doctrine of the Rights of Man as Formulated by Thomas Paine," won a coveted prize. In addition he became an honor student, a member of Phi Beta Kappa, and the recipient of a fellowship for graduate study. His conspicuous career at the university was crowned by the generous Gilder traveling fellowship, which gave him the opportunity to spend a year in Europe immediately before the outbreak of war in 1914.

As a graduate student Bourne majored in sociology, but it was Dewey's instrumentalist philosophy that most stimulated him. Together with William James, Dewey gave him new insights into the fundamental relationship between philosophy and life.

Professor Dewey [he wrote in 1915] has been the first thinker to put the moral and social goal a notch ahead. . . . In its larger implications, Professor Dewey's philosophy challenges the whole machinery of our world of right and wrong, law and order, property and religion, the old technique by which society is still being managed and regulated.

From Dewey he learned that the mind is a tool, or instrument, with which we adjust ourselves to our specific environments; that reason has no divine origin and no key to eternal truth, but was merely " a practical instrument by which we solve problems "; that " words are not invariable symbols for invariable things, but clues to meanings." Most of all Bourne was impressed by Dewey's philosophy of education. The theory that the school was a part of life and must be integrated with it — that one learned by doing — engraved itself upon his mind and spurred him to become one of its most vigorous exponents.

In 1913, while still at Columbia, Bourne published *Youth and Life*, a collection of essays. The imprint of instrumentalism was on almost every page of the book. The social ferment of the time — the vigorous reform movements, the attacks on the Victorian-Puritan morality, the cultural awakening, the enthusiasm of the Progressives at Armageddon — helped to confirm him in his determination to fight for the right of each child to a free and friendly development. Written with force and fluency, his challenging book became a fresh and compelling voice in American literature, articulating clearly and convincingly the rebellious idealism of the younger generation.

Reflecting upon the rigid conventionality of his own social environment, Bourne argued that children were usually crippled morally and spiritually and that only those recovered who had exceptional resiliency.

They enter a bondage from which they can never free themselves; their moral judgment in youth is warped and blighted in a thousand ways, and they pass through life, seemingly the most moral men and women, but actually having never known the zest of true morality, the relish of right and wrong.

To keep the pliant child from growing up into the conventional bigoted man, parents and teachers must avoid burdening him with moral judgments before " he meets the world of vivid contrasts and shocks and emergencies that is youth." He should be given the chance to satisfy his inexhaustible curiosity and interest in his environment — the chance to learn by doing. For there was no shortcut to morality, even as there was no shortcut to knowledge, and there was no relish in right and wrong until one had tasted the give-and-take of life.

Bourne proclaimed the period of youth as the floodtide of life.

The innocence of childhood disappeared in the adolescent's sudden consciousness of being alive and in his troubled urge to self-expression. Youth was always in a state of turbulence, ever falling in love with people and ideas, strongly susceptible to the new and the untried. " Youth does not get ideas, — ideas get him! " Youth should not be too rational, for it was " the rational mind that is constantly being shocked and deranged by circumstances." He must dare! His was the fresh view of the world, his the opportunity for experimentation. " To face the perils and hazards fearlessly, and absorb the satisfaction joyfully, to be curious and brave and eager, — is to know the adventure of life." This satisfaction was the prerogative of the young. " It is they who have constantly to face new situations, to react constantly to new aspects of life, who are getting the whole beauty and terror and cruelty of the world in its fresh and undiluted purity." And they must capitalize on this advantage — one got few ideals after twenty and few new ideas after twenty-five — if they were to serve as the leaven activating society.

A radical himself — " at twenty-five I find myself full of the wildest radicalisms " — Bourne wrote glowingly of the radical ideals of youth. He maintained that it was normal and natural for youth to rebel at the ways of their elders. Their vision fresh and true, their ideals lofty and liberal, they were repelled and outraged by the apparent hypocrisy and cynicism about them. They ached to see justice done, evil overcome — and were forced to take a radical stand in their zeal to set the world aright. " This passion for social justice is one of the most splendid of the ideals of youth. It has the power of keeping alive all the other virtues; it stimulates life and gives it a new meaning and tone." But society, governed by old men who clung to the tarnished ideals of their dead youth, feared the daring of the young rebel. " On the radical there is immediately brought without examination, without reason or excuse, the whole pressure of the organization to stultify his vision and force him back to the required grooves." Yet the radical must resist this pressure if he was to serve the common good. He must dare to fight for his ideals and beliefs, for they " are the germs of the future." In prodding the world along, in gathering unto him the best minds, in keeping bright his vision — in these will he find his great reward.

Among the best essays in the volume are the frank and deeply felt "The Excitement of Friendship" and "The Philosophy of Handicap." In the first he celebrated his grateful satisfaction in and complete dependence on his friends. "A man must get friends," he declared, "as he would get food and drink for nourishment and sustenance. And he must keep them, as he would health and wealth, as the infallible safeguards against misery and poverty of spirit." So dependent was he on his intimate companions that he did not enjoy his walks without one. Nothing, he felt, stimulated his mind so much as good conversation. This theme of friendship was developed further in the sensitive and yet serene discussion of his deformity. The handicapped man, he explained, of whom the world expects little and who is consequently either pitied or ignored, cannot but become timid and distrustful. If he is to keep from sinking into the slough of misanthropy he must enjoy the warmth and hope of social intimacy. This great need of friendship makes him "extraordinarily sensitive to other people's first impression of him. Those who are to be his friends he knows instantly, and further acquaintance adds little to the intimacy and warm friendship that he at once feels for them."

The pages of *Youth and Life* glow with passion and excitement. The writing is easy and forceful, at times even brilliant, but it is not subtle or seasoned. Bourne's intense conviction animates every essay. He despised hypocritical and pretentious people — "pseudos" was his name for them — those who prized conformity and glossed over the evils vitiating their conventional morality. Armed with his greater knowledge of man's achievements, possessed of "a truly religious belief in human progress," he set about to discomfit the forces of the status quo and to array against them the youth of the land. His criticism of the older generation tended to be sweeping and extravagant. Whatever seemed antagonistic to it he praised as worth while and desirable — and all the more so if it reflected favorably on youth. His agitation for social change, however, remained on the literary level. For all his sympathy with the struggle of labor and reformers, he was still the student, brilliant and bold, but not yet the independent and active radical.

In July 1913, Bourne sailed for Europe. Assured of an adequate income for the ensuing year, he planned to take full advantage of his intellectual Grand Tour. What he wanted most of all was to get the feel of European life; to meet liberal writers and social thinkers and to familiarize himself with the new leaven in Western culture.

He was particularly interested in making the acquaintance of the socialist leaders. To him socialism was essentially applied Christianity. He favored " a Religion of Socialism, moving towards an ever more perfect socialized human life on earth." The English Fabians deeply disappointed him. Instead of acting as the leaders of an aggressive socialist movement, most of them impressed him as respectable and ineffectual bourgeois. Much as he admired such individual Englishmen as Shaw, Galsworthy, and Hobson, the " fatuous cheerfulness" of others perturbed and perplexed him. The prevailing emphasis on class irritated him. " The whole country," he complained, " seems very old and weary, as if the demands of the twentieth century were proving entirely too much for its powers, and it was waiting half-cynically and apathetically for some great cataclysm." What he saw of the slums and palaces strengthened his radicalism. He left England certain that its " cruel and unlovely" institutions must give way to a social order of greater justice and equality. " My social philosophy," he confided to a friend, " is working around to a paradoxical desire for Tolstoyan ends through Nietzschean means; socialism, dynamic social religion, through the ruthless application of scientific materialism."

France, where he sojourned for six months, he found spiritually more congenial to him. Life in Paris impressed him as essentially more democratic than that in London. Despite the initial handicap of language he went everywhere, met all kinds of people, read a great deal, and left with a feeling of real affinity for the French people. In Italy he witnessed a three-day general strike.

This "overwhelming expression of social solidarity" impressed him more than the ancient ruins or Renaissance art. Several weeks later, after a brief stop-over in Switzerland, he visited several German cities. The time was late July 1914, and he was greatly upset by the martial spirit of the singing and shouting crowds that gathered daily in ever larger numbers. The thunderclouds of war were gathering fast, and he felt depressed by this irrational mob excitement. "It will give these statesmen who will play their military pawns against each other a splendid excuse for their folly, for they can say that they were pushed into it by the enthusiastic demands of the people." He was in Berlin on August 1 when the Kaiser made his belligerent speech announcing that the German armies were on the march, and the barbaric spectacle deeply horrified him.

Two weeks later he was aboard an ocean liner bound for New York. His Grand Tour had ended in flight from a continent in flames. As he watched the vast expanse of the Atlantic, which shielded his country from foreign entanglements, he felt a surging joy at the thought of home and safety.

The wheels of the clock have so completely stopped in Europe, and this civilization that I've been admiring so much seems so palpably about to be torn to shreds that I do not even want to think about Europe until the war is over and life is running again.

In New York he took modest lodgings with his friend Carl Zigrosser and began the dreaded task of looking for work. His famous black student cape, which he brought with him from Europe and wore to the end of his life, soon became known to the receptionists of editorial offices, but all he was able to do at first was to sell several articles. Towards the end of 1914 the establishing of *The New Republic* provided him with a literary outlet, and he became a frequent contributor. Within a few months his versatility and his cogent pen gained him wide and respectful attention. His articles on modern education were highly provocative; his essays on city planning, Americanization, college reform, and other similar topics, were intelligent and persuasive. Best of all, perhaps, were his literary studies and reviews, which revealed a breadth of view and a sympathetic incisiveness rarely found in the writing of the time.

He was soon earning enough money to be able to live comfortably and to indulge in playing host to an ever-enlarging group of friends. His Tuesday teas became a popular focal point for young intellectuals. Good talk and hard thinking delighted the gnome-like figure who led the conversation. Deep was his joy in his many new friendships. His growing popularity as a critic and radical was attracting all kinds of people to his quarters, and his quick eye readily chose those he knew he would like. Those who remained became his devoted admirers. As Paul Rosenfeld testified extravagantly: " We knew him for one of the rarest, freest, sweetest spirits that have ever come out of this land."

A rising reputation, a good income, dear friends, a strong sense of achievement — nothing soothed the painful thought of his cruelly thwarted sex impulses. All his life he wanted to be like normal people, to love and be loved. Although he counted several gifted girls among his intimate companions, he believed that none would ever be more than a friend. And, until near the end of his life, when he discovered the joy of gratification, this awareness ran like a poison through his thoughts. To Alyse Gregory he wrote,

All my problems are interwoven: if I had one solved, it seems as if they should all be solved. Of course, it seems to me that the key to all of them is love, and the deprivation the one impediment to blossoming. At least I should give anything in the world for an opportunity to test this theory.

And to Mary Messer he confided that all his efforts to think of his women friends on an idealistic plane were mocked by that insatiable desire which, inhibited in him, merely intensified the poignancy of his problem. For, he asserted, he was " a man cruelly blasted by powers that brought him into the world, in a way that makes him both impossible to be desired and yet — cruel irony that wise Montaigne knew about — doubly endowed with desire." In less pessimistic moods, however, he admitted the darkness of this confession; for he was always able to enjoy "philosophy and music, and heaven-sent irony which softens and heals the wounds. . . ."

Bourne's investigations in and reflections on education are to be found in *The Gary Schools,* a brief volume published in 1916, and in *Education and Living,* a collection of essays that appeared a year later. An ardent admirer of John Dewey, he took a professional interest in the newer developments in the public schools. He gave his support to the current clamor for more progressive methods of teaching, and for a closer co-ordination between the schools and the practical world. He envisioned a future in which children in school would acquire not merely intellectual tools but the training for a democratic, rich, and wholesome life.

The public schools he visited pursued the timeworn methods and activities which he had experienced in childhood. Deeply concerned for the well-being of the child, he wrote scathingly of this stultifying atmosphere. He insisted that a child could not be confined to mental activity for five hours a day without injury to its normal growth; that a stimulating and salutary education must also include play, constructive work, socialization, and other non-intellectual activities. He advocated the classroom study of the daily newspaper, greater emphasis on the democratic way of life, the intelligent and intensive use of psychological tests and educational measurements, equal stress on study, work, and play, and the training of all children to the limit of their individual capacities. In 1915 these measures were, if not revolutionary, truly radical.

The schools in Gary, Indiana, provided him with a practical model. In 1915 they had captured the imagination of many progressive educators. Dr. William Wirt, the Gary superintendent of schools, had completely reorganized the town's public schools with a view to adapting them to the needs of its fairly typical industrial population. Differing radically from the conventional curriculum, following closely the educational principles propounded by John Dewey, the Gary system was attacked and praised with equal extravagance. Bourne, sent to Gary by *The New Republic,* studied the schools with care and on his return wrote a series of articles, later expanded into *The Gary Schools,* which established him as the chief exponent of the new educational plan.

What he valued most in the Gary system was its effort to educate the whole being, not merely the mind of the child. " Mr. Wirt believes that by putting in the child's way all the opportunities for vivid development, the child will be able to select those activities for which he is best suited, and thus develop his capacities to their highest power." Under this plan the schools provided a fourfold unity of interest: play and exercise in the open; intellectual study; work in the shop, studio, and laboratory; and social and expressive activity in the auditorium. The longer school day, while enabling the children to participate fully in the school's varied and enriched program, served also to lessen the responsibility of their busy parents and keep the youngsters from loitering in the streets. Moreover, by an ingenious simultaneous use of every part of the school building and by a skillful division of work, the enlarged program was carried out without extra cost to the city.

The Gary plan made no distinction between the utilitarian and the cultural subjects, and as far as possible all courses were taught concretely and in the light of familiar experience. Children were placed with their equals in an effort to keep each group going along at its own normal pace. Character and the moral qualities were trained indirectly as a consequence of the self-reliance which each pupil developed in the pursuit of combined study, work, and play. Bourne summarized:

The Gary school has natural significance because it is the first public school system in successful established operation which has been able to solve the pressing and apparently insoluble problems of the city school; which has kept pace with changing industrial and social conditions, and adapts the school to every kind of child; which synthesizes the best educational endeavors of the day, and . . . marks a distinct advance in democratic education.

The Gary plan was tried out experimentally in various cities. Its successful functioning, as Bourne pointed out caustically, required too great a readjustment on the part of the conservative school administrators, and nowhere was it given a fair trial. Moreover, it soon became a football of politics and ceased to be considered solely on its merits. But by that time the country had become engulfed in war and had no interest other than victory.

The History of a Literary Radical, the posthumous collection edited by Van Wyck Brooks, contains some of Bourne's best-known writings on American culture. The title essay, a vividly sketched self-portrait, traced his literary development from adolescence to maturity and stressed the radical changes in cultural attitudes between the old generation and the new. Ironically enough, his first introduction to the great modern European writers came not in his college studies but at a popular lecture by Professor William Lyon Phelps. He discovered a new world of literature. One book led to another, and all of them produced in his mind a rebelliousness against the dead classics which he had been taught to revere. With other literary radicals he shared the joys of new discoveries, new standards, a new appreciation of America's capacity for cultural greatness.

This lively pride in his native land caused him to protest against our cultural humility. Why, he demanded, should our genius in advertising, " so powerful and universal where soap and biscuits are concerned," fail us when broadcasting our cultural products? Having observed Europe at first hand and with an unawed mind, he saw no reason why we should humble ourselves before it.

Our humility causes us to be taken at our own face value, and for all this patient fixity of gaze upon Europe, we get little reward except to be ignored, or to have our interest somewhat contemptuously dismissed as parasitic.

This attitude, so common among wealthy and fashionable Americans, was not only obsequious and unwarranted but served to discourage our artists and thinkers. Our prime task, therefore, must be to turn our eyes away from Europe and concentrate on our native creative achievements. We have a right to take pride in our best writers and artists, both old and new, who have given clear expression to

American ideals and qualities, our pulsating democracy, the vigor and daring of our pioneer spirit, our sense of *camaraderie*, our dynamism, the big-heartedness of our scenery, our hospitality to all the world.

Only by conserving this American spirit and perpetuating our ideals in artistic form can we hope to achieve our rightful place among the cultures of the world.

Bourne's enthusiasm for our cultural progress led him to examine the then vexing problem of Americanization. In "Trans-National America," an essay of seminal significance, he took a bold stand against the anti-alien intolerance which had become accentuated in 1916, when the article appeared in *The Atlantic Monthly*. Our vociferous chauvinists, he argued, in their insistence upon conformity with American tradition were in truth demanding the assimilation of millions of our population to our Anglo-Saxon way of life. This claim was as unjust as it was unreal. Aliens cannot shed their native cultures together with their foreign clothes. It was indeed because our early settlers insisted on clinging to their English folkways long after they had freed themselves from British rule that our culture assumed a predominantly New England character.

The truth is that no more tenacious cultural allegiance to the mother country has been shown by any other alien nation than by the ruling class of Anglo-Saxon descendants in these American States.

Our "melting pot" theory failed simply because our narrow and rigid New England mold could not possibly contain the variegated cultures of our complex population. Nor was it desirable. "What we emphatically do not want is that these distinctive qualities should be washed out into a tasteless, colorless fluid of uniformity." While many of our immigrants appear to us inferior and undesirable, they have much to contribute to the richness of our cultural pattern. If they are raw materials for our schools, they must be molded not into narrow New Englanders but into socialized Americans.

The promise of America — a richer, freer life for all — excited Bourne's imagination. The United States was to him "a unique sociological fabric," a novel union of men possessed of incalculable opportunities. "We have transplanted European modernity to our soil without the spirit that inflames it and turns all its energy into mutual destruction. Out of these foreign peoples has somehow been squeezed the poison." As a result we have been able, without being aware of it, to establish "the first international nation" in a world which has long dreamed of internationalism in vain.

America is already the first world-federation in miniature, the continent where for the first time in history has been achieved that miracle of hope, the peaceful living side by side, with character substantially preserved, of the most heterogeneous people under the sun.

This transnational character is our great contribution to civilized society. If we are to be true to our destiny we must treasure our cosmopolitan heritage; not confine our culture to the narrowness of the melting pot but broaden it to the variegated vastness of a transnational society.

Meantime Bourne watched with increasing dread as the United States drifted towards intervention in Europe. He believed that our participation in the carnage would be catastrophic. "The war — or American promise: one must choose. One cannot be interested in both. For the effect of the war will be to impoverish American promise." He had no choice. He hated war — the antithesis of everything that was dear to him. So he fought it openly and desperately. Whoever favored war — for whatever reason — he attacked without quarter. By the time we joined the Allies he had alienated many of his friends and most of the editors. *The Atlantic Monthly* was closed to him, *The New Republic* no longer offered assignments, *The Dial's* welcome was brief, and *The Seven Arts* had its subsidy withdrawn largely because it refused to give him up. After

October 1917, all literary outlets were closed to him. A few book reviews and the translation of a book from the French was all he could obtain in the dark months that followed. More and more he had to depend upon his few loyal friends for food and lodging. Yet he continued to maintain his pacifistic principles with a steadfastness and severity reminiscent of the extreme Abolitionists. His mind was never clearer; his logic never keener or more eloquent. To the end of his brief life in December 1918 — he fell victim to an attack of pneumonia — he fought for the American promise with a courage and conviction that placed him with the eminent pacifists of his time.

One of his first major essays against war, appearing in *The New Republic* in July 1916, presented a persuasive, if idealistic, moral equivalent of universal military service. Compulsory militarism, he explained, was a complete negation of true Americanism. In its stead he proposed an application of William James's " conception of a productive army, finding in drudgery and toil and danger the values that war and preparation for war had given." He would have all boys and girls of sixteen enlisted in a universal educational service that would train them for both work and citizenship by setting up as the enemy " our appalling slovenliness, the ignorance of great masses in city and country as to the elementary technique of daily life." For our need, he pleaded, was to learn how to live rather than how to die, how to create rather than how to destroy. Here he was of course the poet, nurtured in nineteenth-century humanitarianism, and not the pragmatist adapting himself to practical situations; but by this time he was done with pragmatism.

The intellectual pacifists, from John Dewey down, who had favored war in 1916 in their zeal to safeguard democracy, received his severest lashings. In a series of passionate and provocative papers in *The Seven Arts*, which James Oppenheim later collected in *Untimely Papers*, he pilloried these teachers and friends for their rationalized apostasy. He was not fooled by their make-believe assertions that they were deliberately leading the nation into " a war that will secure the triumph of democracy and will internationalize the world." No new world order, he declared, could be "built out of the rotten materials of armaments, diplomacy and 'liberal' statesmanship." The deluded intellectuals, pathetically allying themselves with the ruling reactionary groups for the sake of democracy, were certain to be ignored and scorned by them once the war was won. Yet they might have prevailed earlier, when the people were still pacifist and amenable to reason, if they had spent their time and thought in clarification and education, in devising other means than war for carrying through American policy. Instead they had unwittingly become tools of the jingoes. "The intellectuals have still to explain why, willing as they are now to use force to continue the war to absolute exhaustion, they were not willing to use force to coerce the world to a speedy peace." For all their presumed realism they "have forgotten that the real enemy is War rather than imperial Germany."

As the war progressed, Bourne caustically pointed to the justification of his predictions and accusations. Not only were the efforts of the intellectuals to liberalize Allied policy disregarded, but our own strategy was gradually adapted to that of the English and the French.

Those of us who knew a real inexorable when they saw one, and had learned from watching the war what follows the loosing of a war-technique, foresaw how quickly aims and purposes would be forgotten, and how flimsy would be any liberal control of events.

While war was hard on all intellectuals, the pacifists were at least aware of their plight and retained a clear understanding of what was best in American life. Their "skepticism can be made a shelter behind which is built up a wider consciousness of the personal and social and artistic ideals which American civilization needs to lead the good life." In the end, indeed, it would be they who, by holding fast to the values in which war had no part, would serve their country best.

Bourne's strongest castigation was reserved for John Dewey. The latter had been his revered mentor for years. The philosophy of instrumentalism had inspired his thinking on education and culture. When the war in Europe began to cast its ominous shadow across the Atlantic, he expected Dewey, the leading American thinker, to stop the oncoming militarism with a clear and forthright analysis of the fallacies that confused and deluded his followers. He was therefore the more shocked and chagrined to see Dewey confound confusion by complacently accepting intervention and by chiding the pacifists for their nonconformity. Suddenly he perceived his idol's feet of clay and was infuriated.

A philosopher who senses so little the sinister forces of war, who is so much more concerned over the excesses of the pacifists than over the excesses of military policy, who can feel only amusement at the idea that anyone should try to conscript thought, who assumes that the war-technique can be used without trailing along with it the mob-fanaticisms, the injustices and hatreds, that are organically bound up with it, is speaking to another element of the younger intelligentsia than that to which I belong. . . . What I come to is a sense of suddenly being left in the lurch, of suddenly finding that a philosophy upon which I had relied to carry us through no longer works.

Reflection led Bourne to the painful conclusion that instrumentalism had trained a generation of young men who could not distinguish ends from means; who could readily execute orders but lacked the vision to discern the ideas behind these orders. As a consequence, while they busied themselves with the organization of war, the formulation of opinion was assumed by professional patriots and renegade radicals. Dewey's " disciples have learned all too literally the pragmatic attitude towards life, and, being immensely intelligent and energetic, they are making themselves efficient instruments of the war-technique, accepting with little question the ends as announced from above. That those ends are largely negative does not concern them, because they have never learned not to subordinate idea to technique." While Dewey himself had stressed the primacy of values, the unhappy ambiguity in his exposition of the nature of values had caused many of his students to confuse results with product. And while he himself had developed vision and technique together, his teaching had tended to emphasize technique at the expense of vision. Since war inevitably undermined values and favored technique, the pragmatic nature of instrumentalism caused it to " end in caution, regression, and a virtual failure to effect even that change which you so clearsightedly and desirously see."

Although the periodicals were closed to him, Bourne nevertheless continued to write. One of his products was part of a novel which, like his earlier portrait sketches, promised a sensitive and incisive, if not highly creative, work of fiction. Of his many letters of that time — outpourings of his passionate reactions to daily events — the one to Van Wyck Brooks on the formation of a league of youth is perhaps most noteworthy. He wanted both of them to initiate a movement that would lead the youth of the land away from the confusion and compromise of war liberalism and inspire them to work for the fulfillment of the American promise. " It would be an irresponsible gesture," he admitted, " a leap to rally disciples because neither we nor they would stand it any longer." He felt that intelligent youth wanted an idealism unvitiated by acquiescence and based on the fundamental principles of life, liberty, and the pursuit of happiness. The program was to have been elaborated in a series of epistles between the two friends, but the project miscarried — probably because both young rebels realized how few members their league would attract in a time of war.

Bourne's unfinished study of the state, begun shortly before his death, is probably the most important of his writings. An iconoclastic, emotional, almost mystical criticism of the state power, it is in a true sense a development of the earlier attacks by the extreme Abolitionists and individualist anarchists, and particularly that by Thoreau. His chief contention was that the state perpetrated war and fed upon the death of its subjects. " For war is essentially the health of the State," was his ironic refrain. The state began as " the organization of the herd to act offensively and defensively against another herd similarly organized." It served to stress man's gregarious impulse in a time of social crisis, when the individual needed to feel behind him the full power of the community. Symbolizing at once communal strength and parental shelter, the state in time arrogated to itself the power to deal politically with other states. And throughout civilized history such dealings have always ended in war.

The state, Bourne insisted, was not at all the equivalent of the nation. The latter was synonymous with the people and served their intrinsic welfare. Nations never warred with one another, since their interests were never in conflict. States, on the contrary, existed for the sole purpose of waging war and becoming strong at the expense of vanquished states. Governments were their agents and served them by declaring war without consulting the people who did the fighting and the dying. " It is not too much to say that the normal relation of the States is war. Diplomacy is a disguised war, in which States seek to gain by barter and intrigue, by the cleverness of wits, the objectives which they would have to gain more clumsily by means of war."

War is therefore the health of the state in that it unifies the people and completely subjugates them to the will of the government.

Only when the State is at war does the modern society function with that unity of sentiment, simple and uncritical patriotic devotion, cooperation of services, which have been the ideal of the State lover.

At such times the people are united under autocratic control, and dissidents are crushed without mercy. Facts are sunk in the symbol. Thus we reverence not our country but the flag, which is " solely a symbol of the political State, inseparable from its prestige and expansion." This is clearly illustrated by the laws which punish interference with the army and navy much more severely than industrial sabotage, which in our day is actually more dangerous.

Yet the state was no more God-given than any other social institution. It had been exalted by the class which used it as a means of gaining wealth and power at the expense of the nation as a whole.

The sanctity of the State becomes identified with the sanctity of the ruling class and the latter are permitted to remain in power under the impression that in obeying and serving them, we are obeying and serving society, the nation, the great collectivity of all of us.

This sanctity was successfully questioned by our Revolutionary Fathers. In the Declaration of Independence they announced doctrines that were utterly incompatible with the divine right of both kings and states. Unfortunately these doctrines were not given concrete political form. Men did not know how to take advantage of their newly won liberty. War weariness, exaggerated fear of other states, and economic distress caused many of them to sigh for their former political fleshpots. The wealthy conservatives capitalized on this confusion and, " by one of the most successful *coups d'etat* in history," forced state rule back upon the people in the form of our Constitution.

At a time when the current of political progress was in the direction of agrarian and proletarian democracy, a force hostile to it gripped the nation and imposed upon it a powerful form against which it was never to succeed in doing more than blindly struggle.

From a pragmatic standpoint Randolph Bourne was a tragic failure. In possession of all the intellectual qualifications for leadership, well on his way towards a position of power and influence, he deliberately rejected the world at a time of crisis and assumed the role of an outcast crying in the wilderness. With the Kaiser's military might let loose over Europe, with democratic society in grave danger, he quixotically expounded a pacifistic anarchism. It might even be argued that the poison of perversity had early entered his spirit and embittered his entire life's experience. From his first passionate attacks on the folkways and activities of the older generation he proceeded in a contrary direction which logically ended in his uncompromising opposition to a war which the best minds accepted as the lesser of the dire alternatives confronting the country. For all his native gifts, he was only a negative and fanatical eccentric.

History, however, will deal more fairly with him. For he belongs not with the politicians but with the prophets. What matters in his case was not his reaction to daily events nor his judgment of temporal affairs but his energetic stimulation of minds and his vision of the good life. Few Americans possessed his enthusiasm for the deepening and enrichment of our indigenous culture. He early sought to remove the layer of rust and rot which crusted the minds of many Americans. He vigorously assailed the smugness with which this retarding condition was accepted and called upon youth to discard the stiff and prim ways of their elders. Proud of our potential greatness in art and letters, he was impatient with our subservience to Europe. He exhorted us to " turn our eyes upon our own art for a time, shut ourselves in with our own genius, and cultivate with an intense and practical pride what we have already achieved against the obstacles of our cultural humility." His energy, enthusiasm, and sympathy injected into his writing the dynamic appeal which activated and enriched the renascence then in progress.

Together with a more vital cultural growth he sought greater social justice. He believed our continent was rich enough to provide abundantly for all the people, and he wanted everyone to receive his rightful share. Oppression and exploitation, slums and poverty and ignorance — these scabs of inequality offended his soul and he cried out against them with righteous indignation. Culture and justice became the two pillars adorning the edifice of his American promise.

What attracted him [declared Van Wyck Brooks] was the common struggle and aspiration of youth and poverty and the creative spirit everywhere, the sense of a new socialized world groping its way upward. It was this rich ground-note in all his work that made him, not the critic merely, but the leader.

Nor should it be forgotten that he was still in the process of becoming, still in the first flowering of his artistic and intellectual powers, when the war struck at the roots of his being and the "flu" epidemic snuffed out his life.

It was his passionate eagerness for the richer and freer life of the American promise that made him oppose the war so desperately. He knew that war was inimical to culture; that in fighting Prussianism we would expose ourselves to a similar militarism. Because he saw no good reason for our joining a war that did not really concern us, he regarded the efforts of the pro-war liberals as criminal folly. Having no alternative but to oppose them, he did so with all the fierce anger of a visionary at bay. He readily suffered the loss of his reputation, his income, and many of his friends. He continued his Jeremian criticism even after ostracism had driven him into the wilderness. For zeal had sublimated his pacifism into prophecy. His dissenting voice rose accusingly against the moral myopia of the mob and gave expression to a patriotism far nobler than that of the war leaders: a love of country that held fast to the ideal of the ultimate good at a time when practical citizens were concerned solely with matters of immediacy. Paul Rosenfeld well said: "Bourne was the great bearer of moral authority while America was at war. He was our bannerman of values in the general collapse." It was this nobility of vision — so irritating to men of action in times of crisis and yet so vital to the moral health of society — that places Randolph Bourne among the true, if minor, prophets of America.

THE SOCIALISTS

DANIEL DE LEON   EUGENE VICTOR DEBS

JOHN REED

THE SOCIALIST BACKGROUND

T HE " UTOPIAN " SOCIALISTS of the first half of the nineteenth century were mostly humanitarian idealists who preached social justice on religious or moral grounds. Karl Marx and Friedrich Engels, on the other hand, grounded their philosophy of socialism in the science of political economy. Their revolutionary and alarming *Communist Manifesto*, which appeared in 1848, demanded the immediate abdication of the ruling class. Not ideal justice, not the brotherhood of man were their slogans; boldly and bitterly they indicted the prevailing system of capitalism. Their program of action aimed at the abolition of human exploitation and " the forcible overthrow of the whole extant social order." Confident that the hour of revolution was about to strike, they declared open war against the bourgeoisie. Their battle-cry ended with the rallying challenge: " Let the ruling class tremble at the prospect of a communist revolution. Proletarians have nothing to lose but their chains. They have a world to win. *Proletarians of all lands, unite!* "

In this aggressive proclamation the two youthful radicals sketched the basic theories which subsequently made up the foundation stones of Marxian socialism. Their later vital and voluminous writings were devoted to the development of their revolutionary philosophy, in which the materialistic conception of history was of primary significance. As Engels defined it:

[445]

In every historical epoch, the prevailing mode of economic production and exchange and the social organization necessarily following from it form the basis upon which is built up, and from which alone can be explained, the political and intellectual history of that epoch.

From this proposition follows the guiding Marxian principle of the class struggle, which rests upon the assertion that the history of mankind has been a record of continuous " contests between exploiting and exploited, ruling and oppressed classes." Marx, of course, was not the first to discern this social phenomenon. James Madison, to cite but one instance, declared in the tenth issue of *The Federalist* that " those who hold and those who are without property have ever formed distinct interests in society." Marx, however, demonstrated its historical significance and thereby lifted it from a passing observation to a truism of modern social thinking.

Most of *Capital,* of which the first and most important volume appeared in 1867, was devoted to an exposition of the doctrine of surplus value. Marx argued, with an eloquence matching his erudition, that whereas all commodities normally sold at their true value, only the commodity of human labor sold for less. Under capitalism, workingmen received in wages only a fraction of the value created by their labor — usually only enough to enable them to reproduce themselves at a rate warranted by industrial requirements. The remainder of this labor value, distributed as rent, interest, and profits, Marx termed surplus value and claimed that it rightly belonged to the workers who had produced it.

The structure erected by Marx and Engels and their disciples is of course much more intricate and comprehensive than the foregoing simplified summary. Marx took from classical economics the ideas and data which fitted his needs and labored many years to demonstrate factually and devastatingly the evil aspects of the capitalistic system. He condemned the exploitation of workingmen and at the same time asseverated that capitalism was perforce a transitory phase of social development and would be supplanted by the classless co-operative society. " The central thesis of the economic teachings of Mark and Engels," Professor Oscar Jaszi stated,

" is that capitalist society is hopelessly torn by antagonistic forces which will ultimately destroy the whole social fabric, but in such a way that the communist embryo preformed in capitalist society will be set free."

Marx's great achievement was to place the system of capitalism on the defensive. Conservative economists have again and again challenged the validity of Marxian socialism. With the aid of time and altered conditions they have managed to disprove some of its minor claims. None, however, has succeeded in nullifying its major premises. And workingmen the world over, while able to pay only lip-service to Marx's erudite theoretical analysis of capitalism, have eagerly embraced the doctrine of the class struggle and the dream of a co-operative society. In every land they have formed socialist parties and radical trade unions; at first they were frail and ineffective, but in later years they became strong enough to challenge and even to supersede their capitalist governments.

Despite Marx's assumption that the more a country developed industrially the more fertile a field it became for the growth of socialism, the United States has proved relatively barren ground for Marxist propaganda. In the years before the Civil War American workmen were still too few in number, too unaware of themselves as an exploited group, and too conscious of their ability to obtain land cheaply, to concern themselves with the class struggle. In the 1850's and even later American society was in a condition of free fluidity. Men were still fairly equal in the race to achieve economic security; none felt barred from the path that led to affluence. The few trade unions then in existence were disunited, quite feeble, and frequently absorbed in fraternal affairs.

Marxian socialism — socialism and communism were synonymous terms until the Russian Revolution — was first established in the United States by German immigrants. More than a million reached these shores during the 1850's. A number of them were refugees who had participated in the abortive revolutions of 1848 and had to flee for their safety. Among them were William Weitling, Joseph Weydemeyer, and Friedrich A. Sorge, radicals who knew Marx well and worked zealously to achieve a social revolution in their adopted land. In the backrooms of German beer halls they foregathered with those who shared their dreams of a socialistic society. Their talk was grandiose, their factional differences were solemn and emphatic. When Weitling began to advocate a labor exchange bank, he was scorned by the Marxists as a utopian dreamer. In 1853 Weydemeyer formed the General Workingmen's Alliance, but he found himself leader of a stillborn organization. Four years later Sorge was no more successful with his Communist Club. For all their activity and zeal the German socialists made little headway.

The strong industrial spurt after the Civil War, greatly increasing the number of industrial employees and forcing them to labor under extremely bad working conditions, stimulated the growth of radical and trade union movements. William H. Sylvis, a clear-visioned labor leader, devoted himself to building up a mass organization. Largely as a result of his efforts, the National Labor Union was formed in 1866. The demand for the eight-hour workday became its rallying cry. Marx, who kept in close contact with labor activities the world over, spoke optimistically of this event and quoted in *Capital* the following extract from the Union's declaration of principles:

The first and great necessity of the present, to free the labor of this country from capitalistic slavery, is the passing of a law by which eight hours shall be the normal working-day in all the States of the American Union. We are resolved to put forth all our strength until this glorious result is attained.

Sylvis was sympathetic to the aims of socialism and welcomed the Marxian groups into the National Labor Union. In 1869 the Union joined the First International, formed five years previously at Marx's urging, and sent a delegate to its congress in Basle. At this time Sylvis spoke for 640,000 members. His sudden death, however, deprived the Union of its driving force and caused it to disintegrate shortly thereafter.

The affiliated socialist factions remained weak and unstable. Most of their members were of foreign origin. In 1871 the single English-speaking section was joined by Stephen Pearl Andrews, the scholarly individualist anarchist, and the notorious Claflin sisters. These latter published a weekly and printed in its pages the first English translation of the *Communist Manifesto*. But their free-love antics soon scandalized the German socialists and the entire section was expelled from the International.

The American socialist movement was temporarily strengthened by the decision of Marx and Engels to transfer the headquarters of the moribund International to the United States in order to protect it from the disruptive tactics of the Bakunin anarchists. Sorge, the new general secretary, worked heroically to keep the organization alive, but the American social climate proved too alien for the transplanted International. It wilted completely after Marx had advised American socialists against collaborating with bourgeois reformers.

The Socialist Labor party, which was formed in 1877 after several abortive efforts to unite all radical factions, was from the beginning a militant political organization. Strictly Marxist in its principles and aims, it sought to indoctrinate workingmen by means of political education. Its candidates made a relatively good showing in the 1878 campaign, but in subsequent elections their popularity fluctuated radically. Its policy of peaceful propaganda caused it to repudiate the martial *Lehr und Wehr Vereine*. " The question of arming," insisted Philip Van Patten, the party's general secretary, " is with us neither a matter of protection nor an assertion of rights, but a matter of policy, as every clear-minded member knows. The capitalist class is most anxious to force us into the position of an armed mob." This stand against " propaganda of the deed " alienated the members who believed in the effectiveness of sabotage and dynamite. In 1881 the party was reduced to 1500 members and was forced to mark time while the anarchists were having their innings in a campaign of bluster and bravado which was to engulf them in the Haymarket tragedy.

The party remained anemic and inactive throughout the 1880's. Secretary V. L. Rosenberg stated candidly in 1885: "Let us not conceal the truth: the Socialist Labor Party is only a German colony, an adjunct of the German-speaking Social Democracy." The party did combine with labor unions and liberals in backing Henry George for mayor in 1886, but it went its separate way again shortly thereafter. In his correspondence with Sorge, Engels chastised the American socialists for their failure to appreciate the aims and attitudes of the mass of workers. He knew that a number of the leaders of the Knights of Labor, then at its peak of popularity, and of the young but lusty American Federation of Labor were class-conscious radicals, but he also knew that they were too pragmatical to act on their beliefs, except through necessity. "Theoretical ignorance," he wrote, " is characteristic of all young peoples, but so is practical rapidity of development, too. As in England, all the preaching is of no use in America until the actual necessity exists."

In 1889 Daniel De Leon joined the Socialist Labor party and soon galvanized it into militant action. A man of great intellectual development, high idealism, and fanatical purpose, he quickly established himself as the party's most distinguished and determined member. Leadership came to him by default. Under his guidance the party became the center of gravity for all radicals. German, Jewish, and other trade unions favoring socialism welcomed its doctrinal direction. In election campaigns the party manifested a steady growth.

This efflorescence, however, was of short duration. De Leon's dogmatic and domineering behavior soon antagonized union leaders and caused many defections from the party. Nevertheless he persisted in acting according to strict principle. As a Marxist organization, he argued, the party had to engage in active warfare against capitalism. Honest union officials, seeking the weal of the mass of workers, were obliged to join the party in the struggle for a socialist society.

Most labor leaders merely scoffed at such quixotic ratiocination. They were practical men, interested in keeping their jobs at least as much as in furthering the class struggle, and were therefore more attracted by immediate wage increases than by the ultimate benefits of a socialistic commonwealth. Consequently when De Leon began to maneuver for control of the Knights of Labor, he was quickly driven out of the organization. The American Federation of Labor refused to deal with him altogether. Samuel Gompers and his lieutenants insisted on keeping their unions " pure and simple," with no political affiliations of any kind. De Leon retaliated by branding them as traitors to labor and by attacking them on the platform and in his writings. " The social revolution," he declared, " must march over the bodies of each and all of them. . . . Clear the way. Kick the rascals out." His unconstrained invective served only to embitter Gompers against Marxian socialism and thereby to alienate the large body of trade unionists.

De Leon's unbending rigidity likewise brought disruption within the party itself. He never quite understood the mind and motives of the mass of workers. He tended to view them abstractly, from his own idealistic standpoint, and failed to realize their essential eagerness for the immediate small benefits that capitalism could provide. When he insisted on party discipline, many members fell away. The German *Volkszeitung* group was among the first to rebel. In 1896 a number of Jewish intellectuals, angered by the party's refusal to grant them greater journalistic freedom, broke away and issued the *Forward*, which later became the largest Yiddish daily in the world. The most serious split occurred a year after the party had polled over 82,000 votes in the 1898 election, when the so-called " kangaroo exodus " left the organization a purged but proud minority.

De Leon was now rid of all opposition. At his request the chastened party passed a resolution to expel any member who accepted office in "a pure and simple trade or labor organization" and to reject any such official who applied for membership. By this time, however, the Socialist Labor party had become a small sectarian group — loyal to Marxian principles, solemn in its proclamations, persistent in its efforts, yet wholly unattuned to the temper of the people and consequently thoroughly ineffectual.

In 1902 another cleavage took place when the "kanglets" followed the "kangaroos" into the newly formed Socialist party. Three years later, when the Industrial Workers of the World was in process of organization, De Leon eagerly joined the discussions and stamped his strong personality upon its original policies and principles. But in 1908 its convention was taken over by the syndicalist faction. The Socialist Labor party had no choice but to resume its steep and solitary path to the heights of Marxian socialism. After De Leon died in 1914 his mantle fell upon his faithful disciple Arnold Petersen. Under the latter's leadership the small party has managed to survive wars and persecution and to continue its narrow agitational appeal down to the present time.

The Socialist Labor party at no time included all of the country's radicals. Its immigrant membership and alien character deterred a good many Americans who were likewise opposed to industrial exploitation. These dissidents at first hoped to achieve reforms through the Greenback, Populist, and Nationalist parties. When this method of opposition failed, the more determined of them began to grope towards a principle of social justice consonant with prevailing conditions. Some years previously Engels had, unlike De Leon, actually approved such a pragmatic approach to socialism in a letter to Florence Kelley: " Our theory is a theory of development, not of dogma to be learned by heart and repeated mechanically. The less it is hammered into the Americans from the outside and the more they test it through their own experience . . . the more will it become a part of their flesh and blood." Although few American radicals knew that the co-founder of world socialism had sympathized with their unwillingness to subject themselves to an oppressive doctrinal discipline, they proceeded to develop a socialism based on American conditions and requirements.

In the late 1890's Eugene V. Debs emerged as the likeliest leader of this inchoate group of radicals. His experiences as a labor official had led him to accept the philosophy of socialism. "There is no hope for the toiling masses of my countrymen," he declared shortly after Bryan's first defeat, " except by the pathways mapped out by the Socialists, the advocates of the co-operative commonwealth." A pragmatical humanitarian who was eager to put his ideas to the test, he established the Brotherhood of the Cooperative Commonwealth. After discussing its colonization plan with other socialists, he abandoned it as utopian and formed the party of Social Democracy, aiming " to conquer capitalism by making use of our political liberty, and by taking possession of the public power." The organization was at once joined by Jewish socialists from New York and German socialists from Wisconsin. About a year later, however, the party split on the issue of colonization. Debs, Victor Berger, and other confirmed socialists reorganized their faction into the Social Democratic party with the motto of " pure socialism and no compromise." In a newspaper interview early in 1900 Debs stated: "The Social Democratic Party is not a reform party, but a revolutionary party: It does not propose to modify the competitive system but abolish it." At that time the party had 226 branches and 4,536 members — largely as a result of his intensive organizational efforts. It expressed its appreciation by nominating him for the Presidency.

In February 1900, the " kangaroos " met in Rochester, New York, and voted to unite with the Social Democratic party. As a gesture of friendship they also nominated Debs as their candidate. This combination made it possible for the latter to receive nearly 97,000 votes as against 34,000 for the nominee of the Socialist Labor party. After the election the two groups encountered some difficulty in reaching final unity, but ultimately composed their differences and decided to call their organization the Socialist party. Morris Hillquit, an able young " kangaroo," was largely responsible for the merger.

The new party, while containing sizable contingents of foreign birth, consisted largely of young and energetic Americans. Pragmatic idealists, they had not, like so many Europeans, turned socialists after having read Marx's *Capital*. They were therefore quite free of doctrinal training. Although they learned to employ the same cant slogans as those used by the members of the Socialist Labor party, they were primarily concerned with immediate demands and a mass membership. They favored the formation of trade unions, " no matter how small or how conservative," as a means of strengthening the wage-working class. It was their assumption that by co-operating with the existing unions and by fostering new ones they would advance the cause of socialism. This policy early bore fruit when in 1902 the Western Labor Union, with a membership of 150,000, endorsed the principles of the Socialist party. A good many of the unions affiliated with the American Federation of Labor were also friendly toward the party.

During the 1900's the abuses of capitalism and the journalistic campaign against them drove a number of Americans into the socialist camp. Every exposure of human exploitation helped to justify the socialistic criticism of the profit system. Every instance of police brutality toward strikers or judicial connivance favoring corporations resulted in a wave of protests and new converts to socialism. Van Wyck Brooks wrote of this period:

A new breath had blown over the American scene: people felt that the era of big business had reached its climacteric, that a new nation was about to be born out of the social settlements, out of the soil that had been harrowed and swept by the muckrakers, out of the spirit of " service " that animated a whole new race of novelists.

Even in the academic fortresses of conservatism more and more youthful intellectuals heeded the call of conscience and placed the welfare of the people above their own personal ambitions. In 1905 a group of college men, including Jack London and Upton Sinclair, launched the Intercollegiate Socialist Society. Under the able direction of Harry W. Laidler, groups of enthusiastic students soon gathered in the leading universities and colleges to discuss the principles of socialism. During the same period the Rand School of Social Science in New York became a Marxist training center for labor union and socialist organizers.

The Socialist party was broad enough and elastic enough to welcome all the diverse dissidents who applied for admission. Leading muckrakers such as Charles Edward Russell and Allan L. Benson, conscience-stricken rich young men such as J. G. Phelps Stokes and Joseph M. Patterson (later the publisher of the reactionary New York *Daily News*), scholars such as Professor George D. Herron and Robert Hunter, syndicalists like William D. Haywood, and trade unionists of all types — these and many others joined the party and worked hard to increase its effectiveness and prestige. With their help the appeal of socialism became nationwide. Scores of radical periodicals were established. *The International Socialist Review*, in existence since 1900 and ably edited by A. M. Simons, became the intellectual fountainhead of American socialism; J. A. Wayland's *Appeal to Reason*, a militant and typically midwestern weekly, reached a circulation of over a half-million; the Charles Kerr Company issued a large list of socialist books and pamphlets in huge editions. No wonder that the upholders of the status quo were frightened by the prospect. " Socialism," ex-Secretary of the Treasury Leslie M. Shaw declared in 1908, " is taught on every hand and I am alarmed by the general trend of things in this connection."

In that very year, however, the Socialist party received a sudden jolt. After a strenuous campaign, during which Debs toured the country in a " Red Special " at great expense, its vote was very little above that of 1904. It appeared that the converts to socialism were for the most part not disciplined radicals but humanitarians and social rebels easily tempted by the possibility of immediate reforms. Thus many of them, who had voted for Debs when the Democrats put up a plain conservative like Judge Parker, and thereby quadrupled the Socialist party vote, could not in 1908 resist

Bryan's progressive platitudes. Debs, the revolutionary, wanted the party to return to its original status as a workingmen's political organization, but the large majority of the leaders, headed by Hillquit and Berger, preferred to keep the base broad and to intensify their work of " agitation, education, and organization."

With the aid of hundreds of " Jimmy Higginses " — self-effacing and hard-working men and women who devoted themselves to the task of socialistic propaganda — the party rode on the crest of the wave of social idealism which carried many thousands of Americans to the very shores of the co-operative commonwealth. Every means of reaching middle-class liberals was exploited; socialism was presented to them as both a humanitarian and an honorable solution to our social ills.

Similar efforts were also made to win the membership of the American Federation of Labor. Hillquit later averred " that trade unionism and Socialism sprang from the same economic conditions and necessities, that their ultimate goals were consciously or unconsciously identical, that one complemented the other and that both would gain by natural understanding and practical co-operation." To conciliate the conservative labor leaders the Socialist party decided at its 1912 convention to drive the members of the Industrial Workers of the World from its midst. To this end it adopted a constitutional amendment which provided that " any member of the party who opposes political action or advocates crime, sabotage or other methods of violence as a weapon of the working class to aid in its emancipation shall be expelled from membership in the party." A number of trade-union leaders, pleased with the party's new policy, voted for Max S. Hayes, a socialist, when he opposed Gompers for the presidency of the American Federation of Labor — giving him nearly a third of the total vote.

As a result of this augmented activity and opportunistic policy the Socialist party had, according to H. J. Whigham, editor of the then socialistic *Metropolitan*, " tacitly removed the class war as a test of faith." It increased its membership from 58,011 in 1910 to 118,045 two years later — largely by incorporating a number of foreign-language federations. At this time, also, 1039 of its dues-paying members were serving as elected officials, including one Congressman and 56 mayors. In the national elections Debs, opposed by the liberal Woodrow Wilson and the dynamic Theodore Roosevelt, then an outstanding progressive, received 897,011 votes, or nearly six percent of the total — the most a radical party has attained to date.

The expulsion of Haywood and his followers from the Socialist party injured both groups: the Industrial Workers of the World lost the bonds which kept it in balance and the party was deprived of its militant radicalism. Yet this split was logically inevitable. While the socialists who predominated in the party councils were largely of bourgeois origin or inclination, the I.W.W. — " Wobblies " — were mostly migrant or immigrant workers without access to the ballot box, ignored by the conservative craft unions, and driven to desperate measures by aggressive employers and a brutal constabulary. They were marked men and, having nothing to lose, behaved accordingly. At first the organization consisted mostly of western miners, lumberjacks, and farmhands, men of brawn and daring who joined the class struggle with a lusty song; later it received an influx of grossly underpaid textile workers of the East. Although these Wobblies conducted about 150 strikes in the course of their existence, they fought moderately, if persistently, in the face of cruel and sadistic attacks by the police. They won many battles for free speech more by sheer defiance of unwarranted authority than by acts of violence. The prolonged but successful strike of the Lawrence weavers in 1912 brought the Wobblies to the favorable attention of the entire nation. A year later they were similarly prominent in the Paterson silk strike. At this time the organization contained about 75,000 members.

The I.W.W. was severely crippled during World War I. Its open anti-militaristic stand and its refusal to call off strikes, everywhere exposed it to malicious attacks. Its members were beaten and jailed, its halls raided and wrecked, and its very existence was prohibited by numerous anti-syndicalist laws. Finally the federal government rounded up 166 of its leaders, tried 113 under the Espionage Act, and convicted 93. Haywood and a number of others received sentences ranging from ten to twenty years in prison. Not even the hardy I.W.W.'s were able to survive this persecution. Their organized existence has continued spasmodic and spent — maintained by a few faithful members.

The Socialist party appeared at first to function smoothly, as if it had profited from the expulsion of the syndicalist faction. Professor John Graham Brooks, an eminent academic economist, wrote at that time: "There is much reason to believe that Socialism in its most revolutionary character is from now on to have its most fruitful field in the United States." Writers and professional men of all degrees of prominence continued to announce their conversion to the Marxian philosophy. The brilliant, if bohemian, editorial group of *The Masses*, headed by Max Eastman, who had taught philosophy at Columbia University, made their sallies against the faults and foibles of capitalism with a sprightly irresponsibility which pleased many intellectuals. In 1914 the New York East Side, long the stronghold of Tammany Democrats despite the agitation of a number of Jewish radicals, at last sent the Socialist Meyer London to Congress. It looked indeed as if Professor Brooks had spoken truly.

The outbreak of war in 1914 brought sudden disaster to socialist movements everywhere. The failure of the strong socialist parties of Europe to stand up against their bellicose governments and to call a general strike against the war caused not only the rapid disintegration of the Second International, which had grown powerful in its quarter-century of existence, but keen disillusionment among socialists in neutral countries. The American Socialist party, loyal to its principles, promptly condemned war and militarism and urged its members to dedicate themselves to "the task of rebuilding the Socialist International upon such a basis that henceforth it cannot be shaken by the most violent storms of capitalist conflicts." In 1915, fearful of the spread of war to the United States, the party adopted a constitutional amendment stating that "any member of the Socialist Party, elected to an office, who shall in any way vote to appropriate moneys for military or naval purposes, or war, shall be expelled from the party."

No amount of exhortation availed against the torrent of emotional nationalism unloosed by the war. Like most other Americans, socialists began to take sides; the majority, affected by the flood of propaganda, abominated the Kaiser and his arrogant Junkers. As the tide of war neared our shores and the hour of decision held us in the balance, a number of prominent socialists began to insist that Americans must not shirk their duty of saving mankind from German autocracy. The pacifistic Charles Edward Russell advocated this view knowing that it would cost him the party's Presidential nomination in the 1916 campaign. The honor went to Allan L. Benson as a reward for his "conspicuous opposition to war and militarism." The party fought vigorously on the issue of peace, but its total vote shrank by more than a third. As far as the liberals were concerned, the peace could be kept only by the re-election of President Woodrow Wilson.

On the eve of the declaration of war by the United States in April 1917, the Socialist party called an emergency convention in St. Louis. After solemn and prolonged debate the delegates adopted an anti-war proclamation which condemned the murder of millions of workers for the sake of "unholy profits" and opposed the sacrifice of American lives "on the altar of capitalist greed." "We brand the declaration of war by our government as a crime of our capitalist class against the people of the United States and against the nations of the world." A sizable minority, torn by conflicting loyalties, resigned from the party rather than oppose what they believed to be a war to end war. Not a few of them, as if bent on justifying themselves to their own consciences, became almost hysterical in their eagerness to explain the conflict as a crusade to save the world from dire catastrophe.

The United States, dedicated to winning the war, changed almost over night from a tolerant democracy to a de facto dictatorship. The government began to persecute all types of nonconformists ruthlessly. Pacifists and socialists were mistreated with the brutality meted out to Wobblies and anarchists. Their newspapers and magazines were suppressed, their quarters ransacked. About 2000 persons were convicted under the Espionage Act and sentenced to long terms in prison. The work of the Socialist party locals was completely disrupted, though they continued to function underground. Only in a metropolis like New York was the party able to maintain itself and to amass over 145,000 votes, or nearly a quarter of the total, for its mayoralty candidate Morris Hillquit.

While the government was doing its utmost to smash the Socialist party from without, the political eruption in Russia caused it to suffer a schism of even graver consequences. At first all socialists greeted the news of the Czar's abdication with delight. They agreed that the epochal event had changed the character of the war and that the defeat of the Kaiser had become imperative. But the Bolshevik revolution, which rode roughshod over the moderate socialists and boldly formed a workers' republic in defiance of orthodox procedure, confounded many of them. The more conservative leaders refused to condone the wholesale imprisonment and execution of well-known radicals and attacked the Bolshevik rulers for their ruthless and reckless assumption of power. The majority of the members, many of them of Slavic origin, were exhilarated by the realization of the first socialist state and insisted on supporting the Soviets against their enemies. The leftward drift in Europe after the Armistice and the intensified persecution of radicals in the United States served to strengthen their loyalty to the Bolshevik government. They believed that Lenin had initiated the worldwide revolution and preferred his guidance to that of their own leaders.

The formation of the Third International in Moscow on March 6, 1919, precipitated a new split within the American radical movement. Left-wing factions became active in numerous cities. They repudiated the rulings of the national executive committee, issued their own periodicals, and agitated for full co-operation with the

Third International. The committee retaliated by expelling or suspending state and local branches and nullifying the election results in which the moderates were badly beaten. At the emergency convention, held in Chicago at the end of August, the national conservative leaders succeeded with the aid of the police in retaining control of the party organization. The expelled foreign-language groups, claiming to represent true Bolshevism in this country, convened at the same time to form the Communist party. The left-wing majority, having failed either to capture the party or to gain the cooperation of the self-styled Bolsheviks, immediately organized the Communist Labor party. John Reed was one of the leaders of this group and was sent to Moscow to represent the new party at the sessions of the Third International. Two months later both communist factions were driven underground by widespread raids and wholesale arrests and deportations.

The truncated Socialist party, permitted a formal existence by the government, tried valiantly to lay a new foundation for democratic socialism. In 1920 it persuaded the aging Debs, then serving a ten-year sentence in Atlanta, again to become its Presidential nominee. But the 915,000 men and women who voted for him did so more to pay their respects to the imprisoned humanitarian than to indicate any loyalty to the party. The actual membership had fallen from 108,504 in 1919 to 13,484 two years later. Morris Hillquit, the party's astute leader, was well aware of its plight.

The relatively big vote was the last flicker of the dying candle and did not deceive the Socialist. . . . The Socialist Party as such continued to decline catastrophically. It was completely wiped out in a number of states, and all that was left of the erstwhile vigorous and promising movement was a small band of stubborn die-hards, largely concentrated in a few Eastern and Midwestern states.

So feeble was the general interest in socialism after 1920 that when the New York Assembly expelled the five elected socialists by an act of " official lawlessness," only a few liberal lawyers and metropolitan newspapers bothered to express disapproval. To the people at large all "Reds" were vicious agitators and deserved the harsh treatment they received.

With a shrinking membership and predominantly conservative leadership, the Socialist party lacked the strength and enthusiasm to build anew on a Marxian foundation. Instead it began to seek affiliation with labor and liberal elements. After a preliminary meeting earlier in the year, representatives of various groups met in December 1922 to organize the Conference for Progressive Political Action. Hillquit, who attended the sessions, manifested the temper of the Socialist party when he said: " Personally I take the position that progress is always made safely and slowly, step by step." The result of this and subsequent meetings was that in 1924 the new progressive party nominated Senator Robert M. La Follette for the Presidency on an essentially Populist platform. The campaign was intensive and enthusiastic. The socialists relinquished their own ticket and worked for La Follette. When the ballots were counted the Wisconsin liberal received nearly 5,000,000 votes — the largest number ever given to a third party, but too small to satisfy its chief backers. A few months later the important labor leaders left the organization and caused its rapid disintegration. The socialists had no alternative but to resume their former political independence.

In the middle 1920's Norman Thomas emerged as head of the party. A Princeton graduate, a former Presbyterian minister, a persuasive speaker, he readily gained popularity and prestige among both socialists and liberals. But the trend continued strongly in the direction of " normalcy." Nor did it turn towards socialism with the coming of the severe economic depression. In the 1932 election Thomas received a sizable vote, though in the opinion of his followers it seemed — considering the prevailing unemployment and real suffering — disappointingly small. In the subsequent elections most of the liberals and radicals, influenced by campaign issues and by dissension within their own ranks, voted for President Franklin D. Roosevelt. Throughout the 1930's the socialists indeed dissipated their energies in factional fights or in execrating the Russian and American communists. The " rightists " broke away and became venomous and violent at the mere mention of Soviet Russia. Thomas and his followers, confused and discouraged, found themselves caught in the snare of isolationism at the outbreak of World War II. Thereafter the Socialist party remained a political organization in name only.

The " Red " raids which were resumed in November 1919, a year after the war had ended, aimed at the incarceration of individual communists and the destruction of their party organizations. The resulting terror is a dark page in American history. Utilizing a great many *agents provocateurs*, who honeycombed all radical groups and were responsible for much of the propaganda of incitement, the government indulged in an orgy of oppression and brutality. In a short time thousands of suspected communists were arrested and over 500 aliens deported. " It was," according to William Z. Foster, " a real baptism of fire for the Communist movement."

In 1921 the Third International ruled that the two American communist factions should unite into a single party. This they did in December, electing Charles E. Ruthenberg as secretary. With increased governmental tolerance the party abandoned its underground activities and came out into the open under the name of Workers party. In the 1924 election Foster, its Presidential candidate, received 36,386 votes. Bitter factional fights, however, reflecting the Trotsky-Stalin struggle for dominance over the crucial issue of " permanent revolution " versus " socialism in one country," prostrated the party during the ensuing half-decade. Ruthenberg's death in 1927 permitted Jay Lovestone, an energetic but erratic " rightist," to take over the party's leadership. Two years later the Third International deposed him for taking issue with Stalin on a doctrinal matter and promoted Earl R. Browder to his position. (It is of interest to note that Lovestone in 1927 and Browder in 1946 were expelled for the same heresy of " American exceptionalism.") At this time the Communist party had only 7000 members and was flanked by " right " and " left " opposition groups determined to fight the " Stalinites " to the bitter end.

Unlike the Socialist party, which was primarily a political organization and most active during election campaigns, the Communist party was from the outset moved by circumstances and principle to concentrate its energies on defending minority groups and organizing the unskilled workers. At one of its early conventions Ruthenberg reported that, recognizing the immaturity of the class struggle in the United States, the party " has formulated policies for the immediate struggles for political demands which will build up the power of the workers and prepare them for the *revolutionary struggle*." In line with this decision communists helped factory workers and poor farmers in their efforts to improve their economic status. In 1926 they led the strike of the Passaic textile workers with such skill and self-sacrifice as to arouse the respect of liberals everywhere. Two years later they performed a similar service in the embittered Gastonia strike. Wherever labor unrest became manifest they were among the first to offer help and guidance.

The communists were also quick to challenge injustices against radicals and minority groups. Thus, when several young Negroes of Scottsboro, Alabama, were sentenced to die on a trumped-up charge of rape, the communists devoted themselves to their liberation with such zeal — conducting large mass-meetings of protest, collecting signatures and funds — that they succeeded in arousing the conscience of the country against this miscarriage of justice.

The policy of the Communist party in foreign affairs was closely co-ordinated with that of the Third International. The safe and successful development of Soviet Russia was ever the guiding principle. In effect the dominant Bolshevik leaders could do no wrong. Since the United States did not recognize the Soviet government until 1933 and since the diplomats of Europe were almost united in their anti-Russian bias, the American communists joined those of other lands in attacking the enemies of the first socialist republic. They performed this watchdog task with unceasing zeal and thereby exposed themselves to the charge of disloyalty to their own government.

The rise of fascism in Italy and especially in Germany placed all communists on the defensive. Judging it a greater menace to both Soviet Russia and the general communist movement than democratic capitalism, the American communists quickly concentrated their attack upon all forms of reaction at home and abroad. In their newspapers and magazines, in large mass-meetings and by means of pamphlets, they sought to dramatize the danger of fascism to the democratic way of life. More than any other one agency the Communist party exposed the corruption and criminality of the leading Nazis. When General Franco, assisted by Italian and German arms, attacked the liberal Spanish government in 1936, American communists at once saw the threat to world peace and democracy and joined communists in other lands in a common effort to defeat the fascist enemy. They organized and financed the Abraham Lincoln Battalion, called many meetings of protest, and collected funds for Loyalist Spain. Many a communist youth died in battle, and those who survived returned to warn an awakening people of the fascist threat to civilization.

Perhaps the greatest contribution of the communists lay in their undaunted efforts to unionize the mass-production industries. In the early 1930's they gathered the unemployed in meeting halls and on parade to impress upon them their right to work. Wherever they saw the need or the opportunity, they agitated for greater government assistance, for better living conditions, and for improved labor terms. When the New Deal laws facilitated the unionization of labor, the communists took full advantage of the opportunity. Unobtrusive and yet ubiquitous, they made themselves invaluable to the liberal union officials who had formed the Committee on Industrial Organization for the purpose of unionizing the millions of unskilled workers whom the craft unions had long neglected. Though relatively few, the communist agitators and organizers impregnated the Committee with a daring and enterprise that helped it to invade and unionize the industries which had long been noted for their anti-union policies. Within a short time the new unions had millions of members and had succeeded in imposing their terms upon recalcitrant employers. Although some of the corporations fought these unions with the charge of communism, they failed to prejudice their employees against the men who were obviously devoted and enthusiastic industrial unionists.

During the early years of the depression, when our capitalist economy seemed to totter and many men were inclined to heed the prophets of doom, the communists were particularly successful in their appeal to intellectuals. They attracted a number of writers and artists by means of John Reed clubs, by congresses devoted to the ideals and functions of the creative worker, and by their agitation within W.P.A. organizations. Although not many members of these " front " organizations actually joined the party — and some soon reacted violently against all radicalism — the majority gained a social awareness which freshened and deepened their subsequent work.

As already indicated, the Communist party acted as an independent political party more by default than by design. Its leaders knew well enough that they had no chance of political victory in the foreseeable future. Firmly grounded in the doctrines of Marx and Stalin, eager to develop an American class-conscious proletariat, they saw clearly the difficulties of their task. " Many of the great objective difficulties," Foster pointed out, " include the restraining effects of the higher American wage levels, a greater economic opportunity, more formal democratic rights, the diversity of races and nationalities, etc." Obstacles, however, have never yet stopped men determined to achieve a goal. And communists are nothing if not determined.

Very early they sought to ally themselves with labor and liberal groups. In 1922 they were rejected by the Conference for Progressive Political Action. Somewhat later they tried in vain to unite with existing farmer and labor parties. They even made overtures to the Socialist party. None wanted to associate with them for fear of being stigmatized from without and subverted from within. Undaunted, the communists again agitated for a union of all radical and liberal elements during the early 1930's and denounced as " social fascists" those who refused to co-operate with them. In 1936 and again two years later Browder campaigned on the issues of anti-fascism and the people's front. He argued that the Communist party, aware of the great need of a united front, offered as its "main proposal to the American people that they organize themselves in such a Farmer-Labor Party." The American people, however, were not interested. Nor had the liberals and socialists reason to trust the communists in view of their military discipline and pragmatic tactics. For one reason or another they believed the communists were offering them a Trojan horse.

This prejudice against the communists appeared amply justified by their behavior at the outbreak of World War II. Few people knew of the evasive and sham nature of the negotiations early in 1939 between the Western powers and Soviet Russia. The Russians, smarting from the rebuke given to them at Munich the year before, did not trust the British diplomats. Suspecting them of encouraging the Nazis to attack and destroy the Red Army even while the negotiations were proceeding in Moscow, they decided to outsmart the British and sign a Machiavellian pact of friendship with their deadly foe. The mass of mankind was startled and shocked. Even Browder and his followers at first failed to comprehend the nature of the treaty. But they dutifully assumed that whatever Soviet Russia did was right and began to defend her as best they could. Although Poland was already ravaged and the war in the West was entering its "phony" phase, the communists slackened their agitation against the Nazis and inveighed against the British for provoking a war of imperialism. For nearly two years, until the very day that the Germans invaded Soviet Russia, they pursued an isolationist policy and criticized the Roosevelt administration for its imperialistic belligerency.

After June 21, 1941, the communists returned to their prewar tactics. Again they insisted that the Nazis were criminal madmen bent on destroying democracy. The war now lost its imperialistic nature and became a struggle for survival. Complete unity with Russia, they argued, was essential to victory. They devoted themselves to the war effort with undiminished enthusiasm. Regardless of its motivation, the patriotism of the communists was as intensive as it was effective. They defended the no-strike agreement, backed the Roosevelt administration to the limit, and praised the large industrialists for their part in making this country the arsenal of democracy. To achieve victory over the Nazis they were ready, once the Third International was disbanded, to relinquish their party policies and principles. Robert Minor, one of their leaders, asserted that the Communist party " is the most consistent and stubborn fighter for democracy "; that " the American labor movement has a particular duty to support this war for our country's survival "; that " in a time of war crisis like this, the Communist party does not take advantage of the war situation to propose any program that is not acceptable to the country as a whole."

The climax of the communists' effort to adjust themselves to the temper of the American people came with Browder's proposal, after the Teheran Conference, that they liquidate their party and reorganize into an educational society under the name of American Communist Political Association. " Under such a name," he declared, " we will find it much easier to explain our true relationship with all other democratic and progressive groupings which operate through the medium, in the main, of the two-party system, and take our place in free collaboration at their side." As the leader of a highly disciplined party he had no difficulty in getting membership approval for this radical change of tactics. In an interview in PM he stressed the intention of the Association to minimize its disagreements with capitalism and to work with all groups sympathetic to a liberal program. " As far as the issues of the day are concerned, we have more points of similarity than of difference with other progressive groups, and it is our policy to stress the points of agreement rather than the points of difference." In the same interview he favored cartels and monopolies as a means of obtaining postwar full employment and industrial development. " There is in the ranks of big capital an intelligent desire to adjust the practice of capital to the necessities of the democratic advance and a general rise of the well-being of the country." Party discipline forced acquiescence in these views on those who deplored this heretical attitude on the part of their leader, but a large number drifted away from the organization.

Once the Nazis were beaten and the Red Army stood victorious over a prostrate Germany, a number of American communists gagged at further acceptance of Browder's political opportunism. Their chance to act came with the appearance of a critical article by Jacques Duclos, a leading French communist, in which he charged the American party with having blundered into anti-Marxian fallacies. Led by Foster, they began to beat their breasts and to denounce Browder as a traitor to the cause of communism. At a special meeting of the organization they ignominiously deposed their leader of the past sixteen years. They also reconstituted themselves as the Communist party, on a purely Marxian basis. Early in 1946 Browder was expelled from the party for violating its principles and discipline.

After a century of agitation, Marxian socialism has failed to take root in the social thinking of the American people. Alien in origin, weakened by frequent factional quarrels, execrated by powerful opponents who succeeded in making it obnoxious to a large number of workers, it remained relatively ineffectual even in periods of stress and suffering. As Foster admitted, American labor, comparatively well off, has not felt itself driven by penury or oppression to resort to extreme measures. Nevertheless the socialist agitation after 1900, although limited to the political periphery and at no time enlisting more than a small fraction of the population, has helped to stimulate our economic thinking and to instigate social improvements and political reforms which at first seemed revolutionary, if not preposterous, but which in time assumed a normal and desirable inevitability.

How this agitation was pursued by the various socialist groups and what kind of men they were led by are discussed in the following chapters on Daniel De Leon, Eugene V. Debs, and John Reed.

DANIEL DE LEON

APOSTLE OF SOCIALISM

IN 1918, shortly after the Bolshevik Revolution, several American correspondents reported that Lenin had expressed his warm admiration of Daniel De Leon's writings. John Reed, on his return from Russia later that year, declared before the National Executive Committee of the Socialist Labor party:

Premier Lenin is a great admirer of Daniel De Leon, considering him the greatest of modern Socialists — the only one who had added anything to Socialist thought since Marx. It is Lenin's opinion that the Industrial State as conceived by De Leon will ultimately have to be the form of government in Russia.

Lenin apparently nowhere wrote down his opinions on De Leon; there is no evidence that any of De Leon's ideas were incorporated into Lenin's theories and practices; and neither the Communist International nor the American Communist party reprinted any of De Leon's pamphlets. Yet Lenin's reported words recalled an outstanding American Socialist from undeserved obscurity. For by 1918, four years after his death, time had already relegated De Leon to the oblivion reserved for leaders of lost causes. Wholly the intellectual and man of inflexible principle, devoted to ideas and disdaining compromise, caustic and intolerant, he failed to impress his views upon the mass of American workers. His theoretical soundness became affected by the rigidity of orthodox dogma; his acute exegesis of socialism was blurred by polemical wrangling. As a Marxian disciple, however, he towered over his fellow American socialists.

[470]

When Daniel De Leon reached New York in 1872 he had just completed six years of study in Germany and Holland. Born in Curaçao on December 14, 1852, the son of a well-established Spanish-American family, he had decided to make his home in the United States. Knowing Spanish and sympathetic to sufferers of oppression and exploitation, he was readily attracted to a group of Cuban revolutionists and helped edit their Spanish periodical. When the paper was suspended, he obtained a teaching position in a Westchester preparatory school. In 1876 he decided to study law at Columbia University and two years later was graduated with honors. In 1883 he won a prize lectureship in international law at Columbia and kept it for two successive three-year terms. He refused a third term when, because of his activities in behalf of labor, the administration failed to offer him a promised full professorship.

In 1886, perturbed by the bad social conditions in the New York slums and by the clubbing of strikers, he became an ardent participant in Henry George's spectacular mayoralty campaign and scandalized his conservative colleagues at the university by speaking publicly in George's behalf. Once the election was over, however, his inquiring mind quickly perceived the inadequacy of the single-tax theory of economics and in later years he scorned it as " flatulent " and the product of " half-antiquated, half-idiotic reasoning."

His dissatisfaction with the capitalistic system of society, intensified by conditions at Columbia which favored socially acceptable mediocrities over foreigners of ability like himself, caused him to take an interest in the social criticism of his day. A reading of Bellamy's newly published *Looking Backward* stirred his imagination and led him to join the Nationalist movement. Again he was soon disillusioned — his mind was too critical for simple utopias — and perforce drifted toward the inchoate socialist organization which was at that time struggling to make itself heard within the ranks of unionized labor. In 1889, after a reading of some of Karl Marx's writings, he joined the Socialist Labor party.

Not given to doing things by halves, De Leon accepted socialism in dead earnest. Convinced that Marx offered the only practical solution to the ills of society, he dedicated himself to the task of advocating it before the country's working class. First as associated editor and after 1891 as editor of *People*, the organ of the Socialist Labor party, he devoted his acute mind and tremendous energies to the spreading of socialism. Under his direction the periodical became a hard-hitting, straightforward, and clear-cut propaganda medium; his editorials, as later his pamphlets, were superior in quality and cogency to any other similar writings; and his forceful style suffered little from his inability to revise his first drafts or the stenographic copies of his lectures. In 1891 he also became the national lecturer of the party and traveled as far as the Pacific Coast in his tours of agitation. Obviously the intellectual and effective speaker, he impressed his audiences with the vitality of his message.

His great merits dwarfed the older leaders of the party and he quickly established himself as its dominant head. Wholly the idealist and driven by a single-minded determination, he demanded a similar zeal on the part of every professing socialist. Those who differed with him or who failed to conform to strict principle he criticized with fanatical fierceness.

In his efforts to turn socialism into a mass movement he found himself balked by those from whom he had expected warm cooperation — the labor leaders. His point of view and his peremptory approach had immediately antagonized them. Although a few professed a sympathy towards socialism, the majority reviled him as a dreamer and trouble-maker. As officers of craft unions they wanted most of all shorter hours of work and higher wages for their members. The larger interests of labor hardly concerned them. Nor would they tolerate the injection of politics into their unions. Many of them believed in each union for itself and feared any arrangement or tactics that might lessen the chances of immediate gains.

De Leon accused these labor leaders of venality and lack of vision. He regarded them as traitors to the cause of labor and usually referred to them as fakers and ignoramuses. He condemned their craft separatism and their ban on political action as means of abetting the perpetuation of wage slavery. "The pure and simple trade union is not a labor organization but a caricature of capitalism." For the aim of a union of workers must be "the abolition of the wages system of slavery" if it is to be true to its essential purpose. Nor must workmen be misguided by the promise of favorable labor laws, since employers can always find ways of getting around these. "So long as the capitalist class held the government, all such labor laws . . . were a snare and a delusion."

At first De Leon fought the labor officials within the unions. He joined the Knights of Labor and made considerable headway, but in the end his efforts were frustrated and he had to get out. "The trade union leaders," he admitted at the time, "will let you bore from within only enough to throw you out through that hole bored by you." In 1895 he was instrumental in the formation of the Socialist Trade and Labor Alliance under the aegis of the Socialist Labor party — an industrial and class-conscious union. At the next annual convention of the party the Alliance was hailed "as a giant stride towards throwing off the yoke of wage slavery," and socialists were called upon to "consolidate and concentrate the proletariat of America into one class-conscious army, equipped both with the shield of the economic organization and the sword of the Socialist Labor Party ballot." Notwithstanding this brave beginning, the Alliance remained throughout its decade of vain effort an anemic and ineffectual organization. In 1905, when it combined with other labor groups to form the Industrial Workers of the World, it had a membership of 1400.

If De Leon denounced the conservative labor leaders, he despised the pragmatic socialists who invoked Marx without adhering to his doctrines. His thorough study of Marx's writings had convinced him that socialism was based upon the class struggle and could be achieved only by the overthrow of the capitalist system, and he was adamant against any manifestation of what Marx had termed the "cretinism of bourgeois parliamentarianism." "The socialist movement," De Leon declared, "cannot be all things to all men; it can be only one thing, and to only one class — the working class." To be a socialist was in fact to be a revolutionist engaged in active and continuous battle against the capitalist system. Compromise or moderation could not but lead to disaster. "Nothing is gained on the road to palliatives; all may be lost. . . . Not sops, but the unconditional surrender of capitalism, is the battle cry of the Proletarian Revolution."

He therefore demanded that all members of the Socialist Labor party adhere rigidly to the principle of complete unity of theory and tactics; that transgressions be punished according to the gravity of the offense. He attacked without mercy those who refused to subject themselves to party discipline or who favored the doctrine of gradualism. He stigmatized them as reformers — shallow-pated sentimentalists whose platforms he likened to banana peels on which the reformer was bound to slip and bring down the workers with him. "We know him; we have experienced him; we know what mischief he can do; and he cannot get within our ranks if we can help it. He must organize an opposition organization and thus fulfil the only good mission he has in the scheme of nature — pull out from among us whatever reformers may be hiding there."

As a consequence of De Leon's dogmatic idealism, the history of the Socialist Labor party during his quarter-century of leadership was marked by strife and dissension. Few active members were able to measure up to his lofty standard. A number of his devoted colleagues, such as Hugo Vogt, Lucien Saniel, and others, sooner or later rebelled against his obdurate domination. In his defense he explained:

I uniformly go to the full length, fullest length possible, of giving people the opportunity to show what good there is in them, if any, for the movement. All these men who have gone to the dogs gave promise of better things.

Towards the end of the 1890's the larger part of the membership, failing to depose him from the leadership of the party, joined the "kangaroo exodus" and combined with Eugene V. Debs's group in the Middle West to form the Socialist party. A smaller schism occurred three years later when the "kanglets" broke away to unite with the earlier dissidents. This blood-letting became a chronic procedure and kept the party small and anemic.

De Leon accepted these disaffections with philosophic fortitude, declaring comfortingly:

You will never find the revolutionist putting himself above the organization. The opposite conduct is an unmistakable earmark of reformers.

Because he perceived the ideal of socialism with the clarity of utter conviction, he was never able to realize that others were also capable of such implicit faith without necessarily agreeing with him on all points. Having never known the appeal of immediate rewards in the form of higher wages or better working conditions, he condemned such palliatives as insidious sops. At the party's convention in 1900 he was instrumental in eliminating from its platform all immediate demands as well as the right of membership to any official of a craft union. So far as he was concerned, a small but united party promised more for the future of socialism than a large membership interested in hasty palliatives rather than in ultimate goals. Firm adherence to this ideal later caused him to reject his favored son Solon, in whom he had placed fond hopes, when the youth questioned his father's interpretation of Marx's definition of value. In De Leon's mind man was subservient to principle and not otherwise; not even his own son could violate this rule without suffering the consequences.

De Leon's major contribution to the theory of socialism lay in his development of the tactics by which capitalism was to be replaced by a socialist republic. He believed firmly in the doctrine of the class struggle. "Between the Working Class and Capitalist Class there is an irrepressible conflict, a class struggle for life." He also argued that while capitalism was a natural and necessary phase in the evolution of society, it had already reached the end of its usefulness and had become an obstacle to social progress. " Labor alone produces all the wealth," he repeated after Marx, and was therefore entitled to all of it. Only socialism could achieve this economic justice.

Socialism is the logical sequence of economic and sociologic development. It is the movement which overthrows the Political State; rears the Industrial Commonwealth in its place; harmonizes the system of ownership with the collective system of operating the plants of production; and abolishes economic dependency, the foundation of all slavery.

Since capitalism refused to abdicate, and fought as fiercely for its least privilege as for its very existence, it became incumbent upon socialists to achieve their goal by revolutionary means.

Yet De Leon abhorred the reckless use of physical force. To him, revolution was the ripe fruit of disciplined and directed evolution. " No revolutionary class is ever ripe for success," he pointed out, " before it has itself well in hand." To expedite this evolutionary process " to the crisis of revolution," he urged political organization along with industrial unionization. Both were necessary because capitalism was dominant in both fields and must be attacked accordingly. " Without political organization, the labor movement cannot triumph; without economic organization, the day of its political triumph would be the day of its defeat." It should be clearly understood, however, that the political phase was merely the orderly method of attacking capitalism in a democratic society. " The political movement bows to the methods of civilized discussion: *it gives a chance to the peaceful solution of the great question at issue.*" Yet for this very reason it must not yield to the temptation of concessions. " It must be uncompromisingly revolutionary. This fact dictates the conduct of the successful political candidates of labor in the parliaments of capitalism."

De Leon's concept of unionization was closely connected with the ultimate goal of socialism. He believed that laborers naturally seek to unite for mutual benefits.

As sure as a man will raise his hand by some instinct, to shield himself against a blow, so surely will workingmen, instinctively, periodically gather into unions. The Union is the arm that Labor instinctively throws up to screen its head.

Conservative labor leaders, myopic and unscrupulous, concerned more for their jobs than for the welfare of labor, have driven their timid followers into the blind alley of craft unionism. Yet the true direction of unionism is along the broad highway leading to the socialist republic.

The trades union has a supreme mission. That mission is nothing short of organizing by uniting, and uniting by organizing, the whole working class individually — not merely those for whom there are jobs, accordingly, not only those who can pay dues. This unification or organization is essential in order to save the eventual and possible victory from bankruptcy, by enabling the working class to assume and conduct production the moment the guns of the public powers fall into its hands — or before, if need be, if capitalist political chicanery pollutes the ballot box. The mission is important also in that the industrial organization forecasts the future constituencies of the parliaments of the Socialist Republic.

In developing his concept of revolutionary industrial unionism De Leon made clear that it " embraced three domains, closely interdependent, and all three requisite to the whole . . . Form, Tactics, and Goal." He explained that, if the reconstruction of society was to be achieved, all persons engaged in useful occupations must be gathered " into ONE UNION, a Union co-extensive with the Nation's confines." Within this comprehensive union the workers in each industry will be organized into separate constituent unions. Each industrial union will also have its local trade and shop branches, and all will be properly represented by their respective delegates to the governing body of the general industrial union. Workers will thus be so organized within each industry that should the capitalists try to prevent them from assuming power, " they could laugh at all shut-down orders, and carry on production." Under this plan the political state will disappear altogether and be replaced by the socialist industrial republic. " Industrial Unionism is the Socialist Republic in the making; and the goal once achieved, the Industrial Union is the Socialist Republic in operation."

Under socialism industrial constituencies will replace geographical ones. Thus instead of sending Representatives and Senators to Congress on a district and state basis, respectively, the people will elect representatives of various industries. These representatives

would constitute the government, and that government would then own and control those instruments of production that civilization needs. . . . Their legislative work will not be the complicated one which a society of conflicting interests, such as capitalism, requires but the easy one which can be summed up in the statistics of wealth needed, the wealth producible, and the work required.

De Leon did not formulate his theory of industrial unionism in a moment of inspiration; he developed it gradually in the light of Marxian principles and current social conditions. The formation of the Socialist Trade and Labor Alliance in 1895 was a first step in that direction. It was an effort to eliminate the unenlightened and grasping labor officials from union leadership and to provide workers with unions thoroughly imbued with the tactics of socialism. Members of the Socialist Labor party, animated by De Leon's vision of an industrial union which would ultimately grow strong enough to establish the socialist republic, propagated the idea in shops and factories, at meetings and in their writings. But the result was inconsequential. The overwhelming majority of skilled workmen preferred the real, if meager, advantages of the strong craft union to the glowing promises of a feeble industrial union. The new faithful of the Alliance failed to gain new members at the expense of the American Federation of Labor.

Yet the idea of industrial unionism was kept alive by those who perceived the weaknesses of craft unionism. The Knights of Labor, the American Railway Union, and the Western Federation of Miners were crude but earnest efforts to unite large bodies of labor along industrial rather than craft lines. During the early 1900's the issue of industrial unionization was assuming concrete form. While few of the progressive labor leaders who favored it either knew of or sympathized with De Leon's plan, many agreed that an industrial union comprising all workers in an entire industry would certainly be more effective than the loosely affiliated craft unions. Finally a number of the more radical of these men decided to meet in Chicago in order to discuss the ways and means of calling on " the workers of the world" to organize industrially. The conference took place in January 1905, and those present drew up a manifesto which recognized the existence of the class struggle and invited labor representatives to an organizational meeting the following June.

De Leon came to this convention as the head of the delegation sent by the Socialist Trade and Labor Alliance. Because the Alliance had a relatively small membership, it was given little recognition by the sponsors of the conference. Yet De Leon's towering intellectual stature and his firm adherence to basic principles made him, in the words of Professor Paul F. Brissenden, " probably the most striking figure of all " at the sessions which helped to bring forth the lusty Industrial Workers of the World. Although he did not " capture " the convention, he dominated its discussions and succeeded in getting the delegates to abandon the policy of " boring from within " and to include the political clause in the famous Preamble. This achievement was the more notable in view of the fact that the meetings were guided by such outstanding leaders as Eugene V. Debs and William D. Haywood.

In the discussions of principles and tactics Debs sided with De Leon against Haywood. Thus at one point De Leon argued: " You could not first take the men into the union under the false pretense that you were going to raise their wages, and afterwards indoctrinate them. No, you have to indoctrinate them *first*, then bring them in." Haywood disagreed with this view and insisted " that only through the actual class struggle can the working class get its education for the seizure of power." Debs, head of the Socialist party

[479]

and no friend of his socialist rival, stated his position on the question without equivocation: "De Leon is sound on the question of trade unionism, and to that extent, whether I like him or not personally, I am with him."

The Industrial Workers of the World did not of course measure up to De Leon's concept of the revolutionary industrial union which was to destroy capitalism and usher in the socialist republic. But it was the bravest effort labor had yet made in that direction and he hoped for the best. On leaving Chicago he spoke in its behalf in a number of cities, and his address on the I.W.W. Preamble in Minneapolis, outlining the strategic course which organized labor must follow to assure final victory, was at once persuasive and positive and later became one of his most popular pamphlets. He also devoted considerable space in the Daily and the Weekly *People* to the activities and prospects of the I.W.W. and urged his followers to exert themselves to the utmost in its behalf. In the East, members of the Socialist Labor party became the most active workers in the I.W.W. locals.

Dissenting voices began to be heard at I.W.W. meetings soon after the organization was launched. This was inevitable, because the union was an amalgamation of members from such divergent factions as the Socialist Labor party, the Socialist party, anarcho-syndicalist groups, and conservative unionists. Although everyone tried to pull together at the outset, at the second annual convention the different cliques maneuvered for control. De Leon was present, and his insistence on strict adherence to the principles of the Preamble quickened the latent antagonism. Debs's abstention from the conference made De Leon's work all the more difficult and made him seem a trouble-maker.

Haywood was at that time in the Boise, Idaho, jail, where he and two of his fellow labor leaders had been placed by state officials who, having illegally kidnapped them in Colorado, had charged them with the murder of former Governor Steunenberg. De Leon at once joined Debs and others in the campaign for their defense and wrote eneregtically and frequently in their behalf. When Haywood, while in prison, was nominated for governor by the Colorado Socialist party, the Socialist Labor party endorsed him enthusiastically — the first and only time that it favored the candidate of another party. When Haywood was finally freed and became a hero in the eyes of millions of workingmen, De Leon wrote to congratulate him on his acquittal and expressed the hope that he would capitalize on his popularity and assume the leadership of American class-conscious labor. He even declared that the Socialist Labor party would gladly " break ranks " as soon as the I.W.W. organized its own political party. Haywood never acknowledged the letter. Loath to associate himself with the leader of a rival party, he disdained De Leon as a doctrinaire and fanatic.

I was becoming more and more convinced [he wrote in his autobiography] that the Socialist Labor party was so completely dominated by De Leon's prejudices that it could not lend strength to any movement with which it became associated. Whether right or wrong, De Leon always insisted he was right. He made it impossible for any but his devotees to work with him.

The third convention of the I.W.W. went off relatively smoothly. The anarchists' attempt to pass a resolution against the organization's political activities was defeated by a vote of 113 to 15. De Leon spoke cogently and at length for the majority. But the anarchists refused to acquiesce in defeat. On leaving the convention they sought adherents among the syndicalists and socialists. By the time the fourth convention opened they had won over the members of the executive board and were on hand with a large delegation of the " overall brigade " — self-styled " bums " from the West. Completely in control of the meetings, these leaders refused to admit De Leon and others as delegates and proceeded to repudiate the political clause of the Preamble. Another split became unavoidable. The new majority embraced syndicalist " bummery " and thus brought about their subsequent destruction during World War I; the ousted minority of De Leonites formed a new organization, the Workers International Industrial Union — which was in fact the defunct Socialist Trade and Labor Alliance under a new name and which never gained enough members to affect the trend of the American labor movement.

De Leon, disappointed but not discouraged, persisted in his prodigious labors as editor and socialist propagandist. The quick disruption of the first genuine industrial union, after twenty years of intensive effort, must no doubt have hurt him deeply. A master of self-discipline, however, he proceeded to write his daily editorials and to deliver his lectures with his wonted dialectical dexterity. He remained as certain as ever that the advent of the socialist republic was only a matter of time. His rigorous adherence to Marxian principles drove him to denounce everyone in the party who appeared to veer from them. Among those to receive the sting of his condemnation were, as already mentioned, some of his most trusted lieutenants and his eldest son. To the end of his life he valued men only as the agents of ideas; once they ceased to represent the ideas dear to him they seemed to him empty and worthless shells.

Throughout his career as a socialist leader he knew poverty intimately. His salary as editor was small and frequently unpaid — a balance of about $3500 was subsequently paid to his widow — and he had to eke out his living by such extra work as the translation of books. Although he was never able to meet the needs of his family, he refused to write on socialistic topics for commercial periodicals. Yet he had a deep capacity for joyous living and found active contentment in his modest home and fond family.

He died in May 1914, exactly twenty-five years after he had left the cloistered campus for a strenuous existence as an apostle of socialism.

The worst that can be said against Daniel De Leon is that his mind functioned with such fanatical inflexibility as to blind him to the psychological complexities of human nature. He was so certain he was right that he made no allowances for differences of opinion or altered conditions. Under his leadership the Socialist

Labor party became a sect adhering closely to abstract doctrines. Its rigid discipline and complete scorn for the sops required by unenlightened workers stunted its growth and rendered it sterile. Unlike the man from Mars, on whom De Leon called to examine the contradictory nature of socialism on earth, he himself insisted on adjusting facts to theory and not otherwise. His emphasis on principles over men, combined with an irritating air of righteousness — as if Marx's mantle were his personal inheritance — caused him to clash with men of merit and subject the party to chronic discord and a series of schisms. Louis C. Fraina who, though driven from the party, wrote a warmly appreciative article on De Leon at the time of his death, declared that " his wrong judgments of men often led him to harsh measures, rousing unnecessary antagonism." Nor did his free use of sarcastic and offensive epithets mollify opposition.

Yet this criticism gives but the negative aspect of his character and activity. From a positive standpoint he may be said to belong to the small but precious band of visionaries who are completely dedicated to an ideal and seek its realization with all their strength. In this country William Lloyd Garrison comes closest to De Leon in mind and temper. The name of the Abolitionist is revered in the North because circumstances favored his crusade against slavery. Although De Leon's cause — the liberation of the mass of mankind from economic servitude — is at least equally noble in conception, and although he labored in its behalf with exceeding zeal, it failed to gain a following among the men it sought to benefit. American workmen, notwithstanding the great expansion of monopoly capitalism and its power over the economy of the country, continued to regard themselves as men of free and equal stature and therefore failed to appreciate the doctrine of the class struggle. Ready enough to fight for their rights when the occasion demanded and eager to strike for concrete and immediate advantages such as shorter hours and higher wages, they refused to trouble their minds with abstract concepts or ultimate goals. Indoctrinated from childhood by the press, pulpit, and politics to favor the status quo, they recoiled from the thought of turning the social system of their fathers upside down. It was easier for them to revile the idea of socialism as the subversive doctrine of foreign agitators. Because De Leon was the most extreme and most uncompromising of the socialists, his voice remained a cry in the wilderness.

Nevertheless, fame may still snatch him from oblivion — despite the efforts of those socialists who, out of party pique, have either ignored or belittled him. For time is on his side. A man of broad culture and deep learning, he became the first outstanding interpreter of Marxism. He had no sooner embraced socialism than he began to disengage the radical movement from German domination and adapt it to American conditions. His synthesis of the anthropological conclusions of Lewis Henry Morgan with the economic doctrines of Karl Marx and Friedrich Engels, if uncritical and no longer wholly acceptable, was in the 1890's a positive contribution to the study of socialism. An even greater achievement, of course, was his theory of the revolutionary industrial union. As Fraina wrote:

De Leon's name was synonymous with revolutionary Socialism — that Socialism which rejects compromise, recognizes the social value of reform but refuses to deal in reform, and considers revolutionary Industrial Unionism as the indispensable basis of Socialist political action and the revolutionary movement as a whole. De Leon saw clearly the impending menace of State Socialism, particularly within the Socialist movement, and his whole programme was an answer to that menace.

His temperamental deficiencies, which his opponents exaggerated to the extent of impugning his intellectual integrity, manifested themselves only in his truly heroic effort to keep the socialist movement in line with Marxian principles. In this respect he asked for no quarter and gave none. His caustic attacks upon those who differed with him must be explained in the light of his complete devotion to a cause which he held dearer than life and the success of which required complete unity and revolutionary discipline.

Lenin's appreciation of the validity of De Leon's theory of industrial unionism gives promise of similar approbation on the part of future leaders of social revolution. American union officials and pragmatic socialists, perforce cautious and conservative, will probably never cross the Pisgah heights overlooking the economic democracy envisioned by De Leon. But social evolution tends in that direction — tardily and tortuously yet indubitably — and society may one day salute the dreamer who preached the ideal long before it was perceived by men of lesser vision.

EUGENE VICTOR DEBS

EVANGELICAL SOCIALIST

J AMES WHITCOMB RILEY, the Hoosier poet, expressed the sentiment of millions of Americans when he wrote: " God was feeling
mighty good when he created 'Gene Debs, and He didn't have
anything else to do all day." People needed only to meet the lanky
labor leader to like him as their brother. He had, in Riley's lines,

> As warm a heart as ever beat
> Betwixt here and the Judgment Seat.

This love of his fellow men motivated Debs's thought and activity
throughout his life. It impelled him early to become a union organizer, a radical labor leader, a revolutionary socialist, an uncompromising pacifist. From first to last, however, he was simply and
wholeheartedly the humanitarian eager to improve the lot of the
mass of workers — the evangelist preaching the doctrine of economic and social equality.

Eugene Debs was bone and flesh of Middlewestern America. He
was born in Terre Haute, Indiana, on November 5, 1855, the eldest
son of a poor Alsatian grocer who loved good books and cherished
the ideals of American liberty. From him Gene had early learned to
appreciate the dignity of human labor, the goal of social and economic equality. Most people about him indeed exemplified these
virtues and impressed him with their informality and friendliness.
A reading of Victor Hugo and Voltaire, among the books on his

father's shelf, intensified his faith in the generally accepted principles of Jeffersonian democracy.

At fourteen, upon graduation from grammar school, Gene found work in a local factory — scraping paint off old railway cars. " I worked there for a year," he wrote later, " and it almost killed me." Chance made him a locomotive fireman at a dollar a day. He enjoyed the freedom and comradeship of his new position, and his talent for friendship made him liked and respected by the older men. After three years, however, he gave up firing to please his mother; railroad accidents were frequent in those days and Mrs. Debs was too concerned for his safety to restrain her anxiety during his daily runs. Having studied bookkeeping during his evening leisure, he obtained work as a ledger clerk in a wholesale grocery establishment and remained there five years.

The daily routine of his job was a mere chore to young Debs. His ambition soared into higher spheres of achievement. He became very economical with his time and, although he enjoyed being with friends, he devoted many of his free hours to reading and study. His talent for leadership was recognized in 1875 when he was elected president of the Occidental Literary Club, composed of young Hoosiers as hungry for cultural fare as he was. In that capacity he met and was befriended by Wendell Phillips, Robert G. Ingersoll, and other distinguished lecturers. He came to esteem all protagonists of freedom, and Tom Paine, Patrick Henry, and John Brown ranked high among his heroes. As he had frequent occasion to speak in public, he tended to emulate the orators he admired. At first haltingly, but soon with effective fluency, he developed an eloquence which later made him one of the best platform speakers of his time. His oratorical style, at once poetic and passionate, fervent and gentle, held the attention of his hearers even when he assailed them with the barbs of his pointed thoughts.

When he quit his job as fireman he did not cease to think of himself as a railroad man. Early in 1875 he became a charter member and secretary of the Terre Haute lodge of the Brotherhood of Locomotive Firemen. He also helped in the organizing of the brakemen and switchmen. In all his activity he was motivated solely by the altruistic belief that unionization would enable railroad workmen to obtain better working conditions. Although still in his early twenties, he took a prominent part in the work of his lodge. In 1877 he attended the Locomotive Firemen's convention, at which he spoke against strikes and bloodshed and urged the members to behave as respectable men and get what they wanted by honorable means. Two years later, already assistant editor of the *Locomotive Firemen's Magazine,* he declared in convention: " Our organization believes in arbitration. All differences should be settled in this way, for no good has ever or can ever come from resorting to violence and bloodshed." Still later, speaking as one of the popular labor leaders of the Middle West, he asserted: " We are not engaged in any quarrel between capital and labor. . . . All we ask is an honest day's wages for an honest day's work, and we are willing to be considerate and just." It was not till after 1886, when his heart became hardened by repeated rebuffs from the railroad companies, that he justified the strike as a weapon of labor.

Debs was elected City Clerk of Terre Haute in 1879 and was able to give up his job with the grocery firm. A year later he was urged to become secretary-treasurer and editor-in-chief of the Brotherhood of Locomotive Firemen, offices which he accepted in order to save the organization from the complete collapse towards which it had been drifting during the depression of the late 1870's. The heroic task before him excited his enthusiasm and he devoted himself to it with tireless energy and enterprise. Railroad firemen responded to his urging to join the Brotherhood and began to take pride in their membership. In much less time than anyone had expected he succeeded in putting the union on a sound basis. Long afterwards he commented: " I worked that year as I never worked before — it was slavery. For six years I knew no Sunday. I used my salary as City Clerk. I worked one year for nothing and paid out $800 for the Brotherhood."

In 1884 he was elected to the Indiana legislature on the Democratic ticket, but the collusion and callousness of his fellow representatives quickly disgusted him and he refused again to participate in politics. During his year of office he wooed and married Katherine Metzel, who became his lifelong and devoted companion and supporter.

In the course of the 1880's Debs learned from painful experience as a labor official that craft unions divided workmen against one another and thus weakened their bargaining powers with their employers. As the railroads and other large corporations developed monopoly strength, it became necessary for their employees to make a united stand in order to obtain their due demands — and this they could not do as members of unco-operating craft unions. These unions, moreover, discouraged the organizing of the less skilled workers, thereby keeping hundreds of thousands of men out of the Brotherhoods. Speaking in 1905, long after he had left his union, Debs stated:

I aver that the old form of trade unionism no longer meets the demands of the working class. I aver that the old trade union has not only fulfilled its mission and outlived its usefulness, but that it is now positively reactionary, and is maintained, not in the interests of the workers who support it, but in the interests of the capitalist class who exploit the workers who support it.

In later years he was to insist that " the most important fact in all the world for workingmen to take cognizance of is the class struggle," but in the early 1890's this theory had not yet percolated into his conscious thought. The industrial union was then his answer to the vexing problem of strengthening labor against capital. After long heart-searching — " my conscience would not allow it " — he decided to resign from the Brotherhood of Locomotive Firemen, which was paying him a salary of $4000, and to issue a call for the formation of the American Railway Union along industrial lines. " It has been my life's desire," he stated in the announcement, " to unify the railroad employees and to eliminate the aristocracy of labor which unfortunately exists and organize the workers so all will be on an equality." He also promised that if he rose — his salary as president began with $75 a month — " it will be *with* the ranks, not *from* them." So successful was his campaign that within a year the handful of charter members grew to 150,000.

In April 1894, the Great Northern Railroad, controlled by " empire-builder " James J. Hill, announced a cut in wages. Times were hard and work scarce, but the employees rebelled at this latest effort to lower their standard of living, already at a mere subsistence level. Debs shared their resentment and agreed to call them out on strike. The response exceeded his best hopes. At the victory celebration he related:

From the hour the strike commenced, the men were united; they stood shoulder to shoulder — engineers, firemen, brakemen, conductors, switchmen, even the trackmen and the freight handlers, who are generally the first to suffer, stood up as one man and asserted their manhood. . . . As a result of this unification, this show of manliness and courage on the part of the employees, they gained 97½ per cent of what they claimed as their rights.

Mr. Hill's frantic efforts to break the strike were in vain. Debs and his lieutenants managed not only to keep the workers away from their jobs but also to gain the sympathy of the general public. No blood was shed; no rioting or sabotage occurred. After eighteen days, Mr. Hill capitulated and the American Railway Union had won its first strike. Debs's reputation as a labor leader spread across the land with telegraphic speed.

Encouraged by this labor victory, the employees of the Pullman Company, many of whom were members of the American Railway Union, decided to strike against a wage cut of 25 percent and feudal living conditions. George Pullman, a ruthless and vindictive exploiter of labor despite his humble beginnings, was outraged by this show of rebellion and refused to deal with the union. Not even the urging of leading citizens, including Marcus Hanna, caused him to change his mind. When the American Railway Union met in convention a month later, a delegation of the strikers presented their grievances in open meeting and asked for assistance. Their minister, an idealistic young man, spoke so eloquently and depicted the wretched conditions in his parish so graphically that he infuriated his auditors against Mr. Pullman. They began to clamor for a sympathy strike and voted for it even after Debs had advised them against it. Last-minute efforts at arbitration were balked by Mr. Pullman's adamant refusal to meet with his employees. By June 28, three days after the railroad employees began their sympathetic strike against the moving of Pullman cars, 40,000 men had quit work and both passenger and freight service on lines west of Chicago was practically at a standstill.

The railroad companies might have used pressure on Mr. Pullman to force him to arbitrate; instead they insisted on keeping Pullman cars attached to trains according to contract. They believed the strike was giving them an excellent opportunity to break the power of the American Railway Union and determined to make the most of it. Knowing that they could gain their end best under conditions of disorder and duress, they sought to provoke the strikers into acts of violence. Attorney-General Richard Olney, a former railroad attorney and trusted friend, assisted them in this chicane with the power vested in him by President Cleveland. His first move was to appoint Edwin Walker, another railroad attorney, to act for him in the Chicago courts in obtaining a blanket injunction against the strikers under the Sherman Anti-Trust Act. He then requested the federal marshal to engage as many deputies as were needed for the protection of railroad property. According to the official report of the Federal Strike Commission, which made a thorough investigation of the strike, 3600 deputies " were selected by and appointed at the request of the General Managers Association, and of its railroads. They were armed and paid by the railroads, and acted in the double capacity of railroad employees and United States officers." Debs described these deputies more colorfully, yet not inaccurately:

An army of detectives, thugs and murderers were equipped with badge and beer and bludgeon and turned loose; old hulks of cars were fired; the alarm bells tolled; the people were terrified; the most startling rumors were set afloat; the press volleyed and thundered, and over all the wires sped the news that Chicago's white throat was in the clutch of a red mob.

This vandalism on the part of federal officers was made the excuse for sending federal troops into Chicago to restore order. Olney and his associates, bent on breaking the strike rather than on preserving law and order, had deliberately ignored the availability of the local police and the state militia — although Governor Altgeld held thousands of soldiers in readiness outside the city. It was not until the appearance of the federal troops had precipitated rioting and several deaths that the state militia was called in and quickly stopped the disorder.

Several days later Debs and three other union officials were arrested for violation of the injunction and shortly thereafter they were arrested a second time for contempt of court. They were tried for conspiracy before the judge who had helped Walker with the drafting of the injunction. Deb's testimony before the jury was forthright and impressive. After relating the events leading up to the strike, he declared: " Never in my life have I broken the law or advised others to do so." It soon became obvious to many in the courtroom that the jury would favor the defendants — especially after Mr. Pullman had defied the court and fled from the state to avoid being questioned by Debs's attorneys. The evidence was indeed pointing to the guilt of the railroad managers, who had conspired to break the strike by all means at their disposal. At this juncture the judge announced that, owing to the illness of one of the jurors, he was adjourning the trial — indefinitely, as it turned out. Thereupon he sentenced Debs to six months in jail for contempt of court and the other defendants to three months each. Some time later the United States Supreme Court affirmed this sentence by a unanimous vote.

The arbitrary and questionable behavior of the court was condemned by many outstanding liberals. The eminent Judge Lyman Trumbull declared:

The decision carried to its logical conclusion means that any federal judge can imprison any citizen at his own will. If this be true, it is judicial despotism, pure and simple, whatever you may choose to call it.

The government's own investigating commission likewise reproved the court, intimating that the judges had sentenced the strike leaders without troubling to ascertain their guilt. In its carefully detailed and documented report it concluded:

There is no evidence before the commission that the officers of the American Railway Union at any time participated in or advised intimidation, violence or destruction of property.

It was not surprising therefore that Debs accused the government of collusion with the railroads — of helping them to break the strike after it had been practically won. On entering jail he declared that he had "no apologies to make nor regrets to express. . . . There is not a scrap of testimony to show that one of us violated any law whatsoever. If we are guilty of conspiracy, why are we punished for contempt?" Nor was he considered guilty by the mass of workers. On his release from Woodstock prison in November 1895, he was greeted in Chicago by a crowd of over 100,000 admirers who cheered him as their hero. The Chicago *Evening Press* wrote the next day:

Had he been the victorious soldier returned fresh from conquest instead of a convict liberated from prison, his welcome could not have been more spontaneous, enthusiastic, sympathetic.

This extraordinary popularity made Debs a marked man in the eyes of the railroad managers. His efforts to revive the American Railway Union were met at every point by antagonism and intimidation. Railroad detectives followed him everywhere, and the men who dared see him or attend his meetings were fired forthwith. After more than a year of grim persistence he realized the futility of his effort and gave up. On June 18, 1897, he wound up the affairs of the defunct union and personally assumed its debts, amounting to $22,000 — which he paid in full sixteen years later out of fees for lectures on socialism.

[493]

Deplorable labor conditions in the decade after 1885 drove Debs slowly but inevitably towards an acceptance of socialism. Acutely sensitive to injustice and poverty — " when I see suffering about me, I suffer myself " — he grew more and more resentful at the increasing inequality about him. As a conscientious union leader he came in daily contact with labor grievances, unemployment, undeserved misery, His faith in the efficacy of industrial organization gave him a quiet confidence — until he was suddenly confronted by the machinations and ruthlessness of the railroad companies in the Pullman strike.

At this juncture there were delivered, from wholly unexpected quarters, a quick succession of blows that blinded me for an instant and then opened my eyes — and in the gleam of every bayonet and the flash of every rifle *the class struggle was revealed*. This was my first practical lesson in Socialism, though wholly unaware that it was called by that name.

Some months later, testifying before the Federal Investigating Commission, he revealed familiarity with the basic doctrine of socialism when he declared: " I believe in a co-operative commonwealth as a substitute for the wage system." Subsequently, while in jail, he received and read a good many books and pamphlets dealing with social problems. Victor Berger, already a socialist leader, visited him and presented him with a copy of Marx's *Capital*. The prison thus became Debs's college. " I began to read and think and dissect the anatomy of the system in which workingmen, however organized, could be shattered and battered and splintered at a single stroke." By the time he left Woodstock he was a confirmed socialist.

In the political campaign of 1896 he favored Bryan because the radical Democratic platform came closest to his own demands and because he " believed that the triumph of Mr. Bryan and free silver would blunt the fangs of the money power." After the election, however, he definitely turned toward socialism. His first move was to organize The Brotherhood of the Co-operative Commonwealth — a utopian scheme of western colonization. The influence of more experienced socialists caused him to abandon the project and to form the party of Social Democracy. In a circular letter to his friends in the labor movement he wrote:

The issue is Socialism versus Capitalism. I am for socialism because I am for humanity. We have been cursed with the reign of gold long enough. Money constitutes no proper basis of civilization. The time has come to regenerate society — we are on the eve of a universal change.

The colonizers in the party broke away in 1898. Debs and those who remained with him then organized the Social Democratic party. Two years later the party was considerably strengthened by a union with the former members of the Socialist Labor party, who had revolted against Daniel De Leon's domination. In the national elections that year Debs was its nominee for President and polled nearly a hundred thousand votes. The following year the organization assumed its permanent name of Socialist party.

From this point till near the end of his life Debs remained the titular head of the party and was intimately identified with the American radical movement. He led the party's ticket in the next three Presidential elections. His magnetic personality, effective oratory, and tireless energy combined to make him welcome even to those who continued to regard socialism with deep suspicion and to vote for the major parties. According to Upton Sinclair: " Debs's meetings were extraordinary. The largest halls were engaged; admission was charged to all meetings. Yet rain or shine the halls were packed." In the 1908 campaign he and his ever-faithful brother Theodore toured the country in the " Red Special " and remained on it for 65 days. Four years later, despite the confusion and divided loyalties resulting from the candidacies of Theodore Roosevelt and Woodrow Wilson, Debs polled close to a million votes. He begged off making a nationwide campaign in 1916, but four years later, while serving a long prison term in the Atlanta federal penitentiary, he accepted the Presidential nomination and once more received nearly a million votes. In 1924, again at liberty but in poor health, he advised his socialist followers to join with the organized labor and liberal groups in backing the candidacy of the elder Senator La Follette.

Debs rooted the doctrines of socialism deep in his heart. While not of a dogmatic or doctrinaire temperament, being in this respect the opposite of Daniel De Leon, he dedicated himself to his new social vision with a truly evangelical spirit. Uninterested in the dry bones of Marxist theory — being more the missionary than the metaphysician — he developed his vision of the socialist commonwealth in glowing perspective. For years on end, as a journalist and lecturer and political campaigner, he expounded his view of society with zeal and poetic appeal.

In his lectures and writings he popularized the socialist doctrine that capitalism, while a necessary phase in social evolution, had outlived its usefulness and had to give way to the socialist commonwealth. His long and intimate familiarity with capitalistic practices enabled him to demonstrate concretely and persuasively that our economic system was shot through with parasitic corruption. " Capitalism is inherently a criminal system for it is based upon the robbery of the working class and cornerstoned in its slavery." Again and again he assured his attentive auditors that they produced all the wealth but received only a subsistence wage in return, while millionaire wastrels produced nothing and reveled in luxury. The remedy, he asserted, lay in the public ownership of the tools of production. " The working class alone made the tools; the working class alone can use them; and the working class must, therefore, own them." He pointed out, however, that this condition could not be achieved by means of petty and piecemeal reforms; that no reform was genuine which did not aim at the abolition of capitalism. " Government ownership of public utilities," he offered in illustration, " means nothing for labor under capitalistic ownership of government."

In preaching socialism to American workers Debs affirmed that

[496]

its basic aim was not to reform current evils but to abolish the system that produced them — to make social revolution.

Socialism is first of all a political movement of the working class, clearly defined and uncompromising, which aims at the overthrow of the prevailing capitalist system by securing control of the national government and by the exercise of the public powers, supplanting the existing capitalist class government with a socialist administration — that is to say, changing a republic in name into a republic in fact.

To those who feared that socialism would destroy the family, religion, and private property, he offered assurances to the contrary: socialism, by abolishing the class struggle and exploitation, would increase the freedom and well-being of every individual. Thus, while " eighty percent of the people of the United States have no property today," socialism will provide " all the private property necessary to house man, keep him in comfort and satisfy his wants." For socialism was merely that phase of civilization " in which the collective people will own and operate the sources and means of wealth production, in which all will have equal right to work and all will co-operate together in producing wealth and all will enjoy all the fruit of their collective labor."

In the 1900's radicals reveled in talk of revolution, and the term became one of Debs's readiest watchwords. In a May Day address in 1907 he declared: " The most heroic word in all languages is REVOLUTION. It thrills and vibrates; cheers and inspires. Tyrants and timeservers fear it, but the oppressed hail it with joy." In the previous year, on learning of the illegal kidnapping of Moyer, Haywood, and Pettibone, officers of the Western Federation of Miners, and their arrest on the charge of having murdered former Governor Steunenberg of Idaho, he wrote an inflammatory front-page editorial in *Appeal to Reason* in which he warned the mine owners and the public officials serving them against the planned injustice.

Nearly twenty years ago the capitalist tyrants put some innocent men to death for standing up for labor. They are now going to try it again.

Let them dare! There have been twenty years of revolutionary education, agitation and organization since the Haymarket tragedy, and if an attempt is made to repeat it, there will be a revolution and I will do all in my power to precipitate it.

At the time he was strongly condemned by many editors and politicians, and President Theodore Roosevelt referred to him scathingly as an " undesirable citizen." Debs disregarded these attacks and persisted in his encouragement of workers to stand up for their rights. In 1914, during the bloody miners' strike in Colorado, he urged labor unions to provide the strikers with the same kind of high powered rifles as the company gunmen used. " Every district should purchase and equip and man enough Gatling and machine guns to match the equipment of Rockefeller's private army of assassins."

For all his violent speech Debs was, like De Leon, a thoroughly peaceable man. Although he knew that capitalism could not be abolished without a revolution and was ready to precipitate it for the success of socialism, he usually shied away from all forms of violence. " To the extent that the working class has power based upon class consciousness, force is unnecessary; to the extent that power is lacking, force can only result in harm." As a labor leader he never sought to provoke a strike and always tried to settle industrial differences by negotiation and arbitration. And although he was one of the organizers of the Industrial Workers of the World, he was opposed to sabotage and fought the syndicalists within the union.

Debs's faith in socialism strengthened his belief in industrial unionism. Like De Leon, he conceived of both movements as two aspects of the inevitable drive towards the overthrow of capitalism. " There is but one hope," he stated, " and that is the economic and political solidarity of the working class; one revolutionary union, and one revolutionary party." To press this doctrine home he ignored the advice of fellow socialists and spoke out openly and unmistakably in favor of industrial unionization. Over and over he stressed this point of view before his audiences:

You have got to unite in the same labor union and in the same political party and *strike and vote together,* and.the hour you do that, the world is yours.

Almost from the beginning Debs found himself at odds with the parliamentarian socialists who maintained that the party must maintain a neutral position toward trade unions in order to gain adherents from all factions of labor. These intellectuals and dogmatists, while eager to capitalize on Debs's popularity among the mass membership, feared his uncompromising attitude and revolutionary zeal and combined to keep him off the controlling executive committee until near the end of his life. They saw to it also that he did not write the party platform on which he campaigned five times for the Presidency; nor was he ever chosen to represent the party at international socialist conferences. They praised him as their unrivaled mouthpiece, but they arrogated to themselves the power of policy-making.

Debs was not unaware of his anomalous position within the Socialist party, but his deep devotion to the ideal of socialism kept him from making an issue of it. Only when principles were involved did he stand up and fight. He challenged the party functionaries, many of whom were receiving ample incomes as officials of trade unions, when they tried to stop his advocacy of industrial unionism. Indeed, he strongly opposed any dealing with the corrupt and reactionary craft unions. " Not for all the vote of the American Federation of Labor and its labor dividing and corruption breeding craft-unions should we compromise one jot of our revolutionary principles."

In 1911, when the Socialist party was achieving its fastest growth, Debs became deeply perturbed by the policy of compromise with which party organizers sought to gain new members. The influx of middle-class intellectuals troubled him particularly, as he doubted the genuineness of their conversion. Knowing that the executive committee would again insist on his heading the party ticket in the coming election, he wanted to make his position clear and definite.

In an article entitled " The Danger Ahead " he earnestly cautioned his fellow socialists not to seek votes at the cost of principles.

To my mind the working-class character and the revolutionary integrity of the Socialist party are of first importance. All the votes of the people would do us no good if our party ceased to be a revolutionary party, or came to be incidentally so, while yielding more and more to the pressure to modify the principles and program of the party for the sake of swelling the vote and hastening the day of its expected triumph.

He insisted that socialist propaganda must be forthright and fearless, aimed at those who logically should belong to the socialist movement and who could be won over by intelligent reasoning. He consequently urged the party to concentrate upon the ranks of labor. By helping workers to develop their economic powers through efficient industrial organization, he argued, it would gain their political support and thus achieve a solid foundation.

This critical attitude he maintained till near the end of his life. As late as 1920, when asked to head the party's ticket from his cell in the Atlanta prison, he accepted only after again warning the leaders against compromise and opportunism. " There is a tendency in the party to become a party of politicians instead of a party of workers. This policy must be checked, not encouraged. We are in politics not to get votes but to develop power to emancipate the working class." By that time, however, the politicians had taken the party too far along the road of expedience to prevent its disintegration and decline.

The outbreak of World War I in 1914 affected Debs with both sorrow and anger. A gentle humanitarian and a genuine internationalist — " I have no country to fight for; my country is the earth, and I am a citizen of the world " — he regarded the carnage in Europe as the inexcusable folly of rival imperialisms in quest of markets for exploitation. Fearing that this country would be drawn into the conflict unless the people insisted on our remaining neutral, he devoted all his powers to the task of explaining to American workers the madness and cruelty of war.

Capitalist wars for capitalist conquest and capitalist plunder must be fought by the capitalists themselves so far as I am concerned. . . . No worker has any business to enlist in a capitalist class war or fight a capitalist class battle. It is our duty to enlist in our own war and fight our own battles.

He stated that he would rather go to jail or even face a firing squad than favor the warmongers with a single word of approval. Yet he made it clear that he was against the war not because he was a pacifist but because he was a revolutionist.

No, I am not opposed to all wars under all circumstances, and any declaration to the contrary would disqualify me as a revolutionist. When I say I am opposed to all wars I mean ruling-class war, for the ruling class is the only class that makes war. . . . I am opposed to every war but one; I am for that war with heart and soul, and that is the world-wide war of social revolution. In that war I am prepared to fight in any way the ruling class may make it necessary, even to the barricades. That is where I stand and I believe the Socialist party stands, or ought to stand, on the question of war.

When our armies began to march in 1917, the government proceeded to crush all opposition to war with a mailed fist. Freedom of speech, of press, of assembly — these basic rights were scorned by officers of the law and the judiciary as if their exercise were a brash indulgence. As Professor Zechariah Chafee pointed out in *Freedom of Speech*:

The great trouble with the most judicial construction of the Espionage Act is that this social interest has been ignored and free speech has been regarded as merely an individual interest, which must give way like other personal desires the moment it interferes with social interest in national safety.

Debs, an intense libertarian, watched this outburst of intolerance with increasing resentment. He was determined to exercise his inalienable rights as an American citizen regardless of the consequences.

They are trying to send us to prison for speaking our minds [he wrote]. Very well, let them. I tell you that if it had not been for men and women who in the past have had the moral courage to go to prison, we would still be in the jungles.

When a number of his radical friends were imprisoned for saying what he believed, he felt he had no right to be free. After due deliberation he decided to disregard the Espionage Act and speak his mind without restraint.

His opportunity came in June 1918, when he addressed the Ohio state convention of the Socialist party at Canton. Having visited three imprisoned socialists on his way to the meeting, he began his speech with a eulogy of these men. For nearly two hours he discussed the growth and purpose of the socialist movement, the injustices perpetrated on friends of his for speaking their minds on the war, why wars were begun and who died in them, and the hope of labor in the Russian Revolution. He told his audience that capitalist wars resulted only in losses so far as the people were concerned. " The working class who make the sacrifices, who shed the blood, have never yet had a voice in declaring war. The ruling class has always made the war and made the peace."

Debs's arrest followed. At the trial in September he permitted no witnesses to take the stand in his behalf and offered no defense. Nor did he deny any part of his speech. In his talk to the jury he maintained that he had said nothing wrong, that in opposing the war he was in the company of distinguished Americans who had opposed earlier wars, and that every statement he had made was borne out by President Wilson in his book, *The New Freedom*.

From what you have heard in the address of counsel for the prosecution you might naturally infer that I am an advocate of force and violence. It is not true. I have never advocated violence in any form. I always believed in education, in intelligence, in enlightenment, and I have always made my appeal to the reason and to the conscience of the people. . . . I have been accused of obstructing the war. I admit it. Gentlemen, I abhor war. I would oppose war if I stood alone. . . . I have sympathy with the suffering, struggling people everywhere. It does not make any difference under what flag they were born, or where they live, I have sympathy with them all. I would, if I could, establish a social system that would embrace them all.

The jury was duly instructed by the judge and soon reached a verdict of " guilty as charged in the indictment." Two days later Debs took advantage of the opportunity to address the court before being sentenced.

Your honor [he began], years ago I recognized my kinship with all living beings, and I made up my mind that I was not one bit better than the meanest on earth. I said then, and I say now, that while there is a lower class, I am in it; while there is a criminal element, I am of it; while there is a soul in prison, I am not free. . . . In the struggle — the unceasing struggle — between the toilers and producers and their exploiters, I have tried, as best I might, to serve those among whom I was born, with whom I expect to share my lot until the end of my days.

He reiterated his opposition to a system in which a few control most of the wealth and the large masses of workers are kept at a low subsistence level. Such a system, he asserted, had to be replaced by a socialistic commonwealth. " Let the people take heart and hope everywhere," he concluded, " for the cross is bending, the midnight is passing, and joy cometh with the morning."

The judge listened to him patiently, denounced those "who would strike the sword from the hand of this nation while she is engaged in defending herself against a foreign and brutal power," and sentenced Debs to serve ten years in prison. An appeal was at once made to the Supreme Court to invalidate this judgment. A half-year later — four months after the war had ceased — Justice Oliver Wendell Holmes delivered the opinion of the Court upholding the conviction and sentence. He did not apply to this case his famous test of " clear and present danger " which in similar cases was to cause him later to reverse himself. Debs was not surprised.

He accepted the verdict as in keeping with the character of the Court " as a ruling-class tribunal."

Great issues are not decided by courts but by the people. I have no concern in what the coterie of begowned corporation lawyers in Washington may decide in my case. The court of final resort is the people, and that court will be heard from in due time.

In his sixty-fifth year and suffering from lumbago, Debs entered the West Virginia State Penitentiary at Moundsville ready to spend the remainder of his life behind prison bars. His outer acquiescence merely accentuated his boldness of spirit. " I enter the prison doors a flaming revolutionist — my head erect, spirit untamed and my soul unconquerable." This militancy expressed itself in his implicit faith in the Russian Revolution. He heartily supported it " without reservation." Although the subsequent bloodshed in Russia made his " heart ache to think of it," he argued that " during the transition period the revolution must protect itself " and persisted in the belief that out of this violence would emerge the first socialist commonwealth. Later, however, he refused to leave the moribund Socialist party and join the communist faction which made Soviet Russia its chief interest.

As a revolutionist he refused to accept any favors or special privileges from the prison warden. When he was transferred to Atlanta, where he was forbidden to receive the periodicals he had been in the habit of reading and where his health deteriorated, he rejected the offer of influential friends to intercede in his behalf. When some of his admirers petitioned the government for his pardon, he discountenanced their efforts. " To ask a pardon," he explained, " would be to confess guilt." Nor would he accept an unconditional pardon " unless the same pardon were extended to every man and woman in prison under the Espionage Law." His friends soon learned, moreover, that President Wilson, ill and embittered, was determined to keep Debs in prison as long as possible. To his secretary Joseph Tumulty he said: " I will never consent to the pardon of this man. . . . This man was a traitor to his country, and he will never be pardoned during my administration." This was not the attitude of many enlightened Americans, of course, and even the conservative New York *Times* stated editorially in 1920 that " Mr. Debs was convicted for making a socialist speech. No sane person considers him a criminal." Nevertheless the old and ill radical remainéd in the Atlanta penitentiary until the day before Christmas 1921, when he was released by easy-going President Harding. No pardon was given him, and his citizenship was never restored.

Although Debs left Atlanta in poor health, he refused to take refuge in political retirement. There was so much to do! The plight of the socialist movement, broken by the government and bled by factional strife, stabbed him to the quick; the sufferings of the men and women who remained in prison because of their beliefs tugged at his conscience; the very thought of the prison system, which he regarded as " essentially an institution for the punishment of the poor," roused his fiery indignation. He declared optimistically that in many parts of the world socialism was on the march and that no amount of repression would prevent its ultimate triumph. In his articles on his prison experience as well as in his posthumously published book, *Walls and Bars,* he wrote with impassioned eloquence of his hatred of prisons and condemned " the social system which makes the prison necessary by creating the victims who rot behind its ghastly wall."

Even his indomitable spirit, however, could not for long ignore the ravages of illness and old age. The years of incarceration had sapped his vitality. Sojourn in a sanatorium proved of little avail. Nor was his spirit strengthened by the bickering and bitterness within the radical movement. He died on October 20, 1926, in his seventy-first year.

Eugene V. Debs, outstanding American radical, represented the socialistic aspect of the Jeffersonian spirit of democracy as truly as Henry D. Thoreau exemplified its individualistic strain. He was cradled in an atmosphere of freedom and equality. His radicalism, even as that of the Abolitionists and other nonconformists, originated in his love of mankind and hatred of oppression. That it took an economic rather than a religious or political turn was due mainly to the peculiar circumstances in which he found himself. He began to work in a factory at the age of fourteen, and came up against American industrialism during its first efforts at large-scale expansion when its ruthless oppression of labor could not but antagonize many employees and provoke periodic strikes and disorder. Debs early became a union member as a matter of course. Experience taught him that craft-unionism was unable to cope with monopoly capitalism; that only the unionization of an entire industry would give the workers an adequate weapon against oppressive corporations. To this end he resigned his office in the firemen's union and organized the American Railway Union. His radicalism might not have progressed further if he had not been made the victim of the combined might of the federal government and the organized employers. But the injustice and chicane that destroyed the American Railway Union gave him an unforgettable lesson in the Marxian doctrine of the class struggle. His Jeffersonian sense of equality readily led him to embrace socialism as a means of establishing economic democracy — which he perceived as the genuine basis for political democracy.

Possessed of deep faith in the natural goodness of man and of a speaking voice that warmed the heart, he soon became the leading radical orator of his day. He began to propagate the gospel of social and economic equality among the masses of the people — for that was to him the essence of socialism. Professors Perlman and Taft have well characterized him in Volume Four of Commons's *A History of Labor in the United States:*

Debs was the evangelist of socialism for more than a quarter of a century. He had no equal in arousing a labor audience to a high pitch of generous idealism. Through the genuine passion of his humanitarianism, he produced in his hearers the deepest emotion of self-forgetful solidarity with all sufferers regardless of their race, nationality, or country.

JOHN REED

REBEL INTO REVOLUTIONARY

JOHN REED never quite lived down his early reputation as a playboy. Even after he had become a thorough radical and willingly
suffered ostracism, imprisonment, hunger, and death as a consequence, he continued to be regarded as "the playboy of the
Social Revolution." Nor can it be denied that during his long adolescence he was a playboy and prankster, or that he ever lost his
characteristic ebullience of spirit. Yet to stress this part of his personality is to do him a grave injustice: it implies not only a misunderstanding of the inner working of his mind but also a disrespect
for the idealism which led him to martyrdom.

After an ailing and timid childhood, during which he " fed on
fantasy" and dreamt defiance, Reed entered adolescence with a
surplus of physical energy. As a son of the frontier, he took naturally to horseplay and practical jokes as a means of gaining attention. He was also, however, a budding poet and a warm admirer of
his politically insurgent father, who was instrumental in exposing
the land-grabbing of the lumber and railroad companies. In Portland, Oregon, where John Reed was born in 1887, he belonged to
one of the leading families; at Morristown School in New Jersey,
which he entered at the age of sixteen, he was an outsider and on
his own. Eager though he was for social approval, he simply could
not conform to rules. The spirit of the pioneer — a yearning for
complete freedom of action coupled with a craving for acceptance
— moved him to seek success by accentuating his nonconformity.

[507]

His pranks and escapades, while exasperating to the authorities, made him a hero to his fellow students. He spent two happy years at Morristown.

At Harvard, to which he went in 1906, he was for a time " desperately lonely." His persistent efforts to gain friends, to make teams, to join social clubs proved of little avail. He was made to feel that he did not belong, and he was snubbed by those who did. Hurt but determined, he engaged in activities open to outsiders. But the snubs rankled and roused in him the perverse impulse to shock and irritate the " aristocrats." Literary success, while then less precious to him than social prestige, enabled him to spite and scoff at his detractors. His exuberance overflowed in all directions, and he soon became one of the student leaders of the college. Yet his ego continued to feel hurt and resentful. " The more I met the college aristocrats, the more their cold, cruel stupidity repelled me. I began to pity them for their lack of imagination, and the narrowness of their glittering lives — clubs, athletics, society."

Although Reed was an indifferent student, he worked hard at the subjects that interested him and he was strongly influenced by Professor Charles Copeland. He wrote a great deal and composed the lyrics for the senior operetta. As cheer leader at the football games he shocked the conservative snubs by the excitement he generated among the students. He was also a member and officer of several organizations and took an interest in the newly formed Socialist Club, of which Walter Lippmann was the leader. For his boisterous effervescence contained a core of idealism — compounded of the pioneer's inchoate yearnings for freedom and equality and justice — which differentiated him from the mere playboy.

Eager to see the world, he decided to go abroad " for a year's happy-go-lucky wandering." He worked his way across the Atlantic as a " bull-pusher " on a cattle-boat, took walking tours over England and through parts of France and Spain, and wintered in Paris. What impressed him most about the French capital was its spirit of freedom. " You cannot imagine such utter freedom," he wrote to a friend. " Freedom from every boundry, moral, religious, social."

He soon tired of idling away his time, however, and decided to return home " to make a million and get married."

He was shocked to find his father in financial straits and to learn that his parents had gone into debt in order that he and his brother might live the life of a rich man's sons. He felt like a cad and decided to go at once to New York to look for work. Having met Lincoln Steffens while at Harvard and knowing him as a friend of his father, he went to him for advice and assistance. The older man, " full of understanding, with the breath of the world clinging to him," gladly became Reed's friend and confidant. " You can do anything you want to," was his assurance to the aspiring youth; " and I believed him," Reed wrote later. At Steffens's recommendation he was employed as a reader of manuscripts and proofs on *The American Magazine*.

To the zestful youth New York was an enchanting city. His gargantuan curiosity kept him on a never-ending quest for local color. Every section of the metropolis drew him with its special allure. He wandered about the streets with hungry eyes and a quick sympathy. The haze of mystery and alien oddity suffused the squalor and shabbiness of the East Side and gave it a glamour which continued to excite him for months on end. He was equally attracted by the splendor of Fifth Avenue, the strange dishes in " wonderful obscure restaurants," the bohemian life about Washington Square, the gay extravagance of Broadway, the quality of pathos in girls on the streets, the vice and corruption practised in dark alleys and gaudy palaces. He went about with joy and wonder in his heart; the poet in him overflowed with images and metaphors. " In New York I first loved, and I first wrote of the things I saw, with a fierce joy of creation — and I knew at last that I could write."

While time never quite rubbed off the glamour of the great city, he soon became aware of the misery that lay underneath. His acquaintance with radicals of all kinds widened his interest in social problems and gave him a clearer perspective of the working of capitalistic society. But he was no intellectual. Theories and abstract principles seldom moved him to action; his sympathies were quickened by what he saw with his eyes rather than by what he perceived with his mind.

On the whole ideas alone did not mean much to me. I had to see. In my rambles about the city I couldn't help but observe the ugliness of poverty and all its train of evils, the cruel inequality between the rich people who had too many motor cars and poor people who didn't have enough to eat. It didn't come to me from books that the workers produced all the wealth of the world, which went to those who did not earn it.

Meantime he had joined the Harvard Club and the Dutch Treat Club, a gathering place for many of the successful writers and artists, and got on a friendly footing with a large number of people of all sorts. He effervesced with energy and gay spirits and often indulged in pranks and acts of merriment. But he also spent the late hours of the night in writing poems and stories, some of which he published in leading magazines. Repeated rejection slips soon convinced him that, unlike many prosperous authors, he could not truckle to those in power; that, for all his eagerness for acceptance and success, he could not write to order. " A real artist," he insisted, " goes on creating for art's sake whether he achieves publication or not." Indeed, a good share of his writing remains in manuscript.

The death of his father in the summer of 1912 brought him back to Portland, where family matters kept him for three months. In a nostalgic mood he wrote *The Day in Bohemia: or Life among the Artists*, a merry, carefree, satirical set of verses on life in Greenwich Village. Many of his friends are depicted in jolly, well-turned lines. In page after page he appears as the zestful playboy, gamboling, parodying, mimicking, having a gay time thumbing his nose at the great and exaggerating the foibles and fancies of the " geniuses in Manhattan's *Quartier Latin*." These verses were studded with nuggets of fine poetry and enhanced Reed's reputation as a writer.

Shortly after his return to New York he achieved similar success with *Everymagazine, an Immorality Play*, which he wrote and staged for the Dutch Treat Club. Again he was the ironic, irreverent, derisive, irresponsible playboy — but with a difference. For in the meantime he had been feeding on the wormwood of editorial rejection, and the anger of the irritated rebel broke through the poet's laughter. The fact was that he learned only after repeated failure to forgo his craving for popular success. When *The Masses* was launched as a radical monthly, he gladly gave it his best work — which the commercial periodicals wouldn't and couldn't use. In this magazine he could freely express his growing dissatisfaction with things as they were, and he remained intimately associated with it to the very end of his life.

John Reed had his father's sympathy for the underdog, and his uneasy conscience turned his attention to current labor strikes. Inquiry into these social disturbances, he later declared,

brought home to me hard the knowledge that the manufacturers get all they can out of labor, pay as little as they must, and permit the existence of great masses of the miserable unemployed in order to keep wages down; that the forces of the State are on the side of property, against the propertyless.

He ached to remedy this injustice, but did not know how. Meantime the thought that his " happiness was built on the misery of other people " kept him from acquiescing in the social status quo.

Early in 1913 he learned of the silk weavers' strike in Paterson, New Jersey. Aroused by the refusal of the New York newspapers to report the strike and thus acquaint the public with the workers' grievances, Reed and other sympathizers conceived the idea of bringing the strike to New York by means of a pageant in Madison Square Garden. In Paterson, where he went to meet the strikers, Reed was arrested for refusing to leave the vicinity of the factory and sentenced to twenty days in jail. News of his incarceration broke into the metropolitan press and he was released on the fifth day. But he was in the filthy and overcrowded prison long enough to learn to admire the courage and class-consciousness of the arrested strikers and returned to New York determined to make a success of the pageant. He quit his job on *The American Magazine* and for three weeks he labored day and night in training a thousand strikers to sing and act out " the wretchedness of their lives and the glory of their revolt." No effort was spared to insure the effectiveness of the spectacle, and a good deal of money was spent on decorations and other materials. The newspapers and churches gave the undertaking considerable publicity, but much of it was unfavorable.

Nearly all of the fifteen thousand who came to witness the pageant were poor workers unable to afford the higher-priced seats. In admitting them to the expensive sections the managing committee sustained an unexpected loss in receipts. The result was a deficit of some $1500 instead of a hoped-for profit. Regarded as a demonstration of the agony and heroism of the strikers, however, the pageant was a phenomenal success. The performers were splendid in their presentation of the strike scenes, in their singing, and in their dignified and dramatic demeanor. The large audience joined them in the singing with a spontaneity and enthusiasm which excited even the callous reporters. Long after the event witnesses spoke of the pageant as the most memorable spectacle in their experience.

Reed " went to pieces nervously " by the end of the evening. Mabel Dodge arranged for their early passage to Italy, she having meantime become his lover. They lived in the privacy of her villa and for weeks their passion for each other excluded the outside world from their consciousness. Yet Reed could not for long ignore the intermittent pricks of conscience. When he learned of the pageant's deficit and of the failure of the strike, he felt like a coward who had run away from a fight. He could not forget " the exultant men who had blithely defied the lawless brutality of the city government and gone to prison laughing and singing," and it hurt him to think that they had finally to capitulate because he and others like him had failed to support them. Yet he had not the strength to break away. Only towards the end of the summer, while recovering from diphtheria, was he able to heed his uneasy conscience and return to New York to face life again.

For several months Reed floundered, feeling confused and dissatisfied. He took the job of managing editor on *The Masses*, but he knew it was only a stopgap and looked for an opportunity to make full use of his talents as a writer. Much as he sympathized with the workers, he could not see his way to help them materially. Most of all he was troubled by his affair with Mabel. He loved her passionately, but her overwhelming affection and jealous possessiveness made him feel like a prisoner. Finally there came a day when he had to run away pell-mell, leaving her the following note: " Good-by, my darling. I cannot live with you. You smother me. You crush me. You want to kill my spirit. I'm going away to save myself. Forgive me. I love you — I love you." And although he soon returned, penitent and eager for reconciliation, the spell of their passion was broken and their intimacy gradually dissipated.

Towards the end of 1913 Pancho Villa's campaign in Mexico became front-page news and a number of seasoned reporters hurried to the border. At Steffens's recommendation Carl Hovey, editor of *The Metropolitan Magazine*, asked John Reed to go to Mexico as a correspondent. The New York *World* likewise accredited him as its representative. Reed was delighted. It was his big chance and he knew it. While other reporters were satisfied to remain at the border and feed on rumor and prejudice, he wanted to see for himself what the fighting was like — and about. Contemptuous of danger and hardship, he made his way into the heart of the revolution. He attached himself to the army of *compañeros* — the poor carefree peons who adored Villa and fought under him to free the land for the people. He found them " wonderfully congenial " and they accepted him without reserve. Villa at once attracted him. Reed perceived in the coarse and audacious Mexican a modern Robin Hood, the friend of the peons, who was devoting his military talents to the destruction of their centuries-old oppressors.

It was characteristic of Reed to side with the rebel Villa rather than with the reformer Carranza — whom he had met and found indifferent to the needs of the peons. It angered him to hear Americans abuse Mexicans as serfs in need of a whip. "The most humble peon," he wrote in their defense, "has a delicacy of tact and a quick intelligence that are not found among any class of any race that I know. There are no people I have seen who are so close to nature as these people are. They are just like their mud houses, just like their little crops of corn." Indeed, he liked the *pacificos* and the *compañeros* for the very things that irritated the conventional Americans. A peon's conception of freedom struck him as

the only correct definition of Liberty — *to do what I want to do!* Americans quoted it to me triumphantly as an instance of Mexican irresponsibility. But I think it is a better definition than ours — Liberty is the right to do what the Courts want.

Reed's Mexican articles and stories, written with intense sympathy and zest, quickly established him as an outstanding reporter. Some talked of him as the American Kipling. Walter Lippmann declared that Reed had "perfect eyes" and an unfailing memory; "whenever his sympathies marched with the facts, Reed was superb." In article after article he wrote carefully of the men he met, the things they did, the places they occupied, the customs they practised, the battles they fought — and every page possessed the color and clarity which gave his work the vivid reality of literary art. *Insurgent Mexico*, comprising this material, still impresses one with its vitality and verbal beauty.

After four months in Mexico, Reed returned to work valiantly to counteract the agitation for intervention. His articles and interviews were given attentive consideration by men of prominence in the government. He even called on President Wilson in order to tell him what he had found in Mexico. He argued that the struggle below the Rio Grande was "a fight primarily for land," that the peons needed land desperately, and that intervention would destroy the gains of the revolution. So incensed was he against the jingo belligerence of American capitalists that he was ready to join the Mexicans in case of war.

About the time of his return to New York the coal strike in Colorado flared into violence. A tent colony of strikers was attacked and burned to the ground by the state militia, causing the death of two women and nine children. Union members and public-spirited citizens all over the country denounced the outrage and sent money and ammunition to the embattled strikers. It was open class war, and both sides prepared for a last-ditch fight. The editors of *The Metropolitan*, eager to capitalize on Reed's popularity, sent him to Colorado to report the strike. The assignment was highly congenial. He had not forgotten the unheroic ending of his part in the Paterson strike and he wished to make amends. After inspecting the pathetic remains of the destroyed colony, interviewing strikers and local witnesses, and listening to the callous and contumelious talk of public officials and leading citizens, he was surer than ever of the side he favored. Making expert use of official documents and reports, he wrote a factual and unequivocal indictment of the coal companies for ruthlessly exploiting their employees in the sordid quest of profits. The editors of *The Metropolitan* got more than they had bargained for, but they were then still liberal enough to publish the essay as it was written.

The outbreak of World War I in 1914 made it inevitable for Reed to go to Europe as a correspondent. He had no stomach for the assignment. War as such did not interest him. He knew enough of the imperialistic background of the strife between German and British capitalists not to be fooled by newspaper propaganda. From his point of view, the war was " a clash of traders." Much as he despised the mailed-fist tactics of the belligerent Prussian, he was nevertheless repelled by " the raw hypocrisy of his armed foes, who shout for peace which their greed has rendered impossible." He was particularly provoked by those American editors who were swallowing British propaganda whole and were tarring the Germans and painting nimbuses about the heads of the Allies. " We must not be duped by this editorial buncombe about Liberalism going forth to Holy War against Tyranny. This is not Our War."

In France he was not permitted to see the actual fighting. Nor did he find the people imbued with a martial spirit. Everything seemed confused, casual, commonplace. He was confronted by apathy rather than stoicism, by acquiescence instead of idealism; by the dull, mechanical drudgery of war. He found nothing of the spiritual glow which burns in a people fighting for freedom.

In Europe I found none of the spontaneity, none of the idealism of the Mexican revolution. . . . Everything had halted but the engines of hate and destruction.

London, which he also visited, dejected him. The patriotism which was aroused in the people by divers means and which manifested itself in a self-immolating zeal, he found at once "magnificent and infinitely depressing." In his article on England, which *The Metropolitan* never printed, he declared: "Do not be deceived by talk about democracy and liberty. This is not a crusade against militarism but a scramble for spoils. This is not our war."

Later he went to Berlin and from there to the front near Lille. He noted the same docility and indifference among the German soldiers as he had among the Allied troops. Neither seemed to be much disturbed by the inhuman slaughter about them. These impressions moved him to write analytically and critically and not with the vivacity and excitement which distinguished his Mexican articles. He knew that his editors were disappointed, but he could not bring himself to write the sort of colored and unrealistic reporting that filled the American newspapers and magazines.

On his return to New York in January 1915, he was depressed to find most people accepting the Allied version as the true account of the war. In a lecture tour he tried to acquaint his auditors with the facts as he had seen them, but it was obvious that most of them were skeptical. When he met Theodore Roosevelt, his father's hero, in the office of *The Metropolitan* he quarreled with him on the subject of military preparedness. In *The Masses* he wrote:

I hate soldiers. I hate to see a man with a bayonet fixed on his rifle, who can order me off the street. I hate to belong to an organization that is proud of obeying a caste of superior beings, that is proud of killing free ideas, so that it may more efficiently kill human beings in cold blood. . . . Military service plants in your body the germ of blind obedience, of blind irresponsibility.

To keep his job with *The Metropolitan* he wrote such pieces as the ironic article on Billy Sunday, then in his heyday as a popular evangelist. He also composed stories based on his experiences in France and a play on American life which was never produced. Then, when not permitted by the French government to return to the Western Front, he and Boardman Robinson, the illustrator, set out to report the war in Eastern Europe. Their seven months in that region provided them with incidents and escapades to fill a book, *The War in Eastern Europe*, notable for its vivid characterization, incisive interpretation, and broad sympathy. The two rovers saw very little of the fighting, but everywhere they came upon the ravages of war. Typhus was decimating Serbia. Refugees crowded the roads and cities. Rumors and intrigues and spying governed the lives of many people everywhere. Some of the soldiers they met had been fighting so long that they had forgotten the ways of peace. " As we saw them they had settled down to war as a business, and had begun to adjust themselves to this new way of life and talk and think of other things."

Their fantastic excursion into Russia gave them a close view of the graft-ridden and caste-controlled army. They saw at first hand the terrible plight of the millions of soldiers who had to fight almost bare-handed and suffer hunger, cold, and disease because of the incompetence and cupidity of their superior officers.

Graft in Russia is on such a naïvely vast scale that it became almost grotesque. . . . Exposure after exposure revealed that the entire intendency was nothing but a mass of corruption; but the trail always led so far and so high that it had to be choked off.

It was this experience that later quickened Reed's enthusiasm for the Russian Revolution. For he sympathized deeply with the common soldier and civilian; their simple courage and geniality under very trying conditions won his complete admiration.

Russian ideas are the most exhilarating. Russian thought the freest, Russian art the most exuberant; Russian food and drink are to me the best, and Russians themselves are, perhaps, the most interesting human beings that exist.

Reed came back to the United States late in 1915 and devoted himself to completing his articles on Eastern Europe. In December he went to Portland to visit his mother. There he met and immediately fell in love with Louise Bryant. " I think I have found Her at last," he confided to a friend. " She's wild, brave, and straight — and graceful and lovely to look at. . . . I think she's the first person I ever loved without reservation." It did not matter to him that she was then the wife of another; it was enough that she returned his love. Not long after, he welcomed her ecstatically to his New York apartment; and their life together was intimate and intense, if not always harmonious, to the very end.

Throughout the ensuing year Reed marked time. He was still with *The Metropolitan* and he also wrote for other magazines, but his heart was not in commercial writing. Interviewing such celebrities as William Jennings Bryan and Henry Ford and reporting political conventions seemed to him futile chores at a time when the nation was being snared into the vortex of war. For *The Masses* he wrote " At the Throat of the Republic," an angry exposure of the groups backing the preparedness agitation. He also wrote against Mexican intervention and warned the country that war with Mexico would be very costly in the lives of American youths. In the Presidential campaign he joined Steffens and other liberals in urging the people to vote for President Wilson as the man who would keep us out of war. Later he admitted apologetically that he had " supported Wilson simply because Wall Street was against him."

All this time he ached to devote himself to creative writing — novels and poems that he felt surging within him. Several times he actually began a novel, but he failed to proceed. He did write sev-

eral short lyrics, including " Fog," a fine and wistful description of
the sensation of dying, but not the long poem that reverberated in
his imagination. How was one to write fiction and verse with the
world gone mad? At this time he was also physically sick. While in
Serbia he had become seriously ill with a diseased kidney and had
since then suffered several attacks. A summer in Provincetown provided no relief, and he placed himself in the hands of a specialist —
having beforehand legalized his union with Louise. The nephrec-
tomy was successful and he left the hospital after a month.

In January 1917, *The Metropolitan* announced that Reed was
about to leave for China to " hold up the mirror to this mysterious
and romantic country." Events, however, moved fast in those days,
and the trip was prevented by America's entrance into the war.
The Metropolitan no longer had any use for Reed, as his views on
domestic affairs clashed with the new policy of the editors. Nor
were other commercial periodicals interested in his writings. In
need of a job, he accepted employment as a feature writer on the
New York *Mail,* unaware that it was secretly subsidized by the
German government. Although he could not always write as he
wished, he was frequently given opportunities to express himself
freely on topics that appealed to him.

He made no secret of his keen opposition to the war. At a pacifist meeting in Washington on the evening that President Wilson
requested Congress to declare war on Germany, he was the only
one to stand up and declare: " This is not my war, and I will not
support it." To a Congressional committee in 1917 he said: " I am
not a peace-at-any-price man, or a thorough pacifist, but I would not
serve in this war. You can shoot me if you want and try to draft
me to fight — " but he was not permitted to continue. His strongest
attacks on the warmakers he published in *The Masses.*

I know what war means. I have been with the armies of all belliger-
ents except one, and I have seen men die, and go mad, and lie in hospi-
tals suffering hell; but there is a worse thing than that. War means an
ugly mob-madness, crucifying the truth-tellers, choking the artists, side-
tracking reforms, revolutions, and the working of social forces.

During this period he read the writings of Marx and Engels in an effort to learn what had caused the failure of the socialists to stop the war. He thought harder than ever before in his life. He now felt himself wholly on the side of the workers — not merely as a sympathizer but as one of them. His Harvard friends shunned him on the street, and men all about him seemed seized with war-madness, but he was determined to persist in the fight for a better world. To take stock of his life up to that time, as if in preparation for a new start, he wrote "Almost Thirty," a posthumously published essay of frank and discerning self-analysis whose conclusion was:

The whole Great War is to me just a stoppage of the life and ferment of human evolution. I am waiting, waiting for it all to end, for life to resume so I can find my work.

In another effort at striking a personal balance he published *Tamburlaine*, a collection of poems "chosen from among the best byproducts of six happy and exciting years mainly devoted to other things than writing poetry."

When it became apparent that the revolution in Russia was not to be choked off midway, John and Louise Reed became very eager to be present at its logical culmination. Since they could take the trip only as correspondents, they began to interview editors for the assignment. Louise managed to interest a press syndicate, but John had become too notorious a radical to be of use to any commercial periodical. Finally friends of *The Masses* provided the necessary money and the couple left for Russia in August. A month later they reached Petrograd. Reed's exhilaration was intense. He was at once aware that events were moving rapidly towards a climax and he wrote to Boardman Robinson:

Joy where there was gloom, and gloom where there was joy. We are in the middle of things and believe me it's thrilling. There is so much dramatic to write about that I don't know where to begin. For color and terror and grandeur this makes Mexico look pale.

His life in Russia became one continuous round of excitement. He was completely in his element. The bold and unfaltering behavior of the Petrograd workers renewed his faith in the reality of social revolution. After reflecting on the increasing cleavage between those who favored the Soviets and those who opposed them, he confided to Robinson: " I have so far learned one lesson, and that is that the working class and the employing class have nothing in common." His thirst for information and his eagerness to see and hear everything of significance made him attend every important meeting, interview every leader who would talk to him, and note carefully every phase of the unfolding social drama. He made no secret of his sympathy for the Bolsheviki — to the deep chagrin of the American ambassador — and was freely admitted to their headquarters in Smolny Institute. Nor was he a stranger in the offices and halls of the other contending factions, and with unflagging fascination he followed their feeble and futile efforts to stay the tide.

Reed was elated when the Bolsheviki, activated by their determined and dominating leader Lenin, struck for political power. He tried to be everywhere at once, and shuttled between the two opposing forces in his wish to observe every move on both sides. He was being educated fast in the making of a revolution — by the only method he was able to assimilate: concrete action. When Lenin refused to compromise at a time when concession seemed inevitable, Reed was quicker to grasp his great generalship than many of the seasoned Bolsheviki. In an article in *The Liberator* (successor to *The Masses*) he summarized the lessons taught him by the revolution:

That in the last analysis the property-owning class is loyal only to its own property. That the property-owning class will never readily compromise with the working class. That the masses of the workers are not only capable of great dreams but have in them the power to make dreams come true.

Aware that the revolution was shaking the whole world, he assiduously collected data, figures, leaflets, newspapers, reports —

every scrap of documentary evidence which recorded the progress of the epochal event. He was determined to record the greatest social cataclysm in modern history so faithfully and factually as to preclude any hostile attempt at distortion. That he was successful in his undertaking became evident after the publication in 1919 of *Ten Days That Shook the World* — still the best one-volume account of the Bolshevik Revolution.

Once the Kerensky government was overthrown, Reed became impatient to return to the United States. He had learned of his indictment together with the other editors of *The Masses,* and he wanted to join them in facing trial. Even more important was his eagerness to tell his fellow Americans about the lessons of the social revolution. Louise left on January 20, 1918, but he waited another two weeks in order to attend the third All-Russian Congress of Soviets. At Christiania he was held up by the refusal of the State Department to visa his passport. During the month and more that he had to wait until his friends in the United States succeeded in getting him on his way again, he busied himself doing odd jobs for local newspapers. He also began the first draft of a book on the revolution, and composed most of the long poem, "America, 1918." In these warm and vivid verses he, the persecuted social rebel, poured forth his deep and abiding love of his native land and his joyous pride in its pulsating and multifarious metropolis. "Dear and familiar and ever new to me is the city / as the body of my lover. . . ." But the nation which he now perceived across the sea, the war-mad and intolerant nation — "Girt with steel, hard-glittering with power" — which was refusing him entrance, her he lost and loved no more.

Reed reached New York late in April. The first trial of the *Masses* editors had ended in a hung jury the day before his arrival. Still under indictment, however, he was interrogated by government agents for eight hours before he was permitted to land and obtain bail for his release. All his papers were confiscated and kept for months despite his anxious efforts to get them back, and he was thereby prevented from writing his book on the revolution. But if he could not record it formally, he could discuss it orally on the lecture platform. This he did with enthusiasm in a series of meetings that took him as far as the Middle West. In Philadelphia the police closed the hall and he was arrested merely for approaching it; in other cities he was threatened with violence; but he persevered in conveying his dramatic message to thousands of interested listeners.

In vain were his efforts to get commercial magazines to publish his articles on what he regarded as the most momentous story he had ever had to tell. Editors who had competed for his work only two years previously now scorned even to see him. *The Liberator* was of course open to him, and there he published his exciting accounts of revolutionary Russia. There, too, he reported the Chicago mass trial of the I.W.W. By this time he had become so indignant at the ruthless persecution of radicals that he dealt harshly with those of his comrades who counseled prudence, and he resigned from the editorial board of *The Liberator* because he could not bring himself to accept responsibility " for a magazine which exists on the sufferance of Mr. Burleson " — the Postmaster General. When the Allies intervened in Russia, he protested vehemently in public meeting and was promptly arrested. " If people," he insisted, " are to be imprisoned for protesting against intervention in Russia or for defending the workers' republic in Russia, I shall be proud and happy to go to jail." He was the playboy no longer.

At the second *Masses* trial Reed admitted freely that he was opposed to the war and that he was a socialist; but he was less candid, though technically correct, when he denied opposing the recruitment of military forces. Again the jury disagreed, obviously unwilling to convict old-line and well-educated Americans for their radical views. The two other indictments against Reed came to a similar end during the following year.

The government having at last returned his confiscated papers, he began to work furiously on the story of the Bolshevik Revolution. Fortified with many documents, newspapers, and his copious notes, he wrote the book anew. Admittedly a partisan in the struggle for Bolshevik control, he " tried to see events with the eye of a conscientious reporter, interested in setting down the truth," yet eager to forge the truth into a weapon against the enemies of Russia. *Ten Days That Shook the World* was published early in 1919 and at once gained acceptance as a work of exceptional merit. Even the enemies of Bolshevism were unable to impugn its historical veracity; those who sympathized with Russia hailed it as a powerful instrument against reaction. The volume sold widely, and its longevity in a popular edition speaks well for its superiority over similar accounts. Lenin warmly approved of the book and wrote in a foreword:

Unreservedly do I recommend it to the workers of the world. Here is a book which I should like to see in millions of copies and translated into all languages. It gives a truthful and most vivid exposition of the events so significant to the comprehension of what really is the Proletarian Revolution and the Dictatorship of the Proletariat.

In Russia alone the volume has sold into the millions, and its popularity in numerous other translations was equally extraordinary.

With this writing done, Reed again plunged into radical activity. He hoped and at times even believed that a revolution was imminent in the United States — the strongest citadel of capitalism. When he was not championing the Soviets, he was busy strengthening the American radical movement. Vehemently opposed to the conservative socialists who argued that "Socialism is really Jeffersonian democracy," he sought to bring all radicals together on the platform of social revolution. He worked daily far into the night, lecturing, debating, writing and editing for left-wing journals. Never before so busy or so serious, he resented Upton Sinclair's reference to him as "the playboy of the Social Revolution." He knew only too well that revolution was a grave and dangerous undertaking.

After months of sparring and maneuvering for advantage, all the radical factions met in Chicago at the end of August 1919 for the final showdown. The foreign groups began at once to form a separate Communist party. Reed and his fellow American left-wingers tried at first to obtain control of the Socialist party; ousted by the conservatives with the aid of the police and unable to get together with the foreign faction, the Left Wing proceeded to organize the Communist Labor party. Throughout the convention Reed worked diplomatically between meetings and fought for his revolutionary program from the floor.

Late in September he left for Russia as the international delegate of the new party to the meeting of the Communist International. Unable to get a passport, he worked his way to Christiania as a stoker. In "White" Finland he had to remain several weeks in hiding before the radical underground was able to smuggle him to the Russian border. After an absence of nearly two years he was distressed to find the people suffering grievously from cold, hunger, and disease. Exposed to the chaos and exhaustion of a crushing war and a social revolution, blockaded and invaded by foreign forces and torn by civil war, they were enduring terrible hardships. Reed was deeply moved by the heroism and sacrifice which enabled them to achieve a measure of social progress despite these overwhelming odds. He felt that the least he could do was to refuse the privileges accorded to him as a distinguished guest and to share the common physical hardship. After finishing some articles suggested to him by Lenin and others, he went about the country to see for himself what was happening on the farms and in the cities, and described his observations in poignant yet sanguine reports to *The Liberator.*

When he learned about his indictment as an organizer of the suppressed Communist Labor party, he decided to return to the United States to stand trial — disregarding warnings that he faced certain conviction. Early in March 1920 he was arrested in Finland and placed in solitary confinement. News of his incarceration did not reach his friends for more than a month. Their frantic efforts to obtain his release were thwarted by an inimical State Department. Finally the Russian government offered two Finnish prisoners in exchange and Reed was released in June. On his return to Petrograd he was suffering grievously from severe malnutrition: his arms and legs were swollen, his body was covered with sores, and his gums were soft from scurvy. Nursed solicitously by Emma Goldman, who had recently reached Russia after her deportation from the United States, he recuperated slowly.

He was still far from well when he began, as a member of the executive committee, to busy himself with preparations for the second congress of the Communist International. At the sessions he was appointed to the committees on trade unions and minor nationalities. He was actively interested in the problem of dual unionism, and he made a speech on the position of the Negro in the United States. Although he failed to have his way on the subject of unionism, he was re-elected to the powerful executive committee.

A few weeks later he and several other leaders of the Communist International went to Baku to attend the Congress of Oriental Nations. Before leaving he had learned that Louise was about to reach Russia, but he felt it his duty to go. At one of the meetings he spoke against American imperialism. "Don't trust American capitalists. There is but one road to freedom. Unite with the Russian workers and peasants." When he returned to Moscow, Louise "found him older and sadder and grown strangely gentle and esthetic. His clothes were just rags. He was so impressed with the suffering around him that he would take nothing for himself." For a week they enjoyed themselves examining the recent changes in the city, visiting leading officials, attending the opera. Then he became ill. He had taken no precaution against disease and now refused to believe he was in any danger. But his condition grew worse and the doctors found him sick with typhus. On Lenin's order he was immediately removed to the best hospital in Moscow and placed under the care of eminent physicians. But the embargo was still in effect and proper medicines were unobtainable. For more than two weeks Reed fought bravely and with all his strength; but the dread disease ravaged his body and finally he died on October 17, 1920. His friend Robert Hallowell, whose portrait of Reed now hangs in one of Harvard's halls, asserted: "His end might have been different if our State Department had not refused to allow medical supplies to go to Russia."

For a week the body lay in state in the Labor Temple, guarded by soldiers of the Red Guard and honored by thousands of Russians as a hero. A large crowd of workers paid homage to him in the Red Square, and a band played solemn music. The grave was dug by the Kremlin wall, where the " holiest of Russia " lie buried, and a number of leaders who knew him well spoke of his work and his martyrdom.

John Reed was essentially a poet, endowed with acute insight and quickened sympathy. He was also a rebel with an excess of physical exuberance; a Westerner scornful of the class-bound East and yet resentful of its unwarranted snobbery. In adolescence he found release in a kind of frontier humor: a clowning suffused with defiance. Contact with the variegated life of New York, and his Paterson experience in particular, served to direct his rebelliousness against social and economic inequality. The peons in Mexico strengthened his attachment to the poor everywhere, and the cold, cruel mass-murder on the war fronts excited his anger against the capitalist class responsible for it. In the process he developed a fierce love of freedom, a strong hatred of oppression, a keen yearning for a society of free men. When the Russian Revolution reached its climax and the Soviets gained control of the government, he sensed a strong affinity with Bolshevism and embraced it. In working for the social revolution he was living the great poem that he had not the time to write. In dying for it he became a legend and an inspiration to those who followed after him and who also felt the fire of freedom in their hearts.

RADICALISM IN PERSPECTIVE

THE CRITICS AND CRUSADERS discussed in this book have, for all their obvious differences, the common quality of radicalism. A radical may be many things and he may be moved by complex motives, but in the last analysis he is an idealist who feels impelled to right existing wrongs. His rebelliousness may be a form of compensation for suffering from authority or poverty, from thwarted ambition or personal maladjustment. But while others who are similarly conditioned, yet lack the noble impulse, become gangsters or millionaires, clowns or cranks, the radical is driven by a messianic urge to remake the world.

There have always been radicals because society has never been free of inequality and oppression. The majority of men, like Cain, are averse to becoming their brothers' keepers; the small band of critics and crusaders, however, emulate Moses in their zeal to deliver their brethren from bondage. They are quick to become indignant at the shortcomings of society and they try to rectify them in ways congenial to their time and culture. From the very beginning of communal life these radicals have held the mirror up to mankind and pointed to the obvious blemishes.

In a very real sense the United States was conceived and firmly established by the radicals of 1776. It was Samuel Adams and Thomas Jefferson and many others like them who risked their liberty, if not their lives, in their efforts to overthrow British rule and unite the colonies into a nation dedicated to the ideals of the Declaration of Independence. Because Jefferson most eloquently expressed the principles of freedom and equality — ideals consonant with the demands of the prevailing handicraft civilization — he became the patron saint of the radicals who came after him. From his time to ours many Americans have found inspiration in the doctrines of Jeffersonian democracy and have fought for them on the platform, in the polling booth, and on the battlefield. It was a continuous struggle because new wrongs always rose, phoenixlike, out of the ashes of old iniquities; yet these idealists, now few and ineffectual and now numerous and strong, were ever ready to battle for the rights of the poor and the oppressed.

Probably no other wrong in the life of the American republic generated so much altruism and exaltation as Negro slavery. Although the Abolitionists were in a sense the apostles of an emerging industrialism, they were even more — at least individually and consciously — the exponents of a democratic ethics. They believed literally that God made all men free and equal and they could not abide the thought that millions of human beings were living in bondage. They insisted on proclaiming their ideal of freedom with a forcefulness that in the end made it irresistible.

The Abolitionists, like other groups of radicals, were not of one mind. Among them were a number of wealthy men who opposed slavery on moral grounds but who were staid conservatives in everything else. The majority might be classed with their leader Garrison: they were genuine democrats who loved liberty and suspected authority; who revered God and challenged orthodoxy; who abominated chattel slavery in the South and failed to recognize the economic oppression of their neighbors who worked in mills and factories. Their radicalism ended with the adoption of the Thirteenth Amendment. Only a few followed Wendell Phillips in the new crusade against industrial exploitation.

After the Civil War the struggle for economic justice brought about a new realignment of forces: it was no longer Southerners against Northerners but the mass of the people against the powerful corporations. The latter were taking full advantage of the prevailing laissez-faire doctrine and were greedily exploiting an almost virgin continent. In their efforts to get rich quick the financiers and managers of the large companies oppressed their workers in the factory and their customers on the farm; in their eagerness to obtain special privileges they corrupted the agencies of government by means of lobbying and bribery.

Radicals and humanitarians readily took up the cause of economic justice. The fight was long and yielded meager reforms. The reason is twofold. The nature of economic democracy directly affects the very life of modern capitalism, since it implies limitations upon the freedom of enterprise that must ultimately dry up the source of the profit motive. Up to the depression of the 1930's businessmen, riding the crest of industrial development, had little difficulty in brushing aside the attempts to impede their progress. The reformers, moreover, either unaware of the logic of their economic doctrine or yielding to wishful thinking on the effectiveness of palliatives, pursued an obsolescent social philosophy and attacked the symptoms rather than the causes of industrial exploitation. Thus they fought for monetary reforms, for honesty in government, for free land, for free trade, for this law and that. Their agitation, however, failed to check the evils of an agressive capitalism. Corporations continued to grow larger, stronger, and more monopolistic.

The complexity of human nature made it inevitable for the critics of the economic status quo to take divergent paths in their eagerness to reach the goal of social democracy. Although the utopians spent most of their idealism on experiments with Fourieristic phalanxes and perfect communities, not a few continued to dream of a paradise on earth. Edward Bellamy conceived his idealized society within the framework of a socialistic economy. When *Looking Backward* won a large number of eager followers, Bellamy devoted himself to the movement he had initiated with an enthusiasm that quickly exhausted his meager strength. The Nationalist party disintegrated after a few years, but the book which had brought it into being continues to contribute to the agitation for economic equality.

Equally utopian but emphatically individualistic were the early anarchists. They believed that all social wrongs were rooted in governmental authority and that the remedy lay in the curbing of this authority. Let each man live as he wished and permit no man to rule over his fellows — and society will function freely, harmoniously, and advantageously. Thoreau had the vision and the courage to demonstrate the feasibility of the anarchistic way of life. For more than a quarter of a century Benjamin Tucker's *Liberty* advocated the philosophy of individualist anarchism with a gusto that made it stand out among the periodicals of the day. In the 1880's other libertarians, recognizing the cogency of industrial interdependence, advanced a theory of communism which eschewed all centralized authority. Their strong attacks upon capitalistic exploitation and their ominous " propaganda of the deed " subjected them to severe persecution and made the term " anarchism " synonymous with violence and criminality. Nevertheless they persisted in holding high the ideal of freedom from restraint and in fighting for the rights of the oppressed.

Although American economists have not especially distinguished themselves either for originality of thought or for radical ideas, several of them have contributed notably to a realistic understanding of modern economic society. Confronted by conditions which did not square with established theory, these few dissidents evolved principles more consonant with the facts as they found them. Their ideas influenced the thinking of many liberals in and out of government service and thereby contributed considerably to social progress. Thus Henry George's economic agitation, which sought to abolish poverty by stopping the private exploitation of land, for a time assumed the character of a crusade. Brooks Adams, having studied the nature and history of Western civilization, pointed out that the greed and blind selfishness of big business were driving the United States to the abyss of revolution. Thorstein Veblen's writings tore the underpinnings from classical economics and demonstrated the obsolescence of the principles supporting the system of capitalism. Although his books had few readers, there were among them those who gave force and direction to our current economic thinking.

The post-Civil War liberals were Jeffersonian idealists. Suspecting bigness and great wealth and provoked by the get-and-grab methods of the aggressive corporations, they saw the country despoiled of its wealth, the nation robbed of its birthright, and the farmers and laborers deprived of their just share. They worked hard to right these wrongs, but their proposed reforms went against the tide of capitalistic development. For a time their spirited agitation could put only an occasional brake upon the aggrandizement of the powerful monopolies or expose the misfeasance of men in office. Nevertheless, the attacks upon special privileges and corrupt government made by Henry D. Lloyd and John Peter Altgeld in the 1890's and by Robert M. La Follette, the muckrakers and the Progressives after the turn of the century prepared the way for the triumphant New Dealers in the 1930's. In the course of this long struggle for social justice, however, radically altered economic conditions forced the liberals to reject the Jeffersonian tenet of a weak government and embrace the contrary principle advocated by Alexander Hamilton. They found that only a strong central government was in a position to cope with the capitalist leviathan and safeguard the rights of the mass of the people.

The Marxian socialists have been the most persistent and the most radical critics of the status quo. Their agitation proved ineffective because their basic principles of the class struggle and the cooperative commonwealth seemed both pernicious and preposterous to a people imbued with the rightness of the laissez-faire doctrine. Few were ready to scrap a system that enabled a poor man to become a millionaire through his own efforts. For many years, therefore, the socialists received the same treatment as the early Abolitionists: they were either scorned or ignored. After 1900 the widespread social consciousness generated by the muckrakers served to give all radicals a favorable hearing. But the success of the Russian Revolution and the after-effects of World War I gave Marxism a frightening immediacy. The resulting hysteria drove most of the socialists into the underground camp of the communists — the faction that had joined the Third International. Relatively few in number and frequently treated like traitors and outcasts, these radicals nevertheless took a leading part in the struggle for social justice.

Notwithstanding their theoretical confusion and wide practical divergence, the various groups opposing the status quo have achieved notable success in their work to strengthen the democratic base of the American people. One need only recall the grievous conditions existing long after the Civil War — when men labored twelve hours a day for subsistence wages, working conditions were brutal and unsafe, trade unions were few and ineffective, social protection was unknown, farmers were at the mercy of the bankers and the railroads, and corporations practised fraud and chicane at will — to realize that the sum of social legislation enacted in recent years is of a truly revolutionary character. It is at least partly due to the agitation of these critics and crusaders that the American people are at present enjoying a combination of political freedom and economic well-being which is the envy of the world.

What of the future? To consider this question is to deal with conditions that differ fundamentally from those that confronted the radicals of the previous century. Before the 1930's men of wealth were firmly in the saddle. They enjoyed the privileges and powers bestowed upon them by a government functioning under a laissez-faire interpretation of the Constitution. For many decades judges upheld the farce of equality under the law, which presumed a day laborer to be as free and independent as his multimillionaire employer. When state legislatures and the Congress, besieged by burdened workers and farmers, agreed to rectify the egregiously bad practices of the corporations, the courts refused to budge from the letter of the law. They declared unconstitutional acts to shorten the hours of labor or to protect workmen against obvious hazards — insisting that these laws deprived individuals of their inalienable right to work where and when they pleased. By the same reasoning they granted injunctions to employers in labor disputes and sanctioned the use of thugs to break up strikes.

Big business enjoyed these privileges until the early 1930's, when the severe economic depression gave rise to the New Deal. The election of Franklin D. Roosevelt on a liberal platform transferred the government of the country to a body of key men — many of whom had grown up under Thorstein Veblen — who knew that the laissez-faire policy had become completely anachronistic in an age of vast technological and electronic development. It was painfully obvious to them that the individual urban workman, entirely dependent upon his job for his livelihood, was not the equal of the wealthy corporation and must be shielded from exploitation and unemployment; that the small investor and the poor farmer were alike in need of protection from Wall Street and from Main Street respectively. To bring our basic law up to date — that is, to rectify existing inequalities — the Roosevelt administration had Congress enact a number of statutes that, taken together, amount to a social Magna Carta. Workmen and farmers were the chief beneficiaries. The National Labor Relations Act not only permitted employees to organize as they wished but also protected them against unfair practices on the part of their employers. What this meant in effect was that the government ceased favoring capital and looked benevolently upon labor. Shrewd union officials, finding the American Federation of Labor unwilling and unwieldy, quickly formed the Committee on Industrial Organizations (later changed to Congress of Industrial Organizations) for the purpose of unionizing the workers in the mass-production industries. Employing such spectacular methods as the " sit-down " strike and mass picketing, labor organizers soon enrolled millions of members into the new CIO unions. Before long there was considerable general improvement in both wage rates and working conditions. By the end of World War II more than fourteen million union members, conscious of their important part in the amazing rise in production, were determined to get their full share of the nation's augmented income.

The wave of large-scale strikes that spread over the country early in 1946 gave employer groups the opportunity to appeal to an inconvenienced and bewildered public against the unions. Many newspapers and radio commentators attacked organized labor as a menace to " the American way of life." Ignoring the claims of union leaders that their demand for higher wages was merely an attempt to meet the increased cost of living, the spokesmen for business organizations maintained that labor had become too powerful for the good of the country and that the remedy was new legislation that would in effect repeal the National Labor Relations Act. This skillful propaganda and the inept efforts of the government negotiators combined to make labor appear selfish and arbitrary. The coal and railroad strikes, affecting the daily lives of the entire people, finally enabled the enemies of labor to persuade President Truman to turn against the unions.

Conservative union officials such as William Green and John L. Lewis, while continuing to think in terms of " pure and simple " trade unionism and refusing to entertain political gestures in the manner of such progressive Labor spokesmen as Philip Murray, Walter Reuther, and Harry Bridges, found themselves fighting back with the same spirit of aggressiveness. All of them, while differing greatly in their labor ideology, manifested a radical temper in their opposition to antilabor attacks. They and many liberals met this challenge with all the resources at their command. No longer, as in the past, few in number and without influence, they stood their ground with strength and determination. They addressed the members of Congress in the name of millions of voters. Their three political organizations — the CIO Political Action Committee, the National Citizens Political Action Committee, and the Independent Citizens Committee of the Arts, Sciences, and Professions — co-ordinated their activities for greater effectiveness. Their strategy was not merely to hold their gains but to strike out for still greater democracy in industry, for increased liberalism in government, and for more intelligent leadership in world affairs.

The outcome is fairly obvious. Labor is on the defensive and by no means so strong as its opponents insist. But in its favor are the positive trends in social and industrial development. There is no going back: science and invention impel us ever forward; and the problems they originate require fresh methods of treatment. The complexity of modern industrialism, requiring large concentration of workers and a completely urban mode of existence, has given organized labor a tremendous potential power; the operation of any major industry has become so essential to the life of the nation that no government can permit its interruption. As a consequence the doctrines of "free enterprise" and "rugged individualism" have gone the way of human slavery and the horse and buggy. It was well enough, for instance, for the government to serve as a silent partner of the railroads in the strike of 1878, when trains were not yet the basic arteries of the nation's lifeblood; the same attitude on the part of the Cleveland administration in 1894 brought forth the Altgeld-Bryan rebellion; to act similarly in 1946 would invite chaos or revolution. In a highly technological society, social planning and control are both necessary and unavoidable. President Truman's proposal to draft strikers and force them to work was a desperate measure and was as regressive as it would be unworkable. And even that formula is based on government operation of the affected industries — which is not at all what the corporations want.

An examination of the problem of capital-labor relations leads, willy-nilly, to the following alternatives: either big business will be intelligent enough to concede the loss of its special privileges and seek a satisfactory working arrangement with labor — and this seems at present highly unlikely — or, on the failure of industrial peace, the government will be forced to take over and operate the basic industries — as Great Britain, France, and other countries are compelled to do by the logic of unavoidable events. Whether the latter solution will lead to state socialism, a modified fascism, or a liberalized communism is for the future to determine.

[537]

THE INTRANSIGENT NEW DEALERS

GEORGE W. NORRIS   HENRY A. WALLACE

HUGO L. BLACK

THE NEW DEAL BACKGROUND

I N MARCH 1933 FRANKLIN DELANO ROOSEVELT took over the slack reins of government. With him were the ardent New Dealers, men of hope and resolution. In the midst of economic despair they preached the glorious future of an America founded on sound enterprise and social reform. Pragmatic optimists, they immediately proceeded to attack the prevailing economic paralysis and to relieve the widespread misery of the unemployed. Congress was called into special session. For one hundred days it was guided, goaded, and cajoled by Roosevelt and his energetic administrators; in that time it enacted more social and experimental legislation than in any other previous session. Nearly every law was an effort to adapt policy to exigency; the aim was to combine recovery with reform. The net result was an upsurge of confidence in the breasts of millions of Americans.

The special session was only a first giant step toward economic revival and social welfare. In the ensuing five years the Roosevelt Administration and Congress strove boldly and persistently, if not always effectively, to prime the economic pump and to improve the lot of "the underprivileged." The most conspicuous and controversial of the early New Deal laws was the National Industrial Recovery Act. An emergency measure, it sought to stimulate business enterprise and to strengthen labor's bargaining power. Antitrust laws were relaxed to permit nearly 750 industry codes to be drafted and approved. Yet the expected cooperation between employers and workers failed to materialize. Soon it became a matter of carrying water in a leaky pail. By the time the Act was voided by the Supreme Court in 1935 it was in general disfavor. The majority of New Deal laws, however, whether temporary relief measures or permanent economic and social reforms, were greatly appreciated by the mass of Americans. In 1934 and again in 1936 New Deal Democrats were re-elected by unprecedented majorities.

Roosevelt was no radical crusader; his was the vision and the boldness of the solicitous liberal. A master politician and shrewdly practical, he made use of his skills to further the ideals of American democracy. Himself a man of wealth, he execrated the rich who abused their economic power. After nearly two years of unceasing exertion, however, he reported ruefully to Congress: "In spite of our effort and in spite of our talk, we have not weeded out the overprivileged and we have not effectively lifted up the underprivileged." He then redoubled his attempts to enact a body of laws that would curb the one and protect the other. It was an uphill struggle, and some of the measures were either distorted in passage or failed to effect their purpose; but the sum of New Deal legislation was a noble monument of social and economic reform.

The great achievements of the Roosevelt Administration have become solidly established in our national life. The banking reforms and SEC went far to remove the abuses at the financial base of our economic system. The Social Security Act was equally effective in building a foundation of insurance against want for the mass of the people. The National Labor Relations Act became the Magna Carta of organized labor and gave unions the impetus to multiply their membership and greatly strengthen their economic position. A long-sought liberal objective, fathered by Senator Norris, was the establishment of TVA, a vast public-utility enterprise that lifted an entire region out of chronic economic distress and made it a model of planned and prosperous civic development. Finally, various laws for the control of staple crops, the establishment of rural banks and rural electrification, and other ameliorative measures went far to give farmers a standard of living comparable to that prevalent for the rest of the nation.

Roosevelt's unfortunate Court fight, the economic recession soon thereafter, and the increasingly threatening fascist menace in Europe served to suspend the fight for further social reform. The vision of effective economic and political democracy, however, remained bright with Roosevelt and his active New Dealers. In his message to Congress at the beginning of the crucial year of 1941, when the thunderhead of war was darkening the American horizon, Roosevelt requested not only appropriations for unrestricted national defense but also the following "basic things" in American economic and social justice:

Equality of opportunity for youths and others.
Jobs for those who can work.
Security for those who need it.
The ending of special privileges for the few.
The preservation of civil liberties for all.
The enjoyments of the fruits of scientific progress in a wider and constantly rising standard of living.

Engulfment in all-out war forced "Dr. New Deal" to give way to "Dr. Win-the-War." In 1944, however, with the fighting turning definitely in our favor, Roosevelt's thoughts began to ponder the nature of peace and the lot of the millions of uniformed men who would soon need jobs and security. With their welfare in mind he proposed to Congress a declaration of an economic bill of rights. His keynote was postwar security "for all—regardless of station, race, or creed." He sought legislation that would establish for every American the right to work, the rights to adequate wages, to a decent living for the farmer, to do business freely, to a comfortable home, to medical care, to social security, and to a good education.

By that time, however, Congress was in control of conservatives who were not interested in social legislation. Roosevelt made no immediate effort to exert pressure on the legislators. Still deeply involved in the war effort and in the preparations for world peace, he merely presented his blueprint for an economic bill of rights and postponed his drive for its enactment.

His sudden death the following year terminated the New Deal. At first President Harry S. Truman tried valiantly to continue the plans and principles of his great predecessor. But while his words approximated Roosevelt's, he lacked the latter's breadth of view and liberality of spirit. Consequently the Fair Deal, for all its brave front, was but a sickly shadow of the New Deal.

Immediately after the fighting ended in the Pacific, Truman sent a message to Congress recommending Roosevelt's bill of rights. Yet it was delivered with feeble conviction and with a pragmatic implication of compromise. In the end only a watered-down portion of the program was enacted into law. His position as a liberal was also weakened by his lack of rapport with the prominent New Dealers in his administration and by their gradual displacement with inferior men who happened to be his cronies.

In his 1948 campaign for the Presidency Truman, banking on the reservoir of liberalism among the mass of voters at the "whistle stops" and hoping to win many of them away from Henry A. Wallace, promised numerous reforms tending toward the welfare state. Nor did he, once victorious, consider these promises mere campaign oratory. In messages to Congress he advocated the repeal of the Taft-Hartley Act—which he had vetoed without success—and legislation furthering low-cost housing, civil rights, fair employment practices, extended social security, and other social-welfare reforms. His appeal was in vain. The cold war, which began after his break with Stalin, had intensified the conservative trend of the nation. Unable to control the members of his own party, lacking the imagination and spirit to dramatize his legis-lative program, he made little headway with a Congress that chose to ignore some of his proposals and to enact others in so garbled and attenuated a form as to impair their original purpose.

The New Deal failed to achieve the liberal goals it had set for itself. It only partially attained for the mass of Americans what the government had from the first done for the wealthy few. In some measure, however, it reversed the aim of previous administrations by assuming that in legislating to make the masses prosperous it provided a base for a sound and thriving economy. Thus more social and public welfare legislation was enacted under Roosevelt's direction than in all the years of our national existence. More important, a number of these laws have become so firmly established and so generally accepted that their repeal is now unthinkable. One need only mention such measures as SEC, TVA, the Social Security Act, and certain banking and labor laws to realize how thoroughly ingrained they have become in the fabric of our national life.

Equally significant of the New Deal period was the spirit of freedom and tolerance it engendered in every sphere of human activity. Americans, as never before, cherished their rights under the Constitution and knew that the government respected the Bill of Rights. Individuals felt free to think as they pleased and to speak their minds without restraint. This prevailing tolerance was all the more appreciated because of the burgeoning dictatorships abroad. Communist and fascist extremists, few in number and quite ineffectual, were permitted to declaim their doctrines as a matter of course. Indeed, during this period the United States was, at least outwardly, truly a land of the free.

In a nation as large and varied as ours no one point of view can prevail without protest from minority factions. Nor was the New Deal an exception. At first, when it stressed recovery and sought to prime the pump of our disabled economy, criticism was only sporadic and inconsequential. Bankers and businessmen, in financial distress, eagerly accepted the proferred assistance from government agencies. Opposition became vociferous, however, when the Roosevelt Administration sought to eliminate business malpractices and to strengthen the right of workers to join unions of their own choosing.

John J. Raskob, former chairman of the Democratic party and

closely connected with powerful corporations, began in 1934 to organize his fellow industrialists "to protect society from the sufferings which it is bound to endure if we allow communistic elements to lead the people to believe that all businessmen are crooks." With the help of Al Smith and the Du Ponts he succeeded in enlisting the support of leading bankers and corporation officials as well as certain conservative publicists. Named the American Liberty League, this group began an intensive campaign in favor of "individual liberty"—by which term they meant freedom of business enterprise without government control of any kind.

In the political campaigns of 1934 and 1936 the Liberty League strongly opposed New Deal candidates. Yet the effect on the mass of voters was negligible. They had no faith in those whom they considered responsible for the depression and only smiled at the bogey of communism.* Their trust went to a man like Senator William E. Borah who asserted that the Du Ponts were invoking the Constitution because "they had just discovered it," and who maintained that "there is no liberty worthy of the name without economic freedom and social justice."

Roosevelt's counter-attack was sharp and crushing. Irritated by accusations of dictatorship and demagogy, he argued that the country was still in the grip of big business. "A small group had concentrated into their own hands an almost complete control over other people's property, other people's money, other people's labor—other people's lives." It was therefore the "inescapable obligation" of the government to re-establish "a democracy of opportunity." His overwhelming victory in November 1936 put an end to the active existence of the Liberty League.

From the outset of the Bolshevik Revolution fear of communism had agitated certain conservative Americans. Bolshevik excesses and the abolition of private property seemed to them an active threat to the American way of life. A sinister parochialism of

---

* When uncapitalized, the term refers to the political philosophy generally, when capitalized, it refers to the political party.

the few Communists in this country in the 1920's only confirmed their worst fears. In 1930 the House established a special committee, headed by the conservative Hamilton Fish, to investigate communist propaganda with a view to legislating its suppression. A few hearings were held, but the House paid little attention to the results. It had to contend with too much real suffering in the land to worry over the agitation of a few Communists. Two years later Martin Dies introduced a bill to combat communism. It actually passed the House but died in the Senate.

Flamboyant oratory continued on the floor of the House against both communism and fascism. Indeed, with the rise of Hitler the invective was weighted against the German *Bund*. Yet no definite action was taken, since neither of these movements really impinged upon the consciousness of the average American. When Dies reintroduced his bill in 1938, however, and stressed primarily the subversive aspects of Nazi propaganda, the House adopted the resolution, 191 to 41, without serious discussion.

At first Dies spoke with studied decorum. Laying down the rules of conduct for the Committee of Un-American Activities he said, "This is not going to be any 'shooting in the dark' inquiry. We want the facts only and when the hearings start we will know where to go and get them." At the first hearing he reiterated his position:

This committee is determined to conduct its investigation upon a dignified plane and to adopt and maintain throughout the course of the hearings a judicial attitude. . . . We shall be fair and impartial at all times and treat every witness with fairness and courtesy. We shall expect every witness to treat us in the same way. This committee will not permit any "character assassination" or any "smearing" of innocent people.

The initial hearings, devoted to Nazi activities in the United States, were conducted with the promised propriety. When the committee next turned to organized labor, its tactics altered drastically. Instead of adhering to facts as it found them, it sought to demonstrate that CIO unions were under communist domination. It encouraged professional anti-communists to take the witness stand and accepted their malicious and irresponsible accusations as reliable testimony. As *Life* remarked at the time, the committee welcomed anyone who "cared to come in and call anybody a red." When union leaders protested, Dies intensified his attack.

One of Dies's most prominent victims was Governor Frank Murphy of Michigan. Toward the end of his campaign for re-election committee witnesses vilified him as a communist supporter. These hearings made glaring headlines in newspapers over the country, especially in Michigan, and thus contributed to his defeat. When President Roosevelt criticized the committee at a press conference, Dies brazenly accused him of trying to sabotage his investigation of communist subversion. With extraordinary impudence and irrational rancor he viciously fulminated against New Dealers and castigated people he did not like. Paul Y. Anderson, noted political journalist, said in a radio speech: "Some of the most fantastic tales ever heard outside of an insane asylum are gravely accepted by the committee without the faintest effort to discover whether the witnesses are credible or responsible or whether they are actuated by ulterior motives." At the end of the 1938 hearings as many as 483 newspapers and 280 labor organizations were termed 'communist-controlled. Many people regarded the committee hearings as pageants in pathology; many more, fearing fire because of the smoke, appeared impressed.

That a majority of Americans, according to an opinion poll, should favor the continuance of the committee after it had made an egregious spectacle of itself was indicative of the fear and confusion beginning to exercise the nation. The bloom of the New Deal, with its euphoric sense of freedom, was losing its freshness. And the persistent shrill alarm against the danger of communism was taking effect. The reports of cruel extermination of kulaks in the early 1930's and the subsequent purges of leading officials and generals only intensified a widespread aversion to "red totalitarianism." Demagogues like Father Coughlin capitalized on this anxiety by fomenting the dread of communist subversion in the United States. The economic recession in 1938 and the persistent high unemployment evoked the fear that capitalism was perhaps as doomed as the Marxists maintained. To add to the confusion, fascism was dramatically and dangerously on the march in Europe and Asia. Under these circumstances it became psychologically convenient for many Americans to regard the Dies Committee as a clumsy but practical watchdog against communist subversion.

The committee continued to hold sensational hearings during the next two years. The refusal of witnesses to cooperate with it gave Dies the opportunity to spread the communist alarm over the front pages of many newspapers. He warned the nation, without troubling to substantiate his statements, that there were around six million subversives in our midst and constituted a real menace. He also boasted that his revelations have educated the public to detect Fifth-Column tactics. For many months he was the only active member of the committee and concentrated his efforts on the vilification of New Deal officials. After several attacks on Leon Henderson, a forthright government administrator, the latter retorted sarcastically: "My original offer still holds good. I will eat on the Treasury steps any subversive organizations to which Mr. Dies proves I ever belonged. Try again, Mr. Dies." Undaunted, Dies ignored challenges and formal requests of proof. Instead he continued to make irresponsible accusations and to announce sensational inquiries which he never carried out. His defeat for a seat in the Senate, however, and the outbreak of war in alliance with Russia served to suspend the committee's activities until 1945.

The increasingly conservative temper of Congress, which in the House helped to continue the Dies Committee despite its deplorable behavior, also manifested itself in a 1939 amendment to the Hatch Act that prohibited federal employees from belonging to an organization "which advocates the overthrow of our constitutional form of government." The next year Congress made it unlawful for a Communist to be on a federal payroll. In the same year it also passed the Smith Act, the first alien and sedition law since 1798. The Act, enacted with little debate or public discussion, provided for the exclusion of aliens advocating the violent overthrow of the government and made it illegal for anyone to teach or advocate, or be a member of an organization that teaches or advocates, the overthrow of the government by force or violence. At the time the measure received so little publicity that few people knew about its existence until the Justice Department invoked it nearly a decade later.

When the House convened in January 1945, Representative John Rankin made the most of clever parliamentary timing to give the dormant Committee on Un-American Activities permanent status, with himself as its chairman. Rankin lacked Dies's impudence and showmanship but not his zeal and bigotry. Louis Budenz, who had left the Communist party and rejoined the Catholic Church, became his star witness and held forth at numerous hearings on the allegedly subversive activities not only of Communist leaders but also of former New Deal officials. In 1946 hearings were devoted to the Joint Anti-Fascist Refugee Committee, an organization helping Spanish refugees who had fought against Franco forces. Members of the board of directors were questioned at length and the committee's records were requested. When this was refused, mainly on the ground that a number of contributors had relations in Spain whose lives would be endangered by publicity, the board members were cited for contempt of Congress and later convicted and sentenced to jail.

The Republican victory in 1946 gave the chairmanship of the Committee on Un-American Activities to J. Parnell Thomas. By this time the United States and Russia were joined in a cold war. News of spying and subversion was featured in the daily headlines. Gradually the previously passive aversion to communism became active and intense. Thomas took quick advantage of this situation. As arbitrary as his predecessors, he launched upon a much-publicized investigation of subversion. His aim was not so much to expose communism as to implicate New Dealers in what he considered communist activities. His definition of a Communist was "anyone who opposes the work of this committee." He permitted irresponsible and biased witnesses to malign loyal public servants and all types of liberals along with a few known Communists.

Under Thomas's guidance the committee became both a sounding board for every type of neurotic and bigoted witness and a center of alarm against allegedly nefarious and dastardly communist plots. Disregarding the climate of tolerance of the 1930's, when entertaining radical ideas was a common and generally innocent quest on the part of many artists and intellectuals, Thomas attached the communist label to all of them. Nor did he make any allowances for a mere adolescent sally or only a brief and casual association with the left. At no time did he trouble to check on the motivation of his witnesses or on the veracity of his informers; once they pointed a finger at anyone, he gleefully pounced upon the victim as if he were a convicted subversive. The traditional rights of the accused meant nothing to him. To a lawyer seeking to protect his client Thomas said, "The rights you have are the rights given to you by this committee."

Hollywood became one of the committee's most productive targets—assuring it a largess of spicy headlines. Thomas charged that it was infested with Communists. Several pictures made during the war that played up Russia as our valiant ally were used as vicious examples of communist propaganda. A number of "friendly" witnesses offered testimony that ranged from penetrating analyses of communist influence to phrenetic or stupid irrelevancies. Ten of the subpoenaed witnesses, all outstanding actors, writers, and directors, refused to answer questions. They maintained that the committee's activities were unconstitutional and that as American citizens they stood on their right not to respond to questions pertaining to their private beliefs and opinions. All were cited for contempt and found guilty. Professor Robert K. Carr, in his exhaustive study of the committee, is sharply critical of its part in this investigation:

By and large, the Hollywood hearings reveal the committee at its worst. In no other committee undertaking were the motivating forces of politics and the personal prejudices of the committee members more apparent; in no other hearing were the over-all strategy and specific procedures more subject to criticism; no other major investigation of the committee ever ended so anticlimactically or produced so little tangible evidence in support of a thesis which the committee set out to prove.

In the summer of 1948 Elizabeth Bentley and Whittaker Chambers became star witnesses for committees investigating subversion. Their shocking revelations of communist cells and espionage within the Roosevelt Administration were spread over the first pages of the country's newspapers and served Republican committee members with the needed ammunition in the oncoming campaign. At this point Thomas had become implicated in office "kick-backs" that subsequently led to his conviction and imprisonment, but Nixon and Mundt performed well in his stead. Their quarry had become Alger Hiss, whom Chambers accused of espionage activities. Their behavior toward Hiss was contrary to fair procedure. They leaked charges to reporters before giving him an opportunity to answer them; they denounced him repeatedly in a manner to prejudice the public and the grand jury. Indeed they usurped the functions of the grand jury, and Nixon went so far as to castigate the judge who presided at the first Hiss trial for giving the defendant the benefit of reasonable doubt. Whether Hiss was guilty as charged remains a moot matter in the minds of many Americans, but the manner in which the committee proceeded against him was not consonant with our traditional tenets of justice.

Another conspicuous instance of the committee's persecution of individuals was its behavior toward Dr. Edward U. Condon, at the time director of the National Bureau of Standards and one of the nation's eminent scientists. Thomas suspected his loyalty because he had testified in favor of giving atomic control to a civilian board while Thomas strongly urged military supervision. At his first opportunity Thomas denounced Condon as a dangerous man in a position of crucial importance to the nation's survival. Condon's repeated requests to testify under oath at open hearings were disdainfully ignored, but in a committee report he was accused of being "one of the weakest links in our atomic security." At no time of course had the committee documented its charges. Nevertheless he had to undergo several loyalty investigations and remained a marked and harassed man until he resigned from government service to teach in a private university.

The committee resorted to similar harassment of other government employees, scientists, teachers, authors, and others having liberal or radical associations.

The net effect of its improprieties and excesses over a period of nearly twenty years—from the time of Martin Dies to the present unaltered leadership of Francis E. Walter—was a weakening of our traditional concept of criminal justice. It personalized its investigations and considered a witness guilty until and unless he satisfied it as to his innocence and cooperation. It served to create a state of distrust and prejudice not only against dissidents of all kinds but also against the very idea of nonconformity. It repressed the prerogative of intellectual speculation within our universities. It lowered the standards of our federal service, our teachers, and our scientists—causing a pall of conformity and passivity to prevail among them.

Senator Pat McCarran was for many years a powerful and aggressive reactionary. A bitter opponent of the New Deal, he fought against the confirmation of Charles E. Bohlen as ambassador to Russia because he had served in the State Department under Roosevelt and Truman. As chairman of the potent Judiciary Committee he took advantage of the cold-war jitters to force through Congress the passage of the Internal Security Act of

1950. In large measure made up of the earlier Mundt-Nixon bill and other antisubversive proposals, it declares in its preamble that Communists and members of "Communist-front" organizations "in effect repudiate their allegiance to the United States and transfer their allegiance to the foreign country in which is vested the direction and control of the world Communist movement." Among the main features are the provision for large-scale internment of citizens on the outbreak of war, the criminality of any act which would substantially help to make the United States a foreign-controlled dictatorship, the exclusion and deportation of immigrants who are Communists, the registration of any "Communist political organization" and "Communist-front organization," and the creation of a Subversive Activities Controls Board.

In his judiciously critical veto, President Truman explained that the bill sharply curtailed liberal organizations and freedom of expression. "Thus, an organization which advocates low-cost housing for sincere humanitarian reasons might be classified as a Communist-front organization because the Communists regularly exploit slum conditions as one of their fifth-column techniques." But such was the temper of Congress under McCarran's prodding that it overrode the veto by a safe margin. As a congeries of repressive measures the law is one of the worst in our history. Much more than the Smith Act it tends to subvert our basic traditional freedoms. As Professor Zachariah Chafee commented sadly, "It is something quite new to punish men drastically who have done nothing wrong, merely for fear that they might do something wrong. Such a practice is wholly alien to the traditions of English-speaking freedom."

In the same year McCarran also made himself chairman of the subcommittee on Internal Security. He concentrated on Foreign Service officials who had been critical of Chiang Kai-shek and hounded them as disloyal and subversive. His chief target became Professor Owen Lattimore, whose books on Asia had a wide circulation. Senator McCarthy had earlier accused Lattimore of being the "top Russian espionage agent" in this country. After an investigation of this charge, Senator Millard Tydings concluded that it was a "fraud and a hoax perpetrated on the Senate of the United States and the American people." His defeat for re-election later that year, engineered largely by McCarthy, was interpreted by McCarran as approval of a new inquiry—a wishful act to harass a man who had indignantly struck back at his persecutors in *Ordeal by Slander*.

Lattimore was from 1934 to 1941 editor of *Pacific Affairs*, a periodical published by the Institute of Pacific Relations. Long a student of the Far East, he was deputy director of the Pacific operations of the Office of War Information during World War II. He was also political adviser to Chiang Kai-shek and a consultant to several governmental agencies. A free-spoken and sophisticated scholar, versed in Marxist writings but no Marxist, he was sufficiently involved as a New Deal liberal in Chinese affairs to become a ready target for the Chinese Lobby marksmen. His denial of being a Communist persuaded McCarran and the Justice Department that he was perjuring himself.

In February 1952 Lattimore began his new ordeal before the McCarrran subcommittee. For twelve days he was harried and tormented by counsel and members of the committee. They questioned him in relays without giving him the benefit of legal counsel or the opportunity to defend himself in any coherent manner. His opening statement was repeatedly interrupted in an obvious effort to keep him from making an effective refutation of the charges against him. Over and over his inquisitors insisted on categorical answers to questions that required qualification or elaboration. They also tried to trip him on events of ten years back that he could recall only hazily but which they knew about from documents in the Institute's file.

McCarran goaded the Justice Department into obtaining an indictment against Lattimore on seven counts of perjury. Judge Luther W. Youngdahl dismissed four of the counts as invalid and added that there was a serious doubt in his mind "whether any count in this indictment can finally pass the test of materiality." When the Court of Appeals sustained the finding eight to one, United States Attorney Leo A. Rover obtained a new indictment and brazenly requested Judge Youngdahl to disqualify himself as biased. The indignant judge rejected the charge as "scandalous" and again dismissed the counts against Lattimore as "so formless and obscure" that they "would make a sham of the Sixth Amendment." At long last Lattimore emerged a free man—but the damage done to him personally and to the traditional principles of American justice was indeed grave. As he himself pointed out, "McCarthyism insists constantly, emotionally, and menacingly that the man who thinks independently thinks dangerously and for an evil, disloyal purpose."

With our erstwhile ally turned into our dangerous enemy, we became acutely sensitive to individual loyalty and the menace of subversion. This fear played into the hands of the chronic red-baiters. Ignoring the fact that American Communists were a relatively tiny, if noisy, minority and under the constant supervision of FBI informers, Congressmen, publicists, and political bigots vied with one another in magnifying the communist menace and in maligning those suspected of dissidence. Former Representative Clinton D. McKinnon of California stated in 1954:

During the four years I spent as a member of Congress, I became acquainted with many Republican legislators. In the quiet conversations of the cloakroom or office, I have yet to find a responsible Republican who believed our government was endangered by Communists. But on the political platform it was different. Charges of subversion and communism made strong medicine, and they were used for political effect.

The question of loyalty became paramount after 1945. Before 1939 federal employees were assumed to be loyal. Nor could they be questioned concerning their political opinions or activities. The war in Europe and later our own participation in it made caution unavoidable. Yet it was a mere formality until President Truman, hoping to forestall attacks from the Committee on Un-American Activities, issued in 1947 Executive Order 9835, establishing the first loyalty program for the executive branch of the government. Thereafter federal employment was to be denied when "on all the evidence, reasonable grounds exist for the belief that the person involved is disloyal to the Government of the United States." In 1951, with the loyalty agitation on the increase, the program was amended in order to refuse employment to persons about whose loyalty there was "reasonable doubt."

The effect of these restrictions was the opposite of what Truman expected. The congressional committees only exploited this program to justify their charges that the government was infiltrated with subversive officials. To prove their contention they brought to their hearings a parade of former Communists who tailored their testimony to the demagogic aims of the committees. Based on this irresponsible and unchecked evidence, the Committee on Un-American Activities in 1951 listed 624 allegedly subversive organizations, to some of which New Deal employees had belonged. The Attorney General, eager to cooperate, could find only 197 such organizations, and many of them had long ceased to exist. President Truman well stated the consequences of this witch hunt:

It is one of the tragedies of our time that the Security Program of the United States has been wickedly used by demagogues and sensational newspapers in the attempt to frighten and mislead the American people. The McCarthys, the McCarrans, the Jenners, the Parnell Thomases, the Veldes have waged a relentless attack, raising doubts in the minds of people about the loyalty of most employees in government.

In 1953 President Eisenhower, complying with his campaign promises, issued Executive Order 10450 to strengthen earlier loyalty and security regulations. The new program set up as the basic test of employee fitness a finding that such employment "is clearly consistent with the interests of national security." Since loyalty and security boards cannot remain unaffected by the clamor and calumnies of the demagogic press and politicians, they have had to investigate unsupported and malicious charges against many federal employees. Thus they have tended to consider not in the interest of national security such equivocal accusations as contributions to the Spanish Loyalists in the 1930's, association with suspect parents or siblings, opposition to the Mundt-Nixon bill, advocacy of public ownership of basic utilities, and voting for the Progressive party in 1948. Willy-nillly the government sought to exact from its employees a standard of conduct and a conformity of thought that would be considered tyrannical if applied to other citizens. As a consequence morale deteriorated. In the words of Professor Henry Steele Commager, "First-rate men and women will not and cannot work under conditions fixed by those who are afraid of ideas."

In addition to the loyalty programs the government began to prosecute well-known Communists. Stung by the charge that it was "soft" on communism, the Truman Administration in 1948 resorted to the Smith Act in indicting the twelve top Communists. With William C. Foster unavailable because of illness, the eleven defendants were convicted after a protracted and tempestuous trial. The charge was conspiracy to advocate the overthrow of the government by force or violence. When the appeal against the constitutionality of the Smith Act came to the Supreme Court, Chief Justice Fred M. Vinson, for the majority, modified the Holmesian "clear and present danger" doctrine by ruling that the *probable* danger from subversive conspiracy was warrant enough to convict the Communist defendants.

If Government is aware that a group aiming at its overthrow is attempting to indoctrinate its members and to commit them to a course whereby they will strike when the leaders feel the circumstances permit, action by the Government is required. . . . Certainly an attempt to overthrow the Government by force, even though doomed from the outset because of inadequate numbers or power of the revolutionists, is a sufficient evil for Congress to prevent.

The validation of the Smith Act in the *Dennis* case no doubt reflected the effect of the cold war—the Korean fighting was then at its height—upon the majority of the Court. Justices Douglas and Black strongly dissented.

With the *Dennis* ruling in its favor, the Justice Department proceeded to obtain indictments and routine convictions of scores of secondary Communist leaders in different parts of the country. It also prosecuted successfully a number of witnesses found in contempt of Congress and union officials suspected of perjury in denying Communist membership. Most of these cases were appealed to higher courts for reversal.

A good many states similarly sought to suppress alleged subversion within their boundaries. Legislative investigations followed the pattern established by the congressional committees. The Tenney Committee in California was perhaps the most notorious in its irresponsibility and vindictiveness.

Most states also enacted legislation requiring special loyalty oaths of teachers and other public employees. In various cities, and particularly in New York, hundreds of teachers with fine pedagogic records were either dismissed or forced to resign because they had at one time or another associated with the Communist party. Isolated yet significant instances of similar prosecution occurred in Pennsylvania, New Hampshire, and other states. Indeed, during the early 1950's the campaign against alleged disloyalty and subversion assumed hysterical proportions.

In 1950 Senator Joseph R. McCarthy suddenly took over the leadership of the antidemocratic demagogues. A quick-tongued and unscrupulous politician, he scattered his extreme and unwarranted charges with a boldness and ominousness that could not but sound the alarm of danger to an already jittery public. For about four years he rode roughshod over his victims with a studied frightfulness that intimidated those in a position to stand up against him. It was only when he abused the Army and tried to browbeat his fellow Senators that he at last overreached himself.

McCarthy began his political career in Wisconsin as a liberal Democrat. From the first, however, he acted shrewdly and opportunistically. In 1946, when running against Senator Robert M. LaFollette, Jr., for the Republican nomination, he curried favor with pro-communist labor leaders. Aware that they were inimical toward LaFollette because of his outspoken anti-Russian attitude, he took a friendly position toward Russia. "Stalin's proposal for world disarmament is a great thing," he declared, "and he must be given credit for being sincere about it." When he was criticized for accepting Communist support, he retorted cynically: "Communists have the same right to vote as anyone else, don't they?" A good many Democrats also voted for him in the primary on the supposition that he would be easier to defeat than LaFollette in the November election. Once nominated, however, he deliberately attacked his Democratic opponent, a distinguished university professor, as the choice of the *Daily Worker*—and ignored the latter's indignant denial. And McCarthy's opportunism won him the election.

In February 1950 he suddenly sprang into national prominence with a radio speech in Wheeling, West Virginia. There and later in the Senate he asserted that the State Department harbored 205 subversives; that he had in his possession the names of 57 "card-carrying Communists"—or 81 inclusive of "marginal" cases. The larger number he arrived at by simple arithmetic from a statement made by Secretary James F. Byrnes in 1946 that security officers had accused 284 employees as unfit for various reasons and that 79 had been dismissed.

Once in full career, McCarthy disdained answering his critics. Instead he intensified his attacks on communism in government. He accused Secretary of State Dean Acheson of being "pro-communist" and protecting subversives in the State Department. When asked for evidence he merely reiterated his reckless assertions. It should be noted that only one of his list of 81 subversives,

No. 54, to be indicted was Val Lorwin, and he was quickly cleared when it was found that he was in fact an active opponent of communism.

McCarthy's juggernaut went into high gear when he became chairman of the Senate Committee on Government Operations in 1953. One of his first major investigations dealt with the International Information Administration. Although he did not uncover one subversive or produce an iota of evidence of sabotage, he practically wrecked the agency's program. By applying the communist brand to such authors as John Dewey, Sherwood Anderson, Elmer Davis, and many others, he caused a panicky purging of overseas libraries that soon reduced them to feeble propaganda outlets. And he so bullied top officials of the State Department that none dared oppose him openly.

The Army Signal Center at Fort Monmouth, New Jersey, next came under McCarthy's purview. He went there as a one-man committee, questioned employees at closed hearings, and briefed reporters after every session. The impression he gave—and it was spread over daily headlines—was that the place seethed with subversion. "There is no question now from the evidence," he pontificated, "that there has been espionage in the Army Signal Corps." With the cold war reaching hysterical proportions, his ominous innuendo caused a number of employees to lose their jobs. In the words of Alan Barth, "Civilian employees at Fort Monmouth were dismissed or suspended on the flimsiest evidence and vaguest charges, and the Army did nothing to protect them from the Senator's inquisition." Secretary of the Army Robert Stevens did protest that investigation had uncovered nothing subversive, but McCarthy insinuated that he knew better. In the end not one of the charges made against the victimized employees had proved correct and they were later fully reinstated. Meantime production at the center was disrupted and morale was at a low ebb.

McCarthy's arrogance and contumely reached their extremity during the questioning of Brigadier-General Ralph W. Zwicker for having honorably discharged an officer who had previously pled the Fifth Amendment. McCarthy abused General Zwicker shamefully and accused him of being a disgrace to his uniform. The news shocked and outraged many Americans. Few cared to come to the defense of vilified radicals or even liberals, but many considered the tirade against a high-ranking Army officer an intolerable enormity. The resulting Army-McCarthy hearings—a televised spectacle that gripped the country—at last brought home to millions of viewers the warped and wicked aspects of McCarthy's mind. Equally significant was the Senate's own conclusion that McCarthy's improper deportment as chairman of one of its committees was subject to censure. The hearings of the Watkins Committee were by way of contrast a model of decorum and fairness. And the Senate's vote of reproof deprived McCarthy of the impetus to persist in the harm he was causing.

McCarthy had the demagogue's contempt for intellectuals and he disdained the cherished dignity of the individual. He flouted the Bill of Rights as a superfluous appendage dear to fatuous liberals. Those resorting to the Fifth Amendment he sneeringly condemned as "Fifth Amendment Communists." And those whom he considered subversive—anyone not taking his view of communism was in his judgment "doing the work of the Communist party"—he treated with the brute intolerance of the bigot. His attitude created a climate of fear among government workers and kept first-rate men from entering the federal service. Dr. Charles Mayo, eminent head of the Mayo Clinic, spoke for many when he said, "It's getting to be a most difficult thing in this country to accept appointment to government service. You subject yourself to such indignities and insults and untruths."

The Senate's censure of McCarthy served to slow down the search for subversives. The Supreme Court became even more helpful in abating the witch hunt. It began to examine more closely the violations of individual rights. In several notable decisions the majority—perhaps again influenced by the general easement of the cold-war atmosphere—informally so construed the

Smith Act as to reverse its *Dennis* position. "The Statute," explained Justice John M. Harlan, "was aimed at the advocacy and teaching of concrete action for the forcible overthrow of the Government, and not of principles divorced from action"—thereby bringing the Court majority to the views of the dissenting Justices Douglas and Black.

After 1954 the newer appointees to the Court in particular joined these two Justices in the defense of the Bill of Rights. Chief Justice Warren, having spoken for a unanimous Court against segregation, also placed himself unequivocally against the tendency of fighting communism with communistic methods. "The temptation to imitate totalitarian security methods," he stated in a much-publicized article, "is a subtle temptation that must be resisted day by day, for it will be with us as long as totalitarianism itself." Robert M. Hutchins likewise voiced the views of many public-spirited citizens when he protested against violations of our constitutional guarantees. He deplored our recent indoctrination against the principle of presumptive innocence. "When a man is accused, however irresponsibly, of communist inclinations, we feel that if he does not immediately step forward with convincing evidence to the contrary, he admits the charge." Such an individual may be put in the position of a defendant by numerous agencies, "with dreadful consequences in the form of loss of time, effort, money, and reputation"—even though he "eventually wins a clear victory."

Ever since the Supreme Court ruled that the Fifth Amendment permitted witnesses "the claim of privilege against self-incrimination," congressional committees have tended to assume that such claim was a tacit admission of guilt. This contumacious disrespect for a rightful privilege was deplored by serious legal scholars. Dean Erwin N. Griswold of the Harvard Law School expressed their view when he declared that "the Fifth Amendment has been very nearly a lone sure rock in a time of storm" and therefore serves as "a symbol of the ultimate moral sense of the community, upholding the best in us." Chief Justice Warren likewise maintained that the self-incrimination clause must be viewed liberally in favor of the right it sought to protect.

The privilege against self-incrimination is a right that was hard earned by our forefathers. . . . To apply the privilege narrowly or begrudgingly —to treat it as a historic relic, at most merely to be tolerated—is to ignore its development and purpose.

The Warren Court was no doubt aware that back in 1881 Justice F. S. Miller had stated that no person can be punished unless his testimony before either House "is required in a matter into which the House has jurisdiction to inquire"; that Congress does not possess "the general power of making inquiry into the private affairs of the citizen." Chief Justice Warren expounded this view in two important opinions delivered in June 1957. In the *Sweezy* case the conviction was set aside in an eloquent defense of academic freedom and the "political freedom of the individual."

In the *Watkins* case Warren cut the very ground from under the Committee on Un-American Activities when he said, "It would be difficult to imagine a less explicit authorizing resolution. Who can define the meaning of 'Un-American'?" He agreed with defense counsel that there was "no congressional power to expose for the sake of exposure." Since the petitioner was not given sufficient information as to the pertinancy of the questions asked, he was "not accorded a fair opportunity to determine whether he was within his rights in refusing to answer, and his conviction is necessarily invalid under the Due Process Clause of the Fifth Amendment."

If the *Watkins* opinion gave notice to congressional committees that they cannot disregard the constitutional rights of individuals, in the *Jencks* case Justice William J. Brennan held for the majority that the Department of Justice must likewise govern itself within the restrictions of the Bill of Rights. In the lower courts Jencks, a union official, was convicted of falsely swearing that he was not a Communist—mainly on the evidence of two FBI informers. Jencks' counsel, in line with a common rule of criminal law, requested to see the original reports of these witnesses in order to compare them with their oral testimony. This the FBI refused on the ground that the documents must remain secret in the interests of national security. In invalidating the conviction Justice Brennan declared:

We hold that criminal action must be dismissed when the Government, on the ground of privilege, elects not to comply with an order to produce, for the accuser's inspection and for admission in evidence, relevant statements or reports in its possession of Government's witnesses touching the subject matter of their testimony at the trial.

The importance of this decision lies in the curtailment of the unscrupulous use of informers in recent years. J. Edgar Hoover has said that "the confidential informant has become an institution." Dozens of former Communists and other professional anticommunist witnesses have provided so-called expert testimony not only at court trials but also at closed and open hearings of various legislative investigations. In many instances their evidence has been found grossly inaccurate or completely false, yet with disastrous results to the accused. The *Jencks* decision will therefore help to lessen the irresponsible use of professional informers. It should be noted that the effect of a Court ruling is largely dependent on the temper of public opinion. Several years earlier, when McCarthyism was at its worst, Justice Douglas had similarly held in the *Peters* case that "if the sources of information need protection, they should be kept secret"; but once they used them to destroy a man's reputation, they should be put to the test of due process of law. "When we relax our standards to accommodate the faceless informer, we violate our basic constitutional guarantees and ape the tactics of those whom we despise." At that time, however, the ruling was without effect on the legislative inquisitors.

In March 1958 individual rights were further bolstered when the Court ruled by a majority of eight to one that it was illegal for the Armed Services to give draftees less than an honorable discharge because of Communist affiliations before induction—a practice begun after McCarthy had castigated the Army for giving an honorable discharge to an officer who had resorted to the protection of the Fifth Amendment.

Since 1933 the United States has gone through first a remarkable period of democratic reform—years in which individual freedom flourished and social welfare burgeoned—and then a longer period of all-out war followed by a traumatic struggle against an ominous communism. And as in Pharaoh's dream the lean kine devoured the fat, so in our time the spirit of the New Deal was eclipsed in the postwar hysteria. The natural fears engendered by a powerful and ruthless foe, cleverly exploited by unscrupulous demagogues, for a time affected the nation with an irrational intensity. In our frenzied effort to protect ourselves from Communist subversion we tended to trample our cherished traditions of individual freedom. Mark Ethridge, the noted editor, has said that "this period in which we have sacrificed basic freedoms to a fancied security has left wounds that will be a long time healing and scars that will not be erased." The President's Committee on Civil Rights has likewise "found much that was shocking and more that was shameful in the recent record of American civil liberties."

In such an atmosphere of fear and tension there is no tolerance for the critic and crusader. The dedicated dissidents and the devoted humanitarians, who flourished in the permissive decades of the nineteenth century and were esteemed by the New Dealers, became anachronistic eccentrics and dangerous radicals in our own time of illiberality and insecurity. Thus in the chapters that follow Senator Norris, having reached his maximum effectiveness as a crusading liberal in a time of hope and promise, achieved heroic stature as a protagonist of the New Deal. Henry A. Wallace, who for nearly a decade stood closest to Roosevelt, ended his political career as a misfit and rebel in the tension of the cold war. And Justice Black, Roosevelt's first appointee to the Supreme Court and a forthright Jeffersonian, was forced into the unhappy role of persistent dissenter during the postwar decade of bigotry and repression.

[566]

GEORGE W. NORRIS

"THE FIGHTING LIBERAL"

G EORGE W. NORRIS, one of the noblest sons of American liberalism, was for four decades a steadfast and successful protagonist of Jeffersonian democracy. Born in 1861 of pioneer stock, exposed to bleak poverty in his childhood, nurtured on midwestern idealism, he reached manhood with an implicit faith in the hallowed principles of the Declaration of Independence. Like so many of his generation, he left his native Ohio to make a career of law in the newly opened western states and finally settled in Nebraska. There he prospered and began to dabble in politics. An admirer of Lincoln, he had early become a zealous Republican and worked hard for the success of the party.

Having established himself as an able lawyer and popular Republican, Norris was in line for political preferment. He first served successfully as district attorney and then as district judge. Although the Populist tide in Nebraska was running high in 1895, Norris' personal popularity enabled him to win over his active Populist rival—the first time by only two votes but the second by a comfortable majority.

Norris felt a sense of accomplishment in his work on the bench. It was a time of poor crops and unpaid mortgages, and most suits were for the nonpayment of interest. "Only those who lived in the heart of the nation's food-producing regions," he explained, "knew fully the agony of these cycles of crop failure, heavy indebtedness upon the land, and ruinous commodity farm prices." His sympathetic attitude and scrupulous study of each case soon gained him the reputation as a humane and intelligent jurist.

[567]

In 1902 he considered it his Republican duty to accept the proffered nomination to a seat in Congress and was elected after a hard campaign. He went to Washington with a copybook notion of the political process and with a naive belief "that all the virtues of government were wrapt up in the party of which I was a member." Disillusion came quickly. Eager to favor civil service, he soon learned that both parties opposed such legislation for political reasons.

His understanding of the ways of Congress came to him through a series of jolts. He simply could not make party compliance square with a prodding conscience. Again and again he was distressed to find Republicans enmeshed in evils he had ascribed to Democrats. His criticism of spoils and patronage practices met with curt rebuff. The same cold antagonism greeted his effort to lengthen the term of Representatives to four years; an effort that seemed to him highly desirable in view of the fact that "before they are fairly started in the work for which they are elected they are plunged into a campaign for renomination." When he came up for re-election in 1906, the Republican leaders refused to help him. But their opposition made him fight all the harder, and he won then and in subsequent campaigns because the people of Nebraska had come to believe in him and wanted him as their representative in Congress.

In the 1900's Norris was still the unsophisticated idealist. Honest government and the public good were the foundation pillars of his political credo. Irritated by Speaker Joseph Cannon's dictatorial rule, he determined to work for the liberalization of the House rules. Realistic enough not to underestimate Cannon's political prowess, he sought to discomfort him by a stratagem. His first opportunity came in 1910 when House members were to be chosen to participate in a congressional investigation of Secretary of the Interior Ballinger's dismissal of Gifford Pinchot and Louis Glavis, two zealous advocates of conservation. Norris knew that Cannon wanted to clear Ballinger and would appoint men to do his will. Aware of the speaker's habit of leaving the chair at a certain hour,

Norris obtained recognition from the unsuspecting acting Speaker and moved that the members be named by the House as a whole. Aided by his fellow insurgents and abetted by the Democrats, his motion carried 149 to 146—a stinging rebuke to the absent Cannon.

The long-sought maneuver for control in the House came when Norris took advantage of an adventitious ruling by Cannon to present his carefully prepared resolution for the reorganization of the all-powerful Rules Committee. Cannon's adherents, depleted by absences, played for time. Far into the night and all the next day they fought the aroused insurgents with every trick they could muster. But the Norris group were equally alert and determined. Their victory deprived Cannon of his dictatorial powers. A writer in *World's Work* commented: "One man without position against 200 welded in the most powerful political machine that Washington has ever known, has twice beaten them at their own game. Mr. George Norris is a man worth knowing and watching."

Heretofore Norris concerned himself largely with reforming the machinery of politics. After 1910, having won his fifth term by a large majority despite opposition from Republican leaders and in the face of a national Democratic victory, he became affected by the prevailing spirit of progressive insurgency. Senator Robert M. LaFollette in particular stimulated him to grapple with the problems of monopoly and economic equality. When he found that a certain judge, always ruled in favor of a railroad and against small coal-mine owners, he fought for his impeachment and won. He also campaigned against the coffee trust. Long an admirer of Theodore Roosevelt, he joined his newly formed Progressive party in 1912 and gained election to the Senate.

Norris and LaFollette, despised and ignored by the Senate conservatives, were equally devoted to democratic ideals. Yet while LaFollette was militant and grim, driving himself hard and ever insisting on dominance, Norris was moderate and genial, employing shafts of gentle satire against his opponents and accepting temporary defeat philosophically—yet persisting till final victory.

Though both were nominal Republicans, they favored President Woodrow Wilson's liberal program of legislation and even went further than the Democrats in such measures as inheritance taxes, the development of water power, and the public ownership of basic utilities. They were also critical of Wilson's tolerance of political machine methods, particularly in connection with civil service jobs.

A true product of the Middle West, Norris had little interest in foreign affairs and was suspicious of anything that tended to disturb American insularity. Wilson's plea for neutrality in 1914 met with his hearty approval. When Wilson forced Bryan's resignation as Secretary of State and began to advocate military preparedness, Norris joined his pacifistic colleagues in strongly opposing the accelerated war propaganda. To lessen the clamor for war he urged that the manufacture of armor plate and guns be made a government monopoly. "The greatest disgrace of the present century," he insisted, "is that war between civilized nations is still a possibility." He therefore called upon Wilson to seek the establishment of an international court of arbitration.

When Wilson, shortly after his re-election in 1916 on a peace platform, asked Congress for authority to arm merchant ships, Norris joined LaFollette and ten other Senators—Wilson called them angrily "a little group of willful men"—in filibustering the measure to death. The "intellectual lynching" of these dissidents in the press and on the platform caused Norris much anguish. He believed the filibuster was justified and his conscience was clear Yet he did not want to remain in the Senate if he was not representing the will of his constituents.

Anxious to tell them his side of the story and let them decide whether or not he should resign, he engaged the largest hall in Lincoln for a public meeting. On his arrival to the state capital on Sunday, he was visited only by the bravest of his friends, and they came furtively to warn him that he would be mobbed if he attempted to make his address. Years later he wrote in *The Nation*, "I cannot remember a day in my life when I suffered more from a lonely feeling of despondency than upon that particular Sunday."

The following evening he found the hall filled to overflowing—some farmers having come from far distances. When he rose and approached the dais he was greeted with ominous silence. Determined to speak his mind, he began by saying that he had come from Washington to tell them what they could not learn from the newspapers. Whereupon "the people stood up and yelled." Those who had come to jeer were intimidated by this sudden warm response. Cheered and confident, Norris spoke frankly and freely on how he felt about war, the munition makers, Wilson's change of heart; nor did he keep from his audience his insistence on acting subsequently in accord with his conscience. His remarks were repeatedly interrupted with lusty cheers of approval.

Norris returned to Washington with confirmed faith in the rightness of his position. By no means an extreme pacifist, he opposed the war resolution steadfastly but not irreconcilably. Once the fighting began, he supported all war measures. Nevertheless he fought the antiliberal bills with his customary vigor. He maintained that in fighting to make the world safe for democracy we must not trample on our own precious liberties. Loath to seek re-election in 1918, he won by a wide margin despite false accusations and fierce opposition.

At the war's end he welcomed Wilson's idea of a League of Nations, which he envisioned as an agency doing away with the tools of war. "If the world is disarmed," he declared, "and remains disarmed, there will be no more world wars." He urged the establishment of an international court of arbitration and an end to colonial conquest. With this simple and idealistic solution in mind, he followed events at the peace conference in Versailles with increasing perturbation. He was particularly indignant about the secret treaties and the award of Shantung to Japan. Although he opposed only certain parts of the treaty, and greatly disliked allying himself with the conservative group, he could not in conscience vote in its favor.

Throughout the 1920's Norris was in the unhappy position of a political Ishmael. Although nominally a member of the party in power, he found himself intensely at odds with its policies and practices. As chairman of the Committee on Agriculture he fought hard for the farmers, who were suffering from a declining market. He successfully thwarted the seating of Truman Newberry of Michigan; he went to Pennsylvania to campaign against Boss Vare's election to the Senate. Ever vigilant against any bill or amendment that favored a privileged group, he opposed them persistently and courageously.

In 1930 Republican leaders sought his defeat for renomination by putting forth as a rival candidate an obscure grocery clerk of the same name. Their thought was that since under Nebraska law no identification of candidates on the ballot was permissible, all votes for either George W. Norris would automatically become void. Senator Norris was outraged by this act of dirty trickery. He was ready to run as an independent when the state court ruled the rival Norris off the ballot on a technicality. Both party machines then backed the popular Democratic candidate; and the Republicans forged a letter from Tammany Hall in praise of Norris in an effort to alienate voters. The intrepid liberal, however, aided by influential friends from every part of the country, fought back doggedly and won by a comfortable majority.

The high watermark of Norris' Senate activity was his long and ingenious struggle for legislation that resulted in the majestic achievement of TVA. He began the fight in 1920, when as chairman of the Committee on Agriculture he had to take charge of the Muscle Shoals bills. This legislation pertained to the completion of a dam and nitrate plant initiated in 1916 as a war measure but suspended at the time of the armistice. Although the Senate had voted in favor of the project, the House failed to act on it.

The Harding Administration, acting on the principle of "less business in government," placed Muscle Shoals on sale for postwar exploitation. A bid came from Henry Ford—five million dollars for the nitrate plant that had cost over a hundred million to construct. His publicists described the offer glowingly as Ford's benevolent attempt to supply low-cost fertilizer to farmers. Members of Congress, the American Farm Bureau Federation, and Tennessean businessmen joined in their high praise of Ford's public-spirited enterprise. The mere news of his offer started a real estate boom of fantastic proportions.

Norris saw the matter differently. To him Muscle Shoals, once he had familiarized himself with its potentialities for the improvement of the region, was not merely a means of cheap fertilizer but the first step in developing "the entire Tennessee River to its maximum for power, for navigation, and for flood control." It troubled him to note millions of gallons of water roaring over the dam's spillways unattached to generators while thousands of farmers below were without electric power. He was likewise perturbed to discover the continued reliance on the cyanamid process of making nitrogen after the simpler and cheaper Haber method had become available. A reading of the Ford bid gave him no assurance of either cheap power or low-cost fertilizer. His substitute bill for government operation, however, in spite of months of tactical maneuvering, failed of passage.

Early in 1924 the House, acting on President Coolidge's recommendation, voted in favor of the Ford bid. In the Senate, however, prolonged debate resulted in disapproval of the House measure and in favor of Norris's resolution for government operation. By this time the publicized deficiencies of the Ford offer had begun to turn public opinion against it and the bid was withdrawn. That fall Norris promoted his new bill with increased vigor. His strongest opponent in the ensuing debate was Senator Oscar Underwood who accused him of "dreaming dreams." When a vote was finally taken in January 1935, the Underwood substitute bill for private operation was adopted by a vote of 46 to 33. The House leaders, however, made the mistake of sending to conference its earlier measure, which was quite unlike the Senate bill. This gave Norris the opportunity to oppose it on the ground that it contained new matter. With the session nearing its end, he organized a filibuster and thus kept the measure from coming to a final vote.

The fight continued. Norris resigned his chairmanship of the Committee on Agriculture in order to concentrate his efforts in behalf of the Muscle Shoals project. In 1928 he succeeded in having his bill accepted by majorities in both Houses—only to have it nullified by a pocket veto. His caustic comment was that President Coolidge's action "was not only unfair but lacked the courage that a public servant ought to show."

Norris reintroduced his bill at the next session. Maintaining his study of water power, he was able to demonstrate that the electricity used by a Toronto family at a cost of $3.36 from a publicly owned source would amount to $32. in Birmingham and $40. in Nashville. Although the Senate again passed his bill by a sizable majority, the House enacted a contrary measure and the legislation died in conference when Congress adjourned for the 1930 campaign. The next year his bill was successfully adopted in both Houses, but President Hoover immediately vetoed it in a sharply critical statement that government operation would tend "to break down the initiative and enterprise of the American people; that it would destroy equality of opportunity and civilization." Norris considered the veto unjust, but he was not discouraged. He was already looking ahead to Hoover's successor—by then convinced that time was on his side.

Meantime he was campaigning for his Lame Duck Amendment. Long critical of the constitutional proviso—adapted to eighteenth-century conditions—that enabled a defeated Congressman to function as legislator months after the election of his successor, thereby permitting him to barter his vote for a federal job, Norris first offered the Amendment for consideration in December 1922. The Senate approved it overwhelmingly. The House, however, took no action. During the ensuing decade the Senate voted for it five times—only to have the resolution either ignored or killed in the House. In 1932 the Democratic Congress finally voted in favor of the Amendment and within a year the thirty-sixth state ratified it.

In 1926, while in Pennsylvania campaigning against Vare, Norris learned of the oppressive effects of the "yellow dog" contract system upon the state's coal miners. He found that the combination of venal sheriffs, unfriendly courts, and arrogant employers served to develop "a type of bondage that enslaved the miner to a life of toil." He particularly deplored the free use of labor injunctions to keep workers from joining a union.

At his first opportunity he introduced a bill against labor injunctions—going to great trouble to make it as foolproof juridicially as possible. A companion bill was presented in the House by Fiorella La Guardia. In 1930, however, most Congressmen were still antiunion and the measure was defeated. The complexion of the next Congress having altered considerably, the reintroduced bills were adopted almost unanimously. President Hoover's reluctant acquiescence made the Norris-La Guardia Anti-Injunction Act the first of the favorable labor laws in the 1930's.

Early in 1929 Norris learned of Governor Franklin D. Roosevelt's favorable attitude toward public water power. Greater knowledge of the man increased his admiration. When Roosevelt became a candidate for the Presidency, Norris hailed him. This party switch—he had also favored Al Smith in 1928—had become inevitable in view of President Hoover's dogmatic conservatism.

Shortly after his election Roosevelt invited Norris to join him in January on an inspection trip to Muscle Shoals. The two men saw eye to eye and agreed on the widest possible development of the Tennessee region. "I can see my dreams come true," Norris told Roosevelt on receiving a copy of the draft embodying the broad provisions of what was to become the Tennessee Valley Authority.

During his first weeks in office, in the midst of an avalanche of demands upon his time, Roosevelt managed to see Norris several times concerning the bill favoring the Tennessee project. On April 10 he sent to Congress a brief but forceful message requesting the desired legislation. The next day Norris introduced the TVA bill in the Senate; a similar bill was presented in the House. Hearings began at once and both measures were soon enacted by large majorities. On May 14, when the final legislation was signed by the President, Norris felt jubilant.

The Muscle Shoals legislation . . . is a monument to the victorious ending of a twelve years' struggle waged on behalf of the common people against the combined forces of monopoly and human greed. It is emblematic of the dawning of that day when every rippling stream that flows down the mountain side and winds its way through the meadows to the sea shall be harnessed and made to work for the welfare and comfort of man.

TVA was indeed the largest and most comprehensive engineering project ever undertaken by man. No single government agency was ever assigned so gigantic a task or the responsibility for the inclusive development of so vast a region. When the job was finished nearly twelve years later, it comprised the coordinated functioning of 28 dams along a watershed of 40,000 square miles— all operated with the sole aim of providing the maximum good to the people of the region. The use of electricity was made general in the home and factory and on the farm, flood control was established, navigation was greatly accelerated, and the economy and culture of hundreds of thousands of families were tremendously improved and broadened. TVA became in truth the symbol of dynamic democracy intelligently applied.

Norris rightly considered TVA his special responsibility. He helped Roosevelt in the selection of the three directors and kept close contact with them throughout the 1930's. He also combatted the private power companies that sought to belittle the objectives of the gigantic enterprise and to handicap its successful development. Great was his relief and satisfaction when the Supreme Court validated the legislation creating TVA. In Congress Norris made sure that the needed funds were duly appropriated; and he was ever on the alert against a bill or rider tending to affect the project adversely. And the TVA personnel joined with the people of the region to honor him as their patron—giving his name to the first new dam and to the model city built to house the influx of newcomers.

Having achieved the major national reforms he had fought for in Congress, Norris devoted the summer of 1934 to a campaign for the uni-cameral amendment in Nebraska. He had long been critical of the two-house legislative system of government. In 1923 he published an article in which he compared the state organization with a private corporation and pointed out that the legislative system was a relic of monarchial conditions that required checks and balances but was now anachronistic and favored only the politicians. Aware of the hopelessness of reform on a national scale, since small states would never yield their advantage in the Senate, he saw no good reason for perpetuating the two-house state legislature. For the next decade, however, he was too preoccupied in Washington to further the reform in his home state.

Norris had initiative petitions printed at his own expense and organized a corps of volunteers, many of them college students on vacation, to obtain the necessary signatures that would put the amendment on the ballot. The politicians of both parties were furious, and prominent citizens attacked the proposed reform as the death of the American system of government. Despite strong opposition, the volunteers obtained many more signatures than were required by law. Norris himself spoke for the amendment in every part of the state. "If you ever believed me," he told the voters, "believe me now when I say that I have no other interest in this amendment than to make Nebraska a better place in which to live." As before, the people believed him and voted in favor of the unicameral legislature. When it met for the first time on January 5, 1937, Norris was on hand as a honored guest.

In Congress Norris, at the height of his influence, warmly supported the economic and social legislation of the New Deal. Yet he opposed Roosevelt's big-navy program and the patronage policies and machine politics of James Farley. He was incensed when Roosevelt did nothing in 1934 to stop Farley from seeking the defeat of Bronson Cutting, the liberal Republican Senator from New Mexico, and called the action "a blot upon the record of the Roosevelt Administration."

In 1936 Norris was strongly inclined to retire from politics. He left too old and "completely discouraged" by the sordid practices of both major parties. His many friends and admirers, however, insisted that he seek another term. President Roosevelt took the unprecedented step of telling correspondents "on the record" of his eager wish to keep Norris in the Senate. Once more yielding to the dictates of duty, the conscientious Nebraskan consented to run again, but only as an independent. His friends in the Senate and President Roosevelt himself came to Nebraska to speak in his behalf. The latter praised him as "a man who through all these years has had no boss but his own conscience. . . . George Norris's candidacy transcends state and party lines. . . . He is one of our major prophets of America." With the New Deal reaching its peak of popularity in the 1936 election, the independent Norris obtained a comfortable plurality over his two rivals.

Norris favored curbing the conservatism of the Supreme Court. "The people can change the Congress," he asserted caustically, "but only God can change the Supreme Court." He therefore argued for a constitutional amendment to stop "legislation by judiciary." Yet he considered Roosevelt's own effort to modify the personnel of the Court ill-advised and poorly presented. He could not support the measure and was not sorry to see it fail. But he hailed the appointment of Senator Black as the first New Deal Justice.

After 1935 international problems again began to force themselves on Norris's conscience. Anxious to keep the United States out of the future wars in Europe, he favored the passage of the Neutrality Act. The armament disclosures of the Nye Committee confirmed his pacifism. Looking back at World War I, he saw only evil resulting from the catastrophic event: political corruption, new millionaires, crime waves, economic exploitation.

Yet even more than war he abhorred the rising fascist menace. The threat of Hitlerism grew more and more real to him—not only in Europe but in the United States. With the development of the airplane he realized that the oceans were no longer our safeguards and that isolation was becoming impossible. When Hitler's invasion of Poland in 1939 plunged Europe into war, Norris readily, if ruefully, joined Roosevelt in the effort to save the antifascist countries the world over. For him "there was no similarity in the challenge which confronted the American people" in the two wars. Without changing his mind about 1917, he now joined the liberal internationalists in favoring Lend-Lease and other measures helping the democracies. He also campaigned actively for Roosevelt's re-election in 1940 and voted for war after the attack on Pearl Harbor. While the fighting was still at its height he began to discuss the conditions of peace and maintained, as he had after World War I, that permanent disarmament for all nations was "the real cornerstone of the peace"—with the weapons of the defeated enemies destroyed first and those of the victorious allies more gradually.

In 1942 Norris was rounding out his fortieth year in Congress. An octogenarian and yearning for the quiet of retirement, he nevertheless considered it his duty to continue serving his country while it was at war. Conservative politicians in Nebraska again fiercely opposed his re-election. Once more they spread false rumors about him and hammered constantly at the disadvantage of his old age. With the war effort absorbing the attention of Roosevelt and his other friends and with his own campaign limited to a few speeches because of his work in Washington, Norris found himself defeated at the polls for the first time in nearly a half century.

He did not relish defeat, especially in an unfair fight and with an opponent unworthy of him, but he looked forward with pleasure to retirement in McCook. His numerous admirers, however, did not permit him to leave the hurly-burly of politics. In the face of an antidemocratic upsurge stimulated by the war spirit, he readily joined his fellow liberals in a "popular front" against reaction—lending his name, or his presence, or his voice, as the occasion demanded. He also worked on his autobiography, which was published posthumously as *The Fighting Liberal*.

In 1944 he again worked for Roosevelt's re-election and accepted the honorary chairmanship of the National Citizens Political Action Committee. Late in August, however, he was stricken fatally by a cerebral hemorrhage.

George W. Norris never achieved the homage given to the popular hero. He was unquestionably a great. American, but he lacked the quality of self-dramatization. Nevertheless his niche among congressional leaders is secure. No other Senator ever attained his record of constructive legislation. For thirty years he was the Senate's goad and conscience. A typical, yet rare and refined, product of his prairie environment—where democracy prevailed as a pristine, potent force—he proudly adhered to the ideals of the Founding Fathers.

Unlike many of his colleagues in Congress he could not acquiesce in the equivocation of leading politicians. The welfare of the people became the basic criterion; whatever clashed with it he fought without compromise. Among the evils of industrialism he considered the drive and greed of unbridled corporations the antithesis of the public good. "A free people," he argued, "cannot permanently submit to a private monopoly on a necessity of life." Because the control of water power was a dominant issue in his time, he remained adamant in his fight for the public operation of Muscle Shoals.

Characteristically the Middle Westerner in the insularity of his world outlook and hating war as barbarous and futile, he opposed our entrance into World War I with all the force of his native idealism. Twenty years later, however, he viewed world affairs with greater sophistication. Yet his prime interest throughout his active career was the social welfare of the American people, and to this end he devoted himself during his many years in Congress. His honesty of purpose, his warm humanity, his remarkable persistence as a fighter for the public good—these qualities made him one of the most effective liberals in the history of the Senate.

HENRY A. WALLACE

PROTAGONIST OF PEACE AND PLENTY

H ENRY A. WALLACE, born in October 1888, came of a family
inured in the democratic beliefs of the Middle West. His
grandfather grew up in the settled frontier of western
Pennsylvania and later established himself in Iowa, where he
published a weekly for farmers that in time became their lay bible.
No Populist or rabble rouser, he preached the welfare of the
farmer and execrated his unscrupulous exploiters. Henry's father
was more the conventional editor and businessman, but he too was
touched by the spirit of the crusader. As Secretary of Agriculture
under Presidents Harding and Coolidge he strove valiantly, if
futilely, to improve the worsening lot of the American farmer in
the face of Republican indifference. "Young Henry," as the third
Henry came to be called, sat at the feet of his grandfather and
father, absorbing their active interest in the common good.

From early childhood Henry took life seriously and philosophically. Of a reflective bent, he readily interested himself in scientific
speculation, particularly as it related to agriculture. The idea of
increasing the corn crop by hybridization seized upon his youthful
imagination and caused him to experiment with various kinds of
seeds while still in high school. For years he continued his research
until he perfected a hybrid seed and began producing it com-
mercially. The Pioneer Hi-Bred Corn Company, which he founded,
subsequently became a highly successful business enterprise. Simultaneously he wrote regularly for the family weekly, made scientific
studies of farming and the weather, and operated a dairy and

chicken farm. In 1914 he married Ilo Browne and in time became the father of two sons and a daughter.

When his father went to Washington in 1921 to head the Department of Agriculture, Henry assumed the editorship of *Wallaces' Weekly*. He advanced numerous ideas on how to overcome the increasing plight of the farmer in the 1920's. Although his father was a member of the Republican Administration, he frequently wrote editorials highly critical of the government's policies. Having pondered the "Joseph" plan—later termed the "ever normal granary"—as early as 1912, he began to advocate the idea a decade later and urged concurrently the plan of crop controls by the farmers themselves. In his capacities as editor and agricultural economist he made numerous speeches in favor of farm relief by means of these proposed remedies.

All through the 1920's he worked intensively at his editorial and business tasks and at the same time delved in mathematics, genetics, economics, meteorology, and comparative religion. In 1929 he went to Europe in pursuit of his several fields of study and returned more than ever confirmed in this theoretical views. He also became a strong opponent of the tariff.

His studies in agricultural economics and his militant editorials on farm relief gradually made him widely known to students of these subjects. When Franklin D. Roosevelt officially became a candidate for the Presidency, Wallace hailed him as the farmer's friend and worked hard for his election. Favorably impressed by this seemingly diffident and serious-minded Iowan, Roosevelt offered him the Cabinet post his late father had held in a Republican Administration.

Wallace assumed his office as head of the Department of Agriculture with his customary conscientiousness. To deal with the grave crisis, drastic remedies were imperative, and he resorted to them eagerly and hopefully. The Agricultural Adjustment Act, later invalidated by the Supreme Court, was a well-meant but hastily improvised measure to place farmers on a solid economic footing. In an effort to raise prices and control production, Wallace ordered the destruction of ten million acres of growing cotton and the slaughter of six million little pigs. It was a painful act, but he saw no other solution. In reply to his conservative critics —*The Chicago Tribune* referred to him in a streamer headline as "The Greatest Butcher in Christendom"—he stressed that his destructive orders "were not acts of idealism in any sane society. They were emergency acts made necessary by an almost insane lack of world statesmanship during the period 1920 to 1932." He stated further that he could tolerate such acts "only as a clearing up of the wreckage of the old days of unbalanced production."

In his first year in office Wallace traveled 40,000 miles, covering every state in the Union, to see for himself how people lived and what were their immediate needs. He made many speeches, wrote numerous articles and books, and conducted a department of around a hundred thousand personnel. He was not very adroit in dealing with the personal and political rivalries of his associates, but even his caustic critic Dwight Macdonald admitted that on the whole Wallace managed the department very well: "He seems to have impressed his subordinates in those days with his modesty, human decency, competence, energy, and receptivity to new ideas."

Wallace's enthusiasm for the New Deal was genuine and forthright, for it embodied the ideals he had long advocated. Gradually, in his speeches and writings, he became its most eloquent protagonist. Roosevelt liked his earnestness, his devotion, his frankness, and fondly referred to him as "Old Man Common Sense." Yet Wallace was neither extreme nor eccentric in the advocacy of liberalism. As he defined it, "The New Deal places human rights above property rights and aims to modify special privilege for the few to the extent that such modification will aid in providing economic security for the many." In stressing the paramountcy of the general welfare he made clear that "the capitalism of Main Street" must not disregard completely "what the capitalism of Wall Street has taught us."

Pressing world dangers convinced him that it was to the nation's best interest to keep Roosevelt in office for their duration. He was therefore the first Cabinet member to advocate a third term. Roosevelt, on his part, admired Wallace's positive liberalism and insisted on having him as his running mate. The professional politicians balked at the idea of having a man whom they considered an outsider and a visionary in a position to take over the Presidency should Roosevelt break under the extreme strain, but in the end they capitulated.

Roosevelt gave Wallace greater administrative and diplomatic responsibilities than those delegated to any previous Vice President. As the war clouds darkened and preparedness became urgent, he was appointed chairman of the Economic Defense Board, consisting of eight members of the Cabinet, and charged with the duty of buying scarce materials in foreign countries. Later, with the war a reality, the name was changed to Board of Economic Warfare. Even as Secretary of Agriculture, Wallace had foreseen basic shortages of rubber, tin, and other materials not produced in the United States. In 1939 he persuaded Congress to permit him to exchange surplus crops for scarce raw materials. As a result the Commodity Credit Corporation obtained 90,000 tons of rubber with the payment of 600,000 bales of cotton.

Certain that the war would last a long time and that victory required an adequate supply of scarce materials, Wallace was ready to obtain them wherever possible and regardless of cost. Jesse Jones, who as head of RFC served as financier to BEW, frustrated these efforts. A conservative Texan with the banker's cautious mentality, he considered Wallace an impractical dreamer who knew not the value of money and was wasting the nation's finances with harebrained schemes. He was also the bitter enemy of his fellow Texan Milo Perkins, whom Wallace had appointed as executive director of BEW. Consequently Jones in effect vetoed the long-range enterprises of this agency.

In a letter to the Senate Appropriations Committee in June 1943 Wallace, exasperated by Jones's obstructive tactics, charged him with "hampering" the war effort and asked for a separation of BEW from RFC. Jones angrily retorted that Wallace's imputation was full of "malice and misstatements." Wallace defended his accusations in a second letter. Again Jones asserted, rather intemperately, "His tirade is so filled with malice, innuendo, half truth and no truth at all, that considerations of self-respect and of common justice to my associates force me to expose his unscrupulous language." This correspondence, carried on despite the President's request that no such grievances be aired publicly, made sensational headlines in the newspapers. Ten days later Roosevelt removed both from the job of foreign purchases and gave it to Leo Crowley, a prominent businessman and a friend of Jones.

Wallace remained, of course, an important member of the Roosevelt Administration and devoted to the President. His quarrel with Jones, however, strengthened the antagonism of the tradition-bound conservatives. They considered his broad world view and his concern for the mass of mankind as the vapory idealism of a quixotic visionary. They distrusted him because he was not one of them—unlike his predecessor John Garner he neither played poker nor "struck a blow for liberty" with good whiskey—and were therefore determined to keep him from a second term as Vice President. It was obvious to them that Roosevelt would have to be renominated once more and that he would hardly live through a fourth term.

Wallace was aware of this opposition but did not fight back. He merely deplored the bigotry of his enemies, their lack of vision and good will. Much as he wished to succeed politically, he desired even more to promote the social philosophy which he considered essential to the welfare of mankind. Years of intensive reading and reflection had implanted in his conscience a hatred of war, opposition to greed and poverty, a belief in one world and the brotherhood of man.

As Vice President he became, with Roosevelt's warm approval, the fervent spokesman for the philosophy of the New Deal. After

Pearl Harbor he preached the blessings of democracy for all mankind. He argued eloquently that to win the war and achieve lasting peace we must make available to all the fruits of freedom and equality. Early in 1942 he made his famous speech on "The Century of the Common Man":

Some have spoken of the "American Century." I say that the century we are now entering—the century which will come out of this war—can and must be the century of the common man. . . . The people's revolution is on the march, and the devil and all his angels cannot prevail against it. They cannot prevail, for on the side of the people is the Lord.

In articles, speeches, and books he expounded the idea that "we can be decently human and really hard-headed if we exchange our postwar surplus for goods, for peace, and for improving the standard of living of so-called backward peoples." He maintained that after the war we shall not any longer be able to revert to our isolationist position with high-tariff walls around us. After World War I this position proved disastrous; after World War II it will be calamitous because "our surplus will be greater than ever."

He proposed nothing radical. All he asked was that business, labor, agriculture, and government join in a "four-way partnership" with a view to reconciling "the freedom and rights of the individual with the duties required of us by the general welfare." By thus putting our productive resources fully to work and by offering our industrial ingenuity and good will to other peoples we could not only raise our own standard of living but also improve that of the rest of mankind.

The idea of full employment, which had deeply troubled him throughout the meager 1930's, warmed his conscience as he thought of the peaceful era that would follow the defeat of Germany and Japan. Nor did he envision full employment obtained by other than democratic means. In January 1943 he wrote: "We can have full employment in this country without destroying initiative, private capital, or private enterprise. We need the

[586]

driving force of self-interest to get most of the work of the world done."

In 1945 he published a book entitled *Sixty Million Jobs*. This symbolic figure was "synonymous with the peacetime requirements of full employment" for our population at that time. He maintained that we could achieve this goal without inflation or an unbalanced budget. In a detailed exposition of the subject he specified the ways and means of providing jobs for all who wanted them. Among other suggestions he proposed a nationwide budget that would promote full employment by not only doing the things that people wanted done but also by keeping "in readiness the proper short-term programs for emergencies." The development of this budget must of necessity involve the closest kind of cooperation between the government and labor, management and agriculture, so that the final estimates "will rest on the broadest technical and democratic base." The tax policy he proposed was such as to give a maximum of encouragement to private enterprise without putting an unfair burden on the middle- and low-income groups.

Inherent in his plan for full employment was the basic fact that there could be no sixty million jobs unless there were markets for the goods produced by the workers holding these jobs. He therefore stressed that our economic frontiers must be limited not by our geography but by human needs the world over. Nor, he reminded us, should we overlook the challenge of our own human frontiers: those of city slums, undernourishment, health, individual development, and recreation. Job opportunities will of necessity multiply by means of these and other enterprises. He ended the discussion on a spiritual note:

This is both the challenge and the dilemma of democracy—namely, how to get full production, preserve the fundamental freedoms, and then go forward toward objectives which are worthy of man's spirit. In all this there can be no compulsion except that which comes from the earnest search of man's spirit to discover the divine purpose of the universe.

Reviewing Wallace's *Democracy Reborn* in 1944, Mrs. Eleanor Roosevelt commented that his "outstanding and continued theme [was] his belief that whatever is done, must be done for the general welfare of the majority of the people." This belief permeated all his political thinking. In December 1942, in a speech honoring Woodrow Wilson, he projected machinery that would keep nations disarmed and prevent economic warfare. Shortly after Roosevelt had stated that Dr. Win-the-War had replaced Dr. New Deal, Wallace declared at a Jackson Day dinner that the New Deal was not only very much alive but "has yet to attain to its full strength." And though Roosevelt had just cashiered him from BEW, Wallace without a scintilla of rancor praised him as a magnificent New Dealer.

In May 1944 Roosevelt sent Wallace on an important mission to Siberia and China. "The Vice President," he said, "because of his present position as well as his training in economics and agriculture, is unusually well-fitted to bring to me, and to the people of the United States, a most valuable first-hand report." After two months of intensive traveling, inspection, and discussions with various leaders, Wallace returned with his task most ably performed.

He had left the United States fully aware of the handicap his absence from the political scene would be to his renomination. The first to see him on his return in July, shortly before the Democratic convention, were Samuel Rosenman and Harold Ickes. Both told him that if he insisted on another term as Vice President he would split the party. Wallace assured them that he would do the President's bidding. At their first meeting he surprised Roosevelt when he informed him that he had nearly 300 pledged delegates. On his way out he was told by Roosevelt, "I hope it's the same team again, Henry." The President also made public a letter endorsing Wallace's candidacy and stating that if he were a delegate he would vote for him.

If Roosevelt were in the same state of health as in 1940 and not dependent on Congress for approval of his peace and postwar objectives, it is quite likely that he would have fought harder to retain Wallace as his running mate. In July 1944, however, the extreme tension and fatigue of his war leadership was fast undermining his sturdy constitution. He also knew that despite a Gallup poll showing that 65 percent of the voters favored Wallace, the southern politicians and a number of city bosses were savagely opposed to his candidacy. Most of the men close to the President likewise urged him to decide on another nominee. Under these circumstances it was not surprising that he gave half-promises to several and finally agreed to accept Senator Truman.

When Wallace seconded Roosevelt's nomination on the convention floor, he proved himself no politician but a man of integrity and ideals. Although he persisted in his own candidacy, he resorted to none of the maneuvers and ambiguities of the office-seeker. In his seconding speech he extolled the principles of democracy and liberalism to which most delegates at best pay only lip service. Though his own nomination depended on the votes of the southern delegates, he boldly urged the abolition of the poll tax and equal opportunities for all. Norris, the liberal Nestor, highly commended him and said the speech "was an exhibition of statesmanship and courage that I have never seen surpassed. . . . You have grown mightily in my estimation."

On the first ballot for the Vice Presidency Wallace was first with 429½ votes and Truman second with 319½. But the machine swung into action after that and gave Truman a large majority. Wallace took defeat with a good heart. "I really think," he remarked, "that I can do more for the cause of liberalism this way." And all through the campaign he worked as hard for Roosevelt's election as if he were on the ticket with him.

Wallace was told by the President that he could have any office he wished except that of Secretary of State. He chose that of Secretary of Commerce, then held by Jesse Jones. The latter's powerful friends in the Senate united in the fight against Wallace's confirmation. At the hearings Jones gave free rein to his spleen against his successsor. He insisted that Wallace was incompetent and was "willing to jeopardize the country's future with untried ideas and idealistic schemes." Wallace, when testifying, made no effort to placate the Senators. Instead he firmly defended his plans to achieve and maintain full employment and prosperity. "The real issue," he said, "is whether or not the powers of the Reconstruction Finance Corporation and its great subsidiaries are to be used only to help big business or whether these powers are also to be used to help little business and to help carry out the President's commitment of 60,000,000 jobs." Jones's cronies, however, insisted on removing RFC from the jurisdiction of the Department of Commerce and they had their way before Wallace's appointment was confirmed.

As Secretary of Commerce, Wallace attended to his duties with his customary concern. One of his important tasks was to draft the far-reaching employment bill that received Truman's backing and was passed by Congress. From the first, however, he was deeply disturbed by the growing tension between the United States and the Soviet Union. Even before the fighting had ended in 1945, when Russia was still our close and hard-hitting ally, he was distressed by the anti-Russian attitude on the part of influential Americans: "There is altogether too much irresponsible defeatist talk about the possibility of war with Russia. In my opinion, such talk, at a time when the blood of our boys shed on the fields of Europe has scarcely dried, is criminal."

Early in 1946, when General Walter Bedell Smith was appointed our ambassador to Russia, Wallace wrote to President Truman to propose "a new approach along economic and trade lines." It was his belief that if we sincerely offered Russia, badly devastated and impoverished, the economic assistance of which she was in great need, the gesture would break the "diplomatic deadlock" and lead to peaceful negotiation. Somewhat later, at a dinner honoring W. Averell Harriman, retiring ambassador to Russia, Wallace said, "Granting that Russia is wrong on every count, I still say that the United States has nothing to gain, but, on the contrary, everything to lose, by beating the tom-toms against Russia."

In July, unable to still his prodding conscience, Wallace sent Truman a long memorandum concerning our aggravated relations with Russia. He urged him to do his best to allay Russian fears of "capitalistic encirclement." The very idea of a preventive war, he pointed out, was "not only immoral but stupid." The only solution, he continued, "consists of mutual trust and confidence among nations, atomic disarmament, and an effective system of enforcing that disarmament." He opposed the "easy stages" proposal whereby other nations would refrain from attempting to make atom bombs and disclose their uranium resources, while we retained the secret of the atom bomb till full control and inspection were in effective operation. Such a scheme was obviously unacceptable to a proud and suspicious nation like Russia and would only intensify her effort to discover the secret for herself.

Once this happened, the atomic race could be disastrous. "The very fact that several nations have atomic bombs," he asserted, "will inevitably result in a neurotic, fear-ridden, itching-trigger psychology in all the peoples of the world." He further pointed out that our economic abundance, achieved "without sacrificing personal, political, and religious liberties," could surely stand up against the promises of communism. Moreover, "the slogan that communism and capitalism, regimentation and democracy, cannot continue to exist in the same world is, from a historical point of view, pure propaganda."

Truman expressed his appreciation of these views and shelved them. Meantime Wallace was asked by New York liberals to address a political rally at Madison Square Garden. He accepted because he wished to help elect Democratic Congressmen and because it was an opportunity to plead for peace and international amity. Two days before he was to deliver the speech he discussed it with the President—page by page according to Wallace and only a bare mention in the words of Truman.

In the crowded arena and to a nationwide radio audience

Wallace pled for an America vigorously dedicated to peace. The price of peace, he stated, "is the price of giving up prejudice, hatred, fear and ignorance." He made clear that he was "neither anti-British nor pro-British—neither anti-Russian nor pro-Russian." Nor did he believe that "getting tough" ever resulted in anything real or lasting; for "the tougher we get, the tougher will the Russians get." In the interest of peace it was time we understood that "we have no more business in the *political* affairs of Eastern Europe than Russia has in the *political* affairs of Latin America, Western Europe, and the United States." It was necessary for each country to recognize the sphere of interest of the other. He continued:

We must not let our Russian policy be guided or influenced by those inside or outside the United States who want war with Russia. This does not mean appeasement. We most earnestly want peace with Russia—but we want to be met halfway. And I believe we can get cooperation once Russia understands that our primary objective is neither saving the British empire nor purchasing oil in the Near East with the lives of American soldiers. . . .

The response of the audience was mixed. Russian sympathizers hissed the statements critical of the Soviet Union; the liberals applauded the telling points with much enthusiasm. As a consequence radio time was lost and Wallace had to skip passages toward the end. This gave his critics the opportunity to taunt him with the insinuation that he left out the paragraphs he feared his audience would dislike. The next day the newspapers and radio commentators were generally hostile.

On his return to Washington several days later Wallace learned that a newspaper columnist had obtained a copy of his memorandum to Truman and was about to make it public. He therefore conferred at once with Charles Ross, the President's secretary, and the two agreed that it was best to release the memorandum to the press. Publication brought severe criticism from American diplomatic sources. Truman summoned Wallace to the White

House and had him agree not to speak on international affairs while Secretary of State Byrnes was in Paris at a conference of foreign ministers. Meantime Byrnes, taunted by Senator Arthur Vandenberg, complained to the President that Wallace's strictures had weakened his position at the conference and insisted on resigning if Wallace were retained in the Cabinet. The next morning Truman telephoned Wallace and asked for his resignation. That evening the latter, now a free agent, said in a brief radio statement, "I feel that our present foreign policy does not recognize the basic realities which led to two world wars and which now threaten another war—this time an atomic war."

Now separated from government service for the first time in nearly fourteen years, Wallace accepted the editorship of *The New Republic* with the understanding that it was to become a forum for his views on peace and public affairs. For the entire year of 1947 he wrote weekly signed editorials and reports on topics of current interest. Among other things, he frowned upon the formation of Americans for Democratic Action because he felt it served to split the liberal movement and because it had as its "chief emotional drive . . . witch hunting for Communists and hating Russia." Yet he also deplored the position of those liberals who judged "everything solely from the standpoint of 'what will Russia think?' " He expressed the hope that most progressives were not interested in either of these extreme positions.

When the Truman Doctrine was announced in March 1947, Wallace reacted promptly and vigorously. He criticized the subsidy of $400 million to Greece and Turkey as "a program for the destruction, not the extension, of freedom." He warned that people cannot be bought, and regretted our position that "no regime is too reactionary for us, provided it stands in Russia's path." Over the radio he said:

The world is hungry and insecure, and the peoples of all lands demand change. American loans for military purposes won't stop them. President Truman cannot prevent change in the world any more than he can prevent the tide from coming in or the sun from setting. But once America stands for opposition to change we are lost. America will become the most hated nation in the world. . . . . I certainly don't want to see communism spread. I predict that Truman's policy will spread communism in Europe and Asia. You can't fight something with nothing.

He reacted more favorably to the Marshall Plan. It was encouraging to know that Secretary of State George Marshall was aware of the economic needs of European countries and wanted them to cooperate in efforts at recovery. Wallace pointed out, however, the importance of reaching an understanding with Russia and recommended a large loan and a trade agreement.

On the home front he was glad to see that 60,000,000 Americans were actually at work—sooner than he had expected. Truman's loyalty order aroused his indignation. He maintained that in so far as it will tend to punish people for what they think rather than for what they do the order was more shameful than the repressive laws of 1798. His resentment was even greater against the flagrant persecutions of the Committee on Un-American Activities. He accused it of "smears, innuendo, threats and intimidation" against New Dealers, of making no greater distinction between Communists and liberals than it did between evidence and hearsay.

Early in 1947 Wallace went to Europe to deliver several speeches on international affairs. He spoke candidly on American foreign policy and was well received by European liberals. Certain American newspapers and government officials, however, condemned his addresses as bordering on treason. On his return in May he made a highly successful speaking tour over the United States under the auspices of the Progressive Citizens of America. His audiences were everywhere large and enthusiastic, totaling over a hundred thousand who paid admissions to hear him.

Dedicated to the promotion of world peace, he felt exasperated by what he considered Washington's obtuse and harmful foreign policy. After much reflection he concluded that to campaign for the Presidency would be the most effective way of gaining the favorable attention of the American people. He had no illusions of political victory; but he hoped that once he had made clear the urgency of world peace and amity with Russia, his audiences would insist that Washington pursue these ends. In writing he stressed: "*I believe the American people must have an opportunity to express their hopes as well as their fears.*" At the end of 1947 he limited his work on *The New Republic* to a weekly page and devoted himself to the forthcoming campaign.

In announcing his candidacy Wallace declared that both major parties "stand for a policy which opens the door to war in our lifetime and makes war certain for our children." He therefore asked for a large "peace vote" to let the world know "that the United States is not behind the bipartisan reactionary war policy." His announcement ended with a call for "a Gideon's army—small in number, powerful in conviction, ready for action." The answer came from aroused liberals, earnest pacifists, and the motley-graded radicals ranging from the strongly individualistic dissident to the party-wedded Communist. As early as March opinion polls indicated that Wallace was favored by 11 percent of the voters; two months later seasoned politicians predicted that he would receive up to ten million votes.

The Americans for Democratic Action, among whom were a number of the ardent New Dealers of the 1930's, quickly opposed both Wallace and a third party. At its convention in February it "unreservedly condemned" Wallace's third-party candidacy on the ground that it "can serve only to elect an isolationist and reactionary Congress." With this important segment of liberals against him, Wallace had to depend primarily on the Progressive Citizens of America for his political organization.

Meantime in his weekly page and in speeches he was developing the issues of his campaign. Foreign policy was of course his main theme. He deplored the imputation that one must not appeal for an understanding with Russia because that was also the wish of the Communists. "The alternatives," he contended, "were support of the present militaristic bipartisan policy or a retreat to isolationism." He maintained that we must not "leave the advocacy of peace and understanding with Russia solely to a handful of Communists."

With anticommunism in full cry, he argued that civil liberties were the "number one problem in the United States in 1948." In criticism of ADA he said that liberals who were so fearful of communism that they joined hands with "the special interests . . . will, in time, find themselves betrayed and disillusioned. Eventually they will have to take a stand on fundamental issues, and then they will either have to sell their souls or stand up and fight." Actually, he insisted, both parties were in control of "reactionary capitalism"; both were confusing the public by crying "communist in harmony together."

I have no hope that I can stop these cries, but one thing I want to make absolutely clear: I do not accept the support of any person or group advocating the violent overthrow of the government of the United States. I do not accept the support of any person or group which places allegiance to another nation above its allegiance to the United States.

At the same time he declared that he was "utterly and completely against all types of red-baiting" and that he was opposed to any harassment of those who believed in peace with Russia.

In May Wallace made public a letter to Stalin "which set forth a basis for peaceful settlement of differences without sacrificing a single American principle or public interest." It was an eloquent plea to put an end to the cold war by agreeing on general disarmament and the outlawry of the methods of mass destruction; stoppage of export of weapons to other nations; resumption of unrestricted trade; free travel in both countries; free exchange of scientific information; and greater international relief. Stalin's reply intimated that the letter gave a reasonable basis for discussion; Truman ignored it.

When the convention of the "new party" opened in Philadelphia it buzzed with the hallelujah excitement and enthusiasm of a revival meeting. The delegates ranged from old Bull Moosers and aroused pacifists to stanch Communists. As in previous third-party assemblies, there was much singing and a prevailing spirit of fervent exhilaration. Despite the popular-front emphasis, criticism of Russia was discouraged. When a Vermont delegate rose in support of an amendment that would express disapproval of both Russian and American policies, he was voted down by opposition of the floor leaders.

The convention adopted the following nine pledges with great elation: freedom of expression, peace with Russia, elimination of Wall Street from government, lower prices, repeal of the Taft-Hartley Act, control of monopolies and unfair competition, extended social insurance, better education and federal aid, and better government planning. In accepting the nomination Wallace made clear that "the New Party is not pro-Russian or pro-communist, but it will not lend itself in any way to the red-baiting or Russia-baiting of the propaganda-manufacturing pseudo-liberals."

In addition to ADA liberals, the large majority of labor leaders were strongly opposed to Wallace's candidacy. Philip Murray, head of the CIO, was particularly critical because he considered the Progressive party in control of the Communists. Consequently only the few left-wing unions backed Wallace—much to his keen disappointment in view of his devotion to the interests of labor.

Nevertheless the campaign began hopefully. September polls showed that Wallace would get at least three million votes. His zealous supporters were confident that his nationwide speaking engagements would assuredly swell the total vote.

Two factors proved disastrous to Wallace's candidacy. Attacked by both major parties and many liberals as the tool and victim of the Communists, he was unable to overcome the stigma by disclaimers, outspoken as they were, since he refused to make a red-baiting statement. In 1948, however, American indoctrination against communism insisted on outright condemnation of that ideology and all those in any way connected with it. And Wallace was its conspicuous victim that fall.

The communist coup in Czechoslovakia served as egregious proof that communism was on the march the world over and must be stopped. It no doubt alienated millions of voters who were at first favorably inclined toward Wallace because of his close association with Roosevelt but who after the coup turned from him in fear and confusion. These and other liberals flocked to Truman—who was free of the stigma of Communist association and who was campaigning on a platform much like Wallace's on national issues. Thus, by the time of the election only the hard-core radicals and pacifists, together with a few thousand Communists—totaling only a little over a million votes—were all that remained in Gideon's camp. James A. Wechsler, who had spent ten months reporting the Wallace movement, commented vividly on his final impressions of its hapless leader:

In retrospect some of the most lasting images are curiously unpolitical. They are recollections of a shy, white-haired man, incredibly inept in the routines of politics, yet obsessed with a passion for public life; an inarticulate, awkward 60-year-old man taking a terrible physical beating and enduring all sorts of minor indignities; a lonely withdrawn man who must sometimes have experienced deep private doubts about the course of the pilgrimage and yet stubbornly proclaiming his essential righteousness; carrying on as his army dwindled and the nature of his entrapment on a left-wing island became plainer every hour.

Although Wallace's hopes were at a low ebb by November, he was nevertheless deeply disappointed by his poor showing in the election. What perturbed him most was his failure to persuade the mass of Americans of the urgent need to resolve the cold war. With our "tough" policy facing an aggressive and inimical Russian program, the danger of conflict seemed greater than ever. On reflection he perceived that Communist support, exaggerated and execrated by his opponents, had reared an ominous wall between him and millions of Americans who longed for peace and normally would have welcomed his guidance and encouragement. Yet he also knew that he could not have more definitely rejected Communist support and live with his conscience. After the election there remained little more for him to do than to seek the seclusion of his farm and the solace of agricultural experimentation.

For a time he kept in touch with the Progressive party organization, though he took less and less part in its deliberations. In July 1950, having been told by knowledgeable persons that Russia was responsible for the invasion of South Korea, he broke completely with the party when it refused to condemn the Soviet Union for the aggression. He was now fully disillusioned with Russia and favored Truman's immediate armed opposition to the invading North Koreans. Thereafter he has remained aloof from the turmoil and maneuvering of national and world politics.

In 1956, still eager for international amity, he came out in favor of President Eisenhower because he believed that the chances of peace were better with the Republican general than with the liberal Democrat Adlai Stevenson. To justify his political deviation he published an article in *Life* on his "political odyssey." He began by stating that peace remained "the prime necessity." Prior to the development of the hydrogen bomb each side might have had something to gain from a postponement of disarmament. "Now every day's delay in setting up practical inspected disarmament machinery is flirting with violent death; and both sides know it." Unlike a decade ago, however, he now blamed Russia even more than the United States for the dissention between them. With peace still the paramount issue in 1956, however, he decided once more to speak out publicly by favoring Eisenhower because he believed him to be "the man most likely to preserve world peace."

Two years later, in a speech before the Farm Institute in Des Moines, Iowa, he reiterated his confidence in Eisenhower and expounded the idea that before long China's population would be half again as large as it is now and therefore would become a real menace to Russia. With Russia already a "have" country like ourselves, she should welcome an understanding with us if we approached her openly and sincerely. Such an approach will require boldness and imagination to succeed. "The change in both Russia and the United States will come very slowly because both sides have become conditioned by fear, hatred, and distrust . . . and both, at the moment, are determined to surpass each other in destructive power." It was his hope, however, that constructive diplomacy on both sides will assert itself to save the world from a fearful holocaust.

Henry A. Wallace, born seventy years ago, has been "a practical idealist" all his adult life. Of a scientific turn of mind, making his mark as an agricultural economist and achieving notable success in his experimentation with hybrid corn, he was at the same time profoundly attracted to the mystical aspects of life and religion. Of a shy and introspective temperament, his zeal for social justice and world amity has impelled him to crusade for the public welfare and international peace. As the first commercial producer of hybrid corn he amassed a sizable fortune while achieving national recognition as editor of *Wallace's Weekly*. Truman admitted that "Wallace is the best Secretary of Agriculture this country ever had." As Vice President he was given by Roosevelt greater responsibilities than were had by any previous holder of that office. Entering the 1948 campaign with the crippling handicap of Communist support in a time of anticommunist hysteria, he courageously and unflinchingly expounded his views on world peace and the basic principles of individual freedom. Though scorned as a political misfit and mystical visionary by his critics, none has questioned his sincerity and idealism. Whatever his shortcomings, Henry A. Wallace definitely belongs with those Americans who have achieved renown in their fight for the social justice and individual liberties that have characterized the best aspects of American life.

HUGO L. BLACK

DEFENDER OF THE BILL OF RIGHTS

P
RESIDENT ROOSEVELT'S FIRST APPOINTMENT to the Supreme
Court was a highly intricate political problem. His mal-
adroit effort to curb the Court several months earlier had
put many Senators in a recalcitrant mood. He knew they would
refuse to confirm a prominent New Dealer. Yet he was resolved
to name a genuine and aggressive liberal. In a surprise move he
nominated Senator Black of Alabama. Thus Roosevelt once more
revealed himself the master politician: defiantly selecting an ardent
New Dealer and assured of his confirmation by the wonted rule
of senatorial courtesy.

Hugo La Fayette Black, eighth and youngest child of an Alabama petty merchant, was born on February 23, 1886. He grew
up in an environment strongly affected by the spirit of Populism.
Upon graduation from the University of Alabama Law School
he practised for a year in his home town of Ashland and then
moved to Birmingham. Ambitious and gregarious, he joined several
fraternal orders and became an active member of the Baptist
church. In 1911, at twenty-five, he was appointed police judge
and for two years he dealt with the dregs of the Birmingham
poor—mostly Negroes whose ignorance and poverty caused them
to violate the law and become the victims of a vicious prison
system. Black treated them with notable fairness.

Meantime, with a rapidly growing private practice, he was
gaining a reputation as a very effective trial lawyer. Most of his
cases were personal damage suits and his earnings were relatively

high. Eager, however, to gain political advancement, he campaigned successfully for the office of county solicitor. In initiating promised reforms, he ran afoul of men who profited from vested crime and crowded slums. They fought him relentlessly, but he managed to institute certain improvements. He stopped the practice of keeping Negroes in jail longer than necessary, cleaned up the clogged docket, and modified the third-degree methods employed by the Bessemer police.

When war was declared in 1917 he immediately enlisted. On his return to Birmingham after his discharge as captain of artillery, he resumed his private practice. In time he represented the United Mine Workers and other unions in addition to handling some of the most prominent trial cases in the state. In 1921 he married Josephine Foster, a person of high ethical standards and stanch liberalism.

While consolidating his position as one of the prominent lawyers of Birmingham, Black joined the Ku Klux Klan on September 11, 1923, then at the height of its political influence, with a membership of more than two million. In that city, as in many southern towns at that time, most Protestant ministers and prominent businessmen belonged to the Klan, and one of them who was an intimate friend of Black persuaded him to apply for membership. At no time then or since did he have the northern liberal's disdain for the Klan, although he later deplored its intolerance and denounced its acts of violence.

Highly successful as a legal practitioner, with a large annual income, his work did not give him the personal gratification he yearned. When he learned that the aged Oscar Underwood was to retire from the Senate in 1926, he decided to seek that office. Because the Klan's notoriety had increased, he resigned his membership but remained friendly with its local leaders and welcomed their support. For nearly a year he toured the highways and byways of the state in his Model T Ford, shaking hands with voters and advocating legislation that met with their approval. So energetic and effective was his long campaign that in the

August 1926 primaries he won over four rivals—and the nomination was tantamount to election.

Black took his public career very seriously and his study of economics and political science in time made him one of the best-informed men in the Senate. Senator Norris found in him a loyal supporter in the crusade for the public development of Muscle Shoals. Again and again Black stanchly fought proposed conservative legislation. When he sought re-election in 1932 he was strongly opposed by the Klan leaders, having earlier antagonized them by his active support of Al Smith's candidacy. Nevertheless, with the help of organized labor he was once more victorious over his rivals.

Eager to lessen the distress of the current unemployment, he concluded, after considerable study, that the most likely remedy was to spread the available work. On the opening of the Senate session in 1933 he introduced a bill limiting the workweek to thirty hours. With the aid of a vast amount of statistics on economic and industrial conditions he argued that his proposed measure would not only lessen unemployment but also help stabilize industry and thus improve the general economy. He considered his bill preferable to NIRA—which he feared would encourage fascist practices—as a stimulus to recovery, but the more comprehensive National Industrial Recovery Act was backed by the Roosevelt Administration.

Black achieved prominence in the Senate as an investigator. While chairman of a committee to inquire into the operation of mail-carrying contracts he succeeded in uncovering bribery, collusion, and general extravagance in connection with airmail subsidies. He asserted that "huge government expenditures have, in great part, found their way into the pockets of profiteers, stock manipulators, political and powerful financial groups who never flew a plane, who never invented an engine, who never improved an airplane part."

Having been named chairman of the committee to investigate the powerful lobby that fiercely resisted the liberal legislation of the New Deal, he determined to ferret out the facts despite formal barriers and clever dodging. To this end he used the power of his position with the zeal of a reform prosecutor. He ordered searches of files without prior permission, browbeat witnesses, and requisitioned letters and telegrams for "fishing" purposes. His methods were severely criticized, but his retort was that in no other way could he obtain information from men of great wealth who held themselves above the law. And his findings were definite and damning. He and his associates brought to light a vast amount of corrupt and unethical lobbying.

At the end of the investigation Black emerged as the zealous public official who had matched wits with the nation's shrewdest lawyers and industrialists and got what he wanted out of them. Despite the harsh criticism against his methods of inquiry, he succeeded in reversing the tide of public opinion on the holding company bill and helped the enactment of New Deal reforms.

Senator Black's nomination to the Supreme Court surprised certain liberals and outraged his critics. The first could not square their conventional image of a black-robed and dedicated Justice with the aggressive and crusading nominee; the conservatives who had deplored the "terrorism" of the Black Committee considered the appointment a "defiant gesture" and a calamity. The New York *Herald Tribune* expressed this chagrin when it declared editorially that Black's activity on the committee "revealed such an utter lack of judicial spirit, such a complete scorn of constitutional restraints as would make ascent to the Supreme Court a national tragedy." Senator Norris, ill at home, strongly defended Black in a letter to Senator H. F. Ashhurst, chairman of the Judiciary Committee: "I feel greatly grieved at the bitter, unreasonable and sometimes malicious attacks which are being made upon him. His work in the Senate must convince everyone that he possesses a superior ability and undaunted courage which are seldom equalled or surpassed." The question of Black's connection with the Klan was raised but not pursued in the Senate debate and he was promptly confirmed by a vote of 63 to 16. Thereupon he left for a long-postponed vacation in Europe.

On September 13 the Pittsburgh *Post-Gazette,* owned by a severe critic of the New Deal, began to publish Ray Sprigle's series of six articles on Black's Klan membership. Although the stories offered little that was not commonly known in Alabama, they were sensationally reprinted in other newspapers and eminent citizens resumed their attack upon Black and demanded his resignation or impeachment. On his return from Europe he stated his case over the radio with the dignity and objectivity befitting his judicial position: "I did join the Klan. I later resigned. I never rejoined. . . . I have no sympathy with any organization or group which, anywhere or at any time, arrogates to itself the un-American power to interfere in the slightest degree with complete religious freedom." Despite the continuous clamor for his resignation, he never again referred to the matter publicly. He assumed his seat on the bench and his masterly opinions and dissents soon silenced his detractors.

For all its aura of lofty objectivity, the Supreme Court is essentially a political institution. Its members naturally and inevitably deal with social and economic problems in the light of their personal prejudices and predilections. The Court's political complexion at any given time is determined by a combination of the character of its dominant majority and the prevailing public opinion. Yet dissents not infrequently become what one writer called "the most persuasive of precedents." Thus the eloquent calls in the wilderness of Holmes and Brandeis in the 1920's and those of Black and Douglas a generation later exerted an influence more fundamental than the opinions of the then regnant majorities.

Black joined a Court long dominated, if at last precariously, by a majority that respected the rights of property more than the rights of the individual. For half a century it had interpreted the word "person" in the Fourteenth Amendment to include corporations—to the great profit of large-scale business organizations. In effect the rule was: "Your property was what you made it; the liberty to make it your property." Tough-minded, courageous, zealous for the rights of the people, Black was determined to follow the original intent of the Constitution—that of furthering the general welfare. He questioned the judicial rationalization that permitted the deviation of the traditional due process of law from formal procedure to doubtful substance. From the first he strongly dissented from a number of majority opinions favoring corporations that sought to evade state regulations. There was a sharpness in his voice and a validity in his reasoning that put into clear focus the prejudices and precedents encrusted upon the original intent of the basic law.

His experience in Birmingham courts had made him particularly sensitive to the mistreatment of Negroes. In an early case he spoke forcefully in favor of a jury trial for criminal defendants, insisting that states must emphasize it in preference to "judges or masters appointed by judges." And by a jury he meant a jury of one's peers. In *Smith* v. *Texas* he wrote the majority opinion reversing the conviction of a Negro by a white jury. He revealed that although the county in which the trial occurred had a 20-percent Negro population, with half of it poll-tax payers, in eight years prior to the trial only five out of 384 grand jurors were Negroes. Juries thus chosen were not in his view instruments of equal justice. "The Fourteenth Amendment," he stated, "requires that equal protection to all must be given—not merely promised."

The liberalization of the Court by additional Roosevelt appointees favored this view of civil rights. Following earlier dissents by Justices Harlan and Fields, Black maintained for a majority that since the adoption of the Fourteenth Amendment no state could deny or abridge the rights of life, liberty, and property enumerated in the first eight Amendments. Outstanding in this connection was his celebrated opinion in *Chambers et al.* v. *Florida* in 1940. The petitioners claimed that their confessions were obtained under duress—having been questioned intermittently for six days and nights and continuously during the last twenty hours. Moreover, during the interrogation they were not permitted to confer with counsel or to see any friends or relatives. In a review of the evidence Justice Black affirmed that confessions elicited under such conditions violated the very essence of individual liberty. Yet he was not satisfied merely to reverse the convictions. He also spoke out firmly against the use of third-degree methods by police officers, and did it with an impelling eloquence that made his opinion one of the great judicial decisions of our time.

The opinion was at once recognized as a charter of protection for all victims of oppression and intolerance. It was applauded by a good many eminent citizens and forced the police to modify, at least outwardly, their methods of interrogation.

Justice Black's efforts at a broad interpretation of the Fourteenth Amendment are best seen in a long and learned dissent from the majority opinion in *Adamson* v. *California*. The petitioner, convicted of murder in the first degree, appealed on the ground that he was refused the right under the Fifth Amendment not to testify against himself. This appeal the majority denied on the basis of earlier opinions. In his dissent, joined by Justice Douglas, Black related in detail the historical events that had led to the adoption of the Fourteenth Amendment in order to prove that the aim of its first section "was to make the Bill of Rights applicable to the States." He further reviewed the action of the Court in cases from the *Slaughterhouse* opinion in 1873 to the *Twining* ruling in 1908 in order to show that the majority failed "to carry out the avowed purpose of the Amendment's sponsors. . . . Thus the power of legislatures became what this Court would declare it to be at a particular time independently of the specific guarantees of the Bill of Rights." Against this judicial arrogation he protested with all the force of his capable intellect—effectively marshaling the facts relevant to his purpose:

I cannot consider the Bill of Rights to be an outworn eighteenth-century "strait-jacket" as the *Twining* opinion did. . . . In my judgment no nation can lose their liberty so long as a Bill of Rights like ours survives and its basic purposes are conscientiously interpreted, enforced and respected. . . . I fear to see the consequences of the Court's practice of substituting its own concepts of decency and fundamental justice for the language of the Bill of Rights as its point of departure in interpreting and enforcing that Bill of Rights.

Seven years later the seed of this reasoning came into flower with the unanimous ruling of the Court against segregation in the South.

In a series of cases involving the freedom of religion Justice Black spoke on the nature of its inviolability with persuasive clarity. Yet when the *Gobitis* case, concerned with the refusal of children of Jehovah's Witnesses to salute the flag in the classroom, came up for decision in 1940, he and the others on the Court majority were patently influenced by the prevailing patriotism. With France being overrun by the Nazis and with American security presumably in danger, they ruled that the public school authorities had the right to inculcate patriotism by means of the flag salute. Only Chief Justice Stone dissented—with an eloquence that soon persuaded the liberal Justices of their aberration.

Two years later, in *Jones* v. *Opelika,* Justices Black, Douglas and Murphy recanted their error by joining Chief Justice Stone in dissent. They did more. As if in expiation of their patriotic excess, they courageously proclaimed their mistake: "The First Amendment does not put the right freely to exercise religion in a subordinate position. We fear, however, that the opinions in this and in the *Gobitis* cases do exactly that." When the *Barnette* case came up a year later, Justice Robert Jackson spoke for the liberal majority in overruling the previous opinions on the freedom of religion and hailed the broader freedom of the mind with great eloquence.

Justice Black, holding the freedom of conscience synonymous with religious liberty, also dissented from the majority opinion in *In re Summers*, which upheld an Illinois law barring a license to practice law to a conscientious objector. He maintained that this statute, penalizing belief rather than behavior, would not only exclude Quakers from the legal profession but could also be applied to other professions and vocations and was therefore unconstitutional. "Freedom to think, and to worship," he asserted, "has too exalted a position in our country to be penalized on such an illusory basis."

In 1947 he spoke for the majority in another case involving religious freedom. In *Everson* v. *Board of Education* the question was whether the township of Ewing, New Jersey, was acting constitutionally in repaying parents for their children's bus fare to and from public and parochial schools. Justice Black held that in this instance the First Amendment was not violated since free bus rides for children were no different in intent from traffic regulation or fire protection. "The First Amendment," he added, "has erected a wall between church and state. That wall must be kept high and impregnable. We would not approve the slightest breach. New Jersey has not breached it here."

A year later he detected such a breach in *McCullum* v. *Board of Education*. Again the Court's spokesman, he invalidated the Illinois law permitting "released time" from school for religious instruction. He pointed out that here tax-supported property was being used for religious education and school authorities were cooperating closely with the churches.

In keeping with his strong concern for the common good, Justice Black was actively solicitous for the welfare of the worker and the rights of the small businessman. He had little opportunity to deal memorably in this connection, since by the time he joined the Court the Wagner Act had already initiated the spectacular development of organized labor and a number of New Deal laws were curbing the former unrestraint of powerful corporations. His record is nevertheless impressive.

In 1940 he held for the Court, in *Drivers' Union* v. *Lake Valley*

Co., that milk drivers were within their rights in picketing dealers who refused to maintain union standards. A year later he dissented from the majority in *Drivers' Union* v. *Meadowmoor Co.* on the ground that the granted injunction was "too broad and sweeping" and therefore in violation of free speech. This concern for free speech he stated forcefully for the Court in *Bridges* v. *California*. Harry Bridges and the Los Angeles *Times* had made statements prior to court decisions which the judge considered efforts at intimidation and therefore contemptuous. Justice Black disagreed. "No suggestion can be found in the Constitution that the freedom there guaranteed for speech and press bears an inverse ratio to the timeliness and importance of the ideas seeking expression."

In a number of dissents he stressed the rights of labor over those of property, cavalierly disregarding the legalisms and precedents that influenced the majorities. Specifically, his position was that a worker was entitled to compensation in accidents even though partially at fault; that tips given to redcaps could not be considered by employers as part of wages; that a union could picket against nonunion workers even when such picketing was detrimental to their employers; that since the "slack movement" on long freight trains was dangerous to railroad employees, a state had the right to shorten the trains; and that railroad companies could not shirk their responsibilities by specifying exemption on passes given to employees.

In still other cases he was anxious to assure justice to individual workers, weak unions, and petty merchants. Thus he maintained that no man should be deprived of a job because he was not a member of a union; that certain unions, being essentially businesses, were not in a position to claim the benefits of the Norris-LaGuardia Act; that an injured worker was entitled to full compensation even though he was induced to accept a deceptive settlement; that unions cannot strike against the government or practice "featherbedding"; and that it was illegal to prohibit a union organizer to speak without a license.

His insistence on fair treatment and the public good was also evident in his majority opinions and dissents in cases dealing with business practices, patents, taxes, insurance, and other similar matters. In 1942 he allowed the Bethlehem Steel Corporation to retain the excess profits made on legal contracts during World War I. In *Goodyear Co.* v. *Ray-o-Vac Co.* he criticized the practice of patenting minor mechanical improvements in order to obtain "unearned special privileges." He held for the Court in *I.C.C.* v. *Mehling* against the rates which favored grain shipments made to Chicago by rail over those using barges part of the way. He devoted several months to the perusal of many thousands of pages of transcript in *Trade Commission* v. *Cement Institute* and found, for the Court, that the cement companies were guilty of unfair competition and restraint of trade when they agreed to charge the same price for cement in every part of the United States and to stop competition by underselling tactics. He also acted for the majority in *Trade Commission* v. *Morton Salt Co.* when he adjudged the firm guilty of unfair pricing.

Other similar cases in which his philosophy prevailed might be mentioned. In *Associated Press* v. *United States* Justice Black ruled for the majority that the AP by-laws which conferred upon a member the power to deny admission to a competing newspaper served to curb the initiative which brought new newspapers into existence and therefore curtailed the system of free enterprise protected by the Sherman Act. He again spoke for the Court in *United States* v. *Commodities Corporation* in upholding the government's wartime control of prices. In a suit seeking to stop the Tennessee Valley Authority from acquiring private lands, he ruled that the law creating TVA empowered it to transact all the business necessary in its general operation and therefore enabled it "to acquire lands by purchase or condemnation." He also favored the federal government over seacoast states that sued for title to their tidelands oil. He contended that the ocean was of vital consequence to the nation as a whole, that the federal government held its interests in trust for all the people, and that it "was not to be deprived of those interests by the ordinary court rules designed particularly for private disputes over individually owned pieces of property."

Although Justice Black tended to favor the government when its objectives were consonant with the general welfare, he required it to act within the limits of the Constitution and the legislation of Congress. When President Truman sought in 1952 to avert a nation-wide steel strike by an Executive Order directing the Secretary of Commerce to take over the affected steel plants, Black held for the Court that the President had no power to issue such an order and that Congress had in fact specifically denied him such power in labor disputes.

A genuine patriot, Justice Black regards national security of paramount importance. In time of war he is ready to bend freedom to the country's safety and to allow government restrictions not permissible in time of peace. All through World War II he went along with the majority, more than once acting as spokesman, in condemning German spies and subversives and in upholding military restrictions against citizens of Japanese origin on the Pacific Coast. When the majority held that G. S. Viereck did not have to make known the propaganda activities he initiated even though they served his German masters, Black dissented on the ground that Viereck was in fact serving the enemy. In another dissent he maintained that Cramer, who was a Nazi sympathizer, was guilty of treason because he had shielded one of the German saboteurs who had stolen into this country from a German submarine.

Once the danger of invasion was over, he took the position that the law of the land was again supreme. Speaking for the Court in two cases he reversed sentences of civilians by provost court on the ground that the martial law declared in Hawaii after the Japanese attack "was not intended to authorize the supplanting of courts by military tribunals." When California tried to discriminate against Japanese who wanted to return from wartime internment, he asserted their rights in vigorous opinions. In

Oyama v. *California* he voided a state statute prohibiting the ownership of land by aliens who were ineligible for citizenship. He also held in favor of a Japanese commercial fisherman who was refused a renewal of his license on his return after the war. When the Court majority permitted the deportation of an enemy alien in *Ludecke* v. *Watkins,* he protested that as a result of this action "individual liberty will be less secure tomorrow than it was yesterday."

When government agencies began, with the outbreak of the cold war, to deal severely with Communists and political dissidents, Justice Black stood up firmly against their unfair treatment. A fundamental Jeffersonian—cherishing liberty and anxious to preserve it unblemished and unimpaired—he was inclined to tolerate radicals as such and to give alleged subversives the benefit of the doubt. Having meditated deeply on the essentials of democracy, he is sincerely convinced that it is far better to risk the disloyalty on the part of the small Communist minority than to scotch the threat at the cost of the Bill of Rights. For he believes, in the ripeness of wisdom, that in the long run the struggle between capitalistic democracy and Marxist communism will be resolved not on the field of bloody battle but in the hearts of the mass of men—and there the appeal of the Bill of Rights is far more potent than any Communist dogma.

The years of the cold war brought both known Communists and suspected dissidents under the scourge of congressional investigations, inimical laws, and judicial bias. The more important cases arising out of this antisubversive agitation came before the Supreme Court for judication. Repeatedly Justice Black, often joined by Justice Douglas and occasionally by one or more of his colleagues, distinguished himself by vigorous dissents upholding the basic freedoms guaranteed by the Constitution.

Early in the cold war he rejected the ruling that a Communist alien could be kept in jail until his deportability was established. "I can only say," he concluded, "that I regret, deeply regret, that the Court now adds the right to bail to the list of other Bill of Rights guarantees that have recently been weakened to expand governmental powers at the expense of individual freedom."

In *Dennis* v. *United States* the majority dismissed the allegation that jurors in government service could not be impartial in view of the reflection upon their loyalty in case of acquittal. Justice Black disagreed. He insisted that to expect government employees, affected by "the prevailing pattern of loyalty investigations and threatened purges," to serve as impartial jurors in the trial of a Communist, was an unrealistic assumption.

In another dissent he pointed out that for the petitioner to answer questions would have been self-incriminatory. "To-day's holding," he stated, "creates this dilemma for witnesses: On the one hand, they risk imprisonment for contempt by asserting the privilege prematurely; on the other, they might lose the privilege if they answer a single question." This reasoning evidently persuaded the majority in the similar cases of Mr. and Mrs. Blau. "The attempts of the courts below," he held for the Court in Mrs. Blau's case, "to compel petitioner to testify runs counter to the Fifth Amendment as it has been interpreted from the beginning." He also ruled that in convicting Mr. Blau the lower courts erred in failing "to sustain the claim of privilege against self-incrimination." This double judgment made possible for witnesses thereafter to refuse to testify on the ground of self-incrimination without being held in contempt. Ironically, such refusal has come to signify guilt—becoming "Fifth-Amendment Communists"—and has caused many great hardship.

When the Court approved the noncommunist affidavit clause for union officials in the Taft-Hartley Act, Justice Black argued in a lone dissent that the ruling rejected the First Amendment. He pointed out that the validation might be interpreted to exclude such officials from union membership "and in fact from getting or holding any job whereby they could earn a living." Such a condition, he insisted, was arbitrary and discriminatory:

Like anyone else, individual Communists who commit overt acts in violation of valid laws can and should be punished. But the postulate of the First Amendment is that our free institutions can be maintained without proscribing or penalizing political beliefs, speech, press, assembly, or party affiliation. This is a far bolder philosophy than despotic rulers can afford to follow. It is the heart of the system on which our freedom depends.

In the second case of *Dennis* v. *United States* Chief Justice Vinson sustained the Smith Act prohibiting the advocacy of overthrowing the government by force or violence. He reasoned that the "clear and present danger" doctrine might be valid in isolated instances but not "in the context of world crisis after crisis." Since the convicted eleven Communist leaders were presumably prepared forcefully to overthrow the government "as speedily as circumstances would permit," this threat "justifies such invasion of free speech as is necessary to avoid the danger." Justices Black and Douglas dissented spiritedly. They argued that the question at issue was one of free speech and not of violent action. The charge against the petitioners was in fact "a virulent form of prior censorship of speech and the press." Consequently the Smith Act, "authorizing this prior restraint," was "unconstitutional on its face and as applied." And Justice Black concluded wistfully:

Public opinion being what it now is, few will protest the conviction of these communist petitioners. There is hope, however, that in calmer times, when present pressures, passions and fears subside, this or some later Court will restore the First Amendment liberties to the high preferred place where they belong in a free society.

In *Anti-Fascist Committee* v. *McGrath* the majority joined him in holding that the Attorney-General could not list any organization as Communist-controlled without establishing the proof for it. In the present political climate, he stated, such an act was "the practical equivalent of confiscation and death sentence for any blacklisted organization not possessing extraordinary financial, political or religious prestige and influence." When the New York

Feinberg law, prohibiting the employment of teachers who were members of subversive organizations, was validated by the Court majority, Justices Black, Douglas, and Frankfurter strongly dissented. Douglas argued sharply that the law "proceeds on a principle repugnant to our society—guilt by association." Black, concurring, added: "This is another of those rapidly multiplying legislative enactments which make it dangerous—this time for school teachers—to think or say anything except what a transient majority happen to approve at the moment." He also dissented from the majority ruling in *Sacher* v. *United States* against lawyers convicted of contempt in connection with the trial of the eleven Communist leaders. He held that Judge Harold Medina should not have passed on his own charge and that the defendants were entitled to a jury trial.

Black joined Douglas in his dissent from the majority in *Rosenberg* v. *United States*. Both stated that "there were substantial grounds to believe the death sentences of these two people were imposed by the district judge in violation of law." Black added:

It is not amiss to point out that this Court has never reviewed this record and has never affirmed the fairness of the trial below. Without an affirmance of the fairness of the trial by the highest court of the land there may always be questions as to whether these executions were legally and rightfully carried out.

The intensity of the cold-war hysteria slackened considerably after 1954—after both the United States and Russia had reached an atomic stalemate and after the Senate had censured Senator McCarthy. The Supreme Court, liberalized under Chief Justice Warren, resumed a stricter interpretation of the Bill of Rights. Justice Black nevertheless remained as concerned as ever for the sanctity of our basic charter. In *Irvine* v. *California* he dissented on the ground that the petitioner, a gambler, was found guilty on evidence extorted from him in violation of the Fifth Amendment. He was impelled again to dissent in *Barsky* v. *Board of Regents* when the majority validated the legality of the Attorney-General's subversive list. "My view was and is," he explained, "that the list was the equivalent of a bill of attainder which the Constitution expressly forbids."

When Congress, prodded by McCarthy and his sympathizers, passed the Immunity Act as a means of circumventing the Fifth Amendment and compelling unwilling witnesses to testify, Justices Black and Douglas spoke out against the Act in a sharp dissent the first time it came up for a ruling in the Supreme Court. In *Ullmann* v. *United States* they argued "that the right of silence created by the Fifth Amendment is beyond the reach of Congress"; that the action of the majority had removed a protective function of the Fifth Amendment by qualifying the guarantee against self-incrimination.

The Fifth Amendment was written in part to prevent any Congress, any court, and any prosecutor from prying open the lips of an accused to make incriminating statements against his will. The Fifth Amendment protects the conscience and the dignity of the individual, as well as his safety and security against the compulsion of government.

When five of his colleagues in *Jay* v. *Boyd* approved the Attorney-General's regulation authorizing the deportation of aliens on the basis of anonymous information, Black again found himself in the minority. He insisted there was no way to contest the veracity of anonymous accusations, since the information can neither be identified nor questioned. Such information, he declared, cannot be used in a court of law and therefore should not be made the basis of banishment. In our system of government no one's liberty should be taken away by such shortcuts. No amount of legal reasoning by the Court and no rationalization that might be devised "can disguise the fact that the use of anonymous information to banish people is not consistent with the principle of a free country."

In a series of rulings in 1957 the liberalized majority of the Court finally favored the strict interpretation of the Bill of Rights that Justices Black and Douglas had urged so eloquently and so persistently in their numerous dissents. In the *Jencks, Sweezy, Watkins, Schware, Yates,* and other cases the Court in a real sense modified or reversed its former holdings in its interpretation of the Bill of Rights. But the two dissenters, though with the majority in these cases, continued to stress the inviolate nature of our constitutional liberties. In the *Yates* case they would have reversed the convictions of all fourteen petitioners on the ground that the statutory provisions on which their prosecutions were based abridged the freedom of the First Amendment. As in the *Dennis* case, they refused to compromise with principle. And Justice Black declared: Governmental suppression of causes and beliefs seem to me to be the very antithesis of what our Constitution stands for. . . . Unless there is complete freedom of expression of ideas, whether we like them or not, concerning the way government should be run and who shall run it, I doubt if any views in the long run can be secured against the censor. The First Amendment provides the only kind of security system that can preserve a free government.

On March 31, 1958, Justice Black, bolstered by Chief Justice Warren and Justice Douglas, dissented from majority rulings in several cases pertaining to the rights of individuals. In the cases of the Communists Green and Winston he made a frontal attack on the idea that criminal contempts should be treated differently from other criminal cases. The summary trial of criminal contempt, he pointed out, makes the judge "lawmaker, prosecutor, judge, jury and disciplinarian" and no person "should be granted such autocratic omnipotence."

Justice Black's career on the Supreme Court has established him pre-eminently as a twentieth-century Jeffersonian: an impassioned defender of the rights of the individual and a spirited protagonist of justice and equality. A ready supporter of government regulation for the common good, he is an intrepid opponent of any kind of tampering with the basic freedoms established by the Bill of Rights. His gracious and urbane personality combines a lofty idealism with an inflexible will. Acutely intelligent, sincerely democratic, highly learned, he is definitely realistic, impatient with outworn precedent, and forthright in his critical reactions. No chauvinist or isolationist, he cherishes the American form of government because he considers it the highest phase of political development. And he is jealous of any weakening of our democratic principles because he wants the United States to remain a beacon of liberty for all mankind.

His career on the Supreme Court ranks him with the most eminent Justices in the history of that high tribunal. Despite his inauspicious start, he established himself in his first term as a vigorous and valiant interpreter and guardian of the Constitution. His democratic liberalism and his compassion for the weak and oppressed hardened his zeal for the sanctity of the Bill of Rights. He sought to win for the Negro and the alien, the dissident and the Communist, the justice and protection which are their right under the Constitution but which prejudice and agitated fear had withheld from them. And although he has often found himself in the minority—many times the sole dissenter—the forcefulness of his logic and the validity of his protest have the impact of eventual triumph.

BIBLIOGRAPHY

THE ABOLITIONISTS

GENERAL REFERENCES

Beard, Charles A. and Mary R., *The Rise of American Civilization*, New York, 1927

Brooks, Van Wyck, *The Flowering of New England*, New York, 1936

Buckmaster, Henriette, *Let My People Go*, The Story of the Underground Railroad and the Growth of the Abolition Movement, New York, 1941

Commager, H. S., *Theodore Parker*, Boston, 1936

Dumond, D. L., *Anti-Slavery Origins of the Civil War*, Ann Arbor, 1939

Hacker, Louis, *The Triumph of American Capitalism*, New York, 1940

Harlow, R. V., *Gerrit Smith*, New York, 1939

Helper, H. R., *The Impending Crisis in the South*, New York, 1857

Higginson, T. W., *Cheerful Yesterdays*, Boston, 1898

Parrington, V. L., *Main Currents in American Thought*, New York, 1927–1930

Simons, A. M., *Social Forces in American History*, New York, 1911

Symes, Lillian and Clement, Travers, *Rebel America*, The Story of Social Revolt in the United States, New York, 1934

Wilson, Forrest, *Crusader in Crinoline*, The Life of Harriet Beecher Stowe, 1941

WILLIAM LLOYD GARRISON

Birney, William, *James G. Birney and His Times*, New York, 1890

Chapman, J. J., *William Lloyd Garrison*, Boston, 1913

Chertkov, V. G., and Holah, F., *A Short Biography of William Lloyd Garrison*, 1904

Garrison, W. L., *The Liberator: 1831–1865*

—— *Selections from Writings and Speeches*, Boston, 1852

—— *Thoughts on African Colonization*, Boston, 1832

Garrison, W. P. and F. J., *William Lloyd Garrison, 1805–1879; the Story of His Life Told by His Children*, 4 vols., New York, 1885–1889

Johnson, Oliver, *William Lloyd Garrison and His Times*, Boston, 1880

Swift, Lindsay, *William Lloyd Garrison*, New York, 1911

Villard, Fanny Garrison, *William Lloyd Garrison on Non-Resistance, etc.*, New York, 1924

JOHN BROWN

Brown, John, *Words from His Account of His Childhood*, Boston, 1897

Benét, Stephen Vincent, *John Brown's Body*, New York, 1929

Bradford, G., *Damaged Souls*, Boston, 1923

Ehrlich, Leonard, *God's Angry Man*, New York, 1932

Hinton, R. J., *John Brown and His Men*, New York, 1894

Karsner, David, *John Brown, Terrible " Saint,"* New York, 1934

Newton, John, *Captain John Brown of Harper's Ferry*, New York, 1902

Redpath, J., *The Public Life of John Brown*, New York, 1860

Sanborn, J. B., *The Life and Letters of John Brown*, Boston, 1885

Villard, O. G., *John Brown, 1800–1859. A Biography Fifty Years After*, Boston, 1910, New York, 1943

Warren, Robert Penn, *John Brown, The Making of a Martyr*, New York, 1929

WENDELL PHILLIPS

Austin, G. L., *The Life and Times of Wendell Phillips*, Boston, 1884

Coleman, McAlister, *Pioneers of Freedom*, New York, 1929

Martyn, Carlos, *Wendell Phillips: the Agitator*, New York, 1890

Phillips, Wendell, *Speeches, Lectures, and Letters*, First Series, Boston, 1863; Second Series, Boston, 1892

Russell, Charles Edward, *The Story of Wendell Phillips*, Soldier of the Common Good, New York, 1914

Sears, Lorenzo, *Wendell Phillips*, Orator and Agitator, Boston, 1904

Woodberry, G. E., *Wendell Phillips*, The Faith of an American, New York, 1912

THE UTOPIANS

GENERAL REFERENCES

Beard, Charles A. and Mary R., *The Rise of American Civilization*, New York, 1927

Brooks, Van Wyck, *The Flowering of New England*, New York, 1936

Chamberlain, John, *Farewell to Reform*, New York, 1932

Commons, John R. and Associates, *History of Labor in the United States*, New York, 1918

Ely, Richard T., *The Labor Movement in America*, New York, 1886

Fine, Nathan, *Labor and Farmer Parties in the United States*, 1828–1928, New York, 1928

Hillquit, Morris, *History of Socialism in the United States*, New York, 1903

Laidler, Harry W., *A History of Socialist Thought*, New York, 1927.

Mannheim, Karl, *Ideology and Utopia*, An Introduction to the Sociology of Knowledge, New York, 1936

Mumford, Lewis, *The Story of Utopias*, New York, 1922

Noyes, John Humphrey, *History of American Socialisms*, New York, 1870

Parrington, V. L., *Main Currents in American Thought*, 3 vols., New York, 1927–1930

Ross, Harry, *Utopias Old and New*, New York, 1938

Simons, A. M., *Social Forces in American History*, New York, 1911

Symes, Lillian and Clement, Travers, *Rebel America*, The Story of Social Revolt in the United States, New York, 1934

Ware, Norman, *The Labor Movement in the United States*, 1860–1895, New York, 1929

MARGARET FULLER

Anthony, Katharine S., *Margaret Fuller*, A Psychological Biography, New York, 1920

Bell, Margaret, *Margaret Fuller*, A Biography, New York, 1930

Braun, F. A., *Margaret Fuller and Goethe*, New York, 1910

Brooks, Van Wyck, *The Life of Emerson*, New York, 1932

Fuller, Margaret, *Art, Literature, and the Drama*, New York, 1860
—— *At Home and Abroad*, New York, 1856
—— *Love Letters*, New York, 1903
—— *Memoirs*, 2 vols., ed. by R. W. Emerson and others, Boston, 1852
—— *Papers on Literature and Art*, New York, 1846
—— *Summer on the Lakes*, Boston, 1844
—— *Woman in the Nineteenth Century*, Boston, 1845
Higginson, T. W., *Margaret Fuller Ossoli*, Boston, 1884
Howe, Julia Ward, *Margaret Fuller*, New York, 1883
Wade, Mason, *Margaret Fuller, Whetstone of Genius*, New York, 1940
—— *The Writings of Margaret Fuller*, selected and edited, New York, 1941

ALBERT BRISBANE

Brisbane, Albert, *A Concise Exposition of the Doctrine of Association*, New York, 1843
—— *A Mental Biography*, with a Character Study by His Wife, Redelia Brisbane, New York, 1893
—— *General Introduction to Social Sciences*, New York, 1876
—— *The Social Destiny of Man*, New York, 1840
Greeley, Horace, *Recollections of a Busy Life*, New York, 1873
Sotheran, Charles, *Horace Greeley and Other Pioneers of American Socialism*, New York, 1915

EDWARD BELLAMY

Bellamy, Edward, *Dr. Heidendorff's Process*, Boston, 1880
—— *Edward Bellamy Speaks Again*, Yellow Springs, Ohio, 1935
—— *Equality*, Boston, 1897
—— *Looking Backward, 2000–1887*, Boston, 1887
—— *Miss Ludington's Sister, A Romance of Immortality*, Boston, 1884
—— *Six to One: A Nantucket Idyl*, Boston, 1878
—— *Talks on Nationalism*, Boston, 1937
—— *The Blind Man's World and Other Stories*, Boston, 1898
—— *The Duke of Stockbridge, A Romance of Shays' Rebellion*, Boston, 1898
—— *The New Nation*, 1891–1893

Bellamy, Edward, *The Religion of Solidarity*, ed. by A. E. Morgan, Yellow Springs, Ohio, 1940

Johnson, Oliver W., *An Answer to Chaos*, New York, 1933

Morgan, A. E., *Edward Bellamy*, New York, 1944

Russell, Frances, *Touring Utopia*, New York, 1932

Seager, Allan, *They Work for a Better World*, New York, 1939

Vinton, A. D., *Looking Further Backward*, New York, 1890

THE ANARCHISTS

GENERAL REFERENCES

Andrews, Stephen Pearl, *The Science of Society*, Boston, 1895

Bailie, William, *Josiah Warren, The First American Anarchist*, Boston, 1906

Bakunin, Michael, *God and the State*, Boston, 1883

Carr, E. H., *Michael Bakunin*, New York, 1937

David, Henry, *The History of the Haymarket Affair*, New York, 1936

Eltzbacher, Paul, *Anarchism*, New York, 1908

Godwin, William, *Enquiry Concerning Political Justice*, London, 1793

Greene, William B., *Mutual Banking*, New York, 1870

Joad, C. E. M., *Introduction to Modern Political Theory*, London, 1924

Kropotkin, Peter, *The Conquest of Bread*, New York, 1927

—— *Memoirs of a Revolutionist*, Boston, 1899

—— *Mutual Aid*, London, 1902

—— *Revolutionary Pamphlets*, ed. by Roger Baldwin, New York, 1927

Most, John, *The Social Monster*, New York, 1890

Osgood, H. L., " Scientific Anarchism," *Pol. Sci. Quar.*, 18 (1889), 1–36

Plechanov, George, *Anarchism and Socialism*, Chicago, 1908

Russell, Bertrand, *Proposed Roads to Freedom*, New York, 1919

Salter, W. M., *Anarchy or Government?*, New York, 1895

Schaack, Michael J., *Anarchy and Anarchists*, Chicago, 1889

Schuster, Eunice M., *Native American Anarchism*: A Study of Left-Wing American Individualism, Northampton, Mass., 1932

Shaw, George Bernard, *The Impossibility of Anarchism*, Fabian Tracts, No. 45, 1891

Sprading, C. T., *Liberty and the Great Libertarians*, Los Angeles, 1913
Stirner, Max, *The Ego and His Own*, New York, 1907
Symes, Lillian, and Travers, Clement, *Rebel America*, New York, 1934
Vizetelly, E. A., *The Anarchists*, New York, 1911
Warren, Josiah, *True Civilization*, Boston, 1863
Wenley, R. M., *The Anarchist Ideal*, Boston, 1913

HENRY DAVID THOREAU

Atkinson, J. Brooks, *Henry Thoreau, the Cosmic Yankee*, New York, 1927
Browne, Ralph Waldo, *Man or the State?* New York, 1919
Boyd, David, "Thoreau the Rebel Idealist," *Americana*, Vol. 30, 89–118, Somerville, 1936
Canby, Henry Seidel, *Thoreau*, Boston, 1939
Dreiser, Theodore, *The Living Thoughts of Thoreau*, New York, 1939
Gabriel, Ralph H., *The Course of American Democratic Thought*, New York, 1940
Matthiessen, F. O., *American Renaissance, Art and Expression in the Age of Emerson and Whitman*, New York, 1941
Sanborn, F. H., *The Life of Henry David Thoreau*, Boston, 1917
Shepard, Odell, *The Heart of Thoreau's Journals*, Boston, 1927
Thoreau, H. D., *Anti-Slavery and Reform Papers*, ed. by H. S. Salt, London, 1890
—— *The Writings of Henry David Thoreau*, 10 vols., Boston, 1893–1900
—— *The Works of Henry D. Thoreau*, with a biographical sketch by Ralph Waldo Emerson, one-volume edition, New York, 1940
Van Doren, Mark, *H. D. Thoreau, A Critical Study*, Boston, 1916

BENJAMIN R. TUCKER

Liberty, Aug. 1881–April 1908, ed. by B. R. Tucker
Proudhon, Pierre J., *What Is Property?*, trans. by B. R. Tucker, Princeton, Mass, 1876
—— *System of Economic Contradictions*, trans. by B. R. Tucker, Boston, 1887
The Radical Review, May 1877–Feb. 1878, ed. by B. R. Tucker

Tucker, B. R., *The Attitude of Anarchism Toward Industrial Combinations*, New York, 1903
— *Individual Liberty*, ed. by C. L. S., New York, 1926
— *Instead of a Book*, New York, 1897
— *State Socialism and Anarchism*, New York, 1899 (first appeared in *Liberty*, March, 1888)
Yarros, Victor S., *Anarchism*, Boston, 1887
— " Philosophical Anarchism," *Am. Jour. of Soc.* 41:470–83
— " Philosophical Anarchism, Its Rise, Decline, and Eclipse," *Jour. of Soc. Phil.* (Vol. VI), April, 1941, No. 3

EMMA GOLDMAN

Berkman, Alexander, *Now and After, the ABC of Communist Anarchism*, New York, 1929
— *Prison Memoirs of an Anarchist*, New York, 1912
Dell, Floyd, *Women as World Builders*, New York, 1913
Goldman, Emma, *Anarchism and Other Essays*, New York, 1911
— *Living My Life*, New York, 1931
— *My Dissillusionment with Russia*, New York, 1923
— *My Further Disillusionment with Russia*, New York, 1924
— *The Social Significance of the Modern Drama*, Boston, 1914
— " Was My Life Worth Living?," *Harper's* 170:52–8, Dec. 1934
Goldsmith, Margaret, *Seven Women Against the World*, London, 1935
Mother Earth, March 1906–Aug. 1917, ed. by Emma Goldman
Trial and Speeches of Alexander Berkman and Emma Goldman in the U. S. District Court in the City of New York, July 1917

THE DISSIDENT ECONOMISTS

GENERAL REFERENCES

Annals of the Academy of Political and Social Science, CVII, 1923, 333–367
Beard, Charles A. and Mary R., *The Rise of American Civilization*, New York, 1930
Boswell, James L., *The Economics of Simon Nelson Patten*, Philadelphia, 1934

Carnegie, Andrew, *Triumphant America*, New York, 1886

—— *Autobiography*, New York, 1920

Curti, Merle E., *The Growth of American Thought*, New York, 1943

" Economics," *Encyclopaedia of the Social Sciences*

Gabriel, Ralph H., *The Course of American Democratic Thought*, New York, 1940

Hacker, Louis M., *The Triumph of American Capitalism*, New York, 1940

Lloyd, Henry D., " The Story of a Great Monopoly," *Atlantic Monthly*, March 1881

—— *Wealth Against Commonwealth*, New York, 1894

Parrington, V. L., *Main Currents in American Thought*, New York, 1927–30

Patten, S. N., *The Reconstruction of Economic Theory*, Philadelphia, 1912

Sherwood, Sidney, *Tendencies in American Economic Thought*, Baltimore, 1897

Simons, A. M., *Social Forces in American History*, New York, 1911

Tugwell, R. G., " Life and Work of Simon Patten," *Jour. of Pol. Economy*, XXXI, April 1923

Veblen, Thorstein, *The Place of Science in Modern Civilization*, New York, 1919

HENRY GEORGE

Birnie, A., *Single-Tax George*, London, 1939

Brown, H. G., " The Single-Tax Complex," *Jour. of Pol. Economy*, XXXII, 2, April 1924

Geiger, G. R., " The Forgotten Man Henry George," *Antioch Review*, Sept. 1941

—— *The Philosophy of Henry George*, New York, 1933

George, Henry, *The Land Question*, etc., New York, 1881

—— *A Perplexed Philosopher*, New York, 1892

—— *Progress and Poverty*, New York, 1880

—— *Protection or Free Trade*, New York, 1886

—— *The Science of Political Economy*, New York, 1898

—— *Social Problems*, New York, 1883

George, Henry, Jr., *The Life of Henry George*, New York, 1900

Land and Freedom (formerly *The Single Tax Review*)

Marshall, Alfred, *Wealth and Want*, London, 1883

Nock, A. J., *Henry George*, 1939

Post, Louis F., *The Prophet of San Francisco*, New York, 1930

Seitz, Don C., *Uncommon Americans*, New York, 1925

Seligman, E. R. A., *Essays in Taxation*, 10th edition, New York, 1925

The Single Tax Discussion, held at Saratoga, Sept. 5, 1890. Reported for the Am. Soc. Sci. Assoc. and edited by F. B. Sanborn, Concord, Mass., 1890

The Standard

Toynbee, Arnold, *Progress and Poverty*, a Criticism of Henry George, London, 1894

Young, A. N., *The Single Tax Movement in the United States*, Princeton, 1916

BROOKS ADAMS

Adams, Brooks, *American Economic Supremacy*, New York, 1900

—— *The Emancipation of Massachusetts*, Boston, 1887

—— "The Incoherence of American Democracy," an Address to the Bunker Hill Memorial Association, June 17, 1916

—— *The Law of Civilization and Decay*, New York, 1895; new edition with an Introduction by Charles A. Beard, New York, 1943

—— *The New Empire*, New York, 1902

—— *The Theory of Social Revolutions*, New York, 1913

Adams, Henry, *The Degradation of the Democratic Dogma*, with an Introduction by Brooks Adams, New York, 1919

—— *The Education of Henry Adams*, Boston, 1918

—— *Letters*, two volumes, Boston, 1930, 1938

Adams, J. T., *The Adams Family*, New York, 1930

Ford, W.C., "Brooks Adams," *Harvard Graduate Magazine*, XXXV, 1927, 615–27.

Holmes, O. W., *Holmes–Pollock Letters*, Vol. I, Boston, 1942

THORSTEIN VEBLEN

Bates, E. S., "Thorstein Veblen," *Scribner's Magazine*, Dec. 1933

Dorfman, Joseph, *Thorstein Veblen and His America*, New York, 1934

Duffus, R. L., *The Innocents at Cedro*, New York, 1944

Falnes, O. J., " Thorstein Veblen," *Amer. Scandanavian Review*, XXIII, 1935, 24–33

Hobson, J. A., *Veblen*, New York, 1937

Homan, P. T., " Thorstein Veblen," in *American Masters of Social Science*, edited by Howard W. Odum, New York, 1927

Lerner, Max, "What is Usable in Veblen?," *New Republic*, May 15, 1935

Mitchell, W. C., " Thorstein Veblen," *New Republic*, Sept. 4, 1929

Taggart, R. V., " Thorstein Veblen, A Chapter in American Economic Thought," Univ. of Calif. Publications in Economics, VII, No. 1

Veblen, Thorstein, *Absentee Ownership*, New York, 1923

—— *Essays in Our Changing Order*, edited by L. Ardzrooni, New York, 1934

—— *The Engineers and the Price System*, New York, 1921

—— *The Higher Learning in America*, New York, 1918

—— *Imperial Germany and the Industrial Revolution*, New York, 1915

—— *An Inquiry Into the Nature of Peace and the Terms of Its Perpetuation*, New York, 1917.

—— *The Instinct of Workmanship and the State of the Industrial Arts*, New York, 1914

—— *The Place of Science in Modern Civilization*, New York, 1919

—— *The Theory of Business Enterprise*, New York, 1904

—— *The Theory of the Leisure Class*, New York, 1899

—— *The Vested Interests and the Common Man*, New York, 1919

—— *What Veblen Taught*, with an Introduction by W. C. Mitchell, New York, 1936

Wallace, H. A., " Veblen's Imperial Germany and the Industrial Revolution," *Pol. Sci. Quar.*, LV, 1940, 435–45

THE MILITANT LIBERALS

GENERAL REFERENCES

Chamberlain, John, *Farewell to Reform*, New York, 1932

Croly, Herbert D., *The Promise of American Life*, New York, 1912

Curti, Merle, *The Growth of American Thought*, New York, 1943

Destler, Chester McA., "Wealth Against Commonwealth, 1894–1944," *American Historical Review*, Oct. 1944

Faulkner, H. U., *The Quest for Social Justice*, New York, 1931

Filler, Louis, *Crusaders for American Liberalism*, New York, 1939

Gabriel, R. H., *The Course of American Democratic Thought*, New York, 1940

Hicks, John D., *The Populist Revolt*, Minneapolis, 1931

Howe, Frederic C., *The Confessions of a Reformer*, New York, 1925

Ickes, Harold, "Who Killed the Progressive Party?," *American Historical Review*, Jan. 1941

Lloyd, Caro, *H. D. Lloyd, 1847–1903*, New York, 1912

Lloyd, H. D., *Wealth Against Commonwealth*, New York, 1894

Parrington, V. L., *Main Currents in American Thought*, Vol. 3, New York, 1930

Rochester, Anna, *The Populist Movement in the United States*, New York, 1944

Stearns, Harold, *Liberalism in America*, New York, 1919

Whitlock, Brand, *Forty Years of It*, New York, 1914

Woodward, C. Vann, *Tom Watson, Agrarian Rebel*, New York, 1938

JOHN PETER ALTGELD

Altgeld, John Peter, *The Cost of Something for Nothing*, Chicago, 1904

—— *Justice or Persecution*, Springfield, Ill., 1893

—— *Live Questions*, Chicago, 1890, 1899

—— *Oratory, Its Requirements and Reward*, Chicago, 1901

—— *Our Penal Machinery and Its Victims*, Chicago, 1884

Barnard, Harry, "*Eagle Forgotten*": *The Life of John Peter Altgeld*, New York, 1938

Browne, Waldo, *Altgeld of Illinois*, New York, 1924

David, Henry, *The History of the Haymarket Affair*, New York, 1936

Darrow, Clarence, *The Story of My Life*, New York, 1932

Gary, Joseph E., "The Chicago Anarchists of 1886," *Century Magazine*, April 1893

Lindsay, N. V., "The Altgeld Temperament," *The Public*, May 24, 1912

Masters, E. L., "John Peter Altgeld," *The American Mercury*, Feb. 1925

Schaack, Michael J., *Anarchy and Anarchists*, Chicago, 1889
Whitlock, Brand, *Forty Years of It*, New York, 1914
Wish, Harvey, "Governor Altgeld Pardons Anarchists," Ill. State Hist.
   Soc. *Journal*, Dec., 1938

LINCOLN STEFFENS

Filler, Louis, *Crusaders for American Liberalism*, New York, 1939
Hapgood, Hutchins, *A Victorian in the Modern World*, New York, 1939
Howe, Frederic C., *Confessions of a Reformer*, New York, 1925
Steffens, Lincoln, *Autobiography*, New York, 1931
—— *Letters*, 2 vols., ed. by Ella Winter and Granville Hicks, New York,
   1938
—— *Lincoln Steffens Speaking*, New York, 1936
—— *Moses in Red*, Philadelphia, 1926
—— *Out of the Muck*, Riverside, 1913
—— *The Least of These*, Riverside, 1910
—— *The Shame of the Cities*, New York, 1904
—— *The Struggle for Self-Government*, New York, 1906
—— *Upbuilders*, New York, 1909

RANDOLPH BOURNE

Bourne, Randolph, *Education and Living*, New York, 1917
—— *The Gary Schools*, Boston, 1916
—— *The History of a Literary Radical*, New York, 1921
—— Ed., *Towards an Enduring Peace*, New York, 1916
—— *Untimely Papers*, New York, 1919
—— *Youth and Life*, Boston, 1913.
Brooks, Van Wyck, *Emerson and Others*, New York, 1927
Chamberlain, John, *Farewell to Reform*, New York, 1932
Deutch, Babette, *A Brittle Heaven*, New York, 1926
Filler, Louis, *Randolph Bourne*, Washington, 1943
Lerner, Max, "Randolph Bourne and Two Generations," *Twice a Year*,
   1940–41
Oppenheim, James, "The Story of the Seven Arts," *The American
   Mercury*, June 1930
Rosenfeld, Paul, *Port of New York*, New York, 1924

Twice a Year, Vols, II, V–VI, VII

Van Doren, Carl, *Three Worlds*, New York, 1936

Zigrosser, Carl, "Randolph Bourne," *The Modern School*, Jan. 1919

THE SOCIALIST MOVEMENT

GENERAL REFERENCES

Beard, Charles A. and Mary R., *The Rise of American Civilization*, New York, 1930

Berlin, L., *Karl Marx*, London, 1939

Brissenden, Paul, *The I. W. W.: A Study of American Syndicalism*, New York, 1919

Browder, Earl R., *Shall the Communist Party Change Its Name?* New York, 1944

—— *The People's Road to Peace*, New York, 1940

—— *What Is Communism?*, New York, 1936

Commons, John R., *A History of Labor in the United States*, Vol. II, New York, 1918

Fine, Nathan, *Labor and Farmer Parties in the United States, 1828–1928*, New York, 1928

Foster, William Z., *From Bryan to Stalin*, London, 1939

—— *The Fight Against Hitlerism*, New York, 1941

Haywood, William D., *Bill Haywood's Book*, New York, 1929

—— *Evidence and Cross-Examination in the case of U. S. A. vs. Wm. D. Haywood*, undated

Hillquit, Morris, *A History of Socialism in the United States*, New York, 1910

—— *Loose Leaves from a Busy Life*, New York, 1934

Jaszi, Oscar, "Socialism," *Encyclopaedia of the Social Sciences*

Laidler, Harry W., *Socialism in Thought and Action*, New York, 1920

—— *Social-Economic Movements*, New York, 1944

Macy, John, *Socialism in America*, New York, 1916

Marx, Karl, *Capital*, New York, 1906

—— and Friedrich Engels, *The Communist Manifesto*

Minor, Robert, *The Heritage of the Communist Political Association*, New York, 1944

Minor, Robert, *Invitation to Join the Communist Party*, New York, 1943

Oneal, James, *Some Pages of Party History*, New York, 1935

Rogoff, Harry, *An East Side Epic*: The Life and Work of Meyer London, New York, 1930

Ruthenberg, Charles E., *The Workers (Communist) Party*, Chicago, 1926

Sapos, David, *Left-Wing Unionism*, New York, 1926

Symes, Lillian, and Travers, Clement, *Rebel America*, New York, 1934

Todes, Charlotte, *William H. Sylvis and the National Labor Union*, New York, 1942

Wilson, Edmund, *To the Finland Station*, New York, 1940

DANIEL DE LEON

Brissenden, Paul, *The I. W. W.: A Study of American Syndicalism*, New York, 1919

Brooks, John G., *American Syndicalism: The I. W. W.*, New York, 1913

De Leon, Daniel, *Abolition of Poverty*, New York, 1911

—— *Burning Question of Trade Unionism*, New York, 1914, 1932

—— *Fifteen Questions About Socialism*, New York, 1914

—— *Flashlights on the Amsterdam Program*, New York, 1906

—— *Industrial Unionism*, New York, 1920

—— *Marx on Mallock*, New York, 1925

—— *Reform or Revolution*, New York, 1933

—— *Socialist Reconstruction of Society*, New York, 1905

—— *Two Pages from Roman History*, New York, 1903

—— *Ultramontanism*, New York, 1928

—— *Unity*, New York, 1914

—— *What Means This Strike?* New York, 1898, 1941

—— *Daniel De Leon, the Man and His Work*, A Symposium, New York, 1919

Fine, Nathan, *Labor and Farmer Parties in the United States, 1828–1928*, New York, 1928

Fraina, Louis C., "Daniel De Leon," *The New Review*, July 1914

Haywood, William D., *Bill Haywood's Book*, New York, 1929

Hillquit, Morris, *A History of Socialism in the United States*, New York, 1910

Johnson, Olive M., *Daniel De Leon*, New York, 1923

Peterson, Arnold, *Daniel De Leon, Social Architect*, New York, 1941

—— *Daniel De Leon, Social Scientist*, New York, 1945

Raisky, L. G., *Daniel De Leon*, New York, 1932

Simpson, George, "The American Karl Marx," *American Mercury*, Sept. 1944

Socialist Labor Party, 1890–1930, New York, 1931

EUGENE V. DEBS

Bicknell, George, "Eugene V. Debs at Home," *Twentieth Century Magazine*, Aug. 1910

Coleman, McAlister, *Eugene V. Debs; A Man Unafraid*, New York, 1930

Commons, John R., *A History of Labor in the United States*, Vol. IV, New York, 1918

Debs, Eugene V., "Behind Prison Walls," *Century Magazine*, July 1922

—— *Speeches*, with a critical introduction by Alexander Trachtenberg, New York, 1928

—— *The Danger Ahead*, Chicago, 1911

—— *The Growth of Socialism*, Chicago, 1910

—— *Industrial Unionism*, New York, 1905

—— *Unionism and Socialism*, Chicago, 1905

—— *Wall and Bars*, Chicago, 1927

Debs: His Life, Writings and Speeches, Chicago, 1910

Karsner, David, *Debs*, New York, 1919

Painter, Floy Ruth, *That Man Debs and His Lifework*, Bloomington, Ind., 1929

JOHN REED

Bryant, Louise, "Last Days of John Reed," *Liberator*, Feb. 1920

—— *Six Red Months in Russia*, New York, 1918

Eastman, Max, *Heroes I Have Known*, New York, 1942

Hapgood, Hutchins, *A Victorian in the Modern World*, New York, 1939

Hicks, Granville, and John Stuart, *John Reed*, New York, 1937

Lippmann, Walter, "Legendary John Reed," *New Republic*, Dec. 26 1914

Reed, *A Day in Bohemia, or Life Among the Artists*, New York, 1913

—— "Almost Thirty," *New Republic*, April 15 and 29, 1936

—— *Daughter of the Revolution*, New York, 1927

—— *Everymagazine*, an Immorality Play, New York, 1913

—— *Insurgent Mexico*, New York, 1914

—— *Tamburlane*, Riverside, Conn., 1917

—— *Ten Days That Shook the World*, New York, 1919

—— *The War in Eastern Europe*, New York, 1916

Steffens, Lincoln, *Autobiography*, New York, 1930

—— *Letters*, New York, 1938

Williams, Albert Rhys, *Through the Russian Revolution*, New York, 1921

Young, Art, *Art Young, His Life and Times*, New York, 1939

THE INTRANSIGENT NEW DEALERS

GENERAL REFERENCES

Anderson, Jack, and R. W. May, *McCarthy: the Man, the Senator, the "Ism,"* Boston, 1952.

Barth, Alan, *Government by Investigation*, New York, 1955.

——, *Loyalty of Freemen*, New York, 1951.

Barzun, Jacques, *On Human Freedom*, Boston, 1939.

Carr, Robert, K., *The House Committee on Un-American Activities*, New York, 1952.

Chafee, Z., "Thirty-five Years with Freedom of Speech," New York, 1952.

Commager, H. S., et. al., *Civil Liberties under Attack*, Philadelphia, 1951.

Cushman, R. C., *Civil Liberties in the United States*, Ithaca, 1956.

Douglas, W. O., "The Manifest Destiny of America," *The Progressive*, February, 1955.

Dumbauld, Edward, *The Bill of Rights and What It Means Today.* Norman, Okla., 1957.

Fraenkel, O. K., *Our Civil Liberties*, New York, 1944.

Gellhorn, Walter, *The States and Subversion*, Ithaca, 1952.

Griswold, Erwin N., *The Fifth Amendment Today*, Cambridge, Mass., 1955.

Hoffman, H., *Loyalty by Oath*, Wallingford, Pa., 1957.

Hook, Sidney, *Common Sense and the Fifth Amendment*, New York, 1957.

Hutchins, R. M., *The Bill of Rights*, New York, 1956.

Lattimore, Owen, *Ordeal by Slander*, Boston, 1950.

McCarthy, Joe, *McCarthyism: The Fight for America*, New York, 1952.

McWilliams, Carey, *Witch Hunt*, The Revival of Heresy, Boston, 1950.

Millis, Walter, *Individual Freedom and the Common Defense*, New York, 1957.

Newman, E. S., *The Freedom Reader*, New York, 1955.

Ogden, A. R., *The Dies Committee*, Washington, 1945.

Taylor, Telford, *The Grand Inquest*, New York, 1955.

Report of the Special Committee on the Federal Loyalty-Security Program of the Association of the Bar of the City of New York, 1956.

Schaar, J. H., *Loyalty in America*, Berkeley, Calif., 1957.

Spitz, David, *Patterns of Antidemocratic Thought*, New York, 1949.

Stone, I. F., *The Truman Era*, New York, 1953.

Warren, Earl, "The Law and the Future," *Fortune*, 1955.

GEORGE W. NORRIS

Coyle D. C., *Land of Hope*, The Way of Life in the Tennessee Valley, Evanston, Ill., 1941.

Lief, Alfred, *Democracy's Norris*, The Biography of a Lonely Crusader, New York, 1939.

Lillienthal, David E., "Senator Norris and the TVA," *The Nation*, Sept. 23, 1944.

——, *TVA, Democracy on the March*, New York, 1944.

Neuberger, Richard L., and S. B. Kahn, *Integrity, The Life of George W. Norris*, New York, 1937.

Norris, George W., "Electric Light Rates in Ontario, Canada," *Cong. Rec.*, Aug. 22, 1935.

——, *Fighting Liberal*, New York, 1945.

——, "The One-House Legislature," *Annals* of the Acad. of Pol. & Soc. Sci., Sept. 1935.

——, Peace Without Hate, Lincoln, Nebr., 1943.

BIBLIOGRAPHY

——, "Progressives Unite!" *The New Republic*, Sept. 28, 1942.

——, "The Road to Permanent Peace," *The New Republic*, Jan. 17, 1944.

——, "TVA on the Jordan," *The Nation*, May 20, 1944.

——, "Why Henry Ford Wants Muscle Shoals," *The Nation*, Dec. 26, 1923.

Nye, Russell B., *Midwestern Progressive Politics*, East Lansing, Mich., 1951.

Pritchett, C. H., *The Tennessee Valley Authority*, Chapel Hill, 1943.

Selsnick, Philip, TVA, *The Grass Roots*, Berkeley, Calif., 1949.

Villard, O. G., "George W. Norris," *The Forum*, Apr. 1936.

——, *Prophets True and False*, New York, 1928.

HENRY A. WALLACE

Lord, Russell, *The Wallaces of Iowa*, Boston, 1947.

Macdonald, Dwight, *Henry Wallace, the Man and the Myth*, New York, 1948.

The New Republic, 1946-1949.

Timmons, B. N., *Jesse H. Jones*, The Man and Statesman, New York, 1956.

Truman, Harry S., *Memoirs: I. Year of Decision, 1955; II. Years of Trial and Hope*, 1956, New York.

Wallace, Henry A., *Democracy Reborn*, New York, 1944.

——, *New Frontiers*, New York, 1934.

——, "Political Odyssey," *Life*, May 14, 1956.

——, *Sixty Million Jobs*, New York, 1945.

——, *The American Choice*, New York, 1940.

——, *The Century of the Common Man*, ed. by R. Lord, New York, 1943.

——, *The Fight for Peace*, New York, 1946.

——, *Toward World Peace*, New York, 1948.

Wechsler, James A., "My Ten Months with Wallace," *The Progressive*, Nov. 1948.

——, "What Makes Wallace Run?" *The Progressive*, Feb. 1948.

Wise, J. W., *Meet Henry Wallace*, New York, 1948.

HUGO L. BLACK

Black, Hugo L., "I Did Join the Klan," Radio speech, Oct. 1, 1937, *Vital Speeches*, Oct. 15, 1937.

[638]

——, "Inside a Senate Investigation," *Harper's Monthly Magazine*, Feb. 1936.

——, "Lobby Investigation," Radio speech, Aug. 8, 1935, *Vital Speeches*, Sept. 1, 1935.

——, "The Shorter Work Week and Work Day," *Annals* of the Am. Acad. of Pol. & Soc. Sci., March 1936.

——, "The Wages and Hour Bill," Senate speech, July 27, 1937, *Vital Speeches*, Aug. 15, 1937.

——, "To Win the War and the Peace," *The New Republic*, July 27, 1942.

Curtis, C. P., *Lions Under the Throne*, Boston, 1947.

Fairman, Charles, "Does the Fourteenth Amendment Incorporate the Bill of Rights?" *Stanford Law Rev.*, Dec. 1949.

Frank, John P., *Mr. Justice Black*, New York, 1949.

Freund, Paul A., *On Understanding the Supreme Court*, Boston, 1950.

Havighurst, H. C., "Mr. Justice Black," *Nat. Lawyers Guild Quarterly*, June 1938.

Konefsky, S. J., *Chief Justice Stone and the Supreme Court*, New York, 1946.

McCune, Wesley, *The Nine Young Men*, New York, 1947.

McLaughlin, A. C., "The Court, the Corporation, and Conkling," *Am. Hist. Rev.*, Oct. 1940.

Morrison, Stanley, "Does the Fourteenth Amendment Incorporate the Bill of Rights?" *Stanford Law Rev.*, Dec. 1949.

Pritchett, H. C., *The Roosevelt Court*, New York, 1948.

United States Reports, Cases Adjudged in the Supreme Court, 1937-1958, Vols. 302-354, Washington, D. C.

Williams, Charlotte, *Hugo Black*, A Study in Judicial Process, Baltimore, 1950.

INDEX
(up to p. 537)

[641]

INDEX

(to pp. 541-619)

[659]

E DUE

	PRINTED IN U.S.A.